DEAD- POOL

CLASSIC

ADPOOL CLASSIC VOL. 1. Contains material originally published in magazine form as NEW MUTANT #98, DEADPOOL: THE CIRCLE CHASE #1-4, DEADPOOL (1994) #1-4 and DEADPOOL (1997) #1. Sixth printing 2012. BN# 978-0-7851-3124-3. Published by MARVEL WORLDWIDE, INC., a subsidiary of MARVEL ENTERTAINMENT, LLC. OFFICE OF PUBLICATION: 135 West 50th Street, New York, NY 10020. Copyright © 1991, 1993, 1994, 97 and 2008 Marvel Characters, Inc. All rights reserved. $29.99 per copy in the U.S. and $34.99 in Canada (GST #R127032852); Canadian Agreement #40668537. All characters featured in this issue and the distinctive mes and likenesses thereof, and all related indicia are trademarks of Marvel Characters, Inc. No similarity between any of the names, characters, persons, and/or institutions in this magazine with those of any living or ad person or institution is intended, and any such similarity which may exist is purely coincidental. **Printed in Canada**. ALAN FINE, EVP - Office of the President, Marvel Worldwide, Inc. and EVP & CMO Marvel Characters :; DAN BUCKLEY, Publisher & President - Print, Animation & Digital Divisions; JOE QUESADA, Chief Creative Officer; TOM BREVOORT, SVP of Publishing; DAVID BOGART, SVP of Operations & Procurement, Publishing; WAN JAYATILLEKE, SVP & Associate Publisher, Publishing; C.B. CEBULSKI, SVP of Creator & Content Development; DAVID GABRIEL, SVP of Publishing Sales & Circulation; MICHAEL PASCIULLO, SVP of Brand Planning Communications; JIM O'KEEFE, VP of Operations & Logistics; DAN CARR, Executive Director of Publishing Technology; SUSAN CRESPI, Editorial Operations Manager; ALEX MORALES, Publishing Operations Manager; AN LEE, Chairman Emeritus. For information regarding advertising in Marvel Comics or on Marvel.com, please contact John Dokes, SVP Integrated Sales and Marketing, at jdokes@marvel.com. For Marvel subscription uiries, please call 800-217-9158. **Manufactured between 3/26/2012 and 4/9/2012 by R.R. DONNELLEY, INC., SALEM, VA, USA.**

DEAD-POOL

CLASSIC

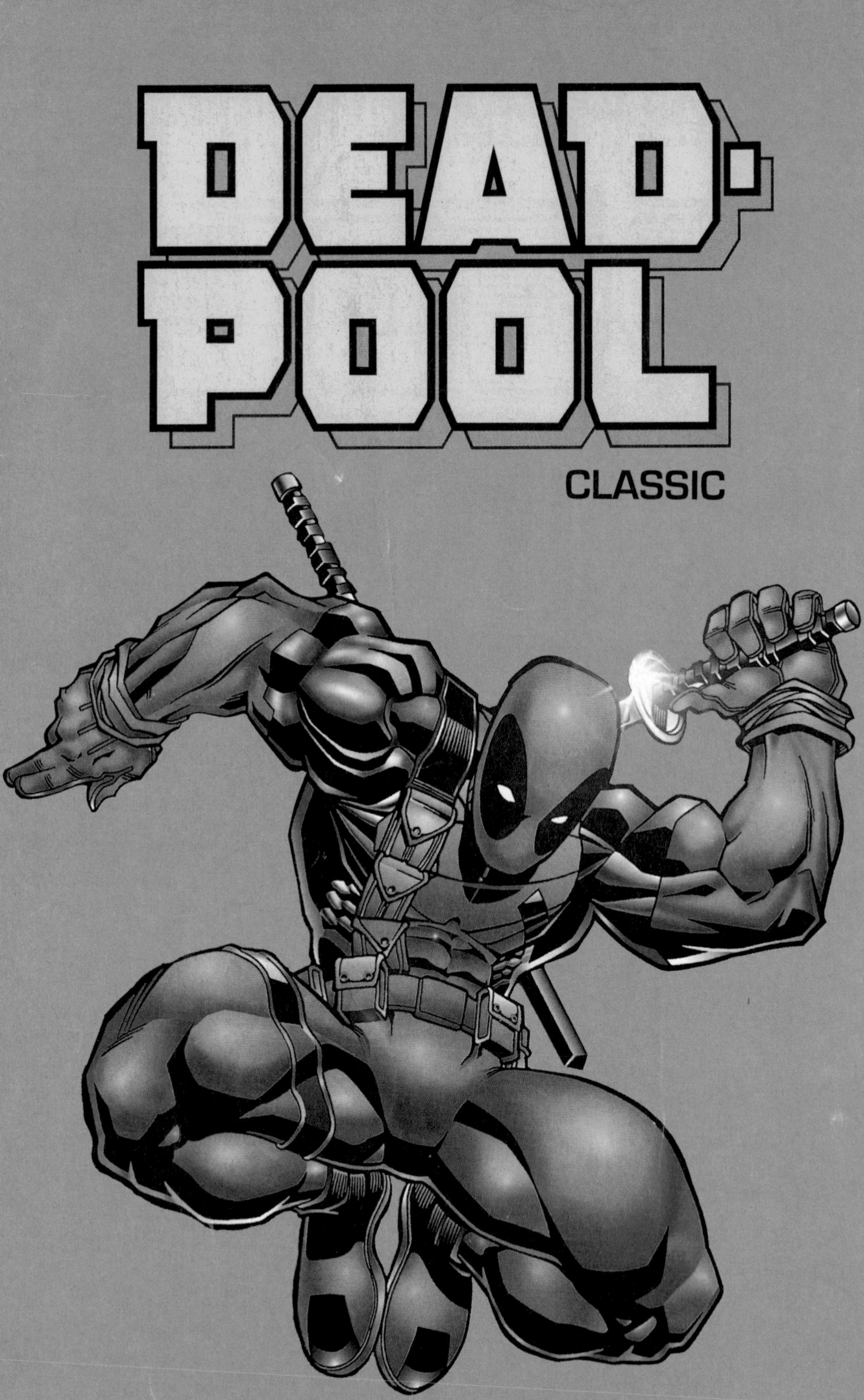

NEW MUTANTS #98

Plotter & Artist: Rob Liefeld
Scripter: Fabian Nicieza
Colorist: Steve Buccellato
Letterer: Joe Rosen
Editor: Bob Harras

DEADPOOL: THE CIRCLE CHASE

Writer: Fabian Nicieza
Penciler: Joe Madureira
Inkers: Mark Farmer & Harry Candelario
Colorist: Glynis Oliver
Letterer: Chris Eliopoulos
Editor: Suzanne Gaffney

DEADPOOL: SINS OF THE PAST

Writer: Mark Waid
Pencilers: Ian Churchill, Lee Weeks & Ken Lashley
Inkers: Jason Minor, Bob McLeod, Bud Larosa & Tom Wegrzyn
Colorists: Dana Moreshead & Mike Thomas
Letterer: Richard Starkings & Comicraft
Editor: Suzanne Gaffney

DEADPOOL #1

Writer: Joe Kelly
Penciler: Ed McGuinness
Inkers: Nathan Massengill & Norman Lee
Colorists: Christian Lichtner & Digital Chameleon
Letterers: Richard Starkings & Comicraft's Dave Lanphear
Editor: Matt Idelson

Front Cover Artists: Rob Liefeld & John Kalisz
Back Cover Artist: Ian Churchill
Book Designer: Carrie Beadle
Production: Jerron Quality Color
Research: Eric J. Moreels
Collection Editor: Mark D. Beazley
Assistant Editors: Nelson Ribeiro & Alex Starbuck
Editor, Special Projects: Jennifer Grünwald
Senior Editor, Special Projects: Jeff Youngquist
Senior Vice President of Sales: David Gabriel
SVP of Brand Planning & Communications: Michael Pasciullo
Editor in Chief: Axel Alonso
Chief Creative Officer: Joe Quesada
Publisher: Dan Buckley
Executive Producer: Alan Fine

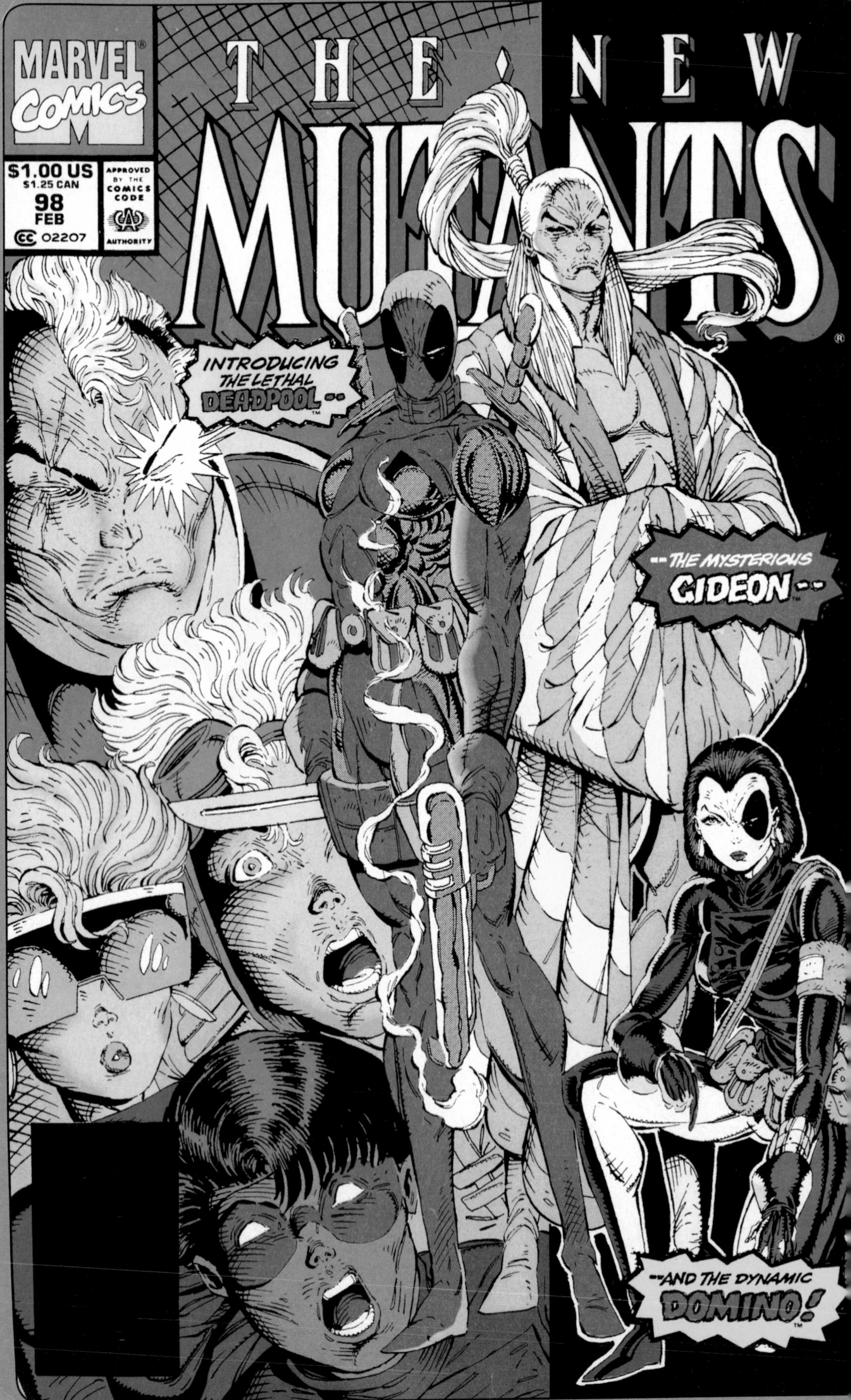
MARVEL COMICS
THE NEW MUTANTS
$1.00 US
$1.25 CAN
98
FEB
02207
APPROVED BY THE COMICS CODE AUTHORITY
INTRODUCING THE LETHAL DEADPOOL--
--THE MYSTERIOUS GIDEON--
--AND THE DYNAMIC DOMINO!

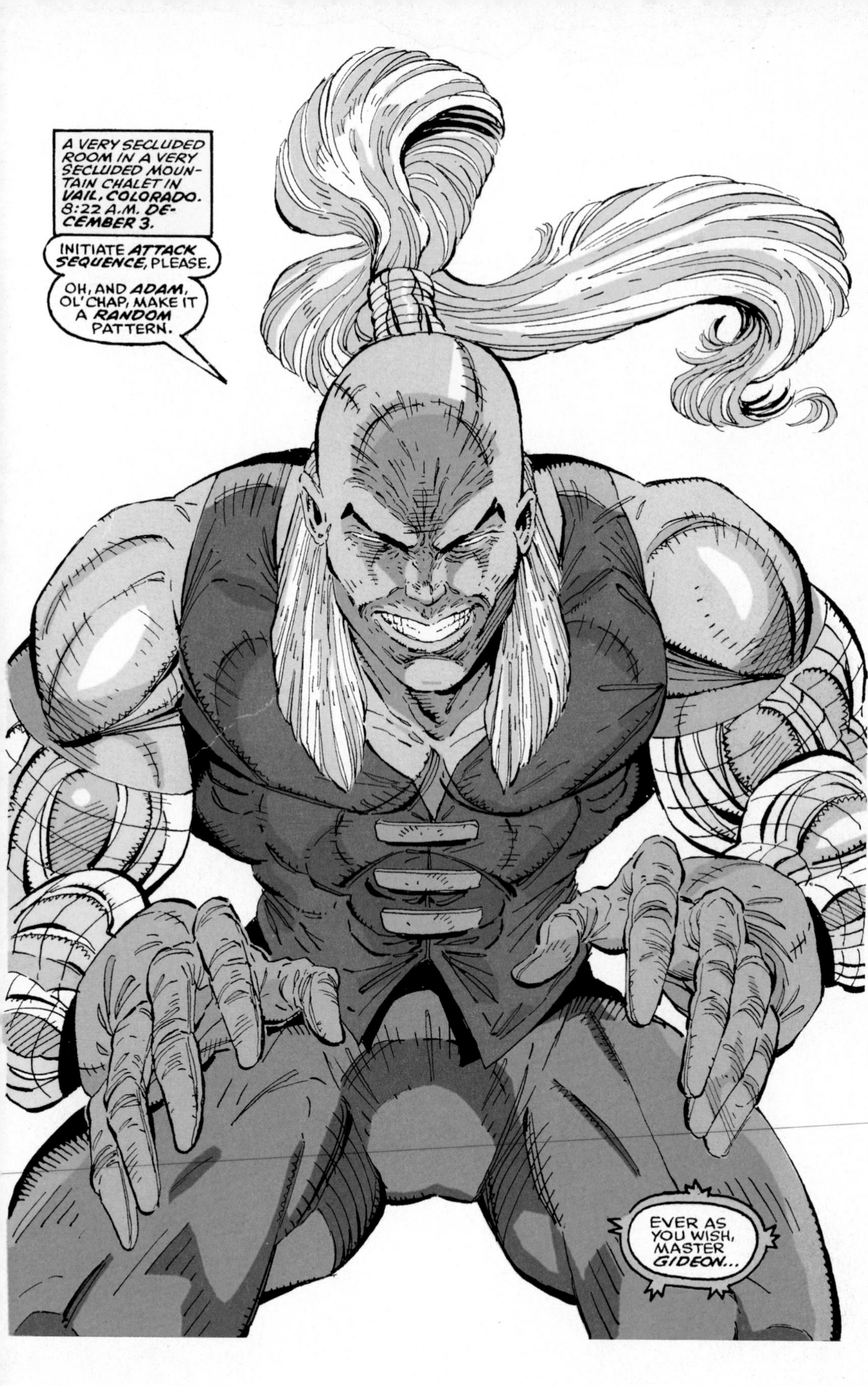
A VERY SECLUDED ROOM IN A VERY SECLUDED MOUNTAIN CHALET IN VAIL, COLORADO. 8:22 A.M. DECEMBER 3.
INITIATE ATTACK SEQUENCE, PLEASE.
OH, AND ADAM, OL' CHAP, MAKE IT A RANDOM PATTERN.
EVER AS YOU WISH, MASTER GIDEON...

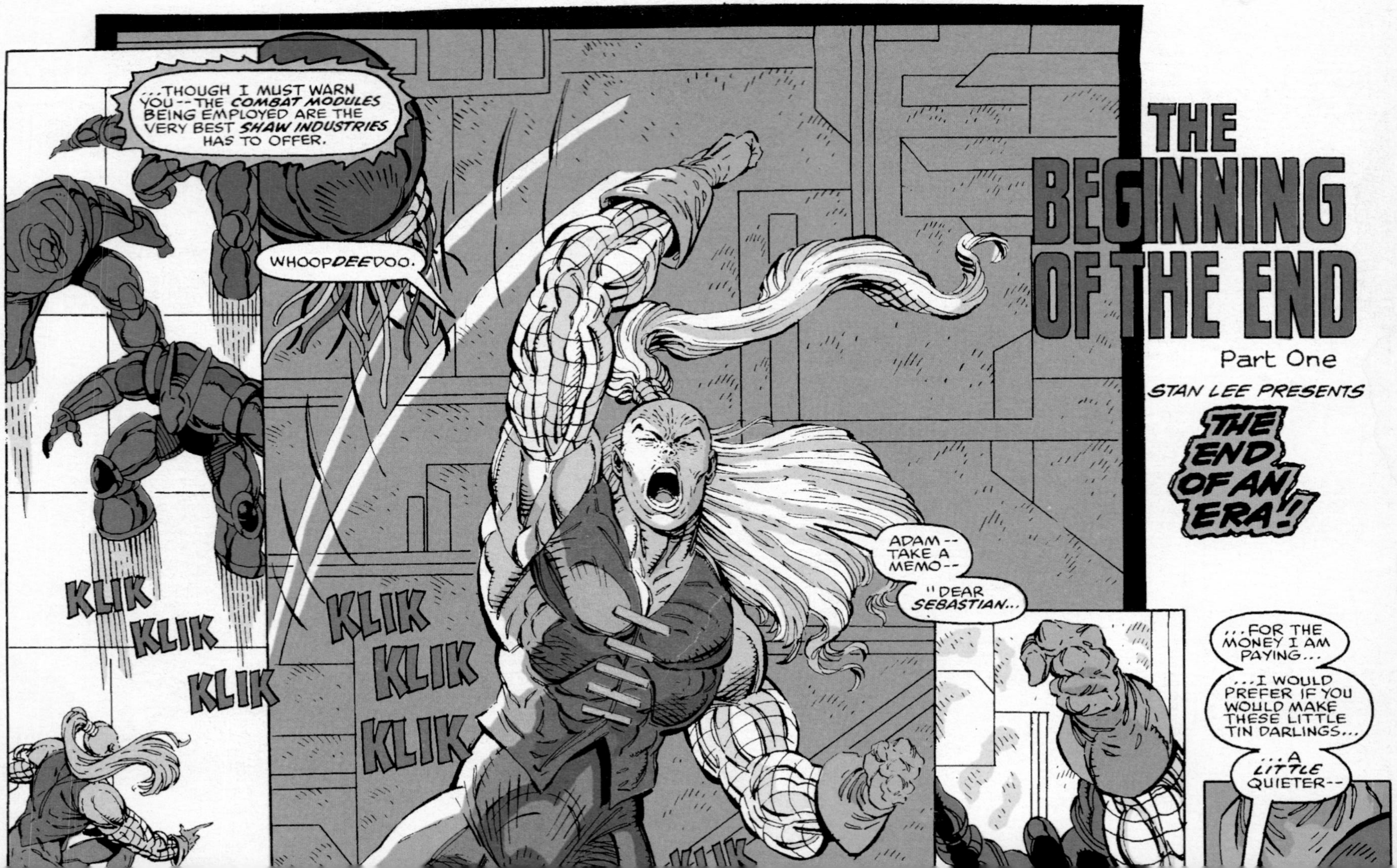
...THOUGH I MUST WARN YOU--THE COMBAT MODULES BEING EMPLOYED ARE THE VERY BEST SHAW INDUSTRIES HAS TO OFFER.
WHOOPDEEDOO.
KLIK
KLIK
KLIK
KLIK
KLIK
KLIK
THE BEGINNING OF THE END
Part One
STAN LEE PRESENTS
THE END OF AN ERA!!
ADAM--TAKE A MEMO--
"DEAR SEBASTIAN...
...FOR THE MONEY I AM PAYING...
...I WOULD PREFER IF YOU WOULD MAKE THESE LITTLE TIN DARLINGS...
...A LITTLE QUIETER--

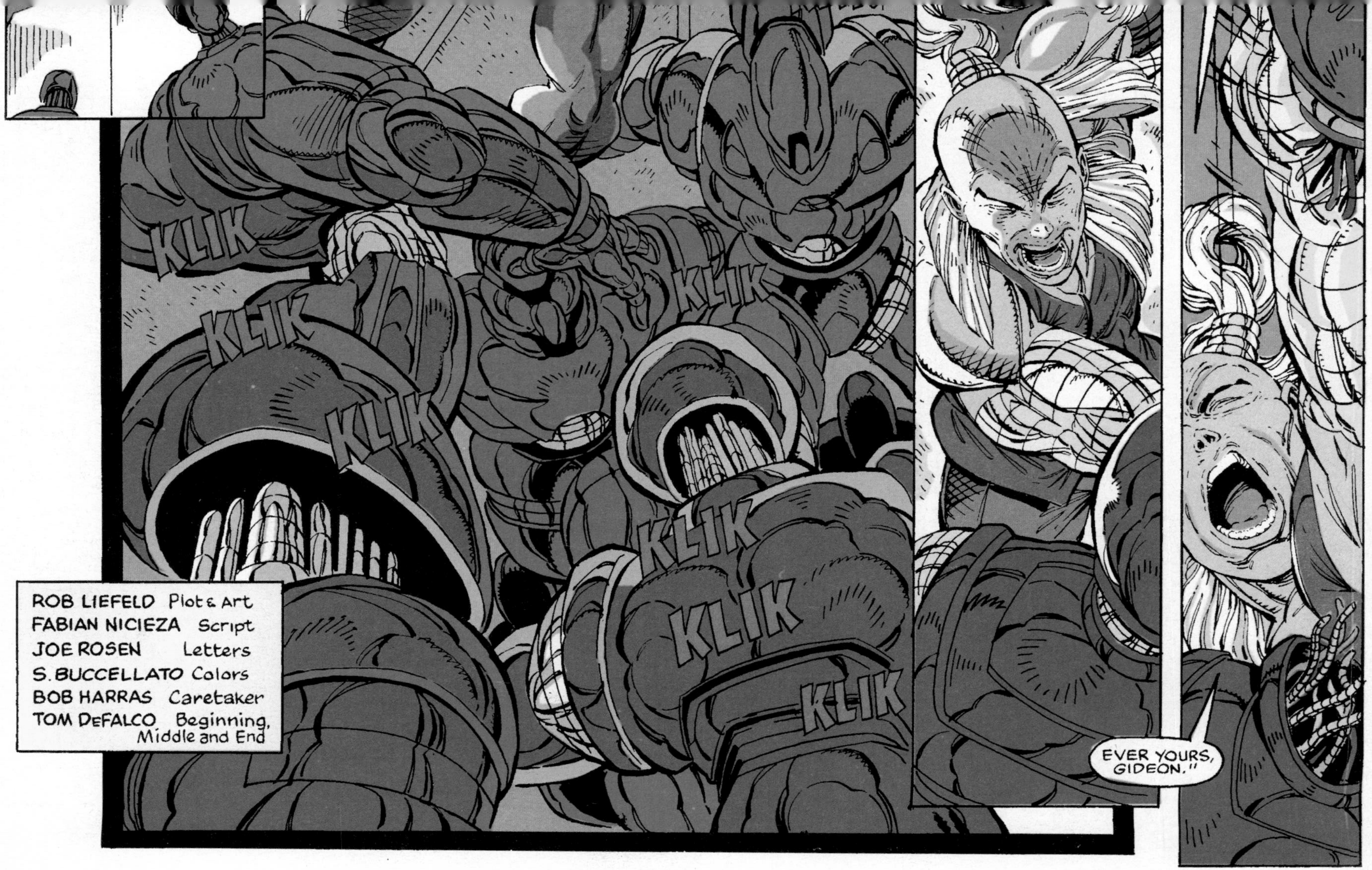
KLIK
KLIK
KLIK
KLIK
KLIK
KLIK
KLIK
ROB LIEFELD Plot & Art
FABIAN NICIEZA Script
JOE ROSEN Letters
S. BUCCELLATO Colors
BOB HARRAS Caretaker
TOM DeFALCO Beginning, Middle and End
EVER YOURS, GIDEON."

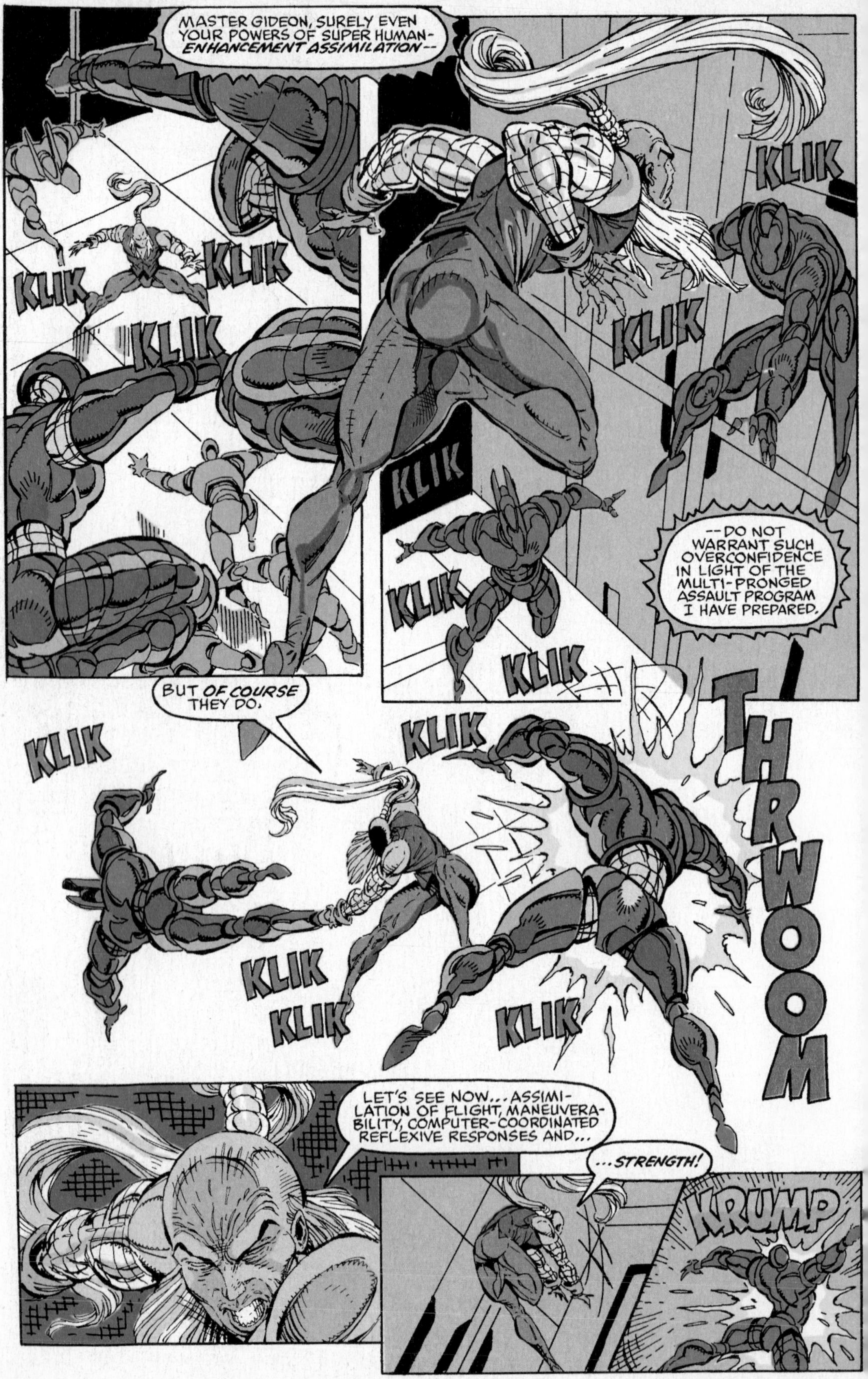

MASTER GIDEON, SURELY EVEN YOUR POWERS OF SUPER HUMAN-ENHANCEMENT ASSIMILATION--
KLIK
KLIK
KLIK
KLIK
KLIK
KLIK
KLIK
KLIK
--DO NOT WARRANT SUCH OVERCONFIDENCE IN LIGHT OF THE MULTI-PRONGED ASSAULT PROGRAM I HAVE PREPARED.
BUT OF COURSE THEY DO.
KLIK
KLIK
THRWOOM
KLIK
KLIK
KLIK
LET'S SEE NOW... ASSIMILATION OF FLIGHT, MANEUVERABILITY, COMPUTER-COORDINATED REFLEXIVE RESPONSES AND...
...STRENGTH!
KRUMP

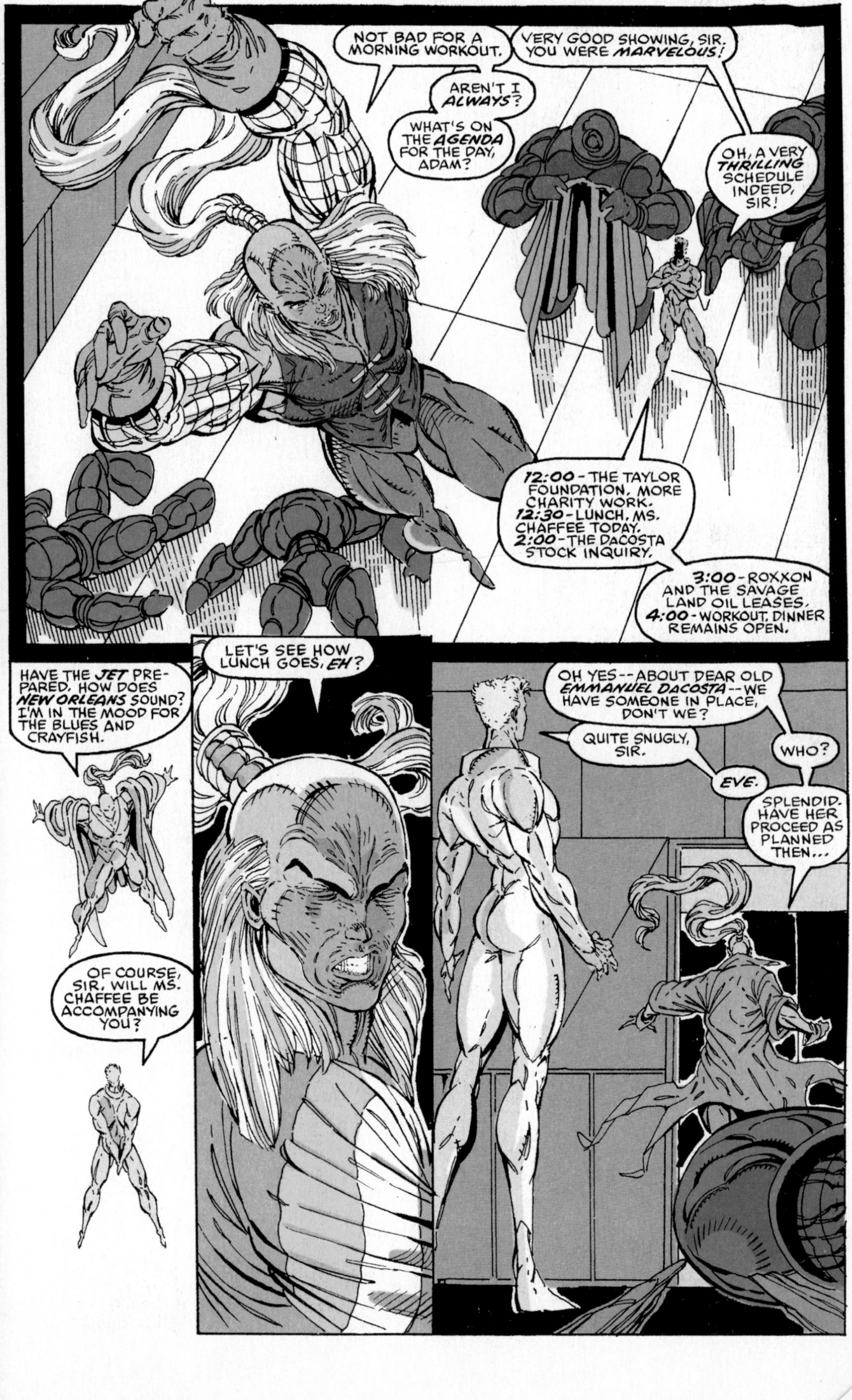
NOT BAD FOR A MORNING WORKOUT.
AREN'T I ALWAYS?
WHAT'S ON THE AGENDA FOR THE DAY, ADAM?
VERY GOOD SHOWING, SIR. YOU WERE MARVELOUS!
OH, A VERY THRILLING SCHEDULE INDEED, SIR!
12:00 - THE TAYLOR FOUNDATION, MORE CHARITY WORK. 12:30 - LUNCH, MS. CHAFFEE TODAY. 2:00 - THE DACOSTA STOCK INQUIRY.
3:00 - ROXXON AND THE SAVAGE LAND OIL LEASES. 4:00 - WORKOUT. DINNER REMAINS OPEN.
HAVE THE JET PREPARED. HOW DOES NEW ORLEANS SOUND? I'M IN THE MOOD FOR THE BLUES AND CRAYFISH.
OF COURSE, SIR. WILL MS. CHAFFEE BE ACCOMPANYING YOU?
LET'S SEE HOW LUNCH GOES, EH?
OH YES--ABOUT DEAR OLD EMMANUEL DACOSTA--WE HAVE SOMEONE IN PLACE, DON'T WE?
QUITE SNUGLY, SIR.
WHO?
EVE.
SPLENDID. HAVE HER PROCEED AS PLANNED THEN...

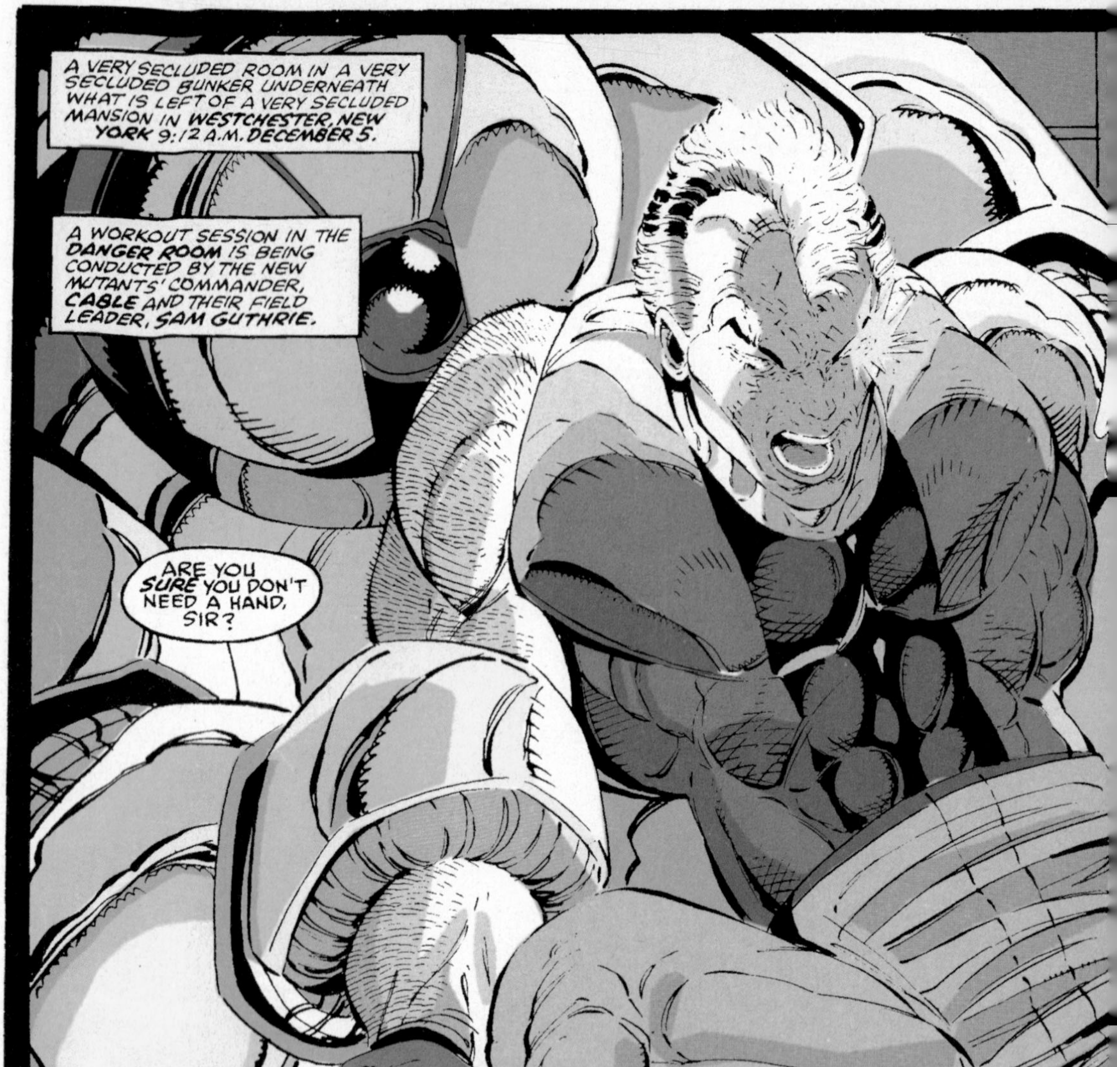
A VERY SECLUDED ROOM IN A VERY SECLUDED BUNKER UNDERNEATH WHAT IS LEFT OF A VERY SECLUDED MANSION IN WESTCHESTER, NEW YORK 9:12 A.M. DECEMBER 5.
A WORKOUT SESSION IN THE DANGER ROOM IS BEING CONDUCTED BY THE NEW MUTANTS' COMMANDER, CABLE AND THEIR FIELD LEADER, SAM GUTHRIE.
ARE YOU SURE YOU DON'T NEED A HAND, SIR?
VERY.

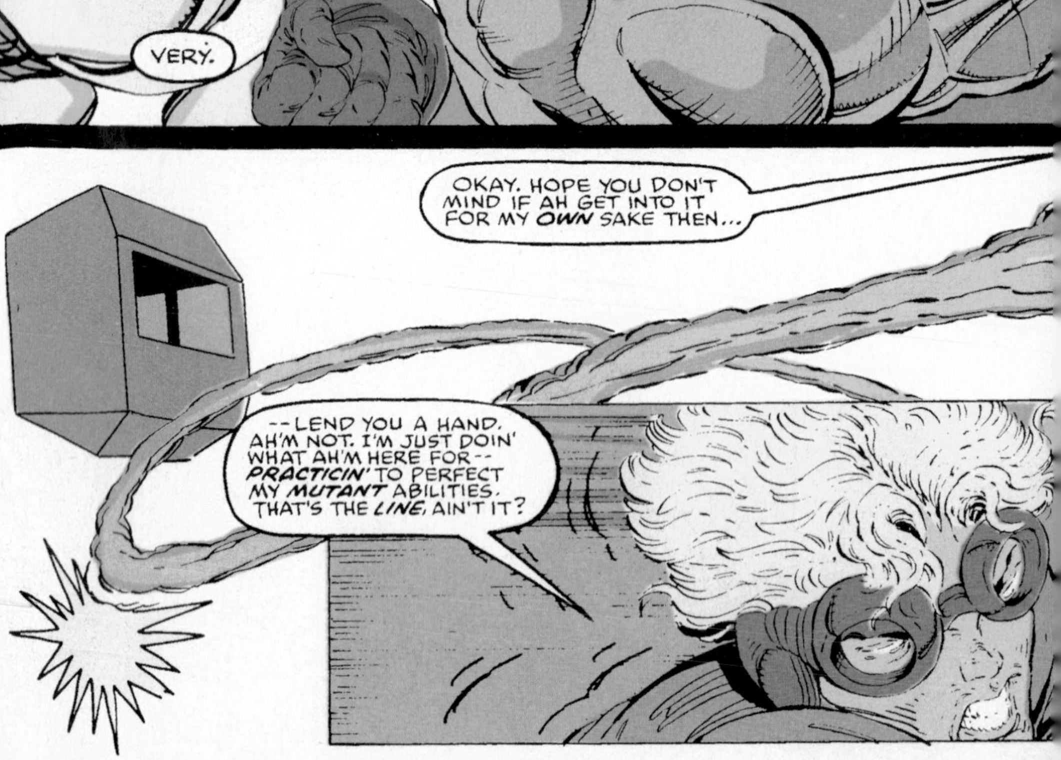
OKAY. HOPE YOU DON'T MIND IF AH GET INTO IT FOR MY OWN SAKE THEN...
--LEND YOU A HAND. AH'M NOT. I'M JUST DOIN' WHAT AH'M HERE FOR--PRACTICIN' TO PERFECT MY MUTANT ABILITIES. THAT'S THE LINE, AIN'T IT?

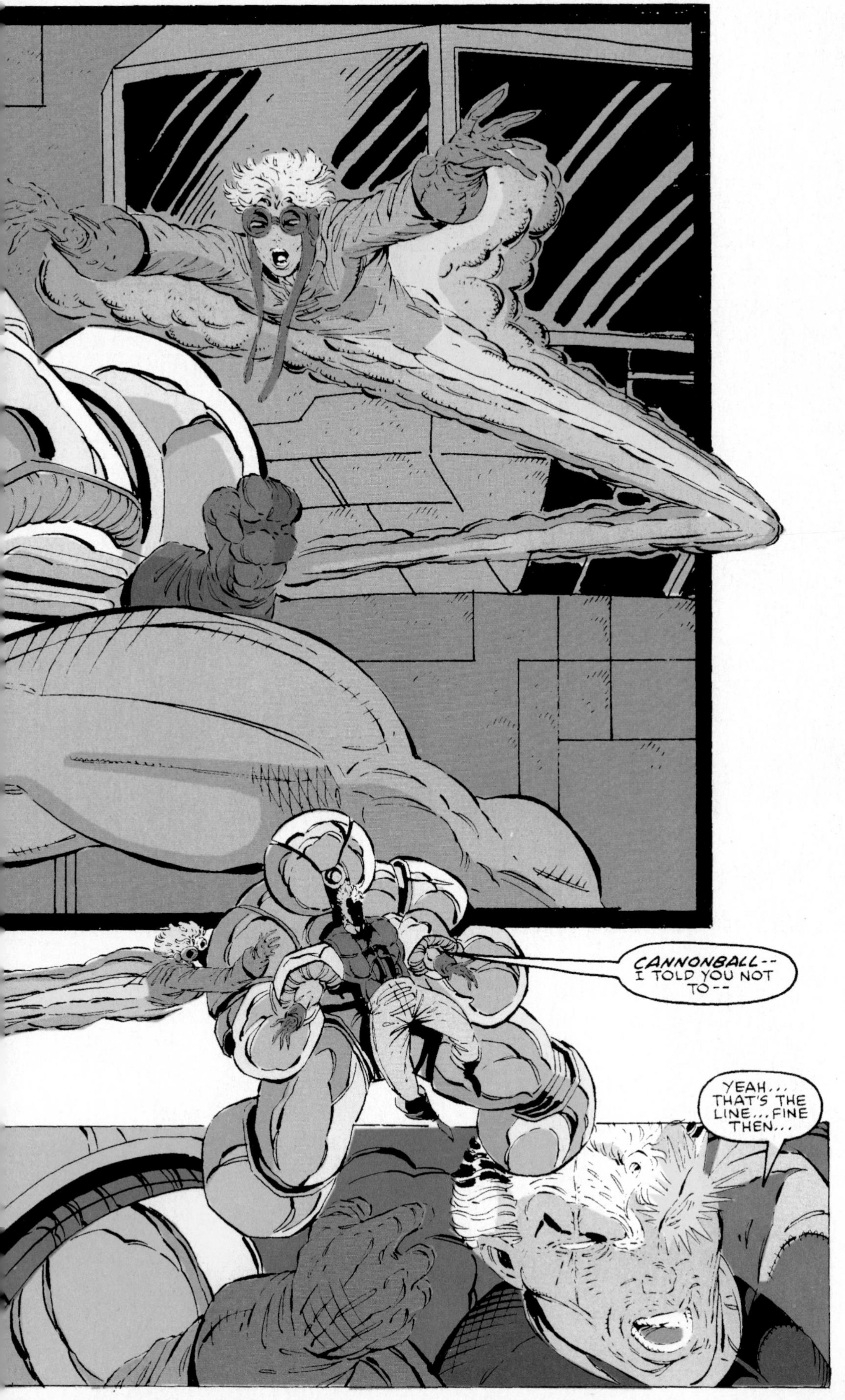
CANNONBALL-- I TOLD YOU NOT TO--
YEAH... THAT'S THE LINE... FINE THEN...

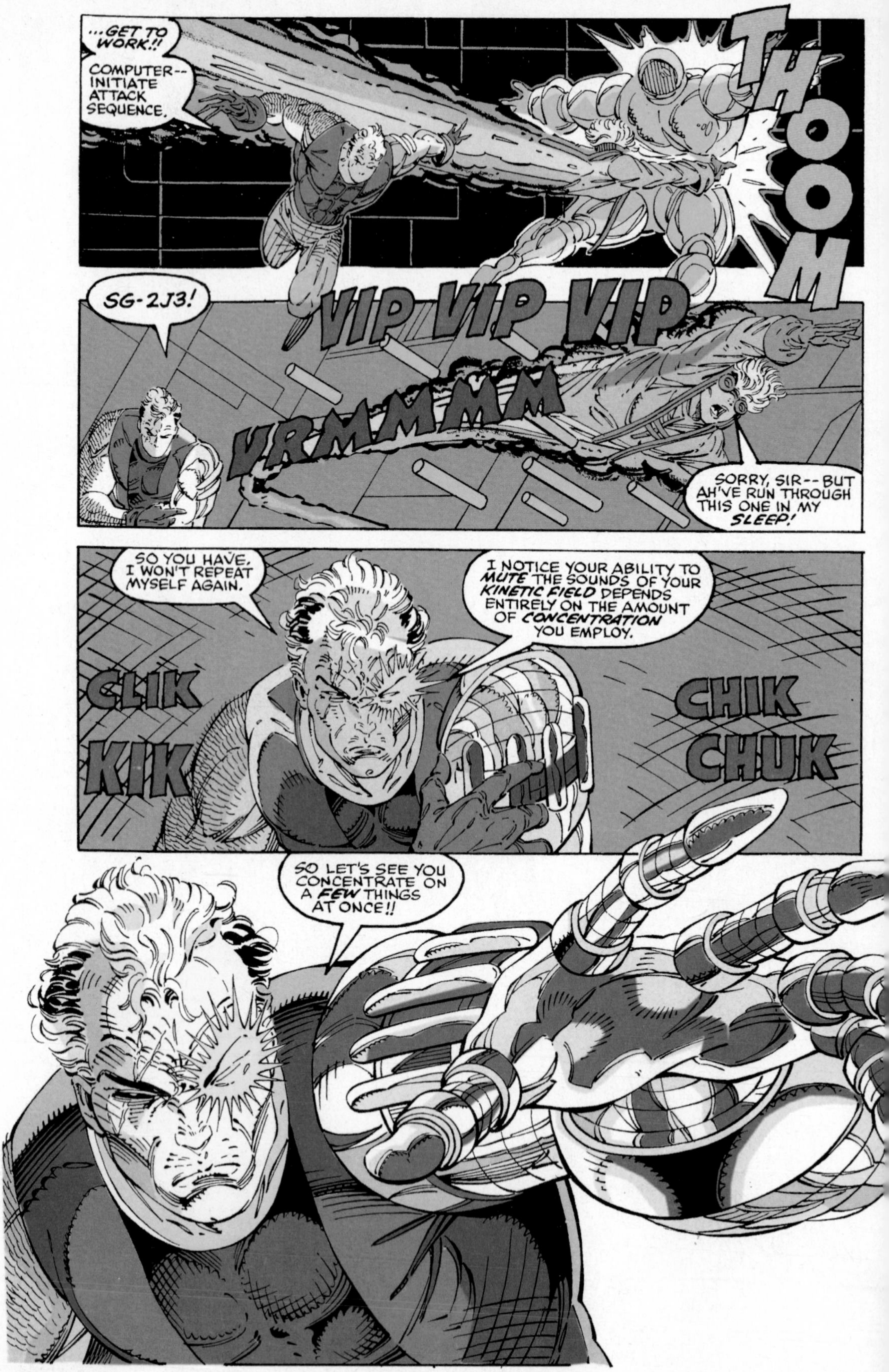
...GET TO WORK!!
COMPUTER-- INITIATE ATTACK SEQUENCE.
THOOM
SG-2J3!
VIP VIP VIP
VRMMMM
SORRY, SIR-- BUT AH'VE RUN THROUGH THIS ONE IN MY SLEEP!
SO YOU HAVE. I WON'T REPEAT MYSELF AGAIN.
I NOTICE YOUR ABILITY TO MUTE THE SOUNDS OF YOUR KINETIC FIELD DEPENDS ENTIRELY ON THE AMOUNT OF CONCENTRATION YOU EMPLOY.
CLIK
KIK
CHIK
CHUK
SO LET'S SEE YOU CONCENTRATE ON A FEW THINGS AT ONCE!!

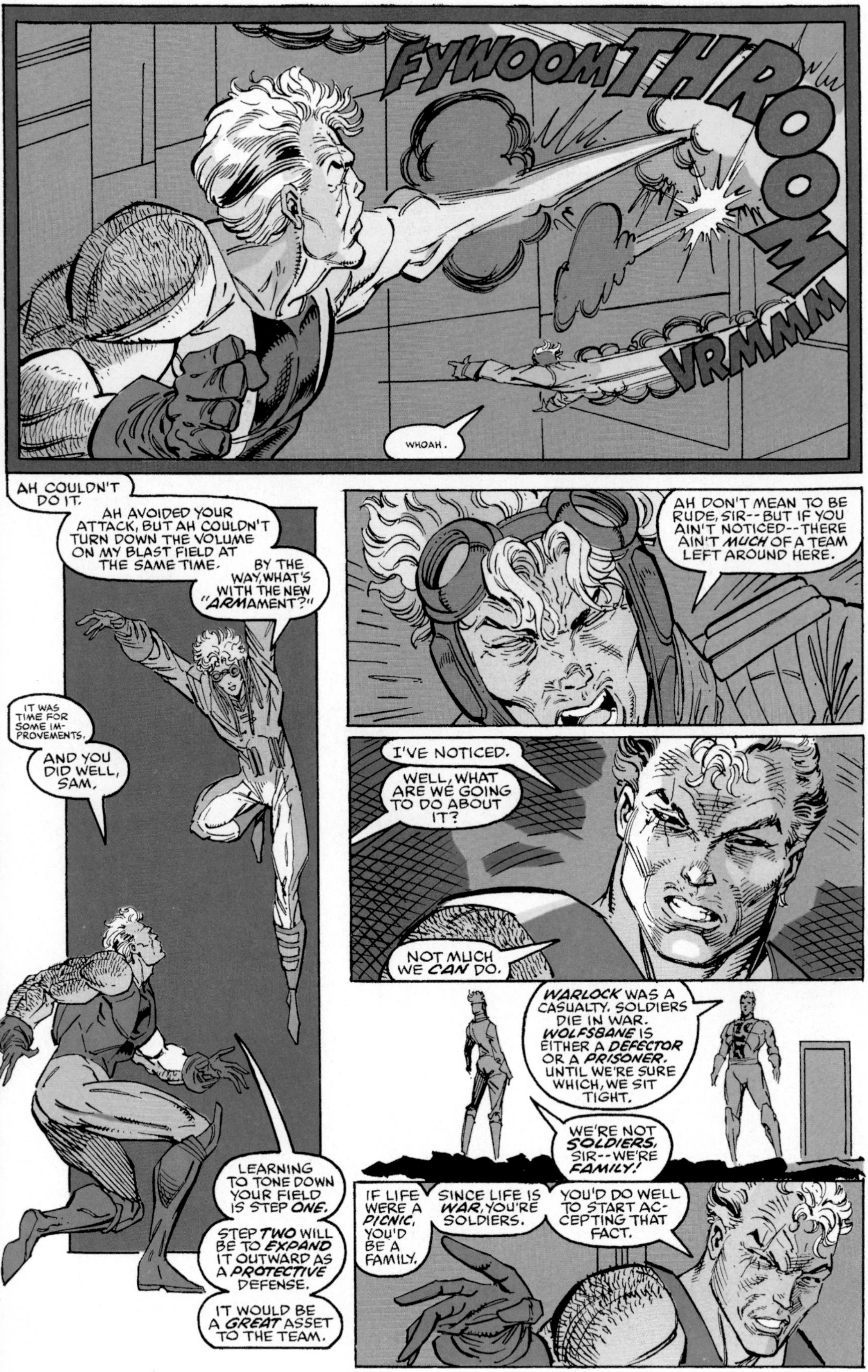

FYWOOM
THROOM
VRMMM
WHOAH.
AH COULDN'T DO IT.
AH AVOIDED YOUR ATTACK, BUT AH COULDN'T TURN DOWN THE VOLUME ON MY BLAST FIELD AT THE SAME TIME.
BY THE WAY, WHAT'S WITH THE NEW "ARMAMENT?"
IT WAS TIME FOR SOME IMPROVEMENTS.
AND YOU DID WELL, SAM.
LEARNING TO TONE DOWN YOUR FIELD IS STEP ONE.
STEP TWO WILL BE TO EXPAND IT OUTWARD AS A PROTECTIVE DEFENSE.
IT WOULD BE A GREAT ASSET TO THE TEAM.
AH DON'T MEAN TO BE RUDE, SIR-- BUT IF YOU AIN'T NOTICED--THERE AIN'T MUCH OF A TEAM LEFT AROUND HERE.
I'VE NOTICED.
WELL, WHAT ARE WE GOING TO DO ABOUT IT?
NOT MUCH WE CAN DO.
WARLOCK WAS A CASUALTY. SOLDIERS DIE IN WAR. WOLFSBANE IS EITHER A DEFECTOR OR A PRISONER. UNTIL WE'RE SURE WHICH, WE SIT TIGHT.
WE'RE NOT SOLDIERS, SIR--WE'RE FAMILY!
IF LIFE WERE A PICNIC, YOU'D BE A FAMILY.
SINCE LIFE IS WAR, YOU'RE SOLDIERS.
YOU'D DO WELL TO START ACCEPTING THAT FACT.

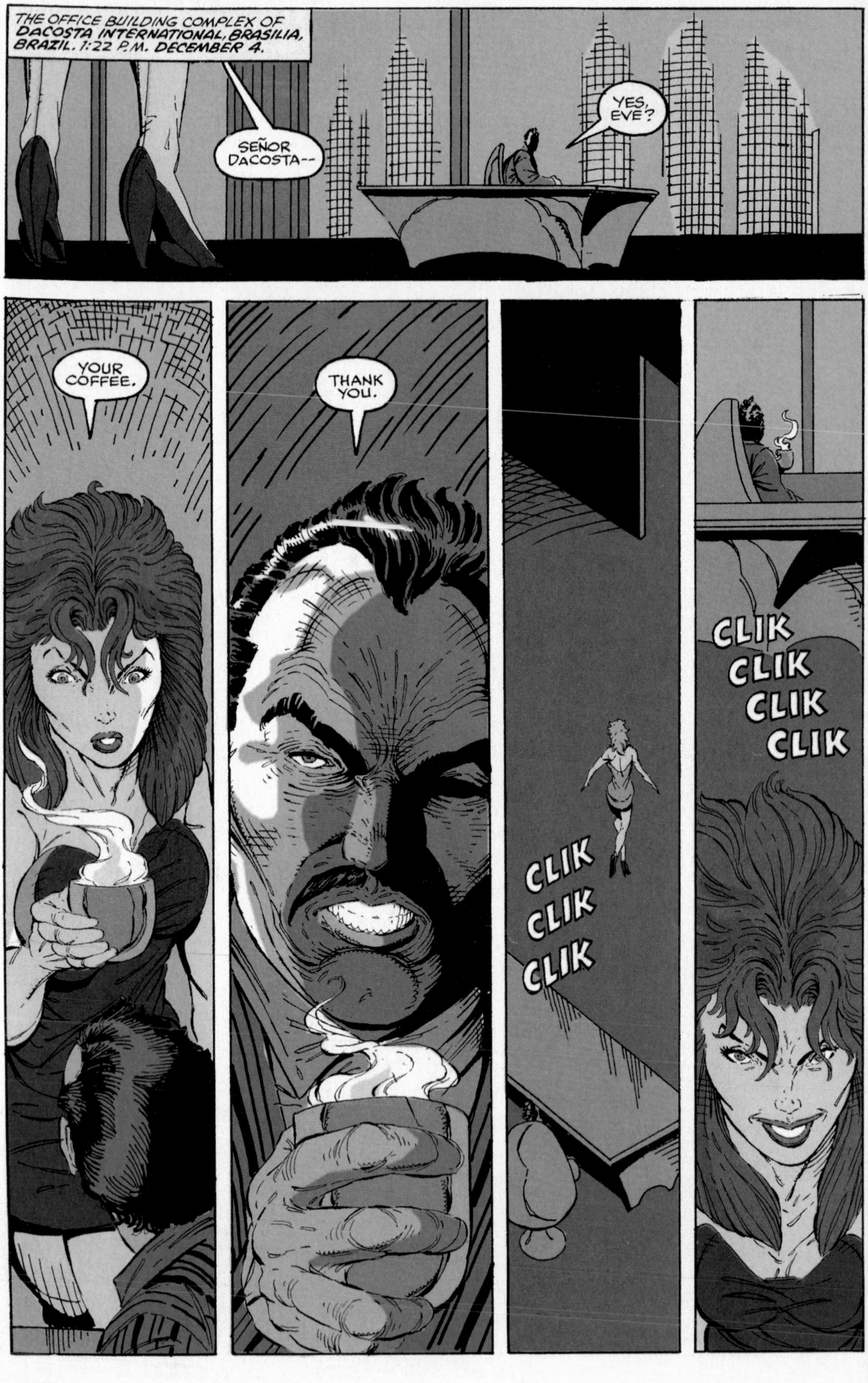
THE OFFICE BUILDING COMPLEX OF DACOSTA INTERNATIONAL, BRASILIA, BRAZIL. 1:22 P.M. DECEMBER 4.
SEÑOR DACOSTA--
YES, EVE?
YOUR COFFEE.
THANK YOU.
CLIK CLIK CLIK
CLIK CLIK CLIK CLIK

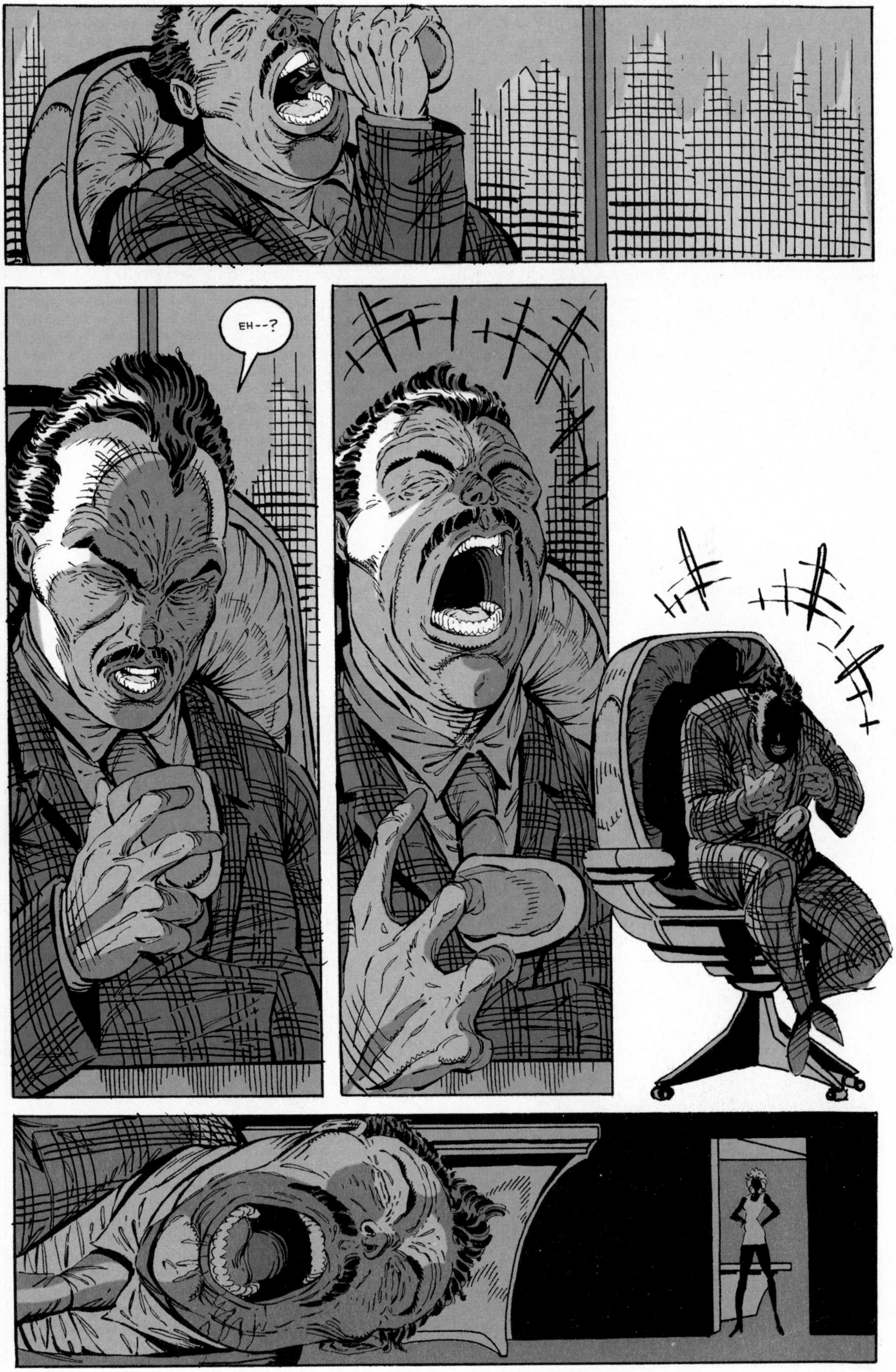
EH--?

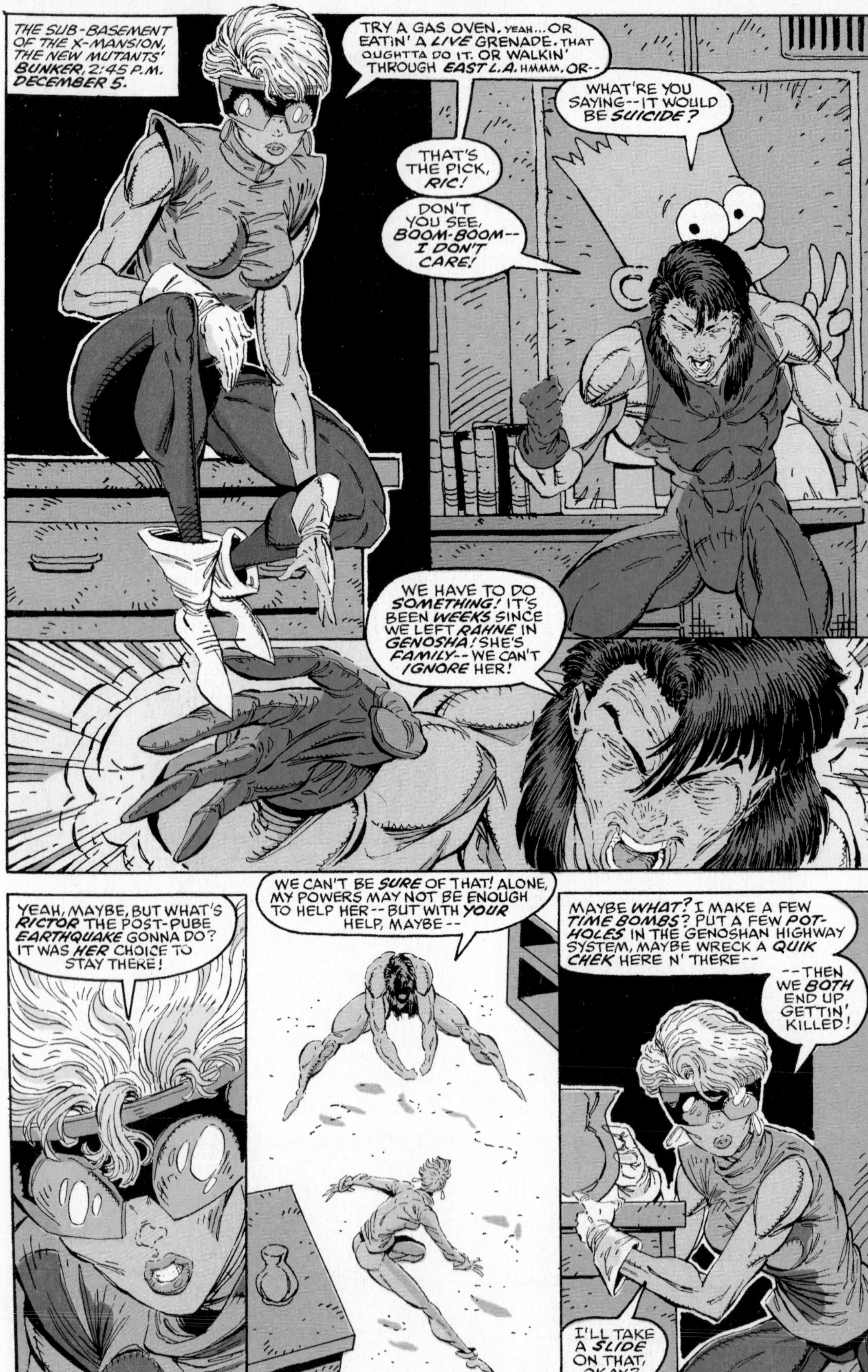
THE SUB-BASEMENT OF THE X-MANSION, THE NEW MUTANTS' BUNKER, 2:45 P.M. DECEMBER 5.
TRY A GAS OVEN. YEAH... OR EATIN' A LIVE GRENADE. THAT OUGHTTA DO IT. OR WALKIN' THROUGH EAST L.A. HMMM, OR--
WHAT'RE YOU SAYING--IT WOULD BE SUICIDE?
THAT'S THE PICK, RIC!
DON'T YOU SEE, BOOM-BOOM-- I DON'T CARE!
WE HAVE TO DO SOMETHING! IT'S BEEN WEEKS SINCE WE LEFT RAHNE IN GENOSHA! SHE'S FAMILY-- WE CAN'T IGNORE HER!
YEAH, MAYBE, BUT WHAT'S RICTOR THE POST-PUBE EARTHQUAKE GONNA DO? IT WAS HER CHOICE TO STAY THERE!
WE CAN'T BE SURE OF THAT! ALONE, MY POWERS MAY NOT BE ENOUGH TO HELP HER--BUT WITH YOUR HELP, MAYBE--
MAYBE WHAT? I MAKE A FEW TIME BOMBS? PUT A FEW POT-HOLES IN THE GENOSHAN HIGHWAY SYSTEM, MAYBE WRECK A QUIK CHEK HERE N' THERE--
--THEN WE BOTH END UP GETTIN' KILLED!
I'LL TAKE A SLIDE ON THAT, OKAY?

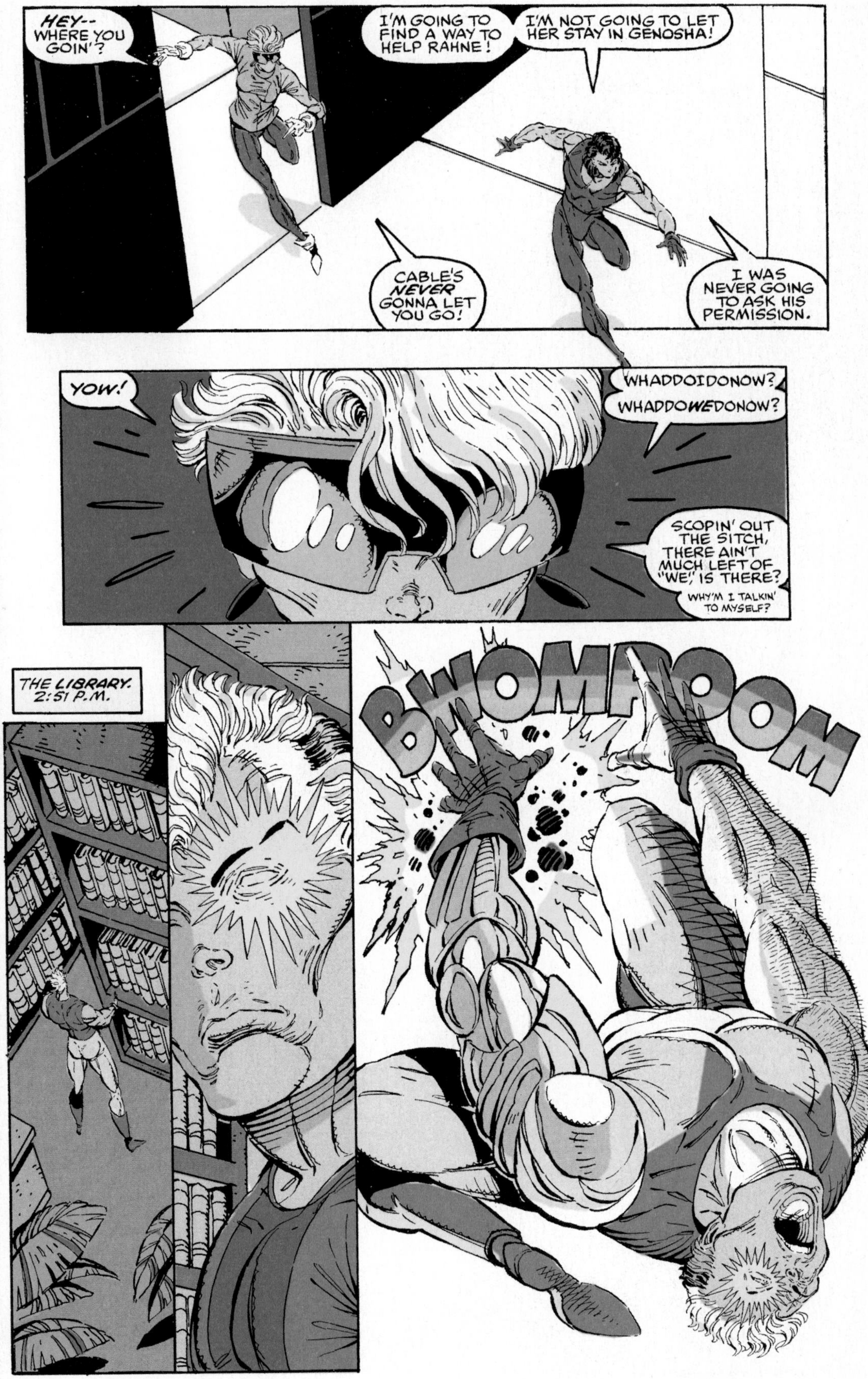

HEY-- WHERE YOU GOIN'?
I'M GOING TO FIND A WAY TO HELP RAHNE!
I'M NOT GOING TO LET HER STAY IN GENOSHA!
CABLE'S NEVER GONNA LET YOU GO!
I WAS NEVER GOING TO ASK HIS PERMISSION.
YOW!
WHADDOIDONOW?
WHADDOWEDONOW?
SCOPIN' OUT THE SITCH, THERE AIN'T MUCH LEFT OF "WE," IS THERE?
WHY'M I TALKIN' TO MYSELF?
THE LIBRARY. 2:51 P.M.
BWOMPOOM

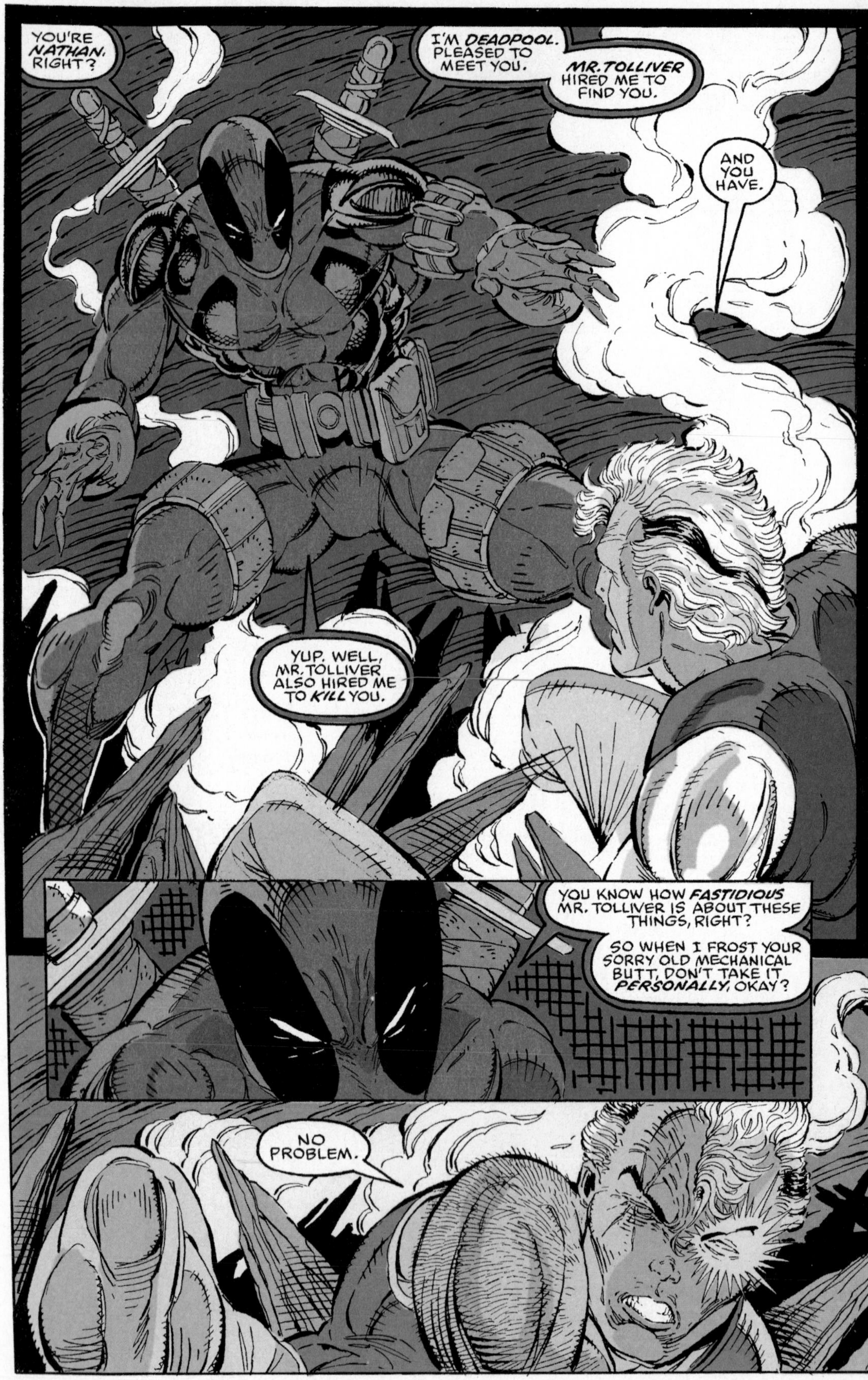
YOU'RE NATHAN, RIGHT?
I'M DEADPOOL. PLEASED TO MEET YOU.
MR. TOLLIVER HIRED ME TO FIND YOU.
AND YOU HAVE.
YUP. WELL, MR. TOLLIVER ALSO HIRED ME TO KILL YOU.
YOU KNOW HOW FASTIDIOUS MR. TOLLIVER IS ABOUT THESE THINGS, RIGHT?
SO WHEN I FROST YOUR SORRY OLD MECHANICAL BUTT, DON'T TAKE IT PERSONALLY, OKAY?
NO PROBLEM.

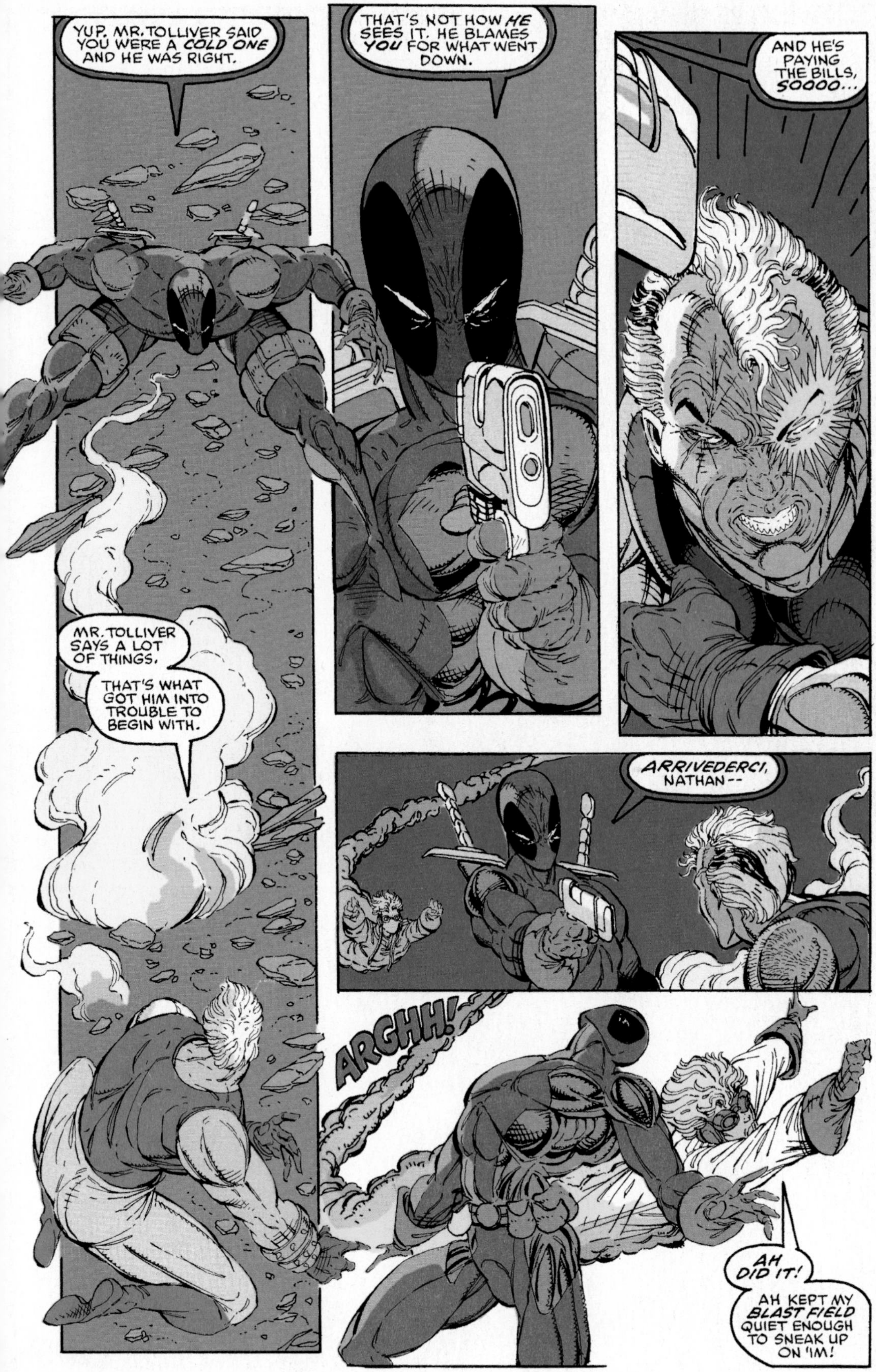
YUP, MR. TOLLIVER SAID YOU WERE A COLD ONE AND HE WAS RIGHT.
MR. TOLLIVER SAYS A LOT OF THINGS.
THAT'S WHAT GOT HIM INTO TROUBLE TO BEGIN WITH.
THAT'S NOT HOW HE SEES IT. HE BLAMES YOU FOR WHAT WENT DOWN.
AND HE'S PAYING THE BILLS, SOOOO...
ARRIVEDERCI, NATHAN--
ARGHH!
AH DID IT!
AH KEPT MY BLAST FIELD QUIET ENOUGH TO SNEAK UP ON 'IM!

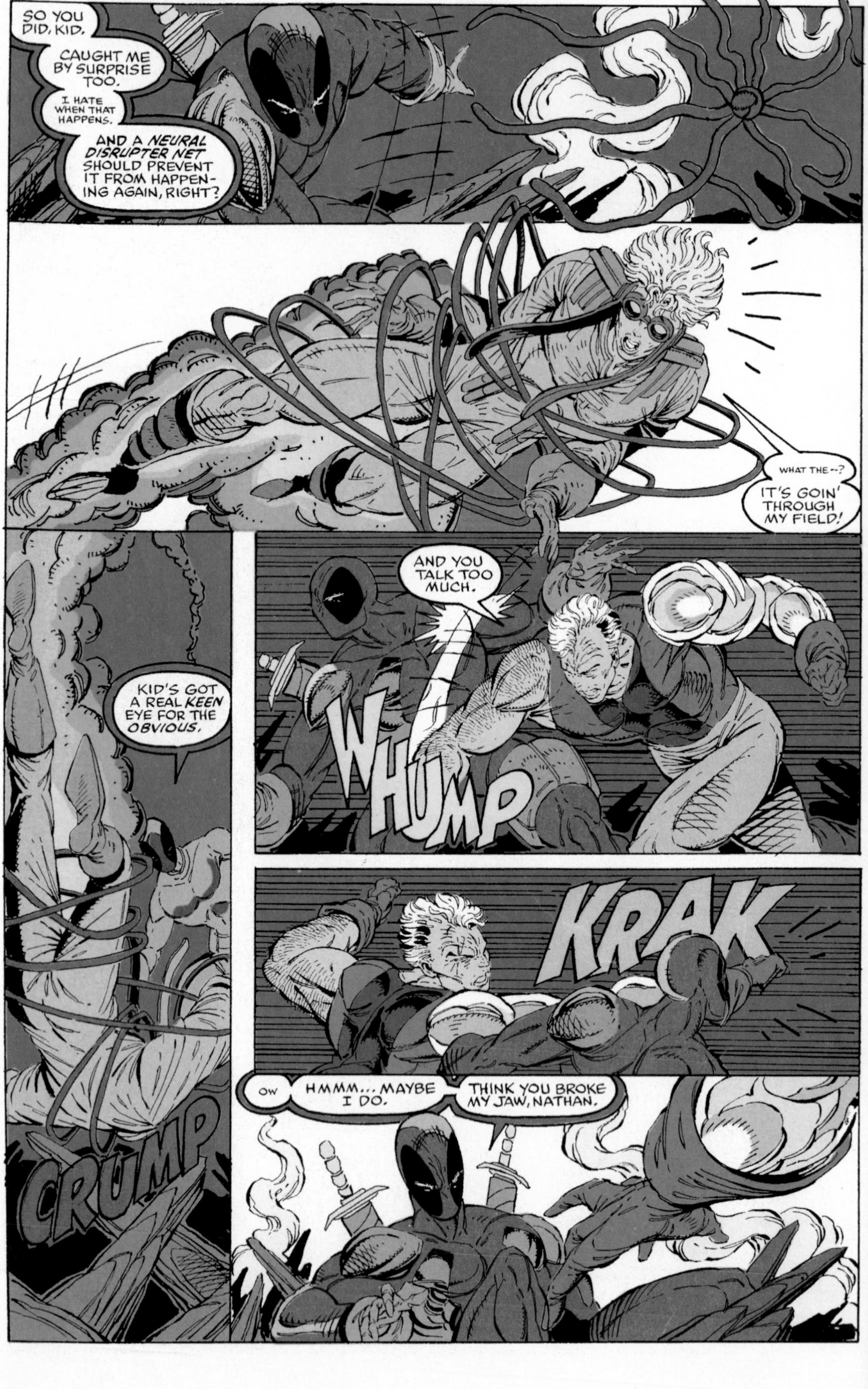
SO YOU DID, KID.
CAUGHT ME BY SURPRISE TOO.
I HATE WHEN THAT HAPPENS.
AND A NEURAL DISRUPTER NET SHOULD PREVENT IT FROM HAPPENING AGAIN, RIGHT?
WHAT THE--?
IT'S GOIN' THROUGH MY FIELD!
KID'S GOT A REAL KEEN EYE FOR THE OBVIOUS.
AND YOU TALK TOO MUCH.
WHUMP
KRAK
CRUMP
OW
HMMM... MAYBE I DO.
THINK YOU BROKE MY JAW, NATHAN.

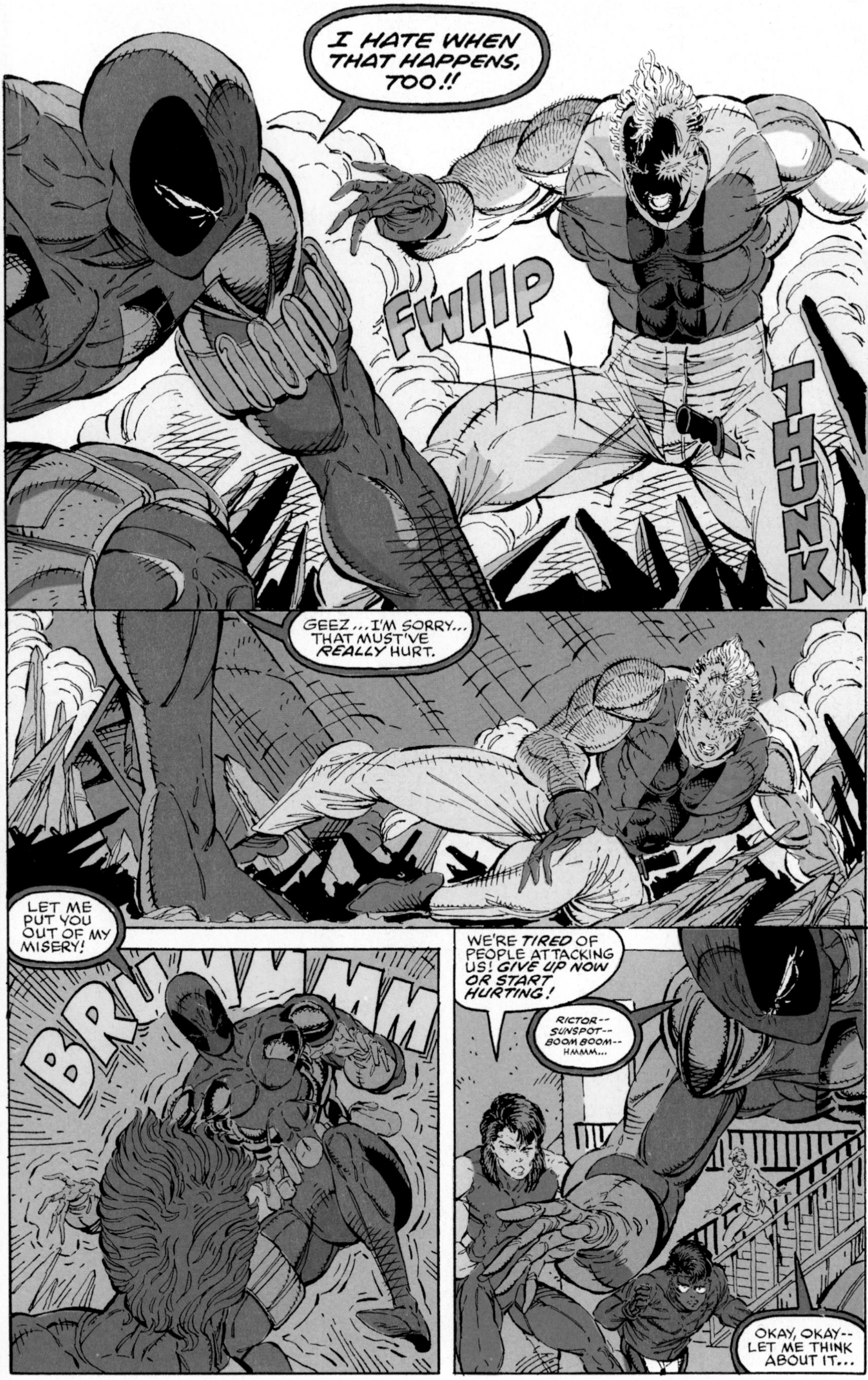
I HATE WHEN THAT HAPPENS, TOO!!
FWIIP
THUNK
GEEZ... I'M SORRY... THAT MUST'VE REALLY HURT.
LET ME PUT YOU OUT OF MY MISERY!
BRUMMMM
WE'RE TIRED OF PEOPLE ATTACKING US! GIVE UP NOW OR START HURTING!
RICTOR-- SUNSPOT-- BOOM BOOM-- HMMMM...
OKAY, OKAY-- LET ME THINK ABOUT IT...

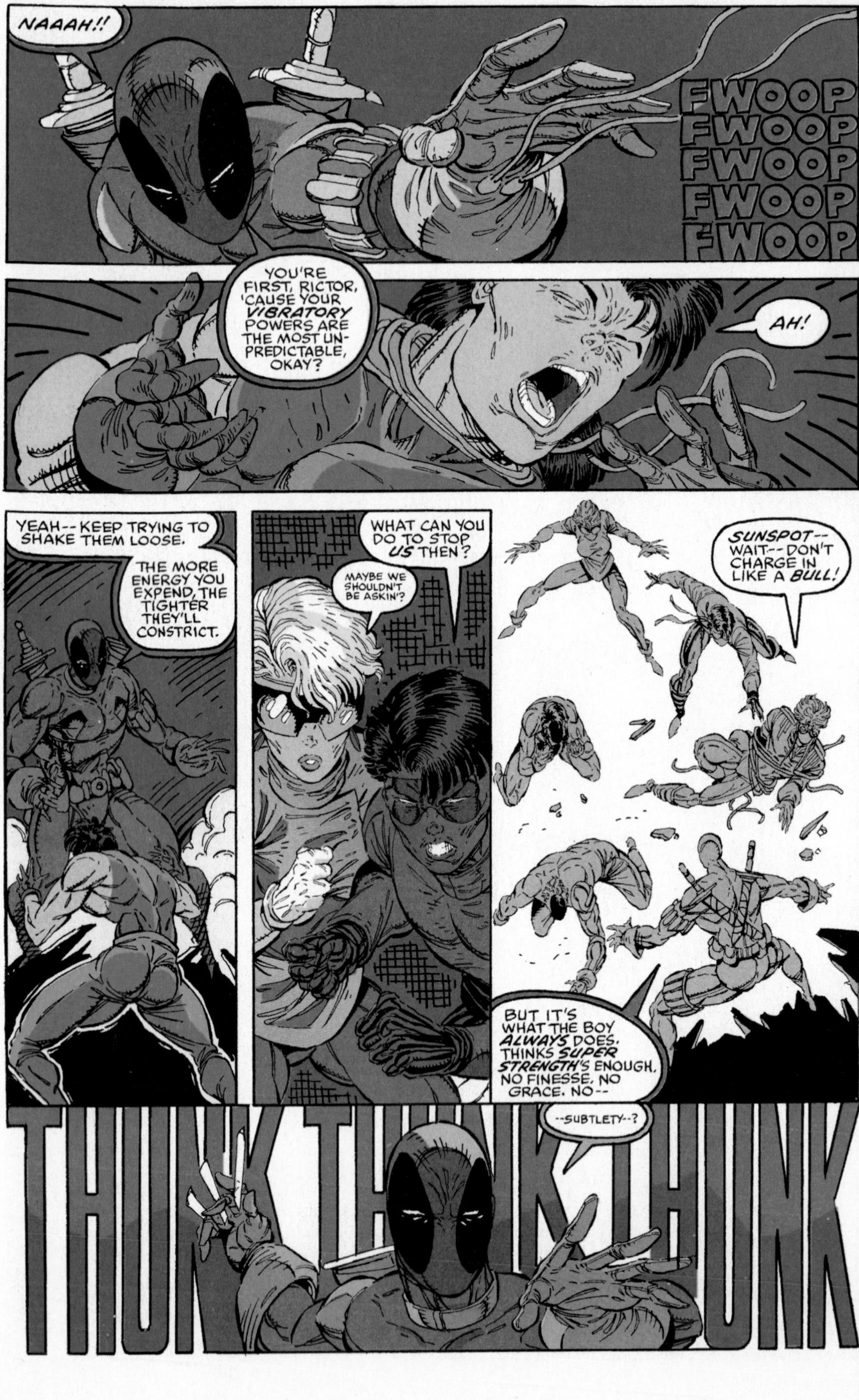
NAAAH!!
FWOOP FWOOP FWOOP FWOOP FWOOP
YOU'RE FIRST, RICTOR, 'CAUSE YOUR VIBRATORY POWERS ARE THE MOST UN-PREDICTABLE, OKAY?
AH!
YEAH-- KEEP TRYING TO SHAKE THEM LOOSE.
THE MORE ENERGY YOU EXPEND, THE TIGHTER THEY'LL CONSTRICT.
WHAT CAN YOU DO TO STOP US THEN?
MAYBE WE SHOULDN'T BE ASKIN'?
SUNSPOT-- WAIT-- DON'T CHARGE IN LIKE A BULL!
BUT IT'S WHAT THE BOY ALWAYS DOES. THINKS SUPER STRENGTH'S ENOUGH. NO FINESSE. NO GRACE. NO--
--SUBTLETY--?

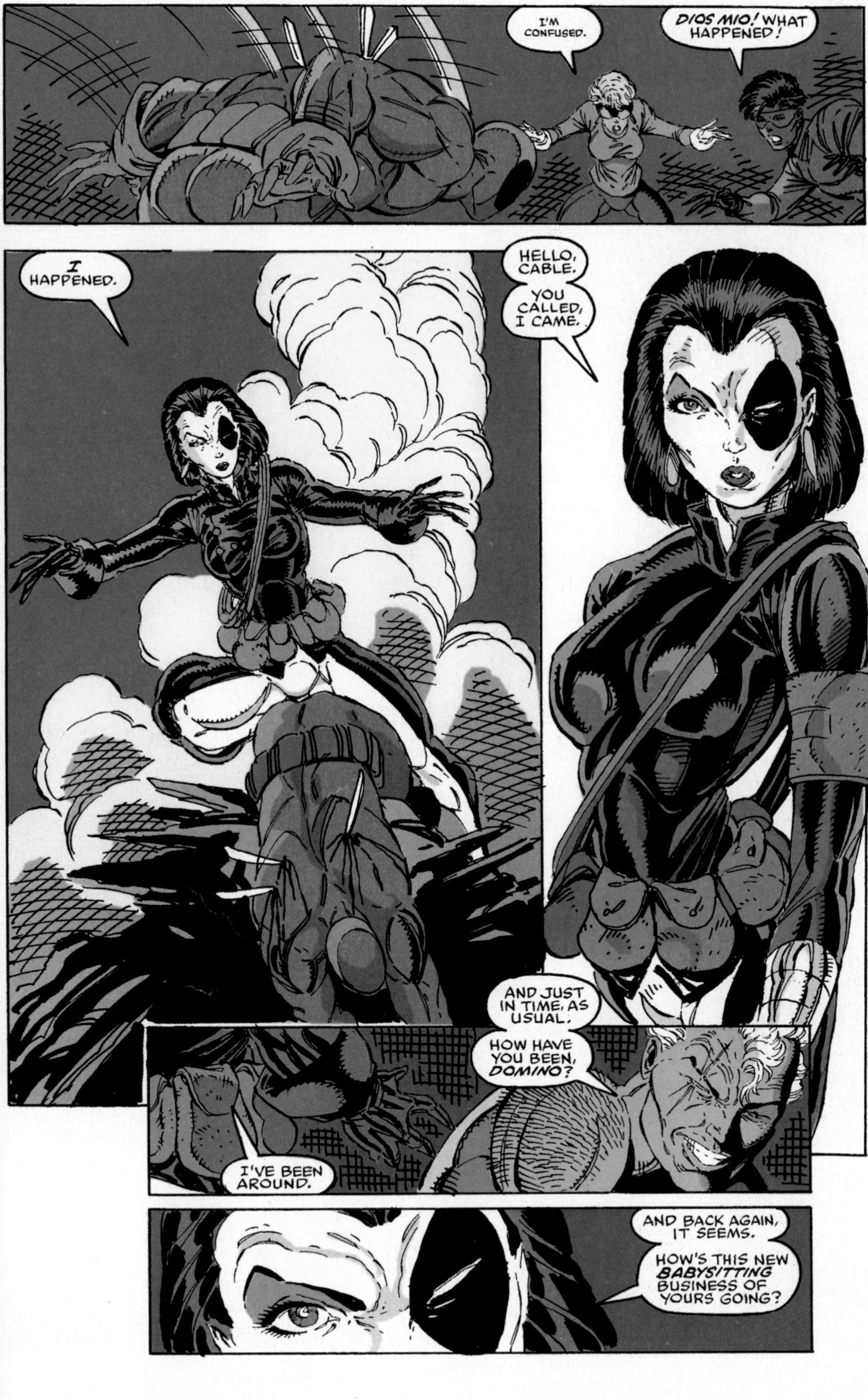
I'M CONFUSED.
DIOS MIO! WHAT HAPPENED!
I HAPPENED.
HELLO, CABLE.
YOU CALLED, I CAME.
AND JUST IN TIME, AS USUAL.
HOW HAVE YOU BEEN, DOMINO?
I'VE BEEN AROUND.
AND BACK AGAIN, IT SEEMS.
HOW'S THIS NEW BABYSITTING BUSINESS OF YOURS GOING?

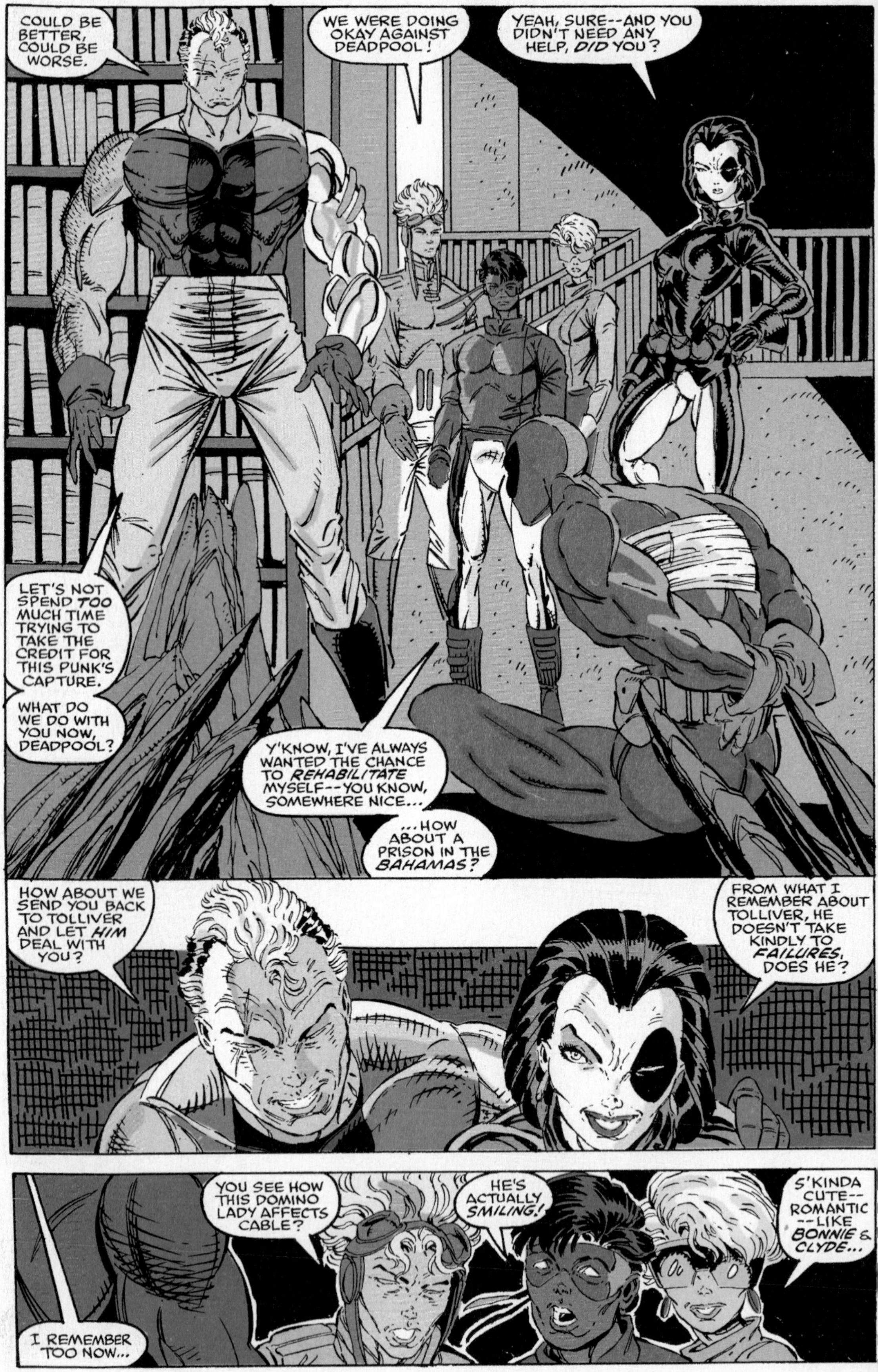
COULD BE BETTER, COULD BE WORSE.
WE WERE DOING OKAY AGAINST DEADPOOL!
YEAH, SURE--AND YOU DIDN'T NEED ANY HELP, DID YOU?
LET'S NOT SPEND TOO MUCH TIME TRYING TO TAKE THE CREDIT FOR THIS PUNK'S CAPTURE.
WHAT DO WE DO WITH YOU NOW, DEADPOOL?
Y'KNOW, I'VE ALWAYS WANTED THE CHANCE TO REHABILITATE MYSELF--YOU KNOW, SOMEWHERE NICE...
...HOW ABOUT A PRISON IN THE BAHAMAS?
HOW ABOUT WE SEND YOU BACK TO TOLLIVER AND LET HIM DEAL WITH YOU?
FROM WHAT I REMEMBER ABOUT TOLLIVER, HE DOESN'T TAKE KINDLY TO FAILURES, DOES HE?
YOU SEE HOW THIS DOMINO LADY AFFECTS CABLE?
HE'S ACTUALLY SMILING!
S'KINDA CUTE-- ROMANTIC --LIKE BONNIE & CLYDE...
I REMEMBER TOO NOW...

11:45 P.M.

BY THE WAY, WHAT'D YOU DO WITH THE CHUMP?

DEADPOOL? OH... BOUND, GAGGED AND... MAILED... BACK TO TOLLIVER.

MAILED?

FEDERAL EXPRESS.

LET ME RUN THROUGH THE LIST OF WHAT LITTLE IS *AVAILABLE* FOR US...

RUSTY COLLINS. ALIGNED WITH THE *MUTANT LIBERATION FRONT.* TOO DIFFICULT TO LIBERATE RIGHT NOW.

RUSTY COLLINS
CODENAME: NONE
MUTATION: PYROKINETIC
LOCATION: UNKNOWN

WHO'S THAT ONE?

SKIDS BLEVINS. ALSO WITH THE MLF. PRETTY USELESS POWER IN BATTLE.

SKIDS BLEVINS
CODENAME: NONE
MUTATION: PROJECTS FRICTIONLESS FORCE FIELD
LOCATION: UNKNOWN

XI'AN COY MANH. KARMA. NOT A TEAM PLAYER. SHE HAS HER OWN AGENDA ANYWAY.

XIAN COY MANH
CODENAME: KARMA

THAT'S A SHAME. TELEPATHS COME IN HANDY.

THE NEXT ONE'S *MAGMA,* RIGHT?

YUP. *AMARA AQUILLA.* SHE'S HOLED UP IN *NOVA ROMA,* THE JUNGLE CIVILIZATION. POWERFUL, BUT SHE'S NOT WORTH THE EFFORT.

MU~~~~~~~C
LOCATION: BRAZIL

LAST UP IS *DANIELLE MOONSTAR, MIRAGE.* SHE BECAME A *VALKYRIE* AND STAYED IN *ASGARD.*

EXCUSE ME?

FORGET ABOUT IT. FORGET ABOUT HER.

DA~~~~~STAR
CO~~~~~AGE
MUT~~~~~ROJECTIVE TELEPATH
LOCATION: EXTRA-DIMENSIONAL

NOT MUCH TO WORK WITH.

I KNOW. I'VE ALREADY TAKEN STEPS TO REMEDY THAT...

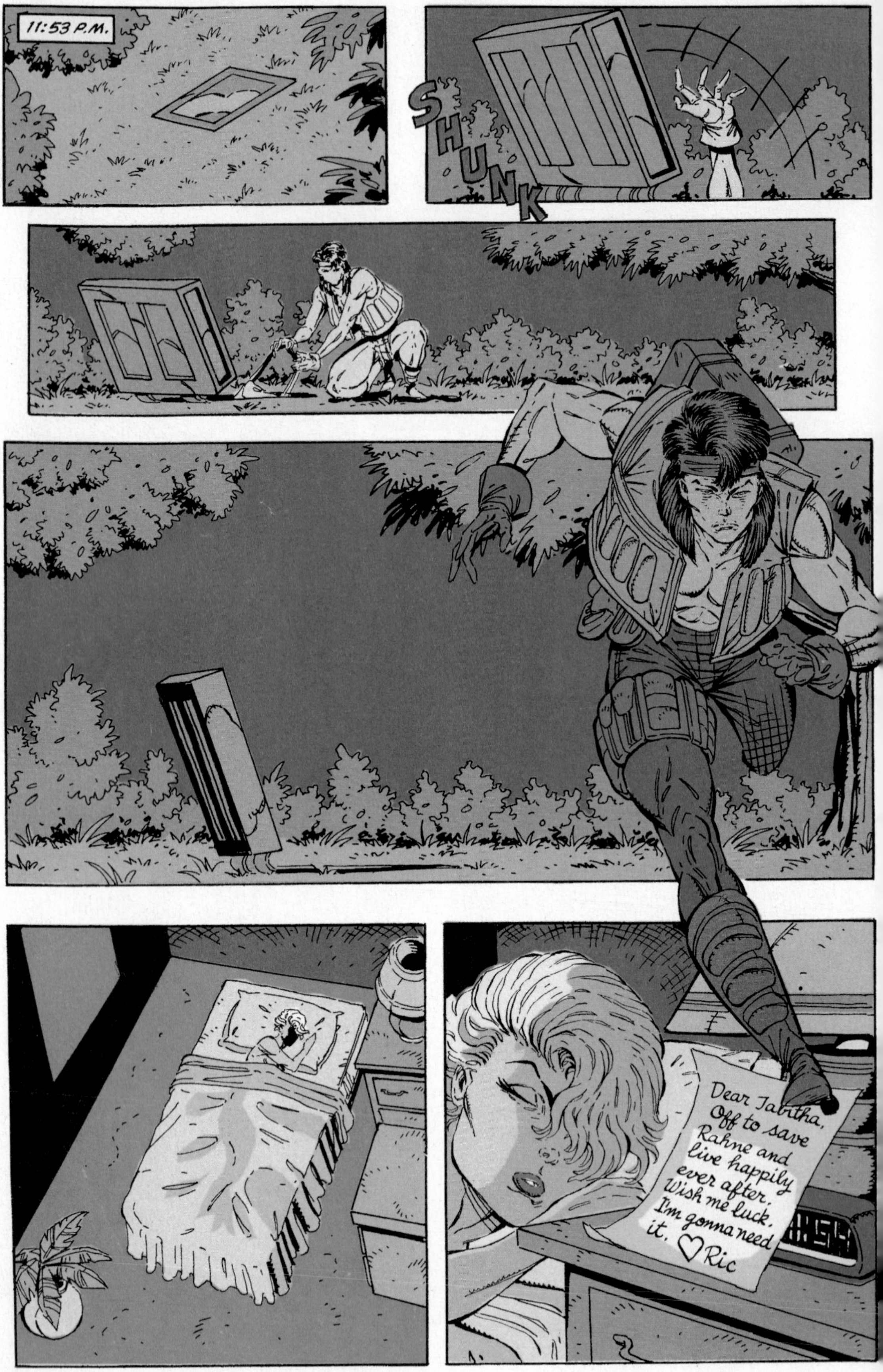
11:53 P.M.
SHUNK
Dear Tabitha,
Off to save
Rahne and
live happily
ever after.
Wish me luck.
I'm gonna need
it. ♡Ric

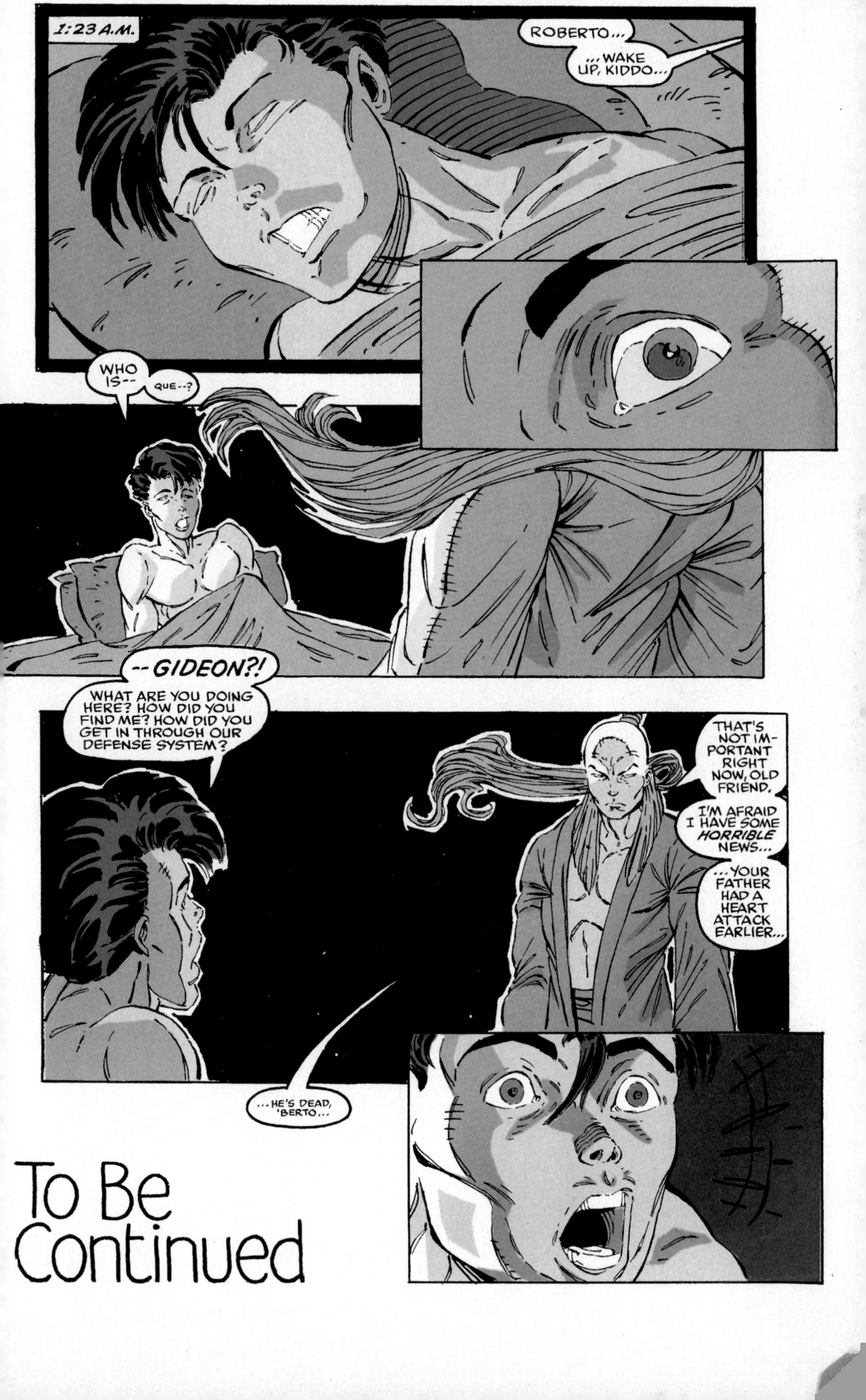

1:23 A.M.
ROBERTO...
...WAKE UP, KIDDO...
WHO IS--
QUE--?
--GIDEON?!
WHAT ARE YOU DOING HERE? HOW DID YOU FIND ME? HOW DID YOU GET IN THROUGH OUR DEFENSE SYSTEM?
THAT'S NOT IMPORTANT RIGHT NOW, OLD FRIEND.
I'M AFRAID I HAVE SOME HORRIBLE NEWS...
...YOUR FATHER HAD A HEART ATTACK EARLIER...
...HE'S DEAD, 'BERTO...

To Be Continued

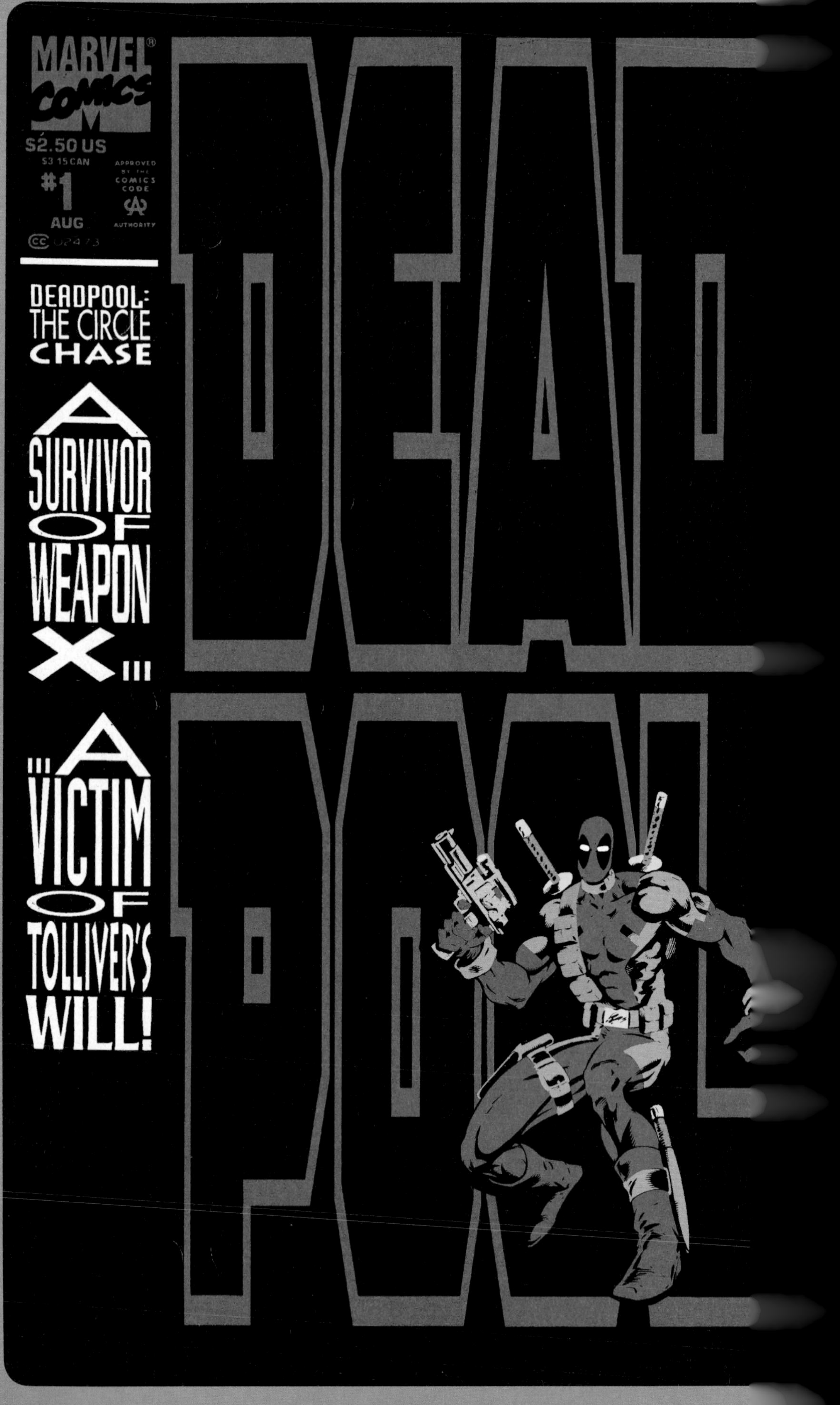

MARVEL COMICS
$2.50 US
$3.15 CAN
#1
AUG
APPROVED BY THE COMICS CODE AUTHORITY
DEADPOOL: THE CIRCLE CHASE
A SURVIVOR OF WEAPON X...
...A VICTIM OF TOLLIVER'S WILL!
DEAD POOL

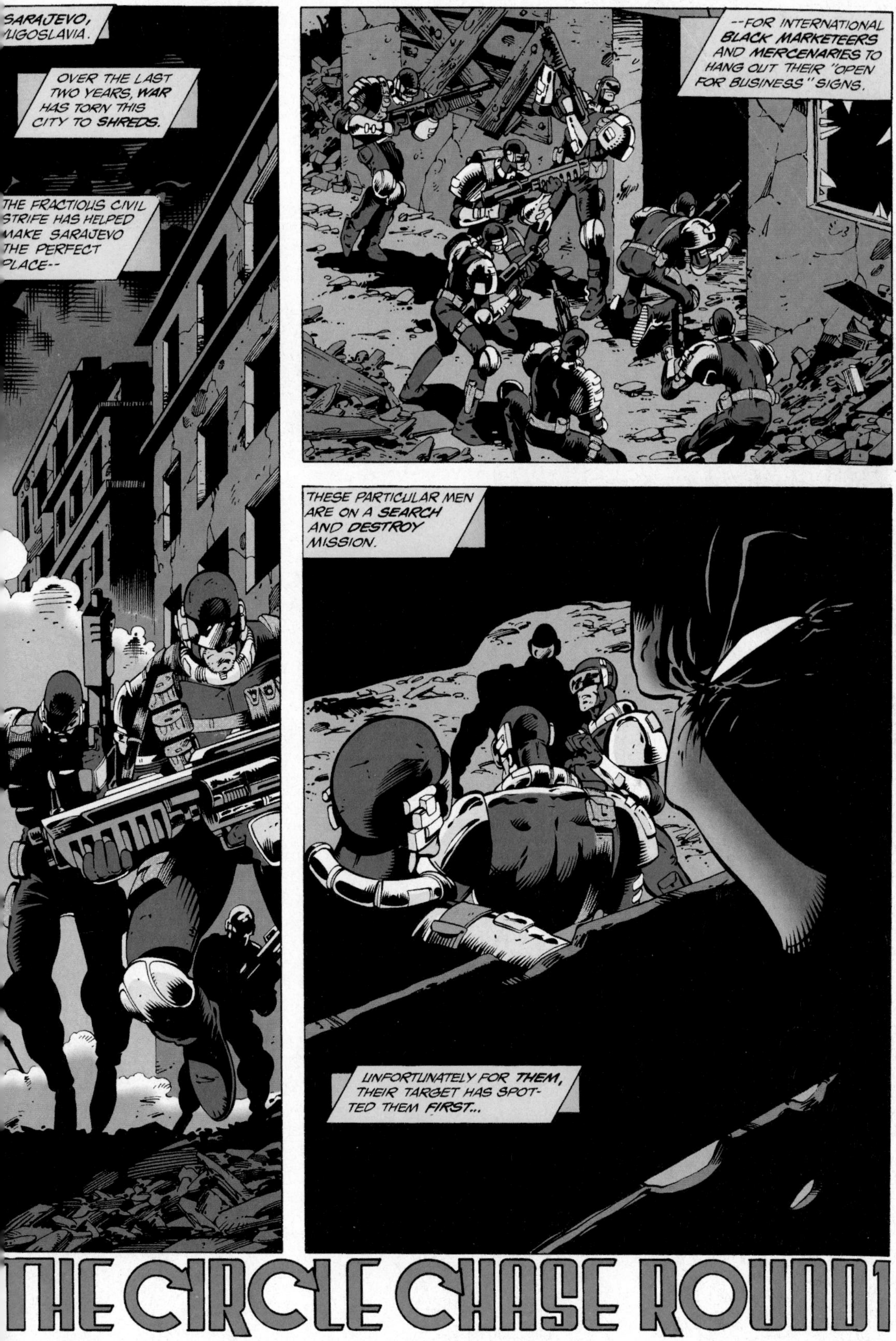
SARAJEVO, YUGOSLAVIA.
OVER THE LAST TWO YEARS, WAR HAS TORN THIS CITY TO SHREDS.
THE FRACTIOUS CIVIL STRIFE HAS HELPED MAKE SARAJEVO THE PERFECT PLACE--
--FOR INTERNATIONAL BLACK MARKETEERS AND MERCENARIES TO HANG OUT THEIR "OPEN FOR BUSINESS" SIGNS.
THESE PARTICULAR MEN ARE ON A SEARCH AND DESTROY MISSION.
UNFORTUNATELY FOR THEM, THEIR TARGET HAS SPOTTED THEM FIRST...
THE CIRCLE CHASE ROUND 1

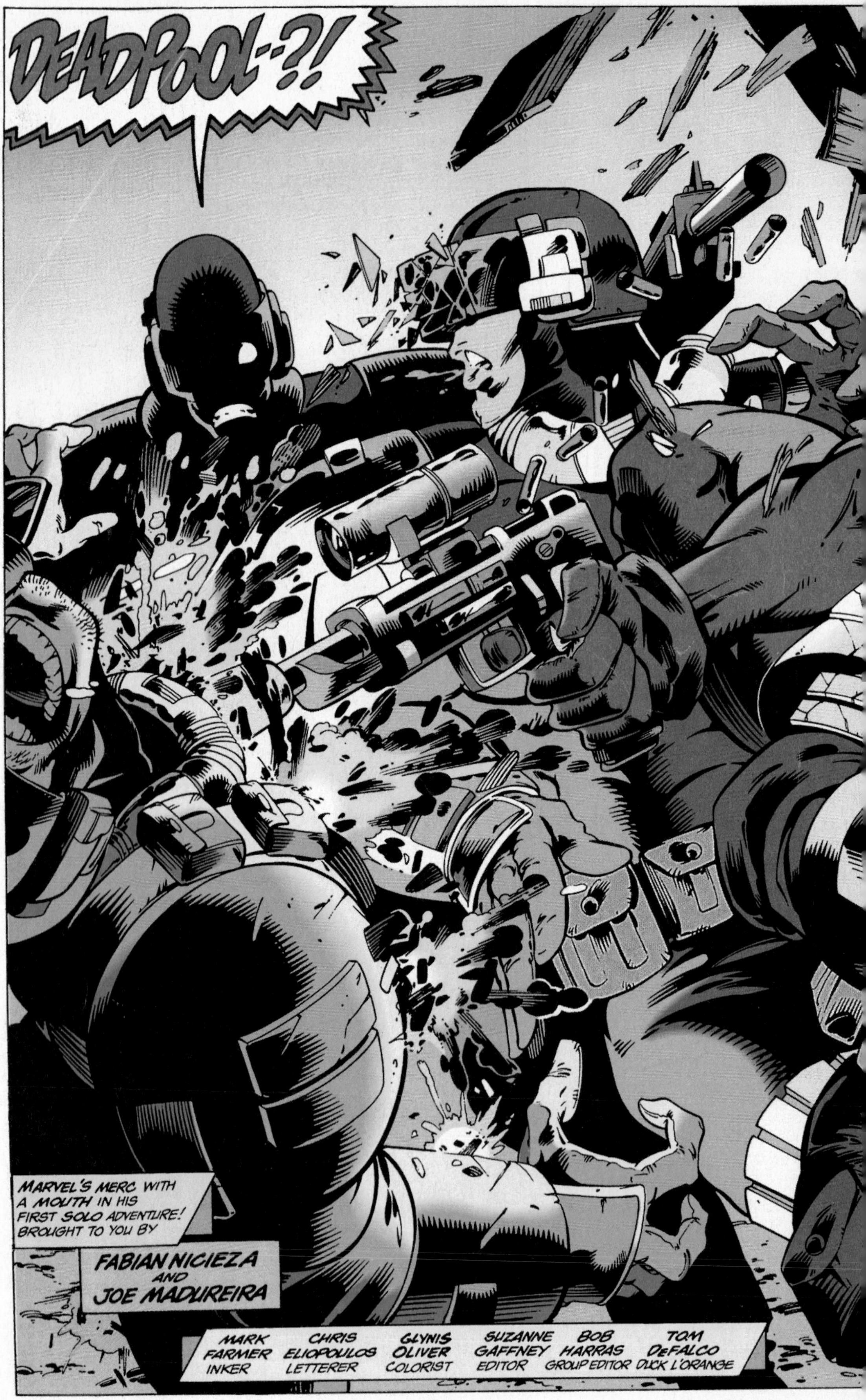
DEADPOOL--?!
MARVEL'S MERC WITH A MOUTH IN HIS FIRST SOLO ADVENTURE! BROUGHT TO YOU BY
FABIAN NICIEZA AND JOE MADUREIRA
MARK FARMER INKER
CHRIS ELIOPOULOS LETTERER
GLYNIS OLIVER COLORIST
SUZANNE GAFFNEY EDITOR
BOB HARRAS GROUP EDITOR
TOM DeFALCO DUCK L'ORANGE

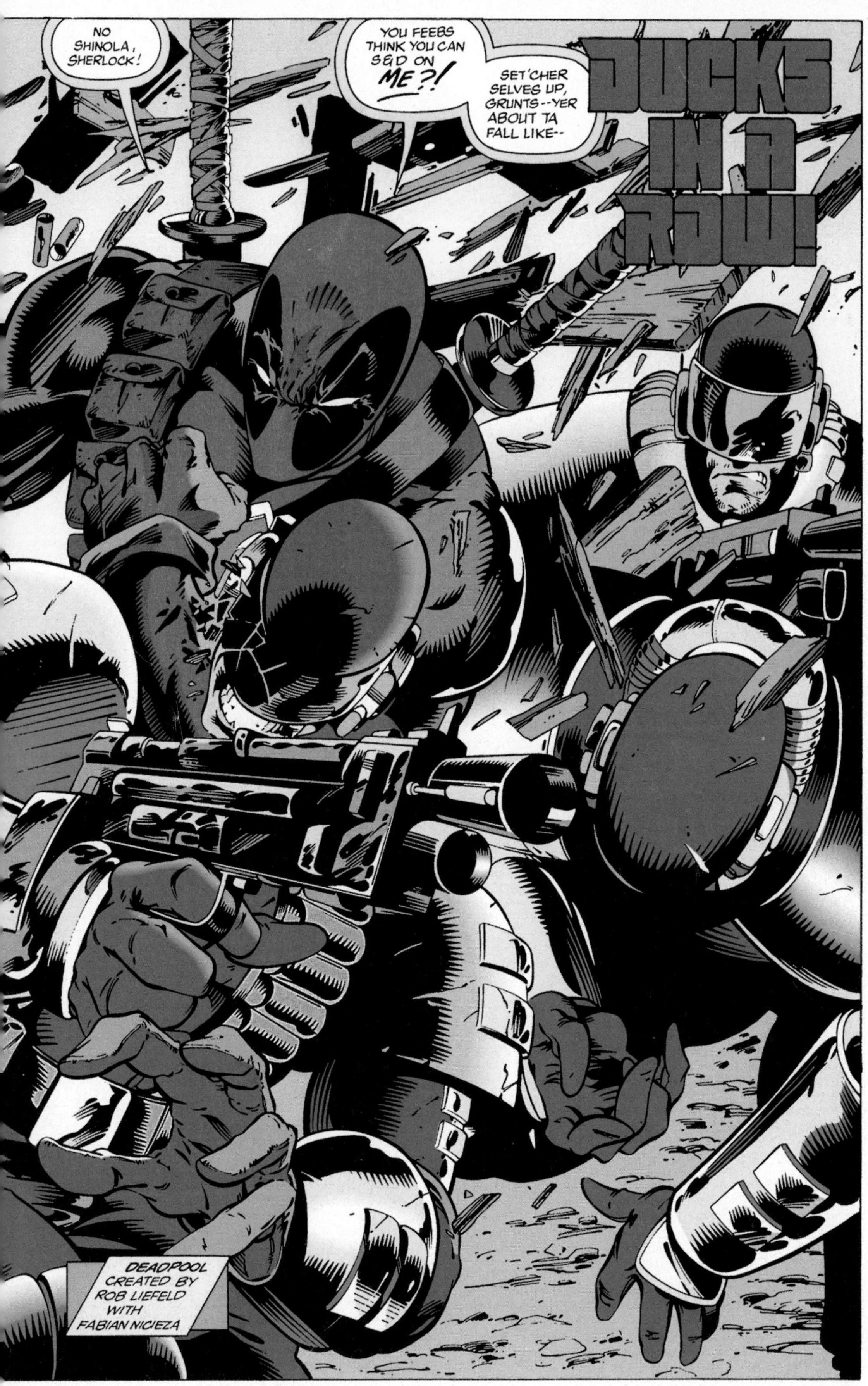
DUCKS IN A ROW!
NO SHINOLA, SHERLOCK!
YOU FEEBS THINK YOU CAN S&D ON ME?!
SET 'CHER SELVES UP, GRUNTS--YER ABOUT TA FALL LIKE--
DEADPOOL CREATED BY ROB LIEFELD WITH FABIAN NICIEZA

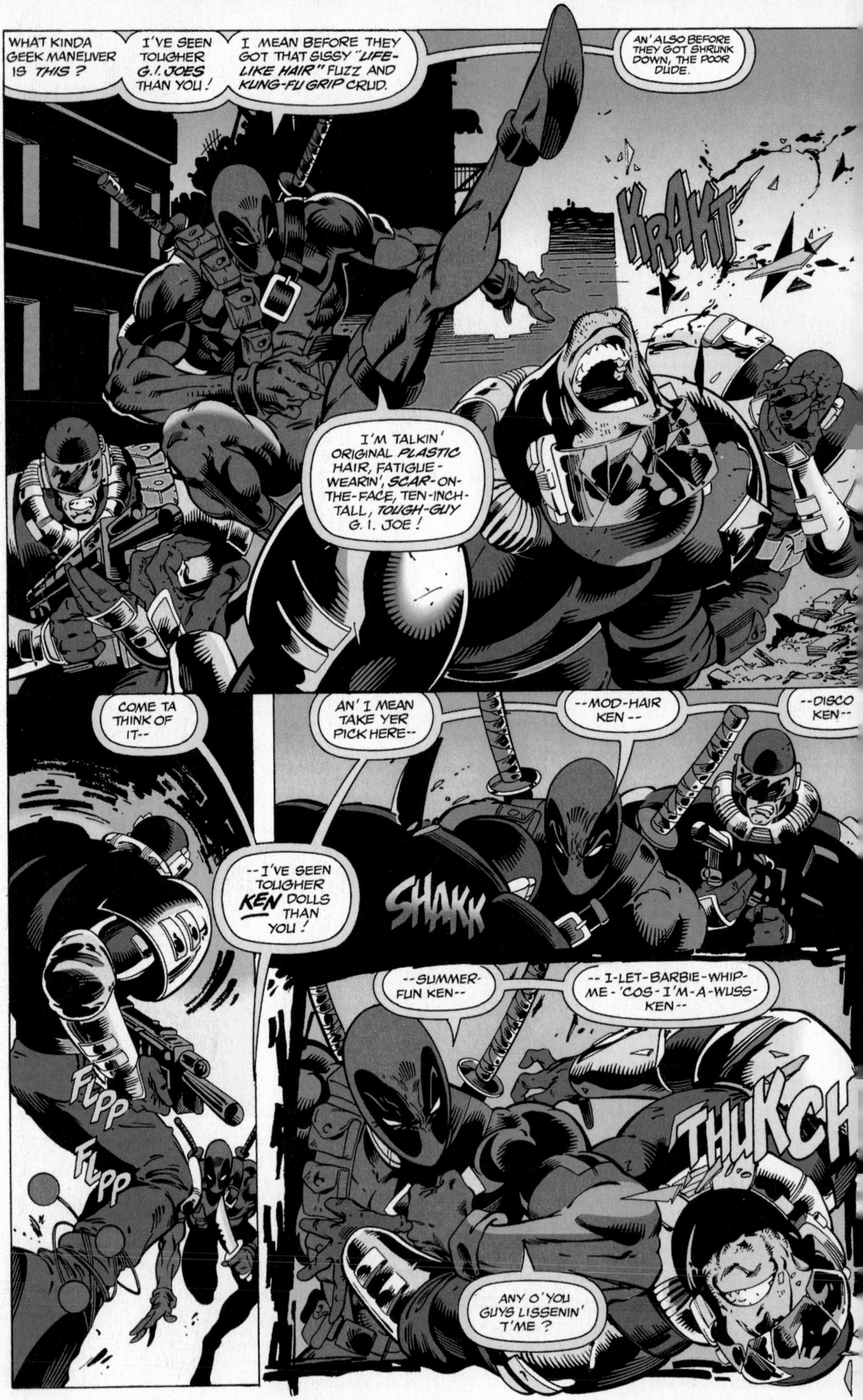
WHAT KINDA GEEK MANEUVER IS THIS?
I'VE SEEN TOUGHER G.I. JOES THAN YOU!
I MEAN BEFORE THEY GOT THAT SISSY "LIFE-LIKE HAIR" FUZZ AND KUNG-FU GRIP CRUD.
AN' ALSO BEFORE THEY GOT SHRUNK DOWN, THE POOR DUDE.
KRAKT
I'M TALKIN' ORIGINAL PLASTIC HAIR, FATIGUE-WEARIN', SCAR-ON-THE-FACE, TEN-INCH-TALL, TOUGH-GUY G.I. JOE!
COME TA THINK OF IT--
--I'VE SEEN TOUGHER KEN DOLLS THAN YOU!
FLPP
FLPP
AN' I MEAN TAKE YER PICK HERE--
--MOD-HAIR KEN--
--DISCO KEN--
SHAKK
--SUMMER-FUN KEN--
--I-LET-BARBIE-WHIP-ME-'COS-I'M-A-WUSS-KEN--
THUKCH
ANY O' YOU GUYS LISSENIN' T'ME?

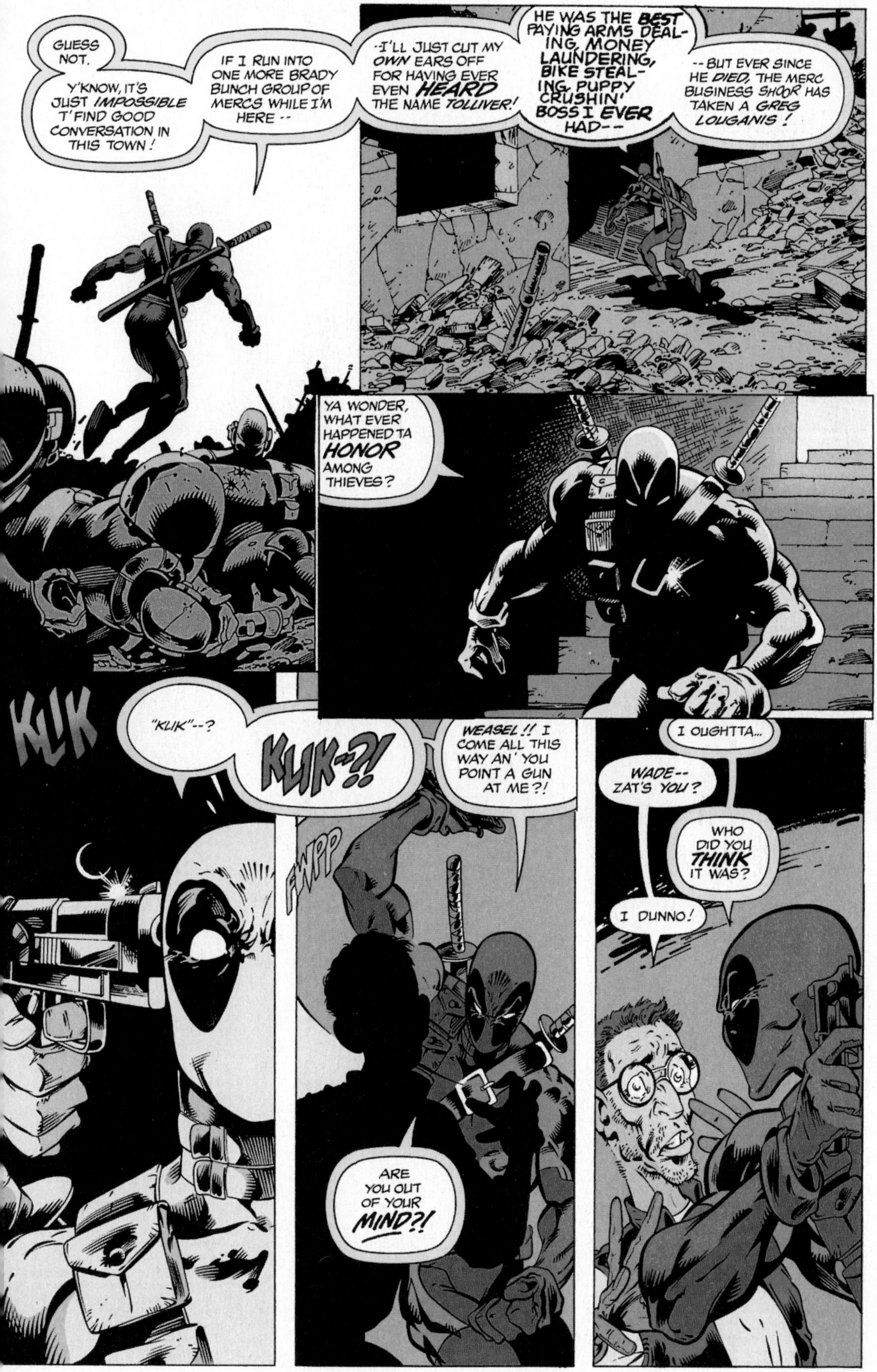

GUESS NOT.
Y'KNOW, IT'S JUST IMPOSSIBLE T'FIND GOOD CONVERSATION IN THIS TOWN!
IF I RUN INTO ONE MORE BRADY BUNCH GROUP OF MERCS WHILE I'M HERE --
-I'LL JUST CUT MY OWN EARS OFF FOR HAVING EVER EVEN HEARD THE NAME TOLLIVER!
HE WAS THE BEST PAYING ARMS DEALING, MONEY LAUNDERING, BIKE STEALING, PUPPY CRUSHIN' BOSS I EVER HAD--
-- BUT EVER SINCE HE DIED, THE MERC BUSINESS SHOOR HAS TAKEN A GREG LOUGANIS!
YA WONDER, WHAT EVER HAPPENED TA HONOR AMONG THIEVES?
KLIK
"KLIK"--?
KLIK--?!
WEASEL!! I COME ALL THIS WAY AN' YOU POINT A GUN AT ME?!
FWIPP
ARE YOU OUT OF YOUR MIND?!
I OUGHTTA...
WADE-- ZAT'S YOU?
WHO DID YOU THINK IT WAS?
I DUNNO!

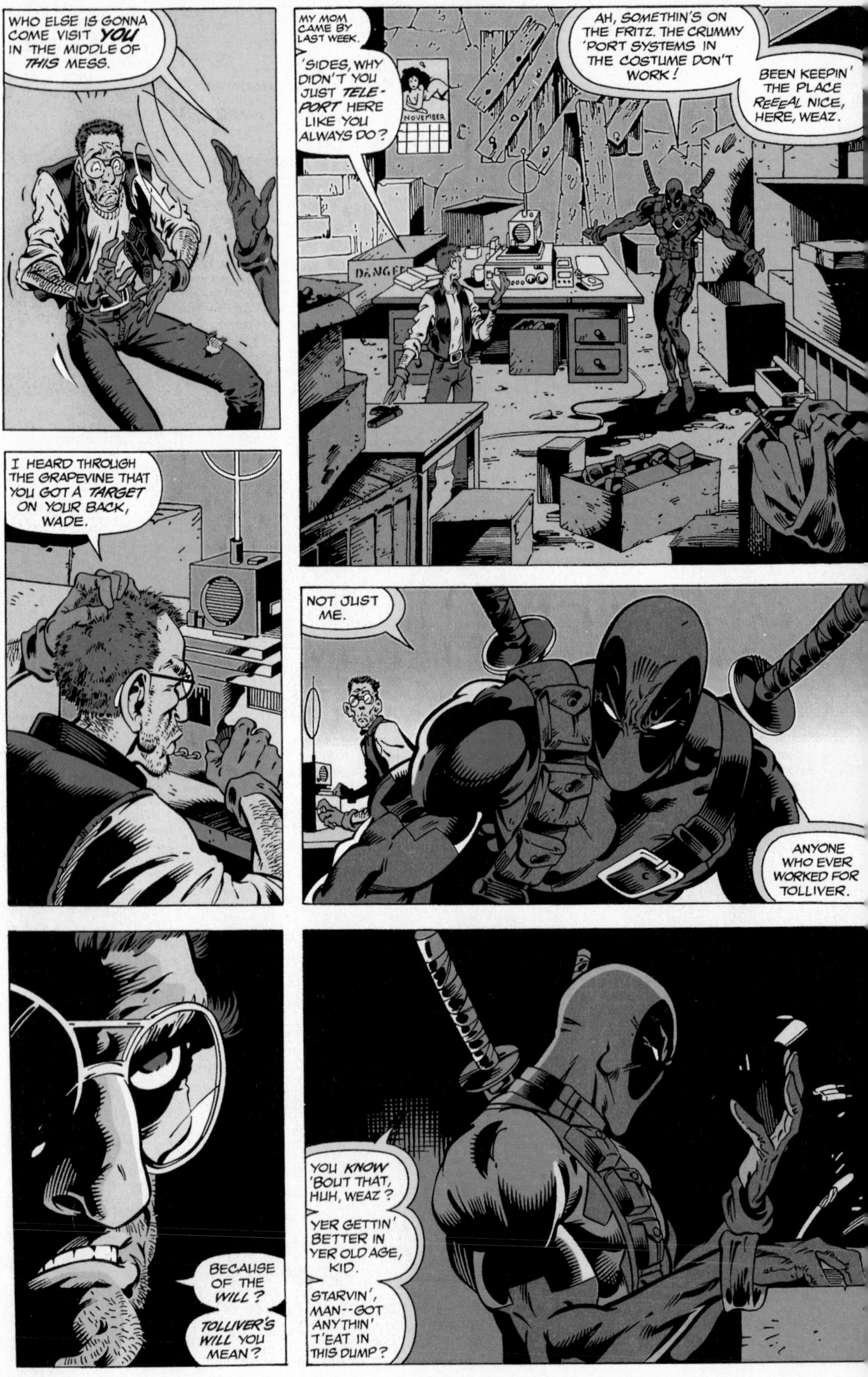
WHO ELSE IS GONNA COME VISIT YOU IN THE MIDDLE OF THIS MESS.
MY MOM CAME BY LAST WEEK.
'SIDES, WHY DIDN'T YOU JUST TELE-PORT HERE LIKE YOU ALWAYS DO?
NOVEMBER
DANGER
AH, SOMETHIN'S ON THE FRITZ. THE CRUMMY 'PORT SYSTEMS IN THE COSTUME DON'T WORK!
BEEN KEEPIN' THE PLACE REEEAL NICE, HERE, WEAZ.
I HEARD THROUGH THE GRAPEVINE THAT YOU GOT A TARGET ON YOUR BACK, WADE.
NOT JUST ME.
ANYONE WHO EVER WORKED FOR TOLLIVER.
BECAUSE OF THE WILL?
TOLLIVER'S WILL YOU MEAN?
YOU KNOW 'BOUT THAT, HUH, WEAZ?
YER GETTIN' BETTER IN YER OLD AGE, KID.
STARVIN', MAN--GOT ANYTHIN' T'EAT IN THIS DUMP?

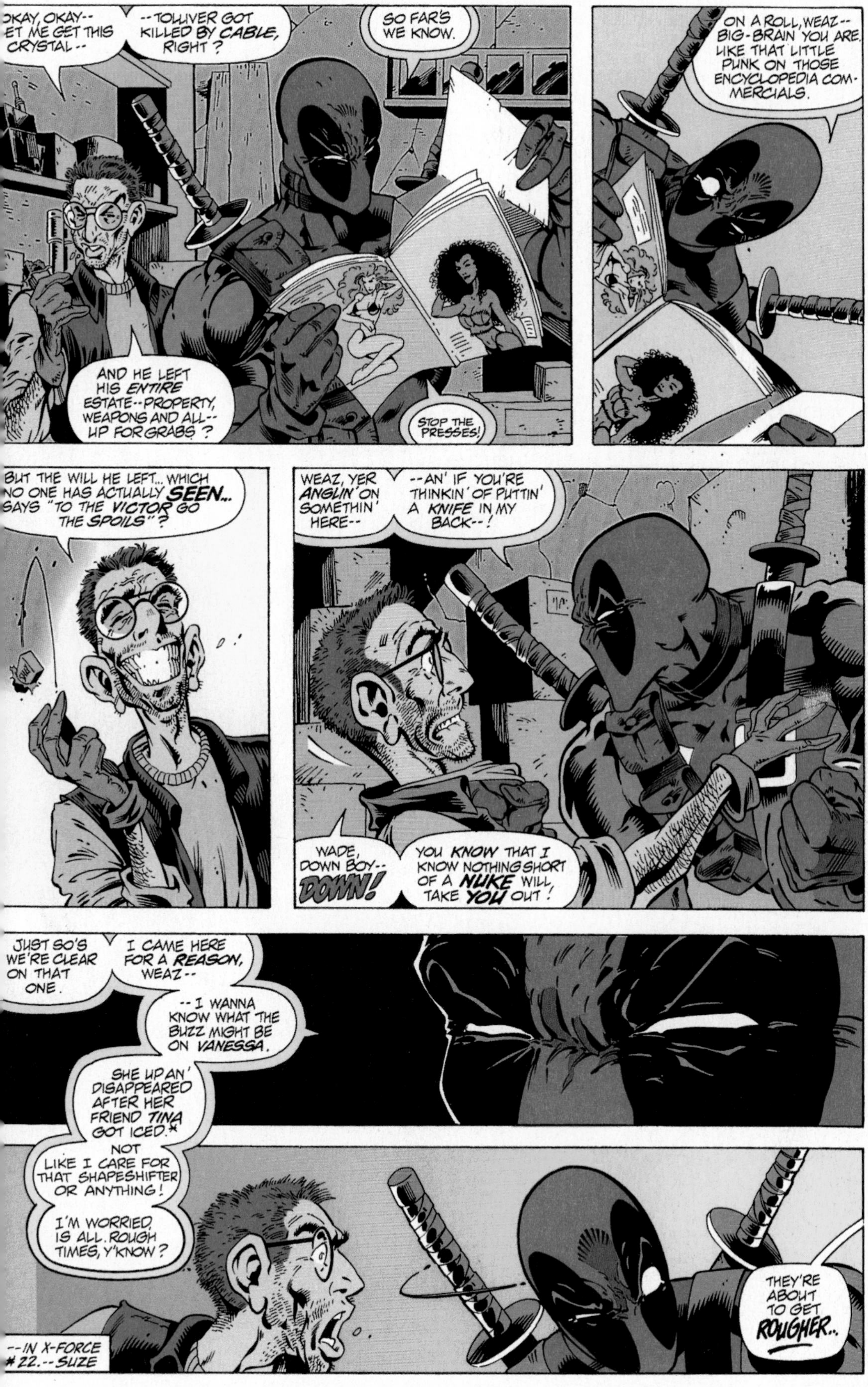

OKAY, OKAY-- ET ME GET THIS CRYSTAL--
--TOLLIVER GOT KILLED BY CABLE, RIGHT?
SO FAR'S WE KNOW.
ON A ROLL, WEAZ-- BIG-BRAIN YOU ARE. LIKE THAT LITTLE PUNK ON THOSE ENCYCLOPEDIA COM-MERCIALS.
AND HE LEFT HIS ENTIRE ESTATE--PROPERTY, WEAPONS AND ALL--UP FOR GRABS?
STOP THE PRESSES!
BUT THE WILL HE LEFT... WHICH NO ONE HAS ACTUALLY SEEN... SAYS "TO THE VICTOR GO THE SPOILS"?
WEAZ, YER ANGLIN' ON SOMETHIN' HERE--
--AN' IF YOU'RE THINKIN' OF PUTTIN' A KNIFE IN MY BACK--!
WADE, DOWN BOY-- DOWN!
YOU KNOW THAT I KNOW NOTHING SHORT OF A NUKE WILL TAKE YOU OUT!
JUST SO'S WE'RE CLEAR ON THAT ONE.
I CAME HERE FOR A REASON, WEAZ--
--I WANNA KNOW WHAT THE BUZZ MIGHT BE ON VANESSA.
SHE UP AN' DISAPPEARED AFTER HER FRIEND TINA GOT ICED.*
NOT LIKE I CARE FOR THAT SHAPESHIFTER OR ANYTHING!
I'M WORRIED, IS ALL. ROUGH TIMES, Y'KNOW?
THEY'RE ABOUT TO GET ROUGHER..
*--IN X-FORCE #22.--SUZE

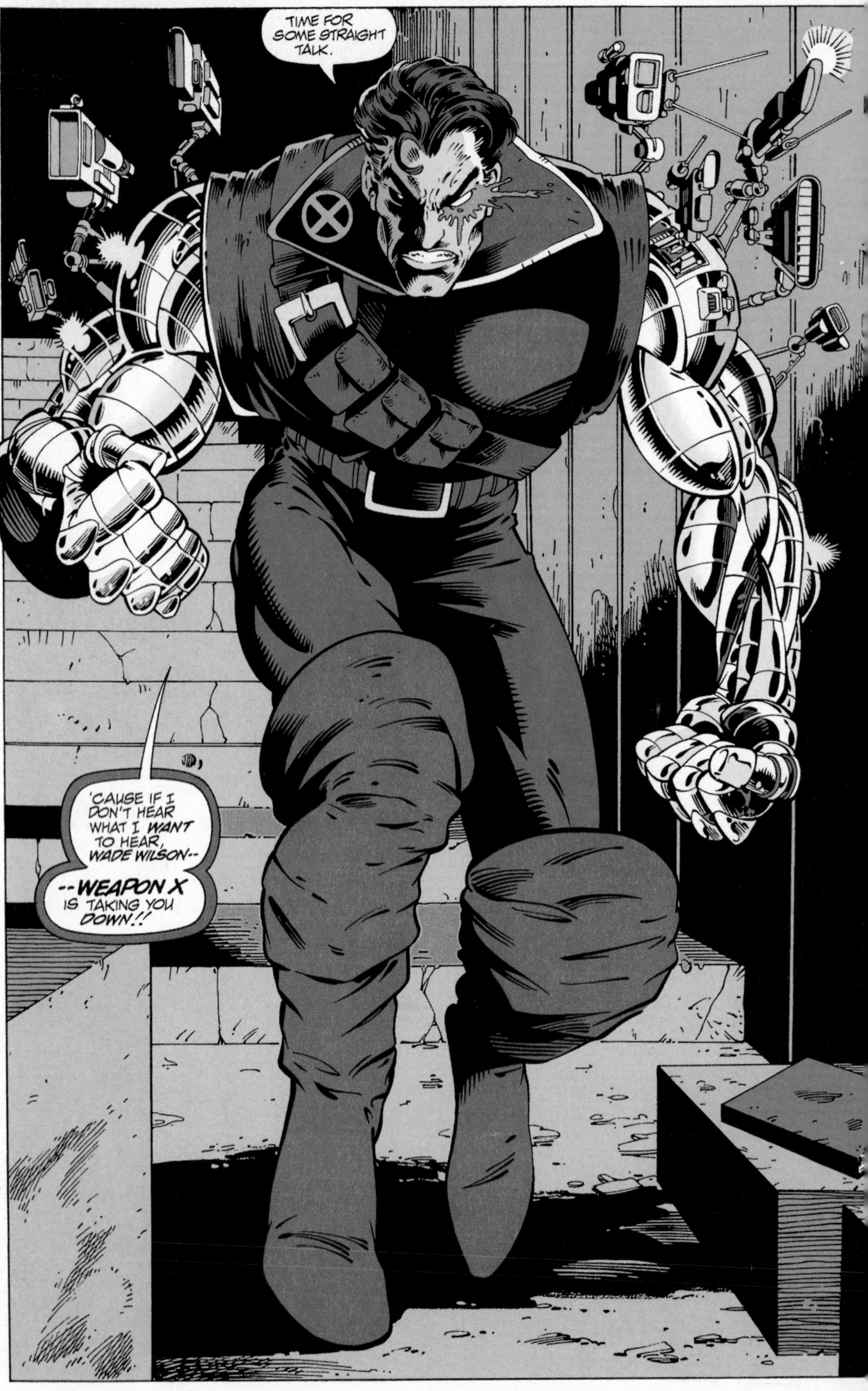
TIME FOR SOME STRAIGHT TALK.
'CAUSE IF I DON'T HEAR WHAT I *WANT* TO HEAR, *WADE WILSON*--
--*WEAPON X* IS TAKING YOU *DOWN*!!

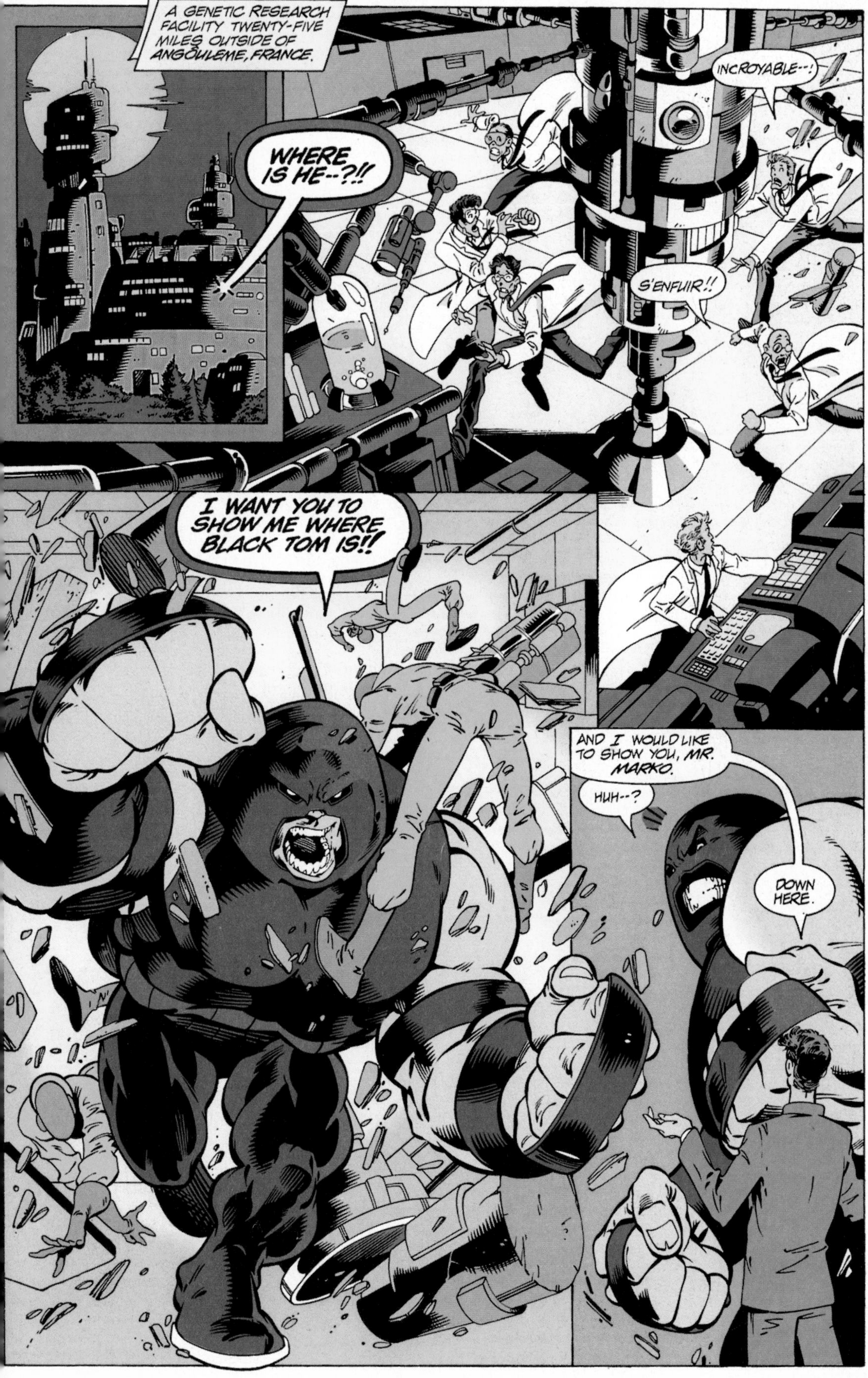

A GENETIC RESEARCH FACILITY TWENTY-FIVE MILES OUTSIDE OF ANGOULEME, FRANCE.
WHERE IS HE--?!!
INCROYABLE--!
S'ENFUIR!!
I WANT YOU TO SHOW ME WHERE BLACK TOM IS!!
AND I WOULD LIKE TO SHOW YOU, MR. MARKO.
HUH--?
DOWN HERE.

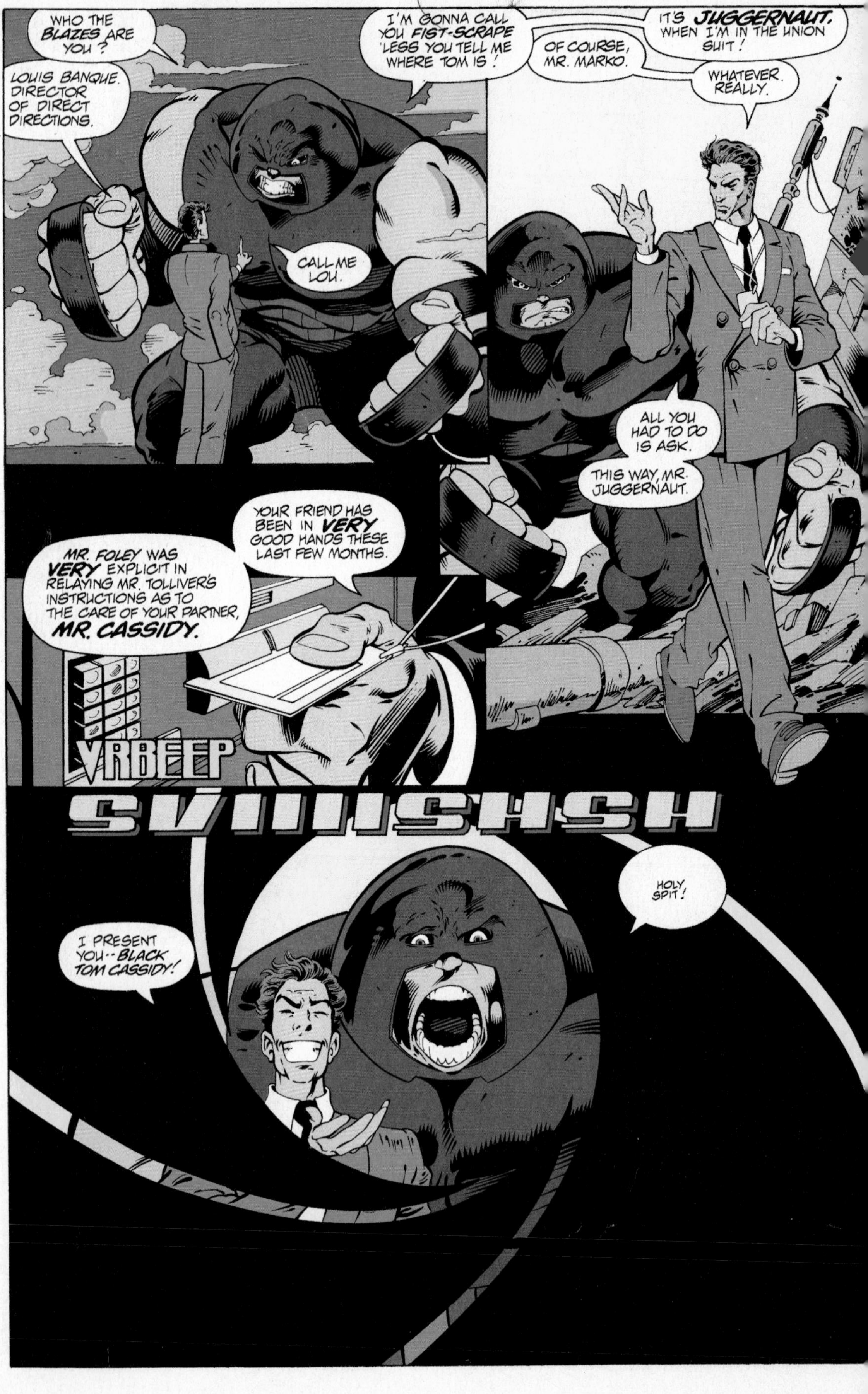
WHO THE BLAZES ARE YOU?
LOUIS BANQUE. DIRECTOR OF DIRECT DIRECTIONS.
CALL ME LOU.
I'M GONNA CALL YOU FIST-SCRAPE 'LESS YOU TELL ME WHERE TOM IS!
OF COURSE, MR. MARKO.
IT'S JUGGERNAUT. WHEN I'M IN THE UNION SUIT!
WHATEVER. REALLY.
ALL YOU HAD TO DO IS ASK.
THIS WAY, MR. JUGGERNAUT.
MR. FOLEY WAS VERY EXPLICIT IN RELAYING MR. TOLLIVER'S INSTRUCTIONS AS TO THE CARE OF YOUR PARTNER, MR. CASSIDY.
YOUR FRIEND HAS BEEN IN VERY GOOD HANDS THESE LAST FEW MONTHS.
VRBEEP
SVIIISHSH
I PRESENT YOU--BLACK TOM CASSIDY!
HOLY SPIT!

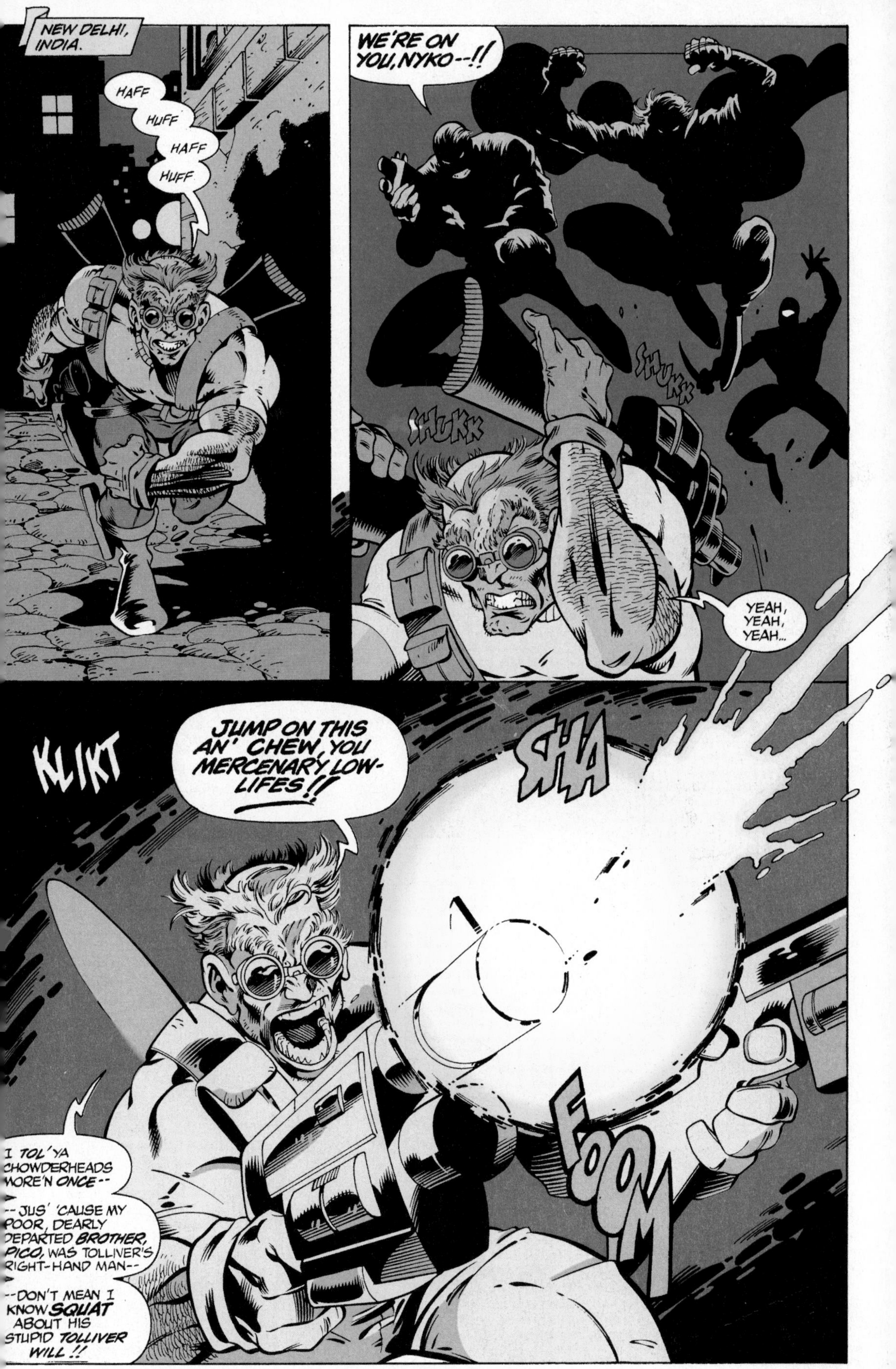
NEW DELHI, INDIA.
HAFF
HUFF
HAFF
HUFF
WE'RE ON YOU, NYKO--!!
SHUKK
SHUKK
YEAH, YEAH, YEAH...
KLIKT
JUMP ON THIS AN' CHEW, YOU MERCENARY LOW-LIFES!!
SHA
I TOL'YA CHOWDERHEADS MORE'N ONCE--
--JUS' 'CAUSE MY POOR, DEARLY DEPARTED BROTHER, PICO, WAS TOLLIVER'S RIGHT-HAND MAN--
--DON'T MEAN I KNOW SQUAT ABOUT HIS STUPID TOLLIVER WILL!!
FOOM

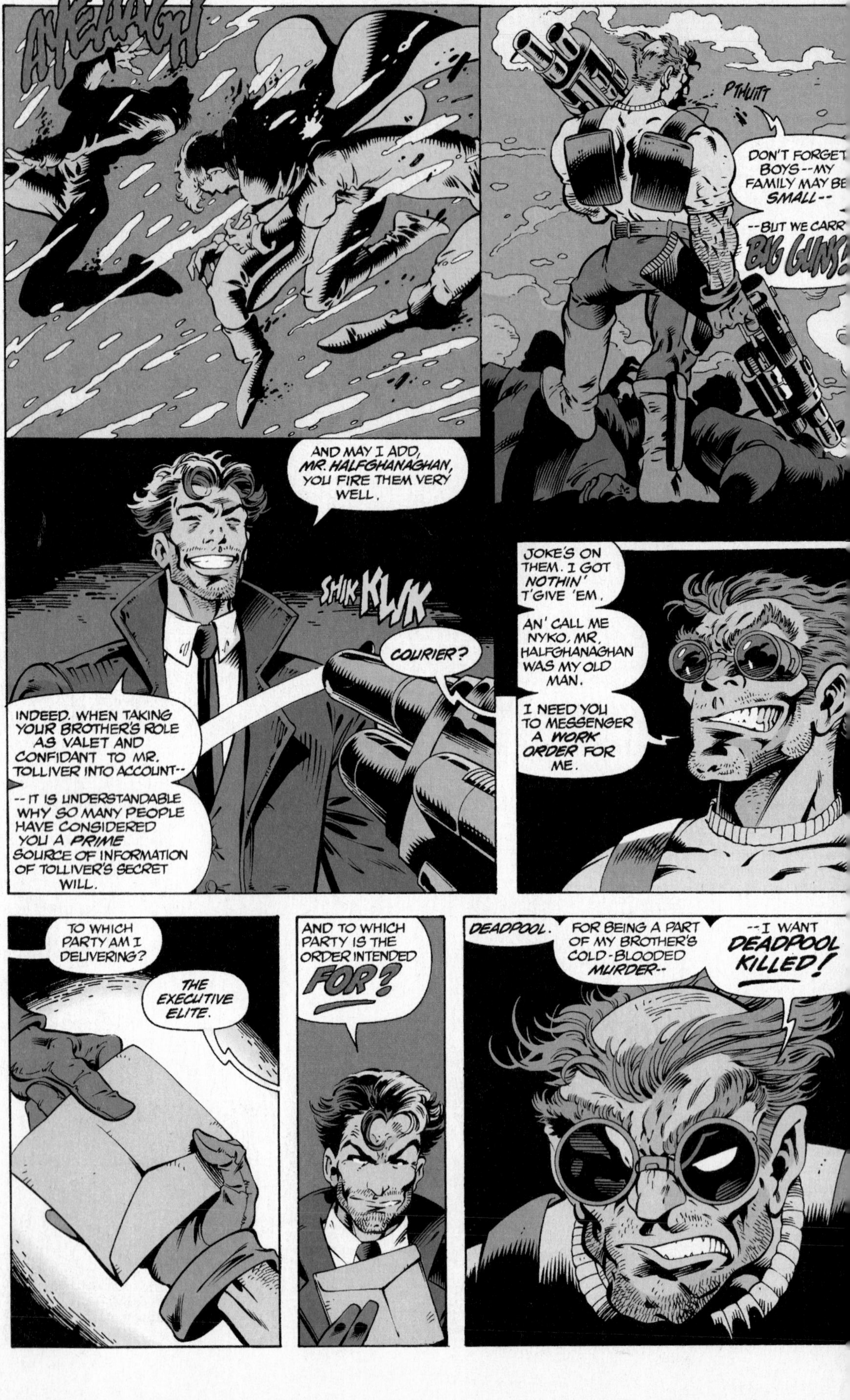
AYEAAGH
PTHUITT
DON'T FORGET, BOYS--MY FAMILY MAY BE SMALL--
--BUT WE CARR BIG GUNS!
AND MAY I ADD, MR. HALFGHANAGHAN, YOU FIRE THEM VERY WELL.
SHIK KLIK
COURIER?
INDEED. WHEN TAKING YOUR BROTHER'S ROLE AS VALET AND CONFIDANT TO MR. TOLLIVER INTO ACCOUNT--
-- IT IS UNDERSTANDABLE WHY SO MANY PEOPLE HAVE CONSIDERED YOU A PRIME SOURCE OF INFORMATION OF TOLLIVER'S SECRET WILL.
JOKE'S ON THEM. I GOT NOTHIN' T'GIVE 'EM.
AN' CALL ME NYKO, MR. HALFGHANAGHAN WAS MY OLD MAN.
I NEED YOU TO MESSENGER A WORK ORDER FOR ME.
TO WHICH PARTY AM I DELIVERING?
THE EXECUTIVE ELITE.
AND TO WHICH PARTY IS THE ORDER INTENDED FOR?
DEADPOOL.
FOR BEING A PART OF MY BROTHER'S COLD-BLOODED MURDER--
--I WANT DEADPOOL KILLED!

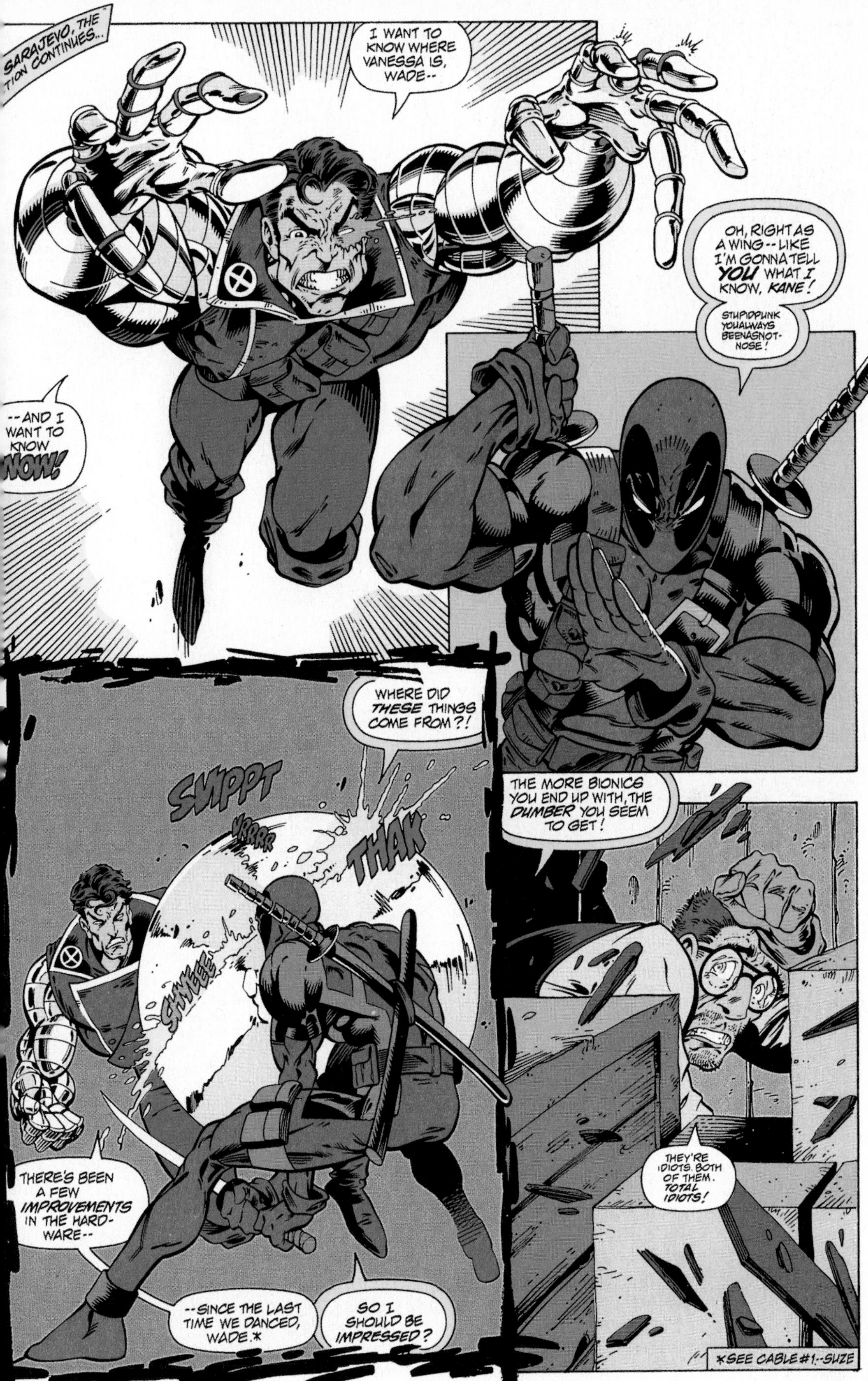
SARAJEVO, THE ...TION CONTINUES...
I WANT TO KNOW WHERE VANESSA IS, WADE--
--AND I WANT TO KNOW NOW!
OH, RIGHT AS A WING--LIKE I'M GONNA TELL YOU WHAT I KNOW, KANE!
STUPIDPUNK YOUALWAYS BEENASNOT-NOSE!
WHERE DID THESE THINGS COME FROM?!
SNPPT
VRRRR
THAK
SHNEE
THERE'S BEEN A FEW IMPROVEMENTS IN THE HARD-WARE--
--SINCE THE LAST TIME WE DANCED, WADE.*
SO I SHOULD BE IMPRESSED?
THE MORE BIONICS YOU END UP WITH, THE DUMBER YOU SEEM TO GET!
THEY'RE IDIOTS. BOTH OF THEM. TOTAL IDIOTS!
*SEE CABLE #1.--SUZE

BRAKKA BRAKKA
BRAKKA
BRAKKA
AH, GO REACH FOR THIS, Y'PUNK PAIN IN MY HEMORRHOIDS!
YOU'VE BEEN FULL OF YOURSELF SINCE WE WERE PUPS BACK AT WEAPON X.
DID YOU LOOSE THESE WITTY-BITTY BUWWETS, WADIE-BOY?
AH, GEEEZ, DO I HATE YOUR SELF-REPAIRING GUTS, OR WHAT?!

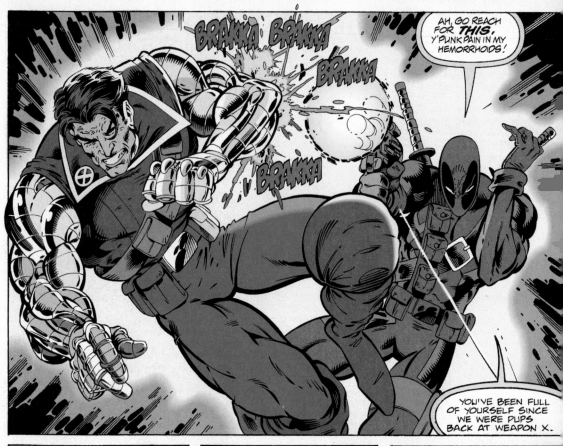

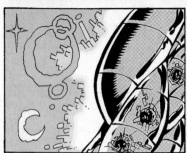

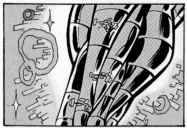

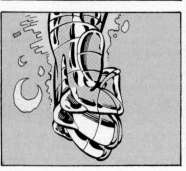

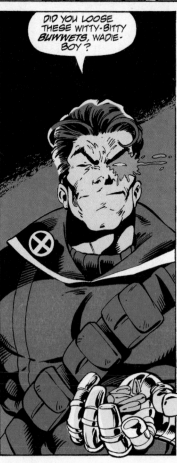

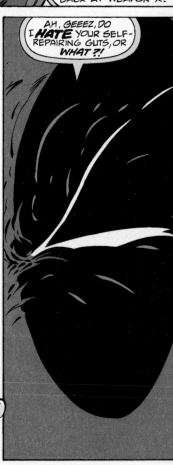

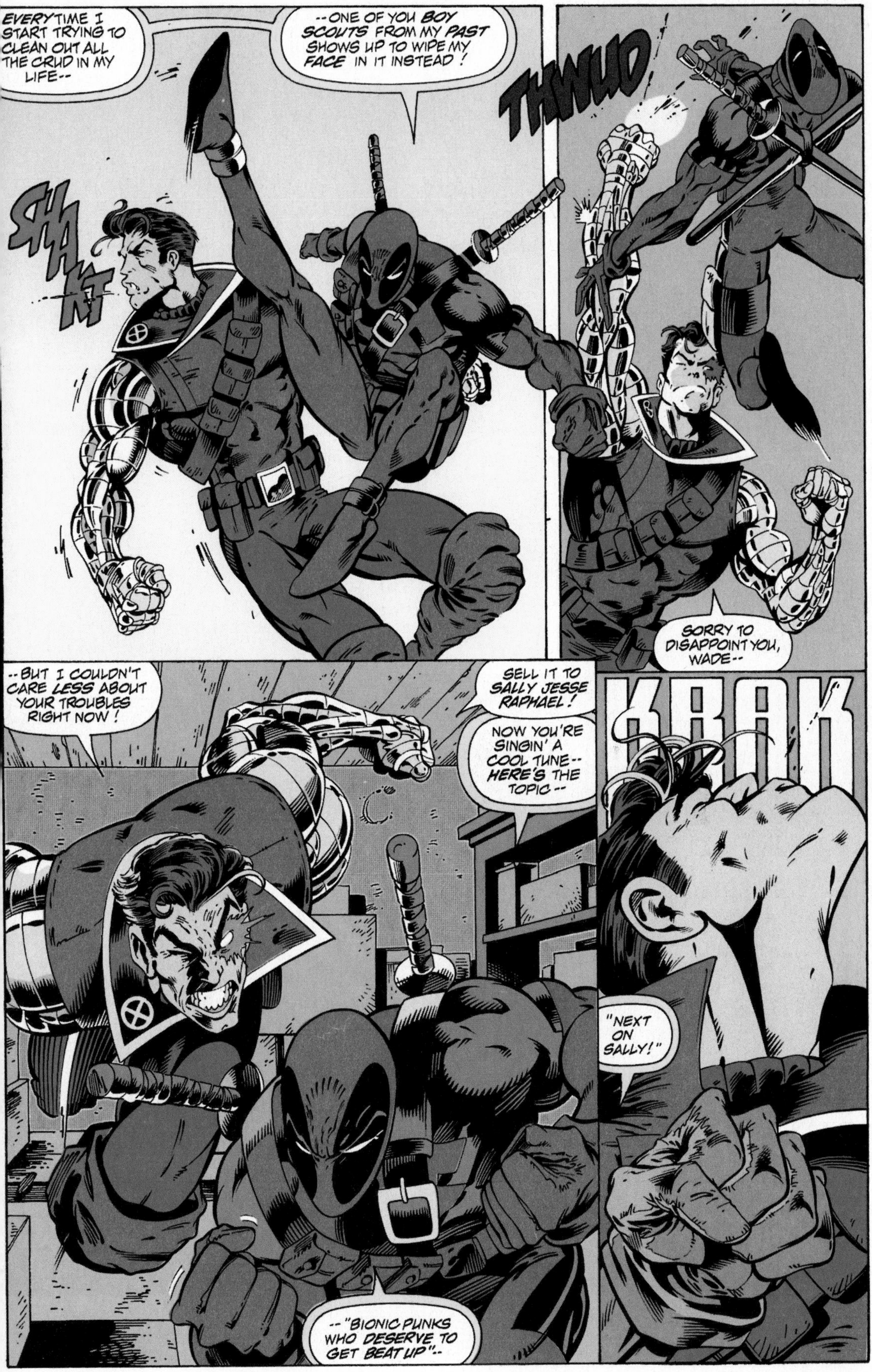
EVERY TIME I START TRYING TO CLEAN OUT ALL THE CRUD IN MY LIFE--
--ONE OF YOU BOY SCOUTS FROM MY PAST SHOWS UP TO WIPE MY FACE IN IT INSTEAD!
SHAKT
THWUD
SORRY TO DISAPPOINT YOU, WADE--
--BUT I COULDN'T CARE LESS ABOUT YOUR TROUBLES RIGHT NOW!
SELL IT TO SALLY JESSE RAPHAEL!
NOW YOU'RE SINGIN' A COOL TUNE-- HERE'S THE TOPIC--
--"BIONIC PUNKS WHO DESERVE TO GET BEAT UP"--
KRAK
"NEXT ON SALLY!"

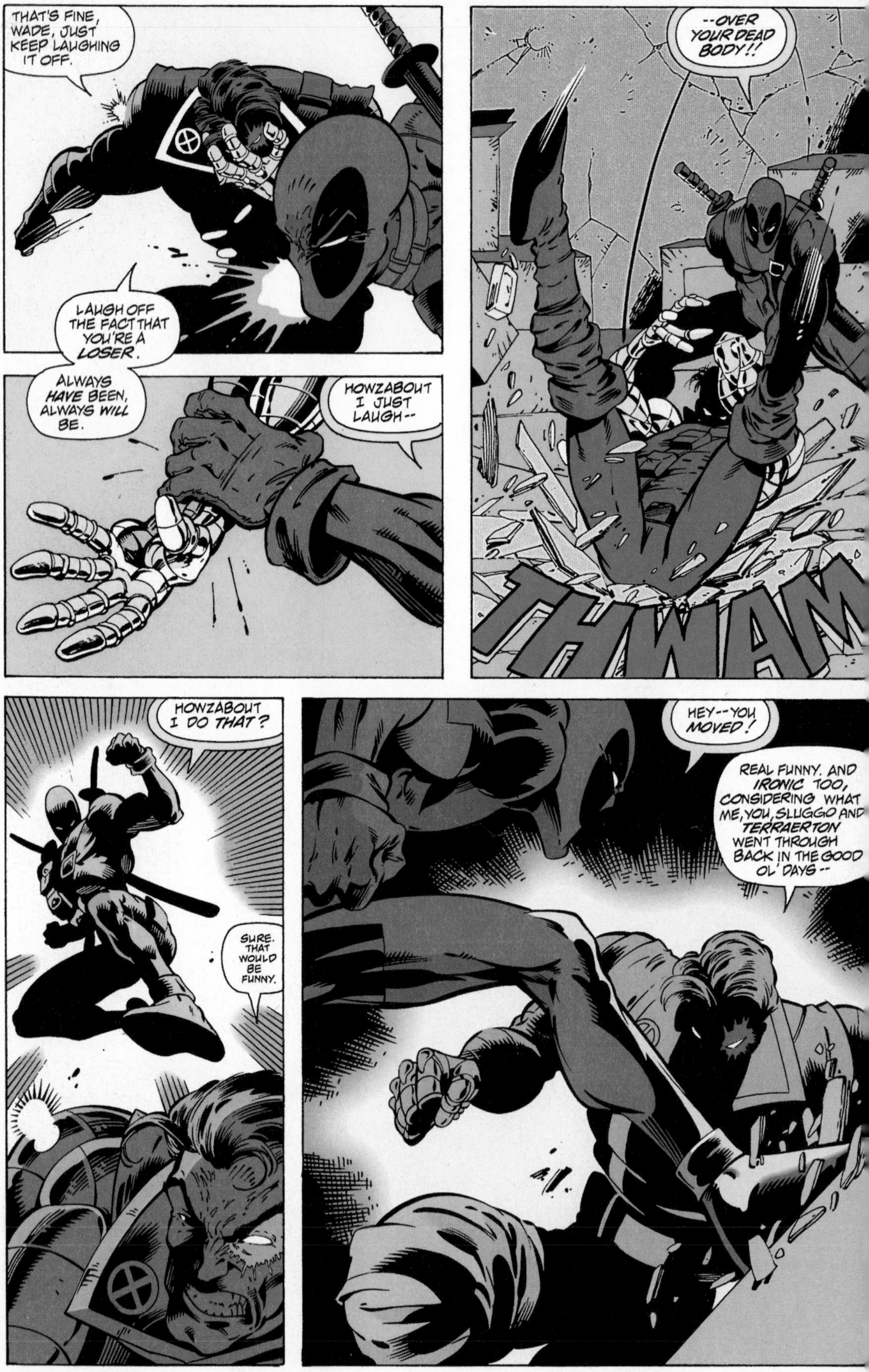
THAT'S FINE, WADE, JUST KEEP LAUGHING IT OFF.
LAUGH OFF THE FACT THAT YOU'RE A LOSER.
ALWAYS HAVE BEEN, ALWAYS WILL BE.
HOWZABOUT I JUST LAUGH--
--OVER YOUR DEAD BODY!!
THWAM
HOWZABOUT I DO THAT?
SURE. THAT WOULD BE FUNNY.
HEY--YOU MOVED!
REAL FUNNY. AND IRONIC TOO, CONSIDERING WHAT ME, YOU, SLUGGO AND TERRAERTON WENT THROUGH BACK IN THE GOOD OL' DAYS--

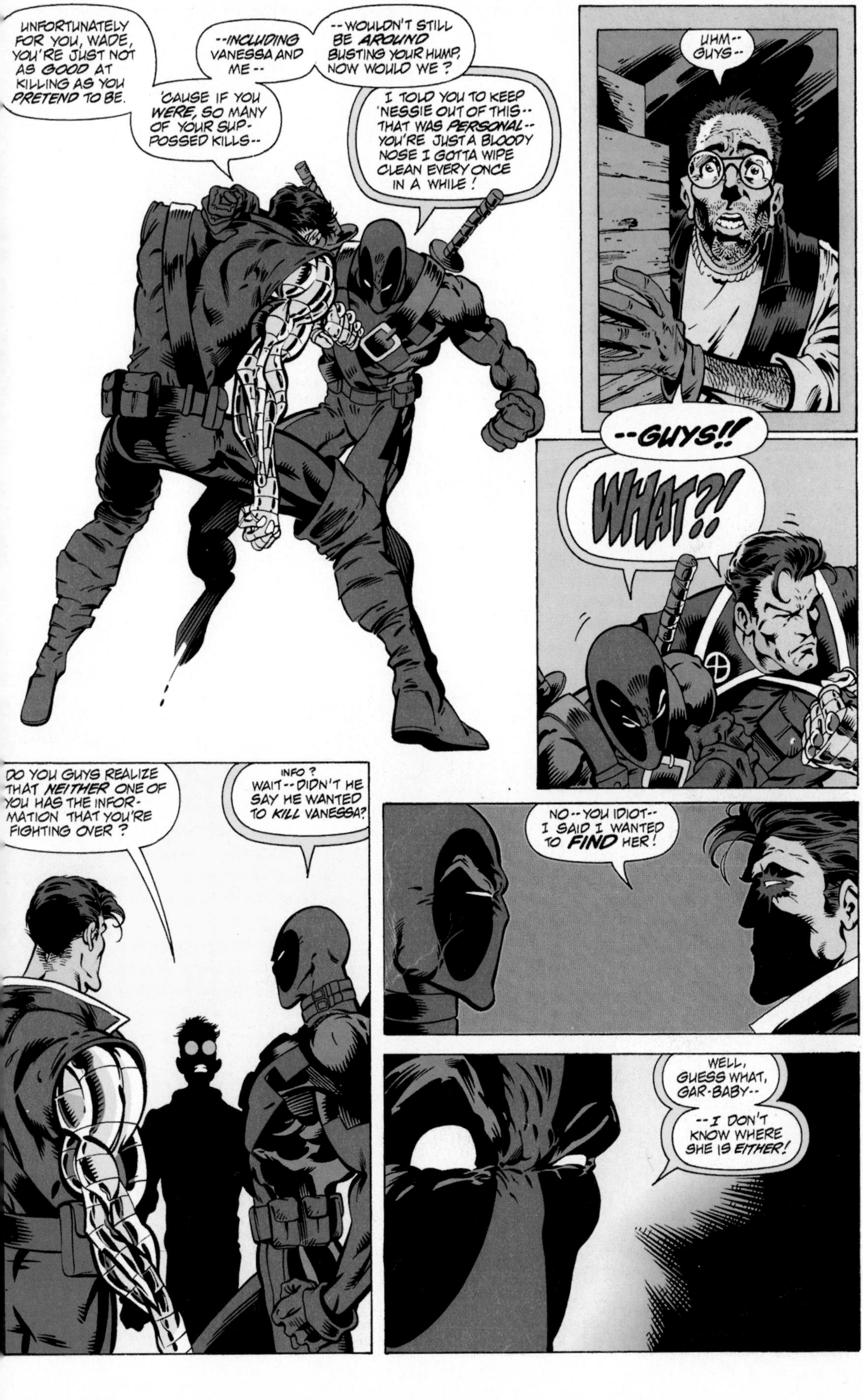
UNFORTUNATELY FOR YOU, WADE, YOU'RE JUST NOT AS GOOD AT KILLING AS YOU PRETEND TO BE.
'CAUSE IF YOU WERE, SO MANY OF YOUR SUP-POSSED KILLS--
--INCLUDING VANESSA AND ME--
--WOULDN'T STILL BE AROUND BUSTING YOUR HUMP, NOW WOULD WE?
I TOLD YOU TO KEEP 'NESSIE OUT OF THIS--THAT WAS PERSONAL--YOU'RE JUST A BLOODY NOSE I GOTTA WIPE CLEAN EVERY ONCE IN A WHILE!
UHM--GUYS--
--GUYS!!
WHAT?!
DO YOU GUYS REALIZE THAT NEITHER ONE OF YOU HAS THE INFOR-MATION THAT YOU'RE FIGHTING OVER?
INFO? WAIT--DIDN'T HE SAY HE WANTED TO KILL VANESSA?
NO--YOU IDIOT--I SAID I WANTED TO FIND HER!
WELL, GUESS WHAT, GAR-BABY--
--I DON'T KNOW WHERE SHE IS EITHER!

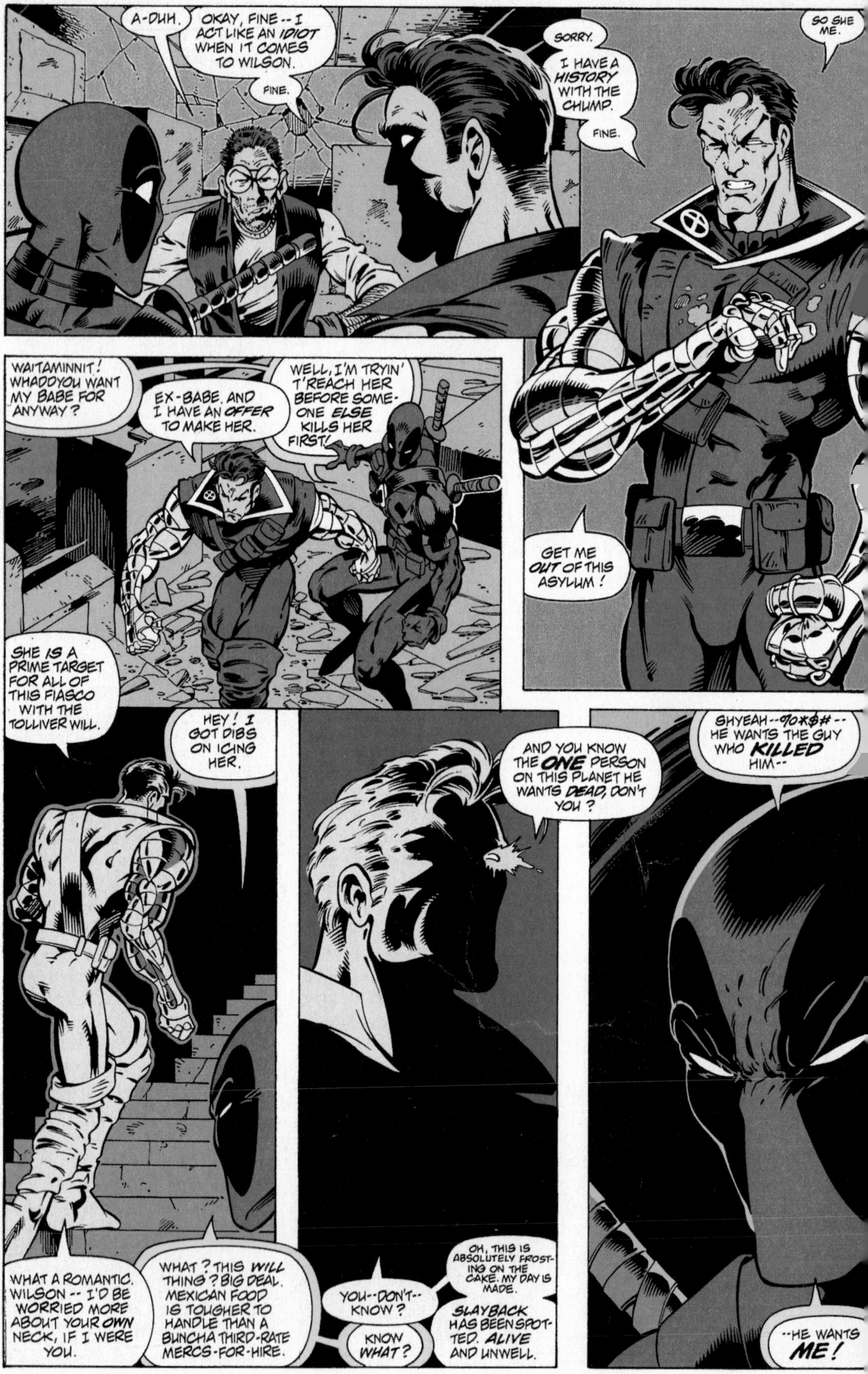

A-DUH.
OKAY, FINE -- I ACT LIKE AN IDIOT WHEN IT COMES TO WILSON.
FINE.
SORRY.
I HAVE A HISTORY WITH THE CHUMP.
FINE.
SO SHE ME.
WAITAMINNIT! WHADDYOU WANT MY BABE FOR ANYWAY?
EX-BABE. AND I HAVE AN OFFER TO MAKE HER.
WELL, I'M TRYIN' T'REACH HER BEFORE SOME-ONE ELSE KILLS HER FIRST!
SHE IS A PRIME TARGET FOR ALL OF THIS FIASCO WITH THE TOLLIVER WILL.
GET ME OUT OF THIS ASYLUM!
HEY! I GOT DIBS ON ICING HER.
WHAT A ROMANTIC. WILSON -- I'D BE WORRIED MORE ABOUT YOUR OWN NECK, IF I WERE YOU.
WHAT? THIS WILL THING? BIG DEAL. MEXICAN FOOD IS TOUGHER TO HANDLE THAN A BUNCHA THIRD-RATE MERCS-FOR-HIRE.
AND YOU KNOW THE ONE PERSON ON THIS PLANET HE WANTS DEAD, DON'T YOU?
YOU--DON'T--KNOW?
KNOW WHAT?
OH, THIS IS ABSOLUTELY FROSTING ON THE CAKE. MY DAY IS MADE.
SLAYBACK HAS BEEN SPOT-TED. ALIVE AND UNWELL.
SHYEAH--%*$# -- HE WANTS THE GUY WHO KILLED HIM--
--HE WANTS ME!

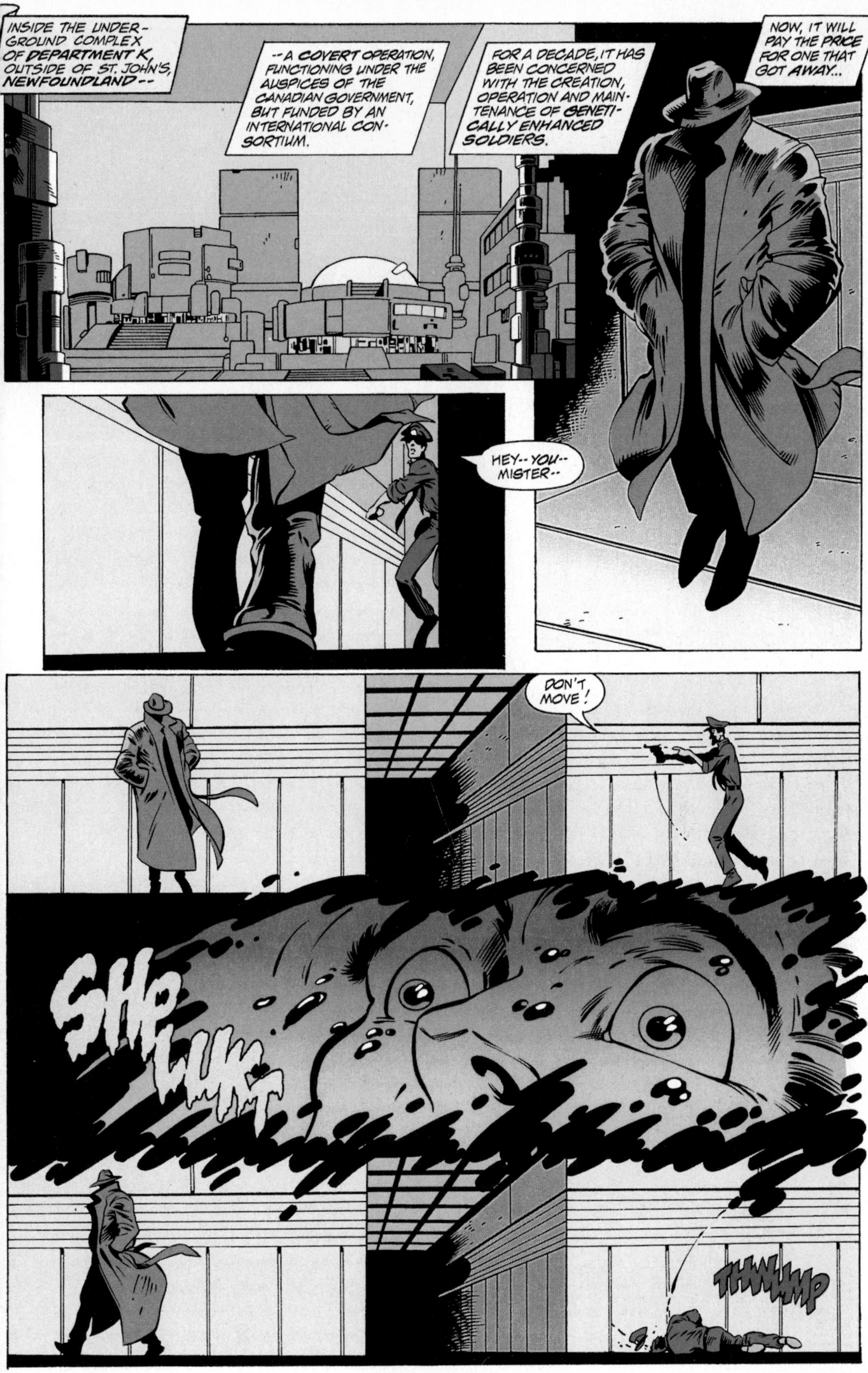
INSIDE THE UNDER-GROUND COMPLEX OF DEPARTMENT K, OUTSIDE OF ST. JOHN'S, NEWFOUNDLAND--
--A COVERT OPERATION, FUNCTIONING UNDER THE AUSPICES OF THE CANADIAN GOVERNMENT, BUT FUNDED BY AN INTERNATIONAL CON-SORTIUM.
FOR A DECADE, IT HAS BEEN CONCERNED WITH THE CREATION, OPERATION AND MAIN-TENANCE OF GENETI-CALLY ENHANCED SOLDIERS.
NOW, IT WILL PAY THE PRICE FOR ONE THAT GOT AWAY...
HEY-- YOU-- MISTER--
DON'T MOVE!
SHPLUNT
THWUMP

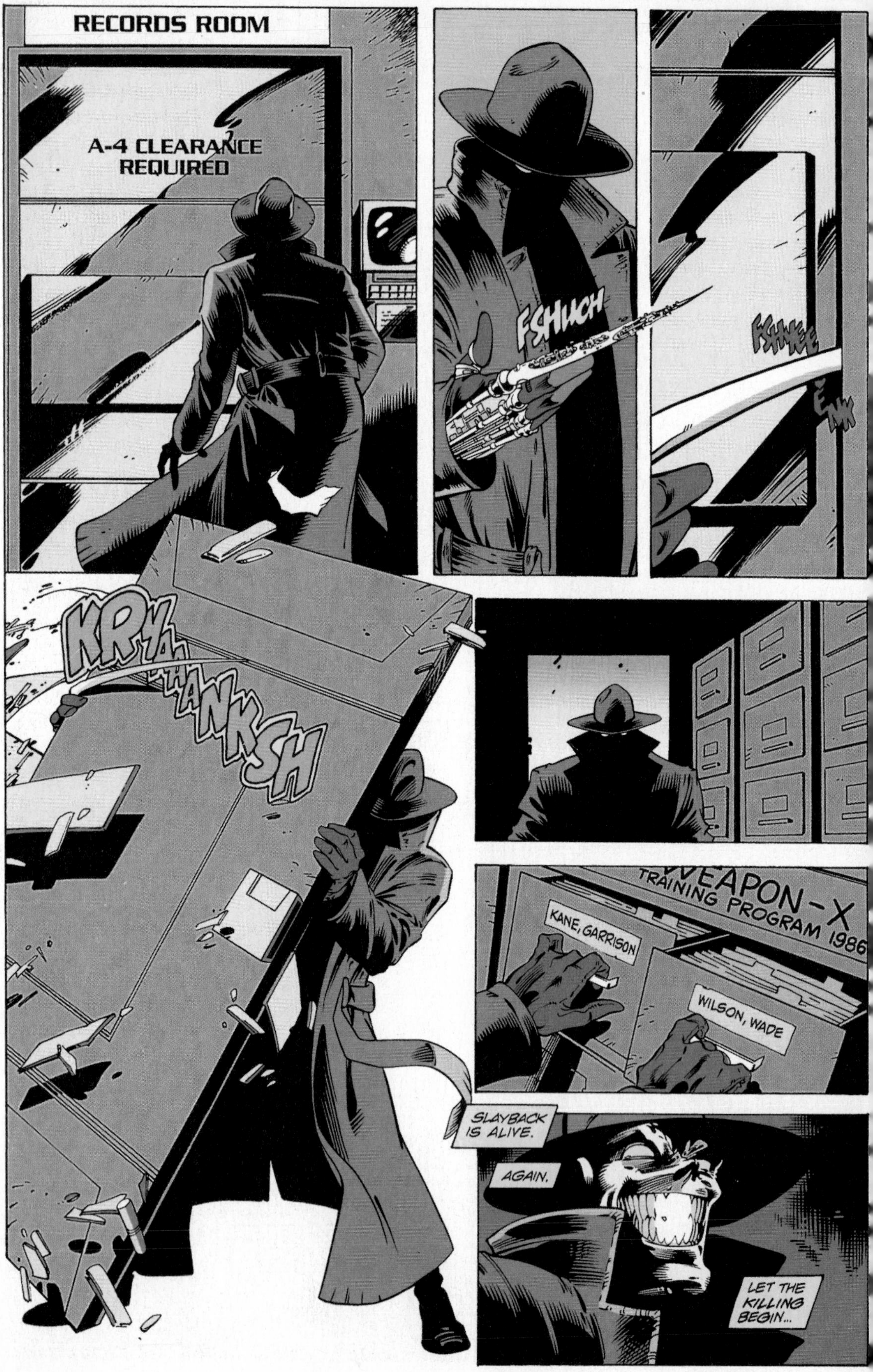
RECORDS ROOM
A-4 CLEARANCE REQUIRED
FSHUCH
FSHNEE
ENK
KRYAAANKSH
WEAPON-X TRAINING PROGRAM 1986
KANE, GARRISON
WILSON, WADE
SLAYBACK IS ALIVE.
AGAIN.
LET THE KILLING BEGIN...

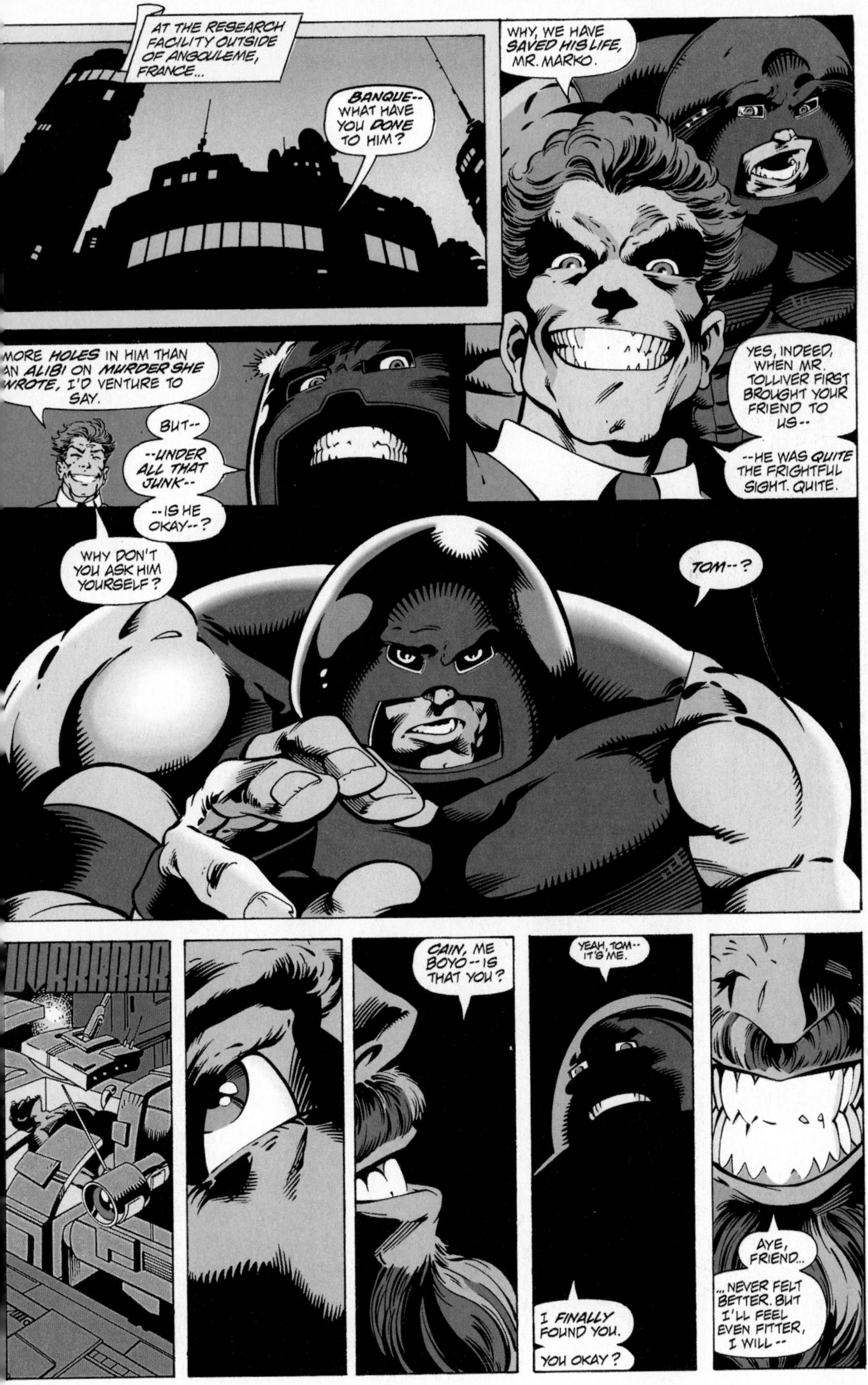

AT THE RESEARCH FACILITY OUTSIDE OF ANGOULEME, FRANCE...
BANQUE-- WHAT HAVE YOU DONE TO HIM?
WHY, WE HAVE SAVED HIS LIFE, MR. MARKO.
MORE HOLES IN HIM THAN AN ALIBI ON MURDER SHE WROTE, I'D VENTURE TO SAY.
BUT--
--UNDER ALL THAT JUNK--
--IS HE OKAY--?
YES, INDEED, WHEN MR. TOLLIVER FIRST BROUGHT YOUR FRIEND TO US--
--HE WAS QUITE THE FRIGHTFUL SIGHT. QUITE.
WHY DON'T YOU ASK HIM YOURSELF?
TOM--?
VVRRRRRR
CAIN, ME BOYO--IS THAT YOU?
YEAH, TOM-- IT'S ME.
I FINALLY FOUND YOU.
YOU OKAY?
AYE, FRIEND...
...NEVER FELT BETTER. BUT I'LL FEEL EVEN FITTER, I WILL--

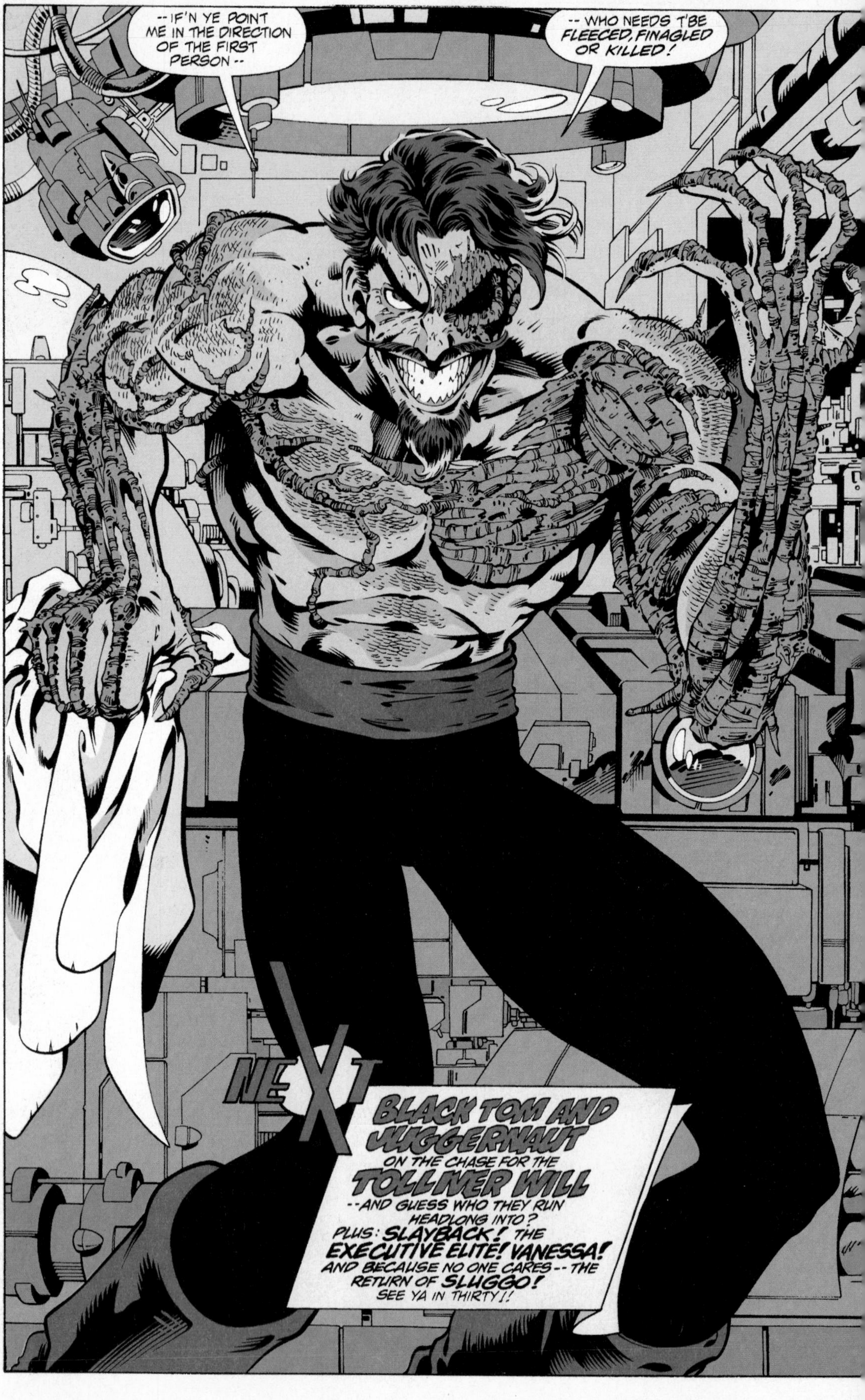
--IF'N YE POINT ME IN THE DIRECTION OF THE FIRST PERSON--
--WHO NEEDS T'BE FLEECED, FINAGLED OR KILLED!
NEXT
BLACK TOM AND JUGGERNAUT ON THE CHASE FOR THE TOLLIVER WILL --AND GUESS WHO THEY RUN HEADLONG INTO? PLUS: SLAYBACK! THE EXECUTIVE ELITE! VANESSA! AND BECAUSE NO ONE CARES-- THE RETURN OF SLUGGO! SEE YA IN THIRTY!!

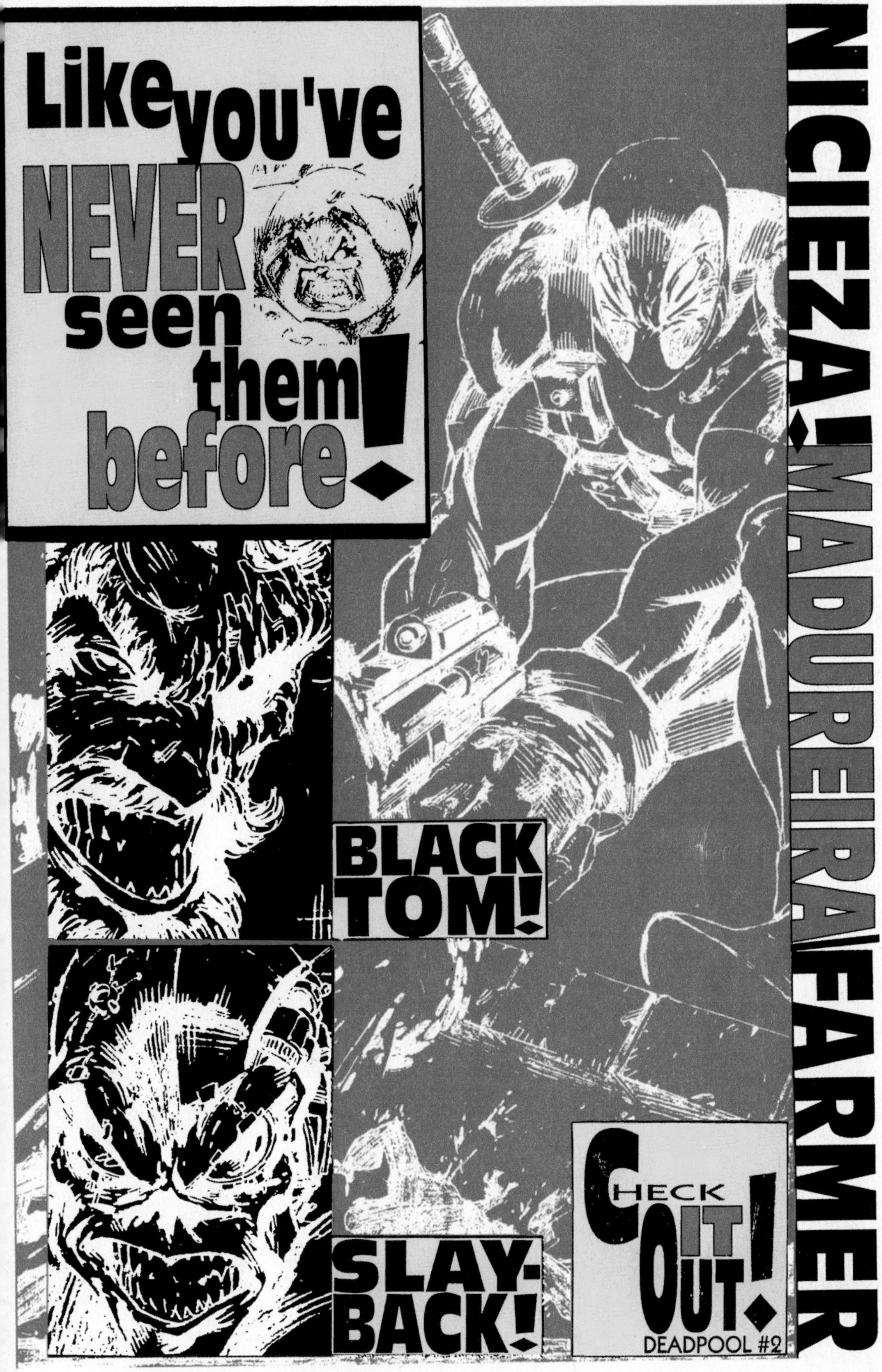
Like you've NEVER seen them before!
BLACK TOM!
SLAY-BACK!
CHECK IT OUT!
DEADPOOL #2
NICIEZA • MADUREIRA/FARMER

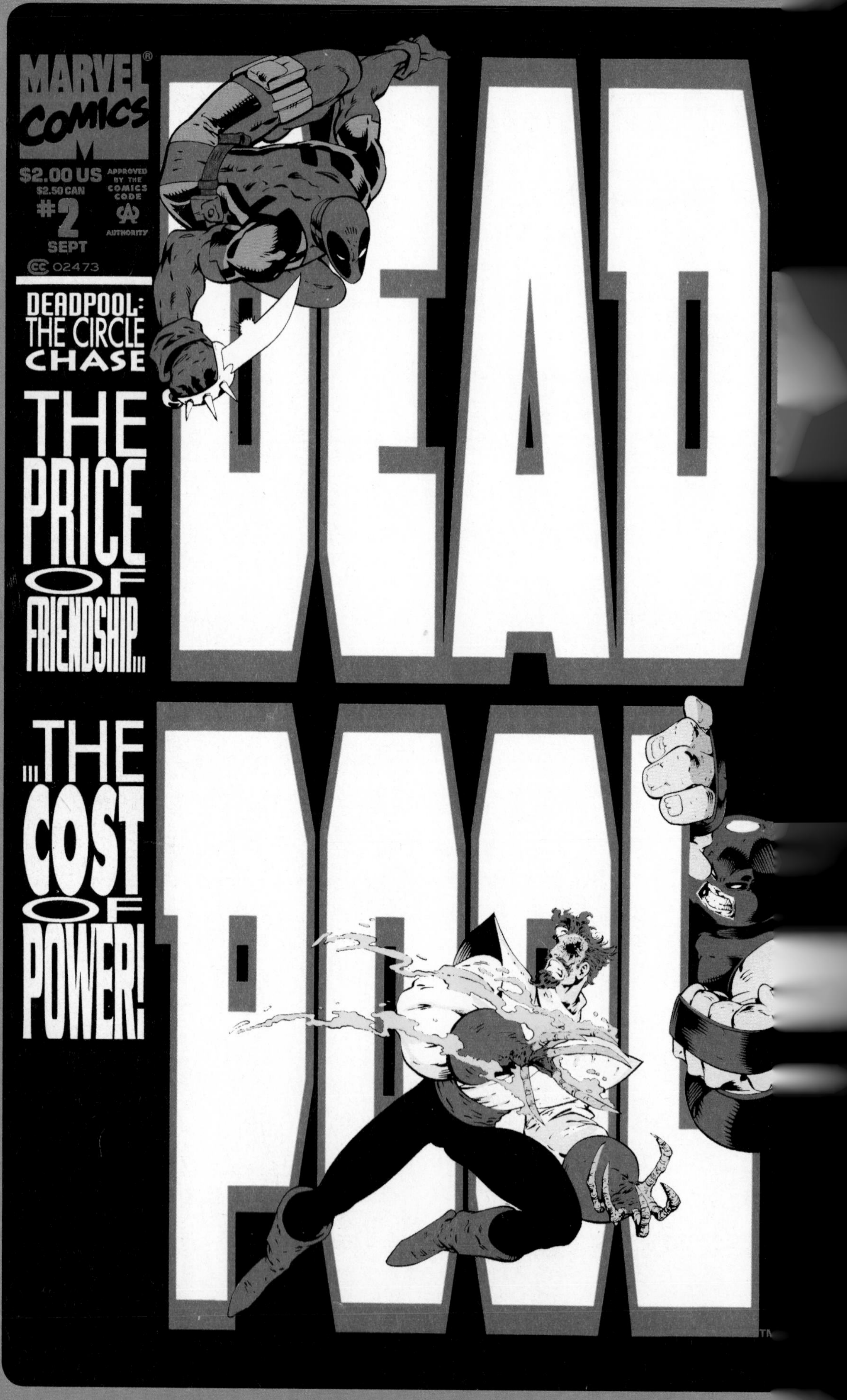
MARVEL COMICS
$2.00 US
$2.50 CAN
#2
SEPT
APPROVED BY THE COMICS CODE AUTHORITY
02473
DEADPOOL: THE CIRCLE CHASE
THE PRICE OF FRIENDSHIP...
...THE COST OF POWER!
DEADPOOL
TM

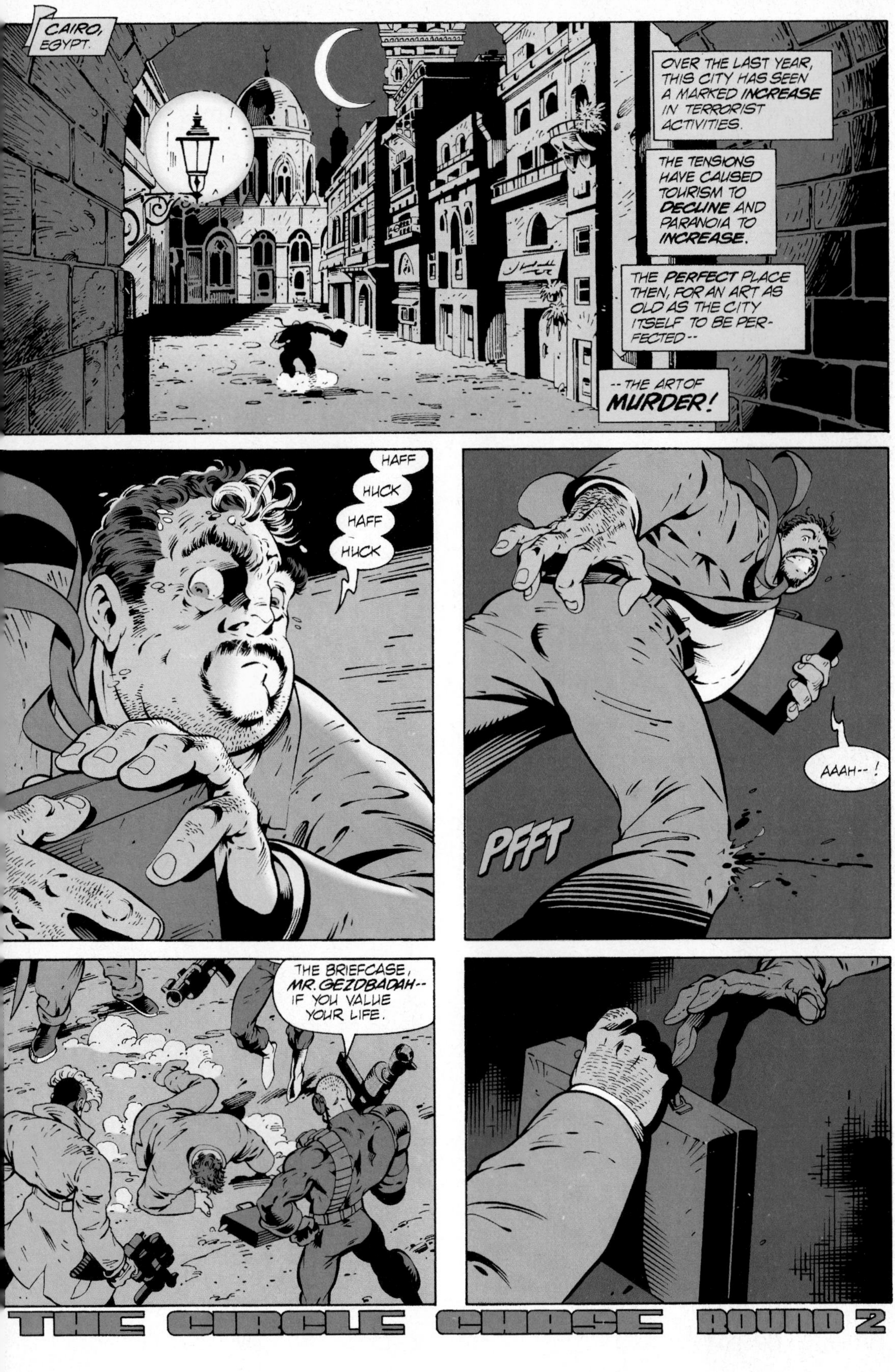
CAIRO, EGYPT.
OVER THE LAST YEAR, THIS CITY HAS SEEN A MARKED INCREASE IN TERRORIST ACTIVITIES.
THE TENSIONS HAVE CAUSED TOURISM TO DECLINE AND PARANOIA TO INCREASE.
THE PERFECT PLACE THEN, FOR AN ART AS OLD AS THE CITY ITSELF TO BE PERFECTED--
--THE ART OF MURDER!
HAFF
HUCK
HAFF
HUCK
PFFT
AAAH--!
THE BRIEFCASE, MR. GEZDBADAH-- IF YOU VALUE YOUR LIFE.

THE CIRCLE CHASE ROUND 2

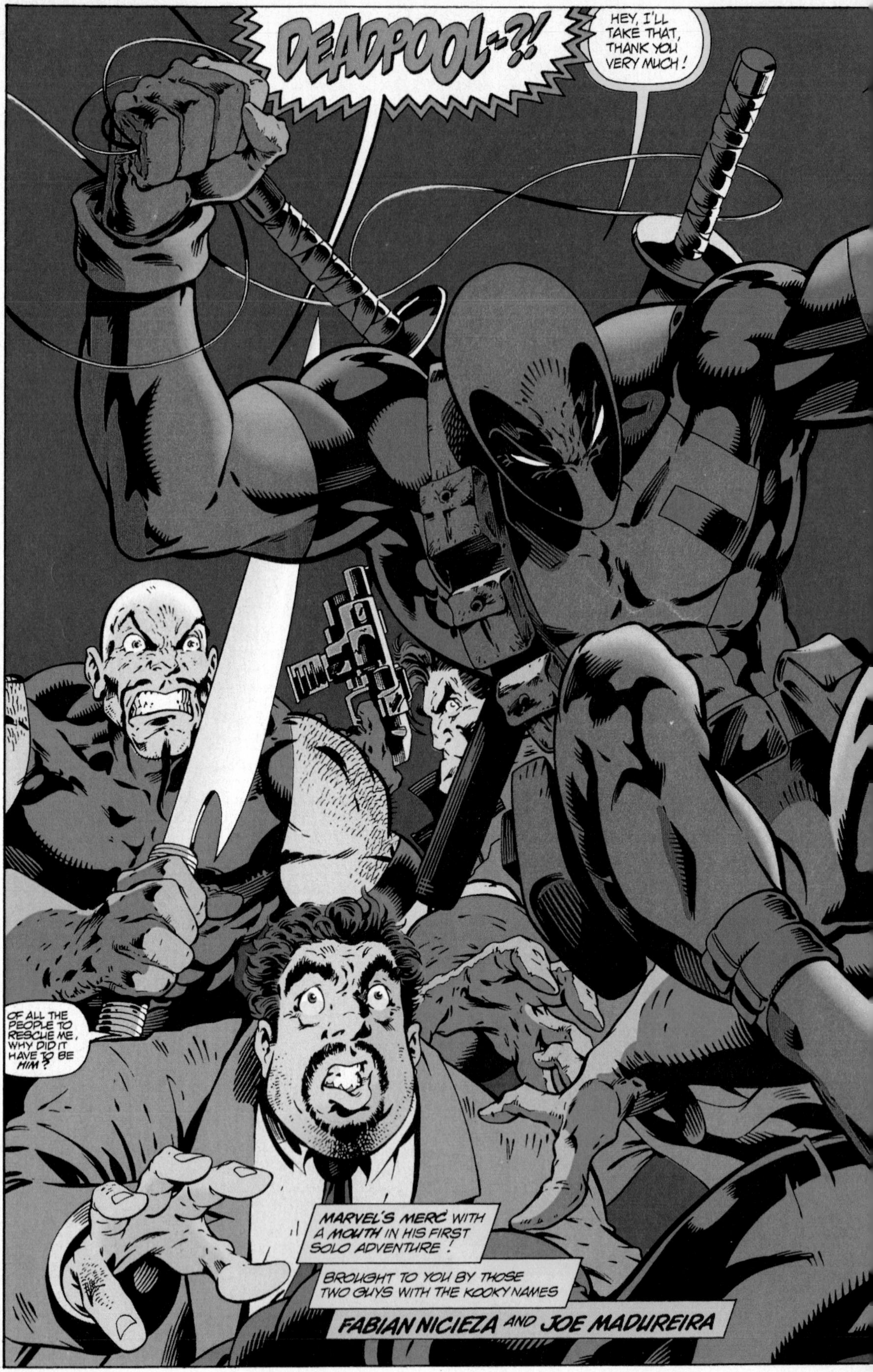
DEADPOOL-?!
HEY, I'LL TAKE THAT, THANK YOU VERY MUCH!
OF ALL THE PEOPLE TO RESCUE ME, WHY DID IT HAVE TO BE HIM?
MARVEL'S MERC WITH A MOUTH IN HIS FIRST SOLO ADVENTURE!
BROUGHT TO YOU BY THOSE TWO GUYS WITH THE KOOKY NAMES
FABIAN NICIEZA AND JOE MADUREIRA

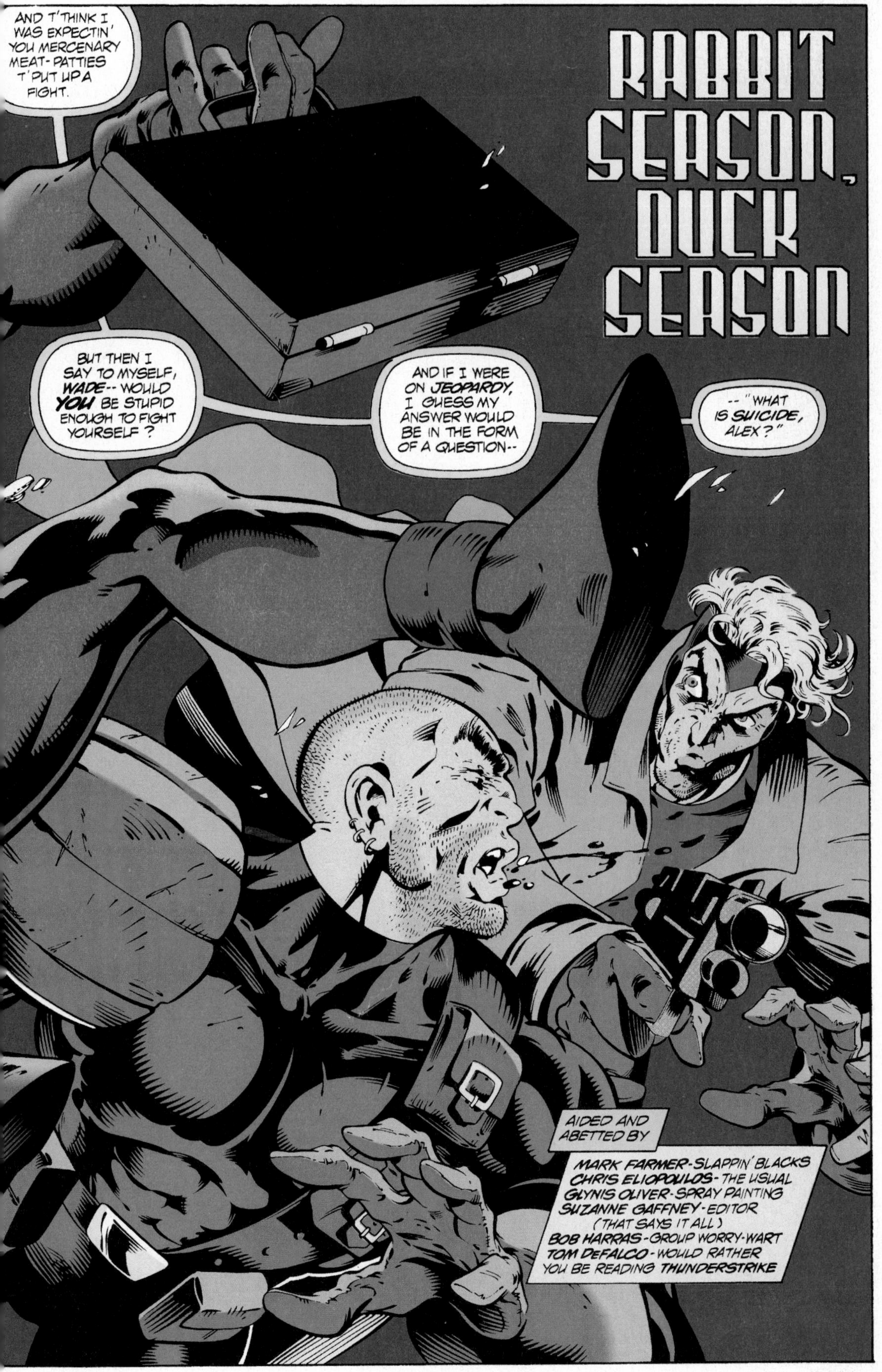
AND T'THINK I WAS EXPECTIN' YOU MERCENARY MEAT-PATTIES T'PUT UP A FIGHT.
RABBIT SEASON, DUCK SEASON
BUT THEN I SAY TO MYSELF, WADE-- WOULD YOU BE STUPID ENOUGH TO FIGHT YOURSELF?
AND IF I WERE ON JEOPARDY, I GUESS MY ANSWER WOULD BE IN THE FORM OF A QUESTION--
-- "WHAT IS SUICIDE, ALEX?"
AIDED AND ABETTED BY
MARK FARMER-SLAPPIN' BLACKS
CHRIS ELIOPOULOS- THE USUAL
GLYNIS OLIVER-SPRAY PAINTING
SUZANNE GAFFNEY-EDITOR (THAT SAYS IT ALL)
BOB HARRAS-GROUP WORRY-WART
TOM DeFALCO-WOULD RATHER YOU BE READING THUNDERSTRIKE

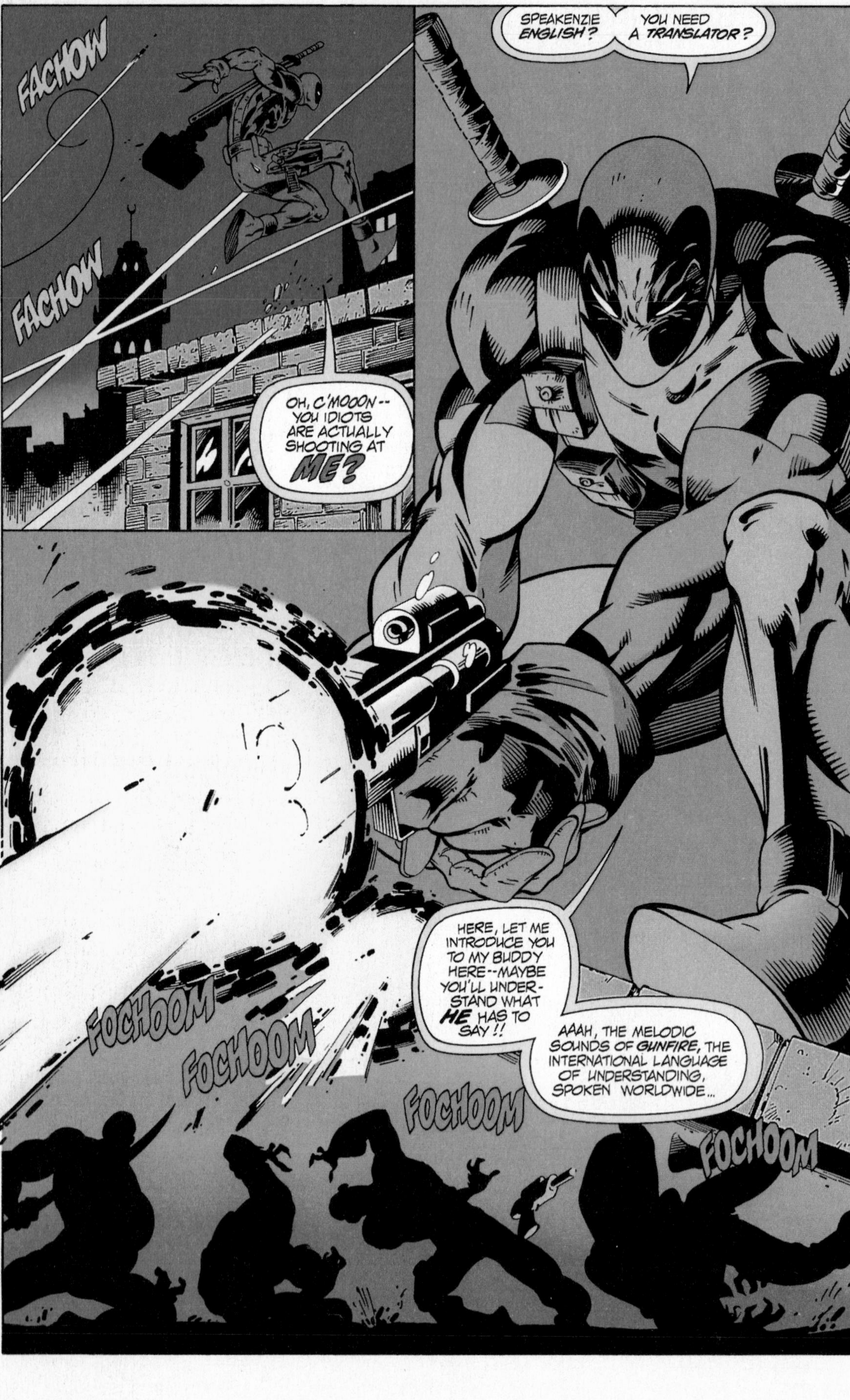
FACHOW
FACHOW
OH, C'MOOON -- YOU IDIOTS ARE ACTUALLY SHOOTING AT ME?
SPEAKENZIE ENGLISH?
YOU NEED A TRANSLATOR?
HERE, LET ME INTRODUCE YOU TO MY BUDDY HERE--MAYBE YOU'LL UNDER-STAND WHAT HE HAS TO SAY!!
FOCHOOM
FOCHOOM
AAAH, THE MELODIC SOUNDS OF GUNFIRE, THE INTERNATIONAL LANGUAGE OF UNDERSTANDING, SPOKEN WORLDWIDE...
FOCHOOM
FOCHOOM

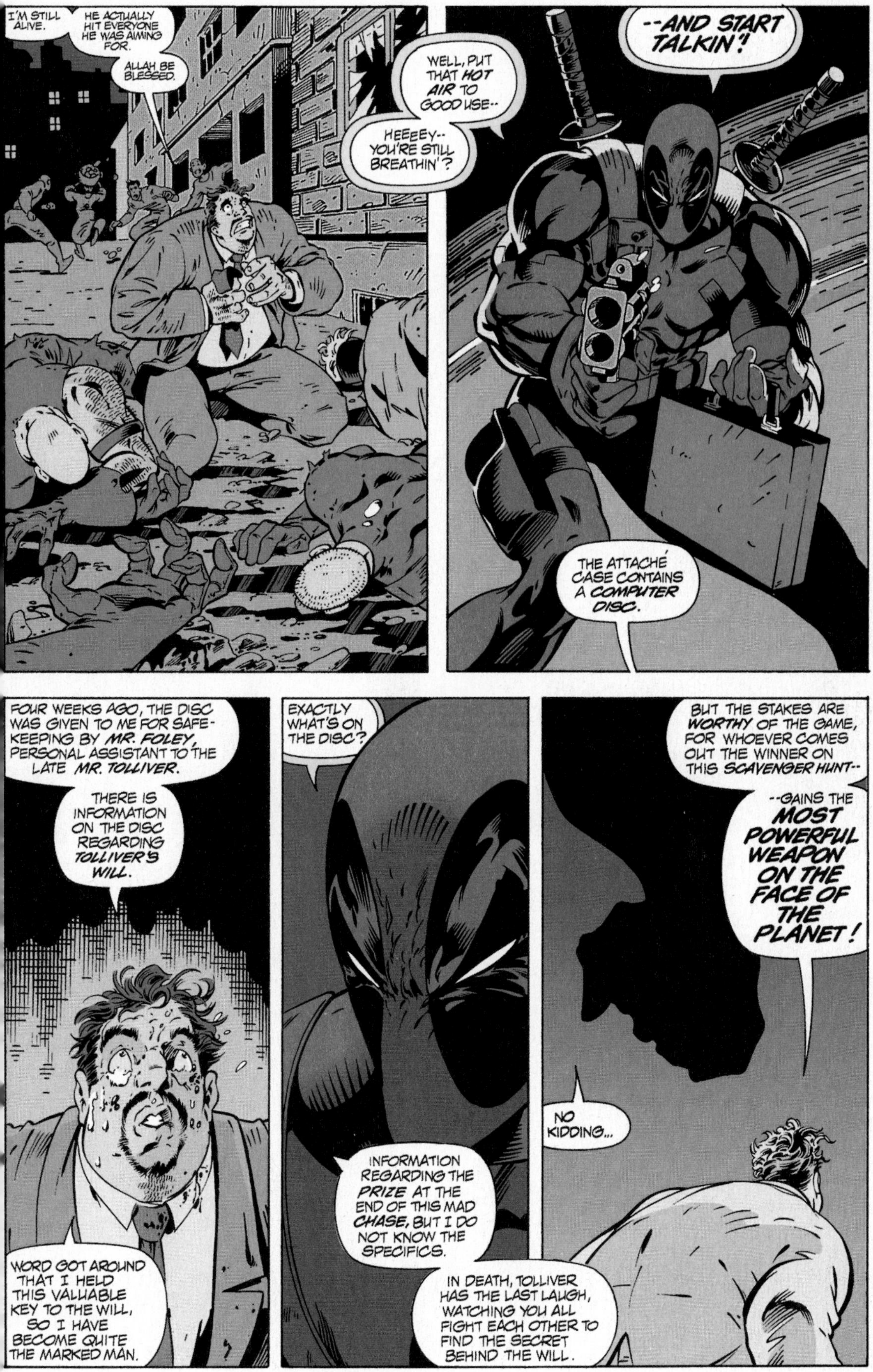
I'M STILL ALIVE.
HE ACTUALLY HIT EVERYONE HE WAS AIMING FOR.
ALLAH BE BLESSED.
WELL, PUT THAT HOT AIR TO GOOD USE--
HEEEEY-- YOU'RE STILL BREATHIN'?
--AND START TALKIN'!
THE ATTACHÉ CASE CONTAINS A COMPUTER DISC.
FOUR WEEKS AGO, THE DISC WAS GIVEN TO ME FOR SAFE-KEEPING BY MR. FOLEY, PERSONAL ASSISTANT TO THE LATE MR. TOLLIVER.
THERE IS INFORMATION ON THE DISC REGARDING TOLLIVER'S WILL.
WORD GOT AROUND THAT I HELD THIS VALUABLE KEY TO THE WILL, SO I HAVE BECOME QUITE THE MARKED MAN.
EXACTLY WHAT'S ON THE DISC?
INFORMATION REGARDING THE PRIZE AT THE END OF THIS MAD CHASE, BUT I DO NOT KNOW THE SPECIFICS.
IN DEATH, TOLLIVER HAS THE LAST LAUGH, WATCHING YOU ALL FIGHT EACH OTHER TO FIND THE SECRET BEHIND THE WILL.
BUT THE STAKES ARE WORTHY OF THE GAME, FOR WHOEVER COMES OUT THE WINNER ON THIS SCAVENGER HUNT--
--GAINS THE MOST POWERFUL WEAPON ON THE FACE OF THE PLANET!
NO KIDDING...

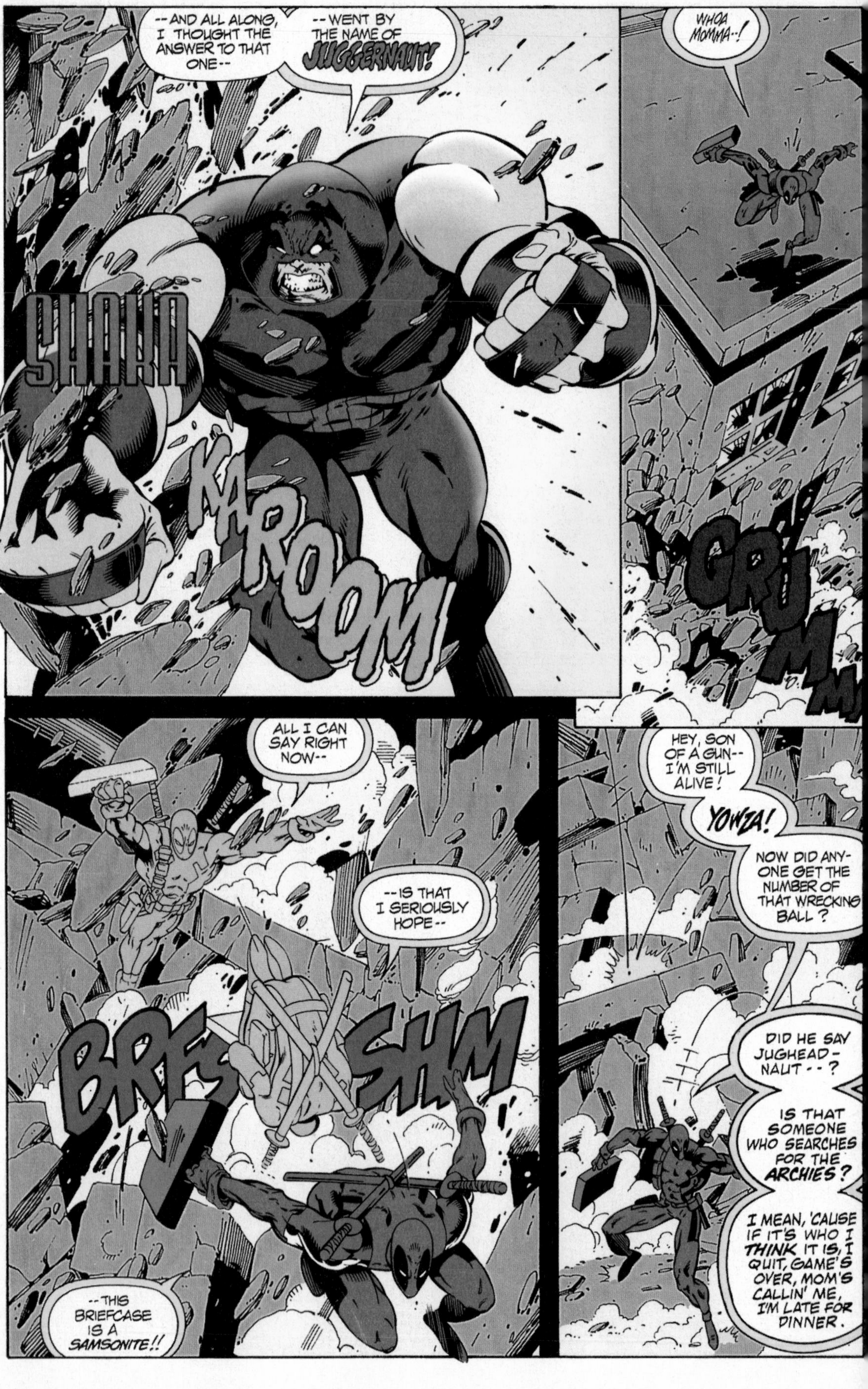

--AND ALL ALONG, I THOUGHT THE ANSWER TO THAT ONE--
--WENT BY THE NAME OF JUGGERNAUT!
SHAKA
KAROOM
WHOA MOMMA--!
GRUMM
ALL I CAN SAY RIGHT NOW--
--IS THAT I SERIOUSLY HOPE--
BRFSSHM
--THIS BRIEFCASE IS A SAMSONITE!!
HEY, SON OF A GUN-- I'M STILL ALIVE!
YOWZA!
NOW DID ANYONE GET THE NUMBER OF THAT WRECKING BALL?
DID HE SAY JUGHEAD-NAUT--?
IS THAT SOMEONE WHO SEARCHES FOR THE ARCHIES?
I MEAN, 'CAUSE IF IT'S WHO I THINK IT IS, I QUIT, GAME'S OVER, MOM'S CALLIN' ME, I'M LATE FOR DINNER.

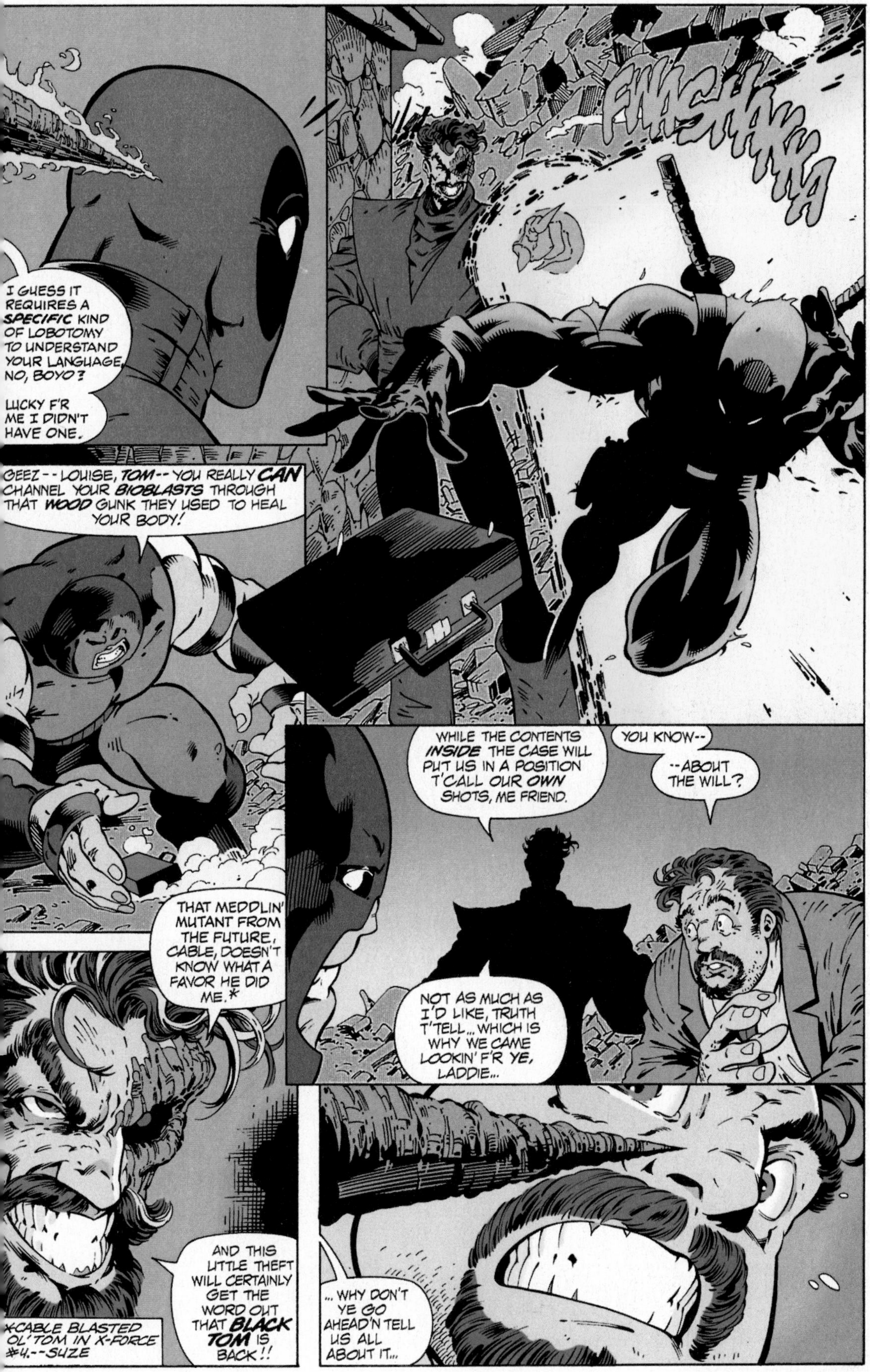
I GUESS IT REQUIRES A SPECIFIC KIND OF LOBOTOMY TO UNDERSTAND YOUR LANGUAGE, NO, BOYO?
LUCKY F'R ME I DIDN'T HAVE ONE.
FWASHAKKA
GEEZ--LOUISE, TOM--YOU REALLY CAN CHANNEL YOUR BIOBLASTS THROUGH THAT WOOD GUNK THEY USED TO HEAL YOUR BODY!
THAT MEDDLIN' MUTANT FROM THE FUTURE, CABLE, DOESN'T KNOW WHAT A FAVOR HE DID ME.*
AND THIS LITTLE THEFT WILL CERTAINLY GET THE WORD OUT THAT BLACK TOM IS BACK!!
*CABLE BLASTED OL' TOM IN X-FORCE #4.--SUZE
WHILE THE CONTENTS INSIDE THE CASE WILL PUT US IN A POSITION T'CALL OUR OWN SHOTS, ME FRIEND.
YOU KNOW--
--ABOUT THE WILL?
NOT AS MUCH AS I'D LIKE, TRUTH T'TELL... WHICH IS WHY WE CAME LOOKIN' F'R YE, LADDIE...
...WHY DON'T YE GO AHEAD'N TELL US ALL ABOUT IT...

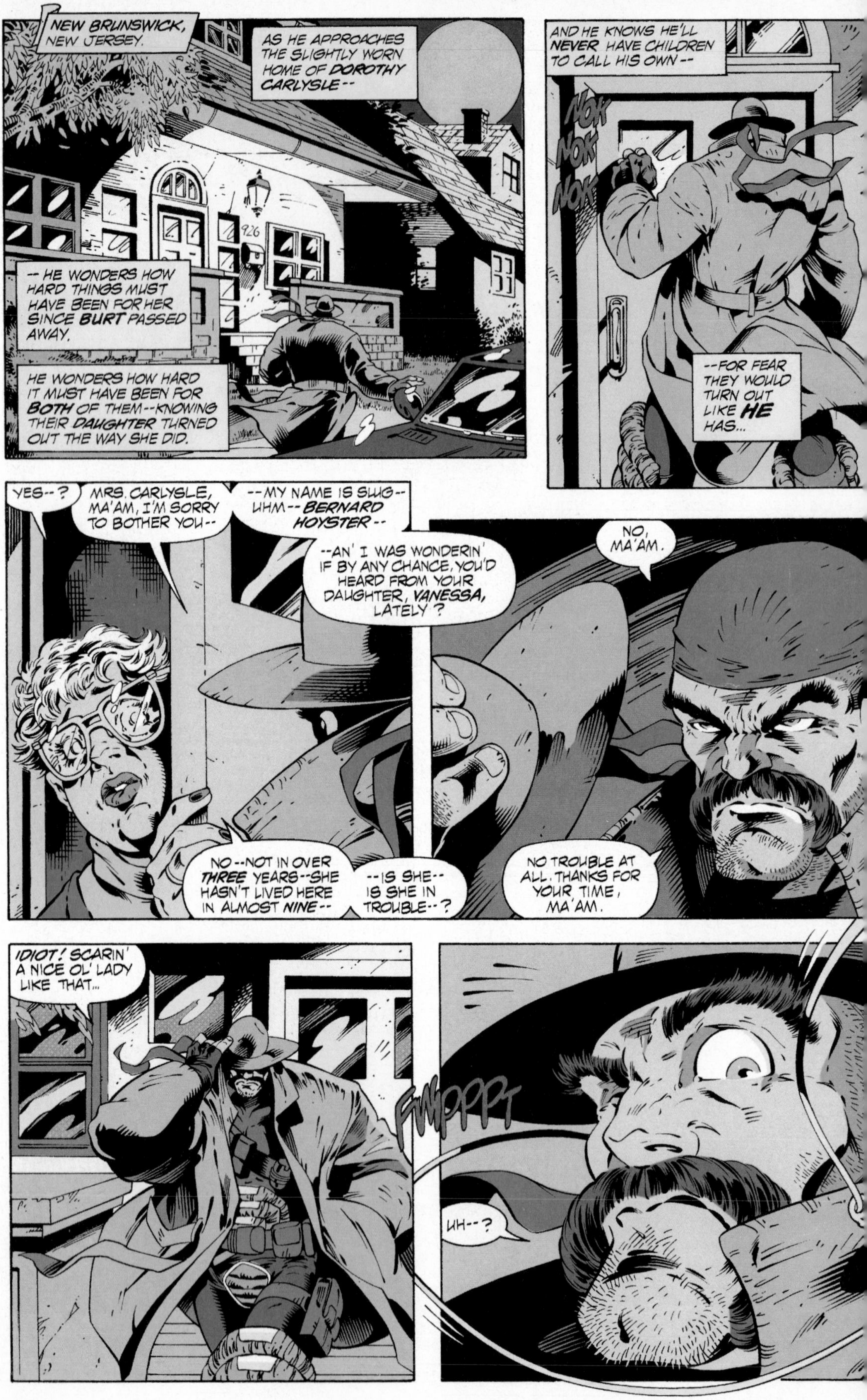
NEW BRUNSWICK, NEW JERSEY.
AS HE APPROACHES THE SLIGHTLY WORN HOME OF DOROTHY CARLYSLE--
--HE WONDERS HOW HARD THINGS MUST HAVE BEEN FOR HER SINCE BURT PASSED AWAY.
HE WONDERS HOW HARD IT MUST HAVE BEEN FOR BOTH OF THEM--KNOWING THEIR DAUGHTER TURNED OUT THE WAY SHE DID.
AND HE KNOWS HE'LL NEVER HAVE CHILDREN TO CALL HIS OWN--
NOK NOK NOK
--FOR FEAR THEY WOULD TURN OUT LIKE HE HAS...
YES--?
MRS. CARLYSLE, MA'AM, I'M SORRY TO BOTHER YOU--
--MY NAME IS SLUG-- UHM--BERNARD HOYSTER--
--AN' I WAS WONDERIN' IF BY ANY CHANCE, YOU'D HEARD FROM YOUR DAUGHTER, VANESSA, LATELY?
NO--NOT IN OVER THREE YEARS--SHE HASN'T LIVED HERE IN ALMOST NINE--
--IS SHE-- IS SHE IN TROUBLE--?
NO, MA'AM.
NO TROUBLE AT ALL. THANKS FOR YOUR TIME, MA'AM.
IDIOT! SCARIN' A NICE OL' LADY LIKE THAT...
FWIPPPT
UH--?

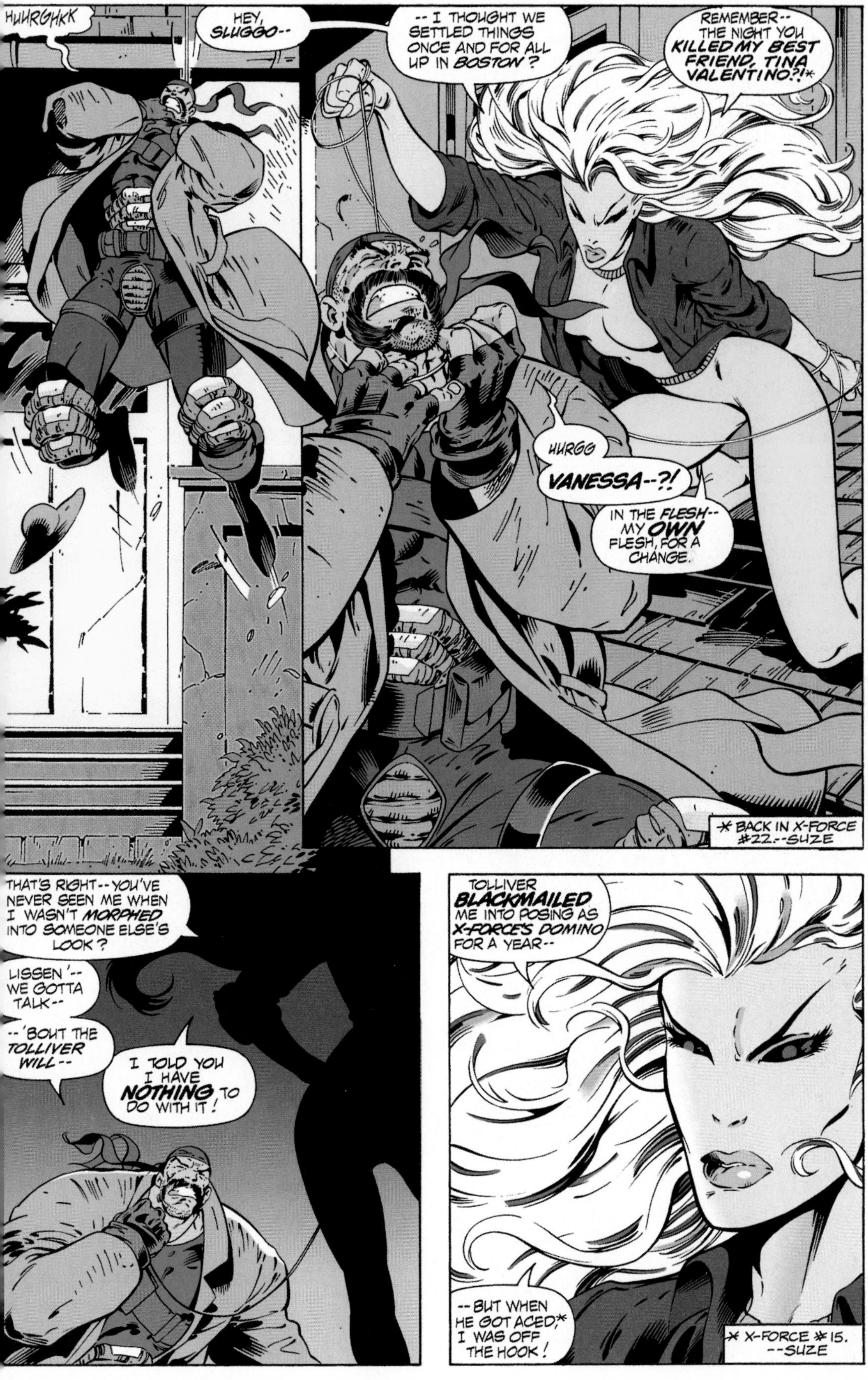
HUURGHKK
HEY, SLUGGO--
-- I THOUGHT WE SETTLED THINGS ONCE AND FOR ALL UP IN BOSTON?
REMEMBER-- THE NIGHT YOU KILLED MY BEST FRIEND, TINA VALENTINO?!*
HURGG
VANESSA--?!
IN THE FLESH-- MY OWN FLESH, FOR A CHANGE.
* BACK IN X-FORCE #22.--SUZE
THAT'S RIGHT--YOU'VE NEVER SEEN ME WHEN I WASN'T MORPHED INTO SOMEONE ELSE'S LOOK?
LISSEN '-- WE GOTTA TALK--
--'BOUT THE TOLLIVER WILL--
I TOLD YOU I HAVE NOTHING TO DO WITH IT!
TOLLIVER BLACKMAILED ME INTO POSING AS X-FORCE'S DOMINO FOR A YEAR--
--BUT WHEN HE GOT ACED,* I WAS OFF THE HOOK!
* X-FORCE #15. --SUZE

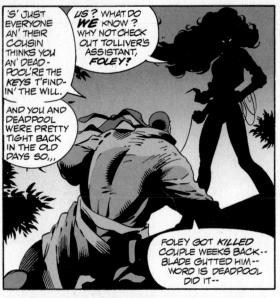

'S' JUST EVERYONE AN' THEIR COUSIN THINKS YOU 'N' DEADPOOL'RE THE KEYS T'FINDIN' THE WILL.

AND YOU AND DEADPOOL WERE PRETTY TIGHT BACK IN THE OLD DAYS SO...

US? WHAT DO WE KNOW? WHY NOT CHECK OUT TOLLIVER'S ASSISTANT, FOLEY?

FOLEY GOT KILLED COUPLE WEEKS BACK-- BLADE GUTTED HIM-- WORD IS DEADPOOL DID IT--

BUT THAT'S WHEN WADE WAS IN BOSTON LOOKING FOR ME.

I KNOW THAT-- AN' SO DO YOU-- BUT NO ONE ELSE DOES--

-- SO PEOPLE'RE GONNA LOOK FOR YOU IN ORDER T'GET T'HIM--

BUT YOU'RE THE ONLY ONE BESIDES TINA WHO KNEW THIS WAS MY PARENTS' HOUSE, RIGHT?

YUH--WADE'S BEEN LOOKIN' ALL OVER FOR YOU.

STUPID JERK... WHERE IS HE NOW, SLUGGO?

WITH THE WEASEL--IN SARAJEVO, I THINK.

HEY-- WHAT'RE YOU DOIN' WITH MY KEYS?

I'M GOING TO NEED THEM TO DRIVE YOUR CAR, SLUGGO.

WHAT ABOUT ME?

WHERE YOU'RE GOING, YOU WON'T NEED A CAR.

WHERE'M I GOIN', 'NESSIE?

TO JAIL, FOR BREAKING AND ENTERING INTO MY MOM'S HOUSE.

WHEN DID I DO THAT?

JUST NOW.

KCHASHSHK

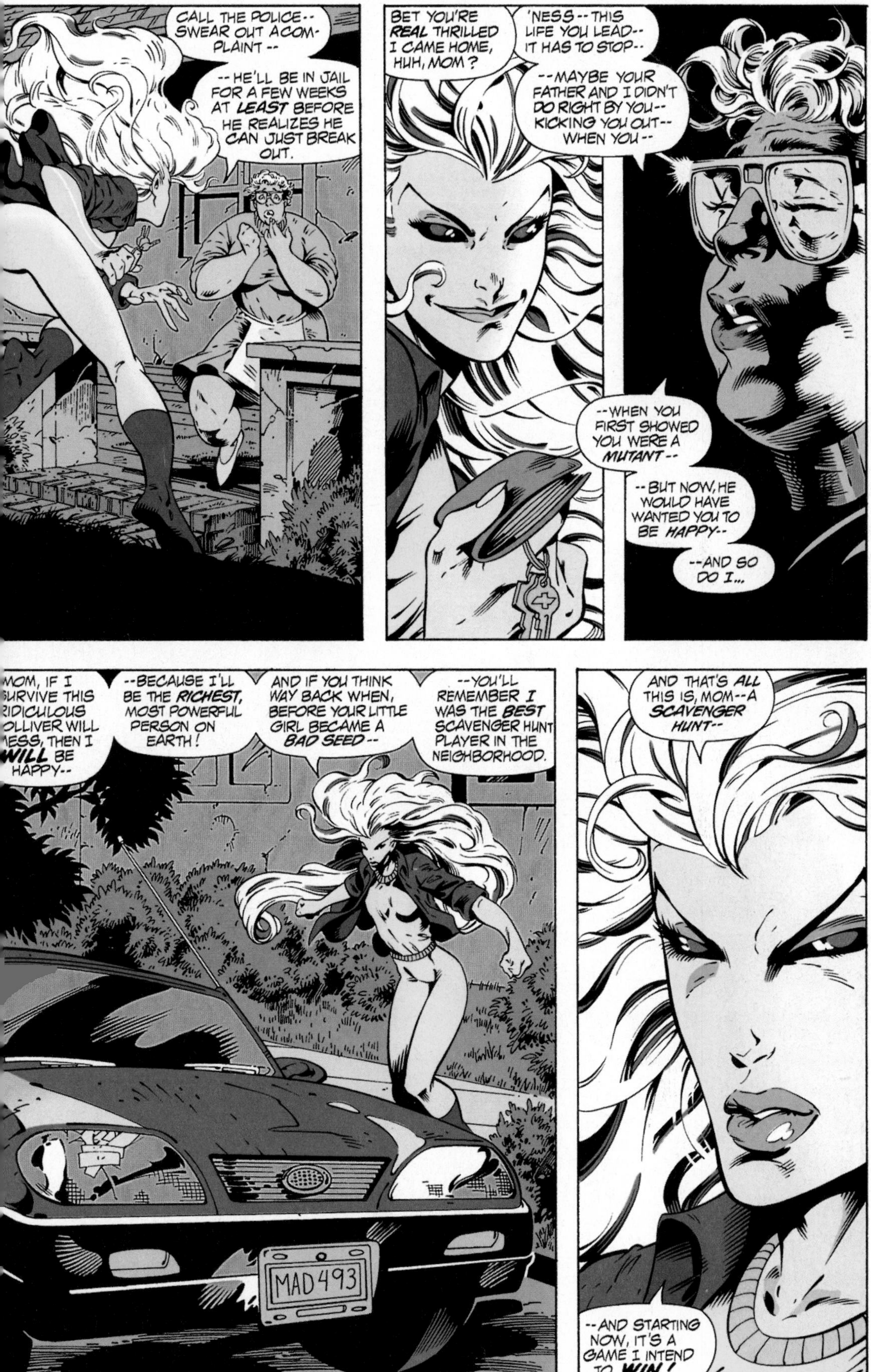
CALL THE POLICE-- SWEAR OUT A COMPLAINT --
-- HE'LL BE IN JAIL FOR A FEW WEEKS AT LEAST BEFORE HE REALIZES HE CAN JUST BREAK OUT.
BET YOU'RE REAL THRILLED I CAME HOME, HUH, MOM?
'NESS -- THIS LIFE YOU LEAD-- IT HAS TO STOP--
--MAYBE YOUR FATHER AND I DIDN'T DO RIGHT BY YOU-- KICKING YOU OUT-- WHEN YOU --
--WHEN YOU FIRST SHOWED YOU WERE A MUTANT --
-- BUT NOW, HE WOULD HAVE WANTED YOU TO BE HAPPY--
--AND SO DO I...
MOM, IF I SURVIVE THIS RIDICULOUS OLLIVER WILL MESS, THEN I WILL BE HAPPY--
--BECAUSE I'LL BE THE RICHEST, MOST POWERFUL PERSON ON EARTH!
AND IF YOU THINK WAY BACK WHEN, BEFORE YOUR LITTLE GIRL BECAME A BAD SEED --
--YOU'LL REMEMBER I WAS THE BEST SCAVENGER HUNT PLAYER IN THE NEIGHBORHOOD.
MAD 493
AND THAT'S ALL THIS IS, MOM--A SCAVENGER HUNT--
--AND STARTING NOW, IT'S A GAME I INTEND TO WIN!

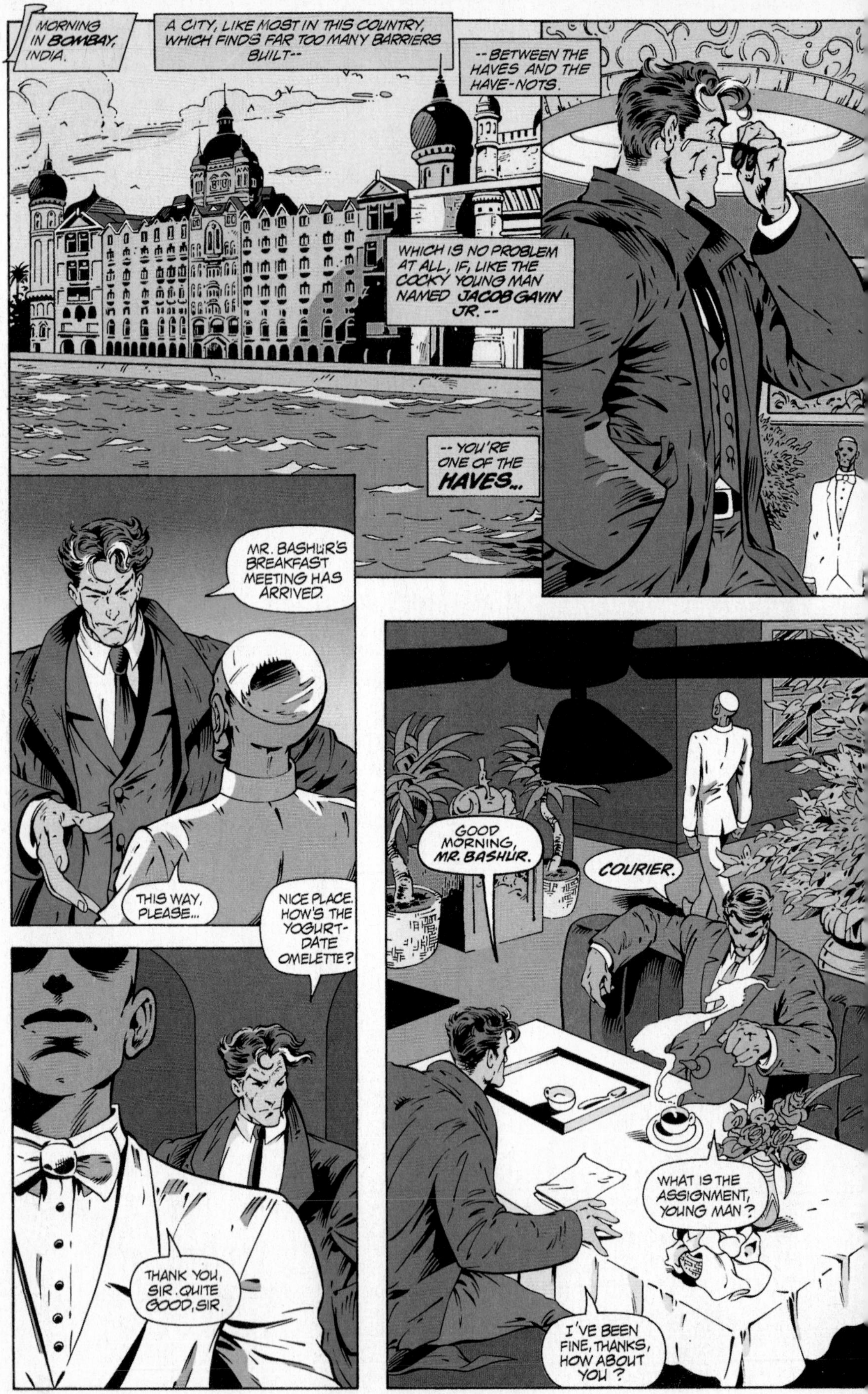
MORNING IN BOMBAY, INDIA.
A CITY, LIKE MOST IN THIS COUNTRY, WHICH FINDS FAR TOO MANY BARRIERS BUILT--
--BETWEEN THE HAVES AND THE HAVE-NOTS.
WHICH IS NO PROBLEM AT ALL, IF, LIKE THE COCKY YOUNG MAN NAMED JACOB GAVIN JR.--
--YOU'RE ONE OF THE HAVES...
MR. BASHŪR'S BREAKFAST MEETING HAS ARRIVED.
THIS WAY, PLEASE...
NICE PLACE. HOW'S THE YOGURT-DATE OMELETTE?
THANK YOU, SIR. QUITE GOOD, SIR.
GOOD MORNING, MR. BASHŪR.
COURIER.
WHAT IS THE ASSIGNMENT, YOUNG MAN?
I'VE BEEN FINE, THANKS, HOW ABOUT YOU?

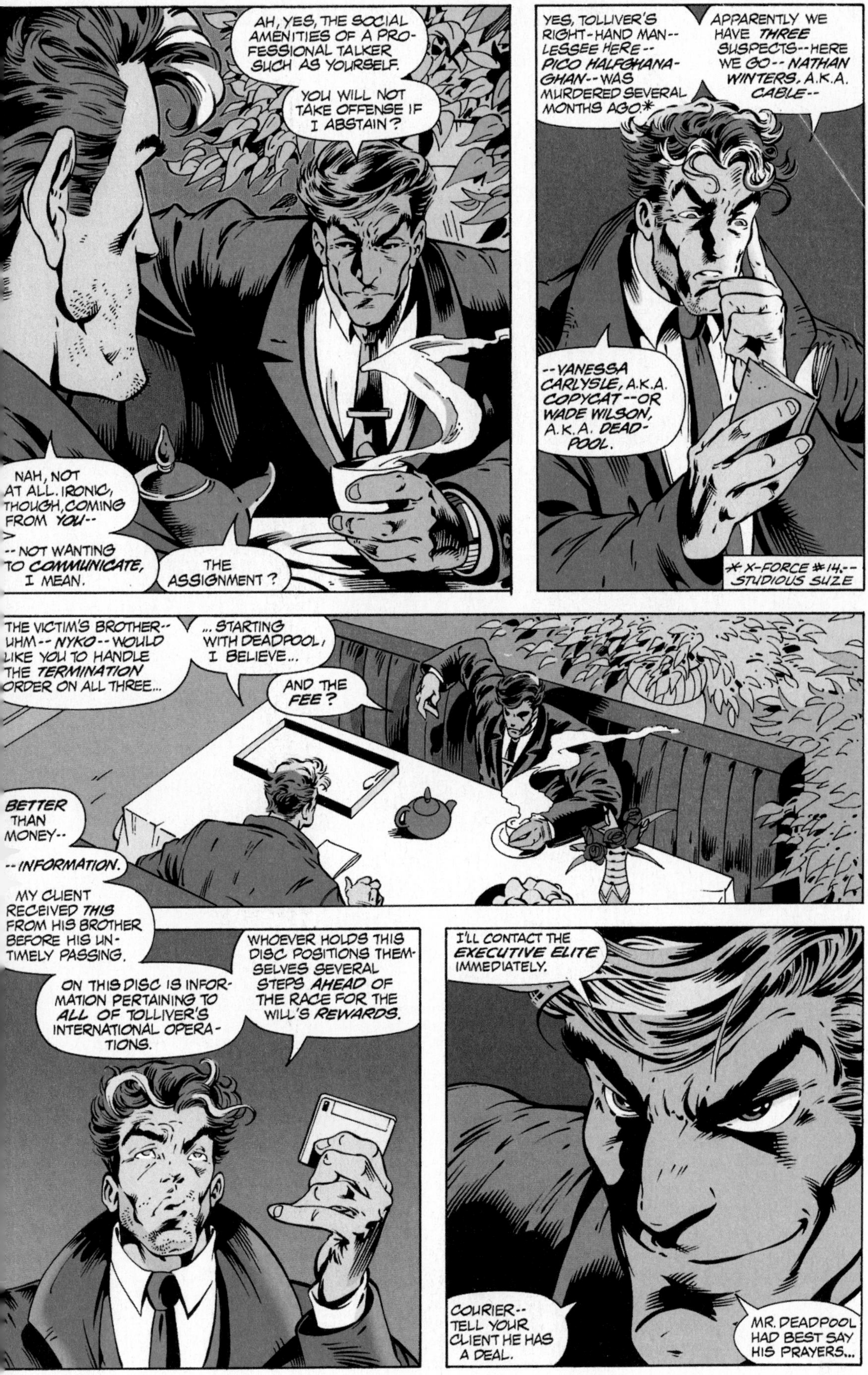
AH, YES, THE SOCIAL AMENITIES OF A PROFESSIONAL TALKER SUCH AS YOURSELF.
YOU WILL NOT TAKE OFFENSE IF I ABSTAIN?
NAH, NOT AT ALL. IRONIC, THOUGH, COMING FROM YOU--
--NOT WANTING TO COMMUNICATE, I MEAN.
THE ASSIGNMENT?
YES, TOLLIVER'S RIGHT-HAND MAN--LESSEE HERE--PICO HALFGHANAGHAN--WAS MURDERED SEVERAL MONTHS AGO.*
APPARENTLY WE HAVE THREE SUSPECTS--HERE WE GO--NATHAN WINTERS, A.K.A. CABLE--
--VANESSA CARLYSLE, A.K.A. COPYCAT--OR WADE WILSON, A.K.A. DEADPOOL.
*X-FORCE #14.--STUDIOUS SUZE
THE VICTIM'S BROTHER--UHM--NYKO--WOULD LIKE YOU TO HANDLE THE TERMINATION ORDER ON ALL THREE...
...STARTING WITH DEADPOOL, I BELIEVE...
AND THE FEE?
BETTER THAN MONEY--
--INFORMATION.
MY CLIENT RECEIVED THIS FROM HIS BROTHER BEFORE HIS UNTIMELY PASSING.
ON THIS DISC IS INFORMATION PERTAINING TO ALL OF TOLLIVER'S INTERNATIONAL OPERATIONS.
WHOEVER HOLDS THIS DISC POSITIONS THEMSELVES SEVERAL STEPS AHEAD OF THE RACE FOR THE WILL'S REWARDS.
I'LL CONTACT THE EXECUTIVE ELITE IMMEDIATELY.
COURIER--TELL YOUR CLIENT HE HAS A DEAL.
MR. DEADPOOL HAD BEST SAY HIS PRAYERS...

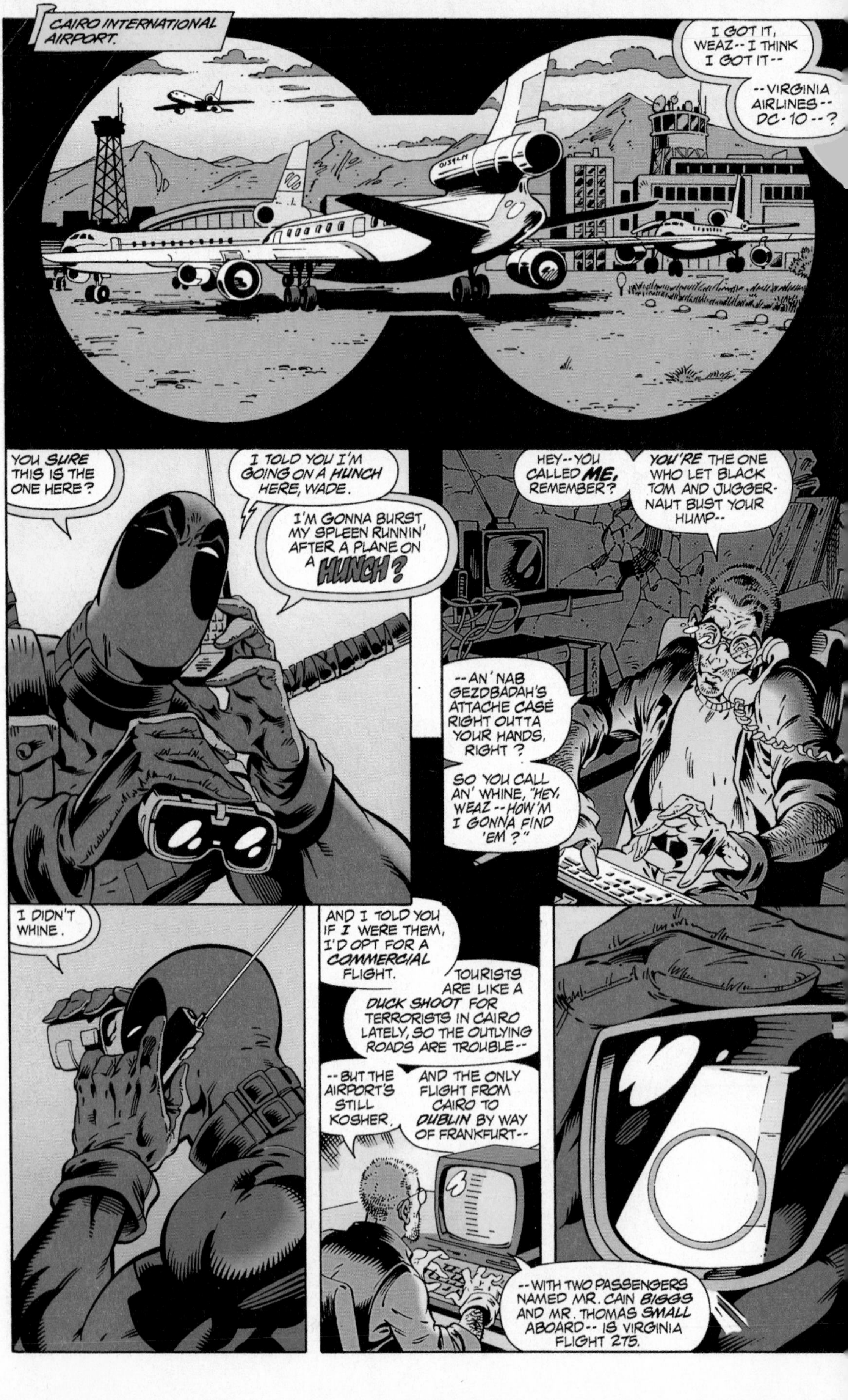

CAIRO INTERNATIONAL AIRPORT.
I GOT IT, WEAZ-- I THINK I GOT IT--
--VIRGINIA AIRLINES-- DC-10--?
YOU SURE THIS IS THE ONE HERE?
I TOLD YOU I'M GOING ON A HUNCH HERE, WADE.
I'M GONNA BURST MY SPLEEN RUNNIN' AFTER A PLANE ON A HUNCH?
HEY--YOU CALLED ME, REMEMBER?
YOU'RE THE ONE WHO LET BLACK TOM AND JUGGERNAUT BUST YOUR HUMP--
--AN' NAB GEZDBADAH'S ATTACHE CASE RIGHT OUTTA YOUR HANDS, RIGHT?
SO YOU CALL AN' WHINE, "HEY, WEAZ--HOW'M I GONNA FIND 'EM?"
I DIDN'T WHINE.
AND I TOLD YOU IF I WERE THEM, I'D OPT FOR A COMMERCIAL FLIGHT.
TOURISTS ARE LIKE A DUCK SHOOT FOR TERRORISTS IN CAIRO LATELY, SO THE OUTLYING ROADS ARE TROUBLE--
--BUT THE AIRPORT'S STILL KOSHER.
AND THE ONLY FLIGHT FROM CAIRO TO DUBLIN BY WAY OF FRANKFURT--
--WITH TWO PASSENGERS NAMED MR. CAIN BIGGS AND MR. THOMAS SMALL ABOARD-- IS VIRGINIA FLIGHT 275.

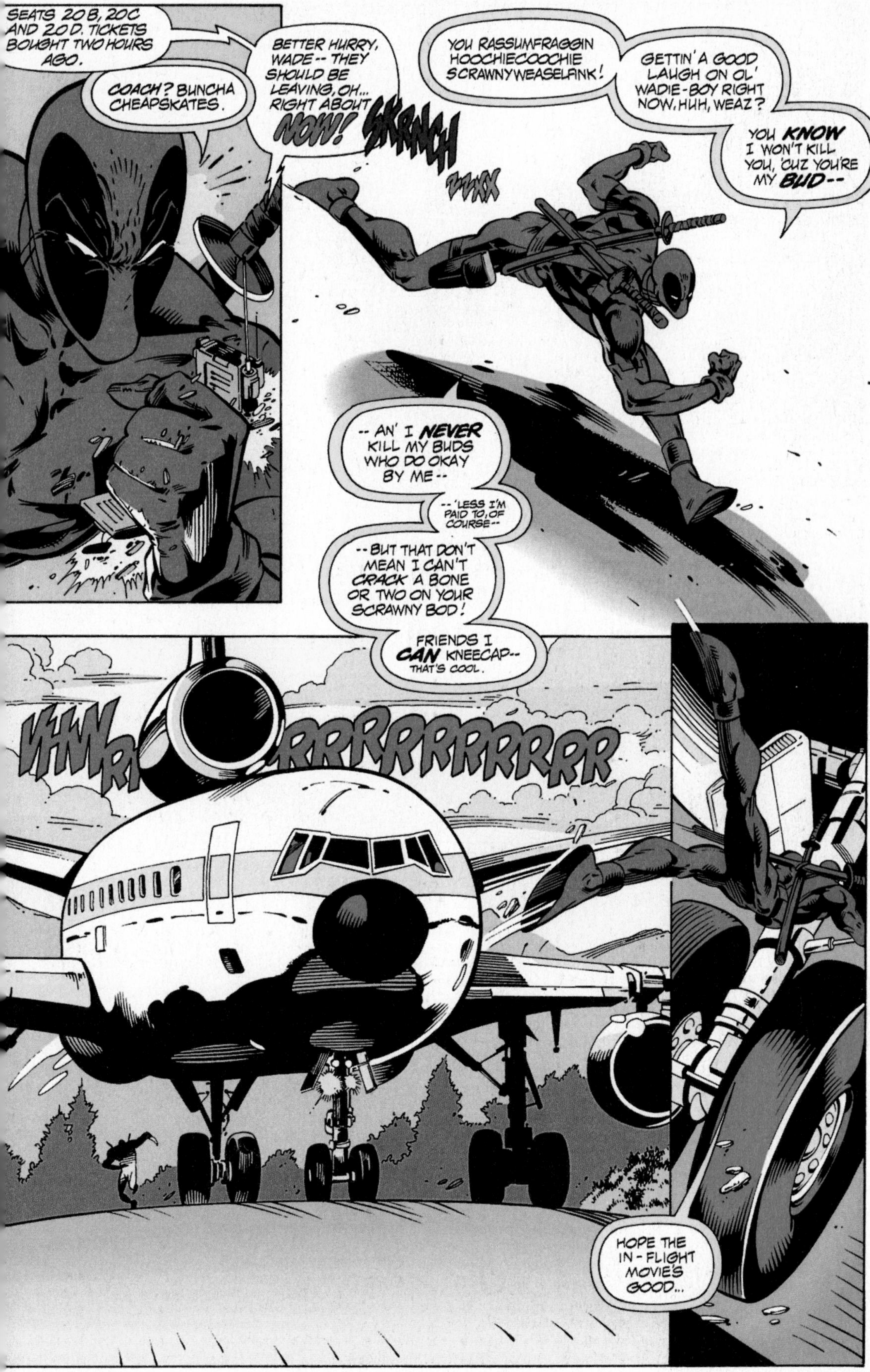
SEATS 20B, 20C AND 20D. TICKETS BOUGHT TWO HOURS AGO.
COACH? BUNCHA CHEAPSKATES.
BETTER HURRY, WADE -- THEY SHOULD BE LEAVING, OH... RIGHT ABOUT NOW!
SKRNCH
ZZZXX
YOU RASSUMFRAGGIN HOOCHIECOOCHIE SCRAWNYWEASELFINK!
GETTIN' A GOOD LAUGH ON OL' WADIE-BOY RIGHT NOW, HUH, WEAZ?
YOU KNOW I WON'T KILL YOU, 'CUZ YOU'RE MY BUD--
-- AN' I NEVER KILL MY BUDS WHO DO OKAY BY ME --
-- 'LESS I'M PAID TO, OF COURSE --
-- BUT THAT DON'T MEAN I CAN'T CRACK A BONE OR TWO ON YOUR SCRAWNY BOD!
FRIENDS I CAN KNEECAP-- THAT'S COOL.
VHWRRRRRRRRRRRRR
HOPE THE IN-FLIGHT MOVIE'S GOOD...

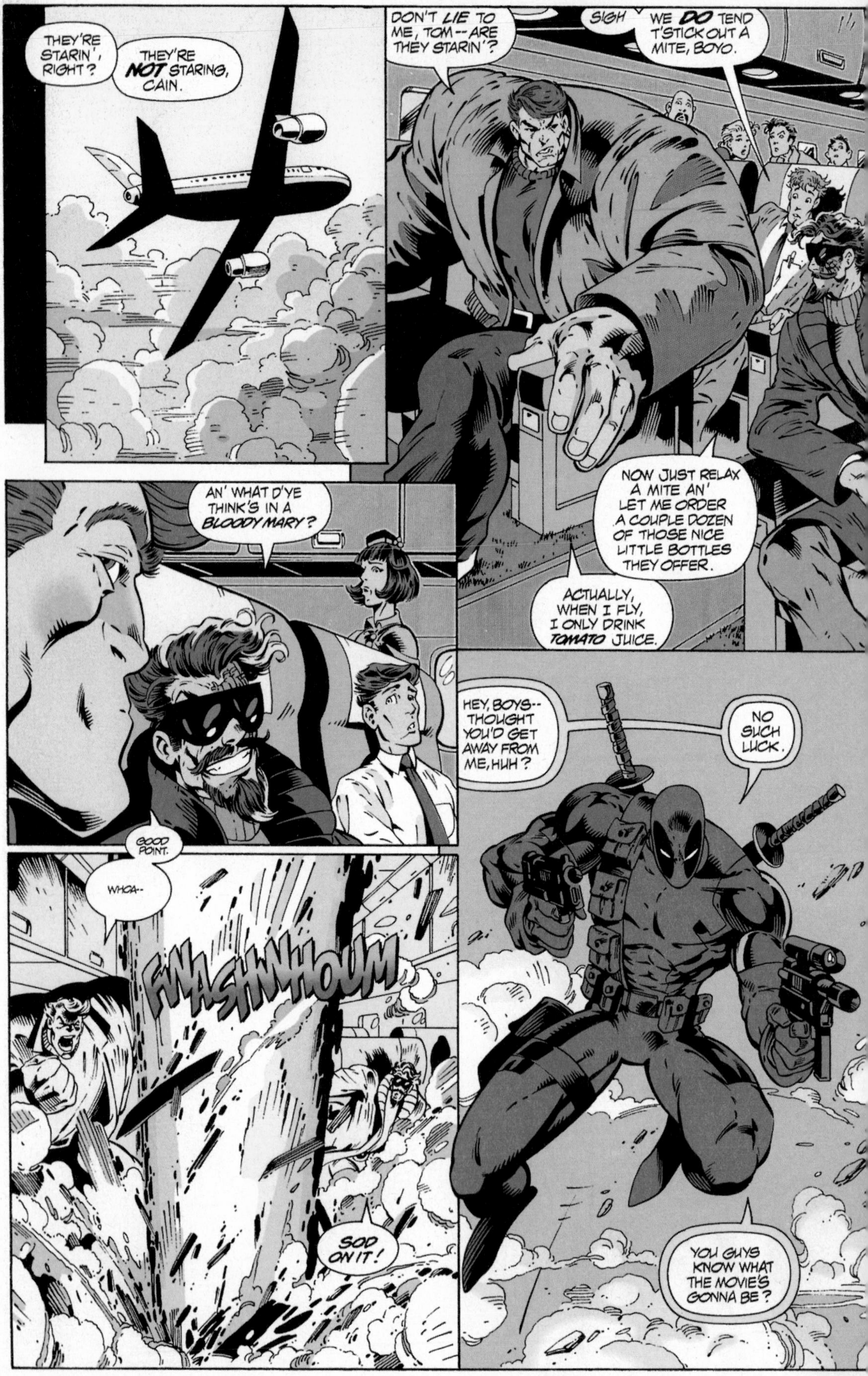

THEY'RE STARIN', RIGHT?
THEY'RE NOT STARING, CAIN.
DON'T LIE TO ME, TOM--ARE THEY STARIN'?
SIGH
WE DO TEND T'STICK OUT A MITE, BOYO.
NOW JUST RELAX A MITE AN' LET ME ORDER A COUPLE DOZEN OF THOSE NICE LITTLE BOTTLES THEY OFFER.
ACTUALLY, WHEN I FLY, I ONLY DRINK TOMATO JUICE.
AN' WHAT D'YE THINK'S IN A BLOODY MARY?
GOOD POINT.
WHOA--
FWASHWHOUM
SOD ON IT!
HEY, BOYS--THOUGHT YOU'D GET AWAY FROM ME, HUH?
NO SUCH LUCK.
YOU GUYS KNOW WHAT THE MOVIE'S GONNA BE?

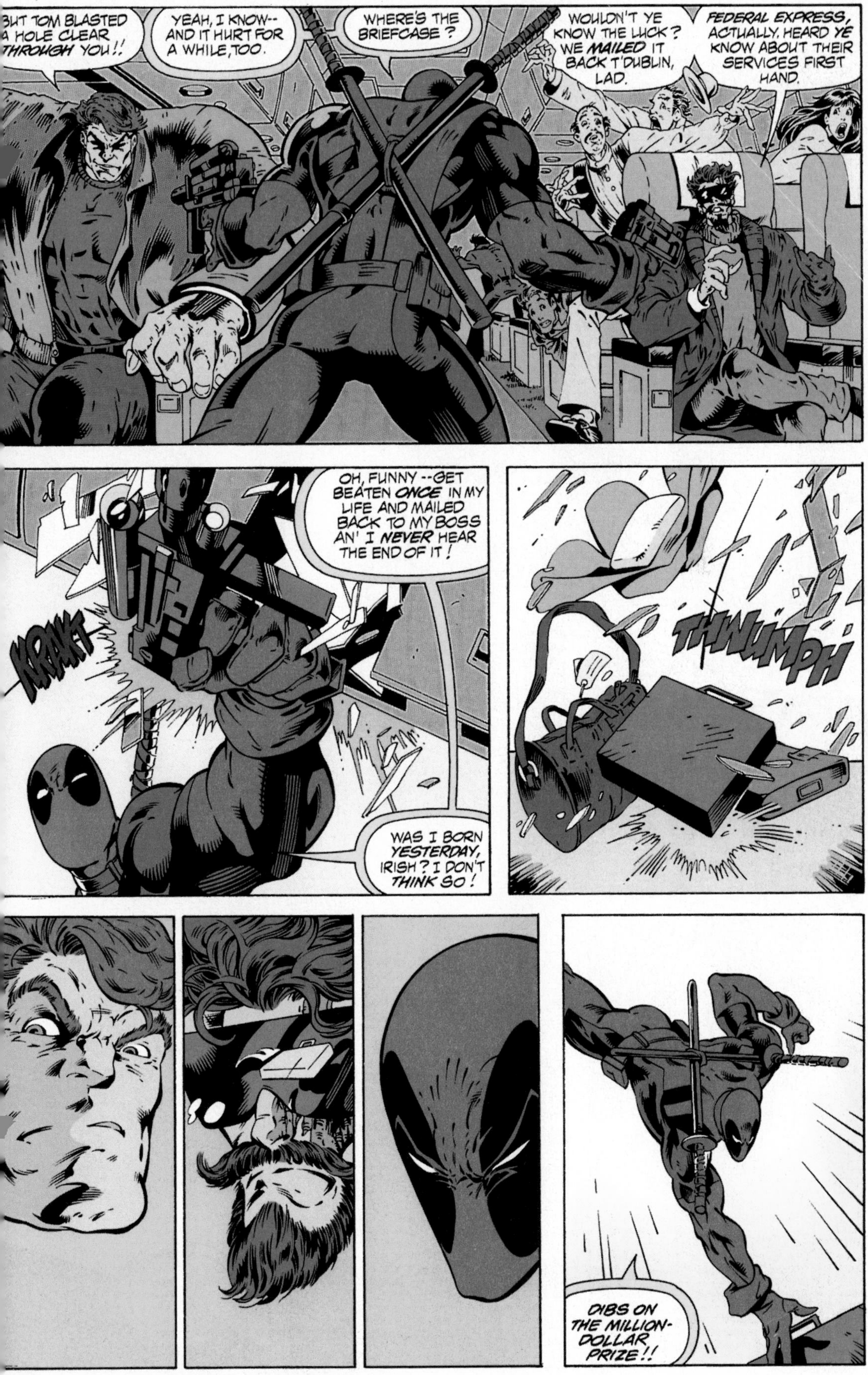
BUT TOM BLASTED A HOLE CLEAR THROUGH YOU!!
YEAH, I KNOW-- AND IT HURT FOR A WHILE, TOO.
WHERE'S THE BRIEFCASE?
WOULDN'T YE KNOW THE LUCK? WE MAILED IT BACK T'DUBLIN, LAD.
FEDERAL EXPRESS, ACTUALLY. HEARD YE KNOW ABOUT THEIR SERVICES FIRST HAND.
OH, FUNNY --GET BEATEN ONCE IN MY LIFE AND MAILED BACK TO MY BOSS AN' I NEVER HEAR THE END OF IT!
KRAKT
WAS I BORN YESTERDAY, IRISH? I DON'T THINK SO!
THWUMPH
DIBS ON THE MILLION-DOLLAR PRIZE!!

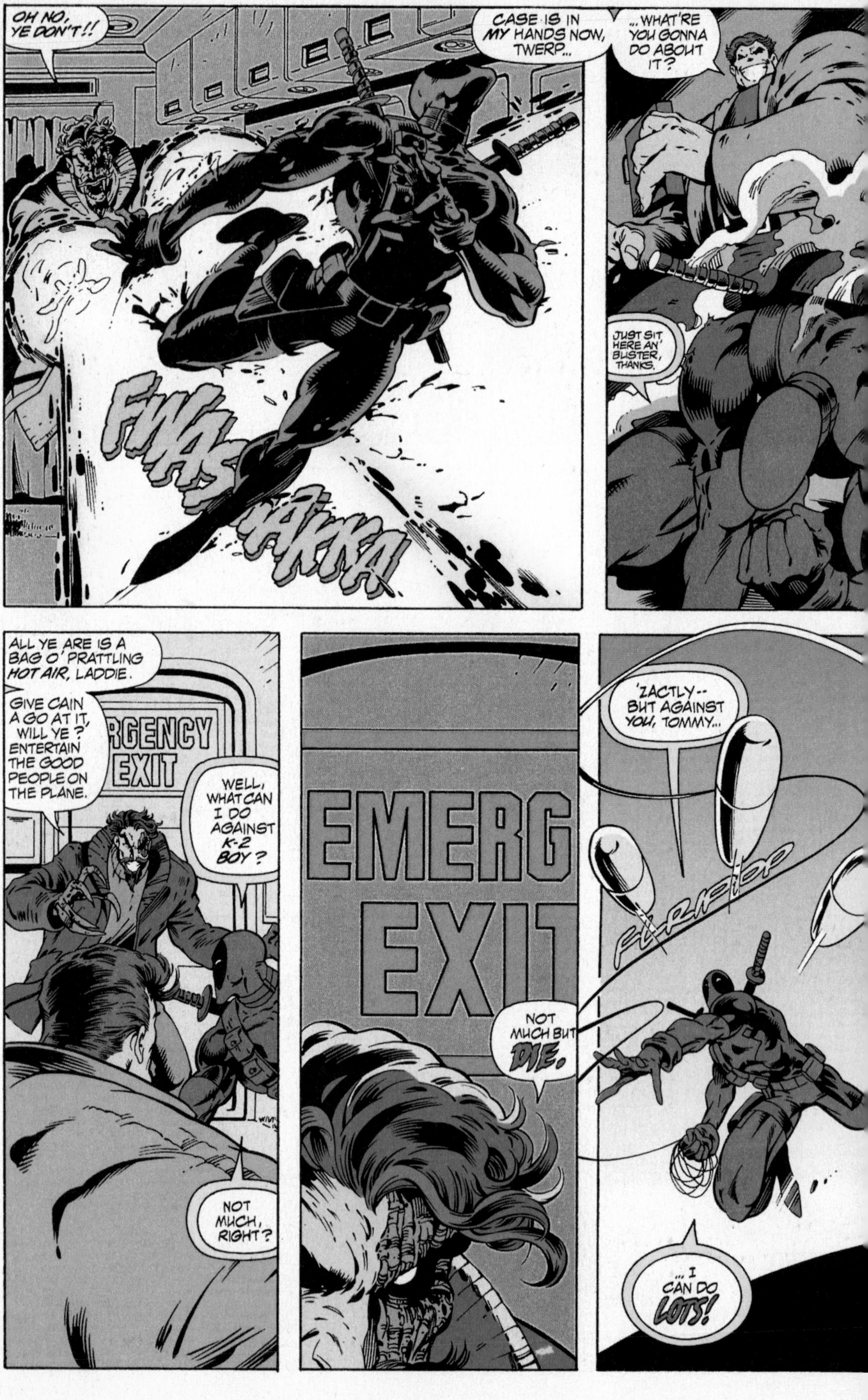
OH NO, YE DON'T!!
CASE IS IN MY HANDS NOW, TWERP...
FWASWAKKA
...WHAT'RE YOU GONNA DO ABOUT IT?
JUST SIT HERE AN' BLISTER, THANKS.
ALL YE ARE IS A BAG O' PRATTLING HOT AIR, LADDIE.
GIVE CAIN A GO AT IT, WILL YE? ENTERTAIN THE GOOD PEOPLE ON THE PLANE.
WELL, WHAT CAN I DO AGAINST K-2 BOY?
NOT MUCH, RIGHT?
EMERG EXIT
NOT MUCH BUT DIE.
'ZACTLY-- BUT AGAINST YOU, TOMMY...
...I CAN DO LOTS!

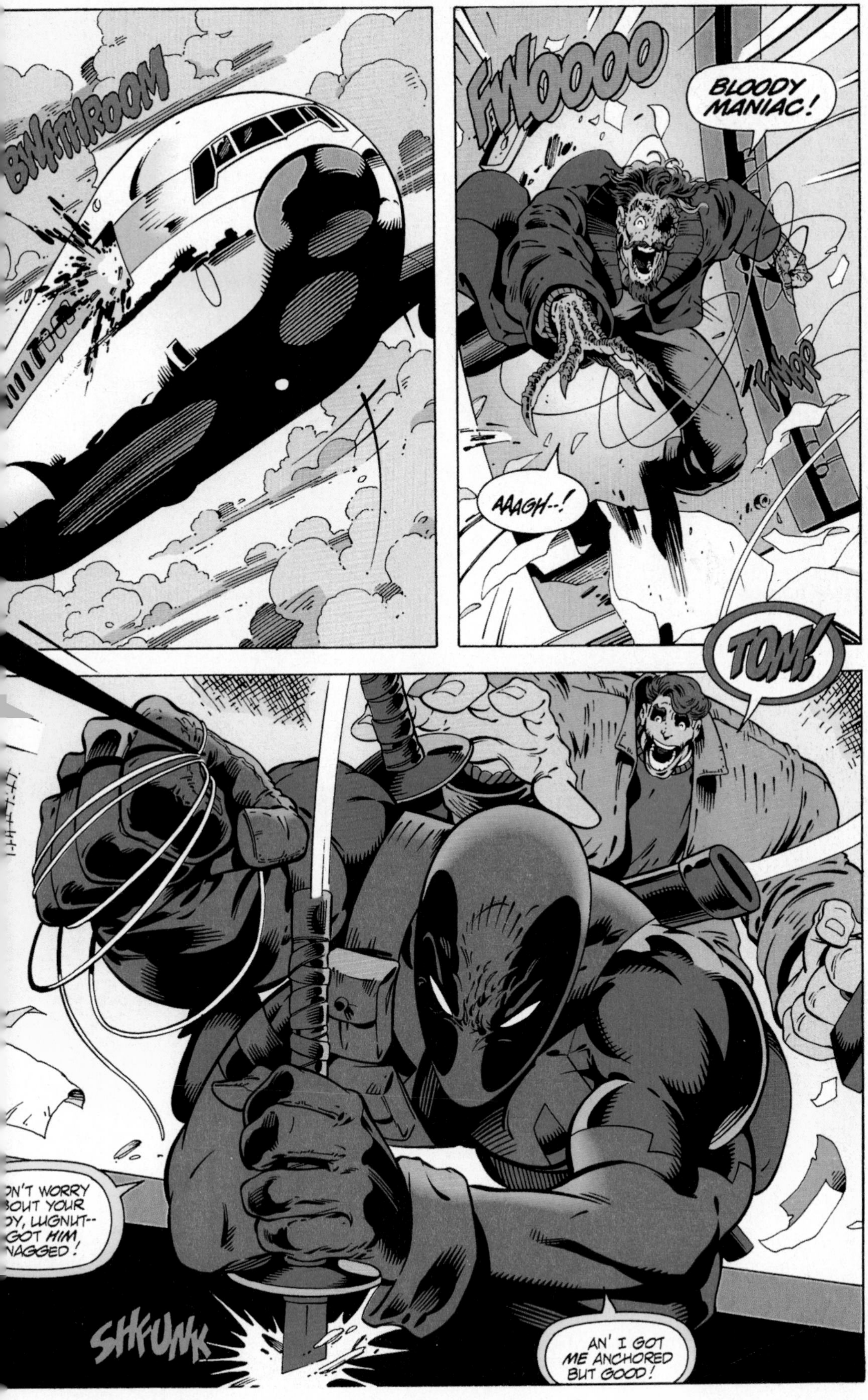
BWATHROOM
FWOOOO
BLOODY MANIAC!
Fwop
AAAGH--!
TOM!
ON'T WORRY BOUT YOUR DY, LUGNUT-- GOT HIM NAGGED!
SHFUNK
AN' I GOT ME ANCHORED BUT GOOD!

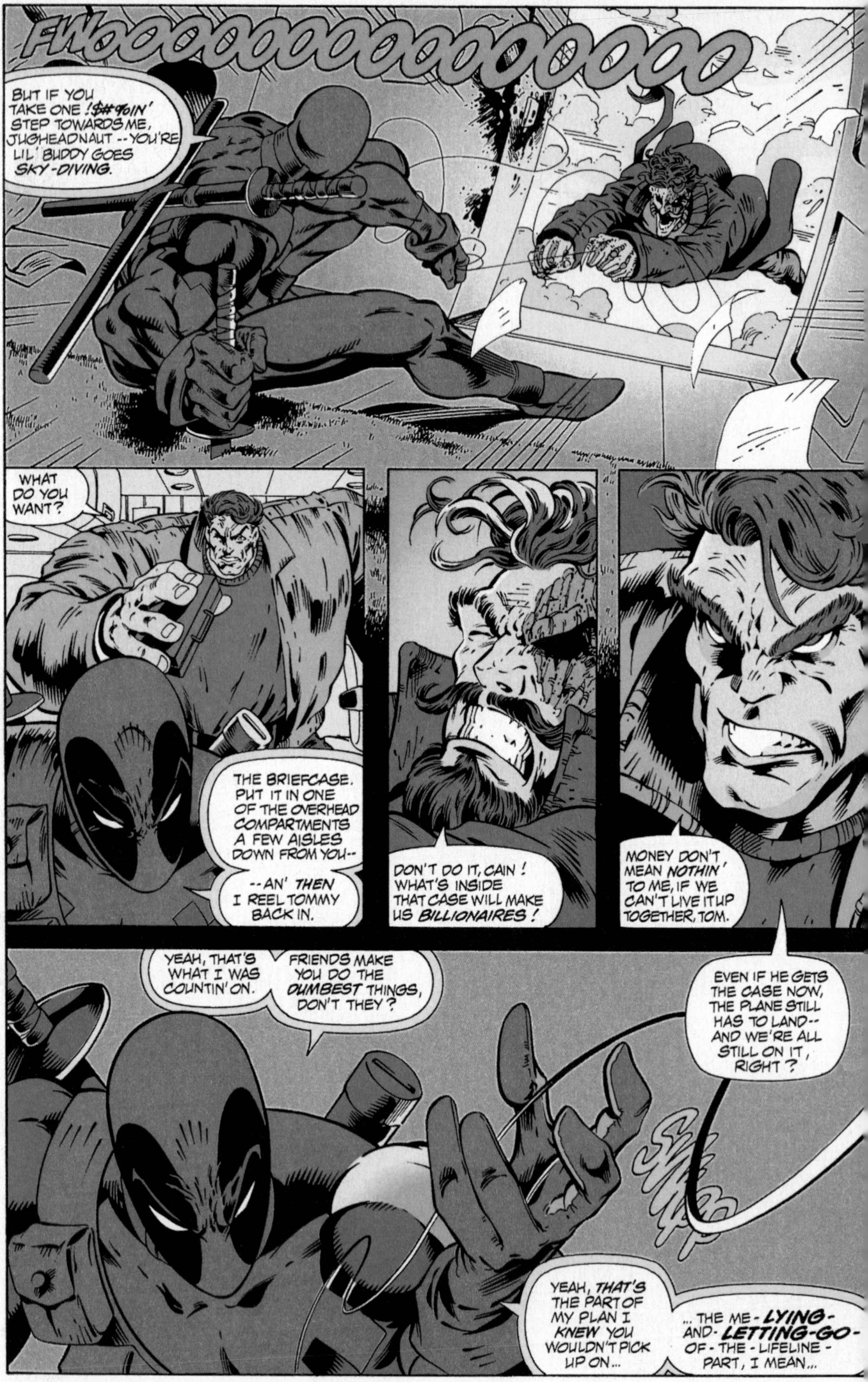
FWOOOOOOOOOOOOOOO
BUT IF YOU TAKE ONE !$#%IN' STEP TOWARDS ME, JUGHEADNAUT -- YOU'RE LIL' BUDDY GOES SKY-DIVING.
WHAT DO YOU WANT?
THE BRIEFCASE. PUT IT IN ONE OF THE OVERHEAD COMPARTMENTS A FEW AISLES DOWN FROM YOU--
--AN' THEN I REEL TOMMY BACK IN.
DON'T DO IT, CAIN! WHAT'S INSIDE THAT CASE WILL MAKE US BILLIONAIRES!
MONEY DON'T MEAN NOTHIN' TO ME, IF WE CAN'T LIVE IT UP TOGETHER, TOM.
YEAH, THAT'S WHAT I WAS COUNTIN' ON.
FRIENDS MAKE YOU DO THE DUMBEST THINGS, DON'T THEY?
EVEN IF HE GETS THE CASE NOW, THE PLANE STILL HAS TO LAND-- AND WE'RE ALL STILL ON IT, RIGHT?
YEAH, THAT'S THE PART OF MY PLAN I KNEW YOU WOULDN'T PICK UP ON...
... THE ME-LYING-AND-LETTING-GO-OF-THE-LIFELINE-PART, I MEAN...

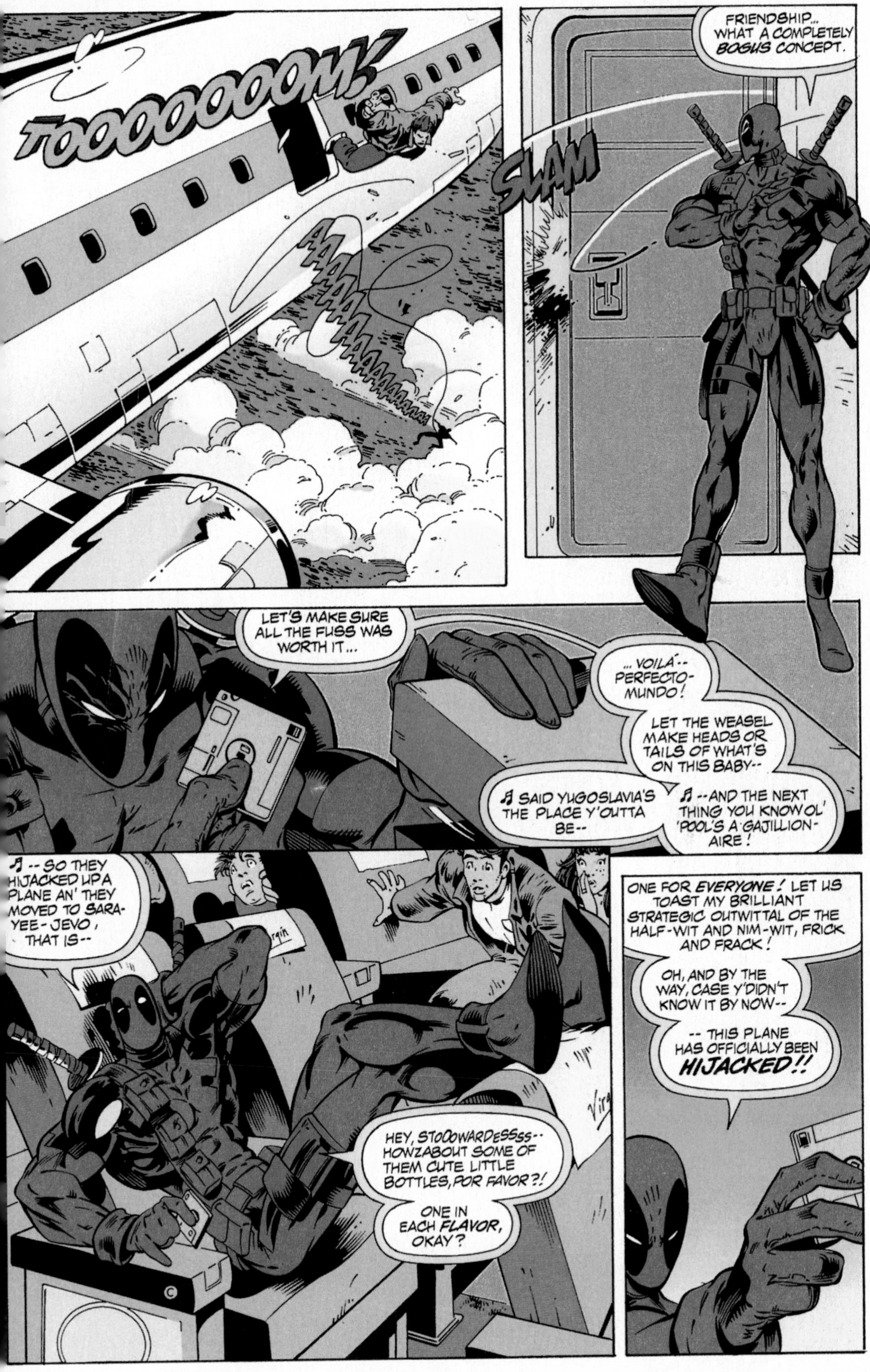

TOOOOOOOOM!
FRIENDSHIP... WHAT A COMPLETELY BOGUS CONCEPT.
SLAM
AAAAAAAAAAAAAAA
LET'S MAKE SURE ALL THE FUSS WAS WORTH IT...
...VOILÁ-- PERFECTO-MUNDO!
LET THE WEASEL MAKE HEADS OR TAILS OF WHAT'S ON THIS BABY--
♫ SAID YUGOSLAVIA'S THE PLACE Y'OUTTA BE--
♫ --AND THE NEXT THING YOU KNOW OL' 'POOL'S A GAJILLION-AIRE!
♫ --SO THEY HIJACKED UP A PLANE AN' THEY MOVED TO SARA-YEE-JEVO, THAT IS--
HEY, STOOOWARDESSss-- HOWZABOUT SOME OF THEM CUTE LITTLE BOTTLES, POR FAVOR?!
ONE IN EACH FLAVOR, OKAY?
ONE FOR EVERYONE! LET US TOAST MY BRILLIANT STRATEGIC OUTWITTAL OF THE HALF-WIT AND NIM-WIT, FRICK AND FRACK!
OH, AND BY THE WAY, CASE Y'DIDN'T KNOW IT BY NOW--
-- THIS PLANE HAS OFFICIALLY BEEN HIJACKED!!

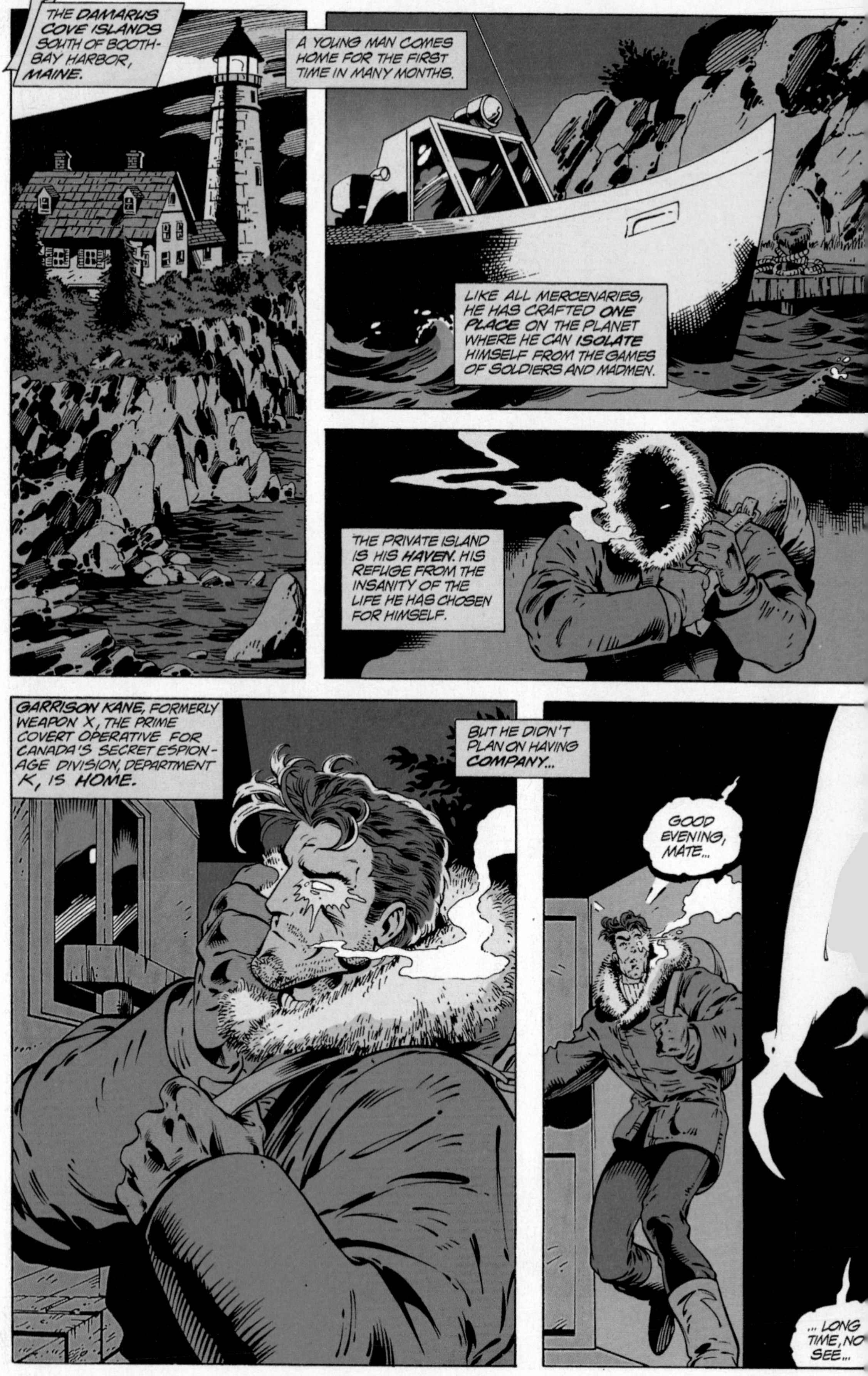
THE DAMARUS COVE ISLANDS SOUTH OF BOOTH-BAY HARBOR, MAINE.
A YOUNG MAN COMES HOME FOR THE FIRST TIME IN MANY MONTHS.
LIKE ALL MERCENARIES, HE HAS CRAFTED ONE PLACE ON THE PLANET WHERE HE CAN ISOLATE HIMSELF FROM THE GAMES OF SOLDIERS AND MADMEN.
THE PRIVATE ISLAND IS HIS HAVEN. HIS REFUGE FROM THE INSANITY OF THE LIFE HE HAS CHOSEN FOR HIMSELF.
GARRISON KANE, FORMERLY WEAPON X, THE PRIME COVERT OPERATIVE FOR CANADA'S SECRET ESPION-AGE DIVISION, DEPARTMENT K, IS HOME.
BUT HE DIDN'T PLAN ON HAVING COMPANY...
GOOD EVENING, MATE...
...LONG TIME, NO SEE...

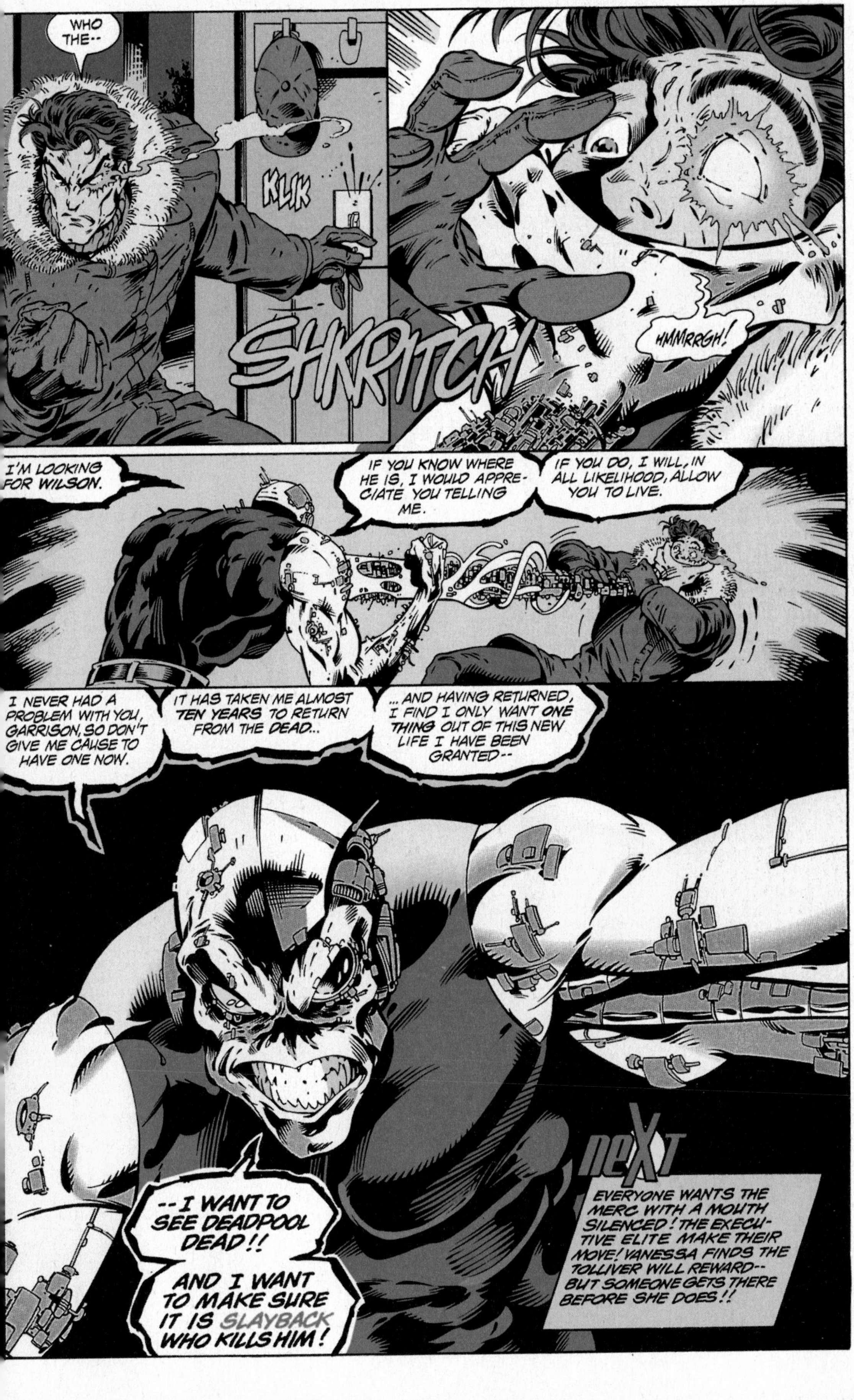
WHO THE--
KLIK
SHRITCH
HMMRRGH!
I'M LOOKING FOR WILSON.
IF YOU KNOW WHERE HE IS, I WOULD APPRECIATE YOU TELLING ME.
IF YOU DO, I WILL, IN ALL LIKELIHOOD, ALLOW YOU TO LIVE.
I NEVER HAD A PROBLEM WITH YOU, GARRISON, SO DON'T GIVE ME CAUSE TO HAVE ONE NOW.
IT HAS TAKEN ME ALMOST TEN YEARS TO RETURN FROM THE DEAD...
...AND HAVING RETURNED, I FIND I ONLY WANT ONE THING OUT OF THIS NEW LIFE I HAVE BEEN GRANTED--
--I WANT TO SEE DEADPOOL DEAD!!
AND I WANT TO MAKE SURE IT IS SLAYBACK WHO KILLS HIM!
neXT
EVERYONE WANTS THE MERC WITH A MOUTH SILENCED! THE EXECUTIVE ELITE MAKE THEIR MOVE! VANESSA FINDS THE TOLLIVER WILL REWARD-- BUT SOMEONE GETS THERE BEFORE SHE DOES!!

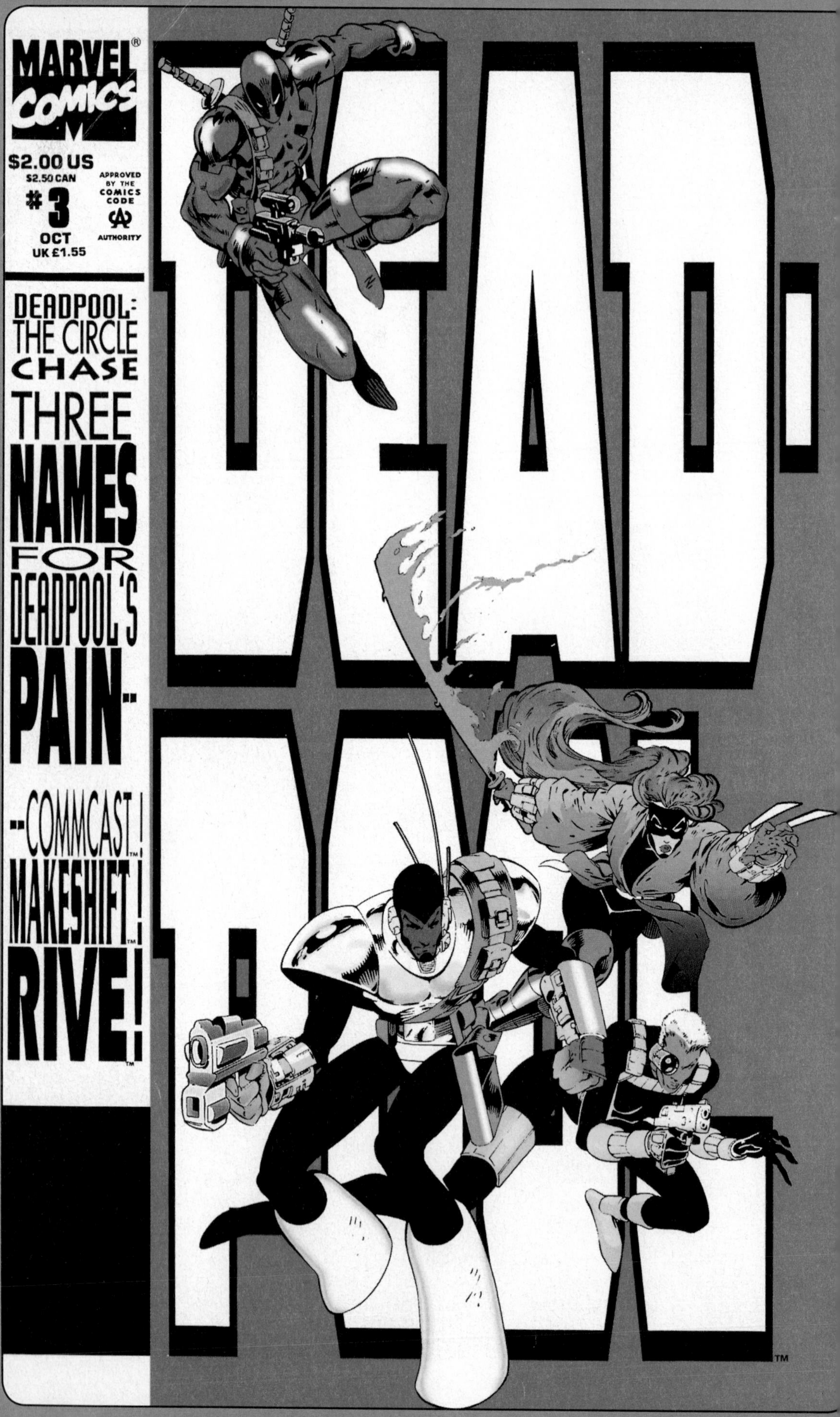

MARVEL® COMICS
$2.00 US
$2.50 CAN
#3
OCT
UK £1.55
APPROVED BY THE COMICS CODE AUTHORITY
DEADPOOL: THE CIRCLE CHASE
THREE NAMES FOR DEADPOOL'S PAIN--
--COMMCAST™! MAKESHIFT™! RIVE™!
DEAD-POOL™

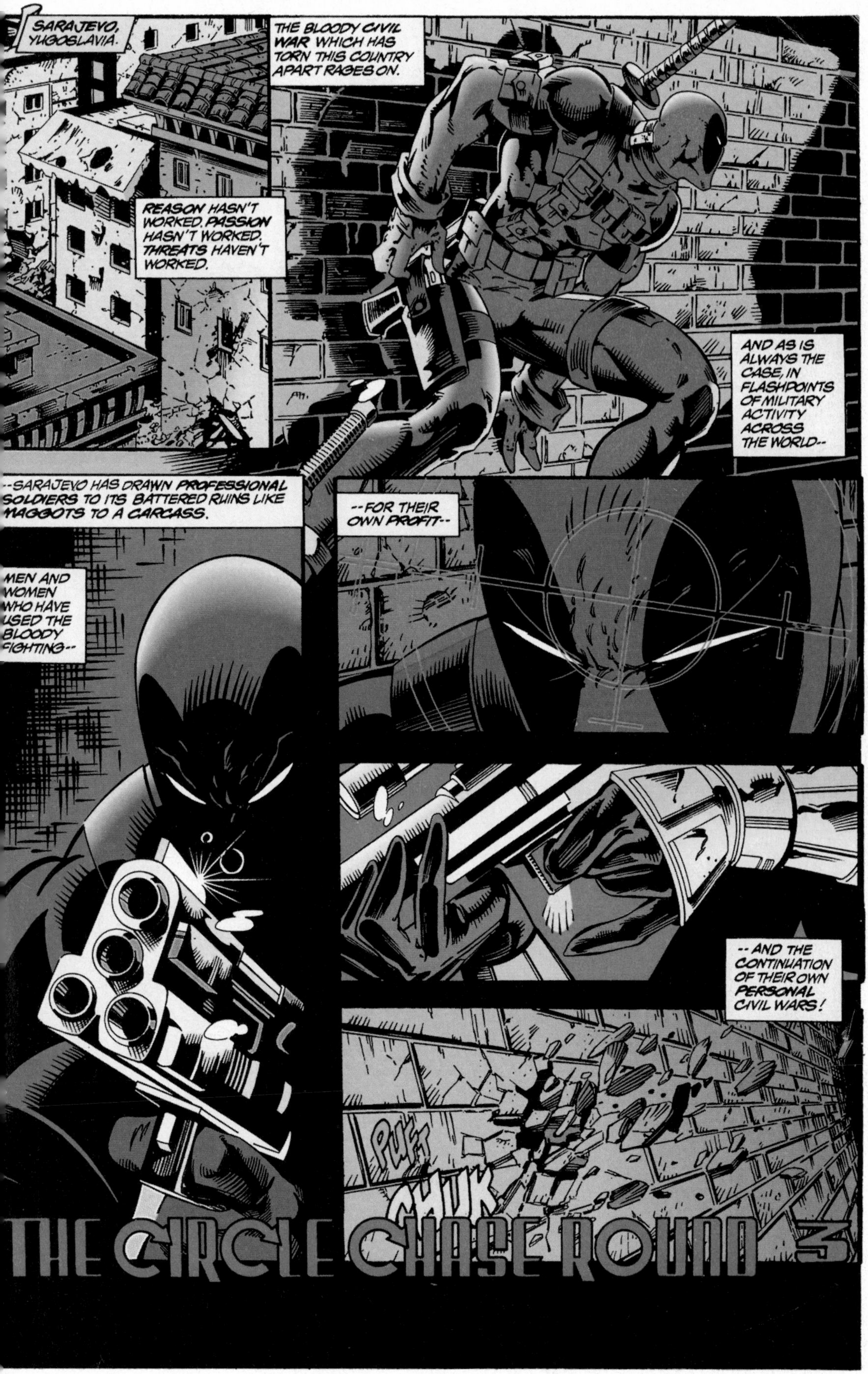

SARAJEVO, YUGOSLAVIA.
THE BLOODY CIVIL WAR WHICH HAS TORN THIS COUNTRY APART RAGES ON.
REASON HASN'T WORKED. PASSION HASN'T WORKED. THREATS HAVEN'T WORKED.
AND AS IS ALWAYS THE CASE, IN FLASHPOINTS OF MILITARY ACTIVITY ACROSS THE WORLD--
--SARAJEVO HAS DRAWN PROFESSIONAL SOLDIERS TO ITS BATTERED RUINS LIKE MAGGOTS TO A CARCASS.
--FOR THEIR OWN PROFIT--
MEN AND WOMEN WHO HAVE USED THE BLOODY FIGHTING--
--AND THE CONTINUATION OF THEIR OWN PERSONAL CIVIL WARS!
PUFT
CHUK
THE CIRCLE CHASE ROUND 3

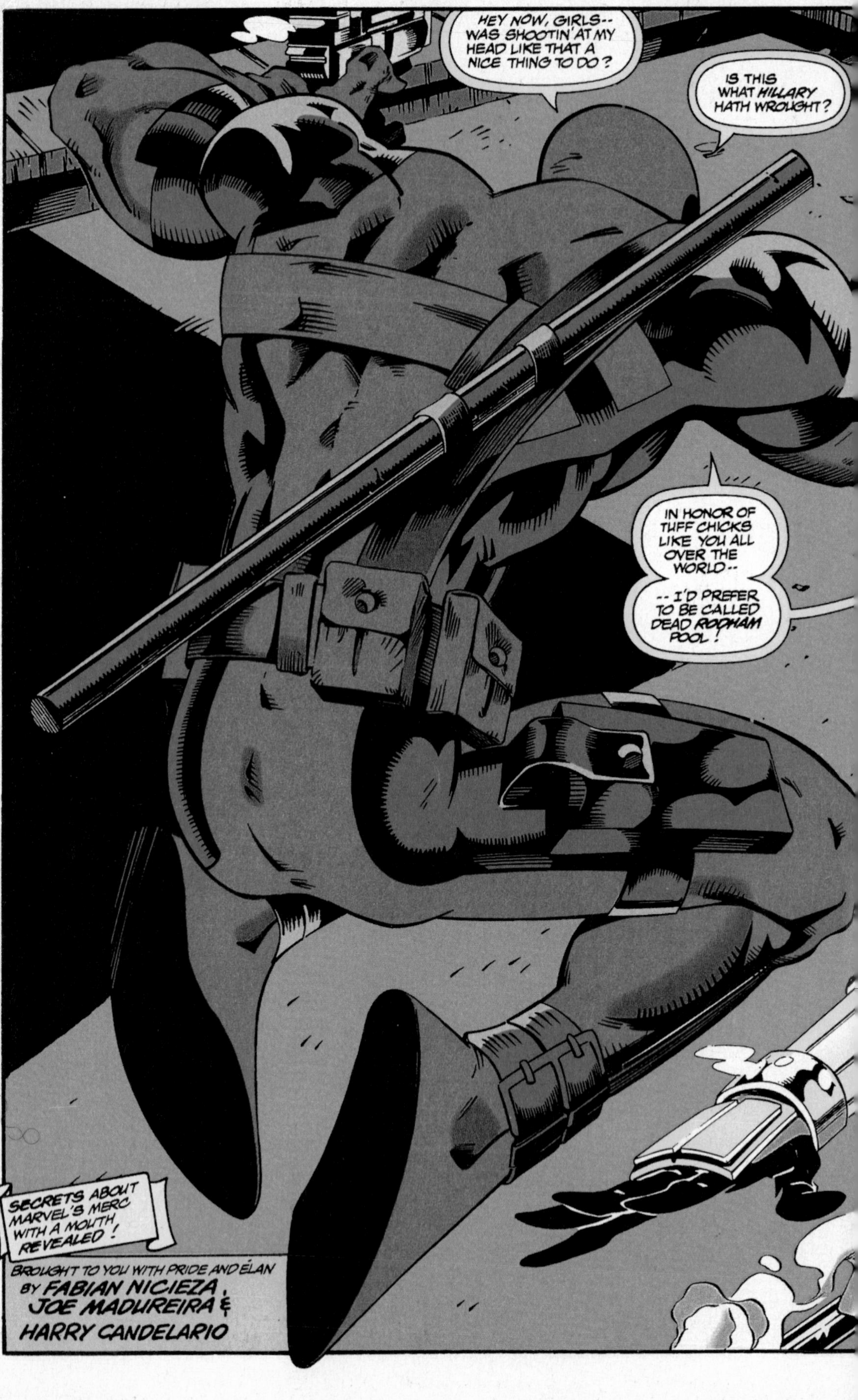
HEY NOW, GIRLS-- WAS SHOOTIN' AT MY HEAD LIKE THAT A NICE THING TO DO?
IS THIS WHAT HILLARY HATH WROUGHT?
IN HONOR OF TUFF CHICKS LIKE YOU ALL OVER THE WORLD--
-- I'D PREFER TO BE CALLED DEAD RODHAM POOL!
SECRETS ABOUT MARVEL'S MERC WITH A MOUTH REVEALED!
BROUGHT TO YOU WITH PRIDE AND ÉLAN BY FABIAN NICIEZA, JOE MADUREIRA & HARRY CANDELARIO

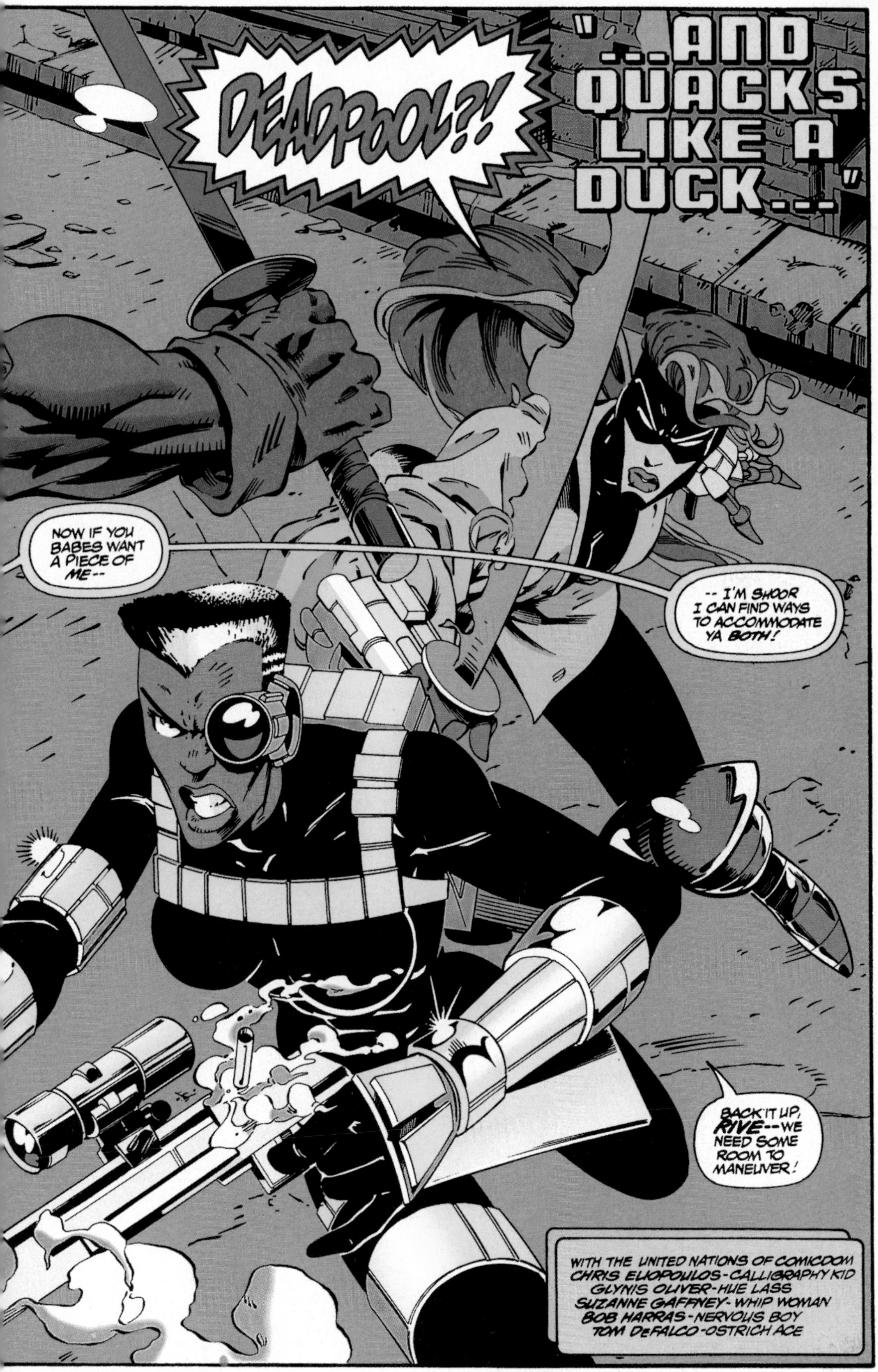
DEADPOOL?!
"...AND QUACKS LIKE A DUCK..."
NOW IF YOU BABES WANT A PIECE OF ME--
-- I'M SHOOR I CAN FIND WAYS TO ACCOMMODATE YA BOTH!
BACK IT UP, RIVE--WE NEED SOME ROOM TO MANEUVER!
WITH THE UNITED NATIONS OF COMICDOM
CHRIS ELIOPOULOS-CALLIGRAPHY KID
GLYNIS OLIVER-HUE LASS
SUZANNE GAFFNEY-WHIP WOMAN
BOB HARRAS-NERVOUS BOY
TOM DEFALCO-OSTRICH ACE

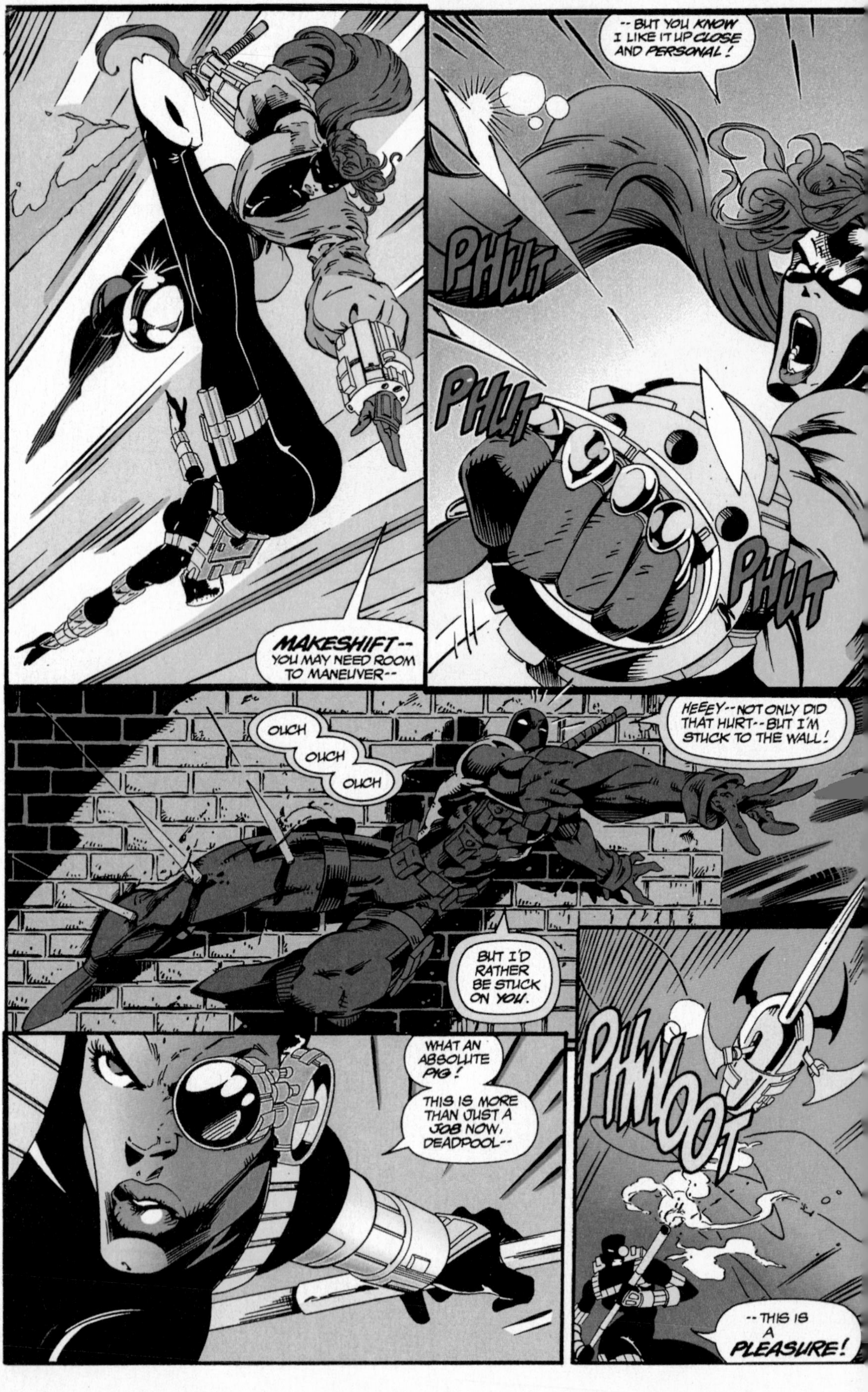

MAKESHIFT-- YOU MAY NEED ROOM TO MANEUVER--
-- BUT YOU KNOW I LIKE IT UP CLOSE AND PERSONAL!
PHUT
PHUT
PHUT
OUCH
OUCH
OUCH
HEEEY--NOT ONLY DID THAT HURT--BUT I'M STUCK TO THE WALL!
BUT I'D RATHER BE STUCK ON YOU.
WHAT AN ABSOLUTE PIG!
THIS IS MORE THAN JUST A JOB NOW, DEADPOOL--
PHWOOT
--THIS IS A PLEASURE!

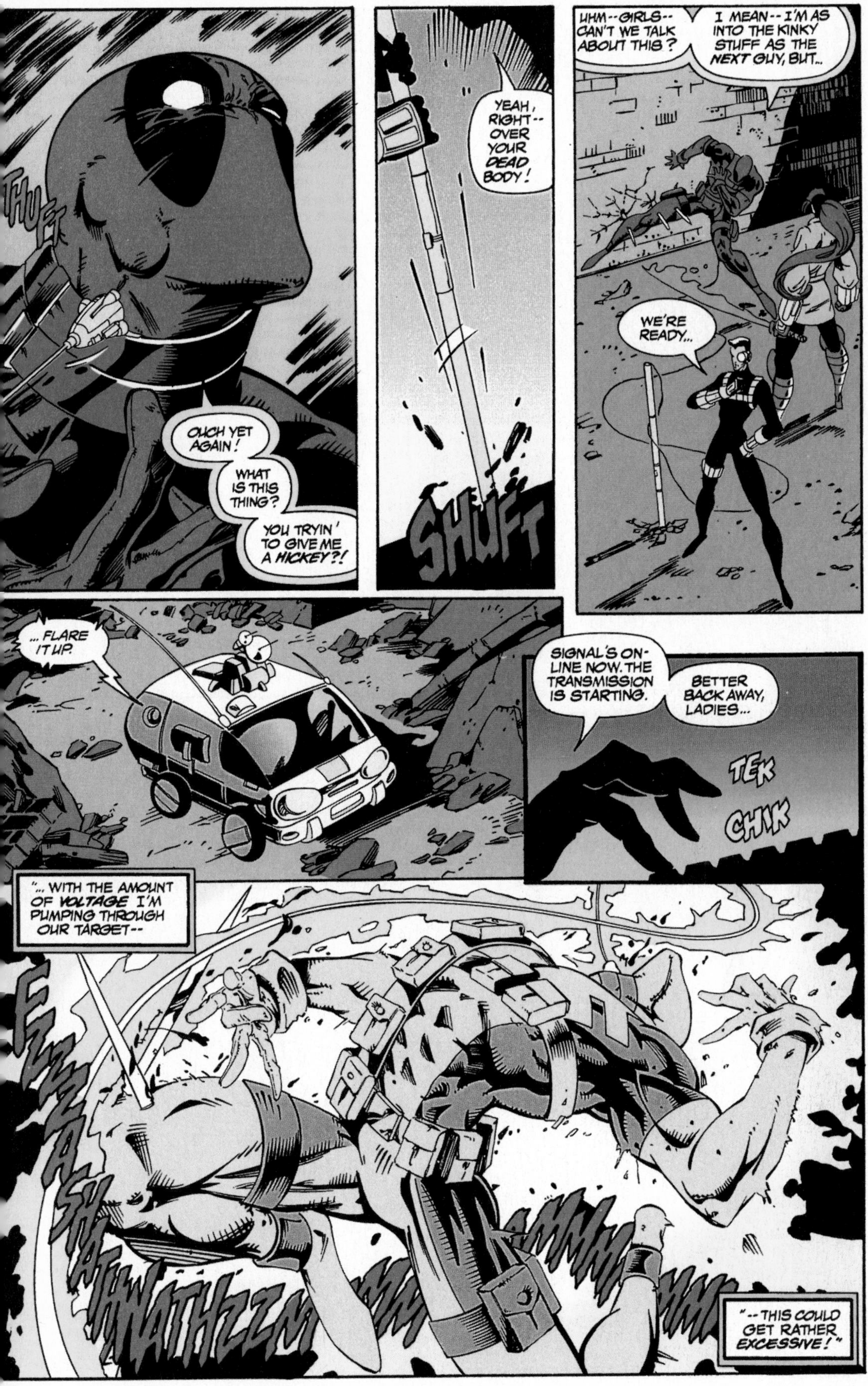
THUFT
OUCH YET AGAIN!
WHAT IS THIS THING?
YOU TRYIN' TO GIVE ME A HICKEY?!
YEAH, RIGHT-- OVER YOUR DEAD BODY!
SHUFT
UHM--GIRLS-- CAN'T WE TALK ABOUT THIS?
I MEAN-- I'M AS INTO THE KINKY STUFF AS THE NEXT GUY, BUT...
WE'RE READY...
...FLARE IT UP.
SIGNAL'S ON-LINE NOW. THE TRANSMISSION IS STARTING.
BETTER BACK AWAY, LADIES...
TEK
CHIK
"...WITH THE AMOUNT OF VOLTAGE I'M PUMPING THROUGH OUR TARGET--
"--THIS COULD GET RATHER EXCESSIVE!"

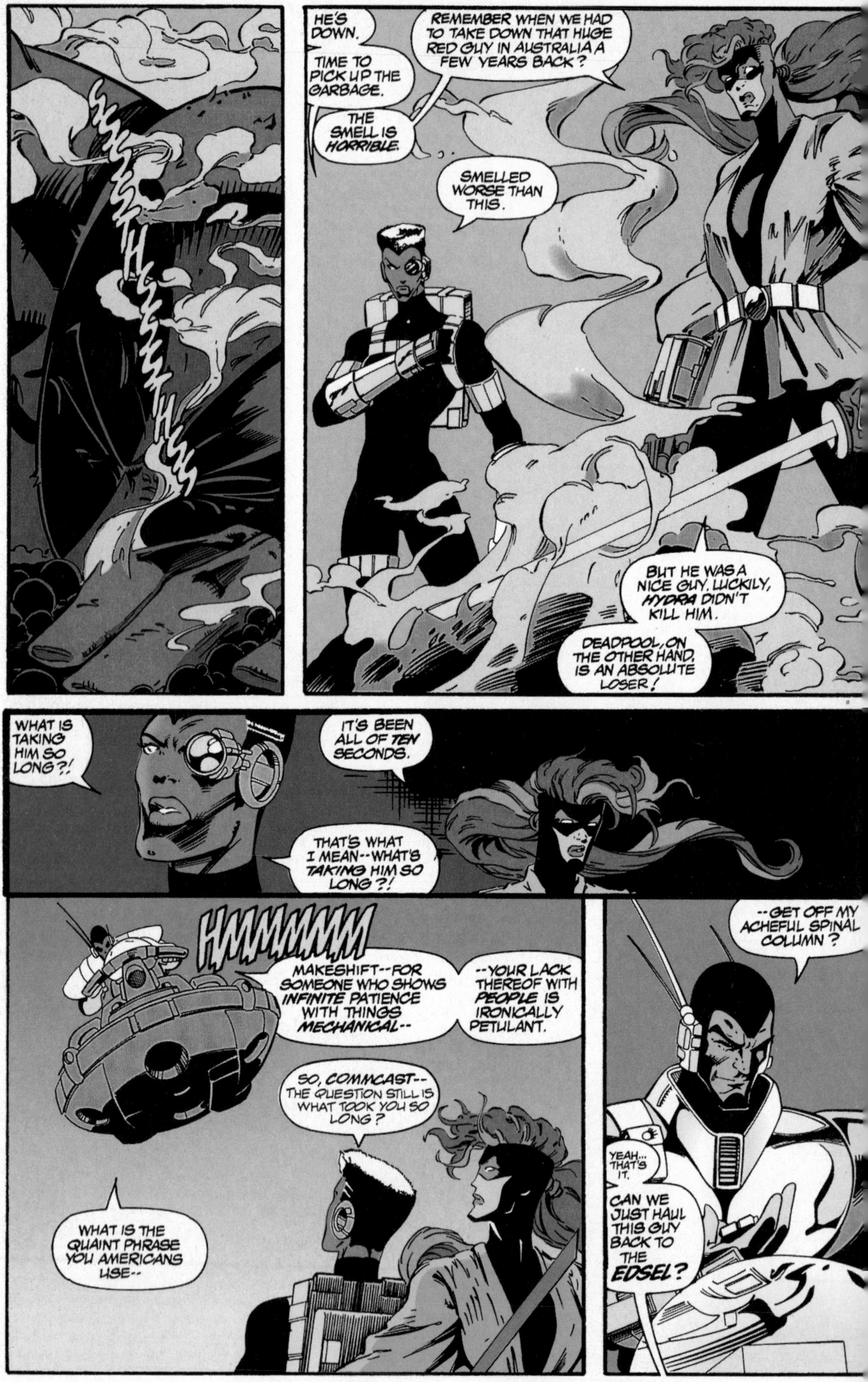

HE'S DOWN.
TIME TO PICK UP THE GARBAGE.
THE SMELL IS HORRIBLE.
REMEMBER WHEN WE HAD TO TAKE DOWN THAT HUGE RED GUY IN AUSTRALIA A FEW YEARS BACK?
SMELLED WORSE THAN THIS.
BUT HE WAS A NICE GUY. LUCKILY, HYDRA DIDN'T KILL HIM.
DEADPOOL, ON THE OTHER HAND, IS AN ABSOLUTE LOSER!
WHAT IS TAKING HIM SO LONG?!
IT'S BEEN ALL OF TEN SECONDS.
THAT'S WHAT I MEAN--WHAT'S TAKING HIM SO LONG?!
HMMMMM
MAKESHIFT--FOR SOMEONE WHO SHOWS INFINITE PATIENCE WITH THINGS MECHANICAL--
--YOUR LACK THEREOF WITH PEOPLE IS IRONICALLY PETULANT.
SO, COMMCAST-- THE QUESTION STILL IS WHAT TOOK YOU SO LONG?
WHAT IS THE QUAINT PHRASE YOU AMERICANS USE--
--GET OFF MY ACHEFUL SPINAL COLUMN?
YEAH... THAT'S IT.
CAN WE JUST HAUL THIS GUY BACK TO THE EDSEL?

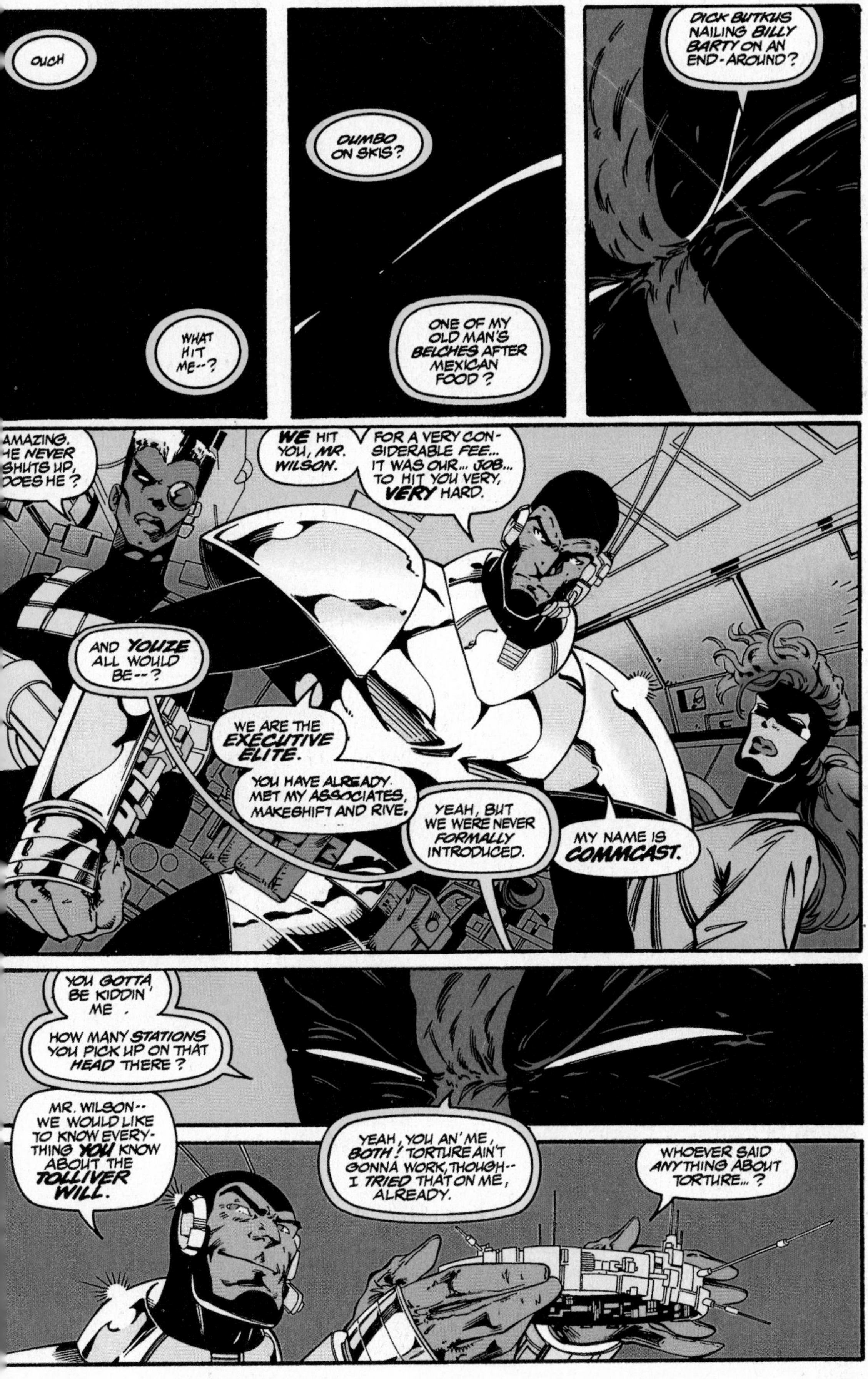
OUCH
WHAT HIT ME--?
DUMBO ON SKIS?
ONE OF MY OLD MAN'S BELCHES AFTER MEXICAN FOOD?
DICK BUTKUS NAILING BILLY BARTY ON AN END-AROUND?
AMAZING. HE NEVER SHUTS UP, DOES HE?
WE HIT YOU, MR. WILSON.
FOR A VERY CONSIDERABLE FEE... IT WAS OUR... JOB... TO HIT YOU VERY, VERY HARD.
AND YOUZE ALL WOULD BE--?
WE ARE THE EXECUTIVE ELITE.
YOU HAVE ALREADY MET MY ASSOCIATES, MAKESHIFT AND RIVE.
YEAH, BUT WE WERE NEVER FORMALLY INTRODUCED.
MY NAME IS COMMCAST.
YOU GOTTA BE KIDDIN' ME.
HOW MANY STATIONS YOU PICK UP ON THAT HEAD THERE?
MR. WILSON-- WE WOULD LIKE TO KNOW EVERYTHING YOU KNOW ABOUT THE TOLLIVER WILL.
YEAH, YOU AN' ME, BOTH! TORTURE AIN'T GONNA WORK, THOUGH-- I TRIED THAT ON ME, ALREADY.
WHOEVER SAID ANYTHING ABOUT TORTURE...?

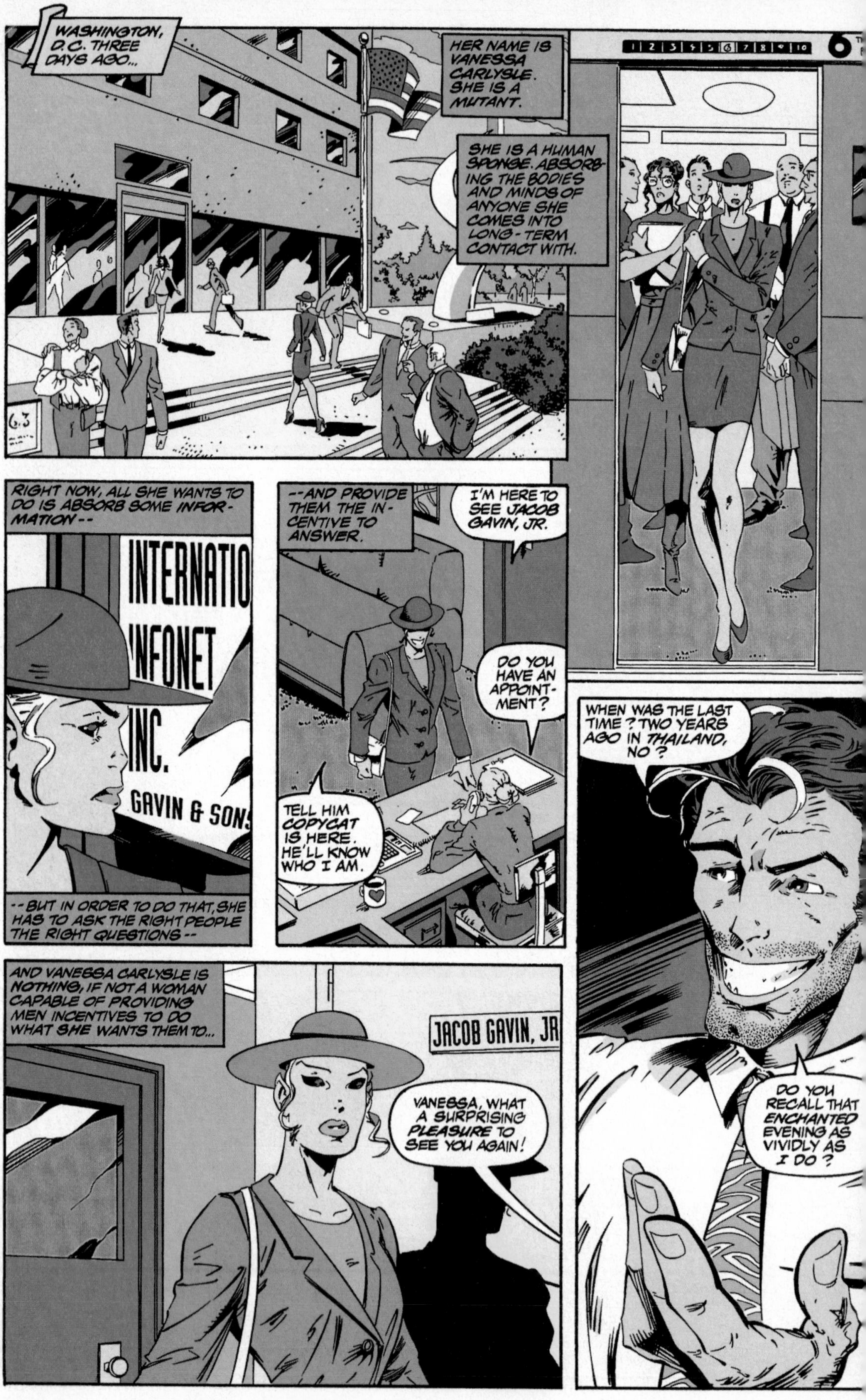

WASHINGTON, D.C. THREE DAYS AGO...
HER NAME IS VANESSA CARLYSLE. SHE IS A MUTANT.
SHE IS A HUMAN SPONGE. ABSORBING THE BODIES AND MINDS OF ANYONE SHE COMES INTO LONG-TERM CONTACT WITH.
1 2 3 4 5 6 7 8 9 10
6
RIGHT NOW, ALL SHE WANTS TO DO IS ABSORB SOME INFORMATION--
INTERNATIO
INFONET
INC.
GAVIN & SONS
--BUT IN ORDER TO DO THAT, SHE HAS TO ASK THE RIGHT PEOPLE THE RIGHT QUESTIONS--
--AND PROVIDE THEM THE INCENTIVE TO ANSWER.
I'M HERE TO SEE JACOB GAVIN, JR.
DO YOU HAVE AN APPOINTMENT?
TELL HIM COPYCAT IS HERE. HE'LL KNOW WHO I AM.
AND VANESSA CARLYSLE IS NOTHING, IF NOT A WOMAN CAPABLE OF PROVIDING MEN INCENTIVES TO DO WHAT SHE WANTS THEM TO...
JACOB GAVIN, JR
VANESSA, WHAT A SURPRISING PLEASURE TO SEE YOU AGAIN!
WHEN WAS THE LAST TIME? TWO YEARS AGO IN THAILAND, NO?
DO YOU RECALL THAT ENCHANTED EVENING AS VIVIDLY AS I DO?

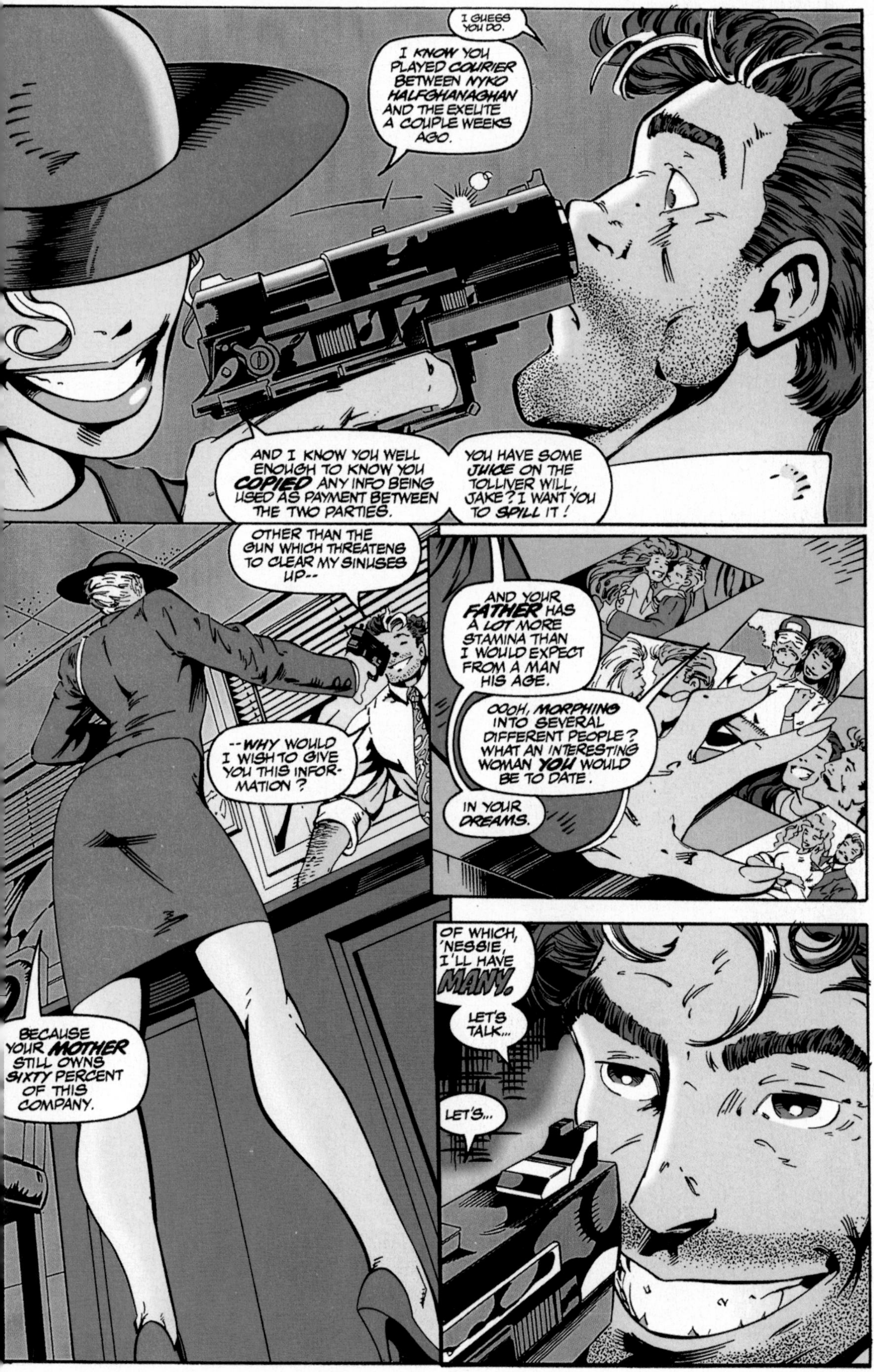
I KNOW YOU PLAYED COURIER BETWEEN NYKO HALFGHANAGHAN AND THE EXELITE A COUPLE WEEKS AGO.
I GUESS YOU DO.
AND I KNOW YOU WELL ENOUGH TO KNOW YOU COPIED ANY INFO BEING USED AS PAYMENT BETWEEN THE TWO PARTIES.
YOU HAVE SOME JUICE ON THE TOLLIVER WILL, JAKE? I WANT YOU TO SPILL IT!
OTHER THAN THE GUN WHICH THREATENS TO CLEAR MY SINUSES UP--
--WHY WOULD I WISH TO GIVE YOU THIS INFORMATION?
BECAUSE YOUR MOTHER STILL OWNS SIXTY PERCENT OF THIS COMPANY.
AND YOUR FATHER HAS A LOT MORE STAMINA THAN I WOULD EXPECT FROM A MAN HIS AGE.
OOOH, MORPHING INTO SEVERAL DIFFERENT PEOPLE? WHAT AN INTERESTING WOMAN YOU WOULD BE TO DATE.
IN YOUR DREAMS.
OF WHICH, 'NESSIE, I'LL HAVE MANY.
LET'S TALK...
LET'S...

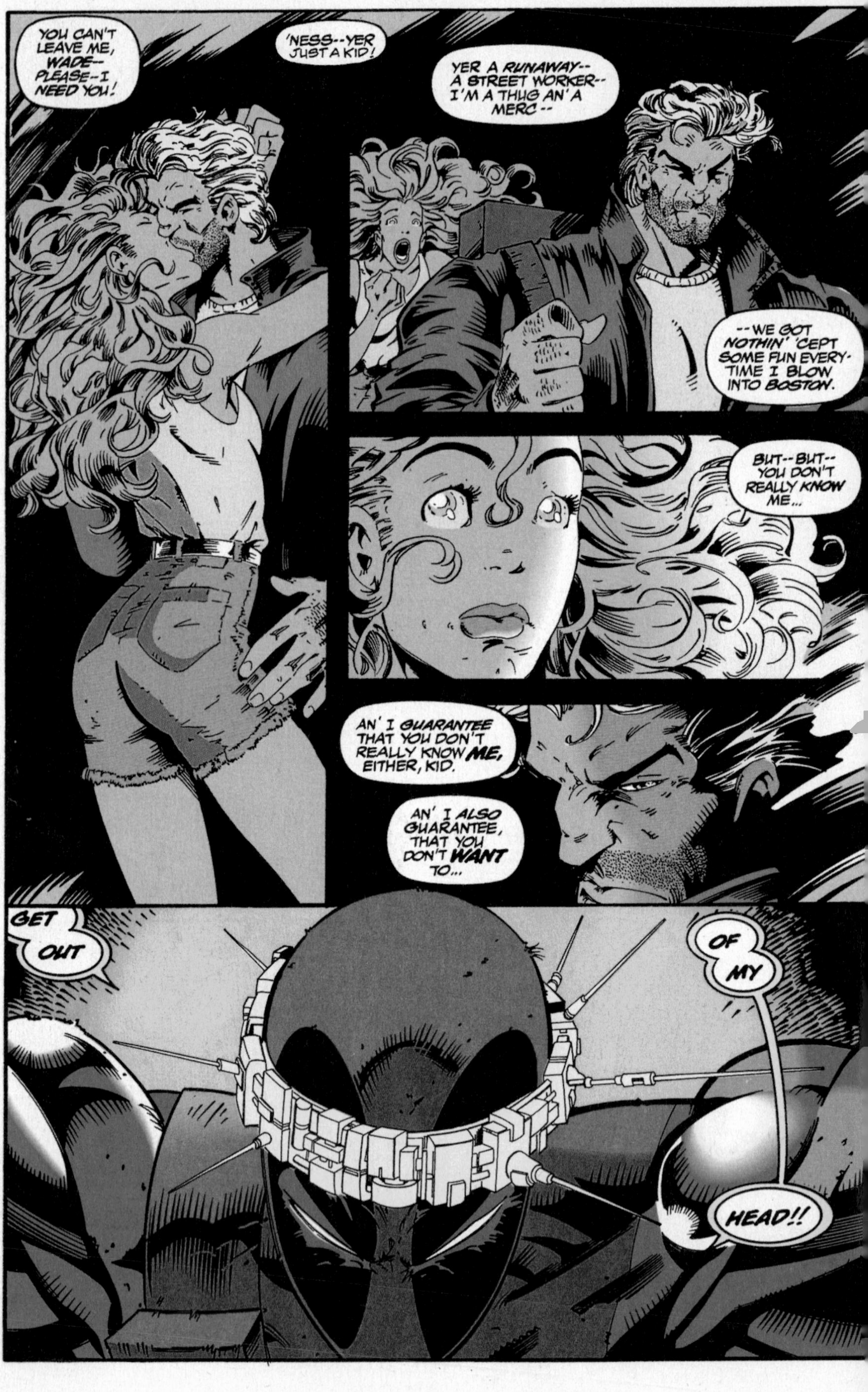
YOU CAN'T LEAVE ME, WADE-- PLEASE--I NEED YOU!
'NESS--YER JUST A KID!
YER A RUNAWAY-- A STREET WORKER-- I'M A THUG AN' A MERC --
--WE GOT NOTHIN' 'CEPT SOME FUN EVERY-TIME I BLOW INTO BOSTON.
BUT--BUT-- YOU DON'T REALLY KNOW ME...
AN' I GUARANTEE THAT YOU DON'T REALLY KNOW ME, EITHER, KID.
AN' I ALSO GUARANTEE, THAT YOU DON'T WANT TO...
GET
OUT
OF
MY
HEAD!!

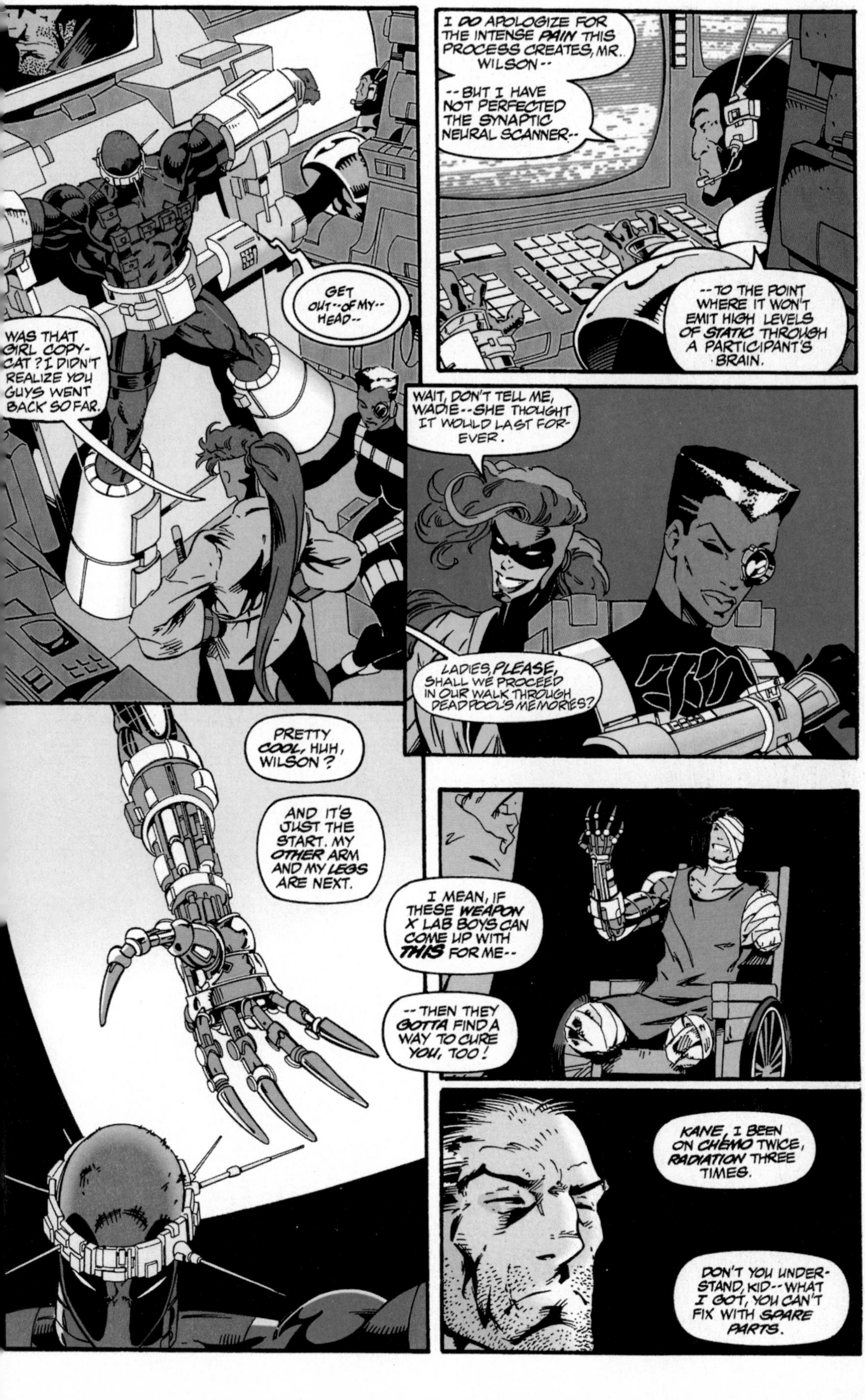
I DO APOLOGIZE FOR THE INTENSE PAIN THIS PROCESS CREATES, MR. WILSON--
--BUT I HAVE NOT PERFECTED THE SYNAPTIC NEURAL SCANNER--
--TO THE POINT WHERE IT WON'T EMIT HIGH LEVELS OF STATIC THROUGH A PARTICIPANT'S BRAIN.
GET OUT--OF MY--HEAD--
WAS THAT GIRL COPY-CAT? I DIDN'T REALIZE YOU GUYS WENT BACK SO FAR.
WAIT, DON'T TELL ME, WADIE--SHE THOUGHT IT WOULD LAST FOREVER.
LADIES, PLEASE, SHALL WE PROCEED IN OUR WALK THROUGH DEADPOOL'S MEMORIES?
PRETTY COOL, HUH, WILSON?
AND IT'S JUST THE START. MY OTHER ARM AND MY LEGS ARE NEXT.
I MEAN, IF THESE WEAPON X LAB BOYS CAN COME UP WITH THIS FOR ME--
--THEN THEY GOTTA FIND A WAY TO CURE YOU, TOO!
KANE, I BEEN ON CHEMO TWICE, RADIATION THREE TIMES.
DON'T YOU UNDERSTAND, KID--WHAT I GOT, YOU CAN'T FIX WITH SPARE PARTS.

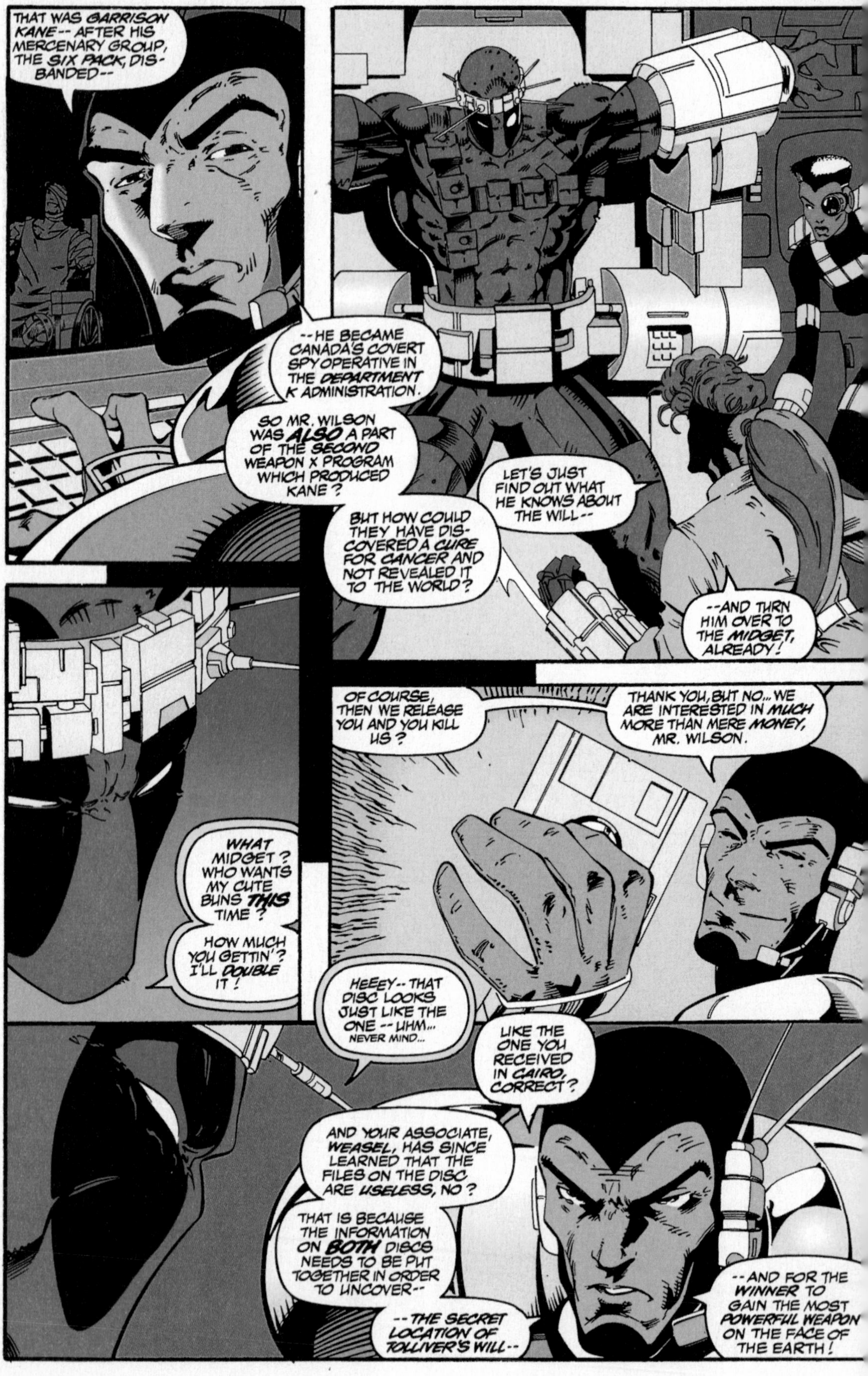

THAT WAS GARRISON KANE-- AFTER HIS MERCENARY GROUP, THE SIX PACK, DISBANDED--
--HE BECAME CANADA'S COVERT SPY OPERATIVE IN THE DEPARTMENT K ADMINISTRATION.
SO MR. WILSON WAS ALSO A PART OF THE SECOND WEAPON X PROGRAM WHICH PRODUCED KANE?
BUT HOW COULD THEY HAVE DISCOVERED A CURE FOR CANCER AND NOT REVEALED IT TO THE WORLD?
LET'S JUST FIND OUT WHAT HE KNOWS ABOUT THE WILL--
--AND TURN HIM OVER TO THE MIDGET, ALREADY!
WHAT MIDGET? WHO WANTS MY CUTE BUNS THIS TIME?
HOW MUCH YOU GETTIN'? I'LL DOUBLE IT!
OF COURSE, THEN WE RELEASE YOU AND YOU KILL US?
THANK YOU, BUT NO... WE ARE INTERESTED IN MUCH MORE THAN MERE MONEY, MR. WILSON.
HEEEY-- THAT DISC LOOKS JUST LIKE THE ONE -- UHM... NEVER MIND...
LIKE THE ONE YOU RECEIVED IN CAIRO, CORRECT?
AND YOUR ASSOCIATE, WEASEL, HAS SINCE LEARNED THAT THE FILES ON THE DISC ARE USELESS, NO?
THAT IS BECAUSE THE INFORMATION ON BOTH DISCS NEEDS TO BE PUT TOGETHER IN ORDER TO UNCOVER--
--THE SECRET LOCATION OF TOLLIVER'S WILL--
--AND FOR THE WINNER TO GAIN THE MOST POWERFUL WEAPON ON THE FACE OF THE EARTH!

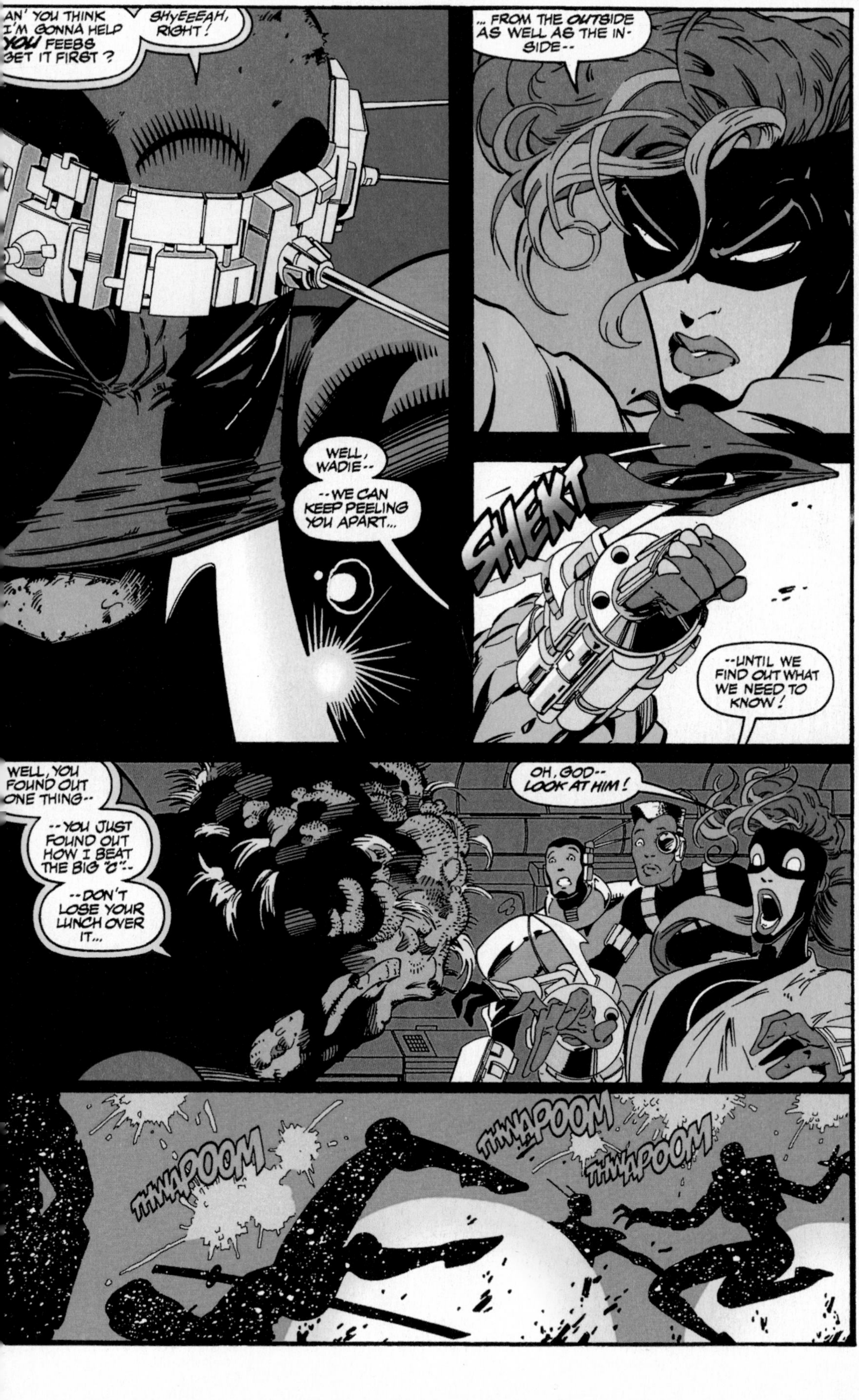
AN' YOU THINK I'M GONNA HELP YOU FEEBS GET IT FIRST ?
SHYEEEAH, RIGHT !
... FROM THE OUTSIDE AS WELL AS THE INSIDE--
WELL, WADIE--
--WE CAN KEEP PEELING YOU APART...
SHEKT
--UNTIL WE FIND OUT WHAT WE NEED TO KNOW !
WELL, YOU FOUND OUT ONE THING--
--YOU JUST FOUND OUT HOW I BEAT THE BIG "C"--
--DON'T LOSE YOUR LUNCH OVER IT...
OH, GOD-- LOOK AT HIM !
THWAPOOM
THWAPOOM
THWAPOOM

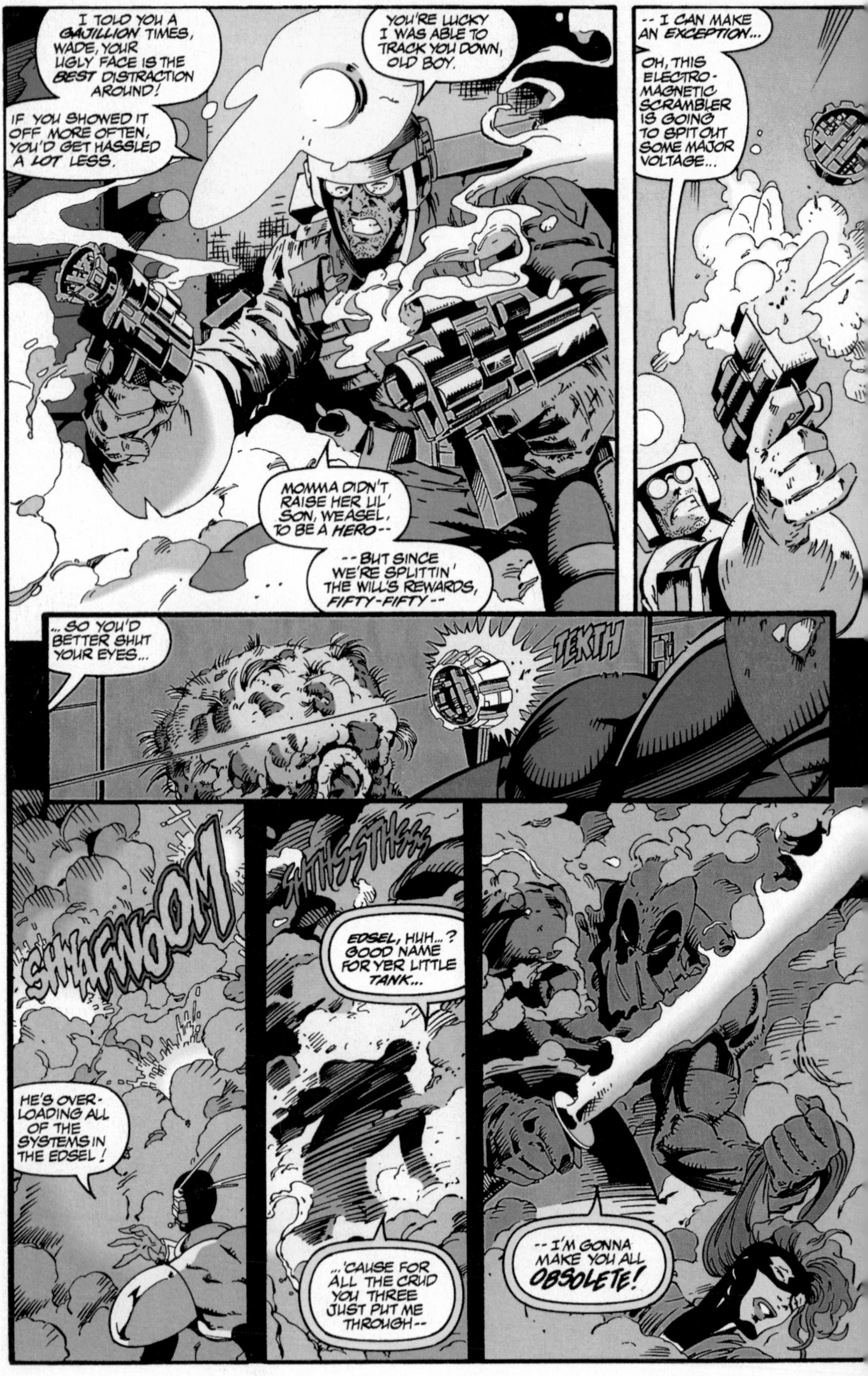
I TOLD YOU A GAJILLION TIMES, WADE, YOUR UGLY FACE IS THE BEST DISTRACTION AROUND!
IF YOU SHOWED IT OFF MORE OFTEN, YOU'D GET HASSLED A LOT LESS.
YOU'RE LUCKY I WAS ABLE TO TRACK YOU DOWN, OLD BOY.
MOMMA DIDN'T RAISE HER LIL' SON, WEASEL, TO BE A HERO--
--BUT SINCE WE'RE SPLITTIN' THE WILL'S REWARDS, FIFTY-FIFTY--
--I CAN MAKE AN EXCEPTION...
OH, THIS ELECTRO-MAGNETIC SCRAMBLER IS GOING TO SPIT OUT SOME MAJOR VOLTAGE...
...SO YOU'D BETTER SHUT YOUR EYES...
TEKTH
SHFAFNOOM
HE'S OVER-LOADING ALL OF THE SYSTEMS IN THE EDSEL!
EDSEL, HUH...? GOOD NAME FOR YER LITTLE TANK...
...'CAUSE FOR ALL THE CRUD YOU THREE JUST PUT ME THROUGH--
--I'M GONNA MAKE YOU ALL OBSOLETE!

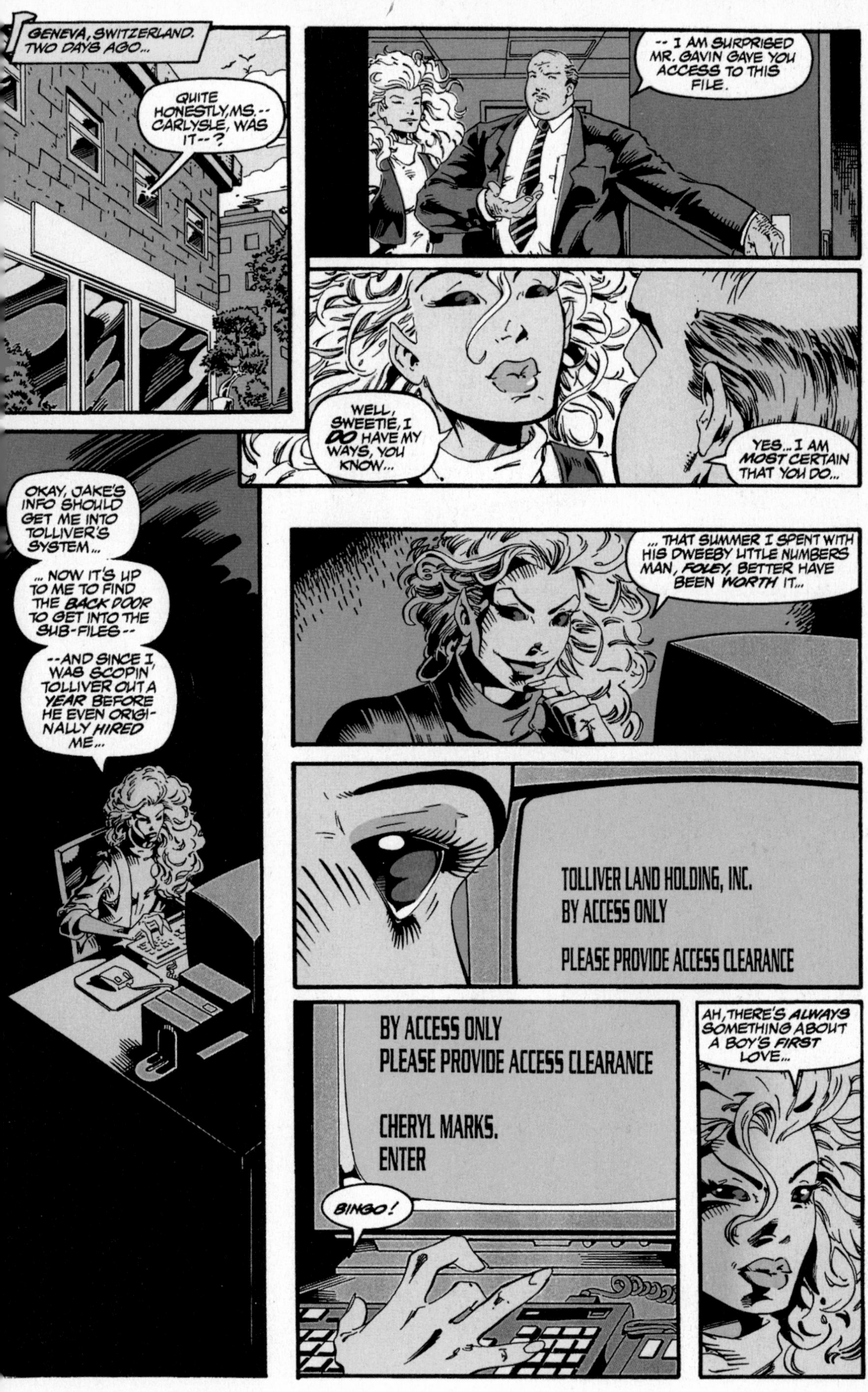
GENEVA, SWITZERLAND. TWO DAYS AGO...
QUITE HONESTLY, MS.-- CARLYSLE, WAS IT--?
-- I AM SURPRISED MR. GAVIN GAVE YOU ACCESS TO THIS FILE.
WELL, SWEETIE, I DO HAVE MY WAYS, YOU KNOW...
YES... I AM MOST CERTAIN THAT YOU DO...
OKAY, JAKE'S INFO SHOULD GET ME INTO TOLLIVER'S SYSTEM...
... NOW IT'S UP TO ME TO FIND THE BACK DOOR TO GET INTO THE SUB-FILES--
--AND SINCE I WAS SCOPIN' TOLLIVER OUT A YEAR BEFORE HE EVEN ORIGINALLY HIRED ME...
... THAT SUMMER I SPENT WITH HIS DWEEBY LITTLE NUMBERS MAN, FOLEY, BETTER HAVE BEEN WORTH IT...
TOLLIVER LAND HOLDING, INC.
BY ACCESS ONLY
PLEASE PROVIDE ACCESS CLEARANCE
BY ACCESS ONLY
PLEASE PROVIDE ACCESS CLEARANCE
CHERYL MARKS.
ENTER
BINGO!
AH, THERE'S ALWAYS SOMETHING ABOUT A BOY'S FIRST LOVE...

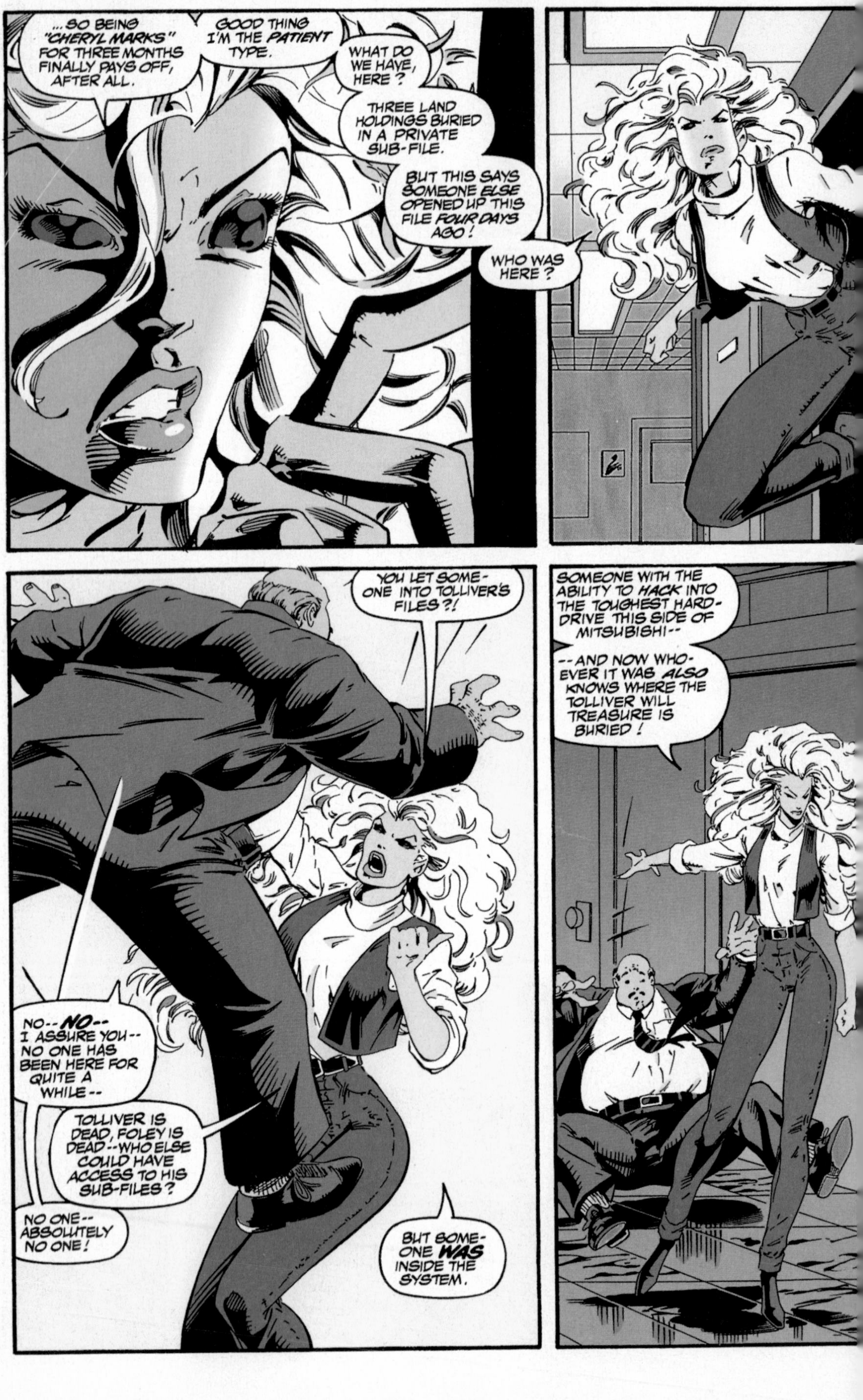
...SO BEING "CHERYL MARKS" FOR THREE MONTHS FINALLY PAYS OFF, AFTER ALL.
GOOD THING I'M THE PATIENT TYPE.
WHAT DO WE HAVE, HERE?
THREE LAND HOLDINGS BURIED IN A PRIVATE SUB-FILE.
BUT THIS SAYS SOMEONE ELSE OPENED UP THIS FILE FOUR DAYS AGO!
WHO WAS HERE?
YOU LET SOME-ONE INTO TOLLIVER'S FILES?!
NO--NO-- I ASSURE YOU-- NO ONE HAS BEEN HERE FOR QUITE A WHILE--
TOLLIVER IS DEAD, FOLEY IS DEAD--WHO ELSE COULD HAVE ACCESS TO HIS SUB-FILES?
NO ONE-- ABSOLUTELY NO ONE!
BUT SOME-ONE WAS INSIDE THE SYSTEM.
SOMEONE WITH THE ABILITY TO HACK INTO THE TOUGHEST HARD-DRIVE THIS SIDE OF MITSUBISHI--
--AND NOW WHO-EVER IT WAS ALSO KNOWS WHERE THE TOLLIVER WILL TREASURE IS BURIED!

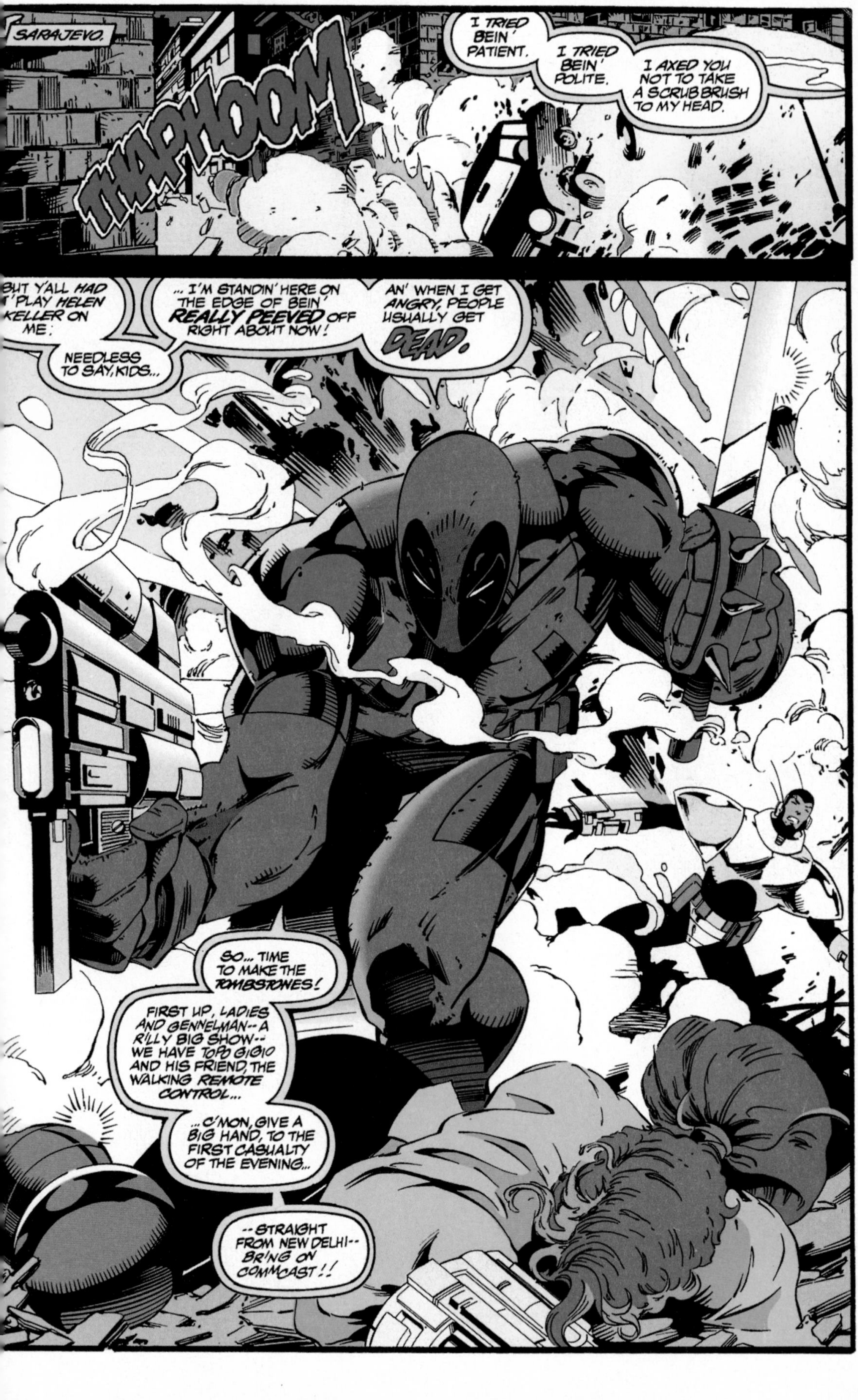
SARAJEVO.
THAPHOOM
I TRIED BEIN' PATIENT.
I TRIED BEIN' POLITE.
I AXED YOU NOT TO TAKE A SCRUB BRUSH TO MY HEAD.
BUT Y'ALL HAD T'PLAY HELEN KELLER ON ME:
NEEDLESS TO SAY, KIDS...
... I'M STANDIN' HERE ON THE EDGE OF BEIN' REALLY PEEVED OFF RIGHT ABOUT NOW!
AN' WHEN I GET ANGRY, PEOPLE USUALLY GET DEAD.
SO... TIME TO MAKE THE TOMBSTONES!
FIRST UP, LADIES AND GENNELMAN-- A R'LLY BIG SHOW-- WE HAVE TOPO GIGIO AND HIS FRIEND, THE WALKING REMOTE CONTROL...
...C'MON, GIVE A BIG HAND, TO THE FIRST CASUALTY OF THE EVENING...
--STRAIGHT FROM NEW DELHI-- BR'NG ON COMMCAST!!

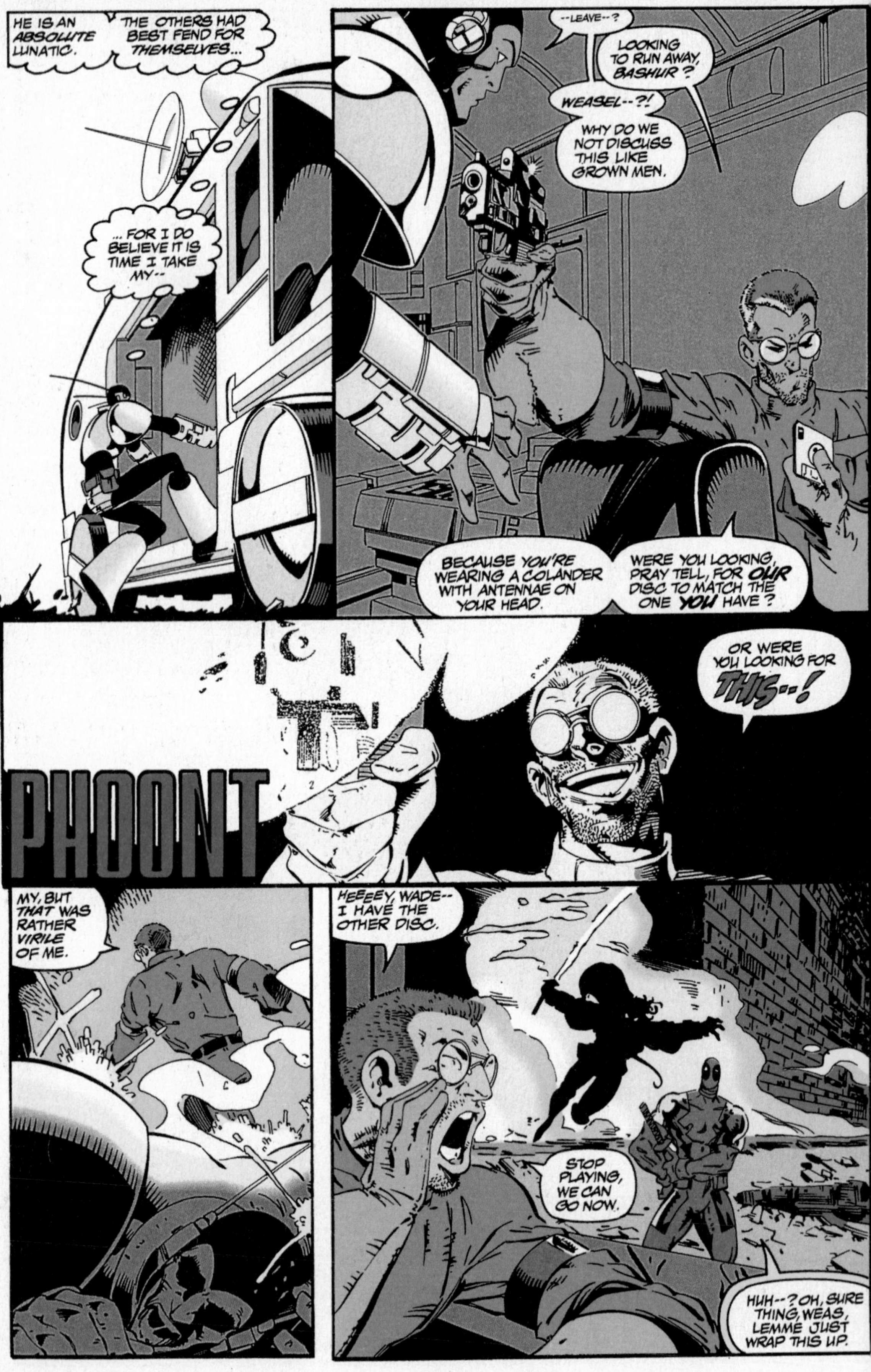
HE IS AN ABSOLUTE LUNATIC.
THE OTHERS HAD BEST FEND FOR THEMSELVES...
...FOR I DO BELIEVE IT IS TIME I TAKE MY--
--LEAVE--?
LOOKING TO RUN AWAY, BASHUR?
WEASEL--?!
WHY DO WE NOT DISCUSS THIS LIKE GROWN MEN.
BECAUSE YOU'RE WEARING A COLANDER WITH ANTENNAE ON YOUR HEAD.
WERE YOU LOOKING, PRAY TELL, FOR OUR DISC TO MATCH THE ONE YOU HAVE?
OR WERE YOU LOOKING FOR THIS--!
PHOONT
MY, BUT THAT WAS RATHER VIRILE OF ME.
HEEEEY, WADE-- I HAVE THE OTHER DISC.
STOP PLAYING, WE CAN GO NOW.
HUH--? OH, SURE THING, WEAS, LEMME JUST WRAP THIS UP.

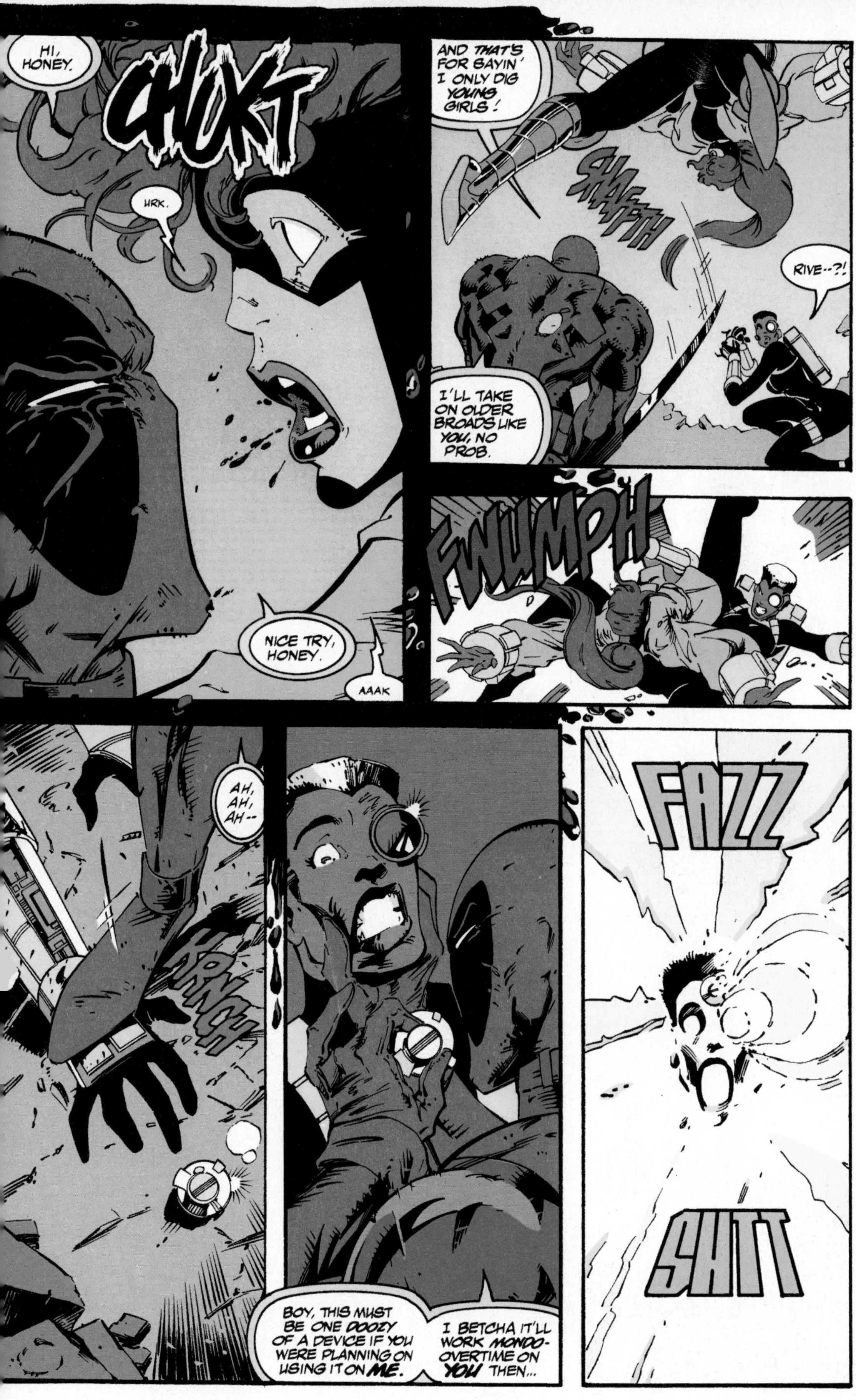
HI, HONEY.
CHUKT
URK.
NICE TRY, HONEY.
AAAK
AND THAT'S FOR SAYIN' I ONLY DIG YOUNG GIRLS!
SHAFFTH
RIVE--?!
I'LL TAKE ON OLDER BROADS LIKE YOU, NO PROB.
FWUMPH
AH, AH, AH--
KRNCH
BOY, THIS MUST BE ONE DOOZY OF A DEVICE IF YOU WERE PLANNING ON USING IT ON ME.
I BETCHA IT'LL WORK MONDO-OVERTIME ON YOU THEN...
FAZZ
SHTT

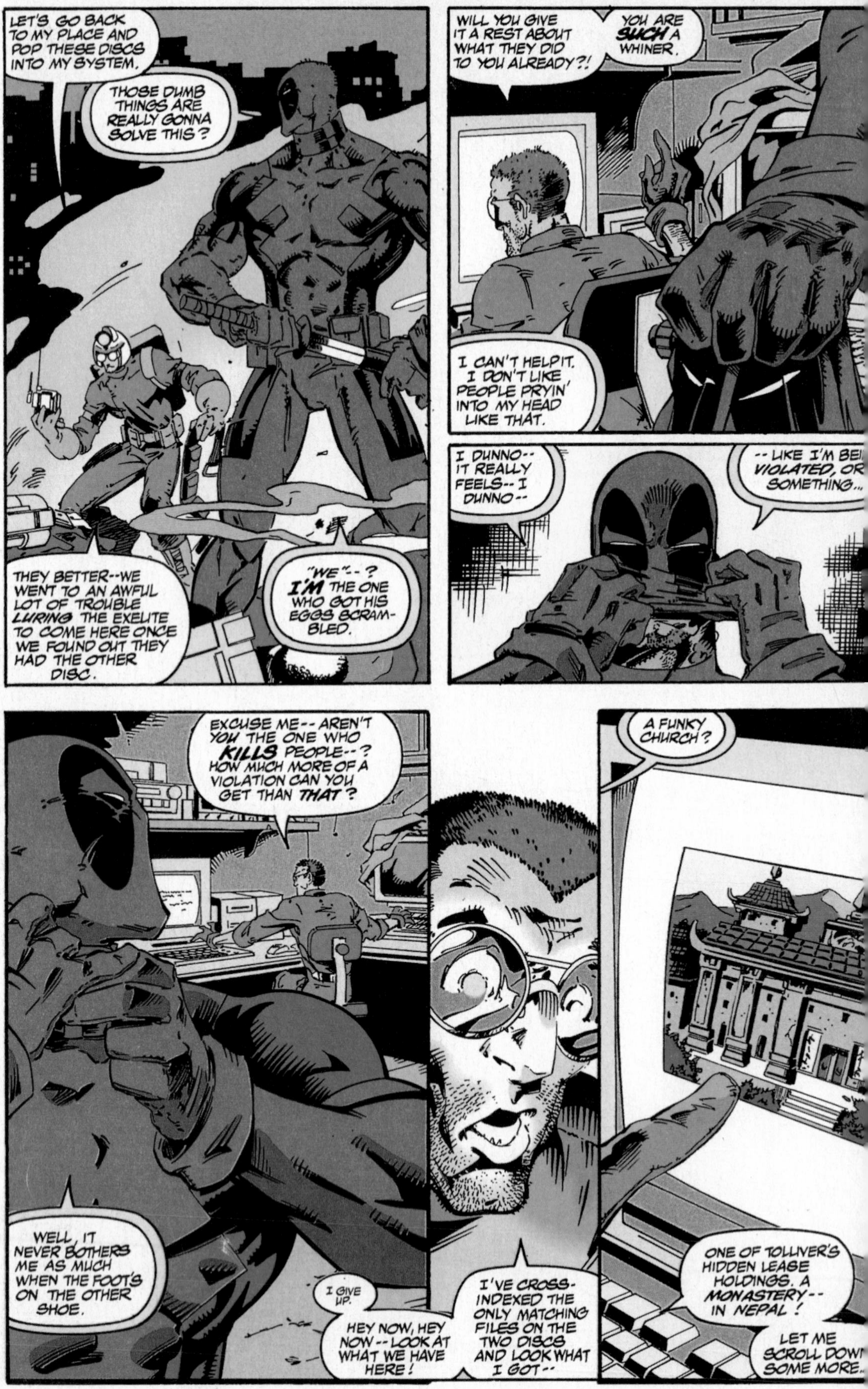
LET'S GO BACK TO MY PLACE AND POP THESE DISCS INTO MY SYSTEM.
THOSE DUMB THINGS ARE REALLY GONNA SOLVE THIS?
THEY BETTER--WE WENT TO AN AWFUL LOT OF TROUBLE LURING THE EXELITE TO COME HERE ONCE WE FOUND OUT THEY HAD THE OTHER DISC.
"WE"--? I'M THE ONE WHO GOT HIS EGGS SCRAMBLED.
WILL YOU GIVE IT A REST ABOUT WHAT THEY DID TO YOU ALREADY?!
YOU ARE SUCH A WHINER.
I CAN'T HELP IT. I DON'T LIKE PEOPLE PRYIN' INTO MY HEAD LIKE THAT.
I DUNNO-- IT REALLY FEELS-- I DUNNO--
--LIKE I'M BEI VIOLATED, OR SOMETHING...
EXCUSE ME--AREN'T YOU THE ONE WHO KILLS PEOPLE--? HOW MUCH MORE OF A VIOLATION CAN YOU GET THAN THAT?
WELL, IT NEVER BOTHERS ME AS MUCH WHEN THE FOOT'S ON THE OTHER SHOE.
I GIVE UP.
HEY NOW, HEY NOW--LOOK AT WHAT WE HAVE HERE!
I'VE CROSS-INDEXED THE ONLY MATCHING FILES ON THE TWO DISCS AND LOOK WHAT I GOT--
A FUNKY CHURCH?
ONE OF TOLLIVER'S HIDDEN LEASE HOLDINGS. A MONASTERY-- IN NEPAL!
LET ME SCROLL DOWN SOME MORE.

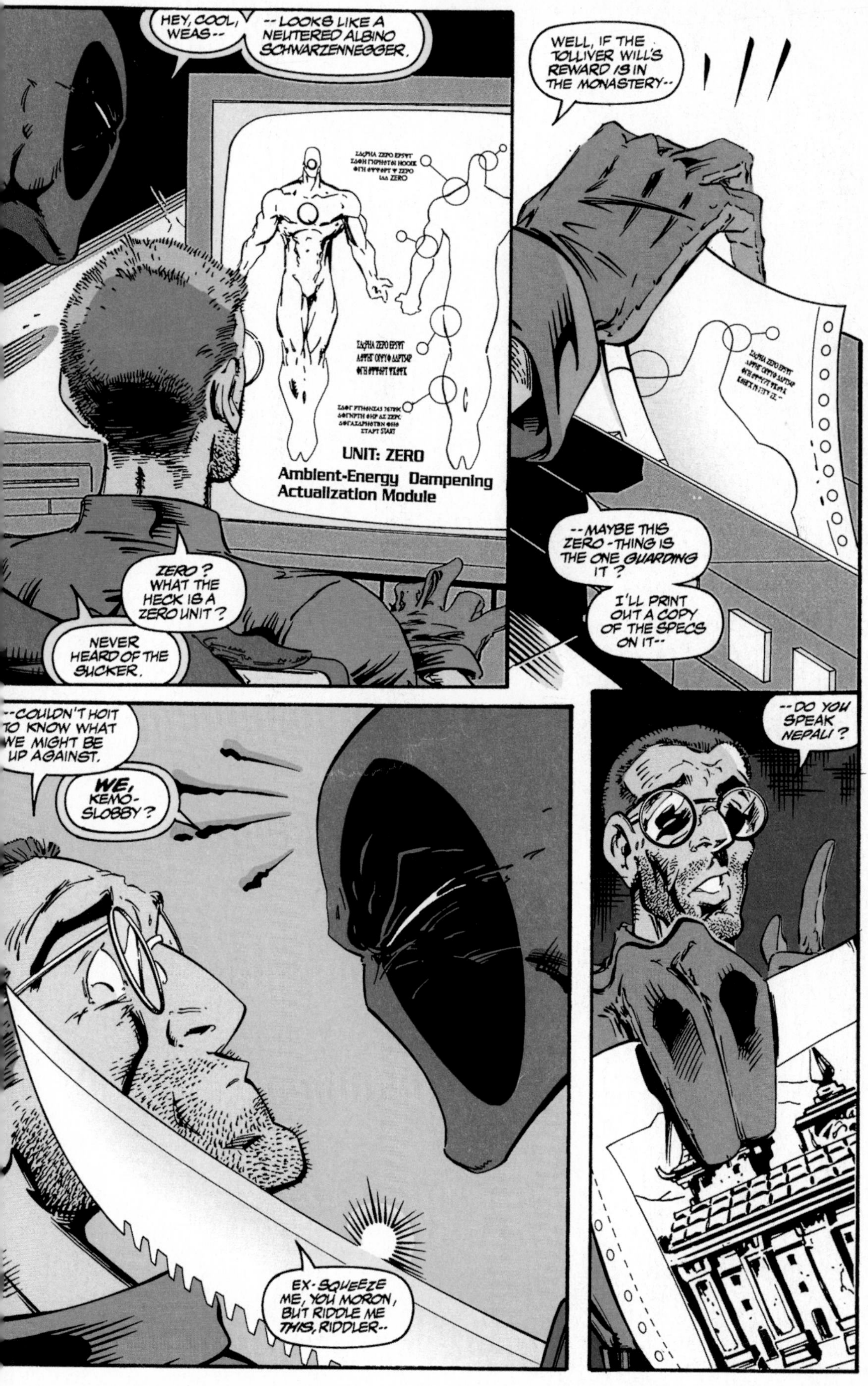
HEY, COOL, WEAS--
--LOOKS LIKE A NEUTERED ALBINO SCHWARZENNEGGER.
UNIT: ZERO
Ambient-Energy Dampening Actualization Module
ZERO? WHAT THE HECK IS A ZERO UNIT?
NEVER HEARD OF THE SUCKER.
WELL, IF THE TOLLIVER WILL'S REWARD IS IN THE MONASTERY--
--MAYBE THIS ZERO-THING IS THE ONE GUARDING IT?
I'LL PRINT OUT A COPY OF THE SPECS ON IT--
--COULDN'T HOIT TO KNOW WHAT WE MIGHT BE UP AGAINST.
WE, KEMO-SLOBBY?
EX-SQUEEZE ME, YOU MORON, BUT RIDDLE ME THIS, RIDDLER--
--DO YOU SPEAK NEPALI?

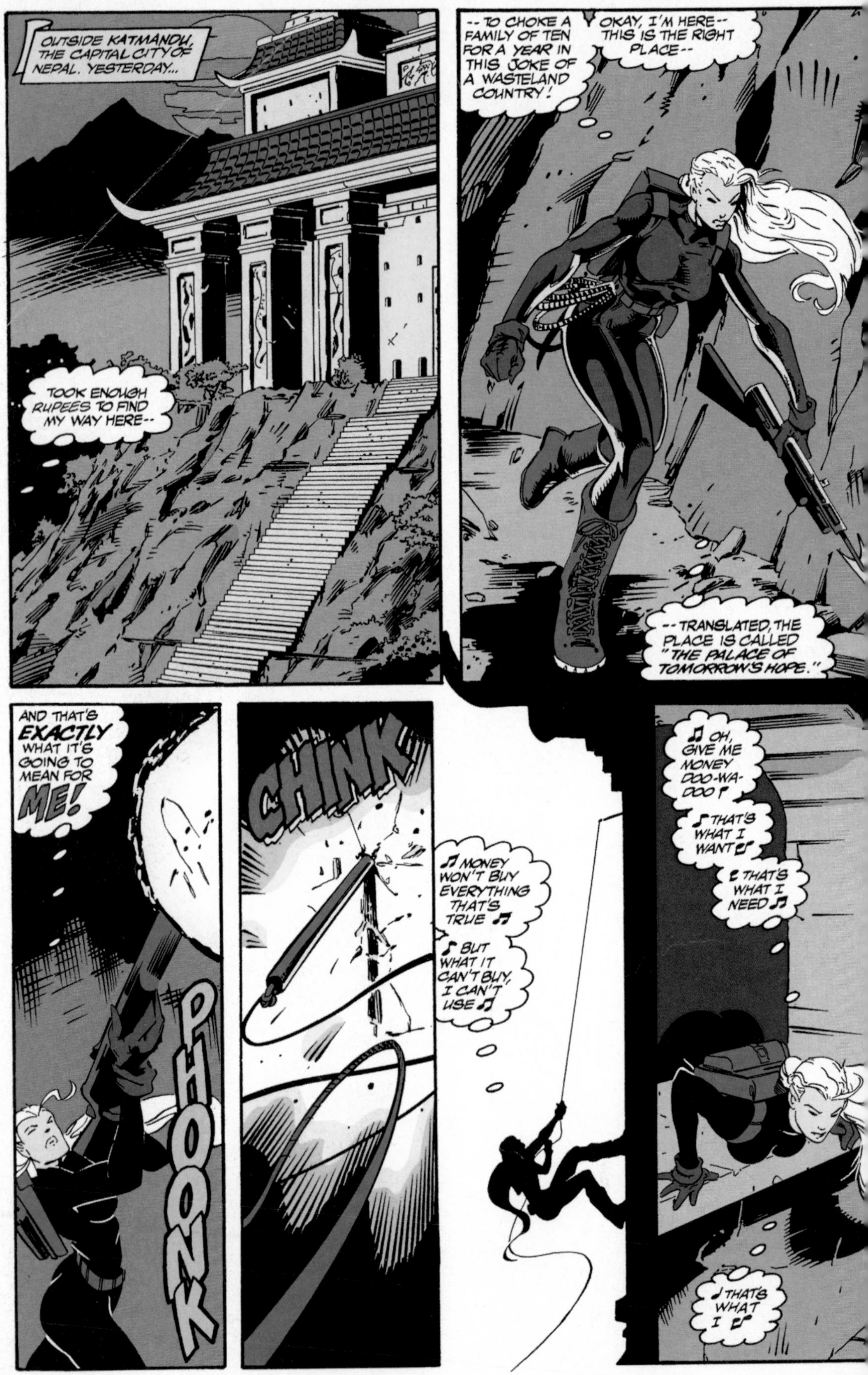
OUTSIDE KATMANDU, THE CAPITAL CITY OF NEPAL. YESTERDAY...
TOOK ENOUGH RUPEES TO FIND MY WAY HERE--
-- TO CHOKE A FAMILY OF TEN FOR A YEAR IN THIS JOKE OF A WASTELAND COUNTRY!
OKAY, I'M HERE-- THIS IS THE RIGHT PLACE--
--TRANSLATED, THE PLACE IS CALLED "THE PALACE OF TOMORROW'S HOPE."
AND THAT'S EXACTLY WHAT IT'S GOING TO MEAN FOR ME!
PHOONK
CHINK
♫ MONEY WON'T BUY EVERYTHING THAT'S TRUE ♫
♪ BUT WHAT IT CAN'T BUY, I CAN'T USE ♫
♫ OH, GIVE ME MONEY DOO-WA-DOO ♪
♪ THAT'S WHAT I WANT ♫
♪ THAT'S WHAT I NEED ♫
♪ THAT'S WHAT I ♪

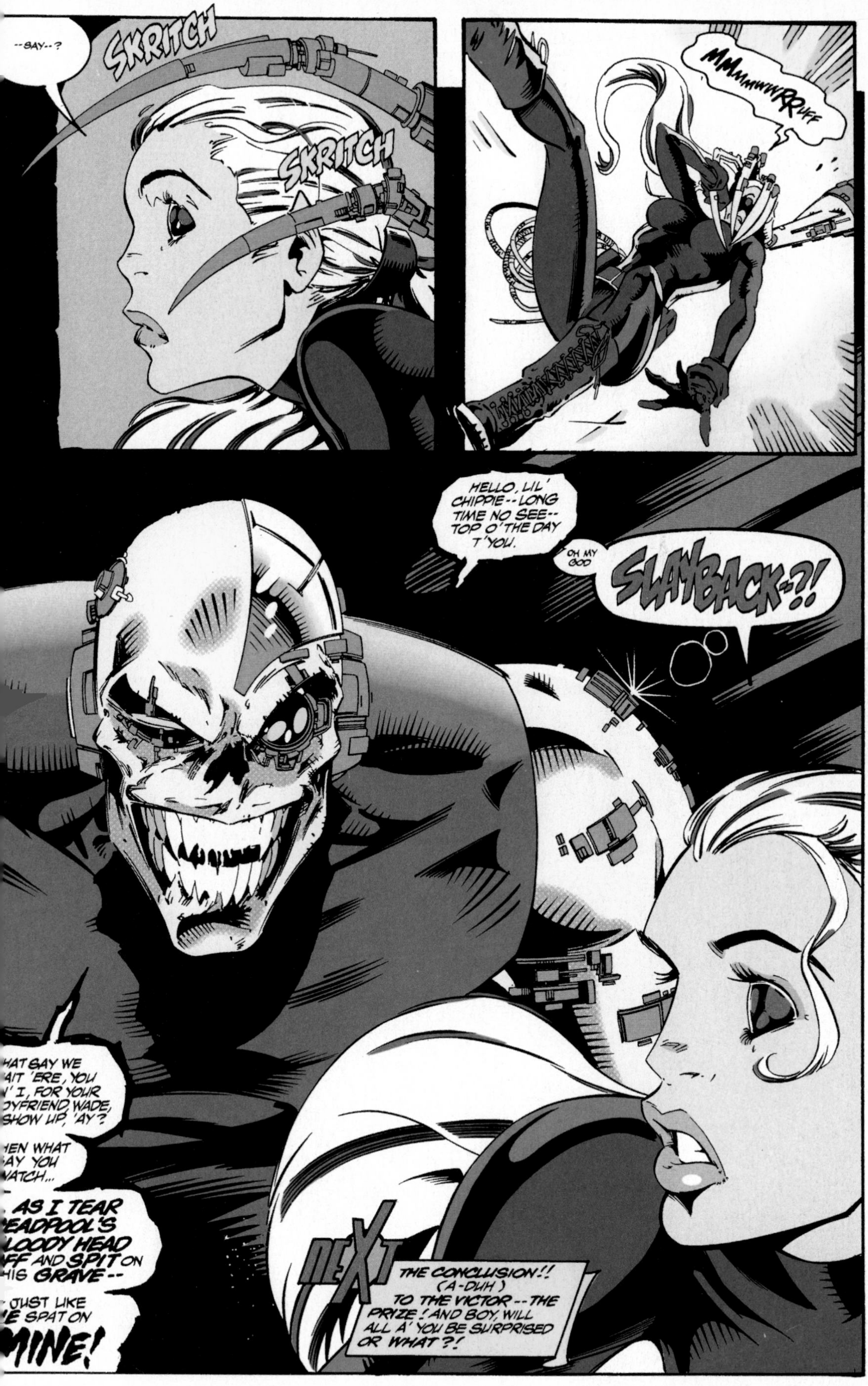
--SAY--?
SKRITCH
SKRITCH
MMMMWWRRUFF
HELLO, LIL' CHIPPIE--LONG TIME NO SEE--TOP O' THE DAY T'YOU.
OH MY GOD
SLAYBACK--?!
HAT SAY WE AIT 'ERE, YOU N' I, FOR YOUR OYFRIEND WADE, SHOW UP, 'AY?
HEN WHAT AY YOU WATCH...
AS I TEAR EADPOOL'S LOODY HEAD FF AND SPIT ON HIS GRAVE--
JUST LIKE E SPAT ON MINE!
NEXT
THE CONCLUSION!! (A-DUH) TO THE VICTOR--THE PRIZE! AND BOY, WILL ALL A' YOU BE SURPRISED OR WHAT?!

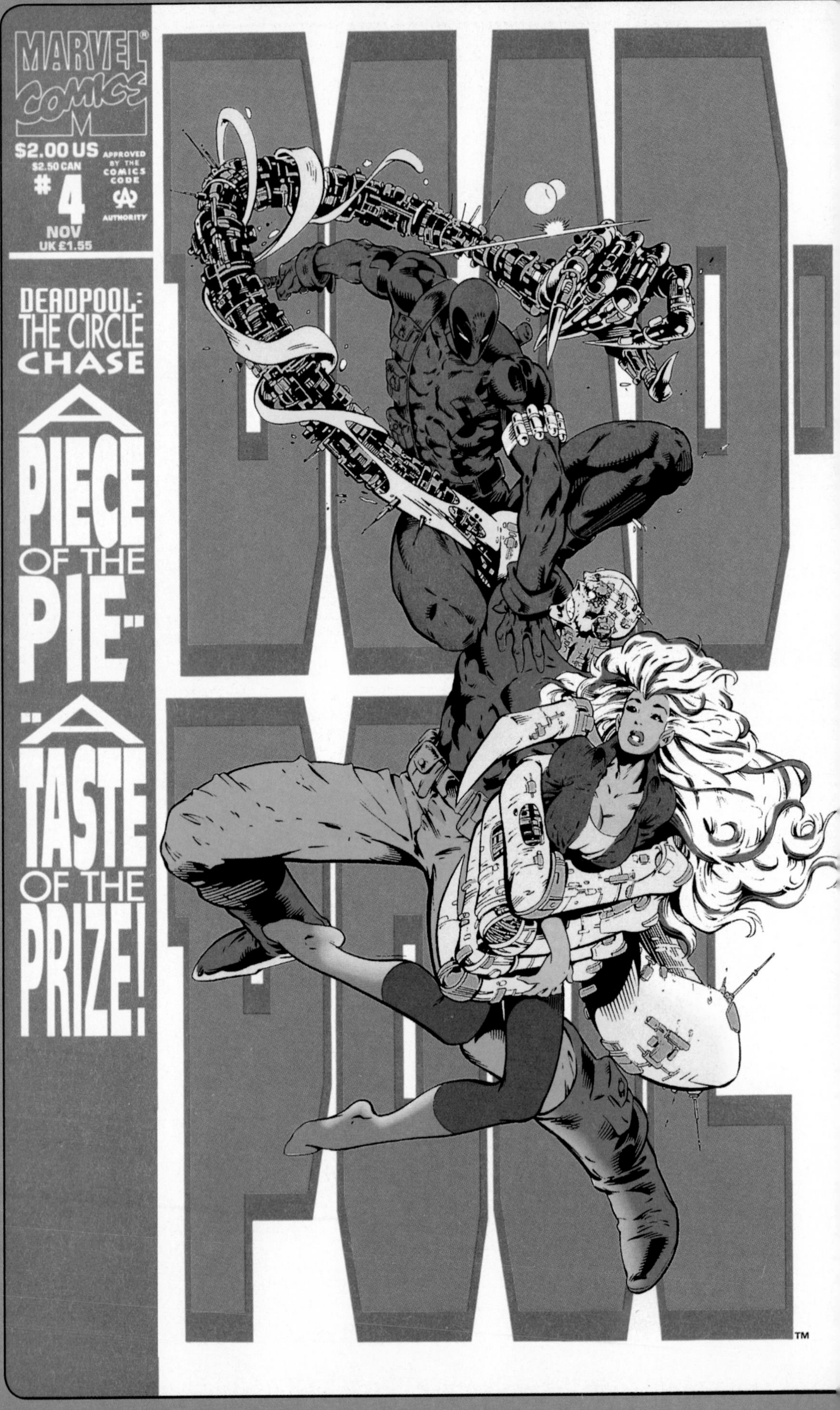

MARVEL COMICS
$2.00 US
$2.50 CAN
#4
NOV
UK £1.55
APPROVED BY THE COMICS CODE AUTHORITY
DEADPOOL: THE CIRCLE CHASE
A PIECE OF THE PIE -- A TASTE OF THE PRIZE!
TM

OUTSIDE OF KATMANDU, THE CAPITAL OF NEPAL, RESTS THE "PALACE OF TOMORROW'S HOPE."

... AND THERE WILL BE PEACE, HARMONY AND LOVE ON EARTH!

A TEMPLE DEVOTED TO PRAYER AND PEACE.

THE EXPECTATION FOR THE SOLEMN MONKS INSIDE IS THAT ONE DAY, THEIR PRAYERS WILL BE ANSWERED...

I HATE EVERYTHING!

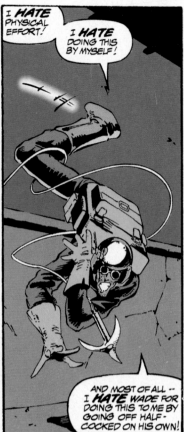

I HATE PHYSICAL EFFORT!

I HATE DOING THIS BY MYSELF!

AND MOST OF ALL -- I HATE WADE FOR DOING THIS TO ME BY GOING OFF HALF-COCKED ON HIS OWN!

STUPID IDIOT DOESN'T KNOW ENOUGH TO BE SCARED OF WALKING INTO A POTENTIAL DEATH TRAP!

COME TO THINK OF IT, I'VE NEVER SEEN THE CHOWDERHEAD AFRAID OF ANYTHING--

-- EXCEPT WHEN HE TALKS ABOUT HIS OLD DAYS WITH THE WEAPON X PROGRAM --

-- AND WHEN HE FIRST THOUGHT HIS OLD BOSS, TOLLIVER, HAD KILLED HIS OLD BABE, VANESSA, A YEAR AGO.

BUT YOU'D THINK AT THE VERY LEAST, HE COULD RESPECT THAT HIS OL' BUDDY--

-- MIGHT BE JUST THE TEENSIEST BIT AFRAID --

--OF BREAKING INTO A TEMPLE--

--WHICH IS HOLDING THE GREATEST WEAPON ON THE FACE...

...OF...

THE CIRCLE CHASE - ROUND 4

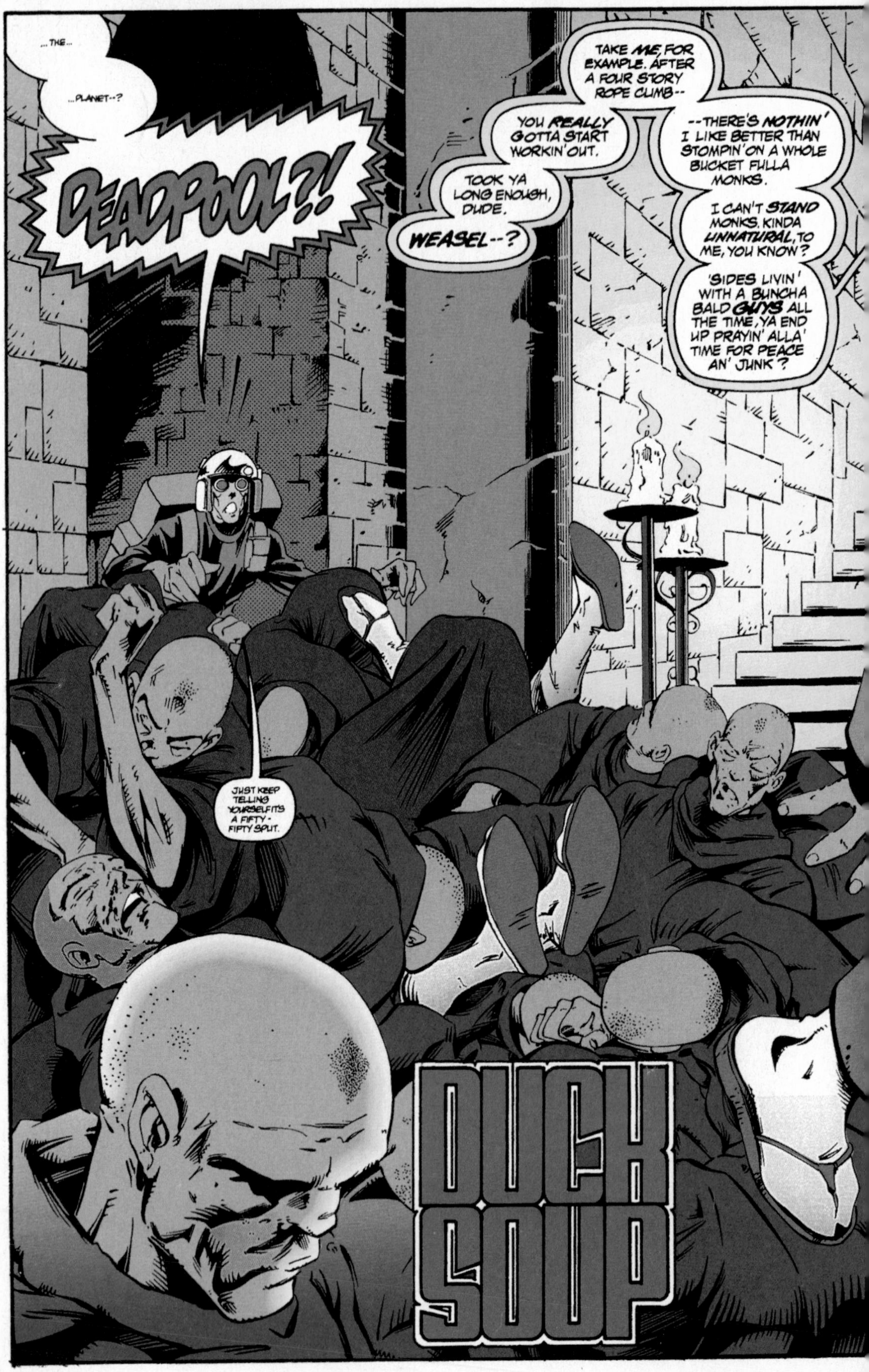
...THE...
...PLANET--?
DEADPOOL?!
WEASEL--?
TOOK YA LONG ENOUGH, DUDE.
YOU REALLY GOTTA START WORKIN' OUT.
TAKE ME, FOR EXAMPLE. AFTER A FOUR STORY ROPE CLIMB--
--THERE'S NOTHIN' I LIKE BETTER THAN STOMPIN' ON A WHOLE BUCKET FULLA MONKS.
I CAN'T STAND MONKS. KINDA UNNATURAL, TO ME, YOU KNOW?
'SIDES LIVIN' WITH A BUNCHA BALD GUYS ALL THE TIME, YA END UP PRAYIN' ALLA' TIME FOR PEACE AN' JUNK?
JUST KEEP TELLING YOURSELF IT'S A FIFTY-FIFTY SPLIT.
DUCK SOUP

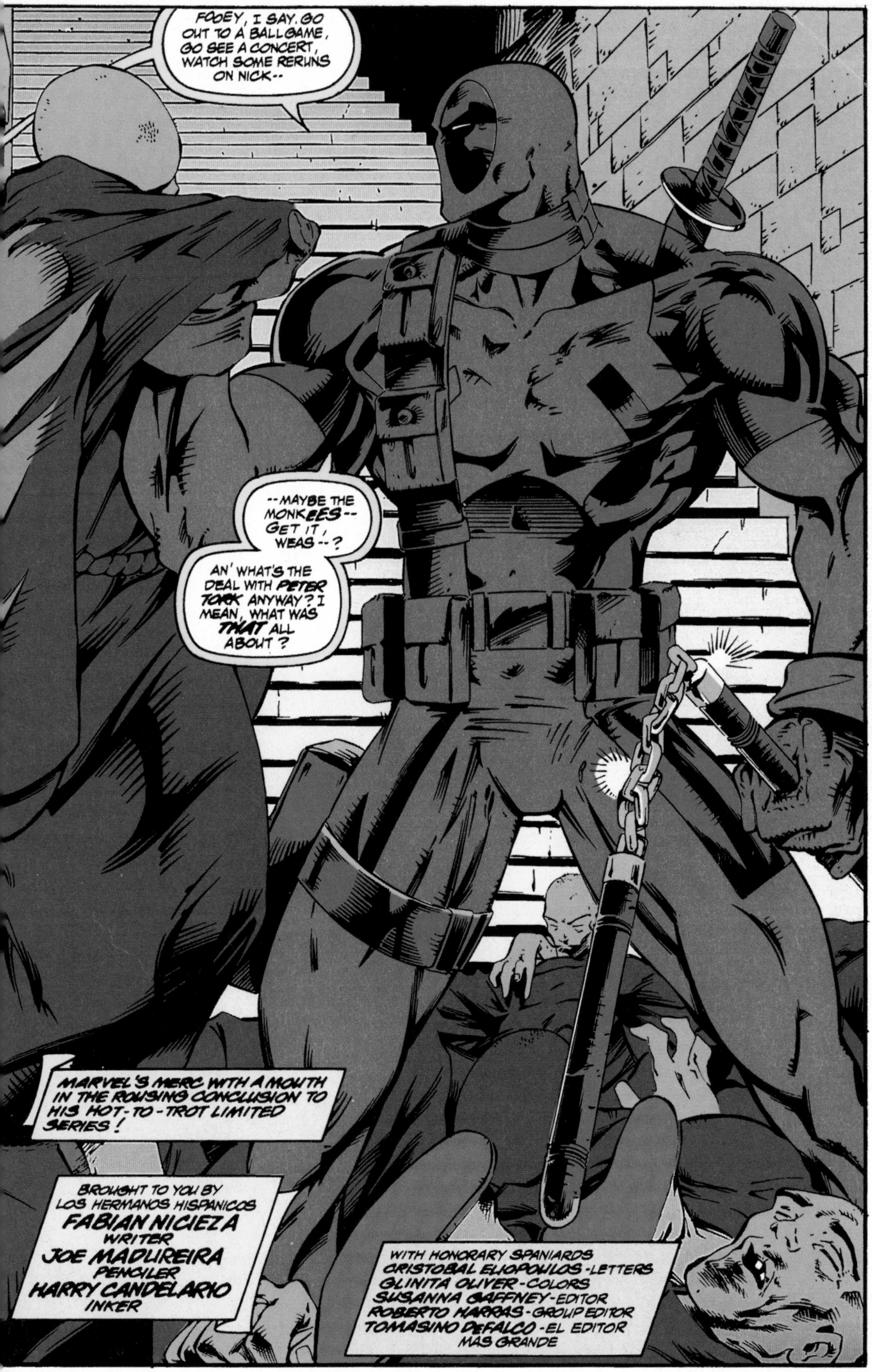

FOOEY, I SAY. GO OUT TO A BALLGAME, GO SEE A CONCERT, WATCH SOME RERUNS ON NICK--
--MAYBE THE MONKEES-- GET IT, WEAS--?
AN' WHAT'S THE DEAL WITH PETER TORK ANYWAY? I MEAN, WHAT WAS THAT ALL ABOUT?
MARVEL'S MERC WITH A MOUTH IN THE ROUSING CONCLUSION TO HIS HOT-TO-TROT LIMITED SERIES!
BROUGHT TO YOU BY LOS HERMANOS HISPANICOS
FABIAN NICIEZA WRITER
JOE MADUREIRA PENCILER
HARRY CANDELARIO INKER
WITH HONORARY SPANIARDS
CRISTOBAL ELIOPOULOS - LETTERS
GLINITA OLIVER - COLORS
SUSANNA GAFFNEY - EDITOR
ROBERTO HARRAS - GROUP EDITOR
TOMASINO DEFALCO - EL EDITOR MAS GRANDE

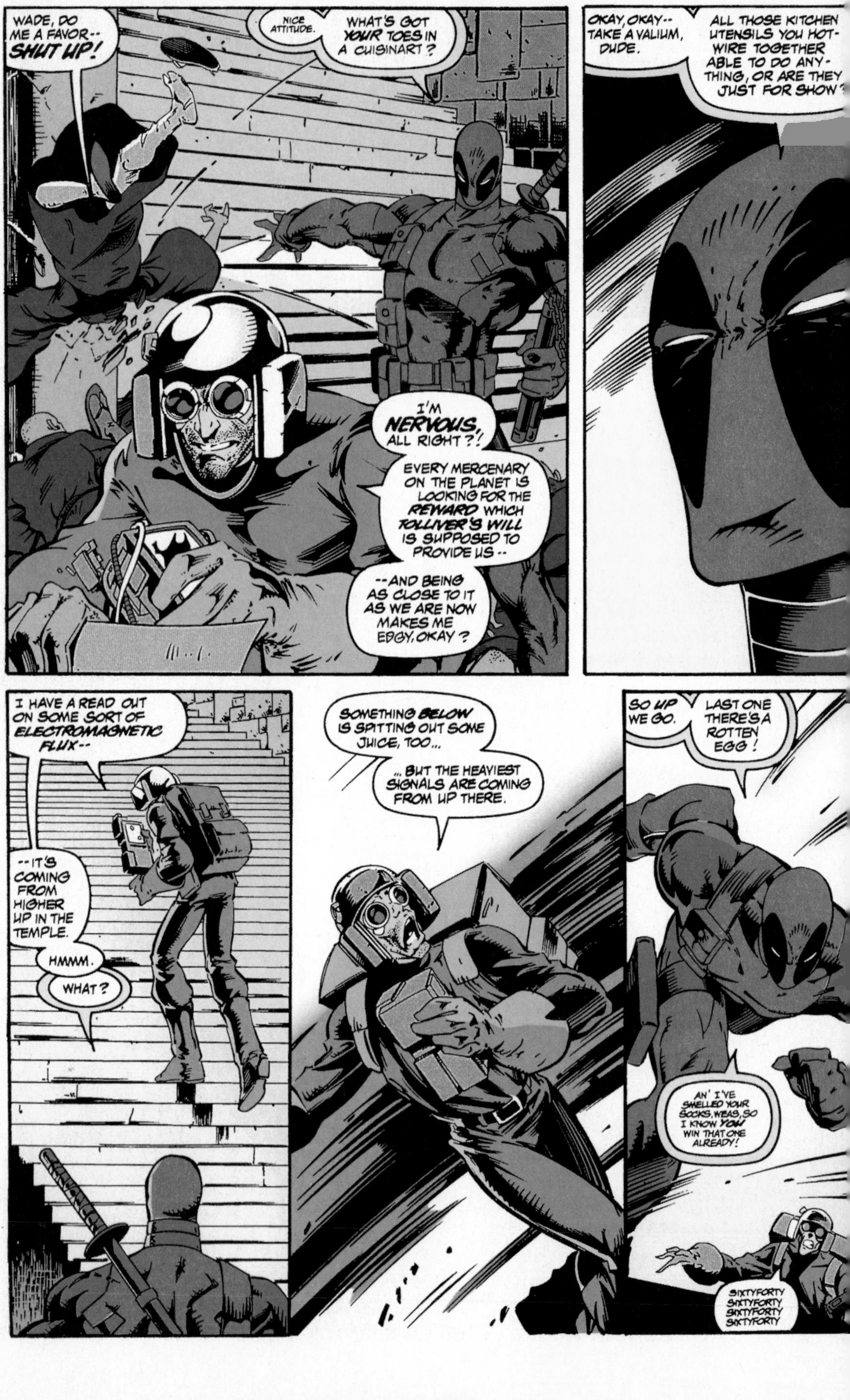
WADE, DO ME A FAVOR-- SHUT UP!
NICE ATTITUDE.
WHAT'S GOT YOUR TOES IN A CUISINART?
I'M NERVOUS, ALL RIGHT?!
EVERY MERCENARY ON THE PLANET IS LOOKING FOR THE REWARD WHICH TOLLIVER'S WILL IS SUPPOSED TO PROVIDE US --
-- AND BEING AS CLOSE TO IT AS WE ARE NOW MAKES ME EDGY, OKAY?
OKAY, OKAY-- TAKE A VALIUM, DUDE.
ALL THOSE KITCHEN UTENSILS YOU HOT-WIRE TOGETHER ABLE TO DO ANYTHING, OR ARE THEY JUST FOR SHOW?
I HAVE A READ OUT ON SOME SORT OF ELECTROMAGNETIC FLUX--
-- IT'S COMING FROM HIGHER UP IN THE TEMPLE.
HMMM.
WHAT?
SOMETHING BELOW IS SPITTING OUT SOME JUICE, TOO...
... BUT THE HEAVIEST SIGNALS ARE COMING FROM UP THERE.
SO UP WE GO.
LAST ONE THERE'S A ROTTEN EGG!
AN' I'VE SMELLED YOUR SOCKS, WEAS, SO I KNOW YOU WIN THAT ONE ALREADY!
SIXTYFORTY SIXTYFORTY SIXTYFORTY SIXTYFORTY

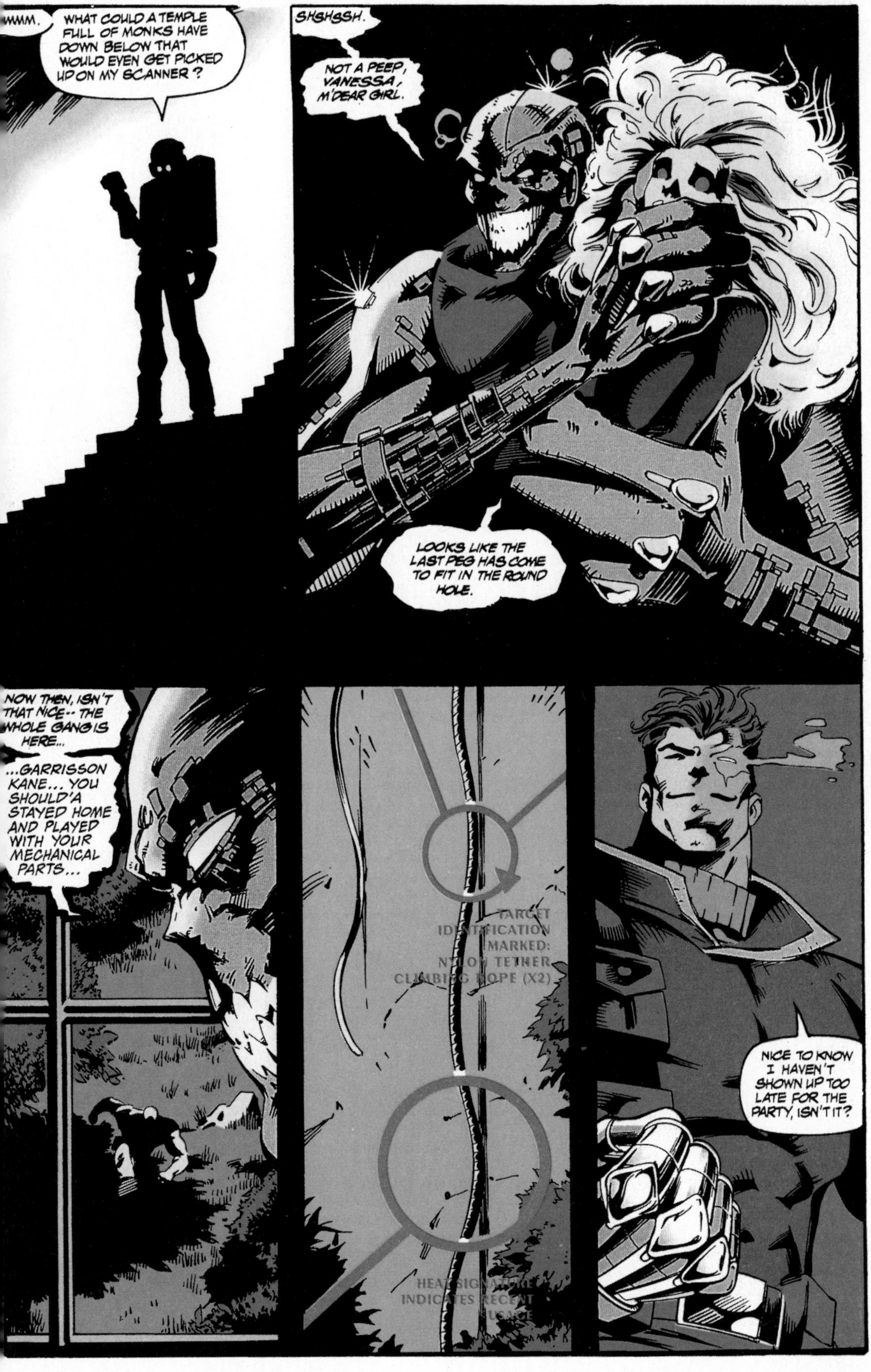
MMM.
WHAT COULD A TEMPLE FULL OF MONKS HAVE DOWN BELOW THAT WOULD EVEN GET PICKED UP ON MY SCANNER?
SHSHSSH.
NOT A PEEP, VANESSA, M'DEAR GIRL.
LOOKS LIKE THE LAST PEG HAS COME TO FIT IN THE ROUND HOLE.
NOW THEN, ISN'T THAT NICE-- THE WHOLE GANG IS HERE...
...GARRISSON KANE... YOU SHOULD'A STAYED HOME AND PLAYED WITH YOUR MECHANICAL PARTS...
TARGET IDENTIFICATION MARKED: NYLON TETHER CLIMBING ROPE (X2)
HEAT SIGNATURE INDICATES RECENT USAGE
NICE TO KNOW I HAVEN'T SHOWN UP TOO LATE FOR THE PARTY, ISN'T IT?

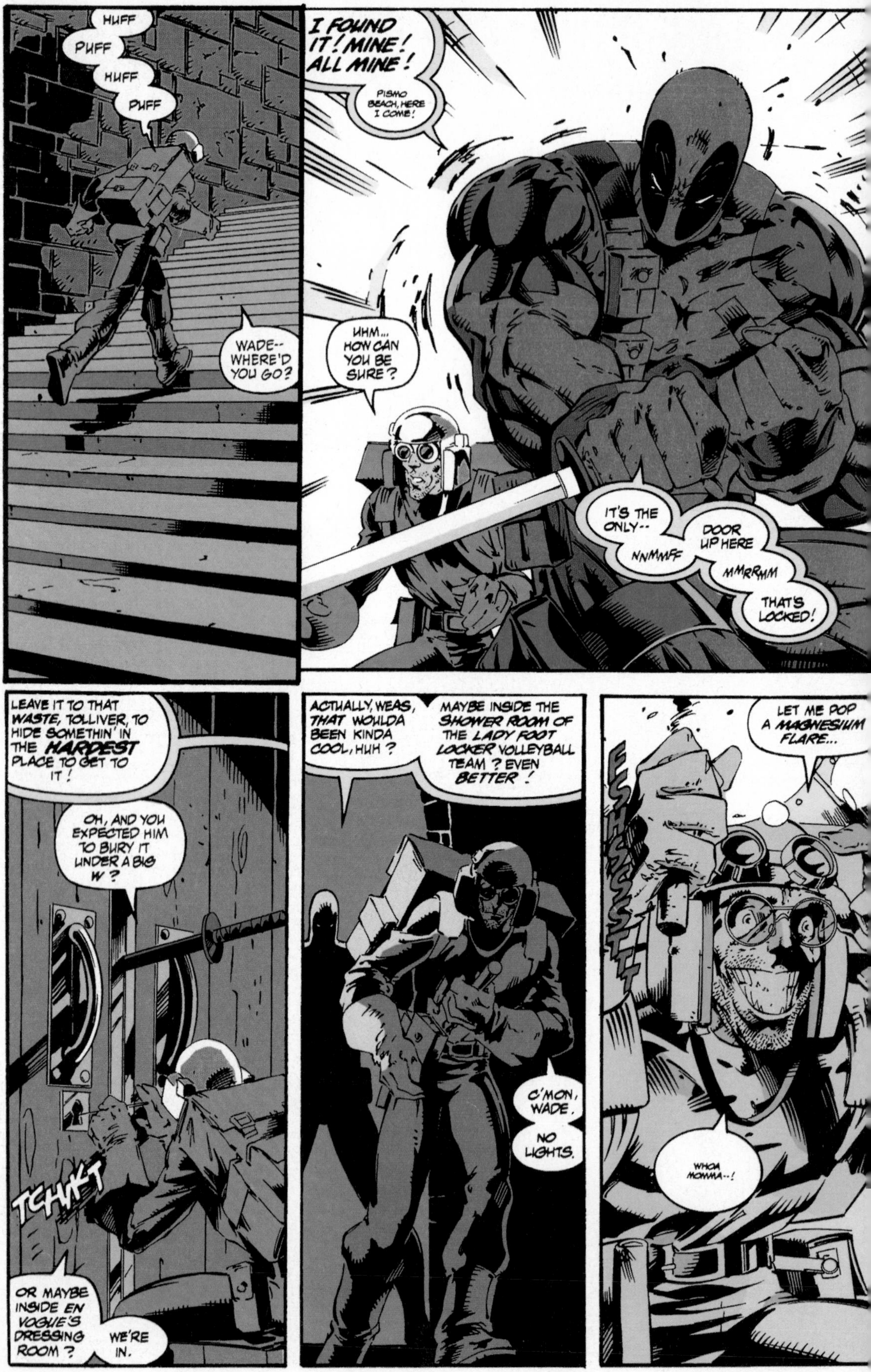
HUFF
PUFF
HUFF
PUFF
WADE-- WHERE'D YOU GO?
I FOUND IT! MINE! ALL MINE!
PISMO BEACH, HERE I COME!
UHM... HOW CAN YOU BE SURE?
IT'S THE ONLY--
NNMMFF
DOOR UP HERE
MMRRMM
THAT'S LOCKED!
LEAVE IT TO THAT WASTE, TOLLIVER, TO HIDE SOMETHIN' IN THE HARDEST PLACE TO GET TO IT!
OH, AND YOU EXPECTED HIM TO BURY IT UNDER A BIG W?
TCHKT
OR MAYBE INSIDE EN VOGUE'S DRESSING ROOM?
WE'RE IN.
ACTUALLY, WEAS, THAT WOULDA BEEN KINDA COOL, HUH?
MAYBE INSIDE THE SHOWER ROOM OF THE LADY FOOT LOCKER VOLLEYBALL TEAM? EVEN BETTER!
C'MON, WADE.
NO LIGHTS.
LET ME POP A MAGNESIUM FLARE...
WHOA MOMMA--!

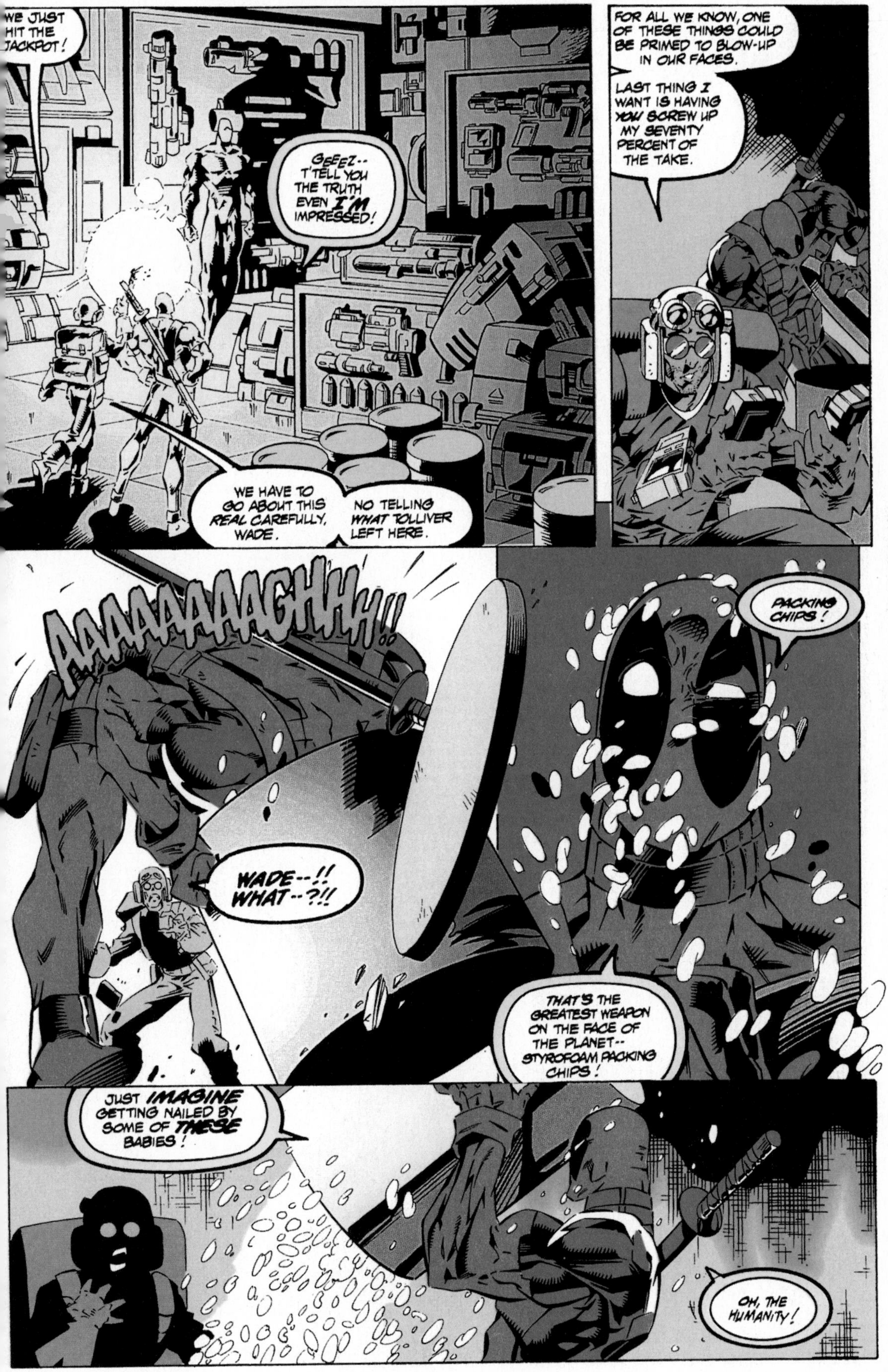
WE JUST HIT THE JACKPOT!
GEEEZ-- T'TELL YOU THE TRUTH EVEN I'M IMPRESSED!
WE HAVE TO GO ABOUT THIS REAL CAREFULLY, WADE.
NO TELLING WHAT TOLLIVER LEFT HERE.
FOR ALL WE KNOW, ONE OF THESE THINGS COULD BE PRIMED TO BLOW-UP IN OUR FACES.
LAST THING I WANT IS HAVING YOU SCREW UP MY SEVENTY PERCENT OF THE TAKE.
AAAAAAAAGHHH!!
PACKING CHIPS!
WADE--!! WHAT--?!!
THAT'S THE GREATEST WEAPON ON THE FACE OF THE PLANET-- STYROFOAM PACKING CHIPS!
JUST IMAGINE GETTING NAILED BY SOME OF THESE BABIES!
OH, THE HUMANITY!

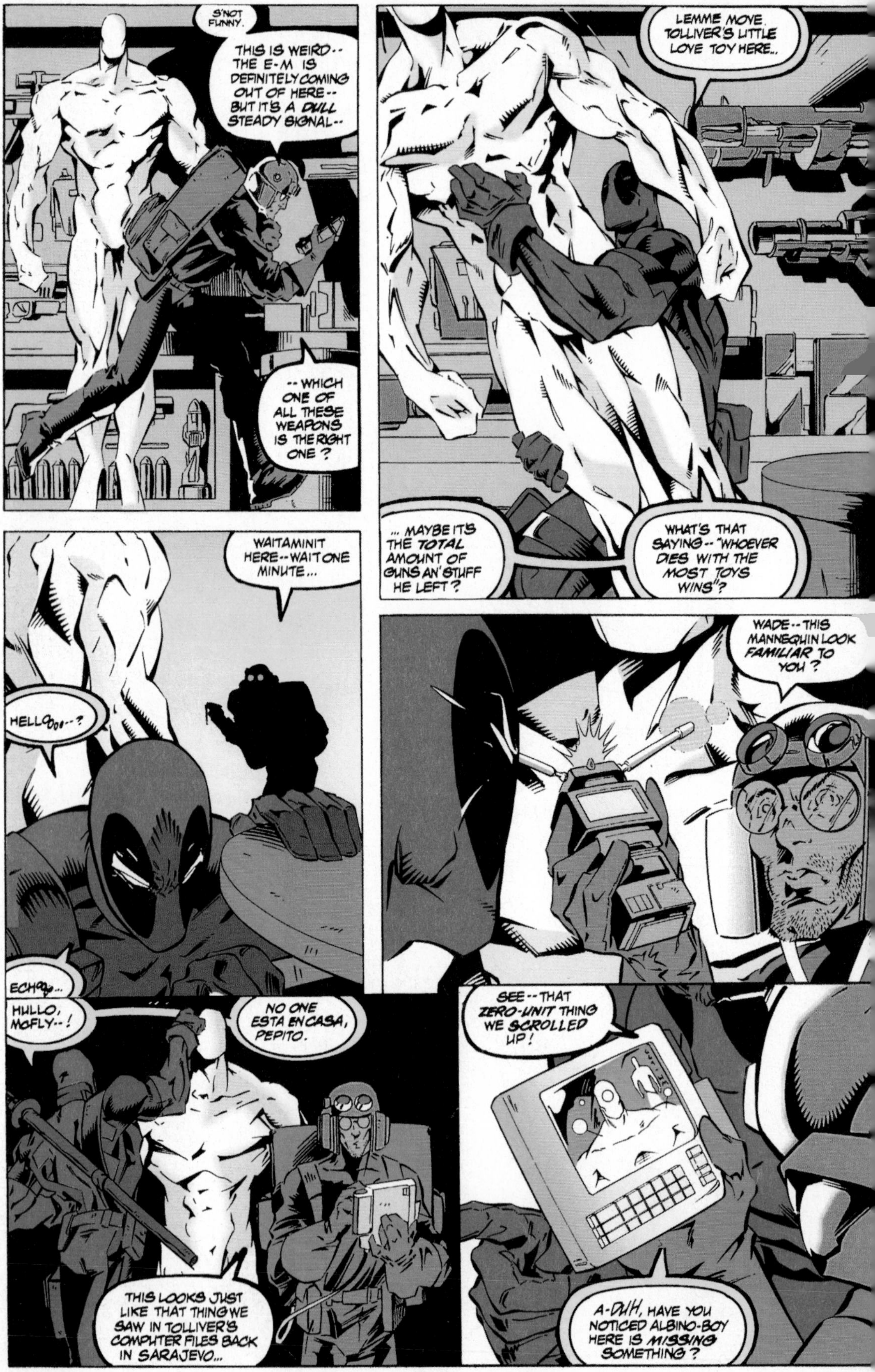
S'NOT FUNNY.
THIS IS WEIRD-- THE E-M IS DEFINITELY COMING OUT OF HERE-- BUT IT'S A DULL STEADY SIGNAL--
--WHICH ONE OF ALL THESE WEAPONS IS THE RIGHT ONE?
LEMME MOVE TOLLIVER'S LITTLE LOVE TOY HERE..
... MAYBE IT'S THE TOTAL AMOUNT OF GUNS AN' STUFF HE LEFT?
WHAT'S THAT SAYING-- "WHOEVER DIES WITH THE MOST TOYS WINS"?
WAITAMINIT HERE--WAIT ONE MINUTE...
HELLOooo--?
ECHOoo...
WADE--THIS MANNEQUIN LOOK FAMILIAR TO YOU?
HULLO, MCFLY--!
NO ONE ESTA EN CASA, PEPITO.
THIS LOOKS JUST LIKE THAT THING WE SAW IN TOLLIVER'S COMPUTER FILES BACK IN SARAJEVO...
SEE--THAT ZERO-UNIT THING WE SCROLLED UP!
A-DUH, HAVE YOU NOTICED ALBINO-BOY HERE IS MISSING SOMETHING?

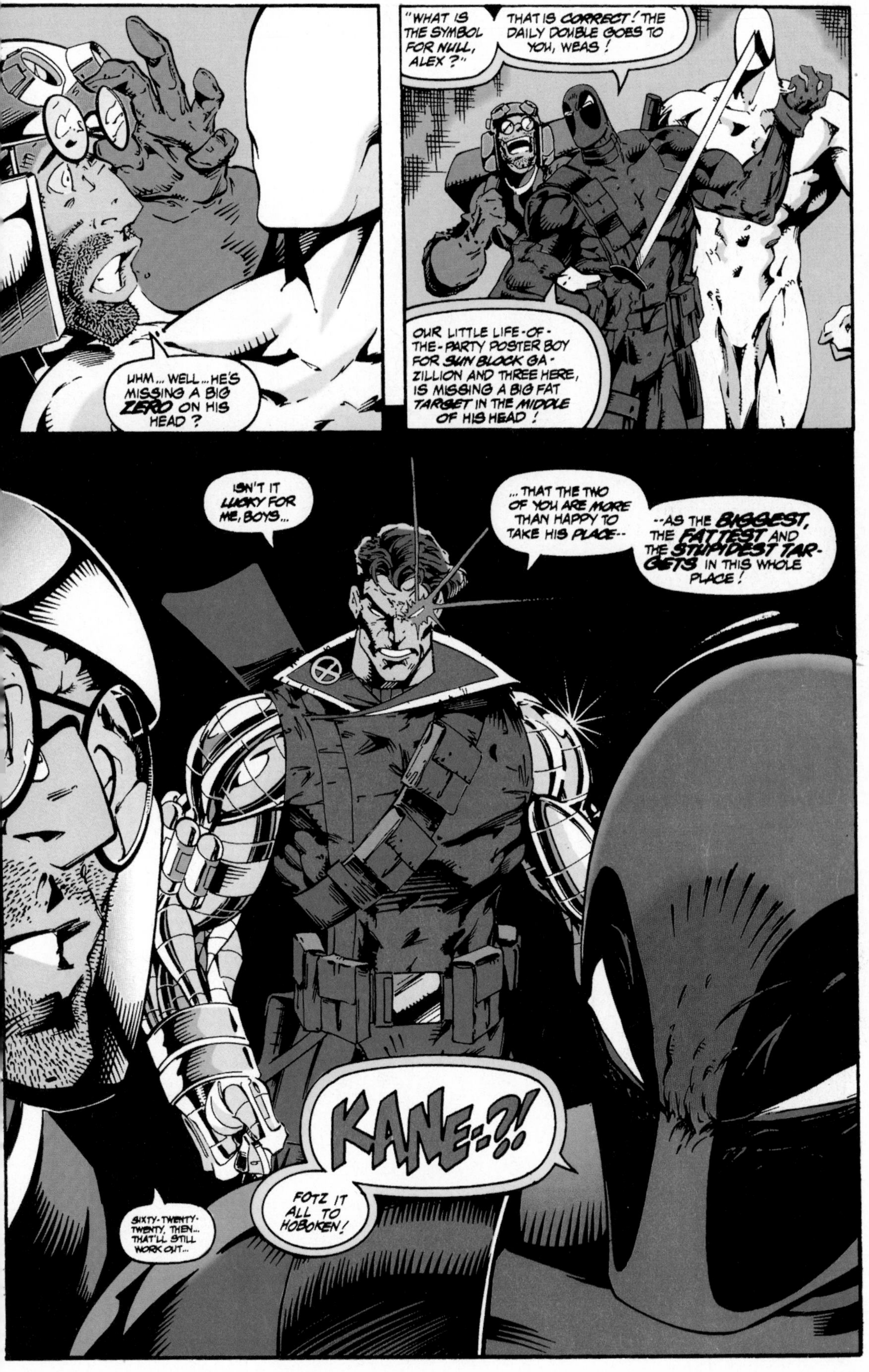
UHM... WELL... HE'S MISSING A BIG ZERO ON HIS HEAD?
"WHAT IS THE SYMBOL FOR NULL, ALEX?"
THAT IS CORRECT! THE DAILY DOUBLE GOES TO YOU, WEAS!
OUR LITTLE LIFE-OF-THE-PARTY POSTER BOY FOR SUN BLOCK GAZILLION AND THREE HERE, IS MISSING A BIG FAT TARGET IN THE MIDDLE OF HIS HEAD!
ISN'T IT LUCKY FOR ME, BOYS...
...THAT THE TWO OF YOU ARE MORE THAN HAPPY TO TAKE HIS PLACE--
--AS THE BIGGEST, THE FATTEST AND THE STUPIDEST TARGETS IN THIS WHOLE PLACE!
KANE-?!
FOTZ IT ALL TO HOBOKEN!
SIXTY-TWENTY-TWENTY, THEN... THAT'LL STILL WORK OUT...

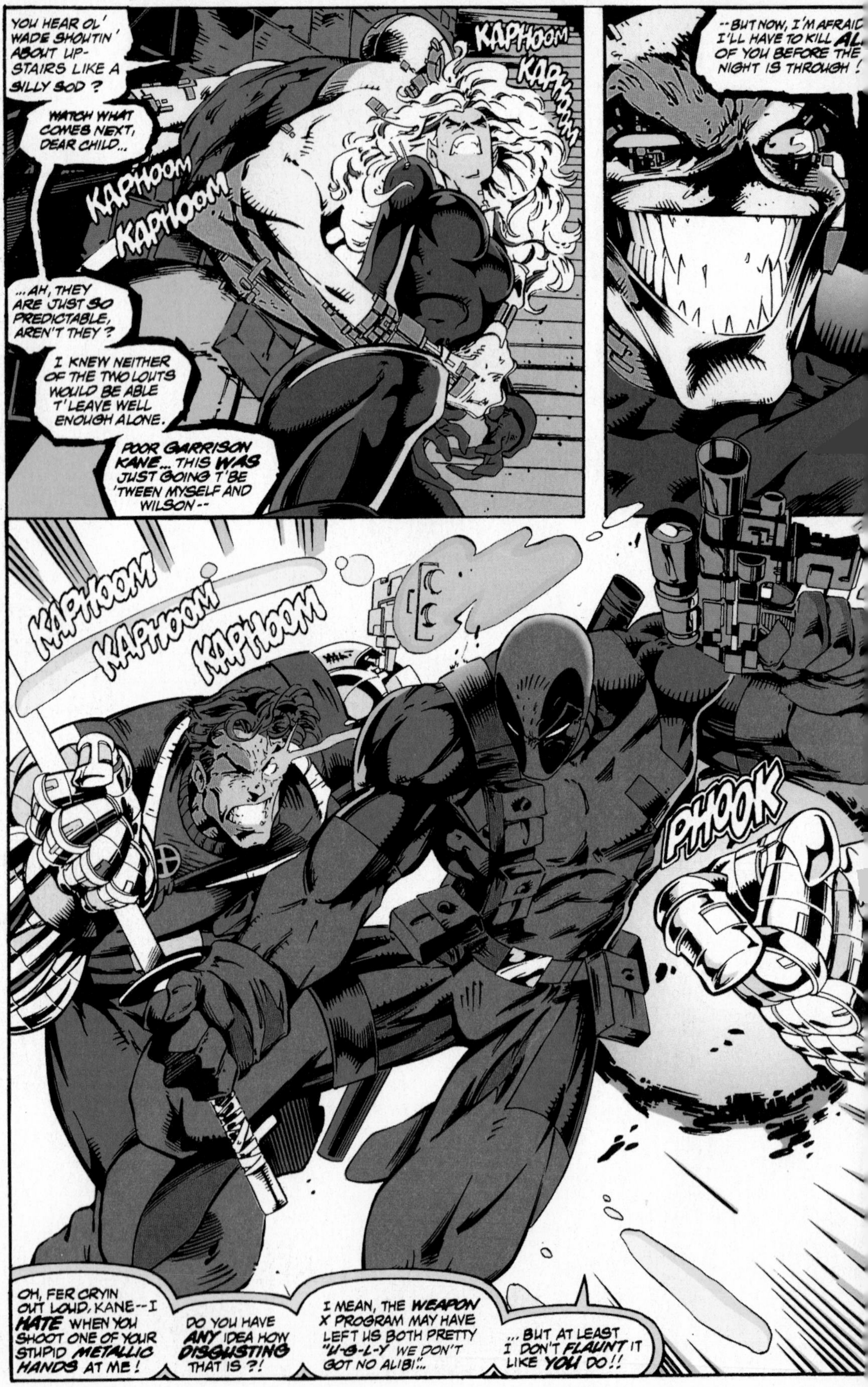

YOU HEAR OL' WADE SHOUTIN' ABOUT UP-STAIRS LIKE A SILLY SOD ?
WATCH WHAT COMES NEXT, DEAR CHILD...
KAPHOOM
KAPHOOM
KAPHOOM
KAPHOOM
...AH, THEY ARE JUST SO PREDICTABLE, AREN'T THEY ?
I KNEW NEITHER OF THE TWO LOUTS WOULD BE ABLE T'LEAVE WELL ENOUGH ALONE.
POOR GARRISON KANE... THIS WAS JUST GOING T'BE 'TWEEN MYSELF AND WILSON --
--BUT NOW, I'M AFRAID I'LL HAVE TO KILL AL OF YOU BEFORE THE NIGHT IS THROUGH !
KAPHOOM
KAPHOOM
KAPHOOM
PHOOK
OH, FER CRYIN OUT LOUD, KANE--I HATE WHEN YOU SHOOT ONE OF YOUR STUPID METALLIC HANDS AT ME !
DO YOU HAVE ANY IDEA HOW DISGUSTING THAT IS ?!
I MEAN, THE WEAPON X PROGRAM MAY HAVE LEFT US BOTH PRETTY "U-G-L-Y WE DON'T GOT NO ALIBI"...
...BUT AT LEAST I DON'T FLAUNT IT LIKE YOU DO!!

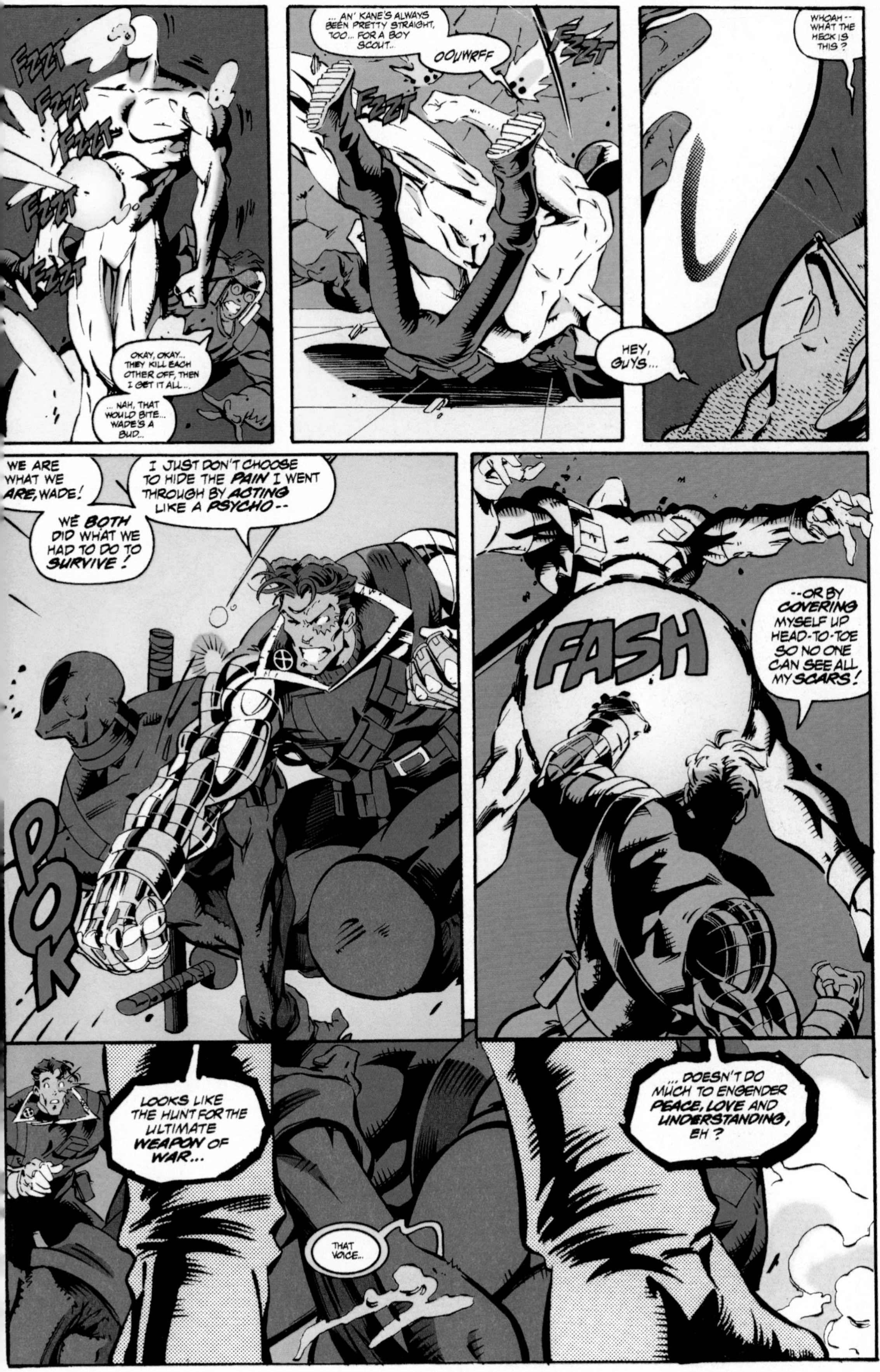
FZZZT
FZZZT
FZZZT
FZZZT
FZZZT
OKAY, OKAY... THEY KILL EACH OTHER OFF, THEN I GET IT ALL...
... NAH, THAT WOULD BITE... WADE'S A BUD...
... AN' KANE'S ALWAYS BEEN PRETTY STRAIGHT, TOO... FOR A BOY SCOUT...
OOUWRFF
FZZZT
FZZZT
HEY, GUYS...
WHOAH -- WHAT THE HECK IS THIS?
WE ARE WHAT WE ARE, WADE!
WE BOTH DID WHAT WE HAD TO DO TO SURVIVE!
I JUST DON'T CHOOSE TO HIDE THE PAIN I WENT THROUGH BY ACTING LIKE A PSYCHO--
POK
FASH
--OR BY COVERING MYSELF UP HEAD-TO-TOE SO NO ONE CAN SEE ALL MY SCARS!
LOOKS LIKE THE HUNT FOR THE ULTIMATE WEAPON OF WAR...
... DOESN'T DO MUCH TO ENGENDER PEACE, LOVE AND UNDERSTANDING, EH?
THAT VOICE...

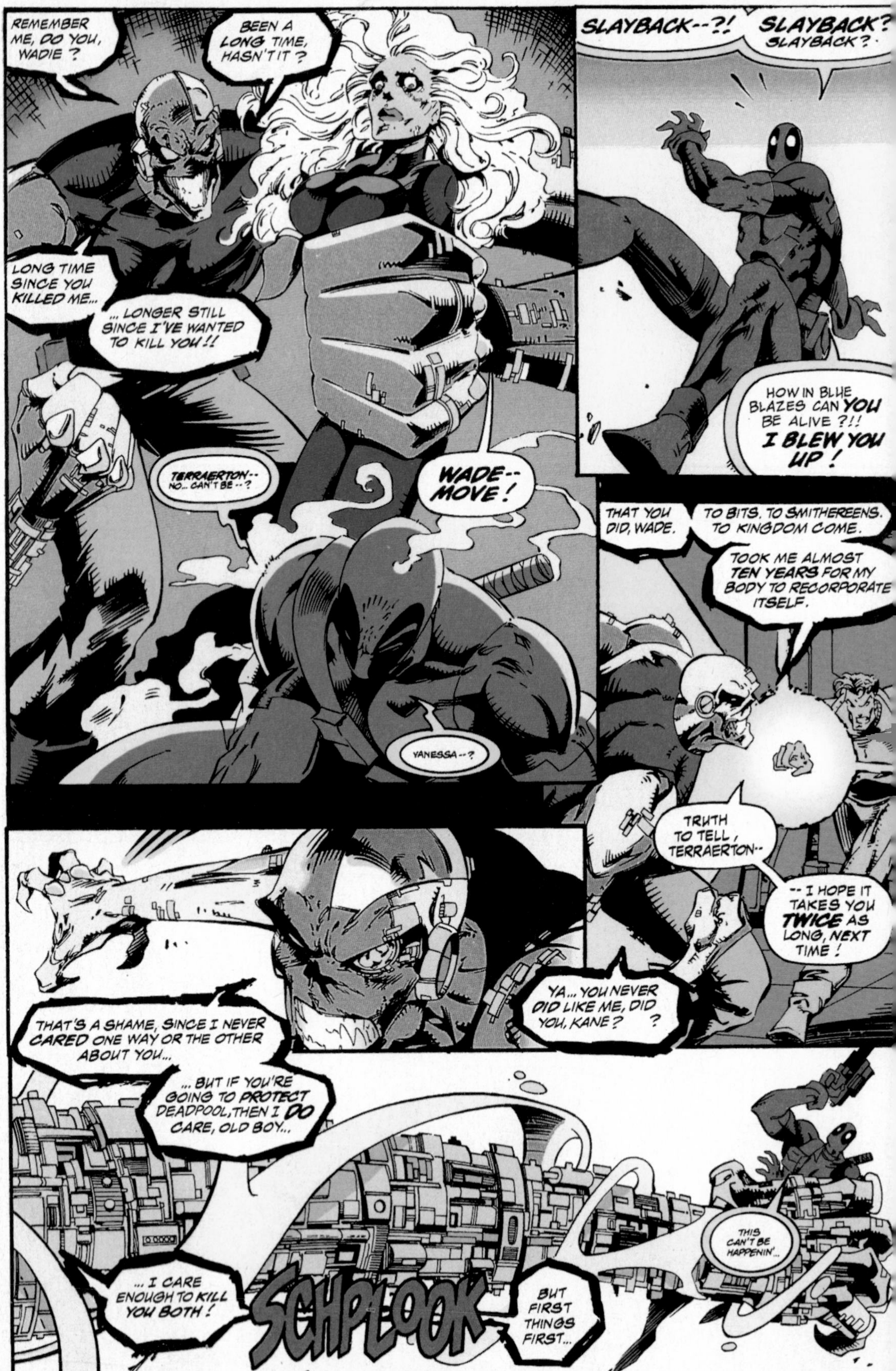
REMEMBER ME, DO YOU, WADIE ?
BEEN A LONG TIME, HASN'T IT ?
SLAYBACK--?!
SLAYBACK? SLAYBACK?
LONG TIME SINCE YOU KILLED ME...
... LONGER STILL SINCE I'VE WANTED TO KILL YOU !!
HOW IN BLUE BLAZES CAN YOU BE ALIVE ?!! I BLEW YOU UP !
TERRAERTON-- NO... CAN'T BE --?
WADE-- MOVE !
VANESSA--?
THAT YOU DID, WADE.
TO BITS. TO SMITHEREENS. TO KINGDOM COME.
TOOK ME ALMOST TEN YEARS FOR MY BODY TO RECORPORATE ITSELF.
TRUTH TO TELL, TERRAERTON--
-- I HOPE IT TAKES YOU TWICE AS LONG, NEXT TIME !
YA... YOU NEVER DID LIKE ME, DID YOU, KANE ?
?
THAT'S A SHAME, SINCE I NEVER CARED ONE WAY OR THE OTHER ABOUT YOU...
... BUT IF YOU'RE GOING TO PROTECT DEADPOOL, THEN I DO CARE, OLD BOY...
... I CARE ENOUGH TO KILL YOU BOTH !
SCHPLOOK
BUT FIRST THINGS FIRST...
THIS CAN'T BE HAPPENIN'...

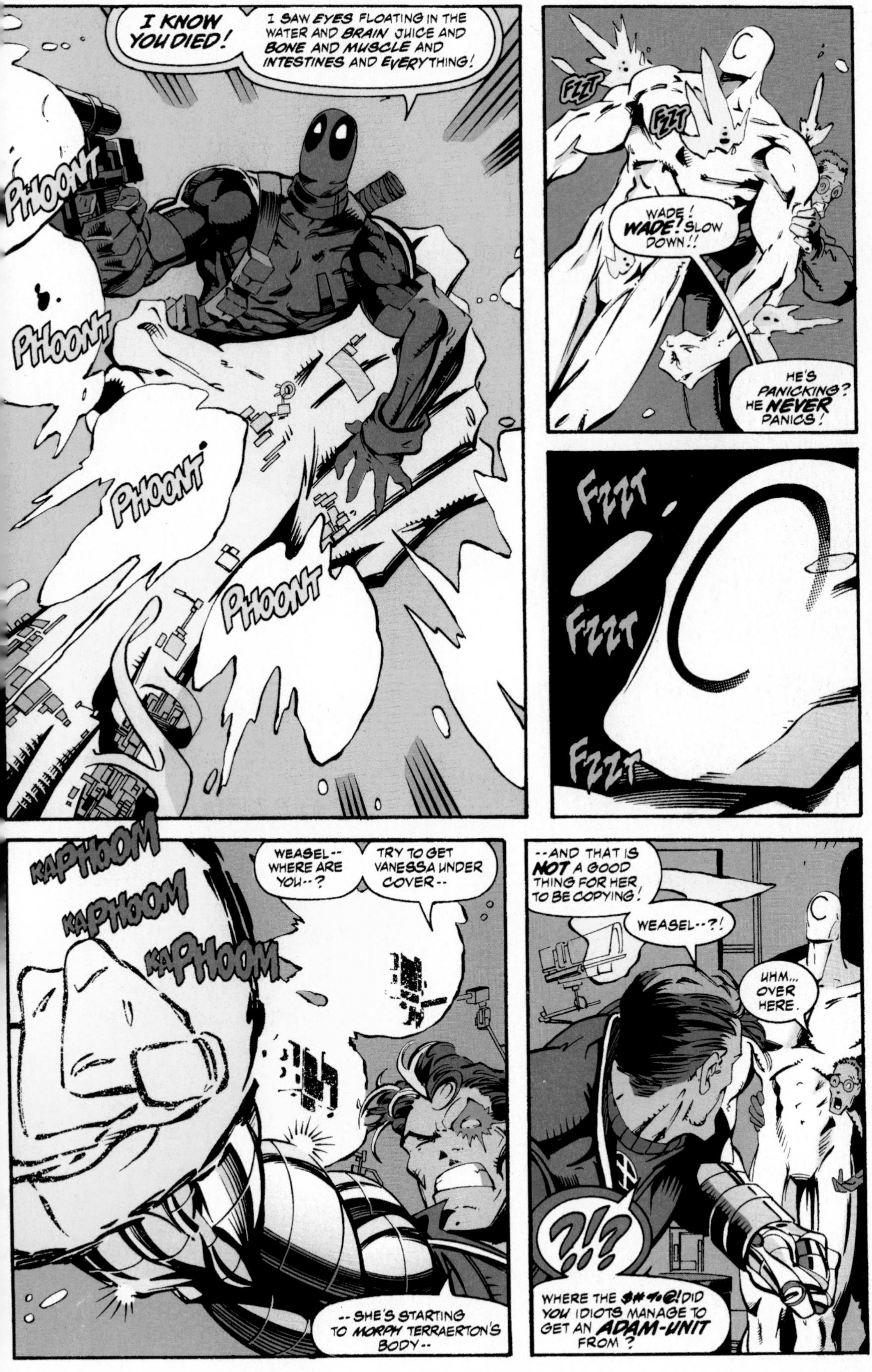
I KNOW YOU DIED!
I SAW EYES FLOATING IN THE WATER AND BRAIN JUICE AND BONE AND MUSCLE AND INTESTINES AND EVERYTHING!
PHOONT
PHOONT
PHOONT
PHOONT
FZZT
FZZT
WADE! WADE! SLOW DOWN!!
HE'S PANICKING? HE NEVER PANICS!
FZZT
FZZT
FZZT
KAPHOOM
KAPHOOM
KAPHOOM
WEASEL-- WHERE ARE YOU--?
TRY TO GET VANESSA UNDER COVER--
--SHE'S STARTING TO MORPH TERRAERTON'S BODY--
--AND THAT IS NOT A GOOD THING FOR HER TO BE COPYING!
WEASEL--?!
UHM... OVER HERE.
?!?
WHERE THE $#%@! DID YOU IDIOTS MANAGE TO GET AN ADAM-UNIT FROM?

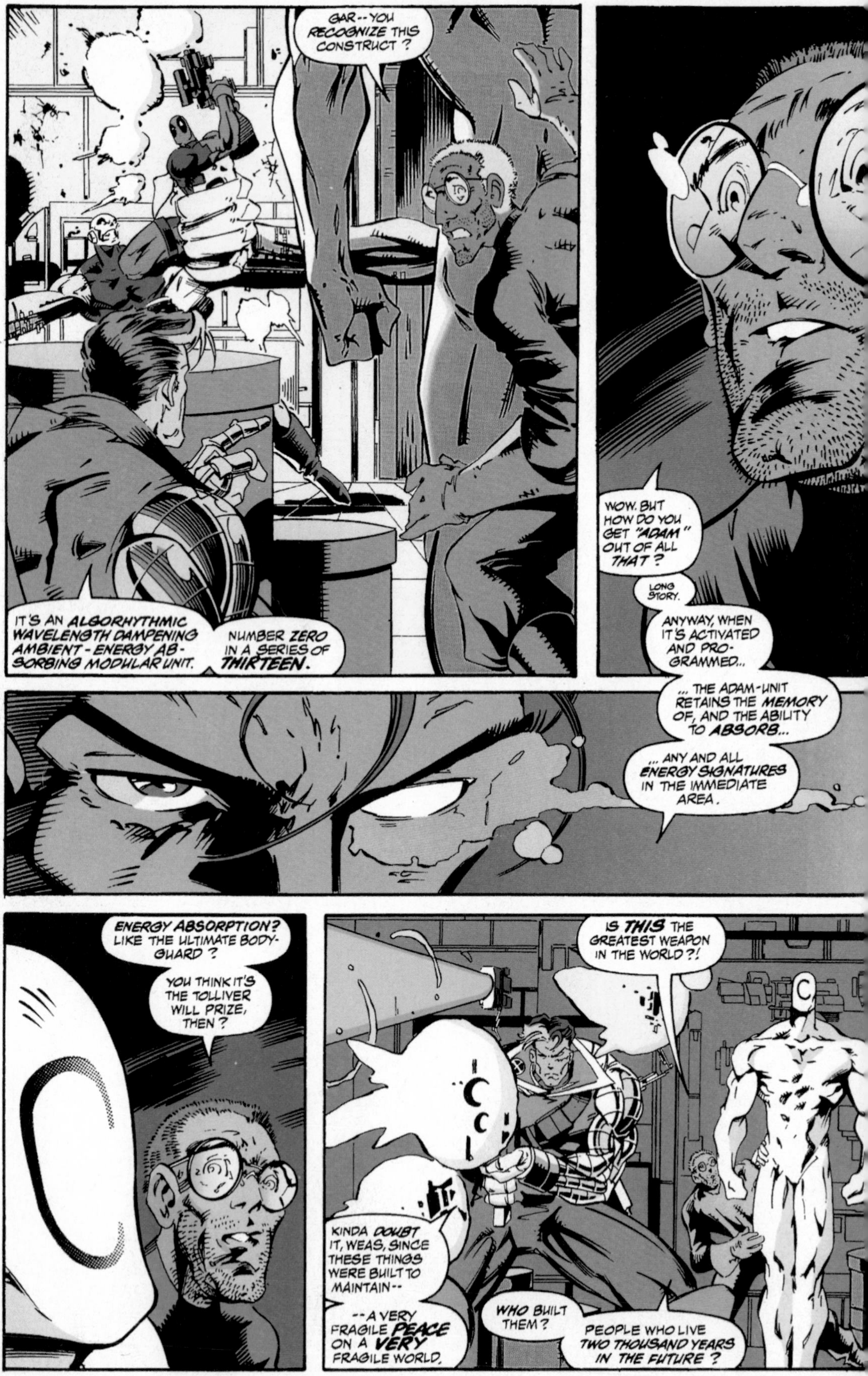
GAR--YOU RECOGNIZE THIS CONSTRUCT ?
IT'S AN ALGORHYTHMIC WAVELENGTH DAMPENING AMBIENT - ENERGY ABSORBING MODULAR UNIT.
NUMBER ZERO IN A SERIES OF THIRTEEN.
WOW. BUT HOW DO YOU GET "ADAM" OUT OF ALL THAT ?
LONG STORY.
ANYWAY, WHEN IT'S ACTIVATED AND PROGRAMMED...
... THE ADAM-UNIT RETAINS THE MEMORY OF, AND THE ABILITY TO ABSORB...
... ANY AND ALL ENERGY SIGNATURES IN THE IMMEDIATE AREA.
ENERGY ABSORPTION? LIKE THE ULTIMATE BODY-GUARD ?
YOU THINK IT'S THE TOLLIVER WILL PRIZE, THEN ?
IS THIS THE GREATEST WEAPON IN THE WORLD ?!
KINDA DOUBT IT, WEAS, SINCE THESE THINGS WERE BUILT TO MAINTAIN--
--A VERY FRAGILE PEACE ON A VERY FRAGILE WORLD.
WHO BUILT THEM ?
PEOPLE WHO LIVE TWO THOUSAND YEARS IN THE FUTURE ?

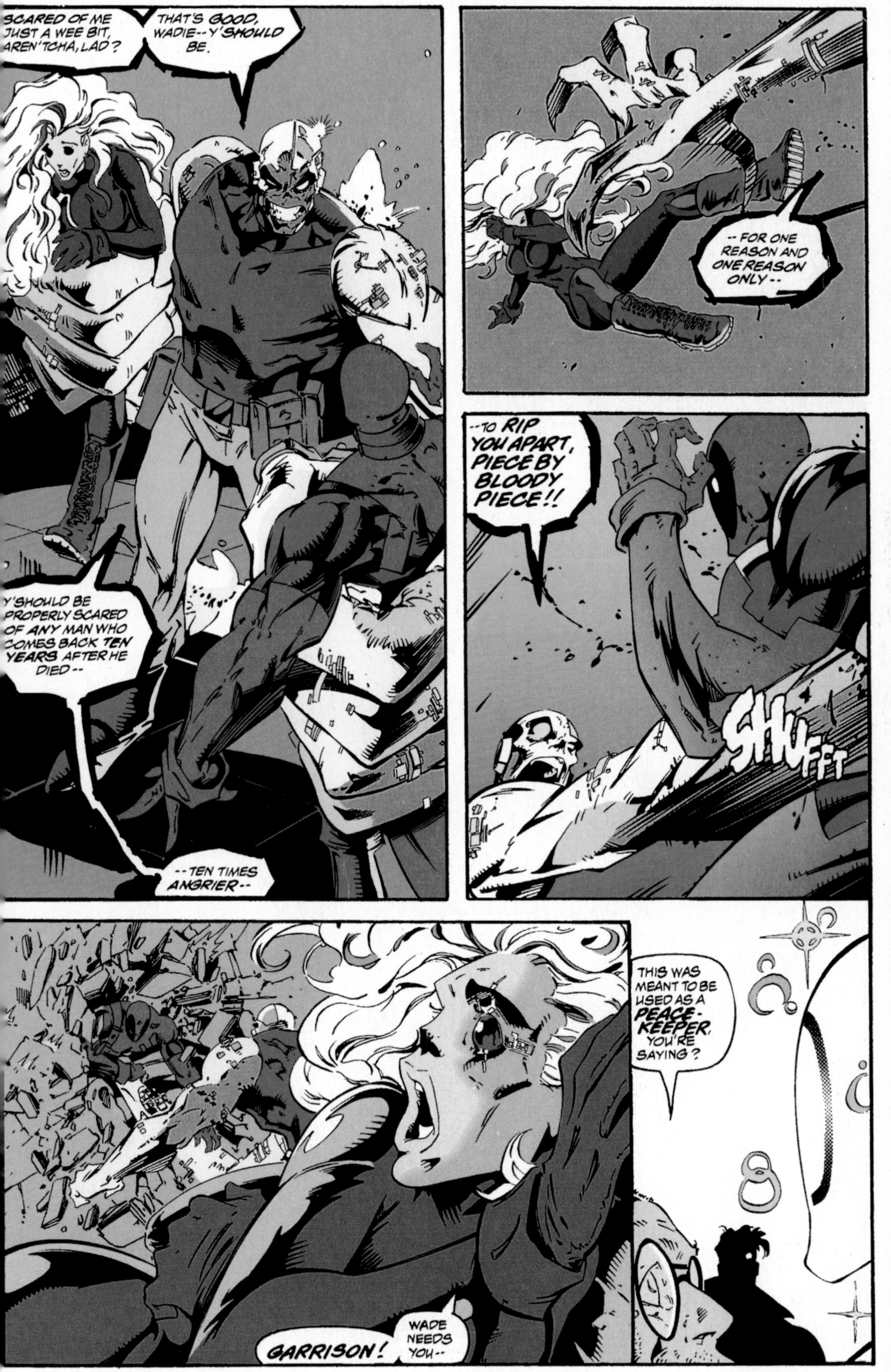
SCARED OF ME JUST A WEE BIT, AREN'TCHA, LAD?
THAT'S GOOD, WADIE--Y'SHOULD BE.
Y'SHOULD BE PROPERLY SCARED OF ANY MAN WHO COMES BACK TEN YEARS AFTER HE DIED--
--TEN TIMES ANGRIER--
--FOR ONE REASON AND ONE REASON ONLY--
--TO RIP YOU APART, PIECE BY BLOODY PIECE!!
SHUFFT
GARRISON!
WADE NEEDS YOU--
THIS WAS MEANT TO BE USED AS A PEACE-KEEPER, YOU'RE SAYING?

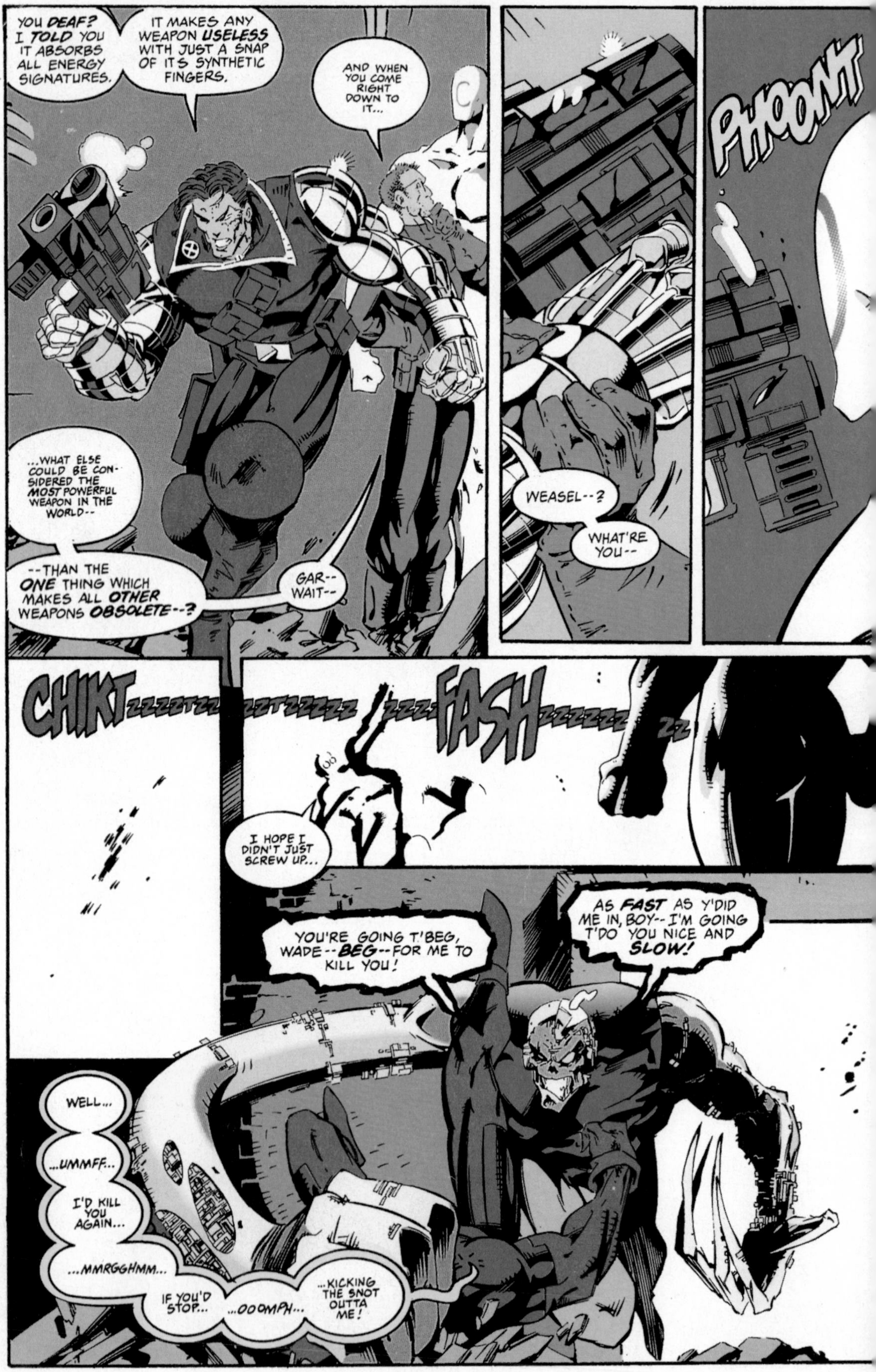
YOU DEAF? I TOLD YOU IT ABSORBS ALL ENERGY SIGNATURES.
IT MAKES ANY WEAPON USELESS WITH JUST A SNAP OF ITS SYNTHETIC FINGERS.
AND WHEN YOU COME RIGHT DOWN TO IT...
...WHAT ELSE COULD BE CONSIDERED THE MOST POWERFUL WEAPON IN THE WORLD--
--THAN THE ONE THING WHICH MAKES ALL OTHER WEAPONS OBSOLETE--?
GAR-- WAIT--
WEASEL--?
WHAT'RE YOU--
PHOONT
CHIKTzzzzzzzzzzzzzzz zzz-FASHzzzzzzzzz
I HOPE I DIDN'T JUST SCREW UP...
AS FAST AS Y'DID ME IN, BOY-- I'M GOING T'DO YOU NICE AND SLOW!
YOU'RE GOING T'BEG, WADE--BEG--FOR ME TO KILL YOU!
WELL...
...UMMFF...
I'D KILL YOU AGAIN...
...MMRGGHMM...
IF YOU'D STOP...
...OOOMPH...
...KICKING THE SNOT OUTTA ME!

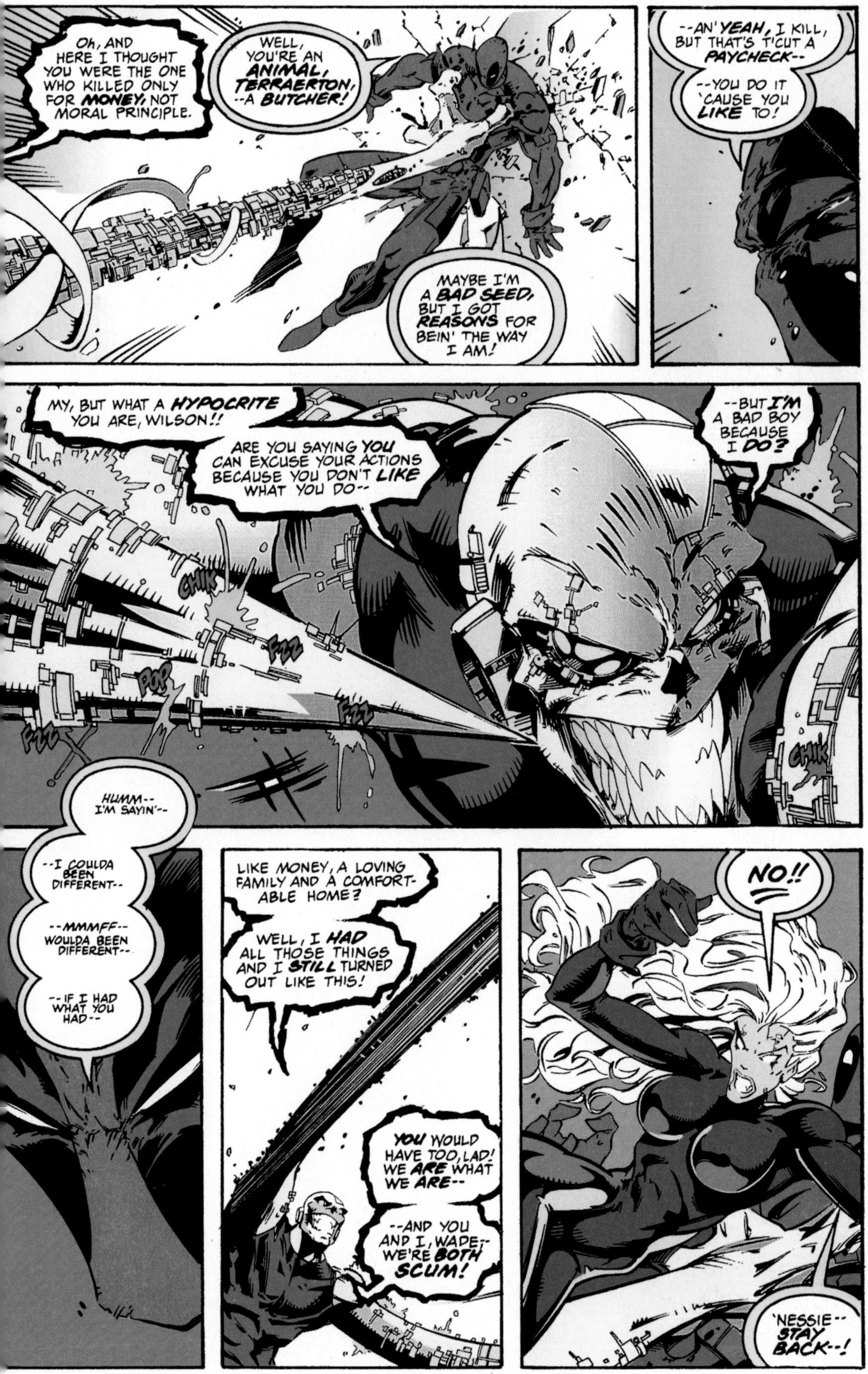

Oh, AND HERE I THOUGHT YOU WERE THE ONE WHO KILLED ONLY FOR MONEY, NOT MORAL PRINCIPLE.
WELL, YOU'RE AN ANIMAL, TERRAERTON, --A BUTCHER!
MAYBE I'M A BAD SEED, BUT I GOT REASONS FOR BEIN' THE WAY I AM!
--AN' YEAH, I KILL, BUT THAT'S T'CUT A PAYCHECK--
--YOU DO IT 'CAUSE YOU LIKE TO!
MY, BUT WHAT A HYPOCRITE YOU ARE, WILSON!!
ARE YOU SAYING YOU CAN EXCUSE YOUR ACTIONS BECAUSE YOU DON'T LIKE WHAT YOU DO--
--BUT I'M A BAD BOY BECAUSE I DO?
CHIK
POP
FZZ
CHIK
HUMM-- I'M SAYIN'--
--I COULDA BEEN DIFFERENT--
--MMMFF-- WOULDA BEEN DIFFERENT--
--IF I HAD WHAT YOU HAD--
LIKE MONEY, A LOVING FAMILY AND A COMFORTABLE HOME?
WELL, I HAD ALL THOSE THINGS AND I STILL TURNED OUT LIKE THIS!
YOU WOULD HAVE TOO, LAD! WE ARE WHAT WE ARE--
--AND YOU AND I, WADE-- WE'RE BOTH SCUM!
NO!!
'NESSIE-- STAY BACK--!

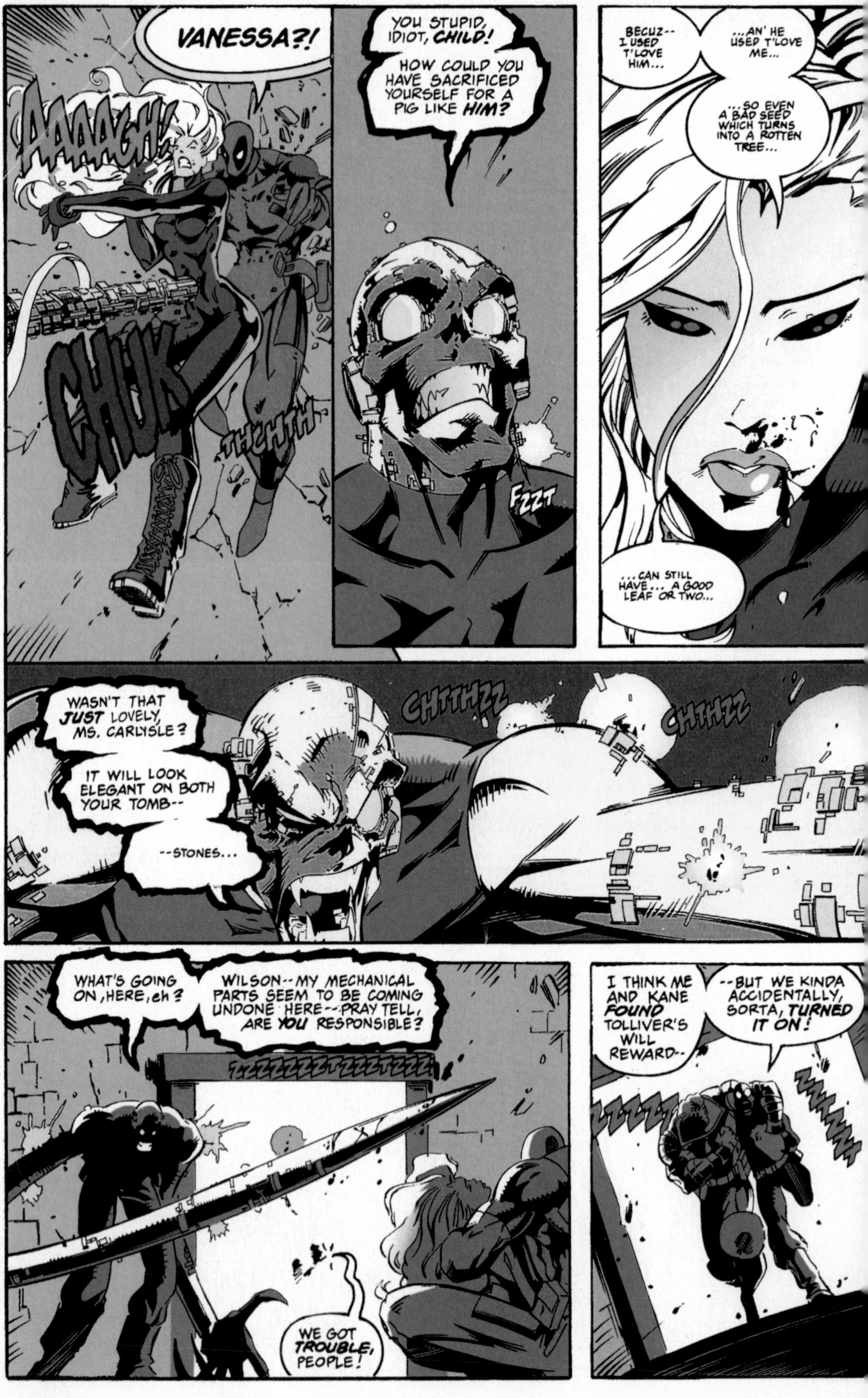
VANESSA?!
AAAAGH!
CHUK
THCHTH
YOU STUPID, IDIOT, CHILD!
HOW COULD YOU HAVE SACRIFICED YOURSELF FOR A PIG LIKE HIM?
FZZT
BECUZ-- I USED T'LOVE HIM...
...AN' HE USED T'LOVE ME...
...SO EVEN A BAD SEED WHICH TURNS INTO A ROTTEN TREE...
...CAN STILL HAVE... A GOOD LEAF OR TWO...
WASN'T THAT JUST LOVELY, MS. CARLYSLE?
IT WILL LOOK ELEGANT ON BOTH YOUR TOMB--
--STONES...
CHTTHZZ
CHTTHZZ
WHAT'S GOING ON, HERE, eh?
WILSON--MY MECHANICAL PARTS SEEM TO BE COMING UNDONE HERE--PRAY TELL, ARE YOU RESPONSIBLE?
WE GOT TROUBLE, PEOPLE!
I THINK ME AND KANE FOUND TOLLIVER'S WILL REWARD--
--BUT WE KINDA ACCIDENTALLY, SORTA, TURNED IT ON!

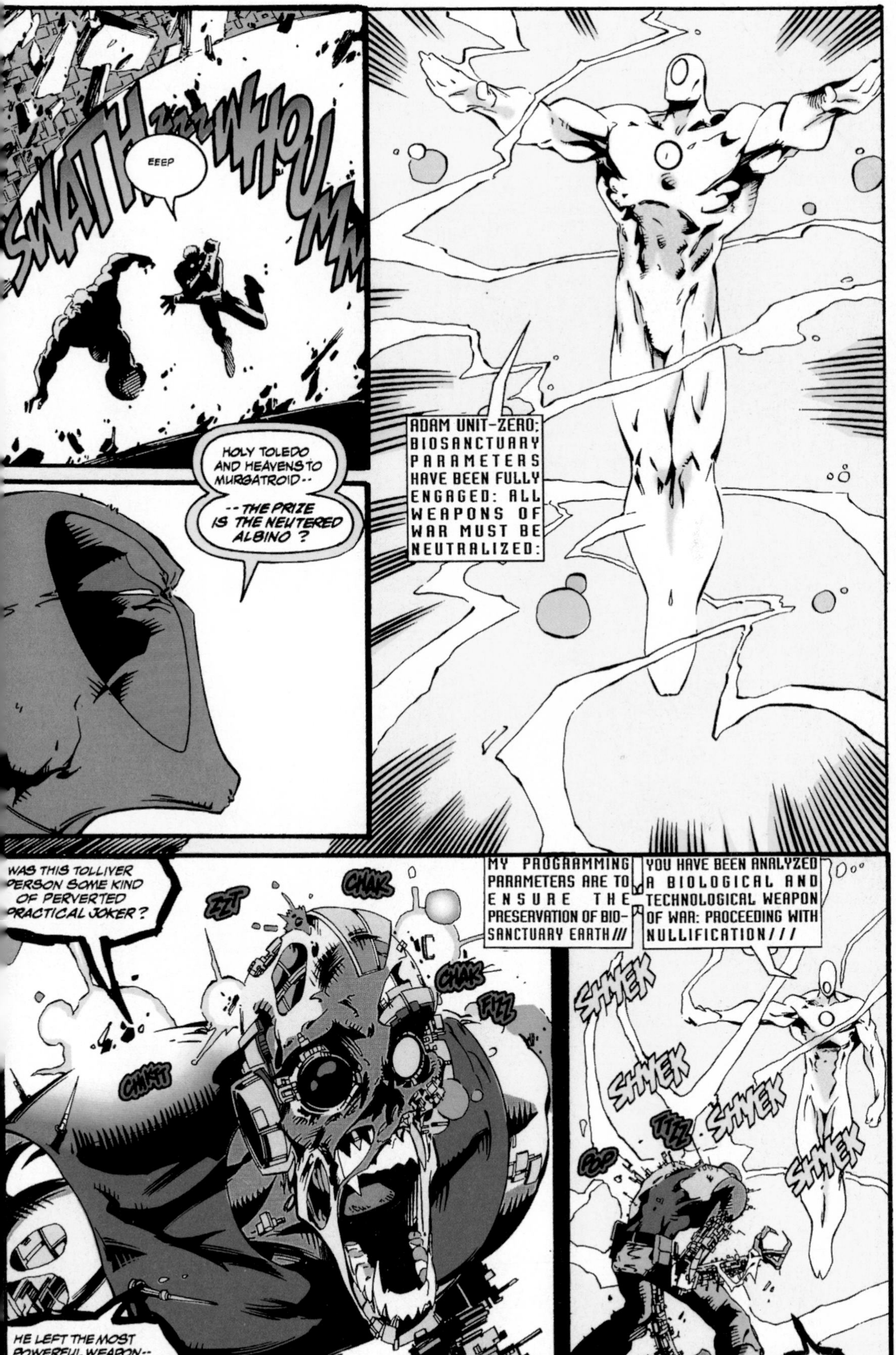
SWATH zzz WHOUMM
EEEP
HOLY TOLEDO AND HEAVENS TO MURGATROID--
--THE PRIZE IS THE NEUTERED ALBINO ?
ADAM UNIT-ZERO: BIOSANCTUARY PARAMETERS HAVE BEEN FULLY ENGAGED: ALL WEAPONS OF WAR MUST BE NEUTRALIZED:
WAS THIS TOLLIVER PERSON SOME KIND OF PERVERTED PRACTICAL JOKER ?
ZZT
CHAK
CHAK
FIZZ
CHKTT
HE LEFT THE MOST POWERFUL WEAPON-- AND IT'S MEANT TO PROMOTE PEACE ?
MY PROGRAMMING PARAMETERS ARE TO ENSURE THE PRESERVATION OF BIO-SANCTUARY EARTH///
YOU HAVE BEEN ANALYZED A BIOLOGICAL AND TECHNOLOGICAL WEAPON OF WAR: PROCEEDING WITH NULLIFICATION///
SHYEK
SHYEK
SHYEK
SHYEK
FZZZ
POP
WHAT THE BLOODY--

KZZZTHSHYEEK

MANOHMAN, THIS GUY'S PSE&G BILL MUST BE *MURDER!*

ANALYZED WEAPON OF WAR HAS BEEN NULLIFIED///

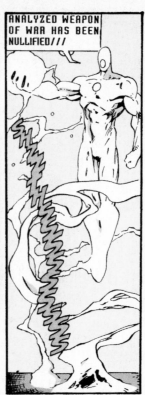

CONTINUING SENSORY SWEEPING SCAN///

POP!

SHYEK

HEY, NOW-- HEY, NOW--

ALTHOUGH SCANNING REGISTRANT CARRIES A WEAPON, HIS IS NOT DEEMED A THREAT TO BIOLOGICAL ORGANISMS///

SHYEK

SHYEK

YOU GOT THAT!

THE FIRST *AND* LAST TARGET I *EVER* HIT WAS STANDING RIGHT IN FRONT OF ME WITH A *COLANDER* ON HIS HEAD!

SHYEK

CONFLICTING SCAN READ OUT: REGISTRANT CONTAINS INCORPORATION OF WEAPONRY INTO BIOLOGICAL MASS: REGISTRANT SHOWS CAPABILITY FOR LETHAL FORCE, BUT BRAINWAVE SCAN INDICATES STRONG INCLINATION TOWARDS SOCIALLY BENEFICIAL BEHAVIOR: DEFER DECISION UNTIL FURTHER CLARIFICATION///

SHYEK

SHYEK

SHYEK

SHYEK

SHYEK

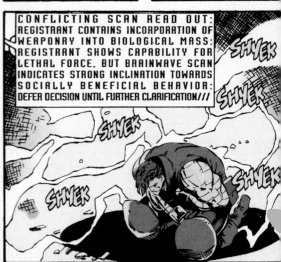

ANALYZED BIOLOGICAL AND TECHNOLOGICAL WEAPON OF WAR: PROCEED WITH NULLIFICATION///

NO...

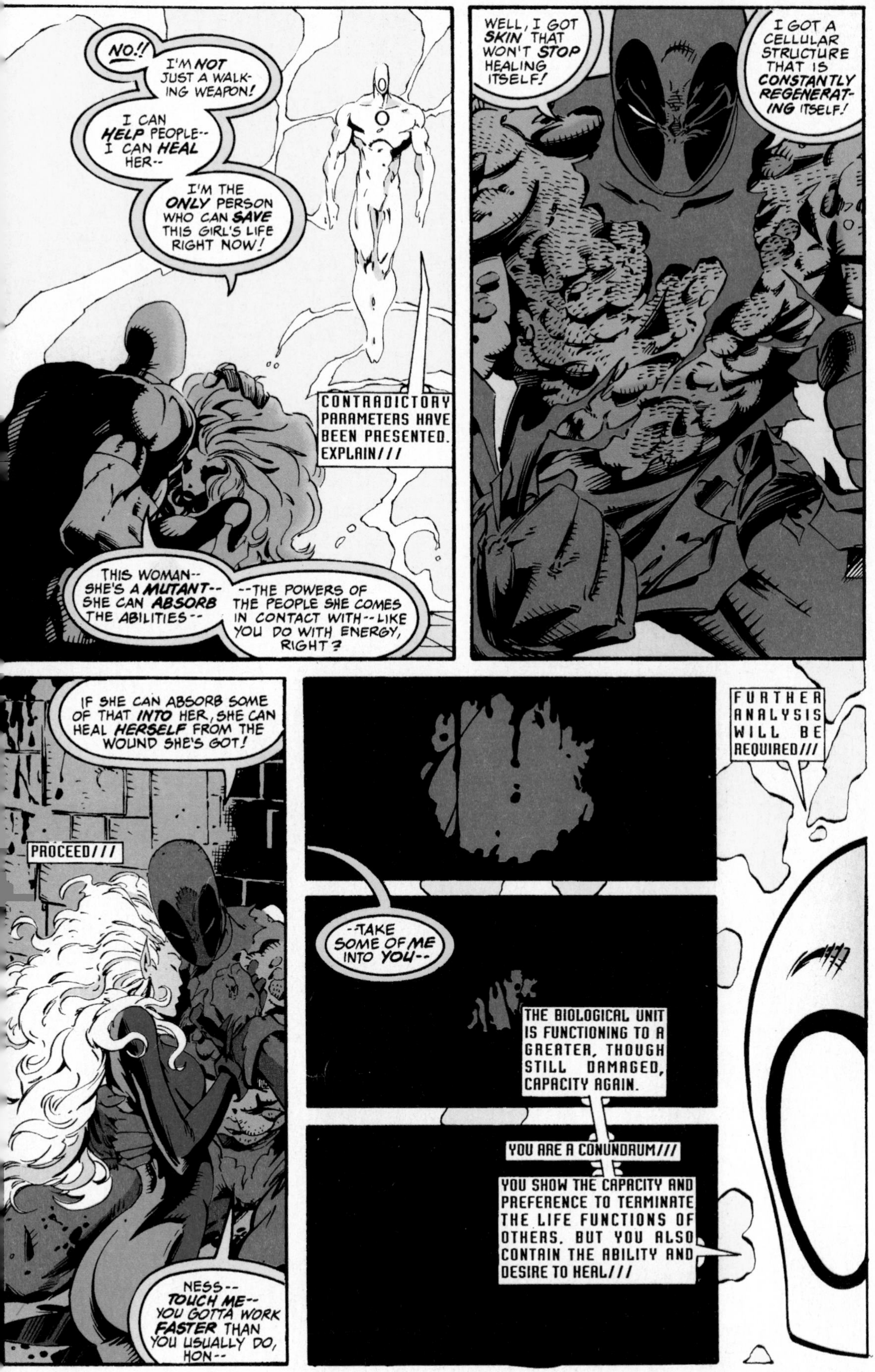
NO!! I'M NOT JUST A WALKING WEAPON!
I CAN HELP PEOPLE-- I CAN HEAL HER--
I'M THE ONLY PERSON WHO CAN SAVE THIS GIRL'S LIFE RIGHT NOW!
CONTRADICTORY PARAMETERS HAVE BEEN PRESENTED. EXPLAIN///
THIS WOMAN-- SHE'S A MUTANT-- SHE CAN ABSORB THE ABILITIES--
--THE POWERS OF THE PEOPLE SHE COMES IN CONTACT WITH--LIKE YOU DO WITH ENERGY, RIGHT?
WELL, I GOT SKIN THAT WON'T STOP HEALING ITSELF!
I GOT A CELLULAR STRUCTURE THAT IS CONSTANTLY REGENERATING ITSELF!
IF SHE CAN ABSORB SOME OF THAT INTO HER, SHE CAN HEAL HERSELF FROM THE WOUND SHE'S GOT!
PROCEED///
NESS-- TOUCH ME-- YOU GOTTA WORK FASTER THAN YOU USUALLY DO, HON--
--TAKE SOME OF ME INTO YOU--
THE BIOLOGICAL UNIT IS FUNCTIONING TO A GREATER, THOUGH STILL DAMAGED, CAPACITY AGAIN.
YOU ARE A CONUNDRUM///
YOU SHOW THE CAPACITY AND PREFERENCE TO TERMINATE THE LIFE FUNCTIONS OF OTHERS. BUT YOU ALSO CONTAIN THE ABILITY AND DESIRE TO HEAL///
FURTHER ANALYSIS WILL BE REQUIRED///

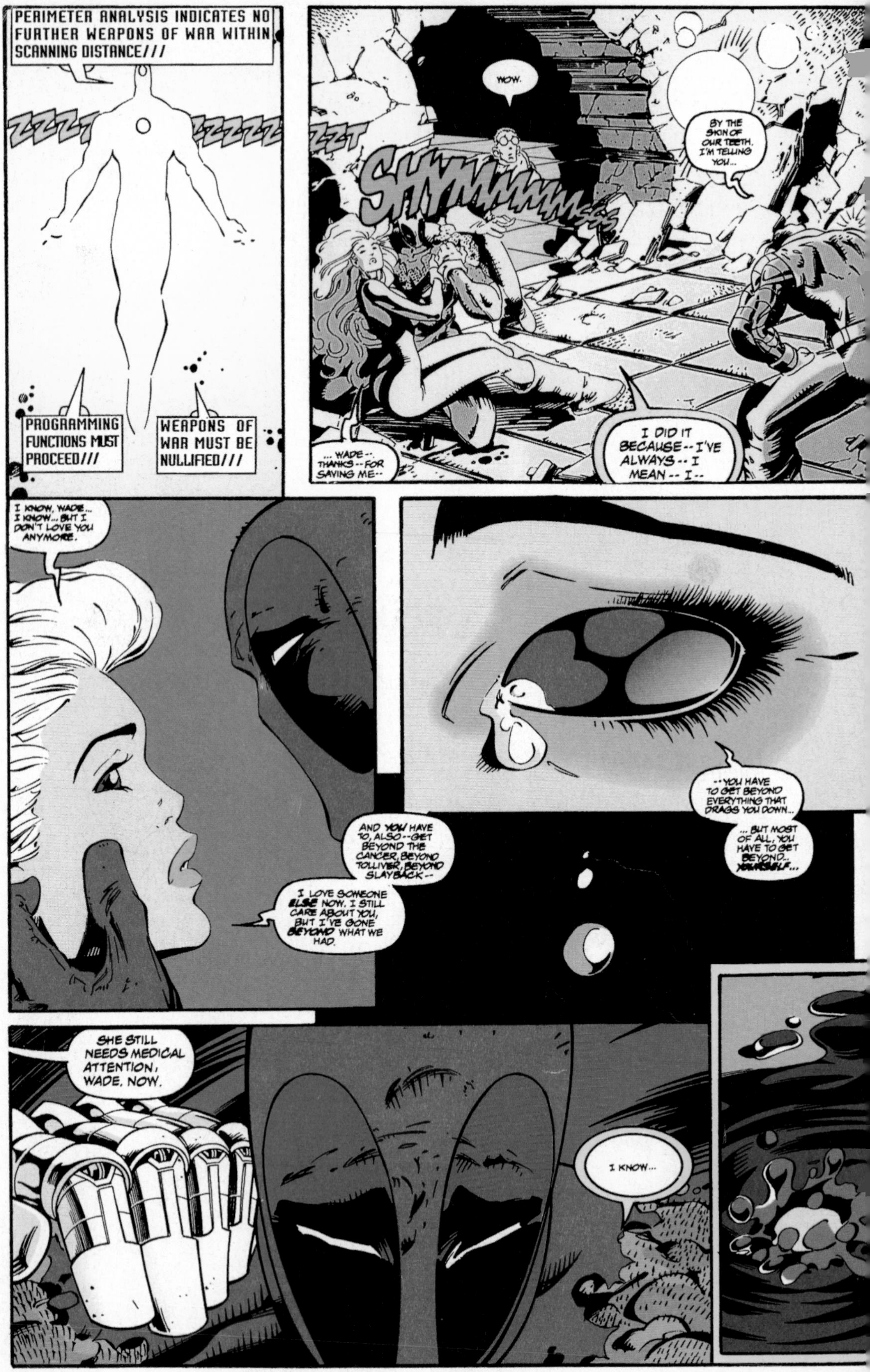

PERIMETER ANALYSIS INDICATES NO FURTHER WEAPONS OF WAR WITHIN SCANNING DISTANCE///
ZZZT
ZZZZZZ
ZZZT
PROGRAMMING FUNCTIONS MUST PROCEED///
WEAPONS OF WAR MUST BE NULLIFIED///
WOW.
BY THE SKIN OF OUR TEETH, I'M TELLING YOU...
SHYMMMMMMSSS
... WADE -- THANKS -- FOR SAVING ME --
I DID IT BECAUSE -- I'VE ALWAYS -- I MEAN -- I --
I KNOW, WADE... I KNOW... BUT I DON'T LOVE YOU ANYMORE.
I LOVE SOMEONE ELSE NOW. I STILL CARE ABOUT YOU, BUT I'VE GONE BEYOND WHAT WE HAD.
AND YOU HAVE TO, ALSO -- GET BEYOND THE CANCER, BEYOND TOLLIVER, BEYOND SLAYBACK --
-- YOU HAVE TO GET BEYOND EVERYTHING THAT DRAGS YOU DOWN...
... BUT MOST OF ALL, YOU HAVE TO GET BEYOND... YOURSELF...
SHE STILL NEEDS MEDICAL ATTENTION, WADE. NOW.
I KNOW...

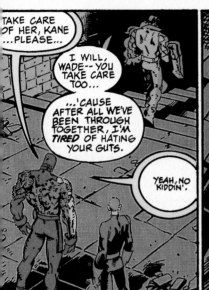

TAKE CARE OF HER, KANE ...PLEASE...

I WILL, WADE-- YOU TAKE CARE TOO...

...'CAUSE AFTER ALL WE'VE BEEN THROUGH TOGETHER, I'M *TIRED* OF HATING YOUR GUTS.

YEAH, NO KIDDIN'.

SHE DON' LOVE ME NO MORE, WEAS.

Ah, *WOMEN*, RIGHT?

NO, IT AIN'T *HER*-- --SHE'S RIGHT --IT'S *ME*...

...I AIN'T EVEN *TRIED* TA BE ANYTHIN' MORE THAN I AM... I AIN'T EVEN *THOUGHT* ABOUT IT!

WHAT DOES THAT SAY ABOUT ME?

BUT WADE, TONIGHT YOU *DID* GO BEYOND THAT-- YOU SHOWED YOU *CAN* DO MORE THAN JUST KILL.

I *DID*, DIDN'T I?

YOU SHOWED YOU'RE *MORE* THAN JUST A FIGHTING MACHINE, A USELESS PIECE OF MURDERING FLESH, A GREEDY BLIGHT ON THE FACE OF--

I *GET* THE IDEA, WEAS!

JUST MAKING SURE...

YOU'RE *RIGHT*, WEAS... I *DID* SHOW SOME GUMPTION TONIGHT.

NICE. SOLID GOLD FOR SURE.

GOTTA BE WORTH A FEW BUCKS.

I *CAN* DO MORE THAN KILL, MAIM, BLEED AND DESTROY.

I FEEL *BETTER* ALREADY!

WHO KNOWS, WEAS, MAYBE THERE'S SOME *HOPE* FOR ME YET?

THE END!

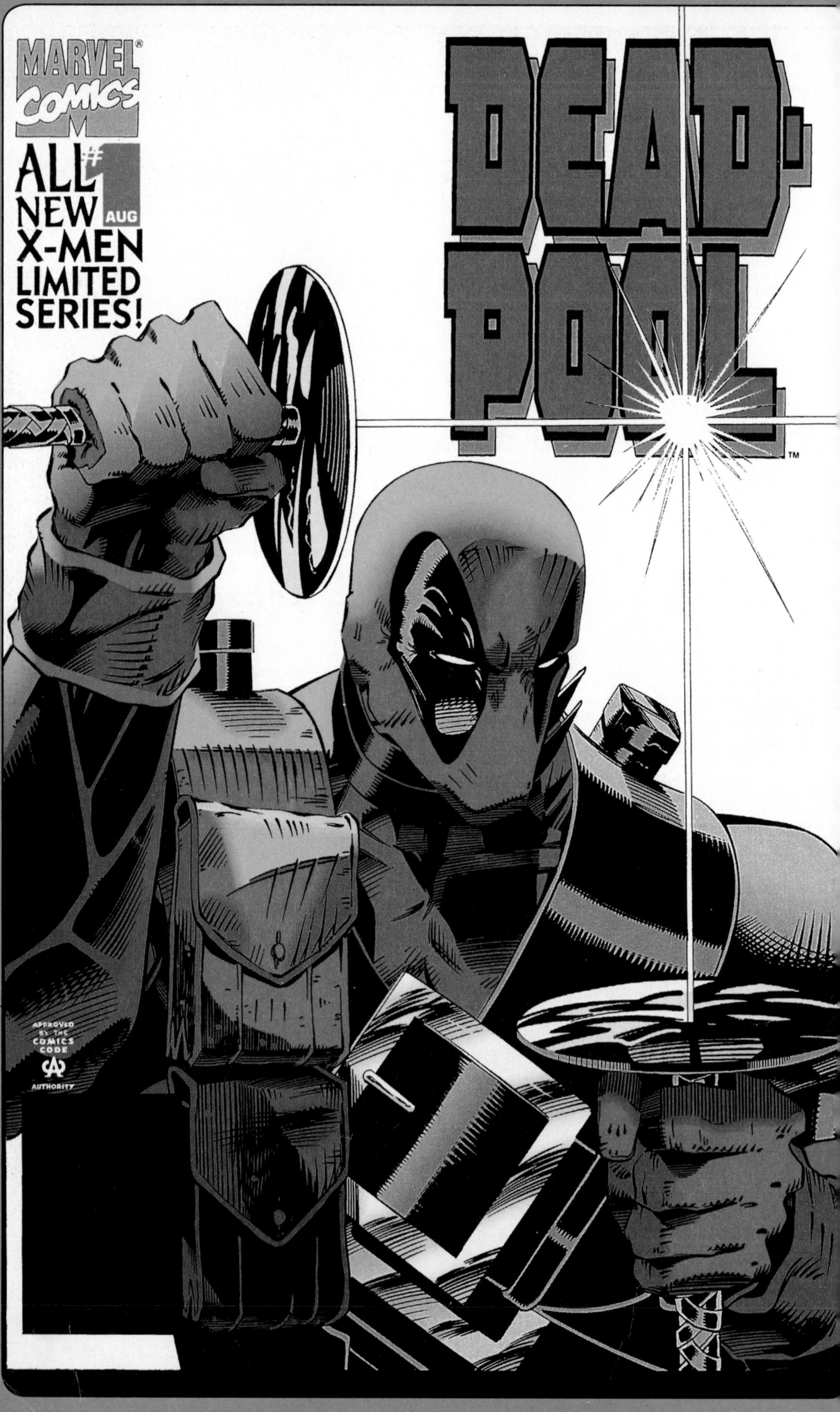
MARVEL COMICS
ALL NEW X-MEN LIMITED SERIES!
#1
AUG
DEAD-POOL
TM
APPROVED BY THE COMICS CODE AUTHORITY

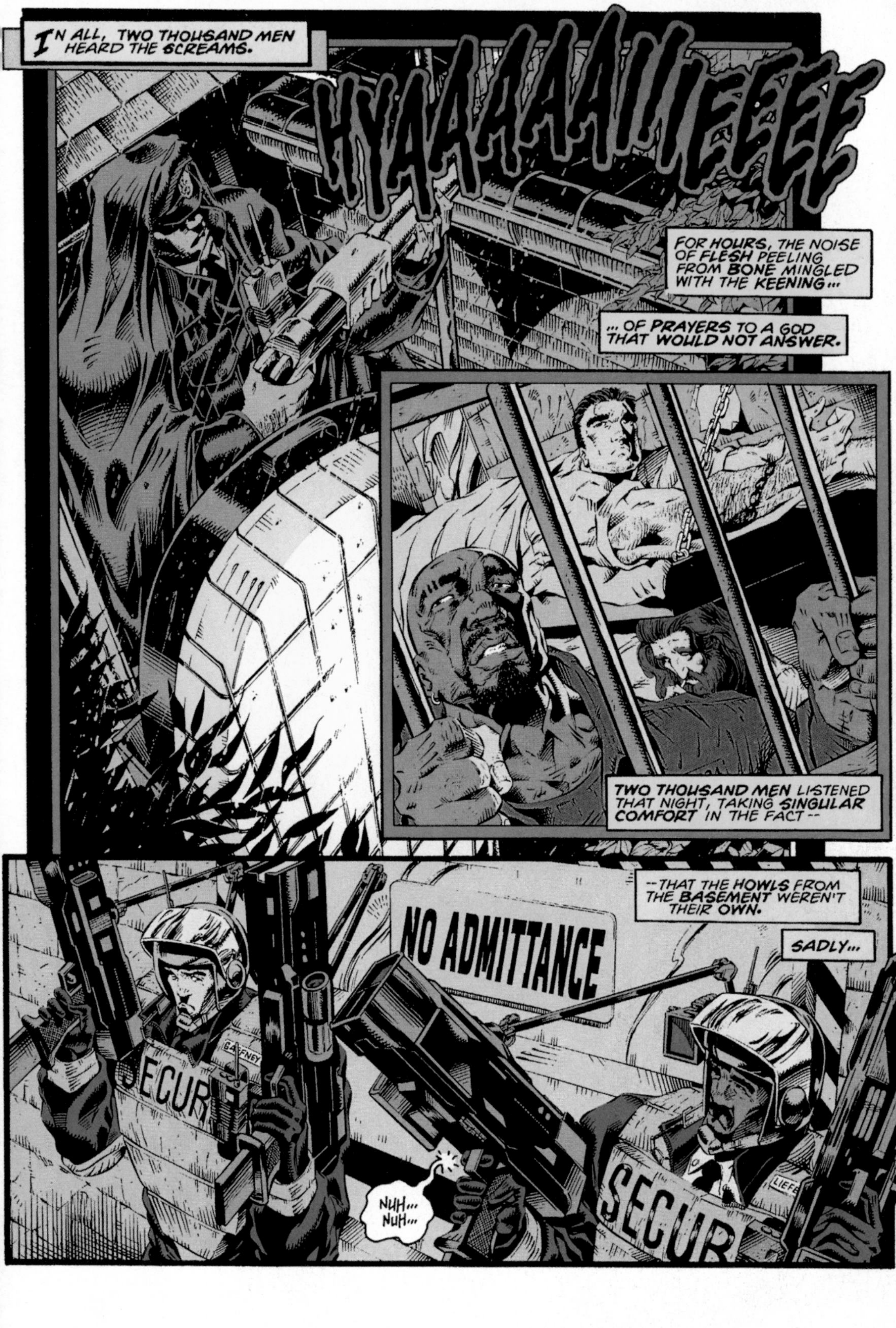
IN ALL, TWO THOUSAND MEN HEARD THE SCREAMS.
HYAAAAAIIIEEEE
FOR HOURS, THE NOISE OF FLESH PEELING FROM BONE MINGLED WITH THE KEENING...
...OF PRAYERS TO A GOD THAT WOULD NOT ANSWER.
TWO THOUSAND MEN LISTENED THAT NIGHT, TAKING SINGULAR COMFORT IN THE FACT--
--THAT THE HOWLS FROM THE BASEMENT WEREN'T THEIR OWN.
SADLY...
NO ADMITTANCE
GAFFNEY
SECUR
NUH... NUH...
SECUR
LIEFE

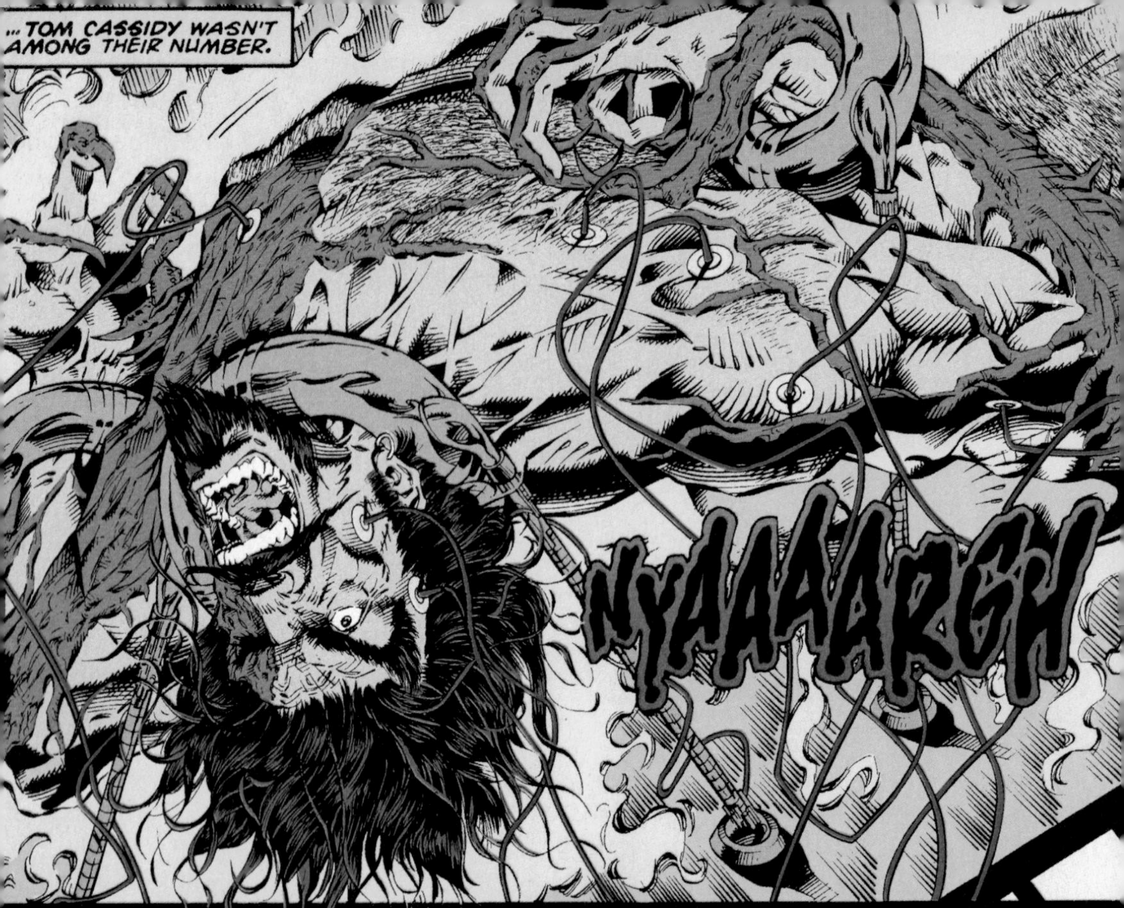
...TOM CASSIDY WASN'T AMONG THEIR NUMBER.
NYAAAARGH

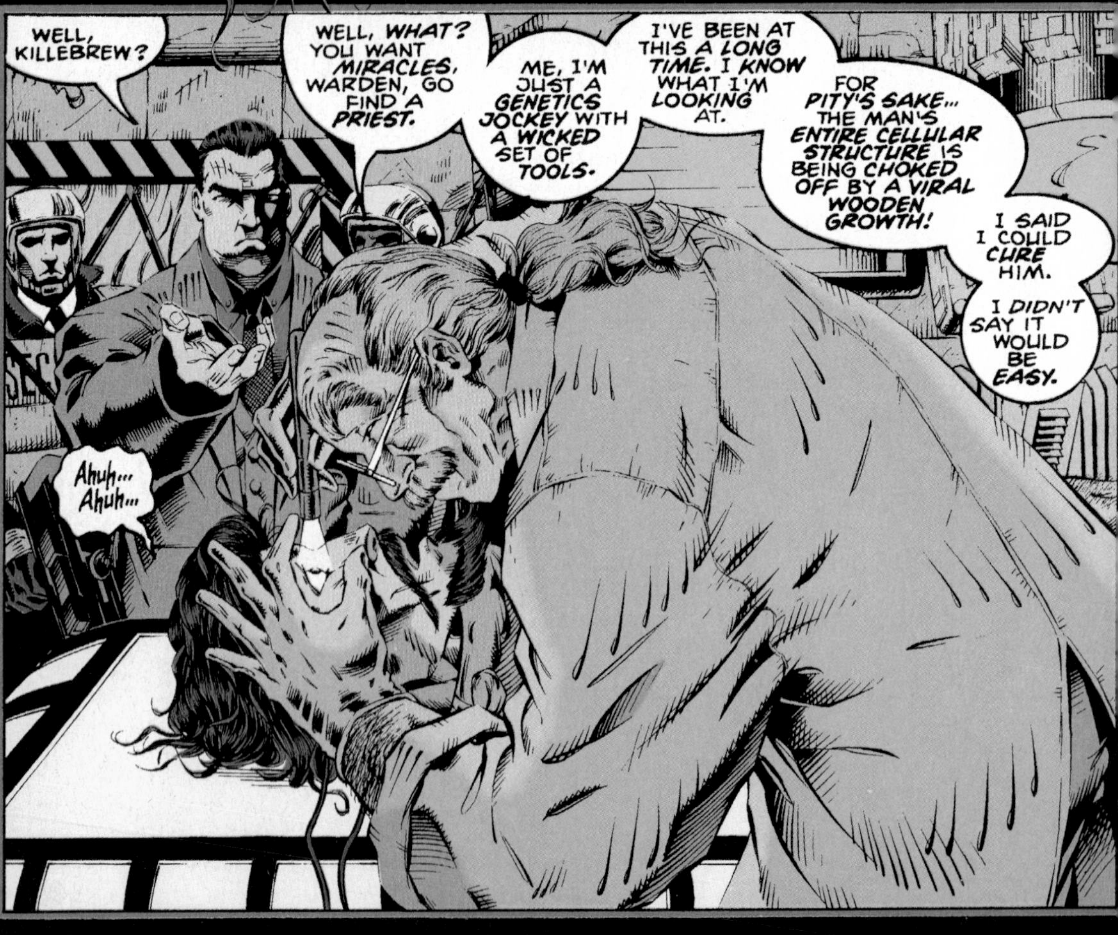
WELL, KILLEBREW?
WELL, WHAT? YOU WANT MIRACLES, WARDEN, GO FIND A PRIEST.
ME, I'M JUST A GENETICS JOCKEY WITH A WICKED SET OF TOOLS.
I'VE BEEN AT THIS A LONG TIME. I KNOW WHAT I'M LOOKING AT.
FOR PITY'S SAKE... THE MAN'S ENTIRE CELLULAR STRUCTURE IS BEING CHOKED OFF BY A VIRAL WOODEN GROWTH!
I SAID I COULD CURE HIM.
I DIDN'T SAY IT WOULD BE EASY.
Ahuh... Ahuh...

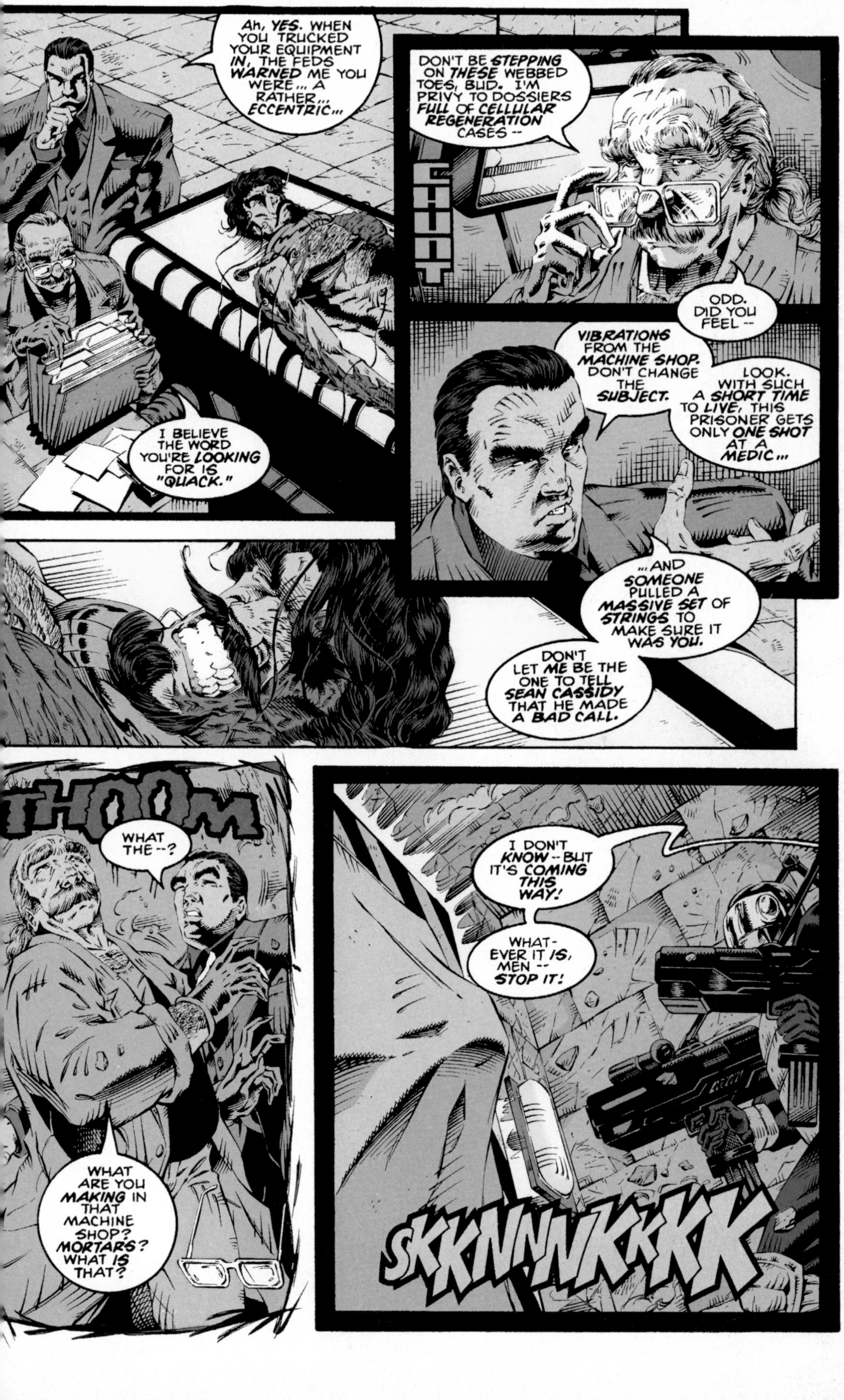
Ah, YES. WHEN YOU TRUCKED YOUR EQUIPMENT IN, THE FEDS WARNED ME YOU WERE... A RATHER... ECCENTRIC...
I BELIEVE THE WORD YOU'RE LOOKING FOR IS "QUACK."
DON'T BE STEPPING ON THESE WEBBED TOES, BUD. I'M PRIVY TO DOSSIERS FULL OF CELLULAR REGENERATION CASES --
ODD. DID YOU FEEL --
VIBRATIONS FROM THE MACHINE SHOP. DON'T CHANGE THE SUBJECT.
LOOK. WITH SUCH A SHORT TIME TO LIVE, THIS PRISONER GETS ONLY ONE SHOT AT A MEDIC...
...AND SOMEONE PULLED A MASSIVE SET OF STRINGS TO MAKE SURE IT WAS YOU.
DON'T LET ME BE THE ONE TO TELL SEAN CASSIDY THAT HE MADE A BAD CALL.
THOOM
WHAT THE --?
WHAT ARE YOU MAKING IN THAT MACHINE SHOP? MORTARS? WHAT IS THAT?
I DON'T KNOW -- BUT IT'S COMING THIS WAY!
WHAT-EVER IT IS, MEN -- STOP IT!
SKKNNNKKKK

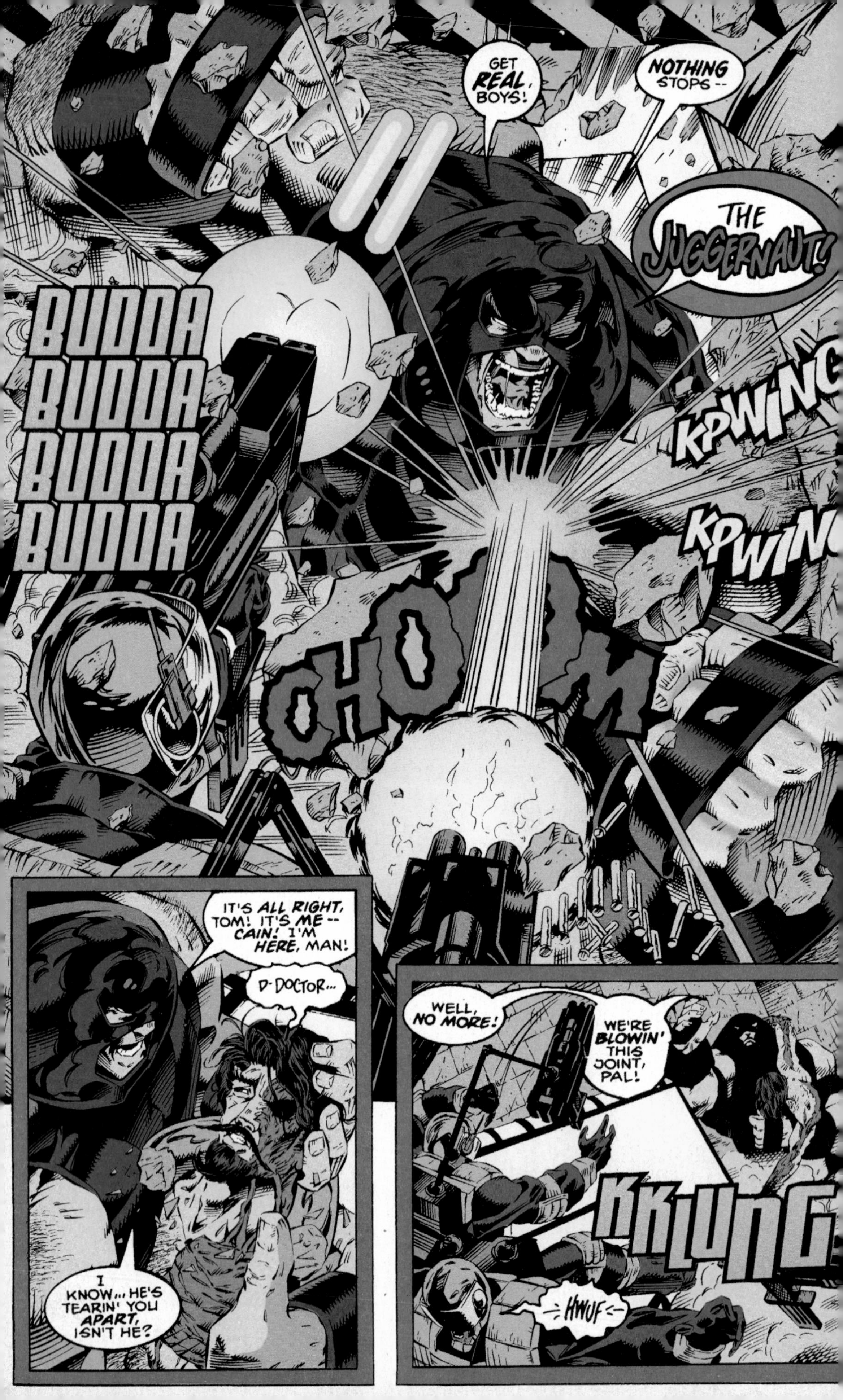
GET REAL, BOYS!
NOTHING STOPS --
THE JUGGERNAUT!
BUDDA BUDDA BUDDA BUDDA
KPWING
KPWING
CHOOM
IT'S ALL RIGHT, TOM! IT'S ME -- CAIN! I'M HERE, MAN!
D-DOCTOR...
I KNOW... HE'S TEARIN' YOU APART, ISN'T HE?
WELL, NO MORE!
WE'RE BLOWIN' THIS JOINT, PAL!
KKLUNG
HWUF

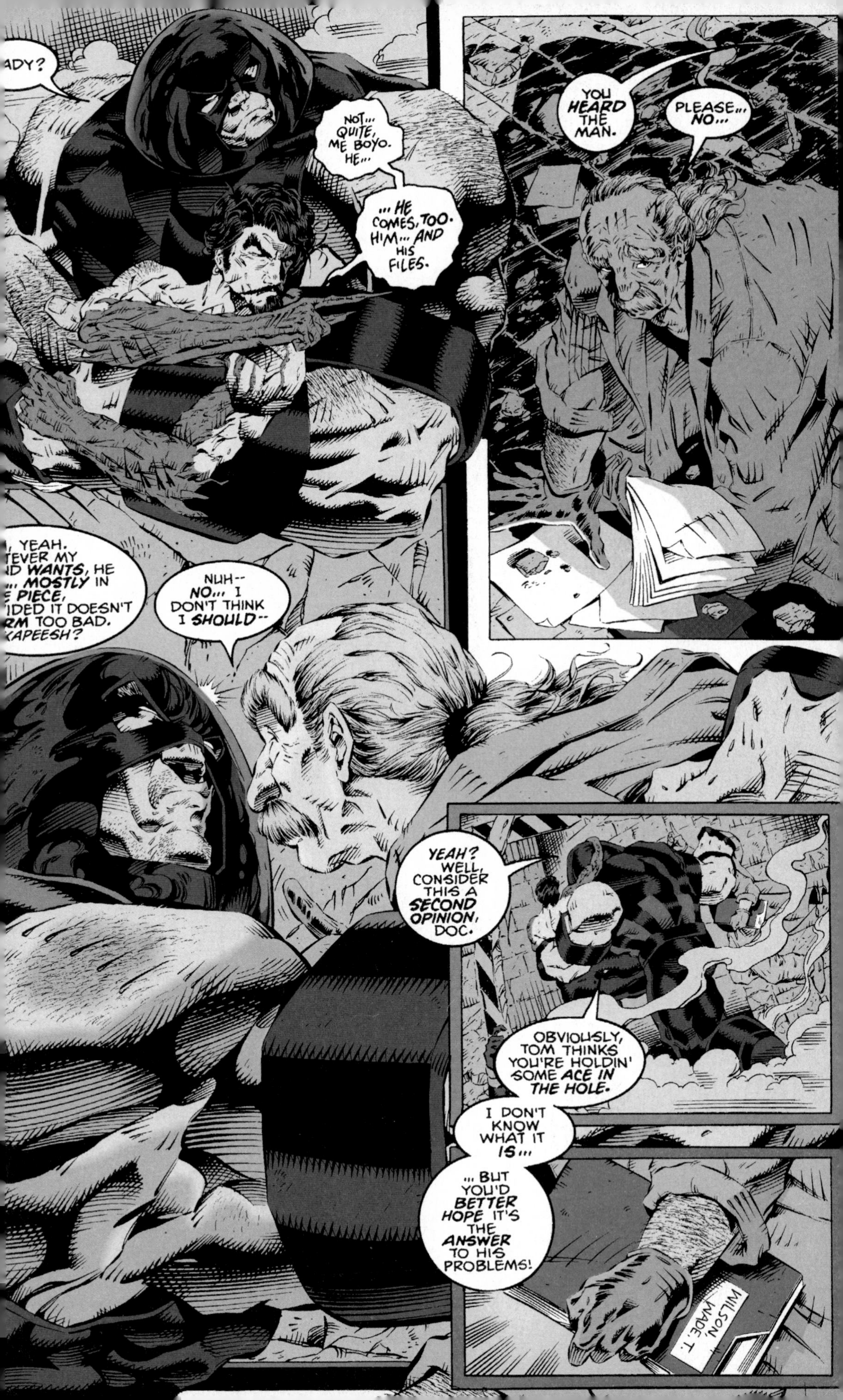

ADY?
NOT... QUITE, ME BOYO. HE...
...HE COMES, TOO. HIM... AND HIS FILES.
YOU HEARD THE MAN.
PLEASE... NO...
, YEAH. TEVER MY ND WANTS, HE ... MOSTLY IN E PIECE, IDED IT DOESN'T RM TOO BAD. KAPEESH?
NUH-- NO... I DON'T THINK I SHOULD--
YEAH? WELL, CONSIDER THIS A SECOND OPINION, DOC.
OBVIOUSLY, TOM THINKS YOU'RE HOLDIN' SOME ACE IN THE HOLE.
I DON'T KNOW WHAT IT IS...
...BUT YOU'D BETTER HOPE IT'S THE ANSWER TO HIS PROBLEMS!
WILSON, WADE T.

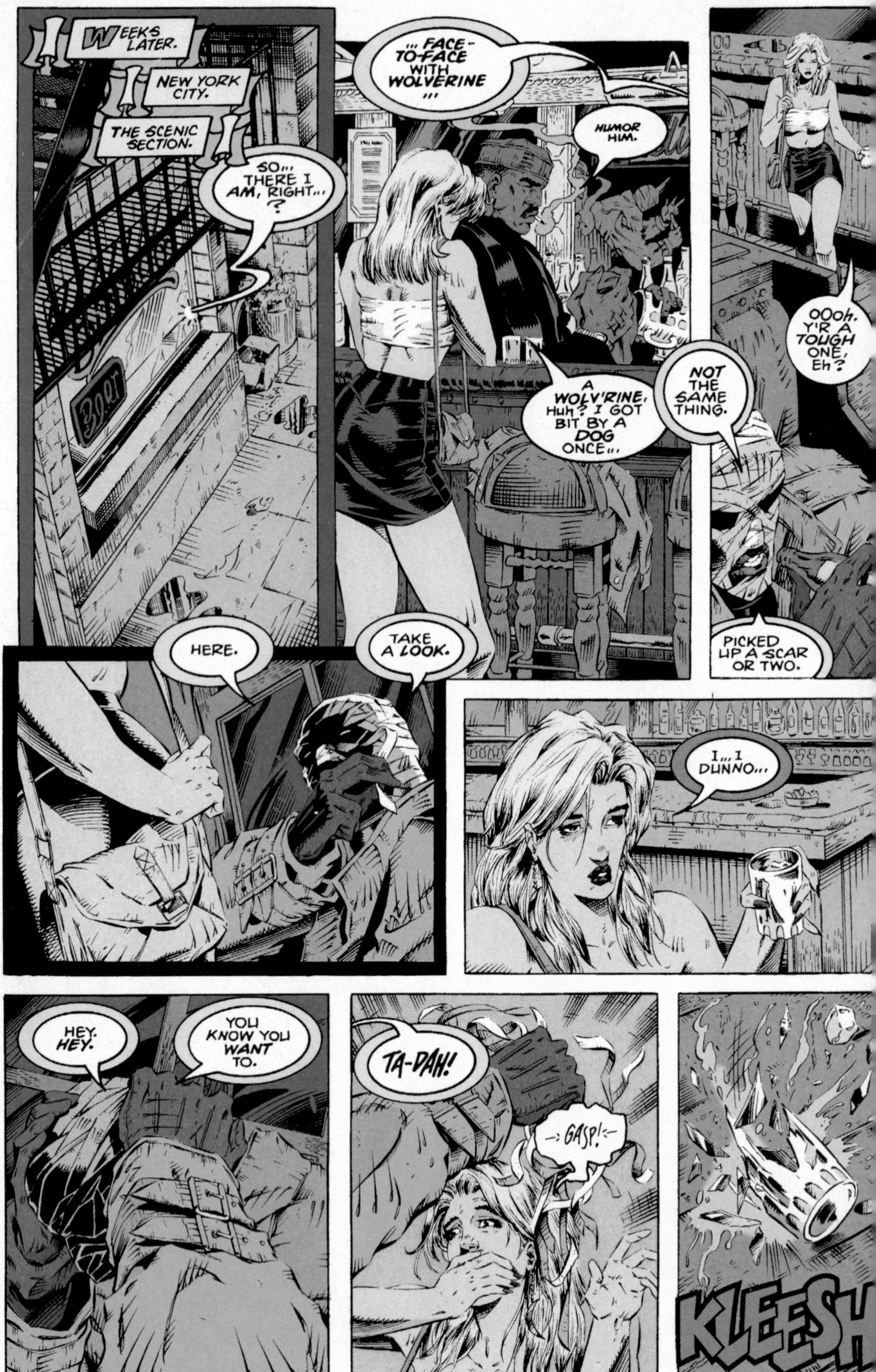

WEEKS LATER.
NEW YORK CITY.
THE SCENIC SECTION.
SO... THERE I AM, RIGHT... ?
... FACE-TO-FACE WITH WOLVERINE ...
HUMOR HIM.
A WOLV'RINE, Huh? I GOT BIT BY A DOG ONCE...
NOT THE SAME THING.
OOOh. Y'R A TOUGH ONE, Eh?
PICKED UP A SCAR OR TWO.
HERE.
TAKE A LOOK.
I... I DUNNO...
HEY. HEY.
YOU KNOW YOU WANT TO.
TA-DAH!
GASP!
KLEESH

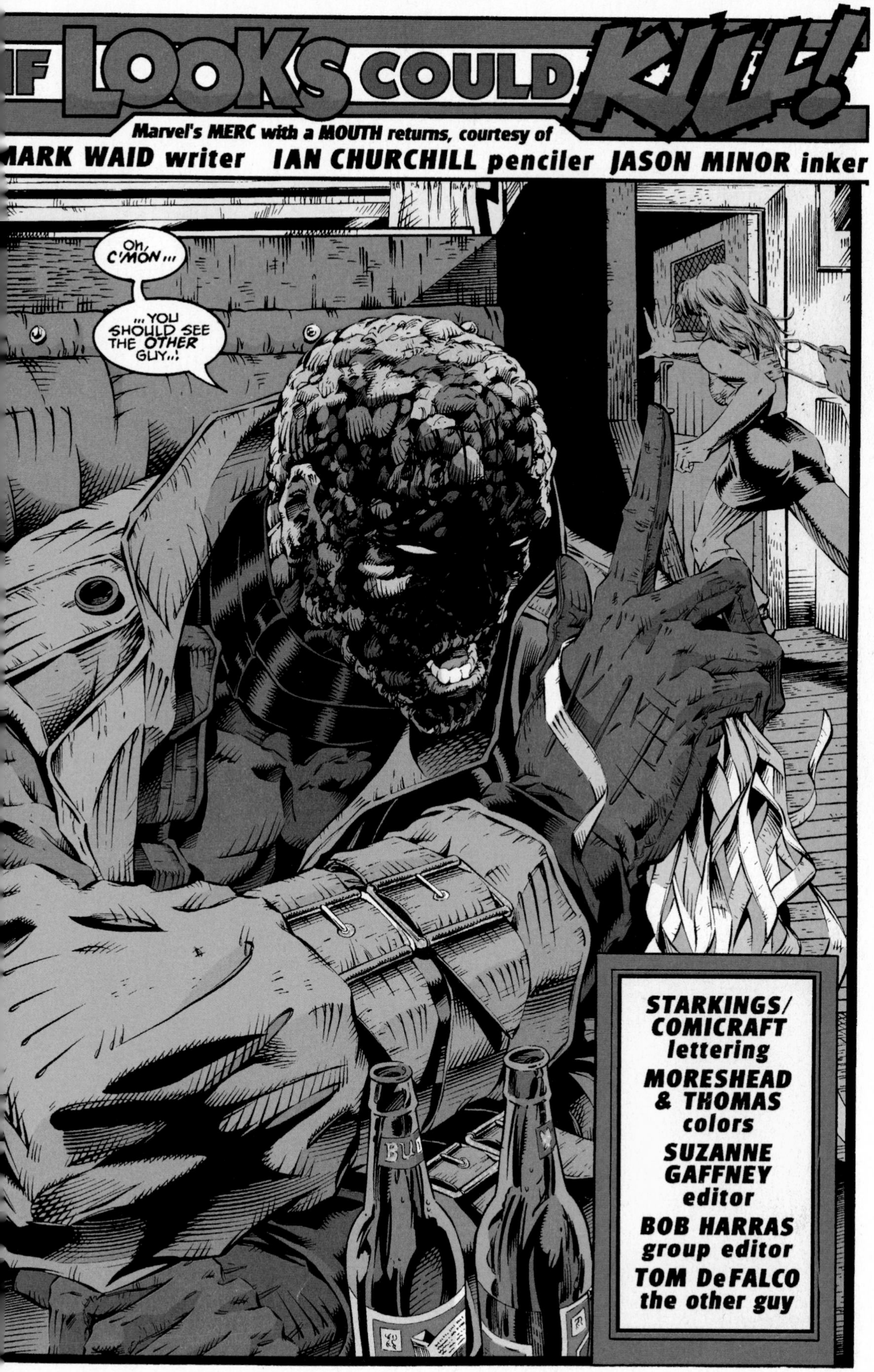

IF LOOKS COULD KILL!
Marvel's MERC with a MOUTH returns, courtesy of
MARK WAID writer IAN CHURCHILL penciler JASON MINOR inker
OH, C'MON...
...YOU SHOULD SEE THE OTHER GUY...!
STARKINGS/ COMICRAFT lettering
MORESHEAD & THOMAS colors
SUZANNE GAFFNEY editor
BOB HARRAS group editor
TOM DeFALCO the other guy

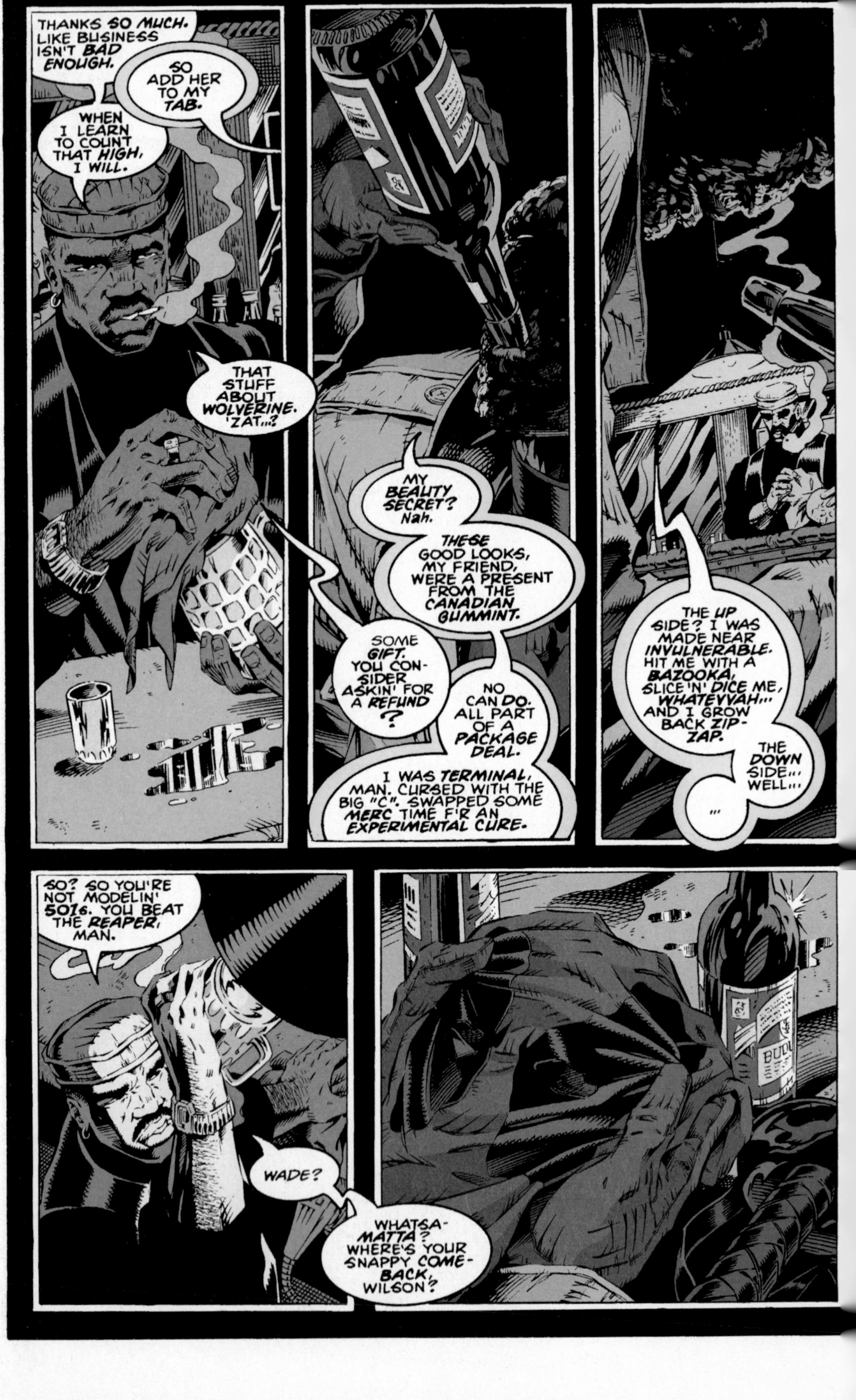
THANKS SO MUCH. LIKE BUSINESS ISN'T BAD ENOUGH.
SO ADD HER TO MY TAB.
WHEN I LEARN TO COUNT THAT HIGH, I WILL.
THAT STUFF ABOUT WOLVERINE. 'ZAT...?
MY BEAUTY SECRET? Nah.
THESE GOOD LOOKS, MY FRIEND, WERE A PRESENT FROM THE CANADIAN GUMMINT.
SOME GIFT. YOU CONSIDER ASKIN' FOR A REFUND?
NO CAN DO. ALL PART OF A PACKAGE DEAL.
I WAS TERMINAL, MAN. CURSED WITH THE BIG "C". SWAPPED SOME MERC TIME F'R AN EXPERIMENTAL CURE.
THE UP SIDE? I WAS MADE NEAR INVULNERABLE. HIT ME WITH A BAZOOKA, SLICE 'N' DICE ME, WHATEVVAH... AND I GROW BACK ZIP-ZAP.
THE DOWN SIDE... WELL...
...
SO? SO YOU'RE NOT MODELIN' 501s. YOU BEAT THE REAPER, MAN.
WADE?
WHATSA-MATTA? WHERE'S YOUR SNAPPY COME-BACK, WILSON?

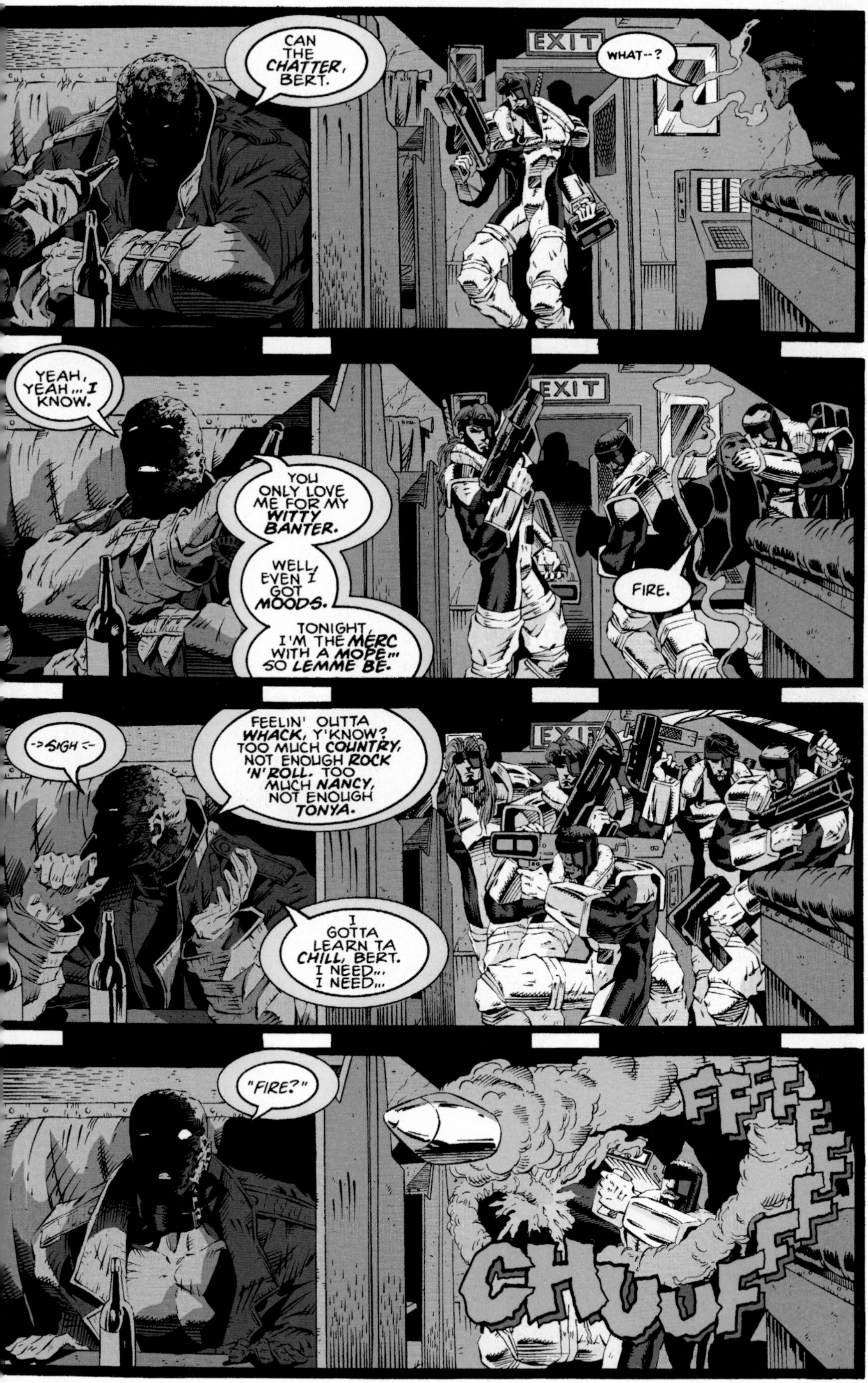
CAN THE CHATTER, BERT.
WHAT--?
YEAH, YEAH... I KNOW.
YOU ONLY LOVE ME FOR MY WITTY BANTER.
WELL, EVEN I GOT MOODS.
TONIGHT, I'M THE MERC WITH A MOPE... SO LEMME BE.
FIRE.
-> SIGH <-
FEELIN' OUTTA WHACK, Y'KNOW? TOO MUCH COUNTRY, NOT ENOUGH ROCK 'N' ROLL. TOO MUCH NANCY, NOT ENOUGH TONYA.
I GOTTA LEARN TA CHILL, BERT. I NEED... I NEED...
"FIRE?"
FFFFFFFF
CHUUFF

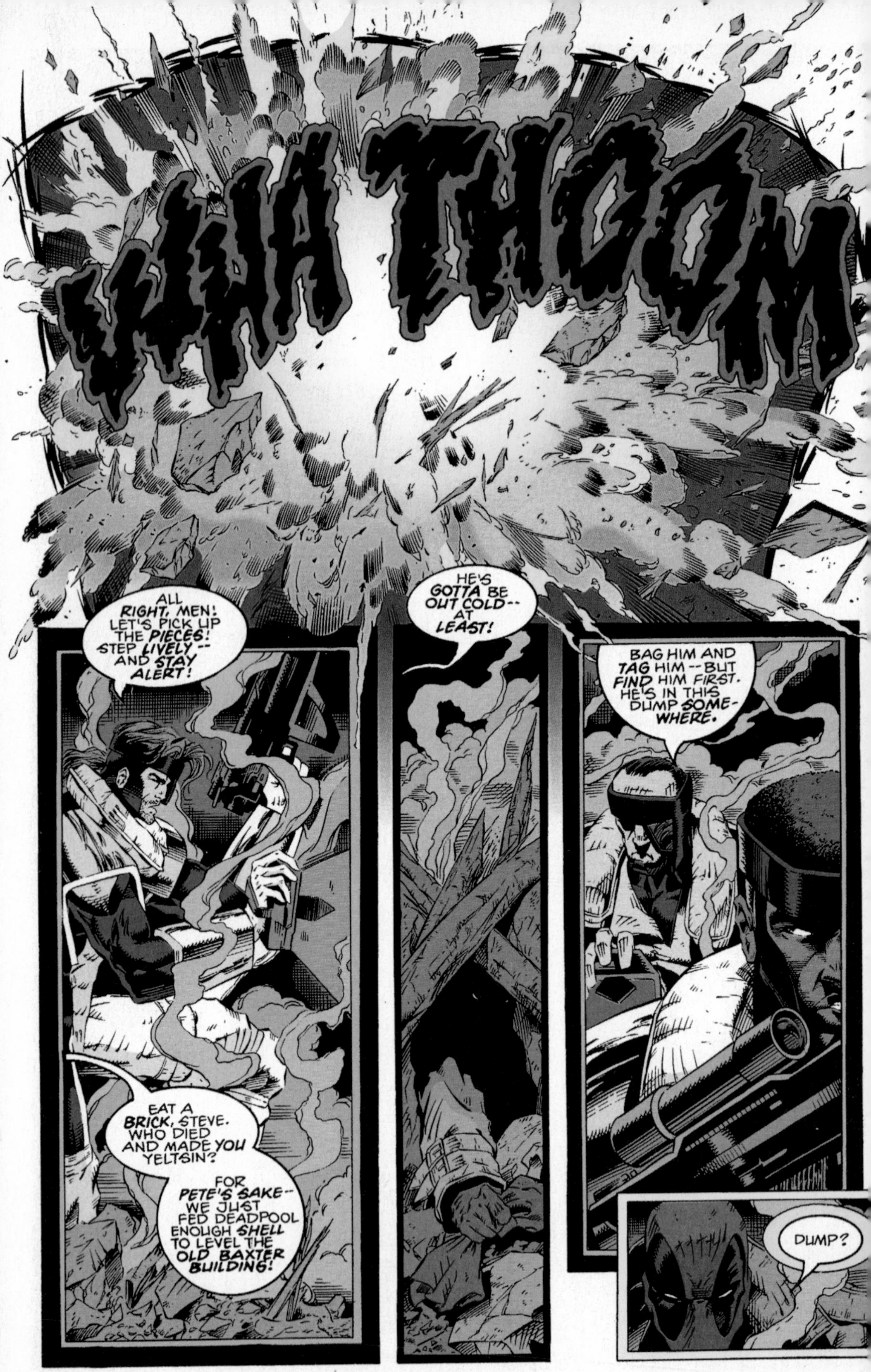

WHA THOOM
ALL RIGHT, MEN! LET'S PICK UP THE PIECES! STEP LIVELY -- AND STAY ALERT!
EAT A BRICK, STEVE. WHO DIED AND MADE YOU YELTSIN?
FOR PETE'S SAKE-- WE JUST FED DEADPOOL ENOUGH SHELL TO LEVEL THE OLD BAXTER BUILDING!
HE'S GOTTA BE OUT COLD-- AT LEAST!
BAG HIM AND TAG HIM -- BUT FIND HIM FIRST. HE'S IN THIS DUMP SOMEWHERE.
DUMP?

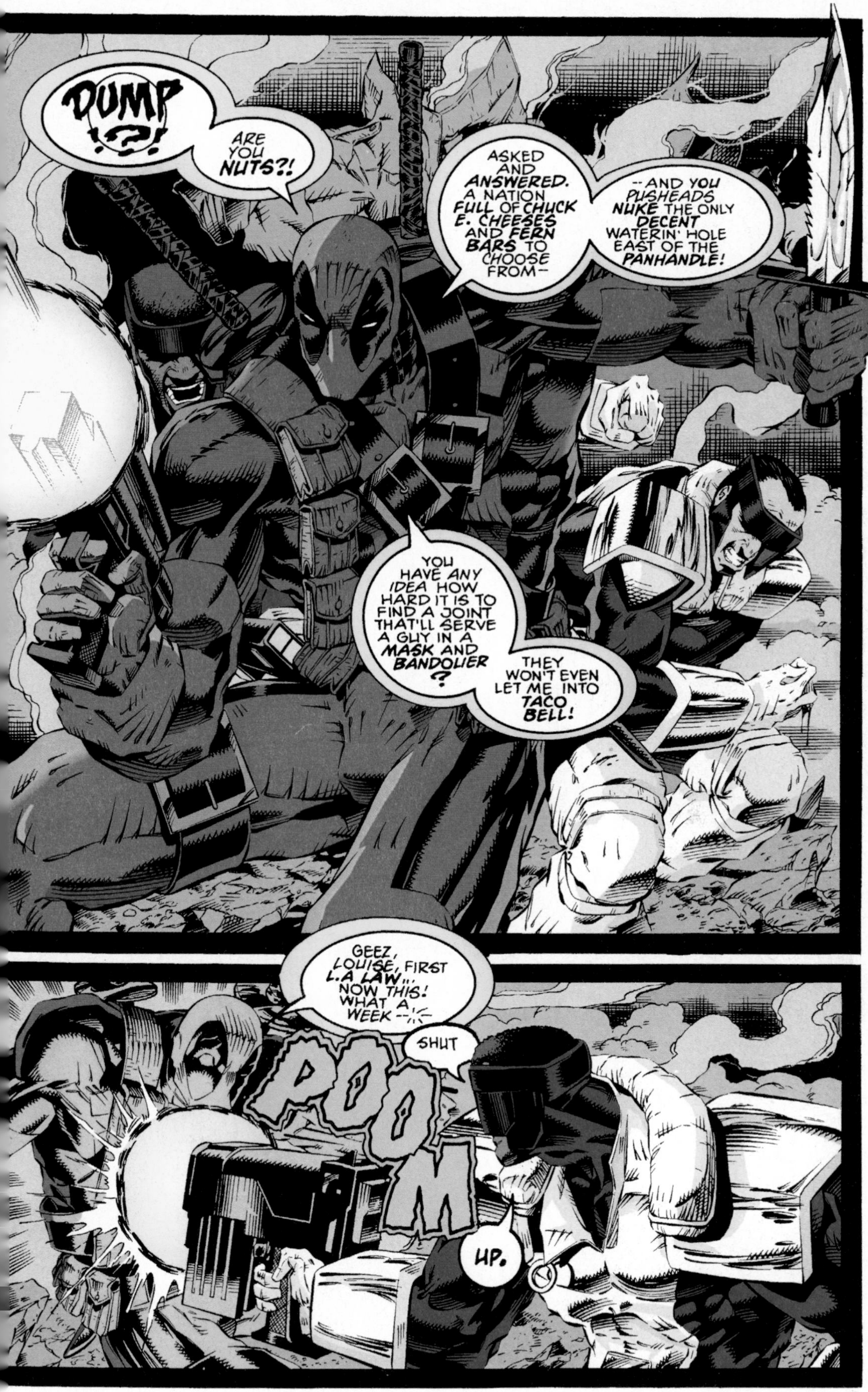
DUMP !?!
ARE YOU NUTS?!
ASKED AND ANSWERED. A NATION FULL OF CHUCK E. CHEESES AND FERN BARS TO CHOOSE FROM--
--AND YOU PUSHEADS NUKE THE ONLY DECENT WATERIN' HOLE EAST OF THE PANHANDLE!
YOU HAVE ANY IDEA HOW HARD IT IS TO FIND A JOINT THAT'LL SERVE A GUY IN A MASK AND BANDOLIER?
THEY WON'T EVEN LET ME INTO TACO BELL!
GEEZ, LOUISE, FIRST L.A LAW... NOW THIS! WHAT A WEEK--
SHUT
POOM
UP.

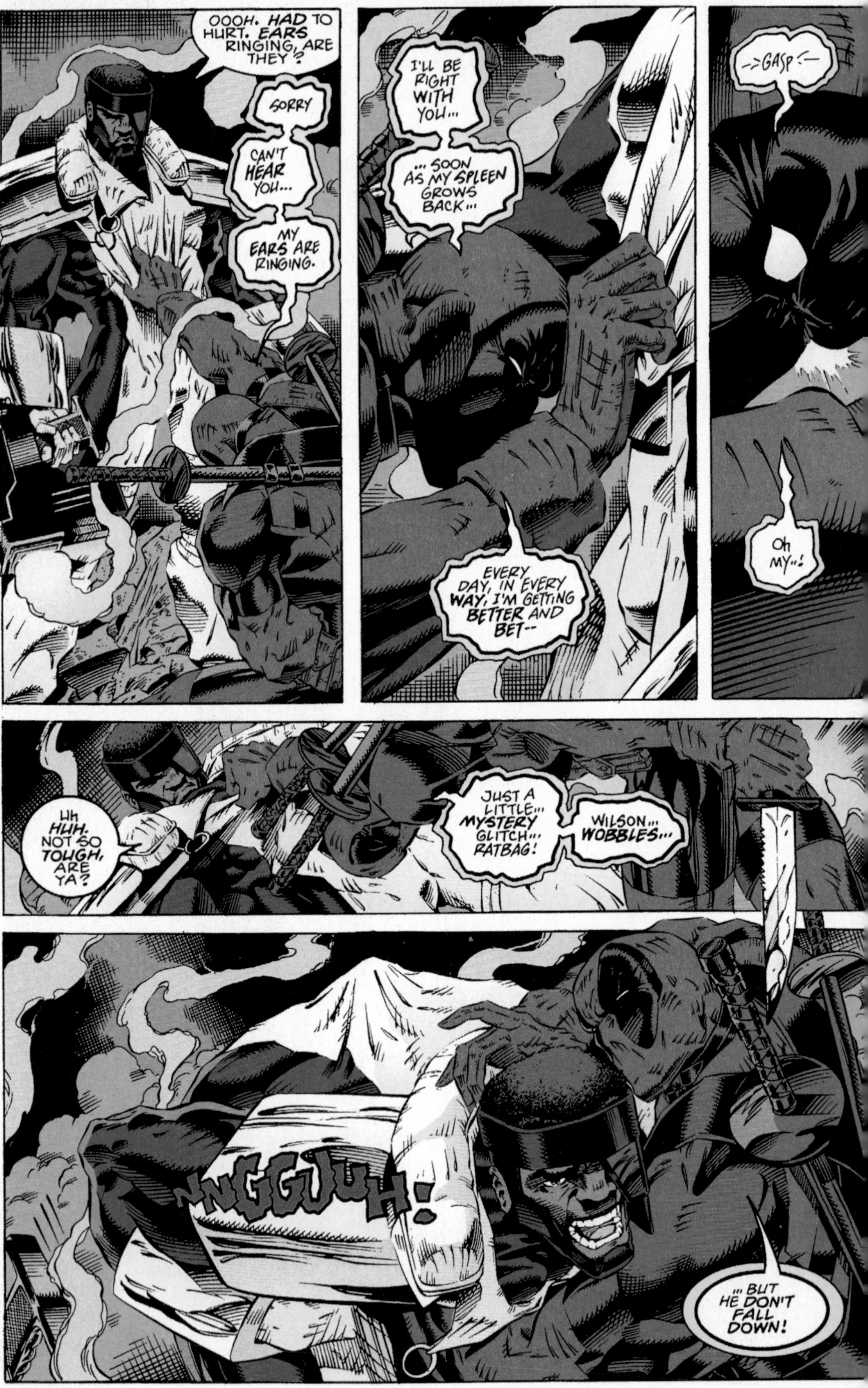
OOOH. HAD TO HURT. EARS RINGING, ARE THEY?
SORRY
CAN'T HEAR YOU...
MY EARS ARE RINGING.
I'LL BE RIGHT WITH YOU...
...SOON AS MY SPLEEN GROWS BACK...
EVERY DAY, IN EVERY WAY, I'M GETTING BETTER AND BET--
--GASP--
Oh MY...!
Uh HUH. NOT SO TOUGH, ARE YA?
JUST A LITTLE... MYSTERY GLITCH... RATBAG!
WILSON... WOBBLES...
NNGGUUH!
...BUT HE DON'T FALL DOWN!

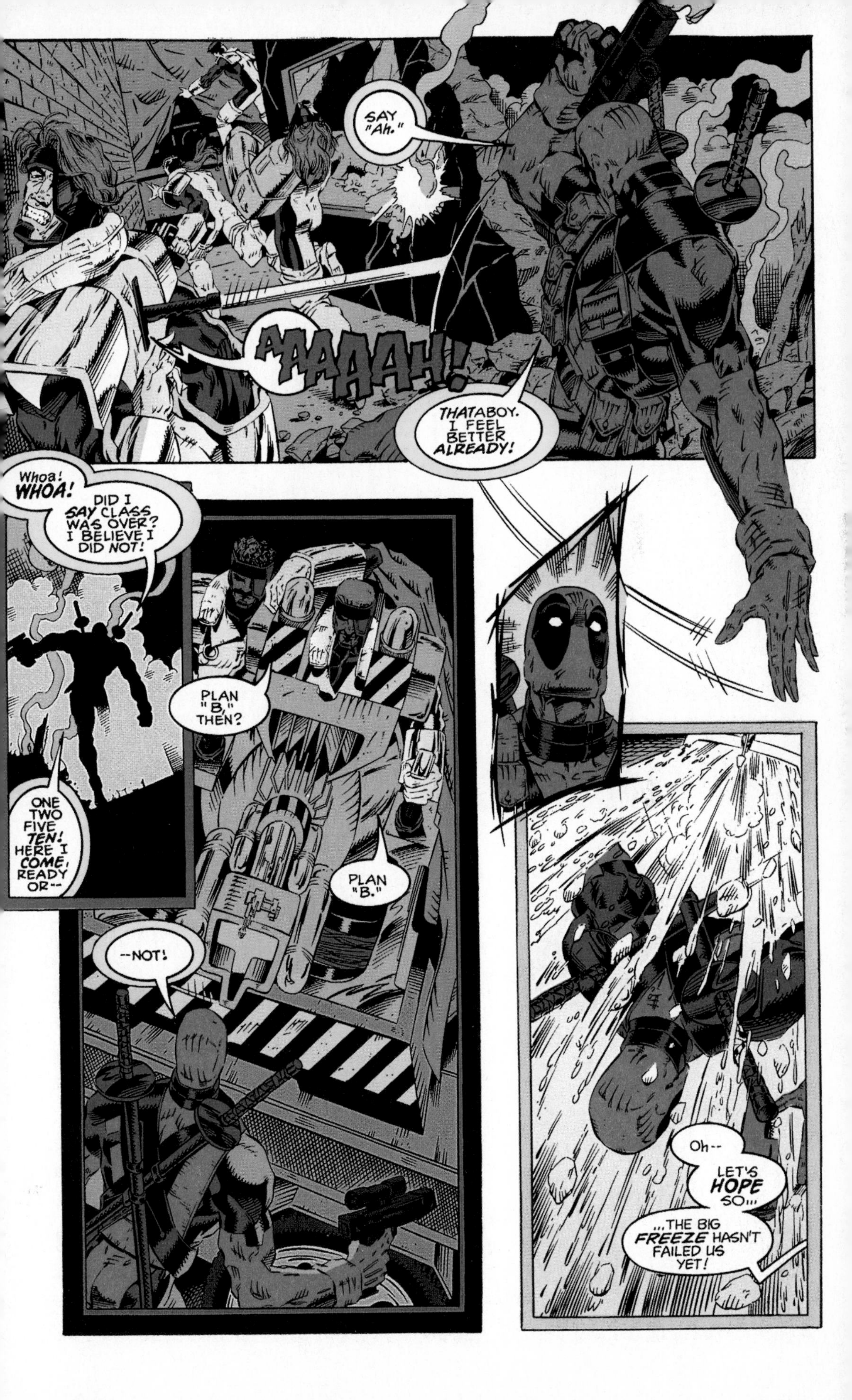
SAY "Ah."
AAAAAH!
THATABOY. I FEEL BETTER ALREADY!
Whoa! WHOA!
DID I SAY CLASS WAS OVER? I BELIEVE I DID NOT!
PLAN "B," THEN?
ONE TWO FIVE TEN! HERE I COME, READY OR--
PLAN "B."
--NOT!
Oh--
LET'S HOPE SO...
...THE BIG FREEZE HASN'T FAILED US YET!

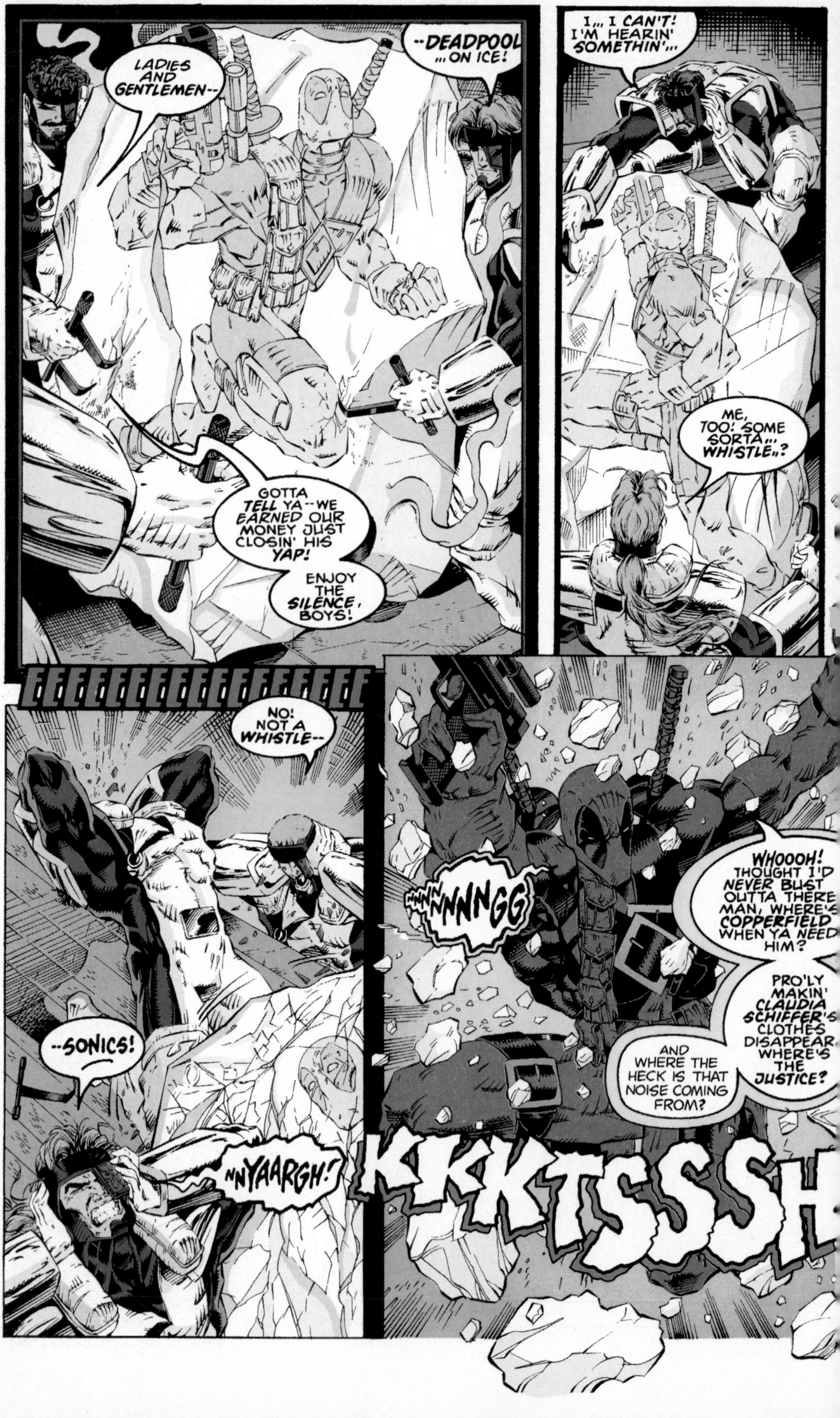
LADIES AND GENTLEMEN--
--DEADPOOL ...ON ICE!
GOTTA TELL YA--WE EARNED OUR MONEY JUST CLOSIN' HIS YAP!
ENJOY THE SILENCE, BOYS!
I... I CAN'T! I'M HEARIN' SOMETHIN'...
ME, TOO! SOME SORTA... WHISTLE...?
EEEEEEEEEEEEEEEEEE
NO! NOT A WHISTLE--
--SONICS!
NNYAARGH!
NNNNNNNGG
WHOOOH! THOUGHT I'D NEVER BUST OUTTA THERE. MAN, WHERE'S COPPERFIELD WHEN YA NEED HIM?
PRO'LY MAKIN' CLAUDIA SCHIFFER'S CLOTHES DISAPPEAR. WHERE'S THE JUSTICE?
AND WHERE THE HECK IS THAT NOISE COMING FROM?
KKKTSSSH

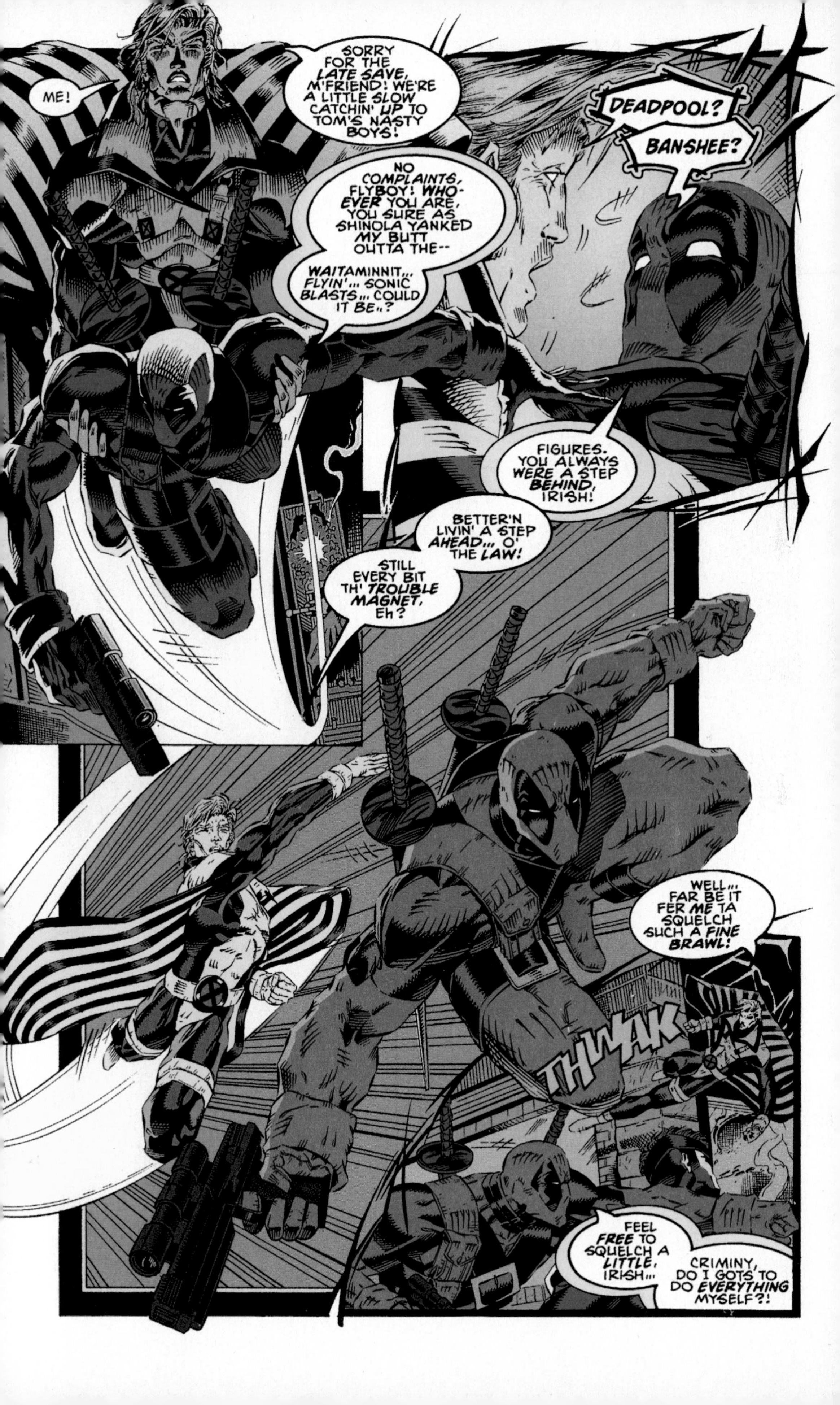
ME!
SORRY FOR THE LATE SAVE, M'FRIEND! WE'RE A LITTLE SLOW CATCHIN' UP TO TOM'S NASTY BOYS!
NO COMPLAINTS, FLYBOY! WHO-EVER YOU ARE, YOU SURE AS SHINOLA YANKED MY BUTT OUTTA THE--
WAITAMINNIT... FLYIN'... SONIC BLASTS... COULD IT BE..?
DEADPOOL?
BANSHEE?
FIGURES. YOU ALWAYS WERE A STEP BEHIND, IRISH!
BETTER'N LIVIN' A STEP AHEAD... O' THE LAW!
STILL EVERY BIT TH' TROUBLE MAGNET, EH?
WELL... FAR BE IT FER ME TA SQUELCH SUCH A FINE BRAWL!
THWAK
FEEL FREE TO SQUELCH A LITTLE, IRISH...
CRIMINY, DO I GOTS TO DO EVERYTHING MYSELF?!

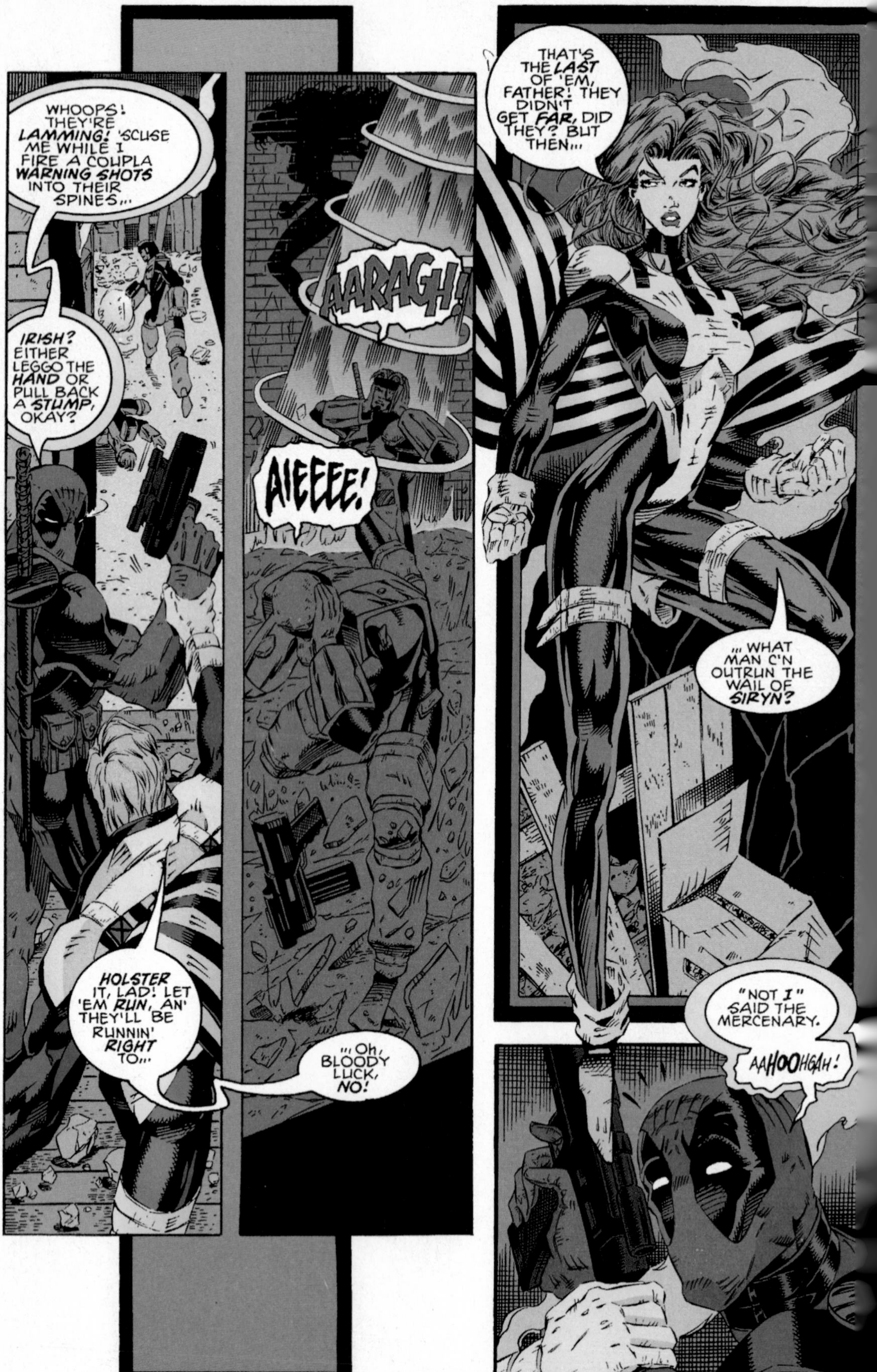
WHOOPS! THEY'RE LAMMING! 'SCUSE ME WHILE I FIRE A COUPLA WARNING SHOTS INTO THEIR SPINES...
IRISH? EITHER LEGGO THE HAND OR PULL BACK A STUMP, OKAY?
HOLSTER IT, LAD! LET 'EM RUN, AN' THEY'LL BE RUNNIN' RIGHT TO...
AARAGH!
AIEEEE!
...OH, BLOODY LUCK, NO!
THAT'S THE LAST OF 'EM, FATHER! THEY DIDN'T GET FAR, DID THEY? BUT THEN...
...WHAT MAN C'N OUTRUN THE WAIL OF SIRYN?
"NOT I" SAID THE MERCENARY.
AAHOOHGAH!

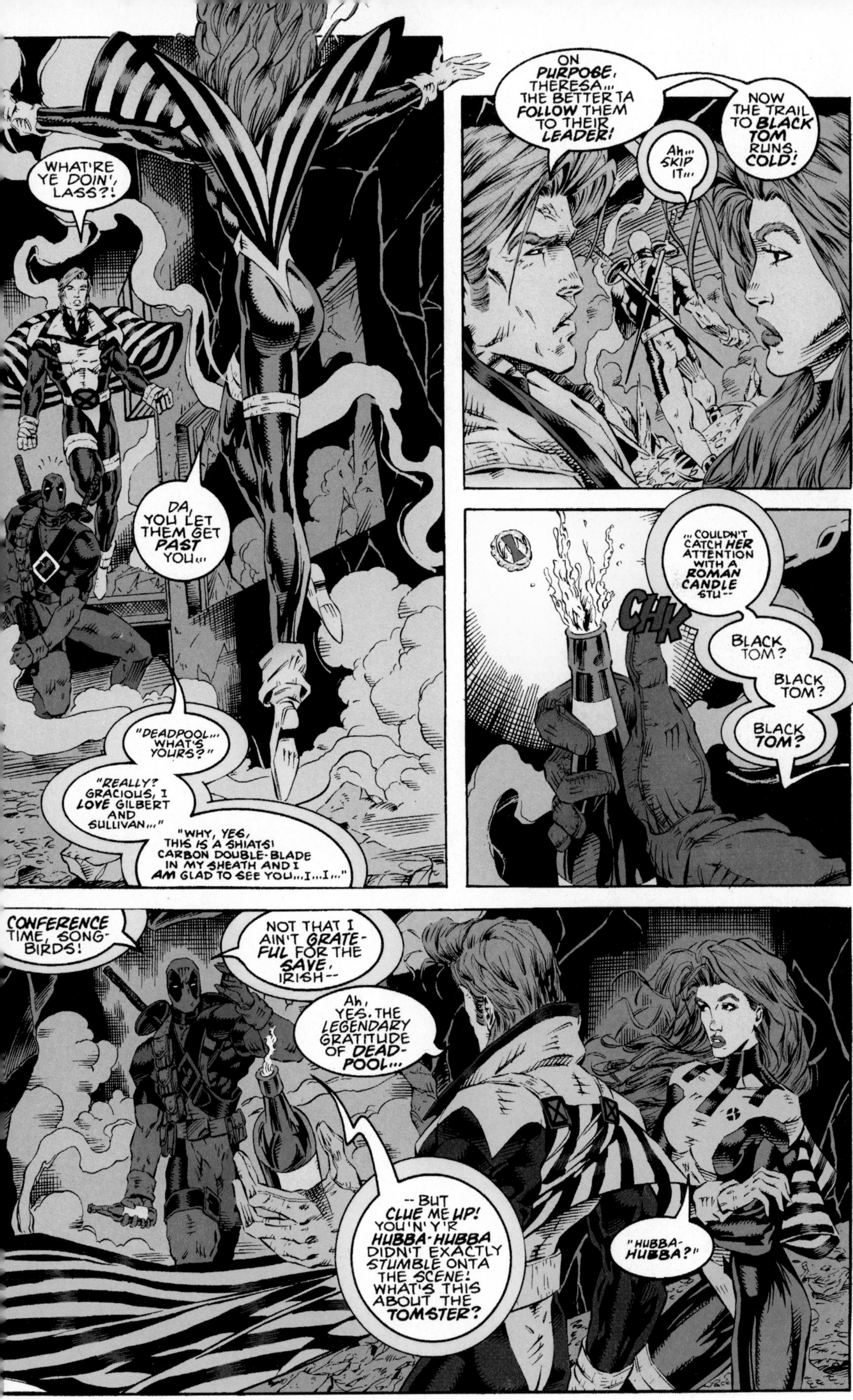

WHAT'RE YE DOIN', LASS?!
DA, YOU LET THEM GET PAST YOU...
"DEADPOOL... WHAT'S YOURS?"
"REALLY? GRACIOUS, I LOVE GILBERT AND SULLIVAN..."
"WHY, YES, THIS IS A SHIATSI CARBON DOUBLE-BLADE IN MY SHEATH AND I AM GLAD TO SEE YOU...I...I..."
ON PURPOSE, THERESA... THE BETTER TA FOLLOW THEM TO THEIR LEADER!
NOW THE TRAIL TO BLACK TOM RUNS COLD!
Ah... SKIP IT...
...COULDN'T CATCH HER ATTENTION WITH A ROMAN CANDLE STU--
CHK
BLACK TOM?
BLACK TOM?
BLACK TOM?
CONFERENCE TIME, SONG-BIRDS!
NOT THAT I AIN'T GRATE-FUL FOR THE SAVE, IRISH--
Ah, YES. THE LEGENDARY GRATITUDE OF DEAD-POOL...
--BUT CLUE ME UP! YOU'N'Y'R HUBBA-HUBBA DIDN'T EXACTLY STUMBLE ONTA THE SCENE! WHAT'S THIS ABOUT THE TOMSTER?
"HUBBA-HUBBA?"

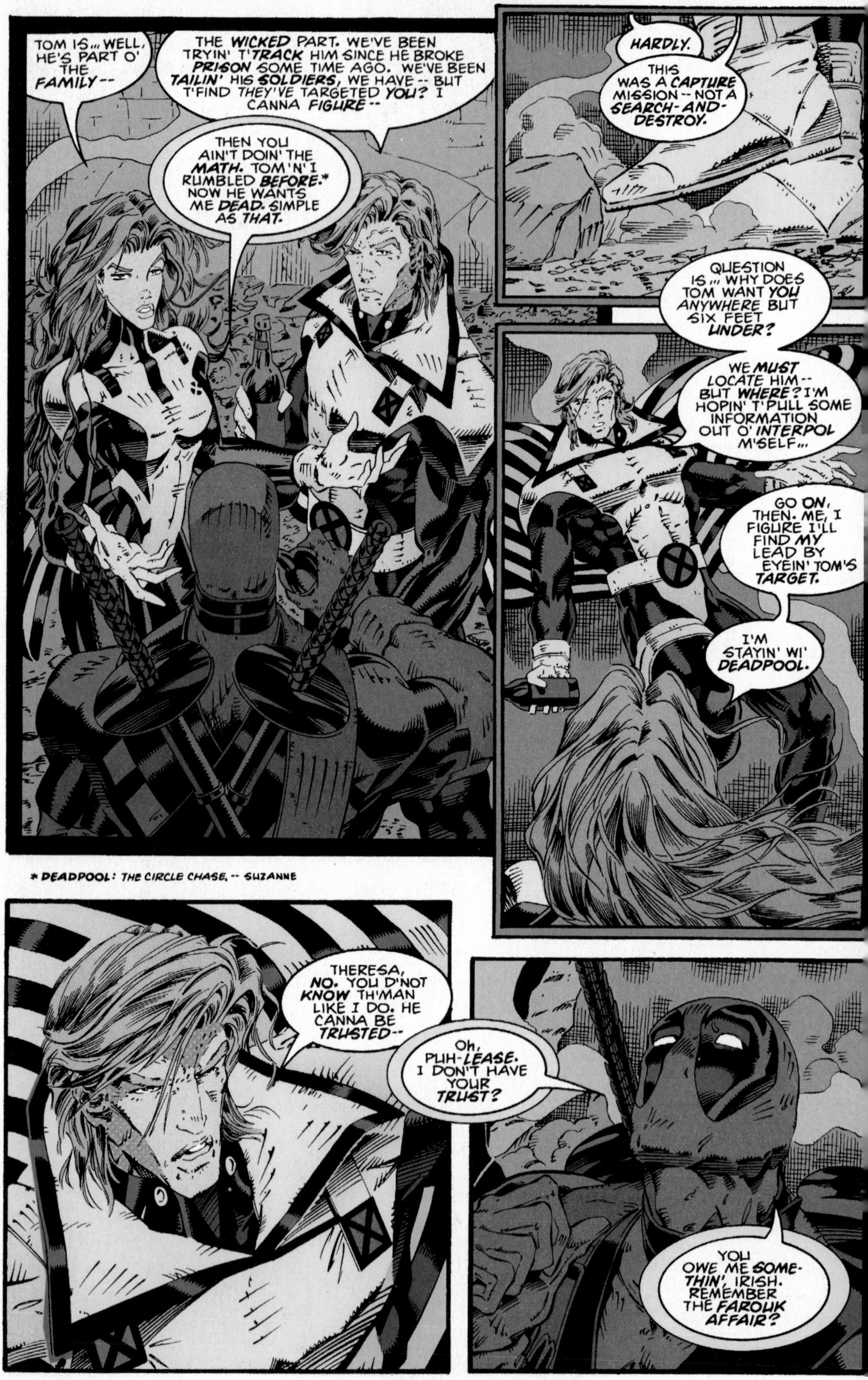
TOM IS... WELL, HE'S PART O' THE FAMILY --
THE WICKED PART. WE'VE BEEN TRYIN' T'TRACK HIM SINCE HE BROKE PRISON SOME TIME AGO. WE'VE BEEN TAILIN' HIS SOLDIERS, WE HAVE -- BUT T'FIND THEY'VE TARGETED YOU? I CANNA FIGURE --
THEN YOU AIN'T DOIN' THE MATH. TOM'N' I RUMBLED BEFORE.* NOW HE WANTS ME DEAD. SIMPLE AS THAT.
* DEADPOOL: THE CIRCLE CHASE. -- SUZANNE
HARDLY.
THIS WAS A CAPTURE MISSION -- NOT A SEARCH-AND-DESTROY.
QUESTION IS... WHY DOES TOM WANT YOU ANYWHERE BUT SIX FEET UNDER?
WE MUST LOCATE HIM -- BUT WHERE? I'M HOPIN' T'PULL SOME INFORMATION OUT O' INTERPOL M'SELF...
GO ON, THEN. ME, I FIGURE I'LL FIND MY LEAD BY EYEIN' TOM'S TARGET.
I'M STAYIN' WI' DEADPOOL.
THERESA, NO. YOU D'NOT KNOW TH'MAN LIKE I DO. HE CANNA BE TRUSTED --
Oh, PUH-LEASE. I DON'T HAVE YOUR TRUST?
YOU OWE ME SOME-THIN', IRISH. REMEMBER THE FAROUK AFFAIR?

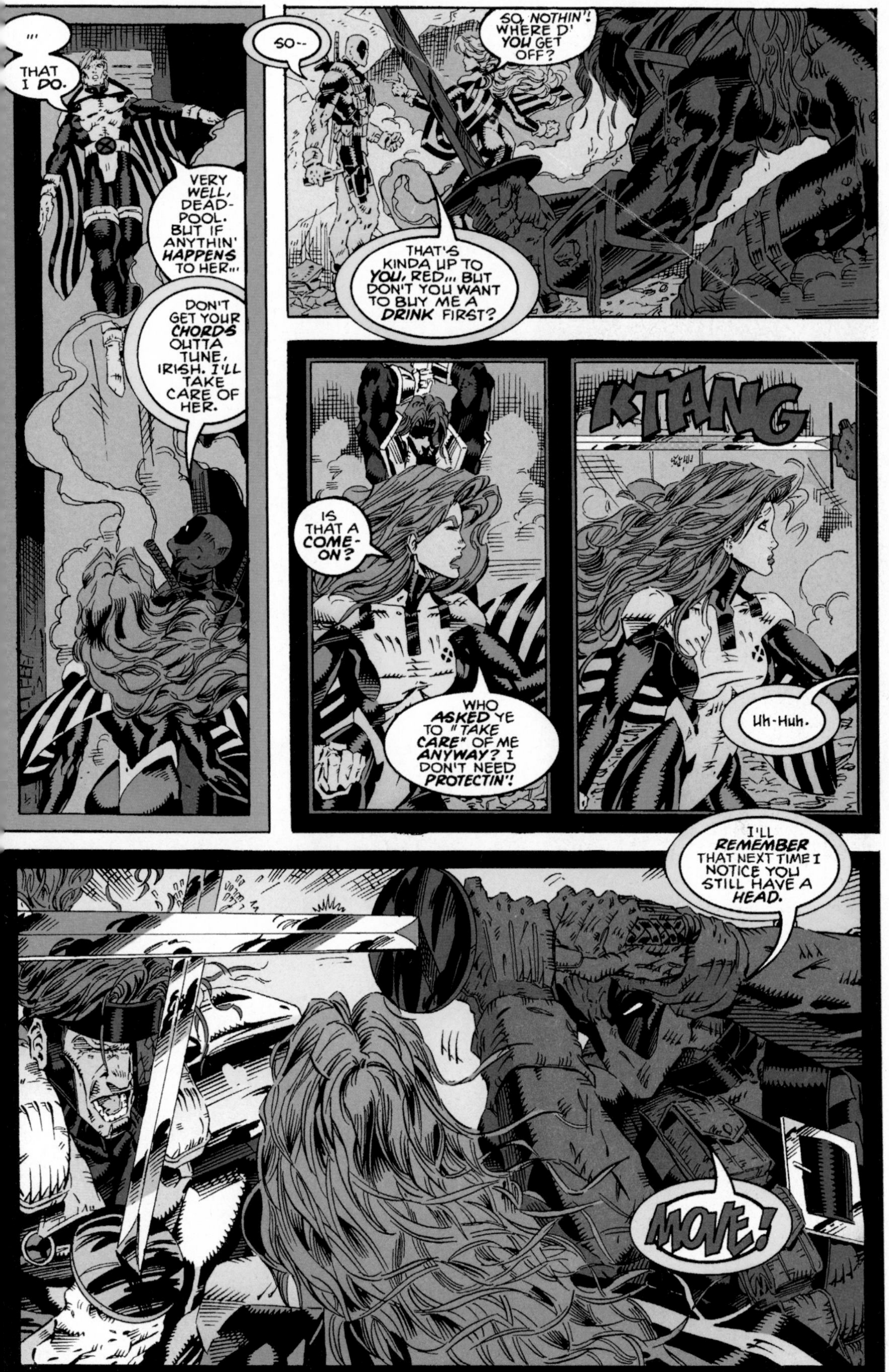
...
THAT I DO.
VERY WELL, DEADPOOL. BUT IF ANYTHIN' HAPPENS TO HER...
DON'T GET YOUR CHORDS OUTTA TUNE, IRISH. I'LL TAKE CARE OF HER.
SO--
SO, NOTHIN'! WHERE D' YOU GET OFF?
THAT'S KINDA UP TO YOU, RED... BUT DON'T YOU WANT TO BUY ME A DRINK FIRST?
IS THAT A COME-ON?
WHO ASKED YE TO "TAKE CARE" OF ME ANYWAY? I DON'T NEED PROTECTIN'!
KTANG
Uh-Huh.
I'LL REMEMBER THAT NEXT TIME I NOTICE YOU STILL HAVE A HEAD.
MOVE!

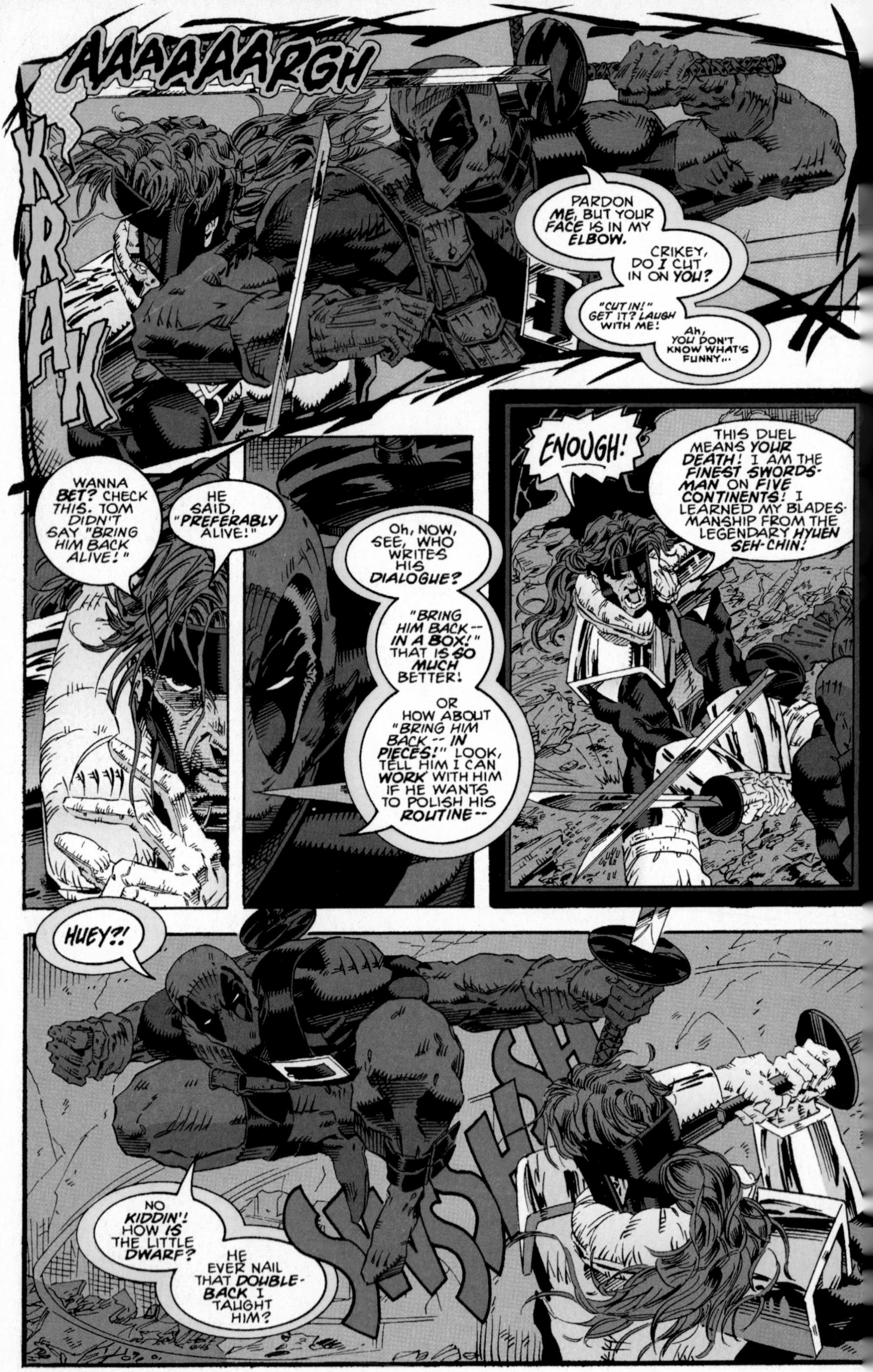
AAAAAARGH
KRAK
PARDON ME, BUT YOUR FACE IS IN MY ELBOW.
CRIKEY, DO I CUT IN ON YOU?
"CUT IN!" GET IT? LAUGH WITH ME!
Ah, YOU DON'T KNOW WHAT'S FUNNY...
WANNA BET? CHECK THIS. TOM DIDN'T SAY "BRING HIM BACK ALIVE!"
HE SAID, "PREFERABLY ALIVE!"
Oh, NOW, SEE, WHO WRITES HIS DIALOGUE?
"BRING HIM BACK-- IN A BOX!" THAT IS SO MUCH BETTER!
OR HOW ABOUT "BRING HIM BACK -- IN PIECES!" LOOK, TELL HIM I CAN WORK WITH HIM IF HE WANTS TO POLISH HIS ROUTINE--
ENOUGH!
THIS DUEL MEANS YOUR DEATH! I AM THE FINEST SWORDS-MAN ON FIVE CONTINENTS! I LEARNED MY BLADES-MANSHIP FROM THE LEGENDARY HYUEN SEH-CHIN!
HUEY?!
NO KIDDIN'! HOW IS THE LITTLE DWARF?
HE EVER NAIL THAT DOUBLE-BACK I TAUGHT HIM?

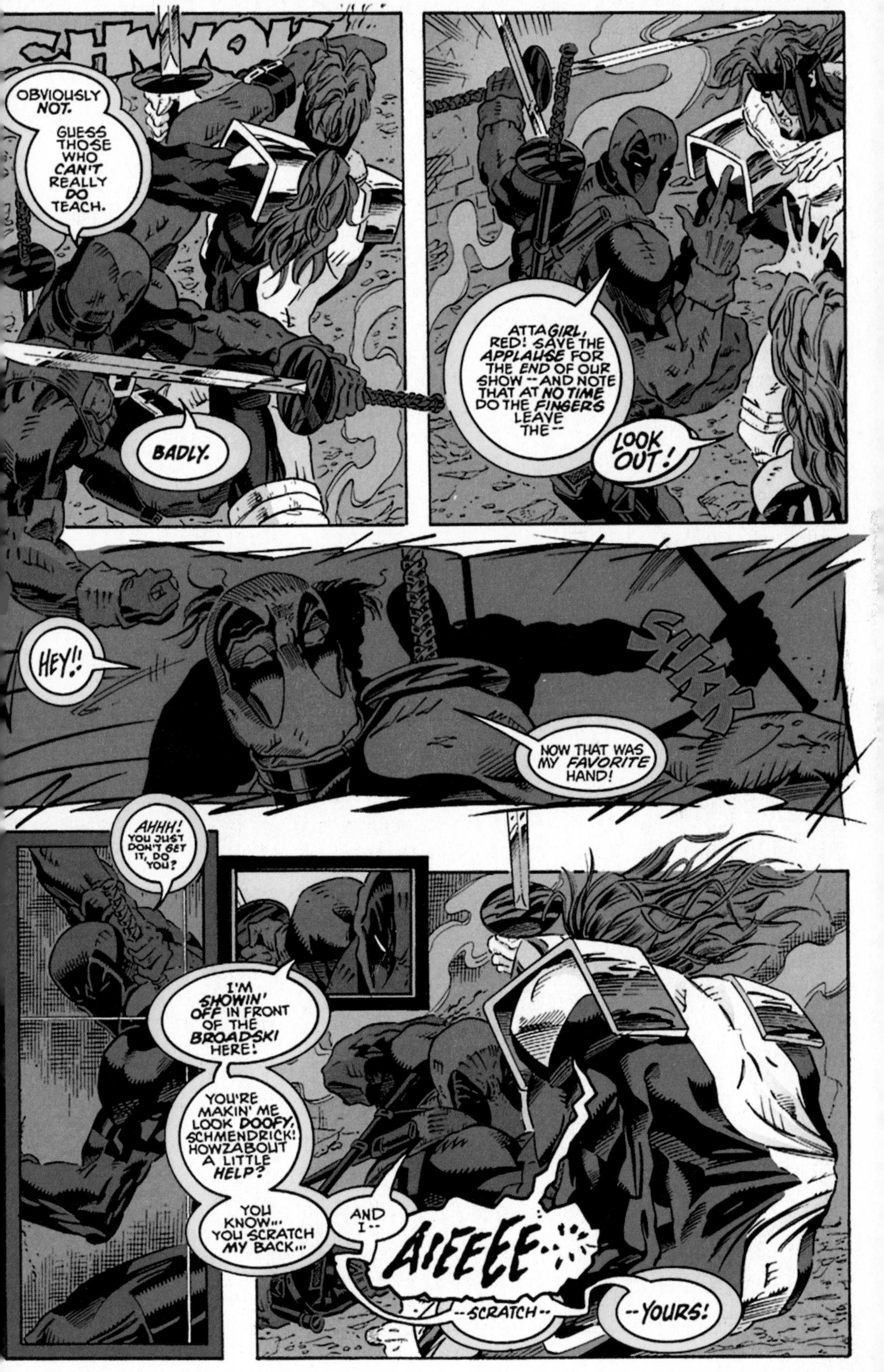
OBVIOUSLY NOT. GUESS THOSE WHO CAN'T REALLY DO TEACH.
BADLY.
ATTA GIRL, RED! SAVE THE APPLAUSE FOR THE END OF OUR SHOW -- AND NOTE THAT AT NO TIME DO THE FINGERS LEAVE THE--
LOOK OUT!
HEY!!
NOW THAT WAS MY FAVORITE HAND!
AHHH! YOU JUST DON'T GET IT, DO YOU?
I'M SHOWIN' OFF IN FRONT OF THE BROADSKI HERE!
YOU'RE MAKIN' ME LOOK DOOFY, SCHMENDRICK! HOWZABOUT A LITTLE HELP?
YOU KNOW... YOU SCRATCH MY BACK...
AND I--
AIEEEE
--SCRATCH--
--YOURS!

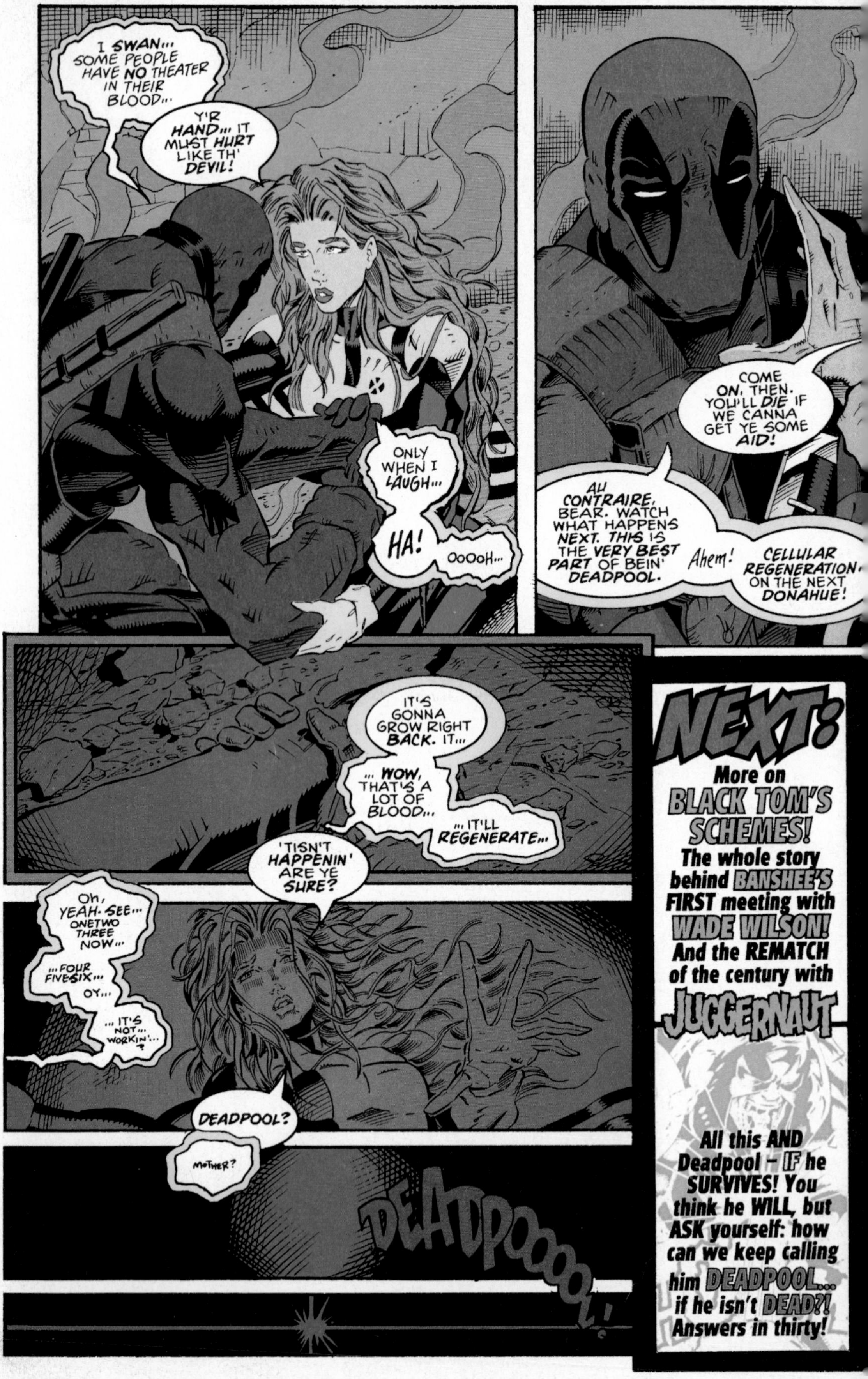

I SWAN... SOME PEOPLE HAVE NO THEATER IN THEIR BLOOD...
Y'R HAND... IT MUST HURT LIKE TH' DEVIL!
ONLY WHEN I LAUGH...
HA!
OOOOH...
COME ON, THEN. YOU'LL DIE IF WE CANNA GET YE SOME AID!
AU CONTRAIRE, BEAR. WATCH WHAT HAPPENS NEXT. THIS IS THE VERY BEST PART OF BEIN' DEADPOOL.
Ahem!
CELLULAR REGENERATION, ON THE NEXT DONAHUE!
IT'S GONNA GROW RIGHT BACK. IT...
...WOW, THAT'S A LOT OF BLOOD...
...IT'LL REGENERATE...
'TISN'T HAPPENIN' ARE YE SURE?
Oh, YEAH. SEE... ONETWO THREE NOW...
...FOUR FIVESIX...
OY...
...IT'S NOT... WORKIN'...?
DEADPOOL?
MOTHER?
DEADPOOOOOL!
NEXT:
More on BLACK TOM'S SCHEMES!
The whole story behind BANSHEE'S FIRST meeting with WADE WILSON!
And the REMATCH of the century with JUGGERNAUT
All this AND Deadpool – IF he SURVIVES! You think he WILL, but ASK yourself: how can we keep calling him DEADPOOL... if he isn't DEAD?! Answers in thirty!

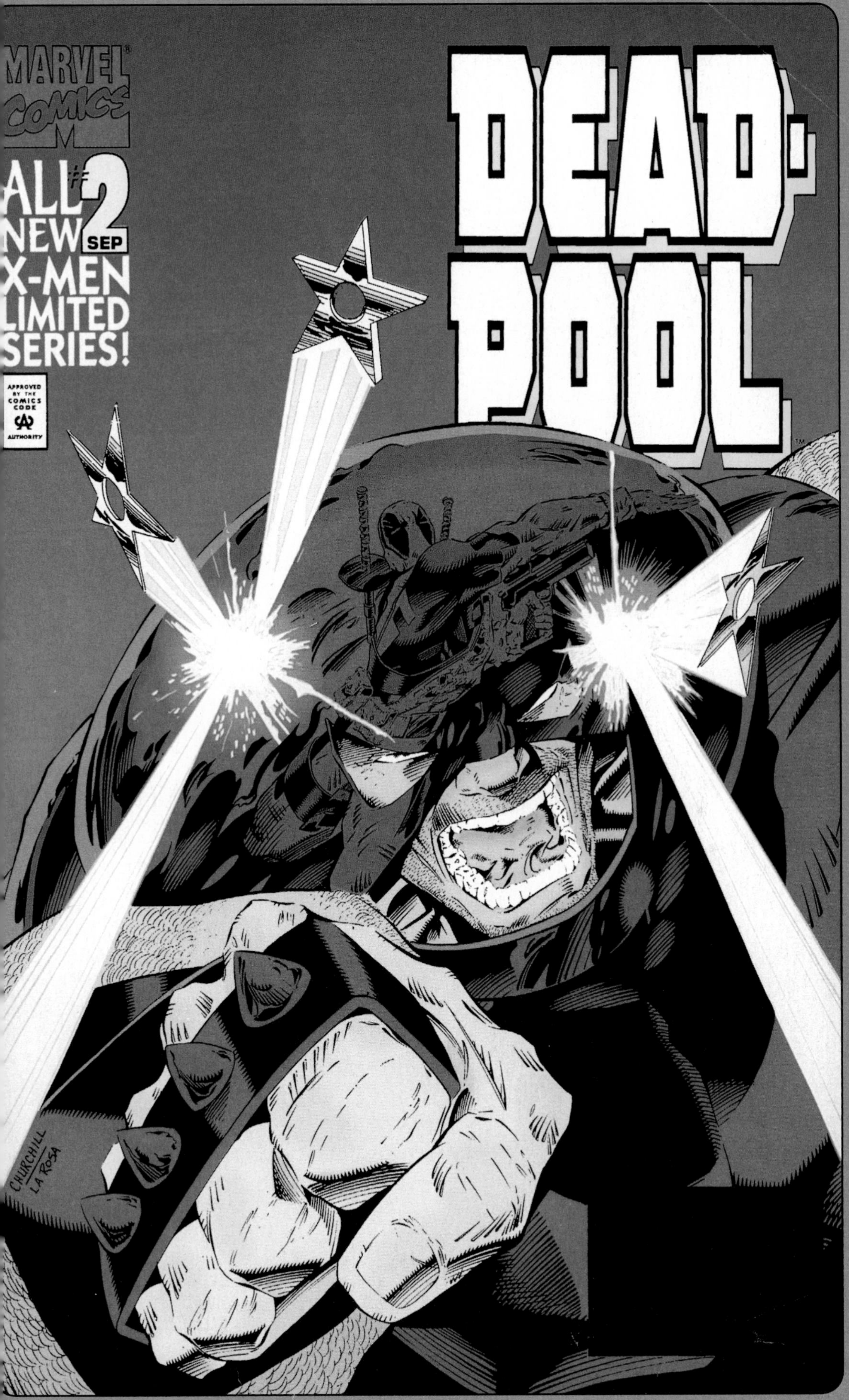

MARVEL COMICS
ALL NEW #2 SEP
X-MEN LIMITED SERIES!
APPROVED BY THE COMICS CODE AUTHORITY
DEADPOOL
CHURCHILL
LA ROSA

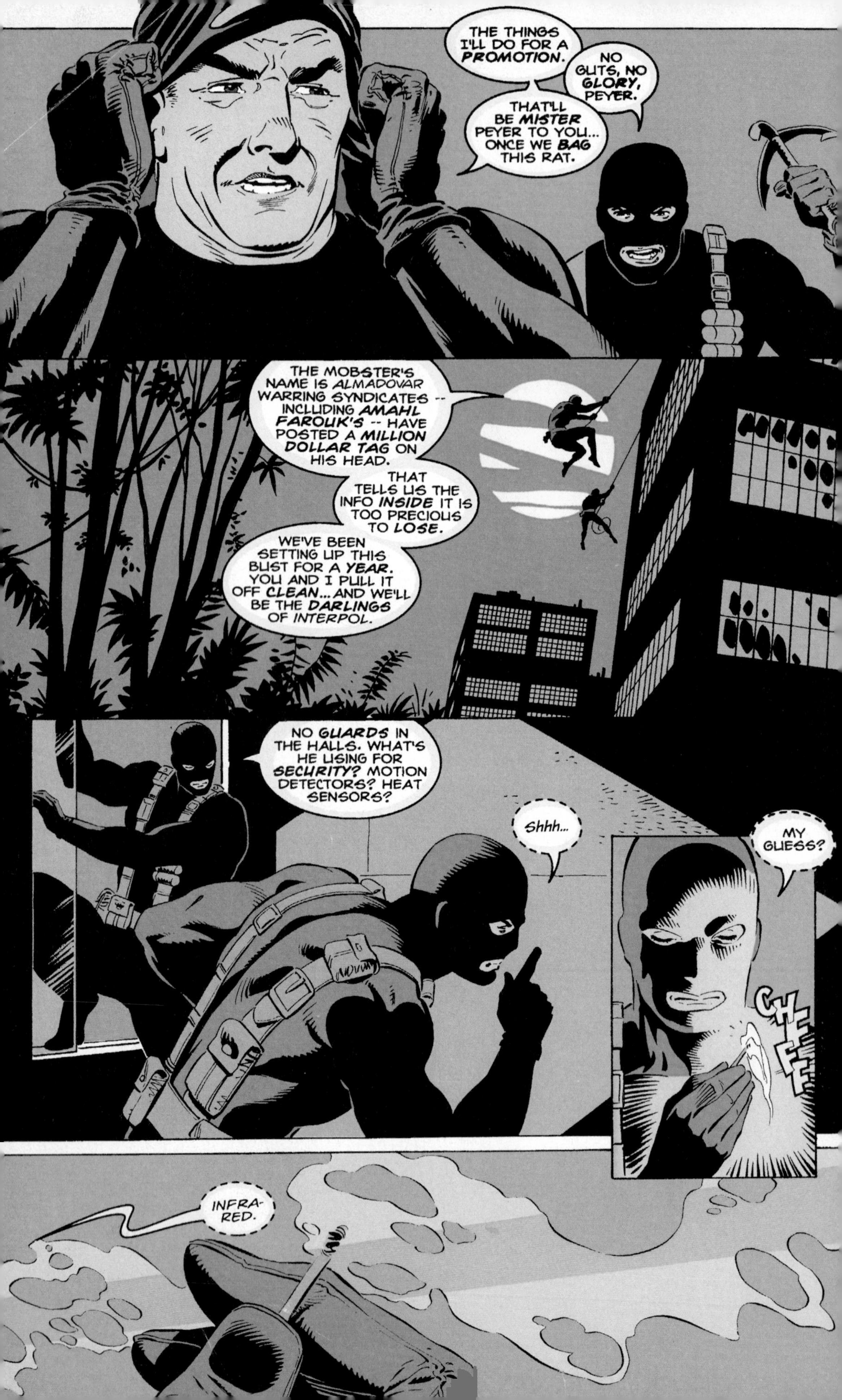
THE THINGS I'LL DO FOR A PROMOTION.
NO GUTS, NO GLORY, PEYER.
THAT'LL BE MISTER PEYER TO YOU... ONCE WE BAG THIS RAT.
THE MOBSTER'S NAME IS ALMADOVAR WARRING SYNDICATES -- INCLUDING AMAHL FAROUK'S -- HAVE POSTED A MILLION DOLLAR TAG ON HIS HEAD.
THAT TELLS US THE INFO INSIDE IT IS TOO PRECIOUS TO LOSE.
WE'VE BEEN SETTING UP THIS BUST FOR A YEAR. YOU AND I PULL IT OFF CLEAN... AND WE'LL BE THE DARLINGS OF INTERPOL.
NO GUARDS IN THE HALLS. WHAT'S HE USING FOR SECURITY? MOTION DETECTORS? HEAT SENSORS?
Shhh...
MY GUESS?
CHFFF
INFRA-RED.

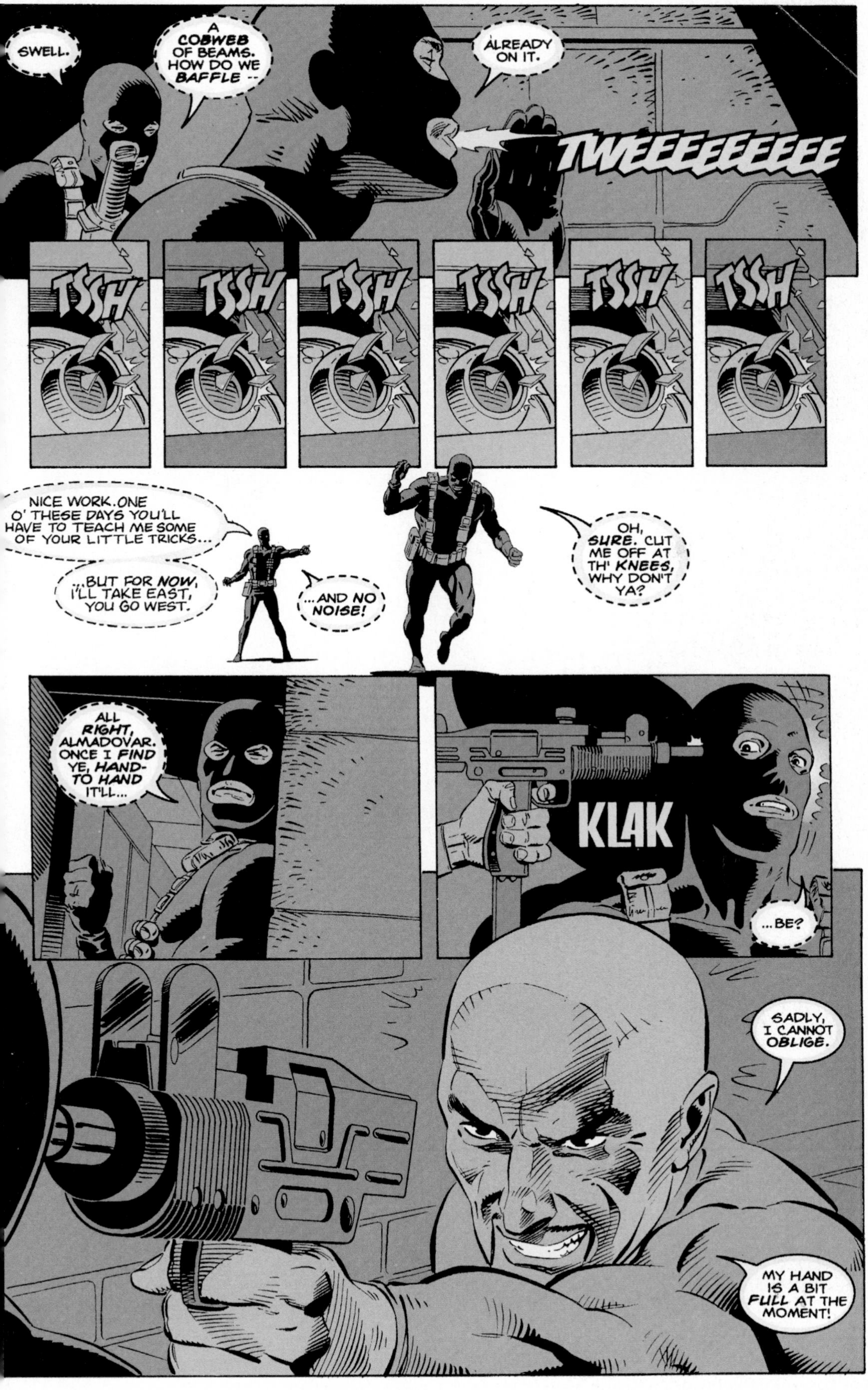
SWELL.
A COBWEB OF BEAMS. HOW DO WE BAFFLE --
ALREADY ON IT.
TWEEEEEEEEEE
TSSH
TSSH
TSSH
TSSH
TSSH
TSSH
NICE WORK. ONE O' THESE DAYS YOU'LL HAVE TO TEACH ME SOME OF YOUR LITTLE TRICKS...
...BUT FOR NOW, I'LL TAKE EAST, YOU GO WEST.
...AND NO NOISE!
OH, SURE. CUT ME OFF AT TH' KNEES, WHY DON'T YA?
ALL RIGHT, ALMADOVAR. ONCE I FIND YE, HAND-TO HAND IT'LL...
KLAK
...BE?
SADLY, I CANNOT OBLIGE.
MY HAND IS A BIT FULL AT THE MOMENT!

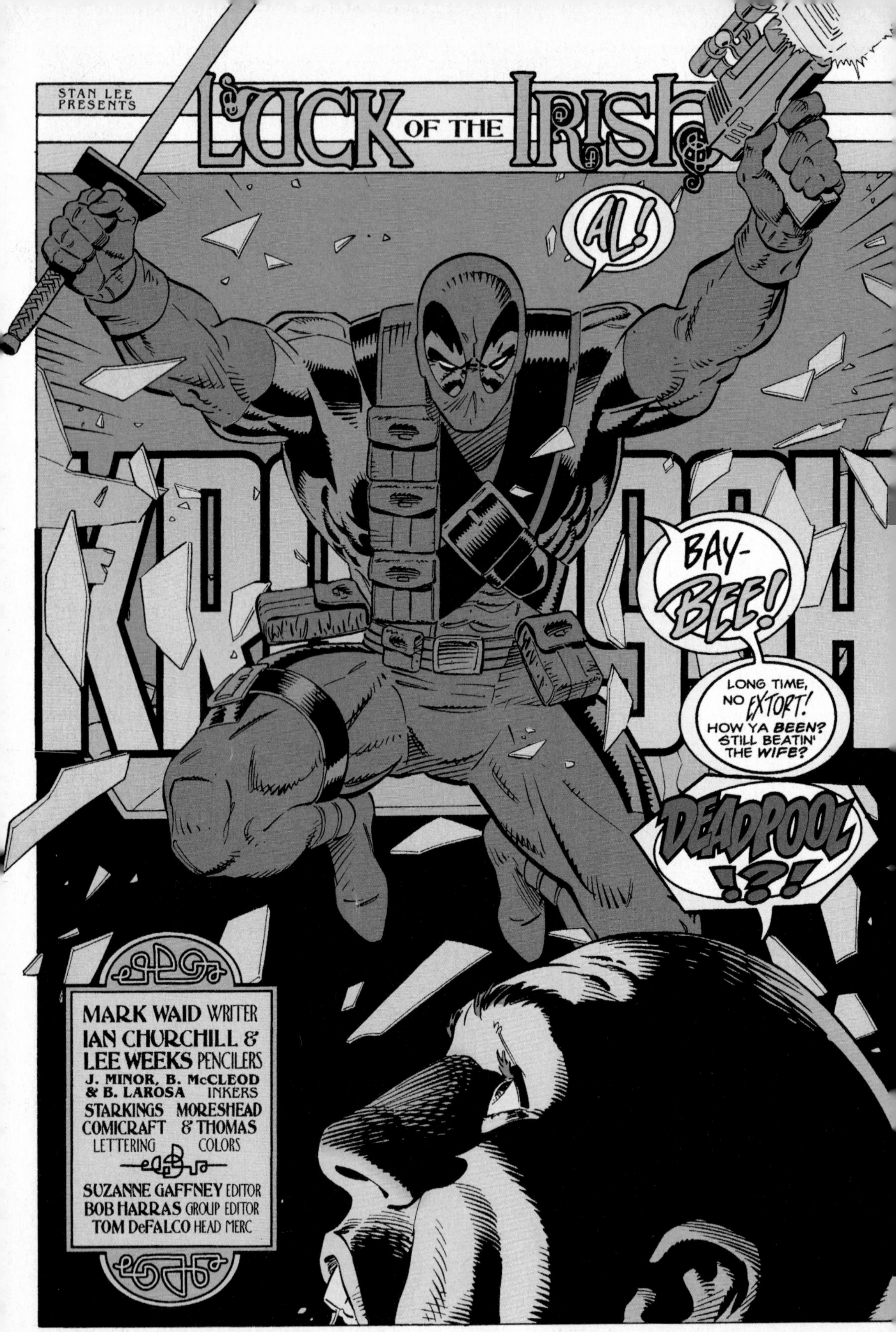

STAN LEE PRESENTS
LUCK OF THE IRISH
AL!
BAY-BEE!
LONG TIME, NO EXTORT! HOW YA BEEN? STILL BEATIN' THE WIFE?
DEADPOOL !?!
MARK WAID WRITER
IAN CHURCHILL & LEE WEEKS PENCILERS
J. MINOR, B. McCLEOD & B. LAROSA INKERS
STARKINGS COMICRAFT LETTERING
MORESHEAD & THOMAS COLORS
SUZANNE GAFFNEY EDITOR
BOB HARRAS GROUP EDITOR
TOM DeFALCO HEAD MERC

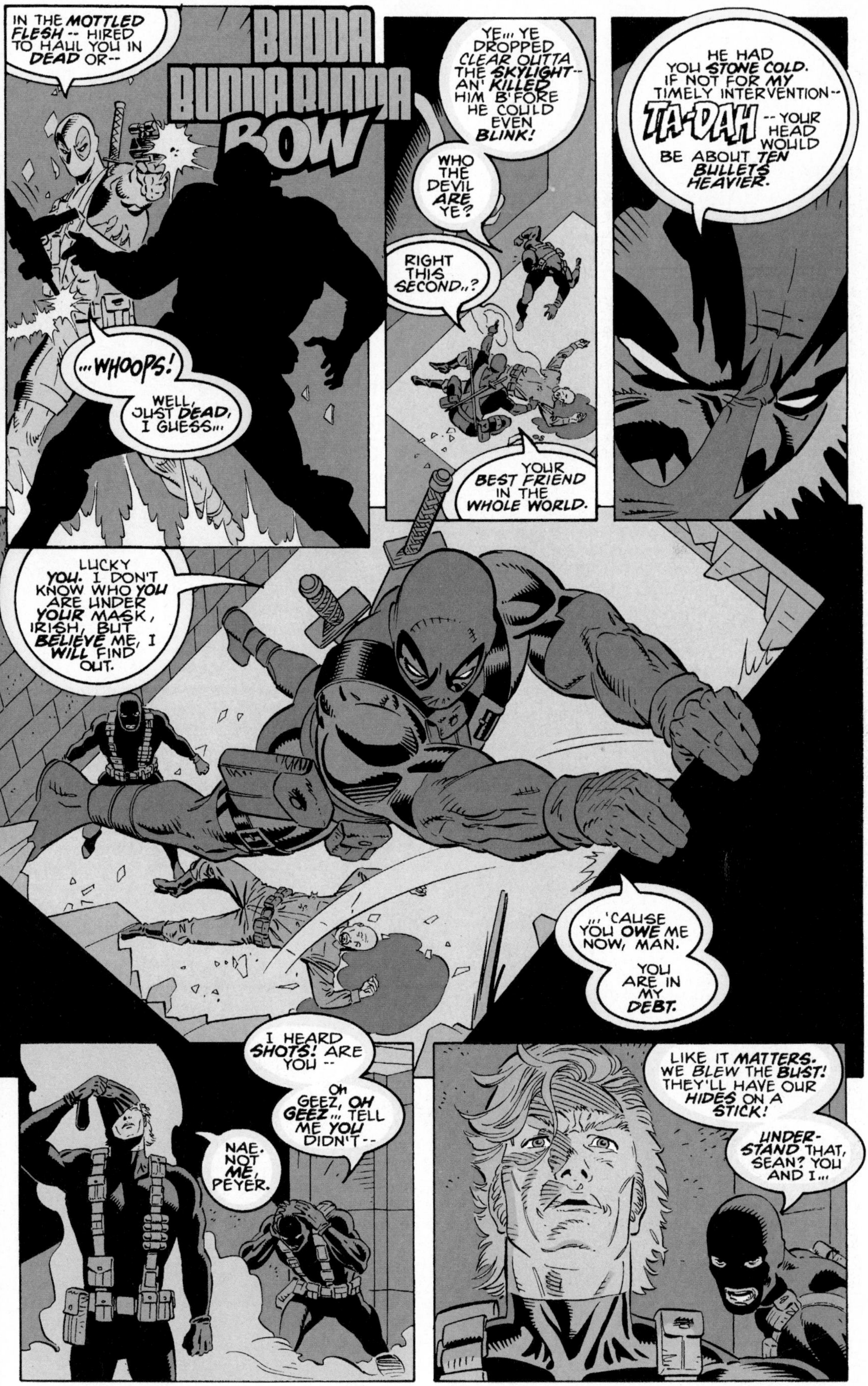
IN THE MOTTLED FLESH -- HIRED TO HAUL YOU IN DEAD OR--
BUDDA BUDDA BUDDA BOW
...WHOOPS!
WELL, JUST DEAD, I GUESS...
YE... YE DROPPED CLEAR OUTTA THE SKYLIGHT-- AN' KILLED HIM B'FORE HE COULD EVEN BLINK!
WHO THE DEVIL ARE YE?
RIGHT THIS SECOND..?
YOUR BEST FRIEND IN THE WHOLE WORLD.
HE HAD YOU STONE COLD. IF NOT FOR MY TIMELY INTERVENTION--
TA-DAH -- YOUR HEAD WOULD BE ABOUT TEN BULLETS HEAVIER.
LUCKY YOU. I DON'T KNOW WHO YOU ARE UNDER YOUR MASK, IRISH, BUT BELIEVE ME, I WILL FIND OUT.
...'CAUSE YOU OWE ME NOW, MAN.
YOU ARE IN MY DEBT.
I HEARD SHOTS! ARE YOU --
OH GEEZ, OH GEEZ... TELL ME YOU DIDN'T--
NAE. NOT ME, PEYER.
LIKE IT MATTERS. WE BLEW THE BUST! THEY'LL HAVE OUR HIDES ON A STICK!
UNDER-STAND THAT, SEAN? YOU AND I...

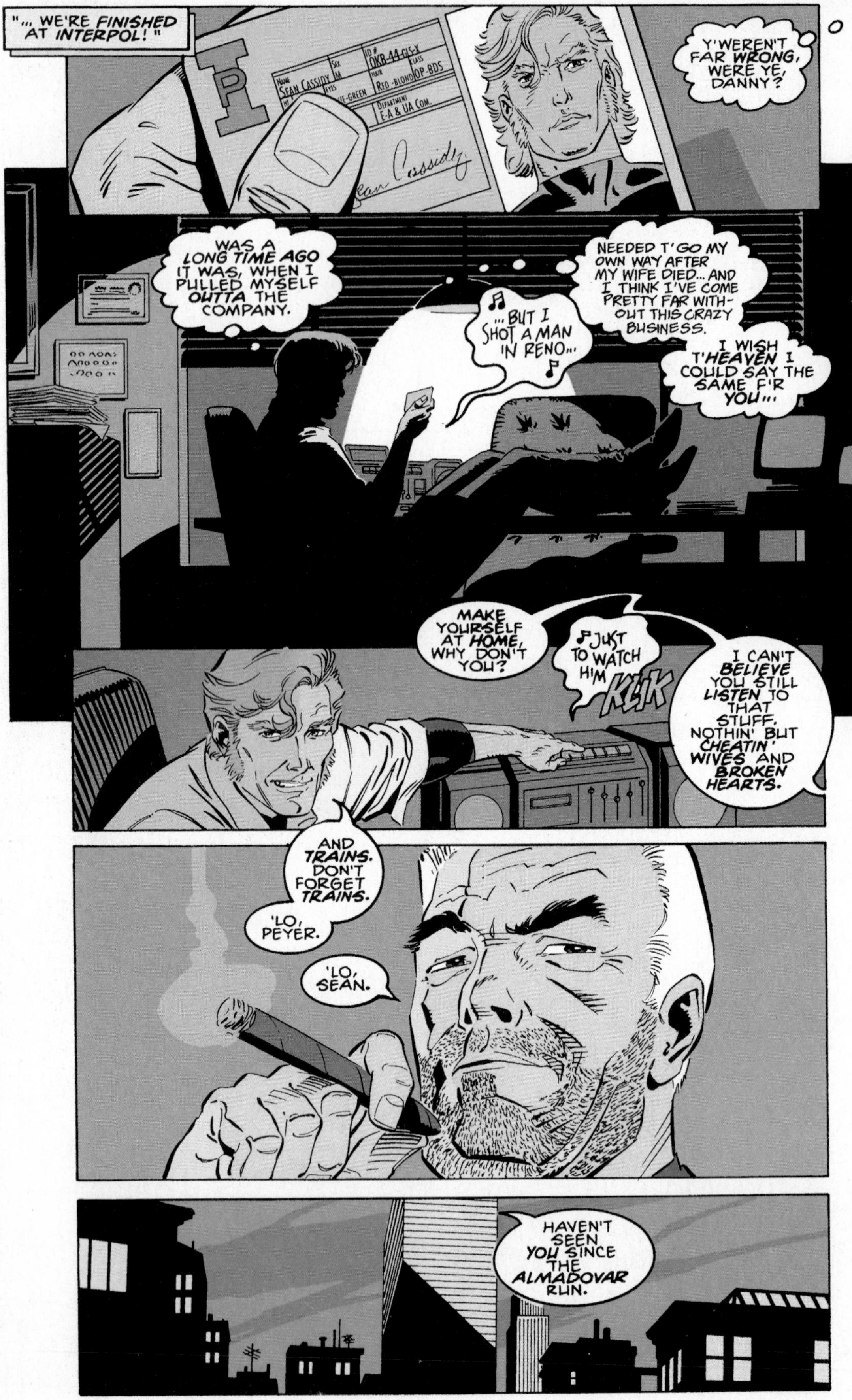
"... WE'RE FINISHED AT INTERPOL!"
Y'WEREN'T FAR WRONG, WERE YE, DANNY?
WAS A LONG TIME AGO IT WAS, WHEN I PULLED MYSELF OUTTA THE COMPANY.
NEEDED T'GO MY OWN WAY AFTER MY WIFE DIED... AND I THINK I'VE COME PRETTY FAR WITHOUT THIS CRAZY BUSINESS.
...BUT I SHOT A MAN IN RENO...
I WISH T'HEAVEN I COULD SAY THE SAME F'R YOU...
MAKE YOURSELF AT HOME, WHY DON'T YOU?
JUST TO WATCH HIM
KLIK
I CAN'T BELIEVE YOU STILL LISTEN TO THAT STUFF. NOTHIN' BUT CHEATIN' WIVES AND BROKEN HEARTS.
AND TRAINS. DON'T FORGET TRAINS.
'LO, PEYER.
'LO, SEAN.
HAVEN'T SEEN YOU SINCE THE ALMADOVAR RUN.

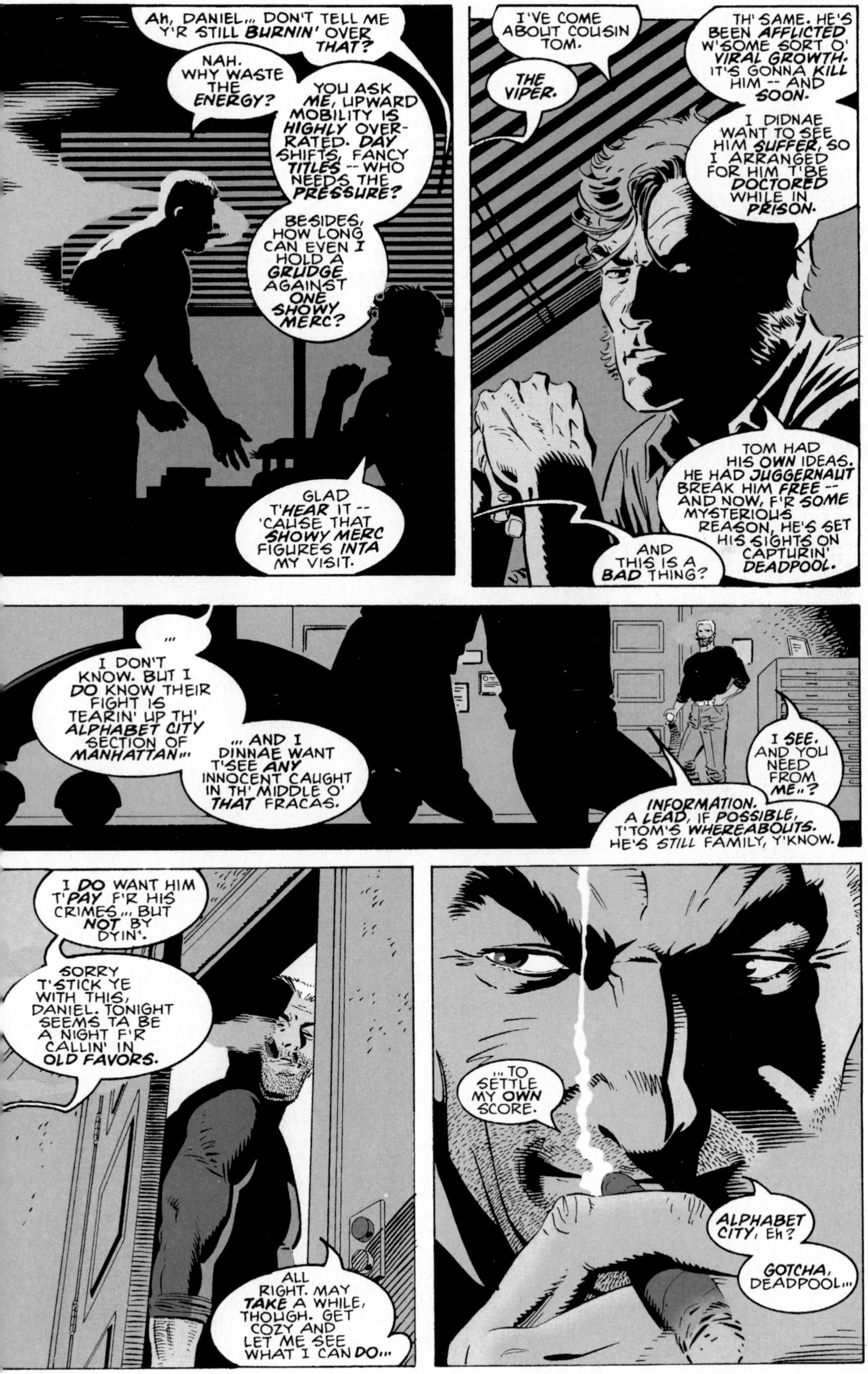

AH, DANIEL... DON'T TELL ME Y'R STILL BURNIN' OVER THAT?
NAH. WHY WASTE THE ENERGY?
YOU ASK ME, UPWARD MOBILITY IS HIGHLY OVER-RATED. DAY SHIFTS, FANCY TITLES -- WHO NEEDS THE PRESSURE?
BESIDES, HOW LONG CAN EVEN I HOLD A GRUDGE AGAINST ONE SHOWY MERC?
GLAD T'HEAR IT -- 'CAUSE THAT SHOWY MERC FIGURES INTA MY VISIT.
I'VE COME ABOUT COUSIN TOM.
THE VIPER.
TH' SAME. HE'S BEEN AFFLICTED W'SOME SORT O' VIRAL GROWTH. IT'S GONNA KILL HIM -- AND SOON.
I DIDNAE WANT TO SEE HIM SUFFER, SO I ARRANGED FOR HIM T'BE DOCTORED WHILE IN PRISON.
TOM HAD HIS OWN IDEAS. HE HAD JUGGERNAUT BREAK HIM FREE -- AND NOW, F'R SOME MYSTERIOUS REASON, HE'S SET HIS SIGHTS ON CAPTURIN' DEADPOOL.
AND THIS IS A BAD THING?
...
I DON'T KNOW. BUT I DO KNOW THEIR FIGHT IS TEARIN' UP TH' ALPHABET CITY SECTION OF MANHATTAN...
...AND I DINNAE WANT T'SEE ANY INNOCENT CAUGHT IN TH' MIDDLE O' THAT FRACAS.
I SEE. AND YOU NEED FROM ME..?
INFORMATION. A LEAD, IF POSSIBLE, T'TOM'S WHEREABOUTS. HE'S STILL FAMILY, Y'KNOW.
I DO WANT HIM T'PAY F'R HIS CRIMES... BUT NOT BY DYIN'.
SORRY T'STICK YE WITH THIS, DANIEL. TONIGHT SEEMS TA BE A NIGHT F'R CALLIN' IN OLD FAVORS.
ALL RIGHT. MAY TAKE A WHILE, THOUGH. GET COZY AND LET ME SEE WHAT I CAN DO...
...TO SETTLE MY OWN SCORE.
ALPHABET CITY, EH?
GOTCHA, DEADPOOL...

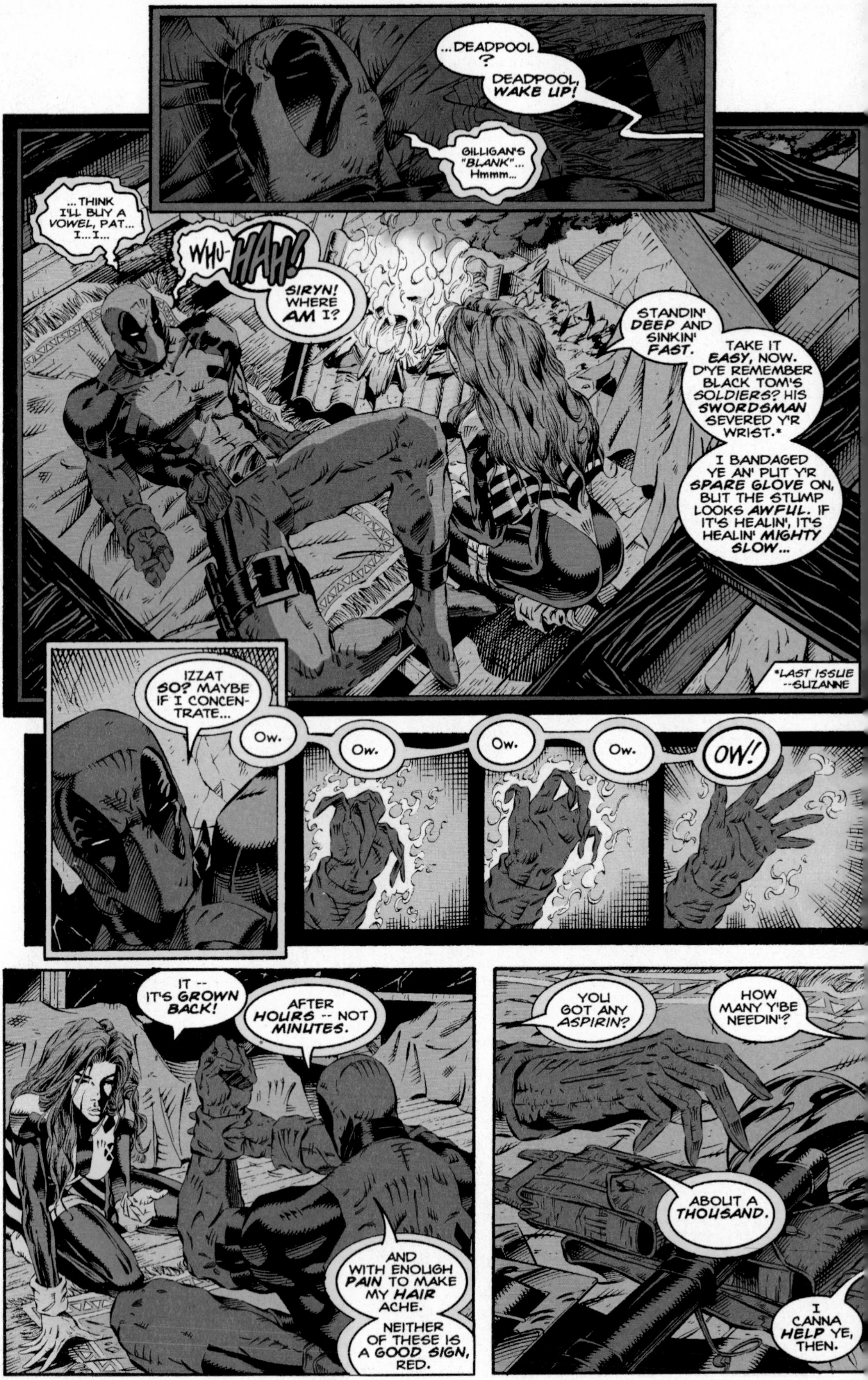
...DEADPOOL ?
DEADPOOL, WAKE UP!
GILLIGAN'S "BLANK"... Hmmm...
...THINK I'LL BUY A VOWEL, PAT... I...I...
WHU-HAH!
SIRYN! WHERE AM I?
STANDIN' DEEP AND SINKIN' FAST.
TAKE IT EASY, NOW. D'YE REMEMBER BLACK TOM'S SOLDIERS? HIS SWORDSMAN SEVERED Y'R WRIST.*
I BANDAGED YE AN' PUT Y'R SPARE GLOVE ON, BUT THE STUMP LOOKS AWFUL. IF IT'S HEALIN', IT'S HEALIN' MIGHTY SLOW...
*LAST ISSUE --SUZANNE
IZZAT SO? MAYBE IF I CONCEN-TRATE...
Ow.
Ow.
Ow.
Ow.
OW!
IT -- IT'S GROWN BACK!
AFTER HOURS -- NOT MINUTES.
AND WITH ENOUGH PAIN TO MAKE MY HAIR ACHE.
NEITHER OF THESE IS A GOOD SIGN, RED.
YOU GOT ANY ASPIRIN?
HOW MANY Y'BE NEEDIN'?
ABOUT A THOUSAND.
I CANNA HELP YE, THEN.

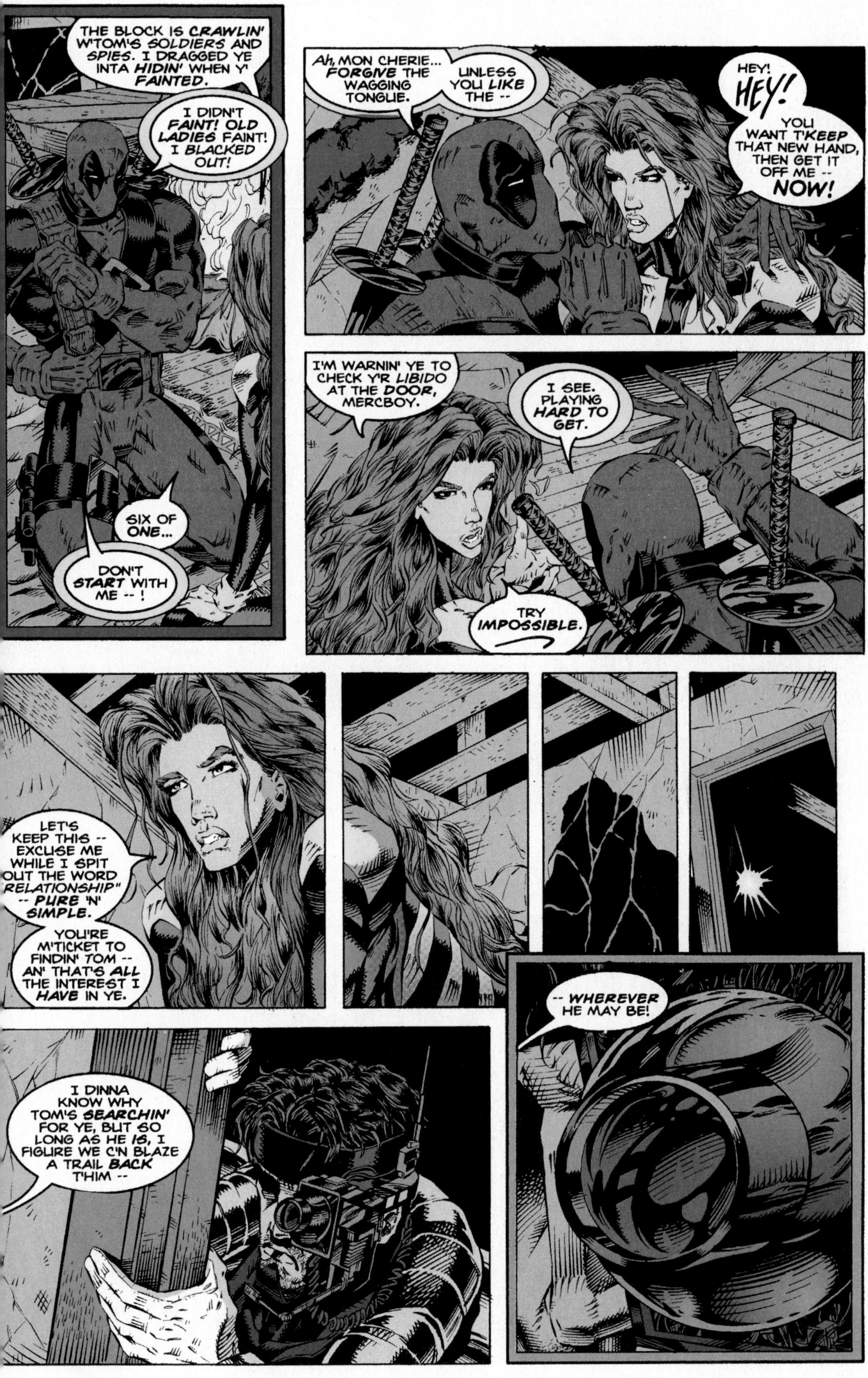
THE BLOCK IS CRAWLIN' W'TOM'S SOLDIERS AND SPIES. I DRAGGED YE INTA HIDIN' WHEN Y' FAINTED.
I DIDN'T FAINT! OLD LADIES FAINT! I BLACKED OUT!
SIX OF ONE...
DON'T START WITH ME -- !
Ah, MON CHERIE... FORGIVE THE WAGGING TONGUE.
UNLESS YOU LIKE THE --
HEY! HEY! YOU WANT T'KEEP THAT NEW HAND, THEN GET IT OFF ME -- NOW!
I'M WARNIN' YE TO CHECK Y'R LIBIDO AT THE DOOR, MERCBOY.
I SEE. PLAYING HARD TO GET.
TRY IMPOSSIBLE.
LET'S KEEP THIS -- EXCUSE ME WHILE I SPIT OUT THE WORD "RELATIONSHIP" -- PURE 'N' SIMPLE.
YOU'RE M'TICKET TO FINDIN' TOM -- AN' THAT'S ALL THE INTEREST I HAVE IN YE.
I DINNA KNOW WHY TOM'S SEARCHIN' FOR YE, BUT SO LONG AS HE IS, I FIGURE WE C'N BLAZE A TRAIL BACK T'HIM --
-- WHEREVER HE MAY BE!

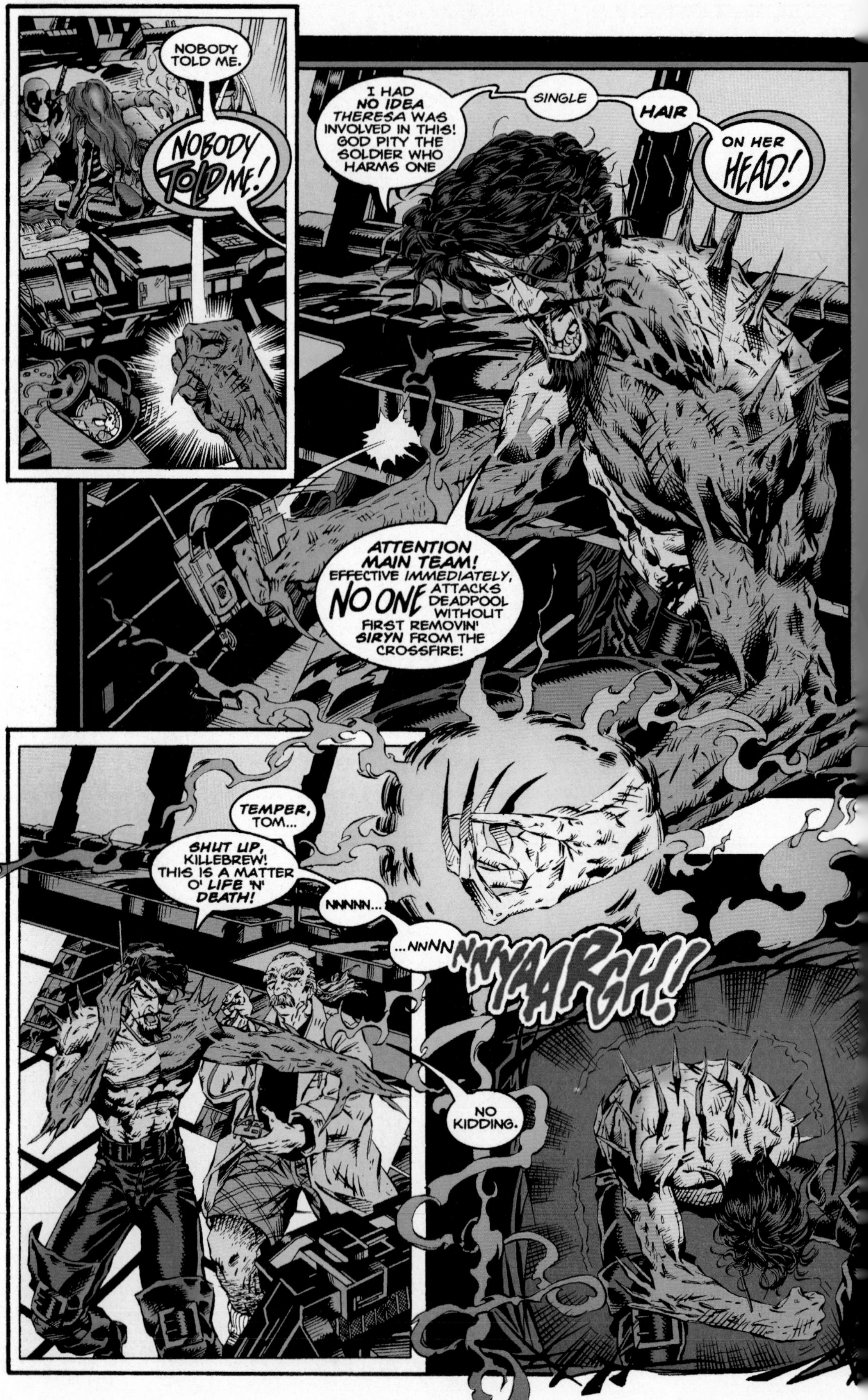

NOBODY TOLD ME.
NOBODY TOLD ME!
I HAD NO IDEA THERESA WAS INVOLVED IN THIS! GOD PITY THE SOLDIER WHO HARMS ONE
SINGLE
HAIR
ON HER HEAD!
ATTENTION MAIN TEAM! EFFECTIVE IMMEDIATELY, NO ONE ATTACKS DEADPOOL WITHOUT FIRST REMOVIN' SIRYN FROM THE CROSSFIRE!
TEMPER, TOM...
SHUT UP, KILLEBREW! THIS IS A MATTER O' LIFE 'N' DEATH!
NNNNN...
...NNNNNNYAARGH!!
NO KIDDING.

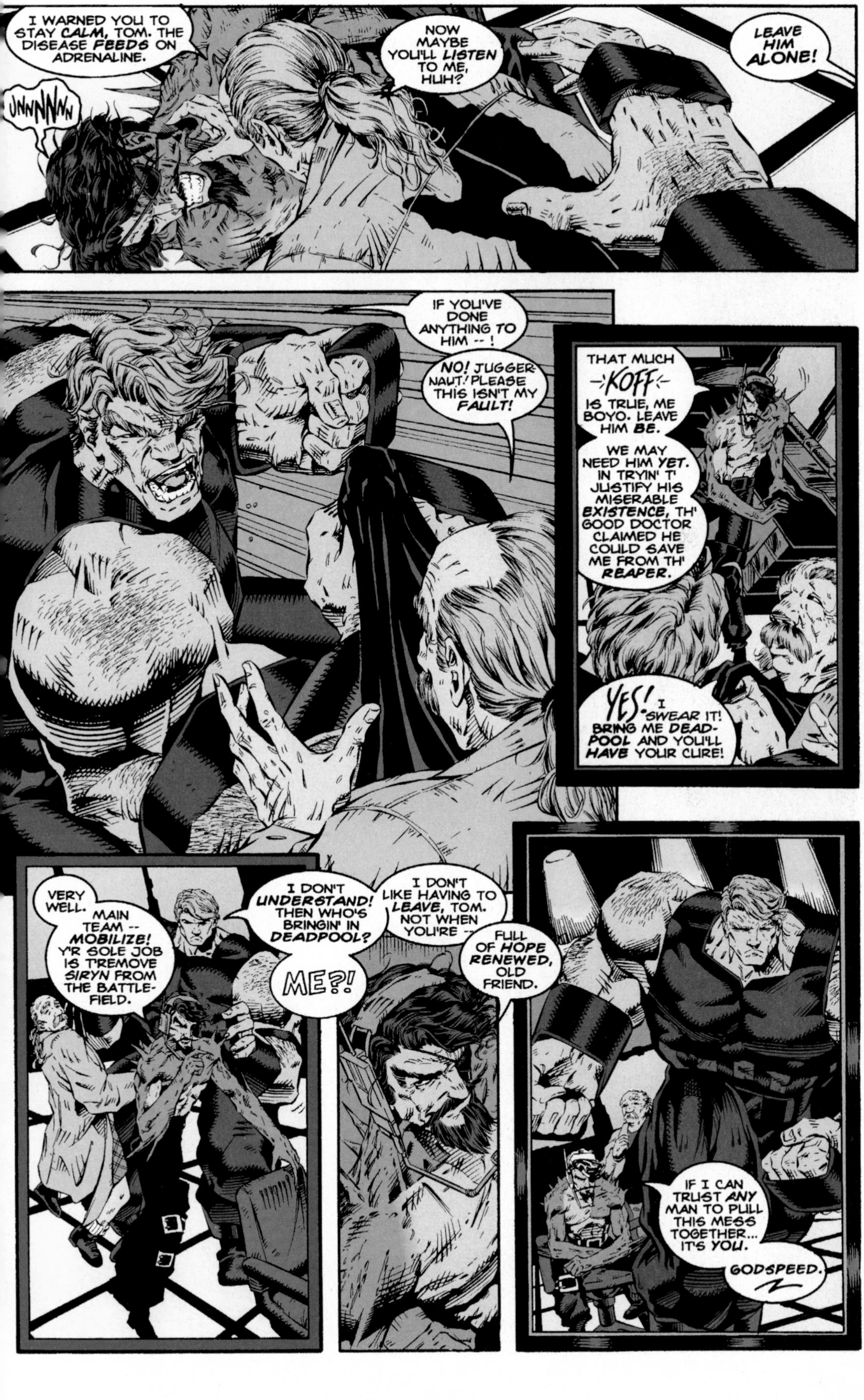
I WARNED YOU TO STAY CALM, TOM. THE DISEASE FEEDS ON ADRENALINE.
NOW MAYBE YOU'LL LISTEN TO ME, HUH?
LEAVE HIM ALONE!
UNNNNNN
IF YOU'VE DONE ANYTHING TO HIM -- !
NO! JUGGERNAUT! PLEASE THIS ISN'T MY FAULT!
THAT MUCH -KOFF- IS TRUE, ME BOYO. LEAVE HIM BE.
WE MAY NEED HIM YET. IN TRYIN' T' JUSTIFY HIS MISERABLE EXISTENCE, TH' GOOD DOCTOR CLAIMED HE COULD SAVE ME FROM TH' REAPER.
YES! I SWEAR IT! BRING ME DEADPOOL AND YOU'LL HAVE YOUR CURE!
VERY WELL. MAIN TEAM -- MOBILIZE! Y'R SOLE JOB IS T'REMOVE SIRYN FROM THE BATTLEFIELD.
I DON'T UNDERSTAND! THEN WHO'S BRINGIN' IN DEADPOOL?
ME?!
I DON'T LIKE HAVING TO LEAVE, TOM. NOT WHEN YOU'RE --
FULL OF HOPE RENEWED, OLD FRIEND.
IF I CAN TRUST ANY MAN TO PULL THIS MESS TOGETHER... IT'S YOU.
GODSPEED.

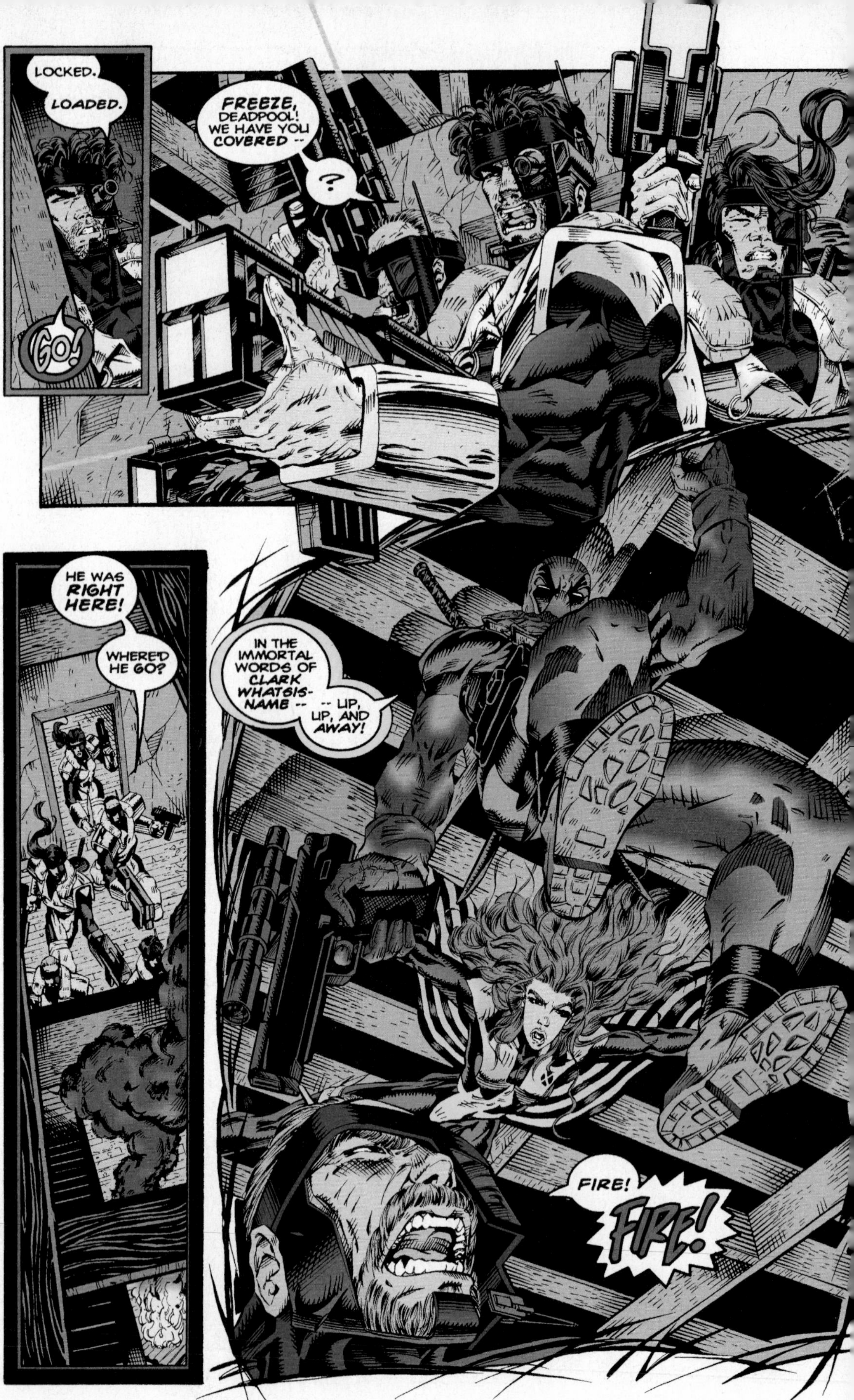

LOCKED.
LOADED.
GO!
FREEZE, DEADPOOL! WE HAVE YOU COVERED --
?
HE WAS RIGHT HERE!
WHERE'D HE GO?
IN THE IMMORTAL WORDS OF CLARK WHATSIS-NAME --
-- UP, UP, AND AWAY!
FIRE!
FIRE!

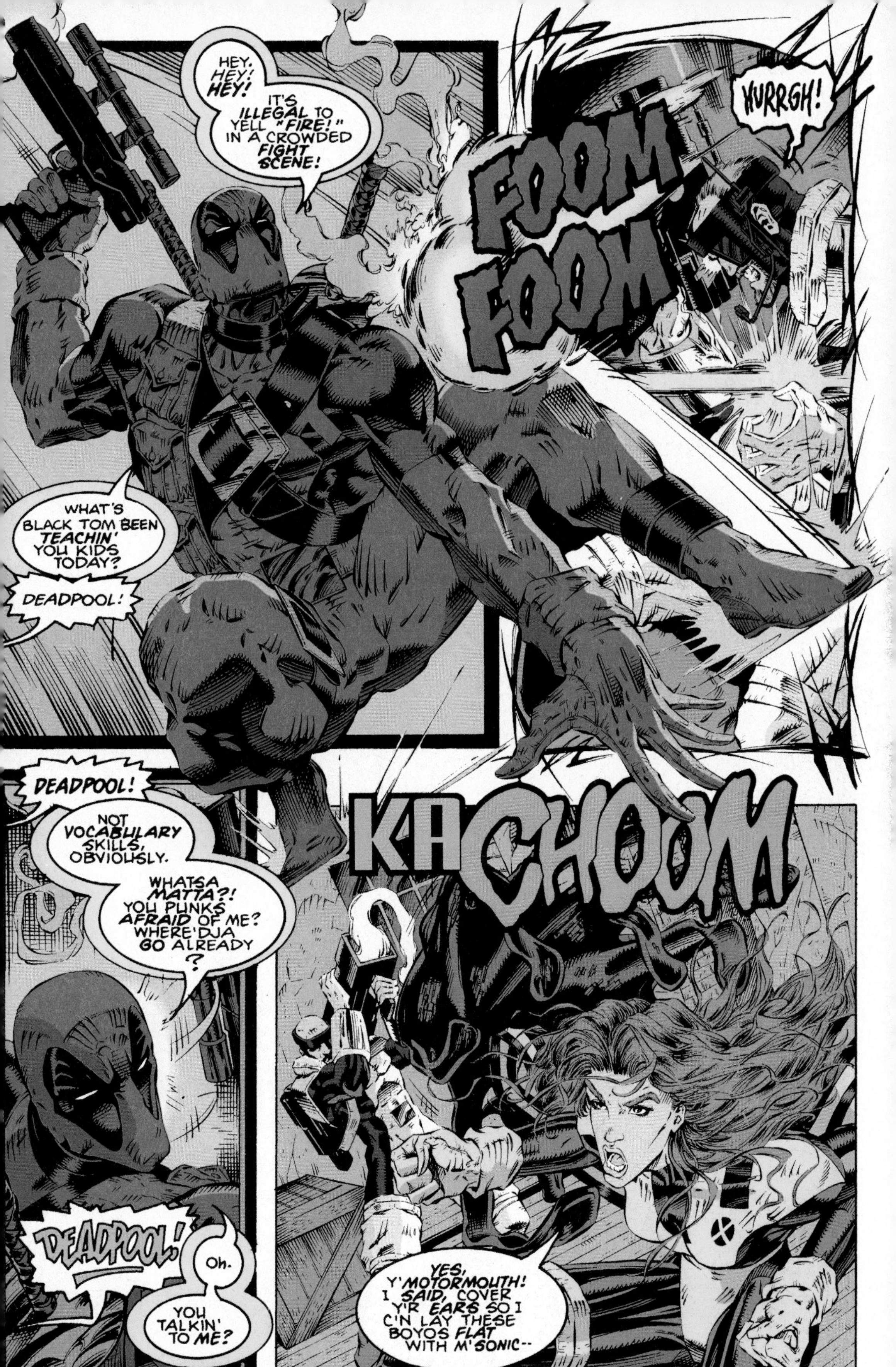
HEY. HEY! HEY! IT'S ILLEGAL TO YELL "FIRE!" IN A CROWDED FIGHT SCENE!
HURRGH!
FOOM FOOM
WHAT'S BLACK TOM BEEN TEACHIN' YOU KIDS TODAY?
DEADPOOL!
DEADPOOL!
NOT VOCABULARY SKILLS, OBVIOUSLY.
WHATSA MATTA?! YOU PUNKS AFRAID OF ME? WHERE'DJA GO ALREADY ?
KACHOOM
DEADPOOL!
Oh.
YOU TALKIN' TO ME?
YES, Y'MOTORMOUTH! I SAID, COVER Y'R EARS SO I C'N LAY THESE BOYOS FLAT WITH M'SONIC--

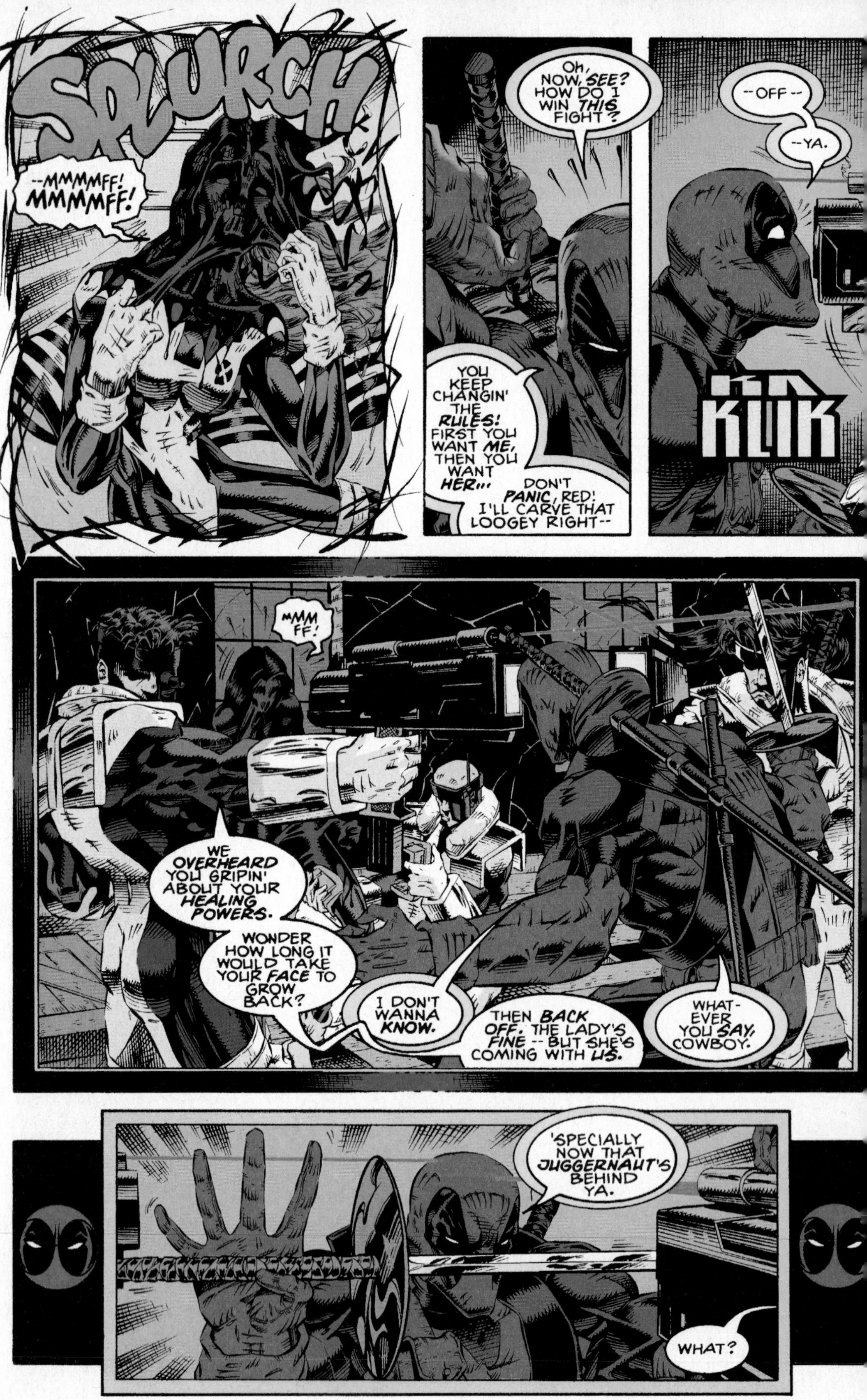
SPLURCH
--MMMMFF! MMMMFF!
Oh, NOW, SEE? HOW DO I WIN THIS FIGHT?
YOU KEEP CHANGIN' THE RULES! FIRST YOU WANT ME, THEN YOU WANT HER...
DON'T PANIC, RED! I'LL CARVE THAT LOOGEY RIGHT--
--OFF--
--YA.
KLIK
MMMFF!
WE OVERHEARD YOU GRIPIN' ABOUT YOUR HEALING POWERS.
WONDER HOW LONG IT WOULD TAKE YOUR FACE TO GROW BACK?
I DON'T WANNA KNOW.
THEN BACK OFF. THE LADY'S FINE -- BUT SHE'S COMING WITH US.
WHAT-EVER YOU SAY, COWBOY.
'SPECIALLY NOW THAT JUGGERNAUT'S BEHIND YA.
WHAT?

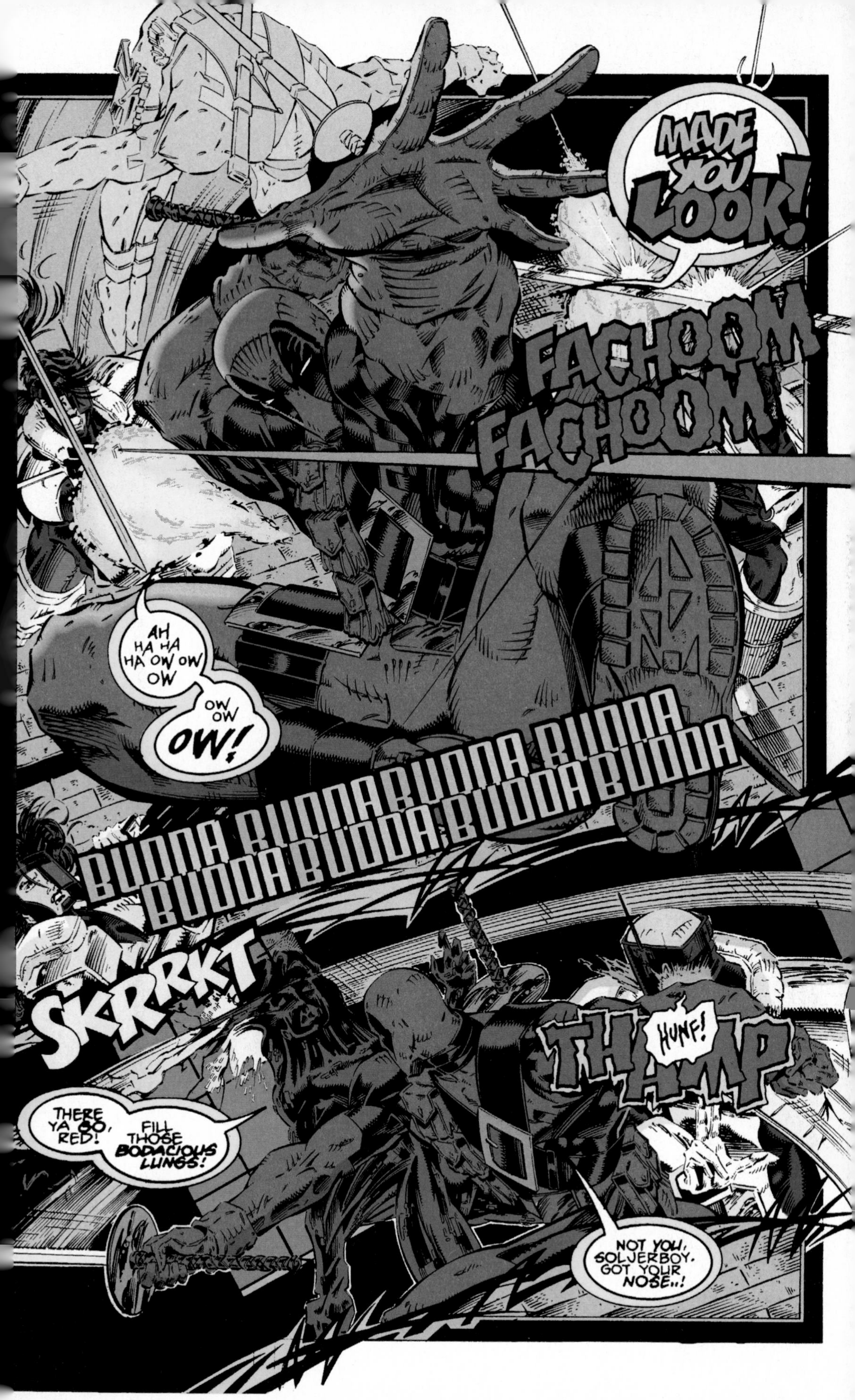
MADE YOU LOOK!
FACHOOM FACHOOM
AH HA HA HA OW OW OW
OW OW OW!
BUDDA BUDDA BUDDA BUDDA BUDDA BUDDA BUDDA BUDDA
SKRRKT
THAMP
HUNF!
THERE YA GO, RED!
FILL THOSE BODACIOUS LUNGS!
NOT YOU, SOLJERBOY. GOT YOUR NOSE..!

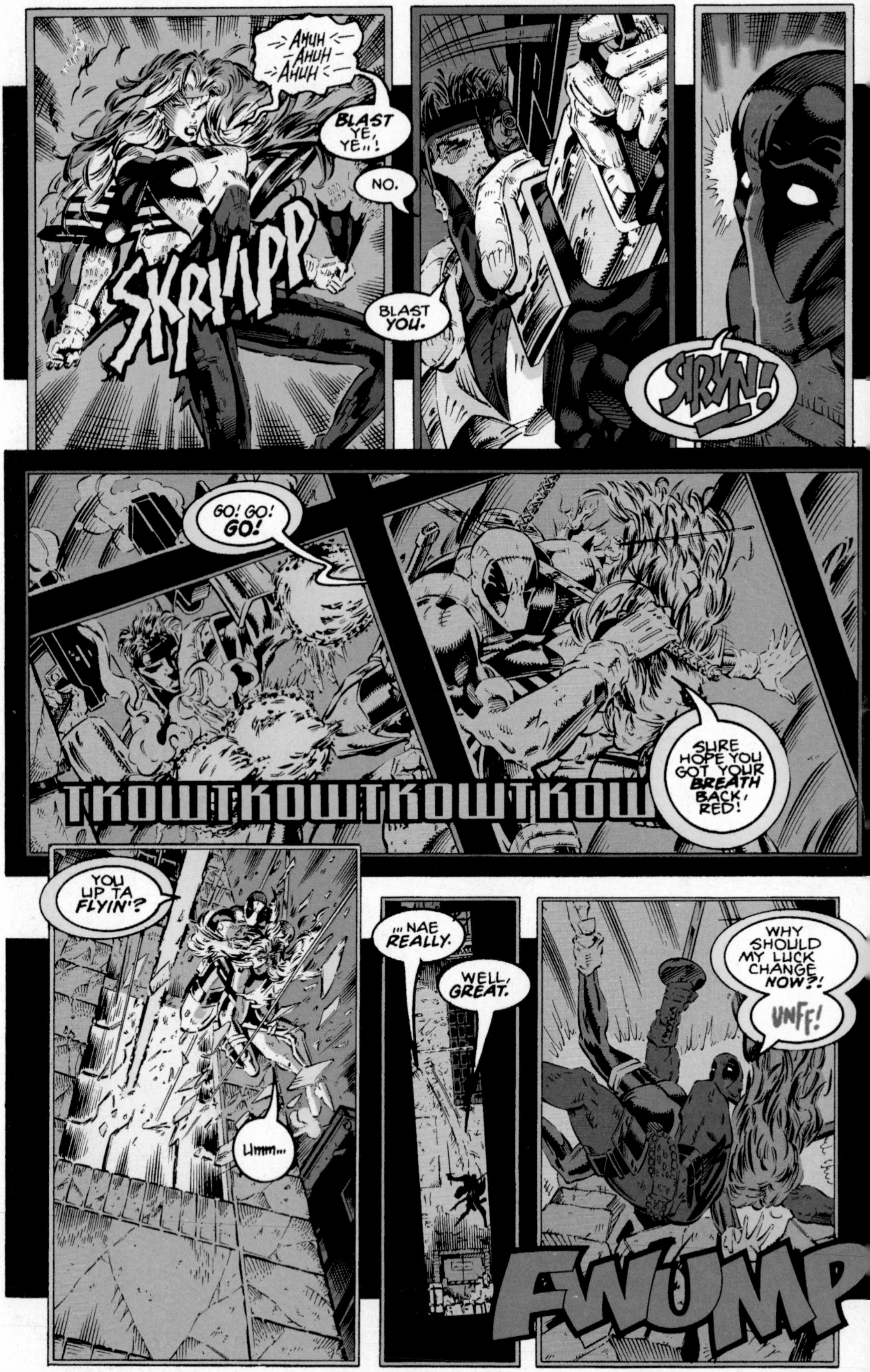

AHUH AHUH AHUH
BLAST YE, YE..!
NO.
SKRIIPP
BLAST YOU.
SRYN!
GO! GO! GO!
TKOWTKOWTKOWTKOW
SURE HOPE YOU GOT YOUR BREATH BACK, RED!
YOU UP TA FLYIN'?
Umm...
...NAE REALLY.
WELL, GREAT.
WHY SHOULD MY LUCK CHANGE NOW?!
UNFF!
FWUMP

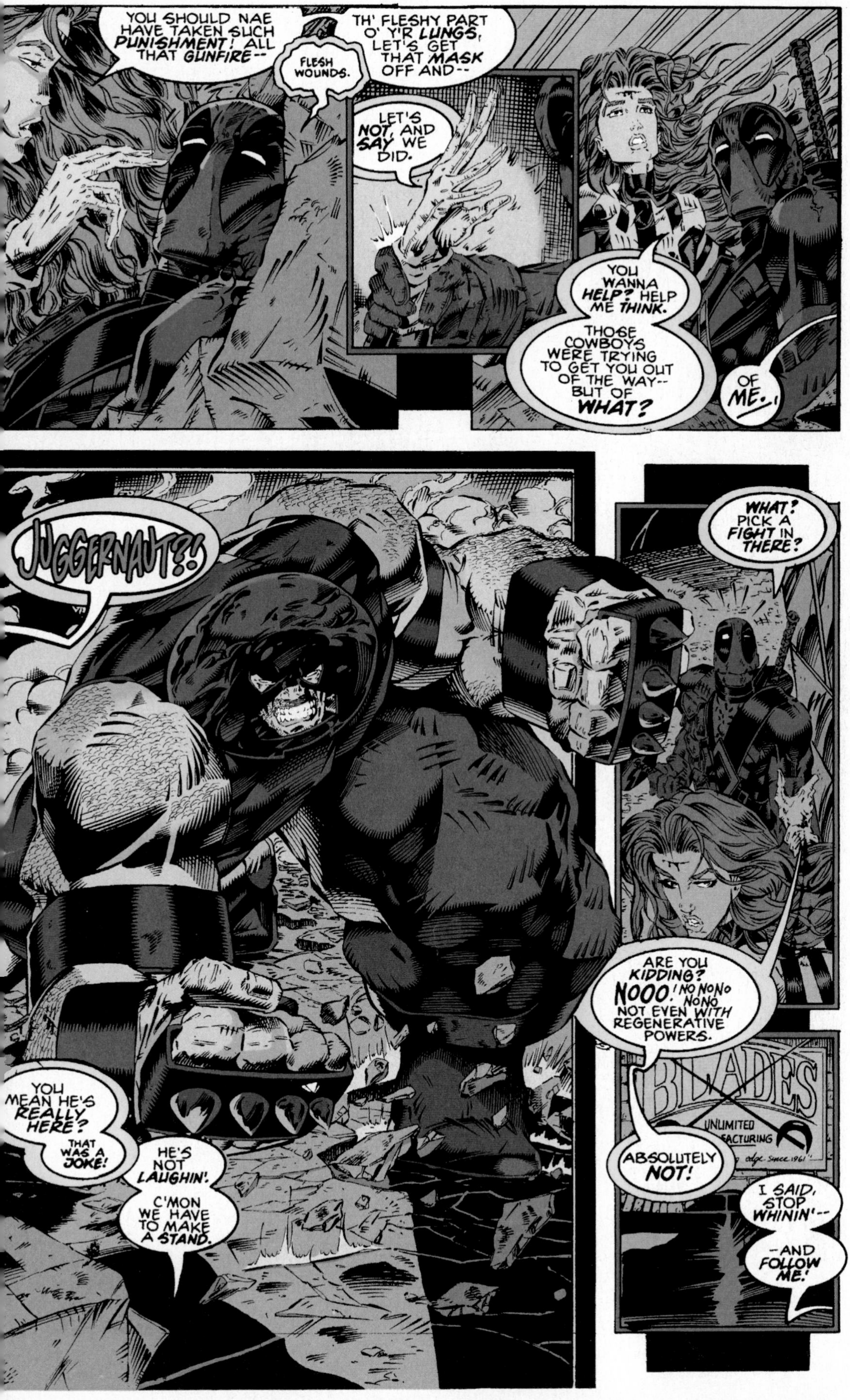
YOU SHOULD NAE HAVE TAKEN SUCH PUNISHMENT! ALL THAT GUNFIRE--
FLESH WOUNDS.
TH' FLESHY PART O' Y'R LUNGS, LET'S GET THAT MASK OFF AND--
LET'S NOT, AND SAY WE DID.
YOU WANNA HELP? HELP ME THINK.
THOSE COWBOYS WERE TRYING TO GET YOU OUT OF THE WAY-- BUT OF WHAT?
OF ME..!
JUGGERNAUT?!
WHAT? PICK A FIGHT IN THERE?
ARE YOU KIDDING? NOOO! NO NO NO NO NO NOT EVEN WITH REGENERATIVE POWERS.
BLADES
UNLIMITED
FACTURING
edge since 1961
ABSOLUTELY NOT!
YOU MEAN HE'S REALLY HERE?
THAT WAS A JOKE!
HE'S NOT LAUGHIN'.
C'MON WE HAVE TO MAKE A STAND.
I SAID, STOP WHININ'--
--AND FOLLOW ME!

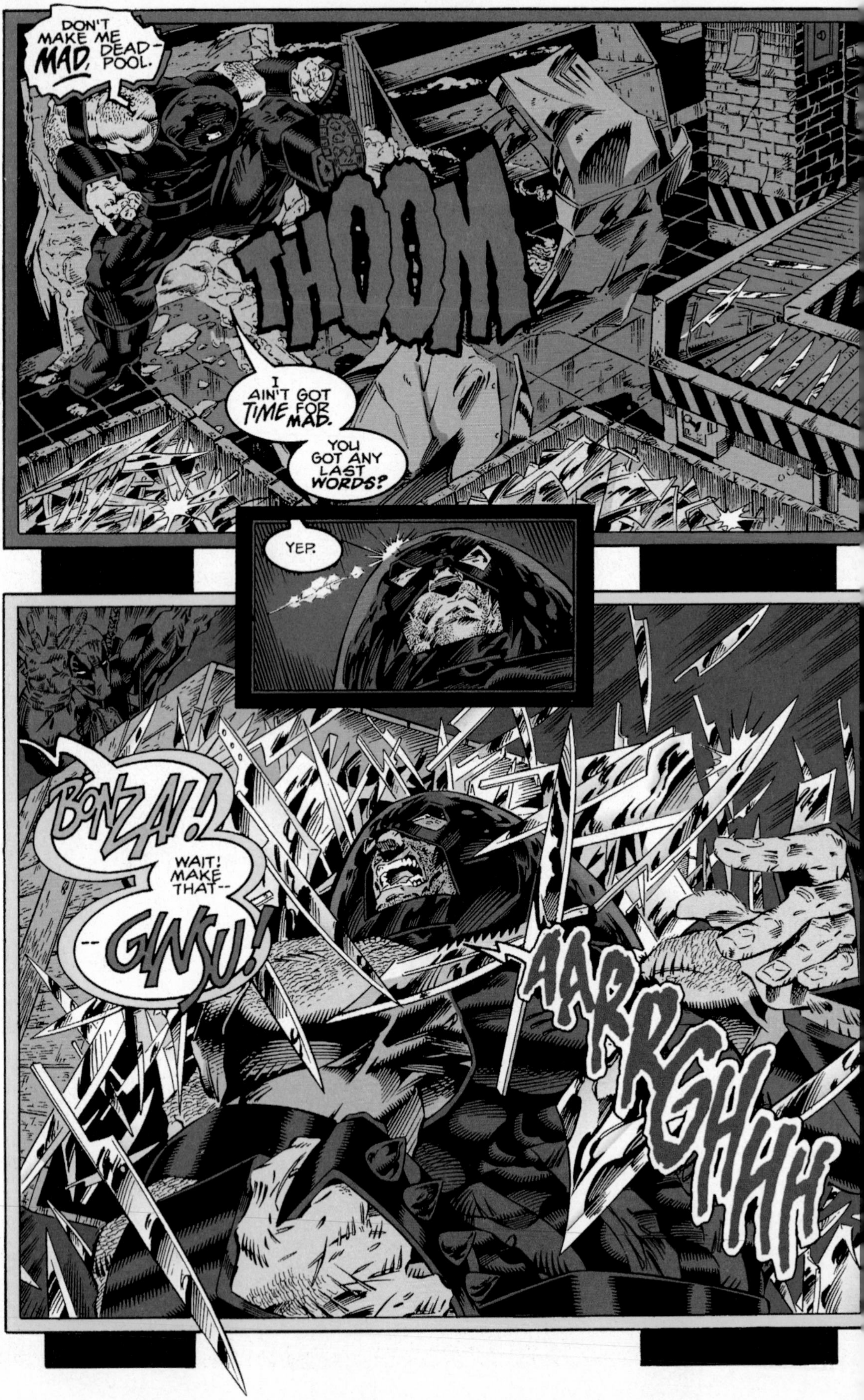

DON'T MAKE ME MAD, DEAD-POOL.
THOOM
I AIN'T GOT TIME FOR MAD.
YOU GOT ANY LAST WORDS?
YEP.
BONZAI!
WAIT! MAKE THAT--
--GINSU!
AARRGHHH

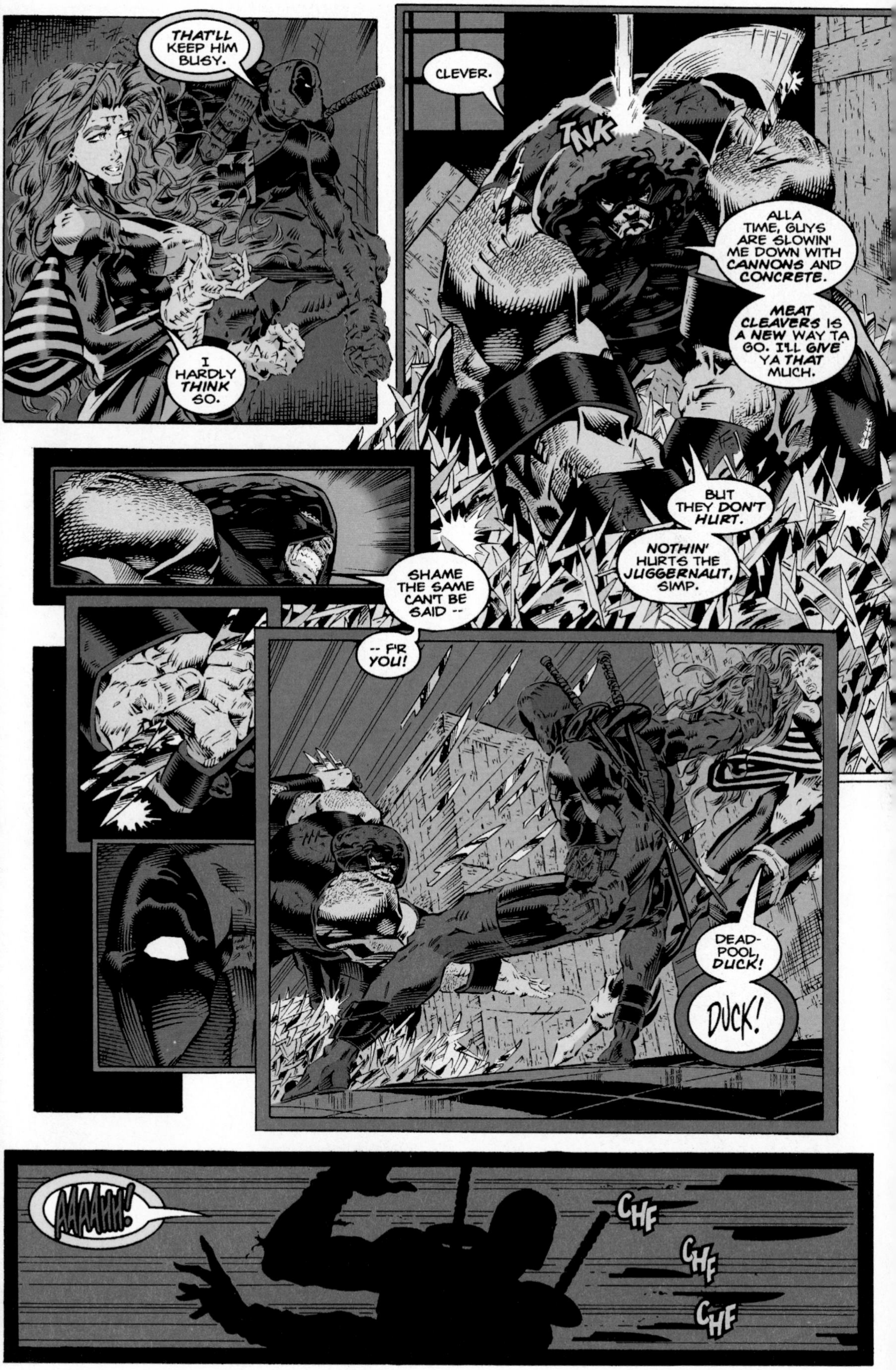
THAT'LL KEEP HIM BUSY.
I HARDLY THINK SO.
CLEVER.
TNK
ALLA TIME, GUYS ARE SLOWIN' ME DOWN WITH CANNONS AND CONCRETE.
MEAT CLEAVERS IS A NEW WAY TA GO. I'LL GIVE YA THAT MUCH.
BUT THEY DON'T HURT.
NOTHIN' HURTS THE JUGGERNAUT, SIMP.
SHAME THE SAME CAN'T BE SAID --
-- F'R YOU!
DEAD-POOL, DUCK!
DUCK!
AAAAHH!
CHF
CHF
CHF

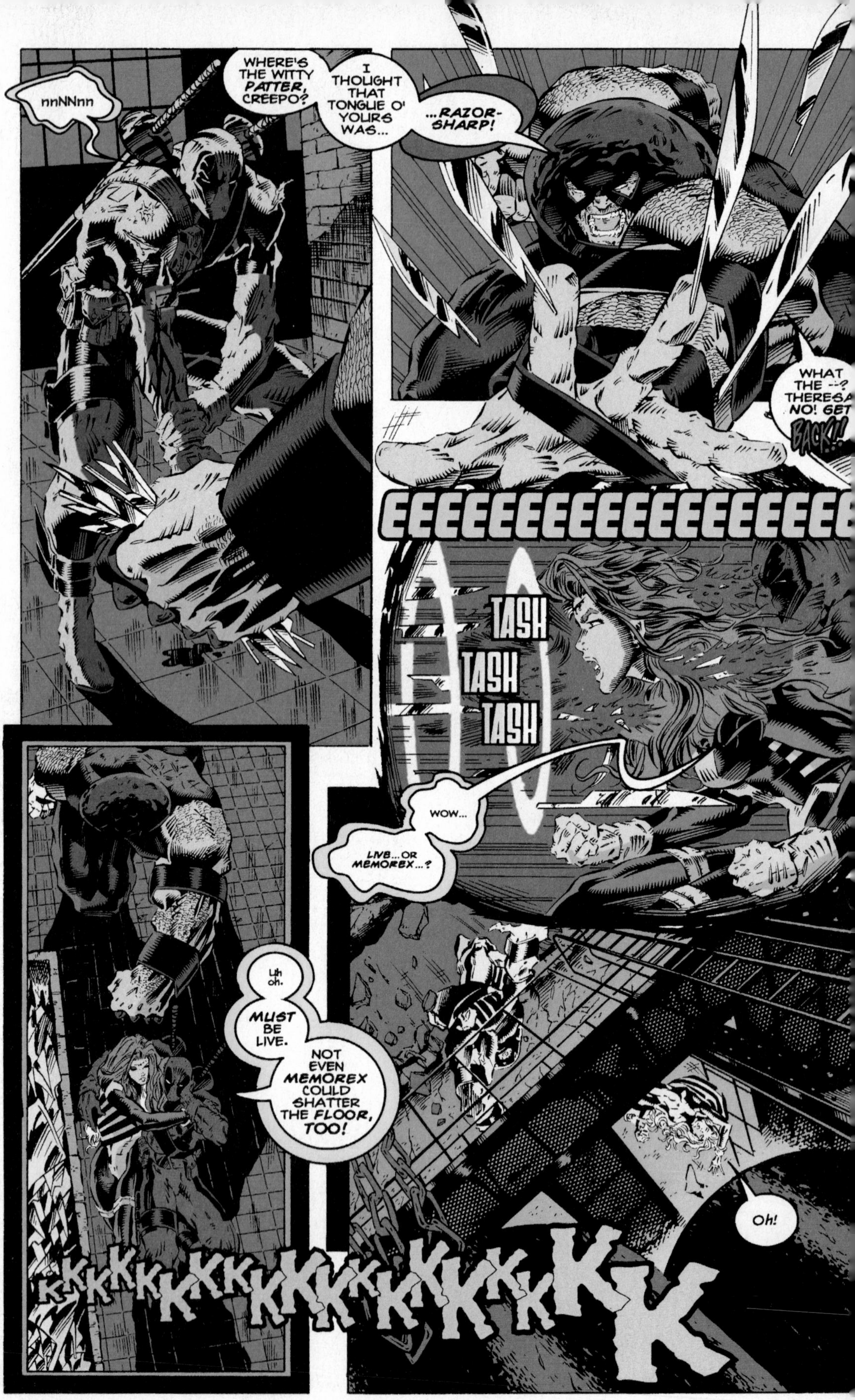

nnNNnn
WHERE'S THE WITTY PATTER, CREEPO?
I THOUGHT THAT TONGUE O' YOURS WAS...
...RAZOR-SHARP!
WHAT THE --? THERESA! NO! GET BACK!!
EEEEEEEEEEEEEEEEEE
TASH TASH TASH
WOW...
LIVE...OR MEMOREX...?
Uh oh.
MUST BE LIVE.
NOT EVEN MEMOREX COULD SHATTER THE FLOOR, TOO!
Oh!
KKKKKKKKKKKKKKKKKKKKK

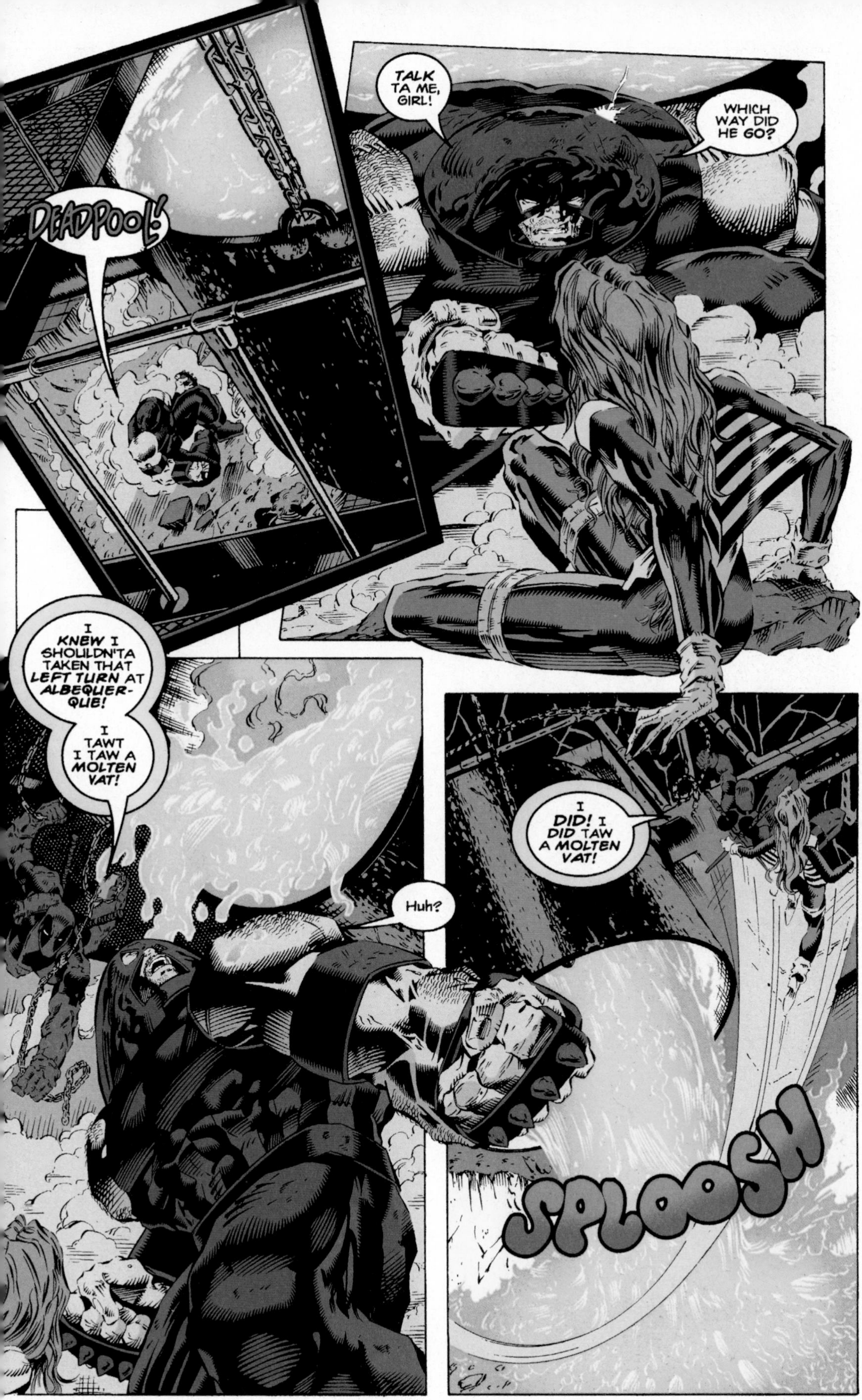
DEADPOOL!
TALK TA ME, GIRL!
WHICH WAY DID HE GO?
I KNEW I SHOULDN'TA TAKEN THAT LEFT TURN AT ALBEQUERQUE!
I TAWT I TAW A MOLTEN VAT!
Huh?
I DID! I DID TAW A MOLTEN VAT!
SPLOOSH

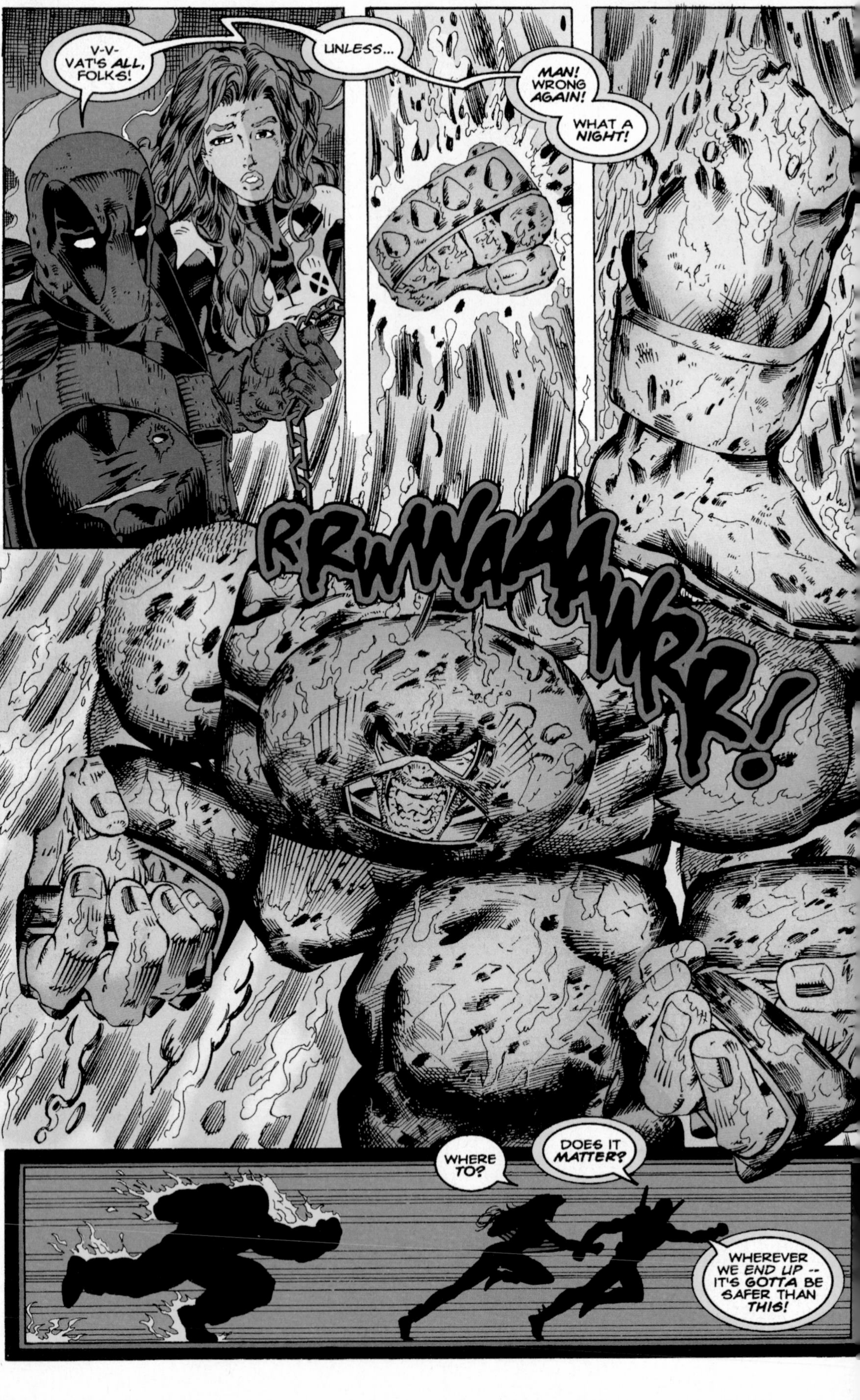

V-V-VAT'S ALL, FOLKS!
UNLESS...
MAN! WRONG AGAIN!
WHAT A NIGHT!
RRWAAAWRR!
WHERE TO?
DOES IT MATTER?
WHEREVER WE END UP -- IT'S GOTTA BE SAFER THAN THIS!

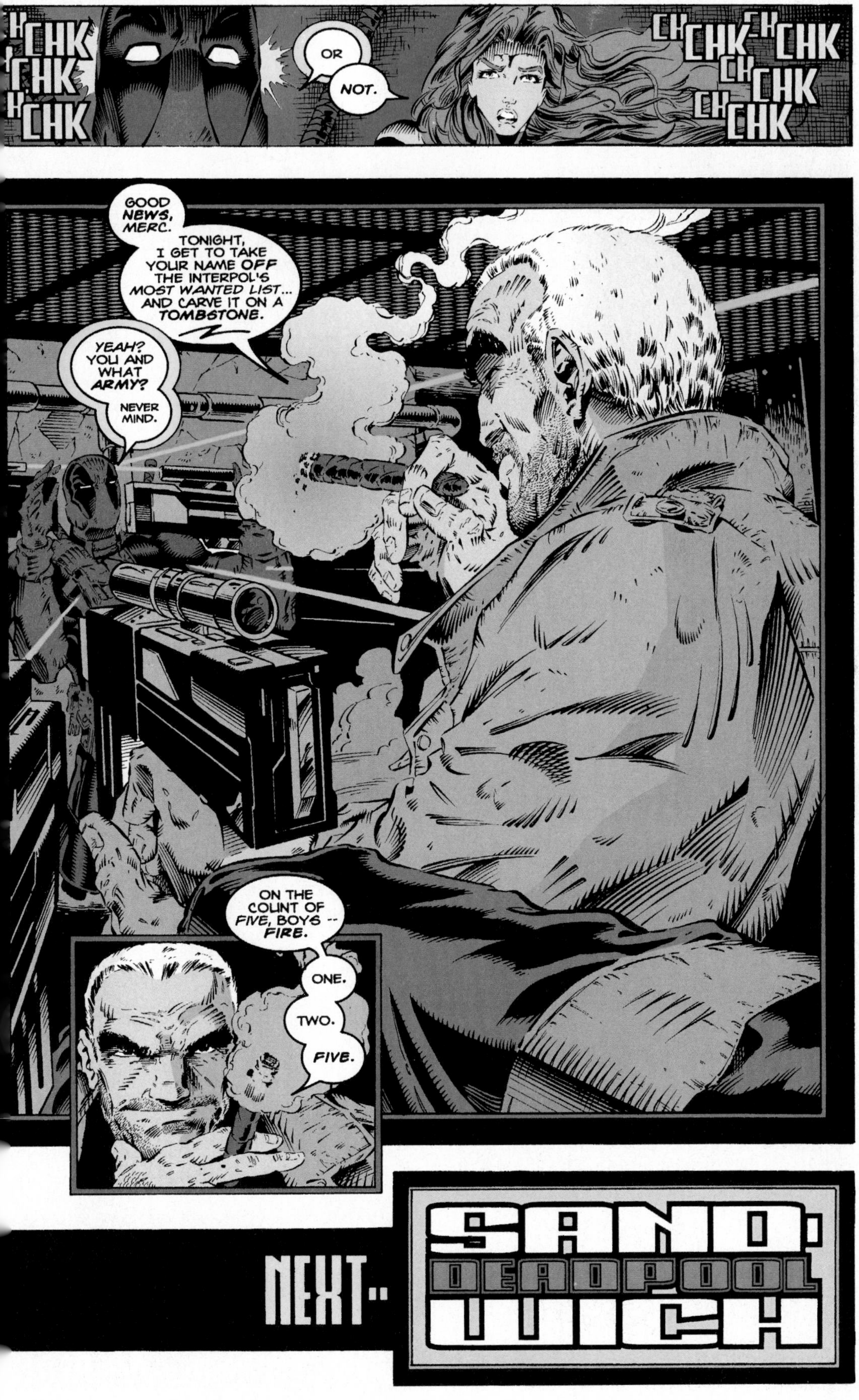
CHK
CHK
CHK
OR
NOT.
CHCHK CHCHK
CHCHK
CHCHK
GOOD NEWS, MERC.
TONIGHT, I GET TO TAKE YOUR NAME OFF THE INTERPOL'S MOST WANTED LIST... AND CARVE IT ON A TOMBSTONE.
YEAH? YOU AND WHAT ARMY?
NEVER MIND.
ON THE COUNT OF FIVE, BOYS -- FIRE.
ONE.
TWO.
FIVE.
NEXT..
SAND:
DEADPOOL
WICH

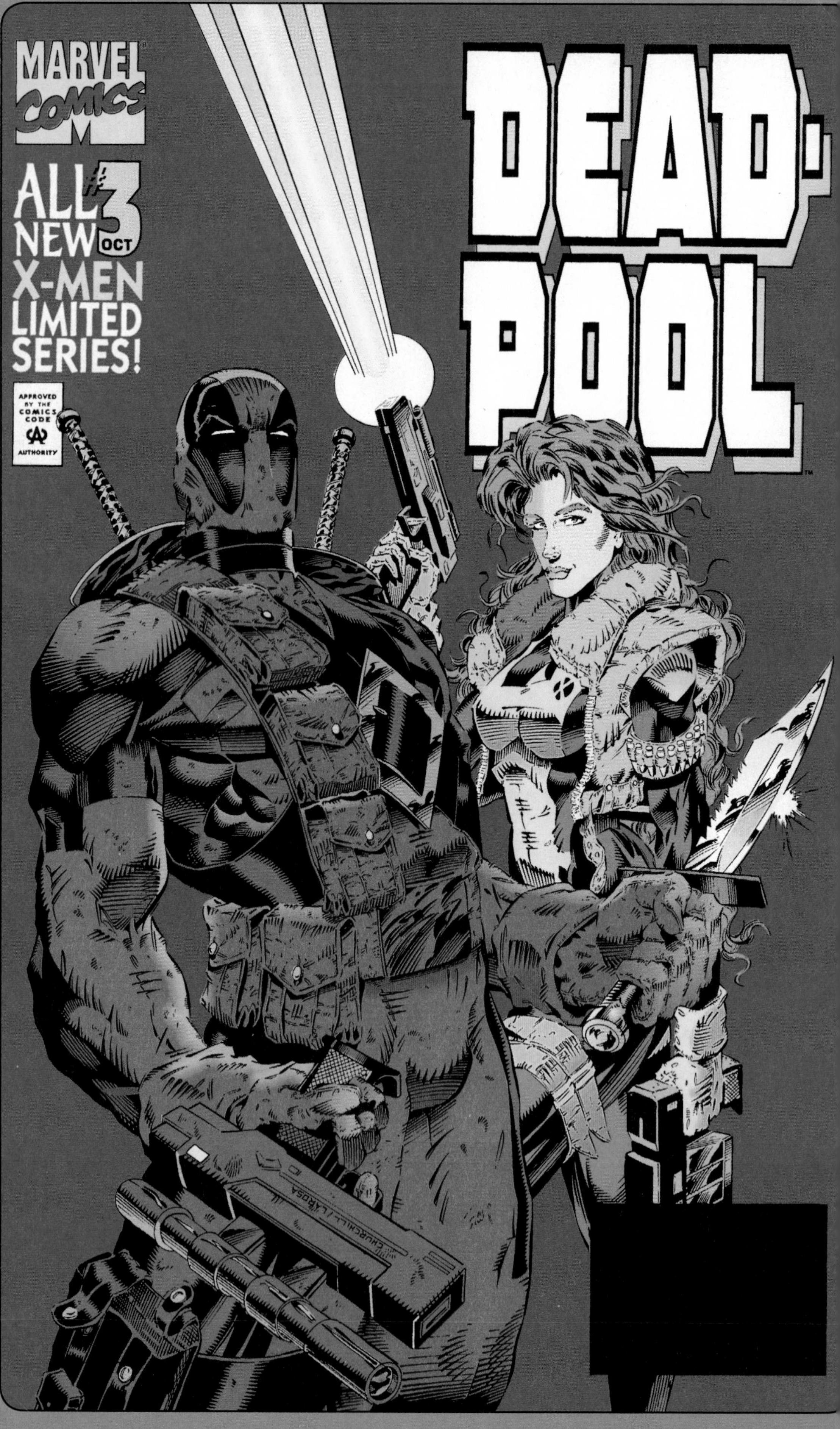
MARVEL COMICS
ALL NEW #3 OCT
X-MEN LIMITED SERIES!
APPROVED BY THE COMICS CODE AUTHORITY
DEAD-POOL™
CHURCHILL/LAROSA

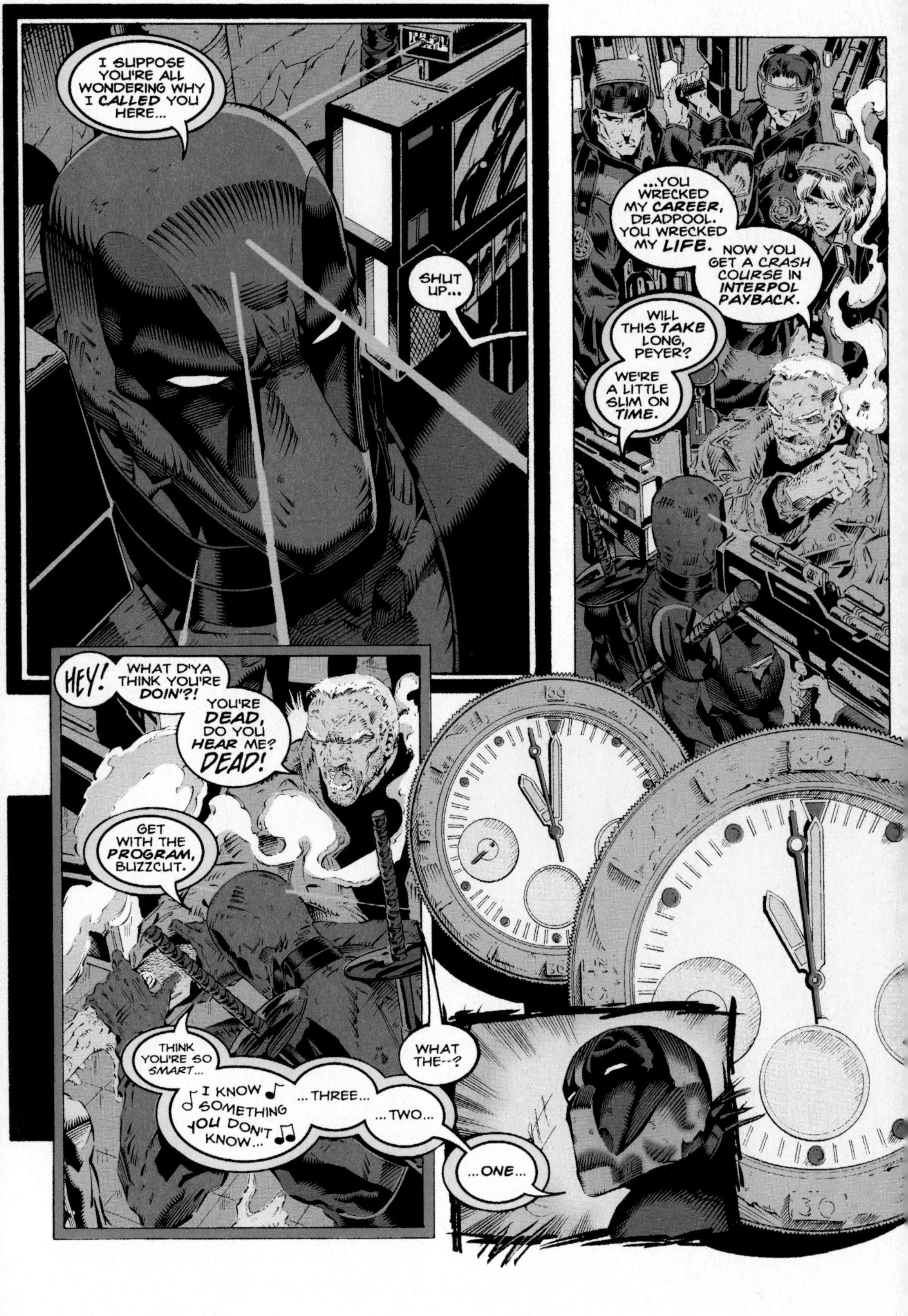
I SUPPOSE YOU'RE ALL WONDERING WHY I CALLED YOU HERE...
SHUT UP...
...YOU WRECKED MY CAREER, DEADPOOL. YOU WRECKED MY LIFE.
NOW YOU GET A CRASH COURSE IN INTERPOL PAYBACK.
WILL THIS TAKE LONG, PEYER?
WE'RE A LITTLE SLIM ON TIME.
HEY!
WHAT D'YA THINK YOU'RE DOIN'?!
YOU'RE DEAD, DO YOU HEAR ME? DEAD!
GET WITH THE PROGRAM, BUZZCUT.
THINK YOU'RE SO SMART...
I KNOW SOMETHING YOU DON'T KNOW...
WHAT THE--?
...THREE...
...TWO...
...ONE...

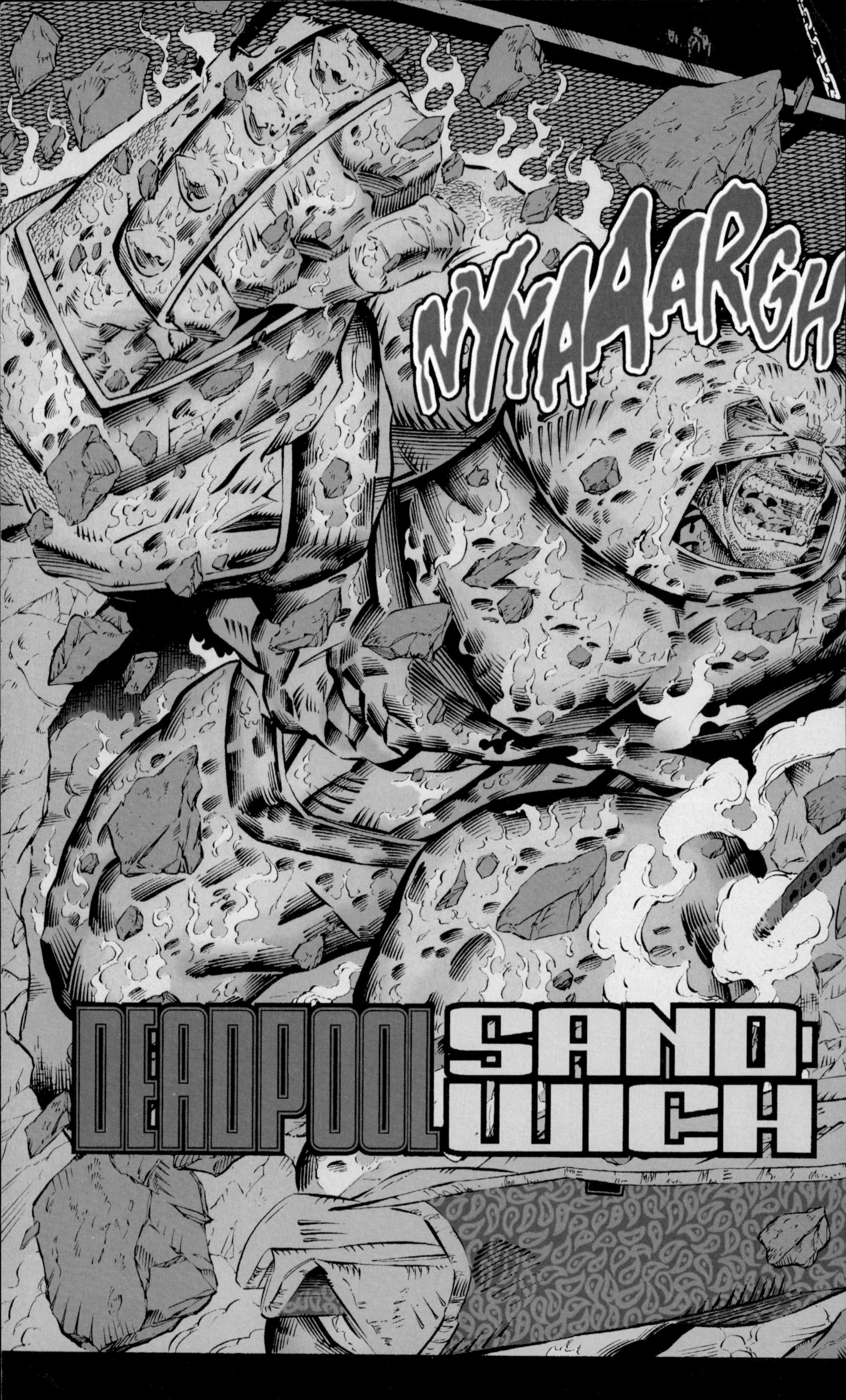
NYYAAARGH
DEADPOOL
SAND-WICH

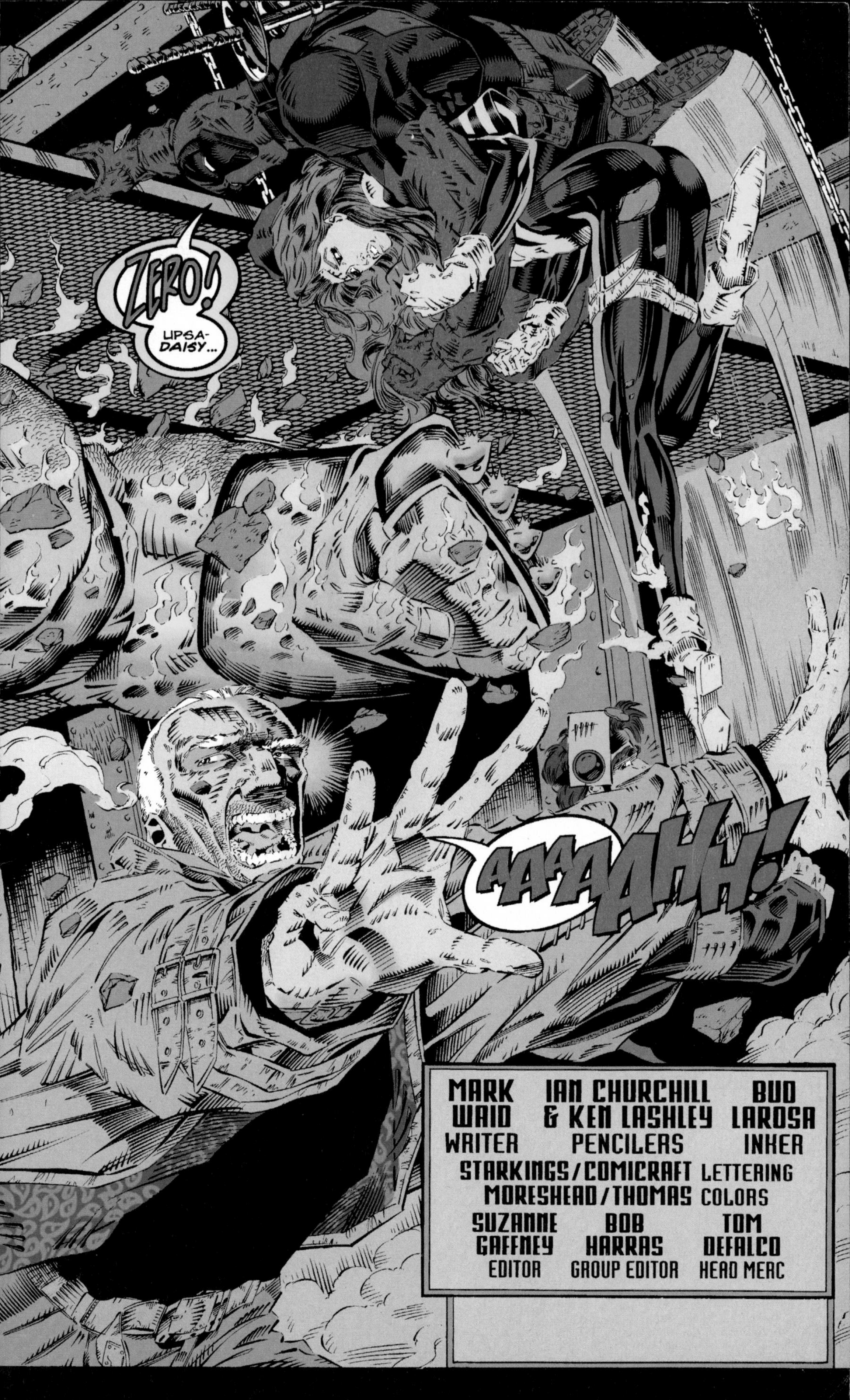
ZERO!
UPSA-DAISY...
AAAAAHH!

MARK WAID WRITER
IAN CHURCHILL & KEN LASHLEY PENCILERS
BUD LAROSA INKER
STARKINGS/COMICRAFT LETTERING
MORESHEAD/THOMAS COLORS
SUZANNE GAFFNEY EDITOR
BOB HARRAS GROUP EDITOR
TOM DEFALCO HEAD MERC

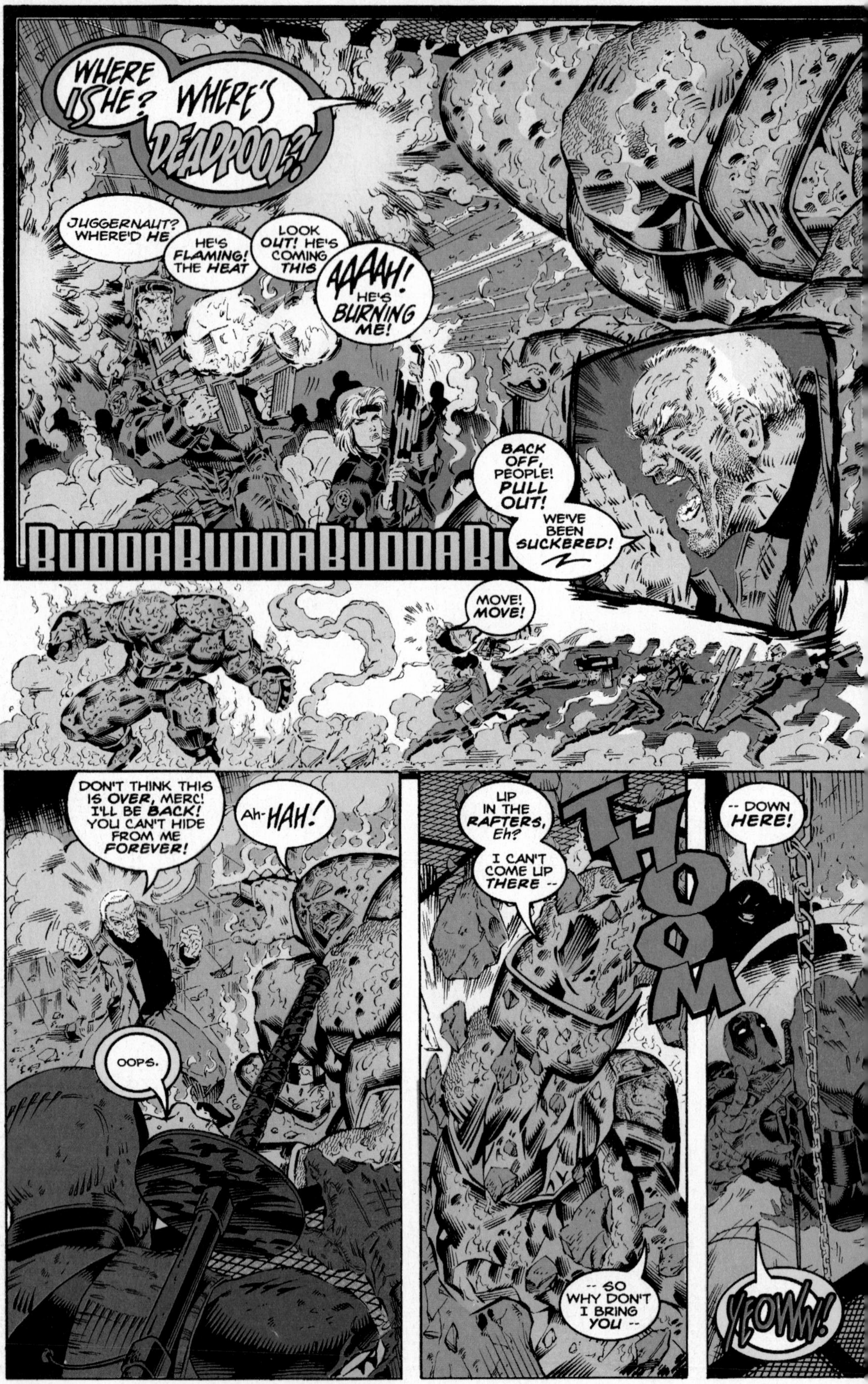
WHERE IS HE? WHERE'S DEADPOOL?!
JUGGERNAUT? WHERE'D HE
HE'S FLAMING! THE HEAT
LOOK OUT! HE'S COMING THIS
AAAAH! HE'S BURNING ME!
BUDDABUDDABUDDABU
BACK OFF, PEOPLE! PULL OUT!
WE'VE BEEN SUCKERED!
MOVE! MOVE!
DON'T THINK THIS IS OVER, MERC! I'LL BE BACK! YOU CAN'T HIDE FROM ME FOREVER!
Ah-HAH!
OOPS.
UP IN THE RAFTERS, Eh?
I CAN'T COME UP THERE --
-- SO WHY DON'T I BRING YOU --
THOOOM
-- DOWN HERE!
YEOWW!

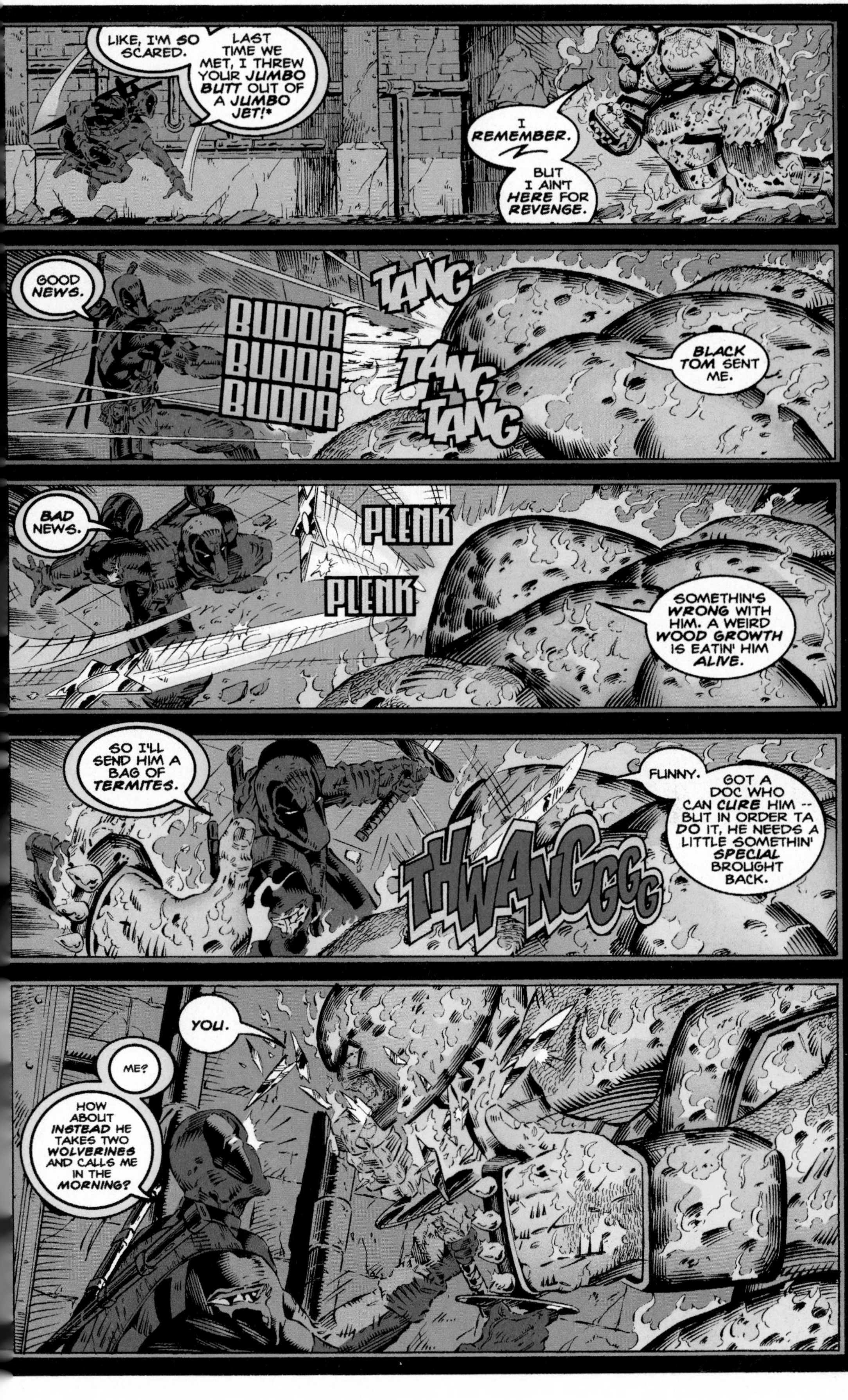
LIKE, I'M SO SCARED.
LAST TIME WE MET, I THREW YOUR JUMBO BUTT OUT OF A JUMBO JET!*
I REMEMBER.
BUT I AIN'T HERE FOR REVENGE.
GOOD NEWS.
BUDDA BUDDA BUDDA
TANG
TANG TANG TANG
BLACK TOM SENT ME.
BAD NEWS.
PLENK
PLENK
SOMETHIN'S WRONG WITH HIM. A WEIRD WOOD GROWTH IS EATIN' HIM ALIVE.
SO I'LL SEND HIM A BAG OF TERMITES.
FUNNY.
GOT A DOC WHO CAN CURE HIM -- BUT IN ORDER TA DO IT, HE NEEDS A LITTLE SOMETHIN' SPECIAL BROUGHT BACK.
THWANGGGG
YOU.
ME?
HOW ABOUT INSTEAD HE TAKES TWO WOLVERINES AND CALLS ME IN THE MORNING?

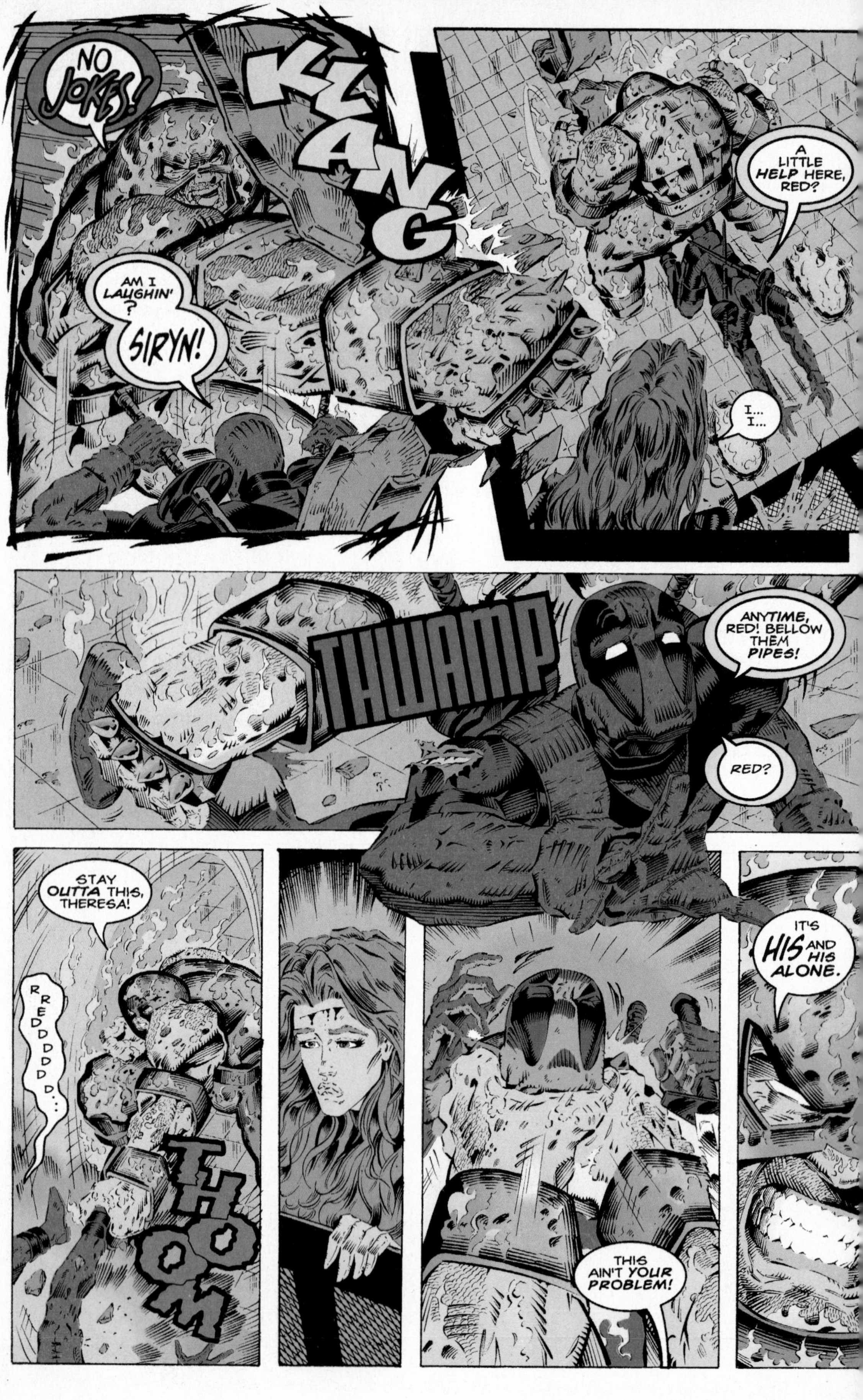
NO JOKES!
KLANG
AM I LAUGHIN'? SIRYN!
A LITTLE HELP HERE, RED?
I... I...
THWAMP
ANYTIME, RED! BELLOW THEM PIPES!
RED?
STAY OUTTA THIS, THERESA!
RREDDDDD D...
THOOM
THIS AIN'T YOUR PROBLEM!
IT'S HIS AND HIS ALONE.

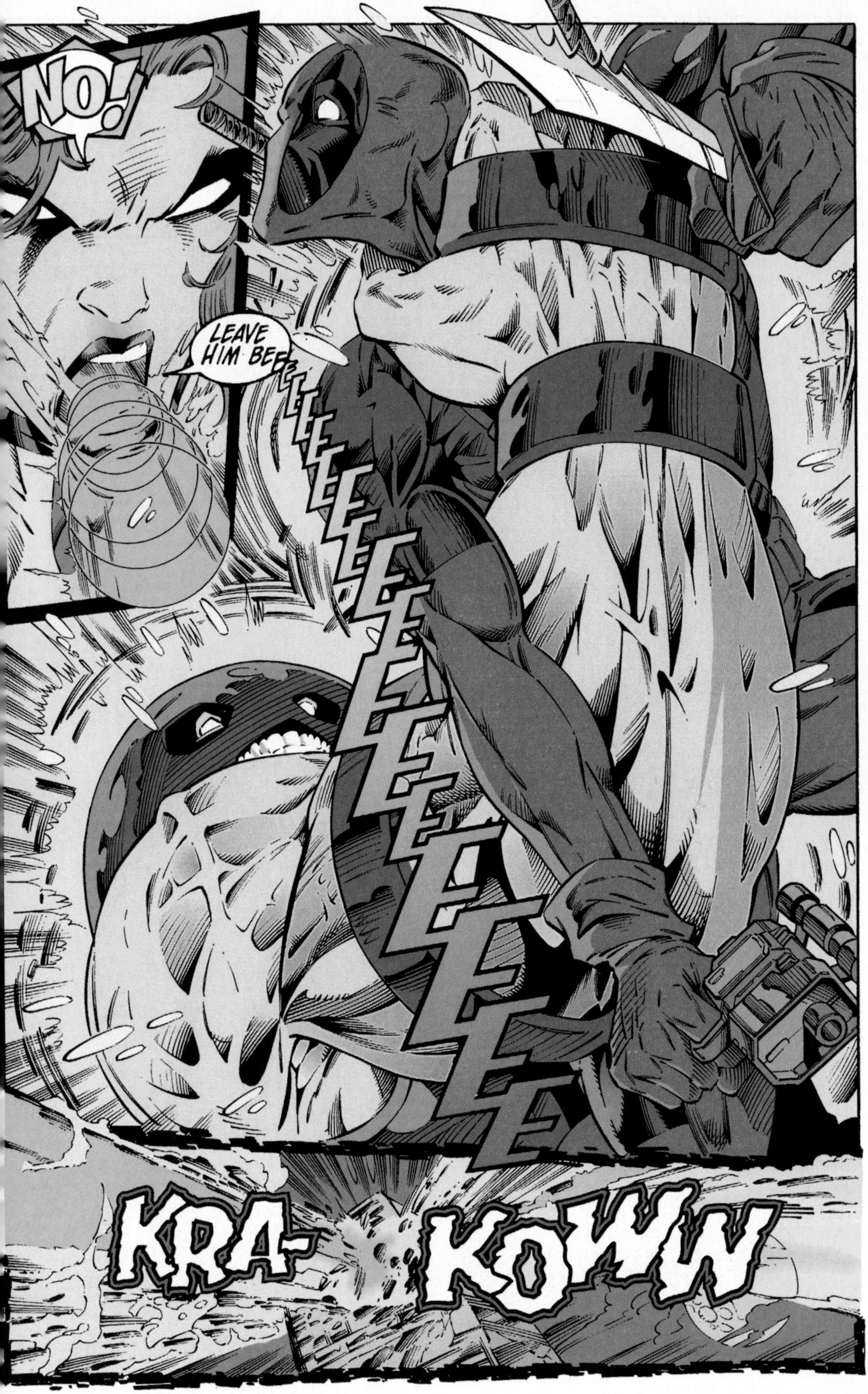
NO!
LEAVE HIM BEEEEEEEEEEEEEEEEE
KRA-KOWW

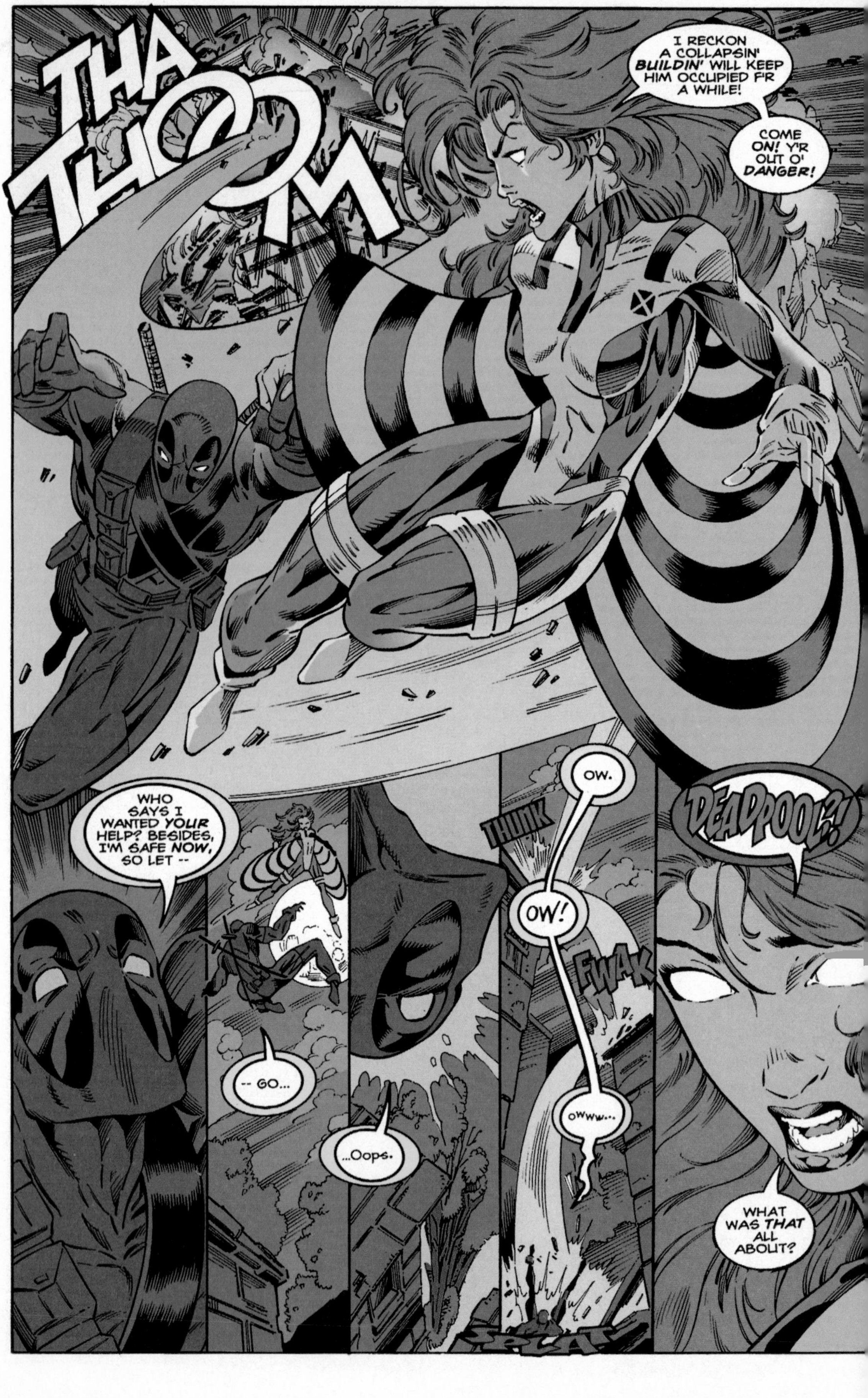
THA THOOM
I RECKON A COLLAPSIN' BUILDIN' WILL KEEP HIM OCCUPIED F'R A WHILE!
COME ON! Y'R OUT O' DANGER!
WHO SAYS I WANTED YOUR HELP? BESIDES, I'M SAFE NOW, SO LET --
-- GO...
...Oops.
THUNK
OW.
OW!
FWAK
owww...
DEADPOOL?!
WHAT WAS THAT ALL ABOUT?

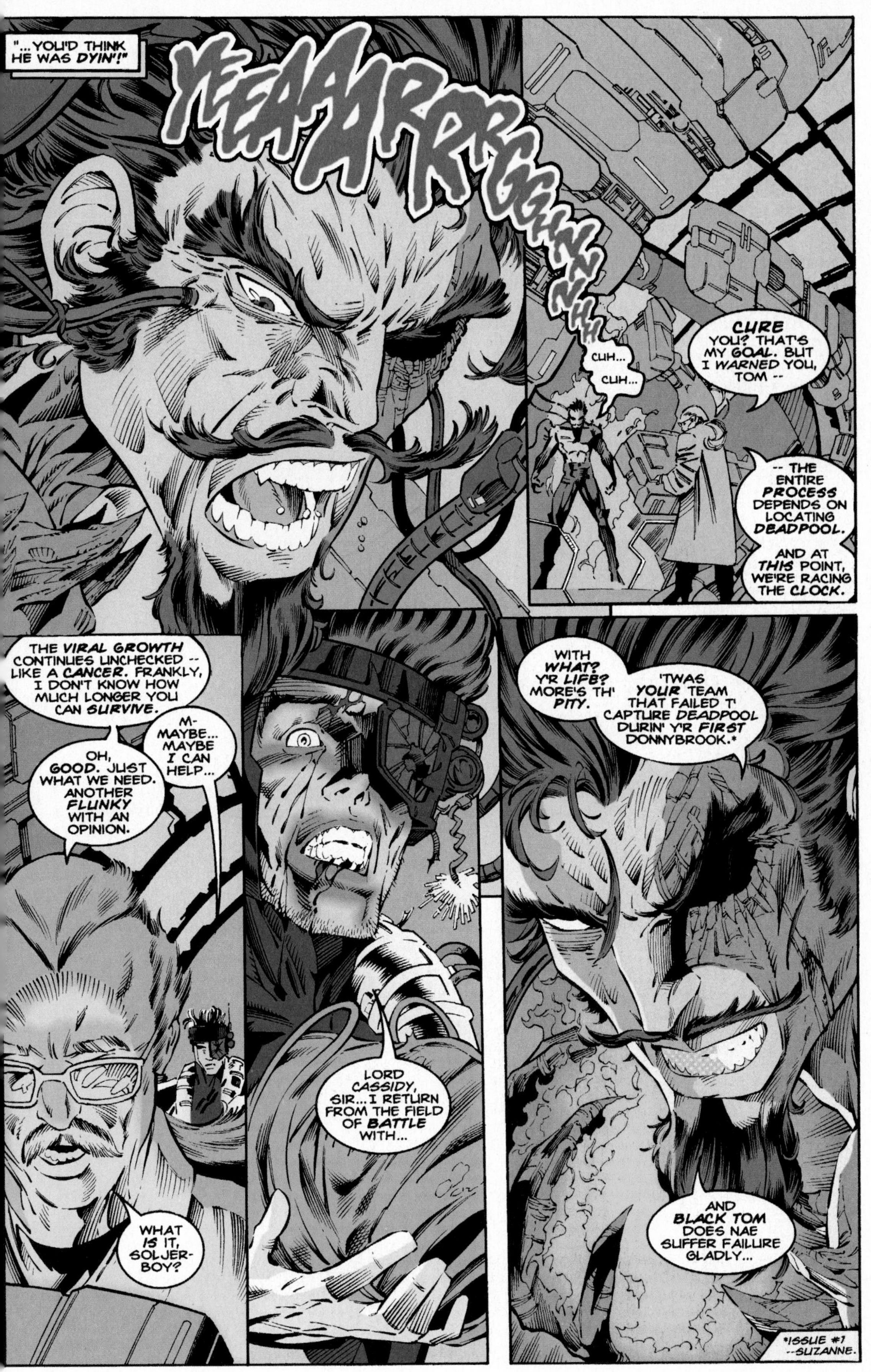
"...YOU'D THINK HE WAS DYIN'!"
YEAAARRRGGHHNNHH
CUH... CUH...
CURE YOU? THAT'S MY GOAL. BUT I WARNED YOU, TOM --
-- THE ENTIRE PROCESS DEPENDS ON LOCATING DEADPOOL.
AND AT THIS POINT, WE'RE RACING THE CLOCK.
THE VIRAL GROWTH CONTINUES UNCHECKED -- LIKE A CANCER. FRANKLY, I DON'T KNOW HOW MUCH LONGER YOU CAN SURVIVE.
M-MAYBE... MAYBE I CAN HELP...
OH, GOOD. JUST WHAT WE NEED. ANOTHER FLUNKY WITH AN OPINION.
WHAT IS IT, SOLJER-BOY?
LORD CASSIDY, SIR... I RETURN FROM THE FIELD OF BATTLE WITH...
WITH WHAT? Y'R LIFE? MORE'S TH' PITY.
'TWAS YOUR TEAM THAT FAILED T' CAPTURE DEADPOOL DURIN' Y'R FIRST DONNYBROOK.*
AND BLACK TOM DOES NAE SUFFER FAILURE GLADLY...
*ISSUE #1 --SUZANNE.

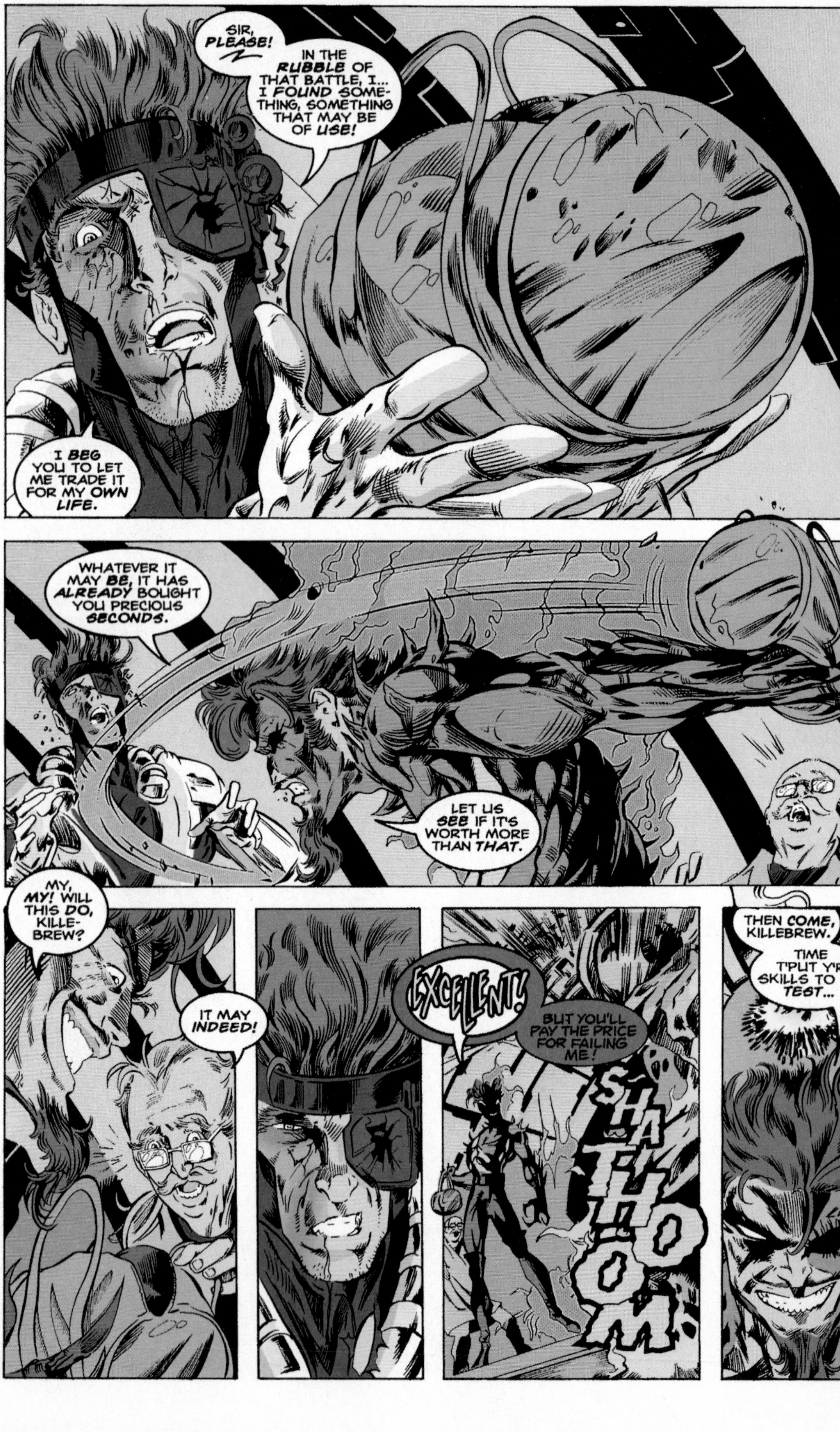
SIR, PLEASE!
IN THE RUBBLE OF THAT BATTLE, I... I FOUND SOMETHING, SOMETHING THAT MAY BE OF USE!
I BEG YOU TO LET ME TRADE IT FOR MY OWN LIFE.
WHATEVER IT MAY BE, IT HAS ALREADY BOUGHT YOU PRECIOUS SECONDS.
LET US SEE IF IT'S WORTH MORE THAN THAT.
MY, MY! WILL THIS DO, KILLEBREW?
IT MAY INDEED!
EXCELLENT!
BUT YOU'LL PAY THE PRICE FOR FAILING ME!
SHA THOOOM!
THEN COME, KILLEBREW.
TIME T'PUT Y'R SKILLS TO TH' TEST...

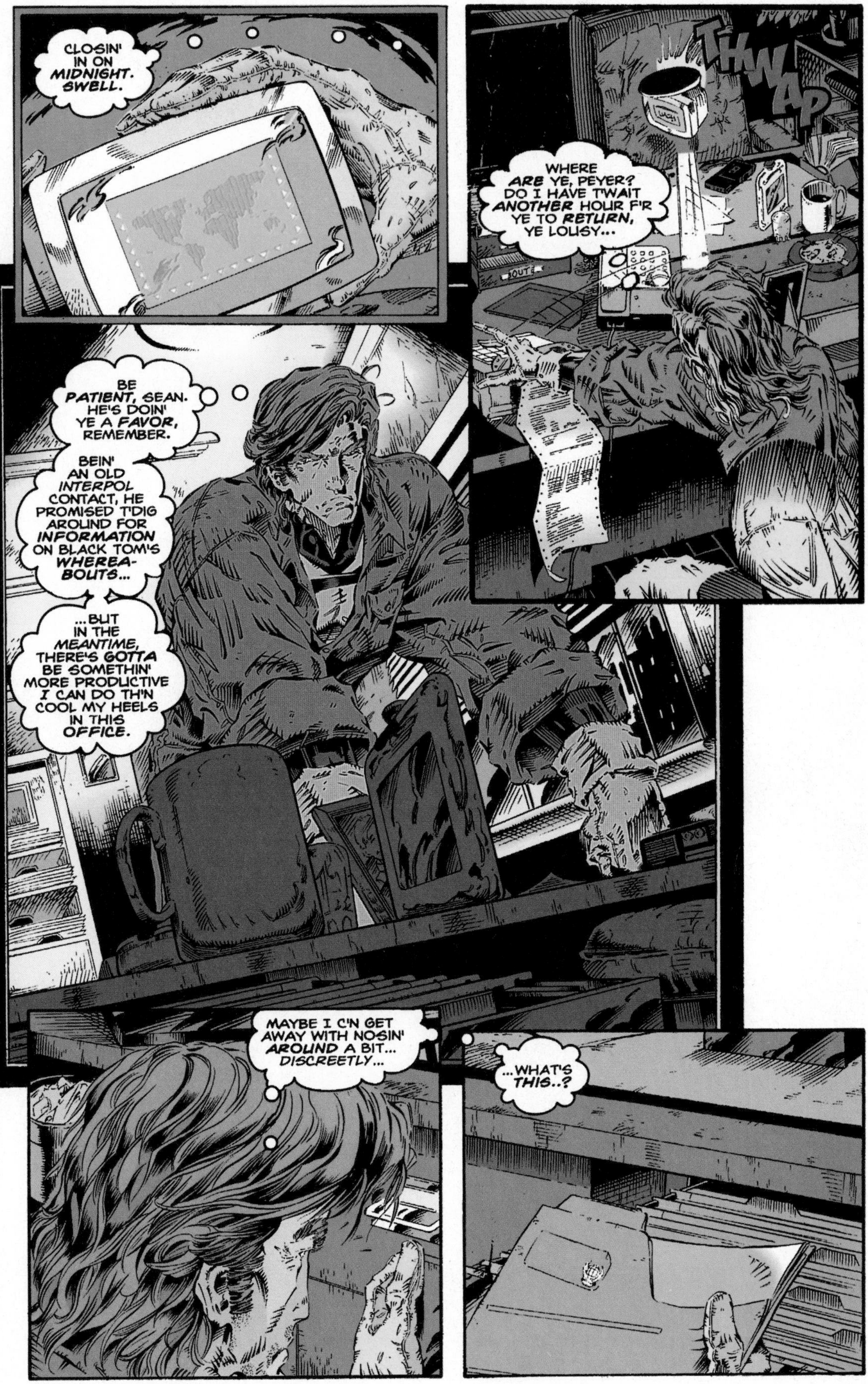
CLOSIN' IN ON MIDNIGHT. SWELL.
THWAP
WHERE ARE YE, PEYER? DO I HAVE T'WAIT ANOTHER HOUR F'R YE TO RETURN, YE LOUSY...
BE PATIENT, SEAN. HE'S DOIN' YE A FAVOR, REMEMBER.
BEIN' AN OLD INTERPOL CONTACT, HE PROMISED T'DIG AROUND FOR INFORMATION ON BLACK TOM'S WHEREABOUTS...
...BUT IN THE MEANTIME, THERE'S GOTTA BE SOMETHIN' MORE PRODUCTIVE I CAN DO TH'N COOL MY HEELS IN THIS OFFICE.
MAYBE I C'N GET AWAY WITH NOSIN' AROUND A BIT... DISCREETLY...
...WHAT'S THIS..?

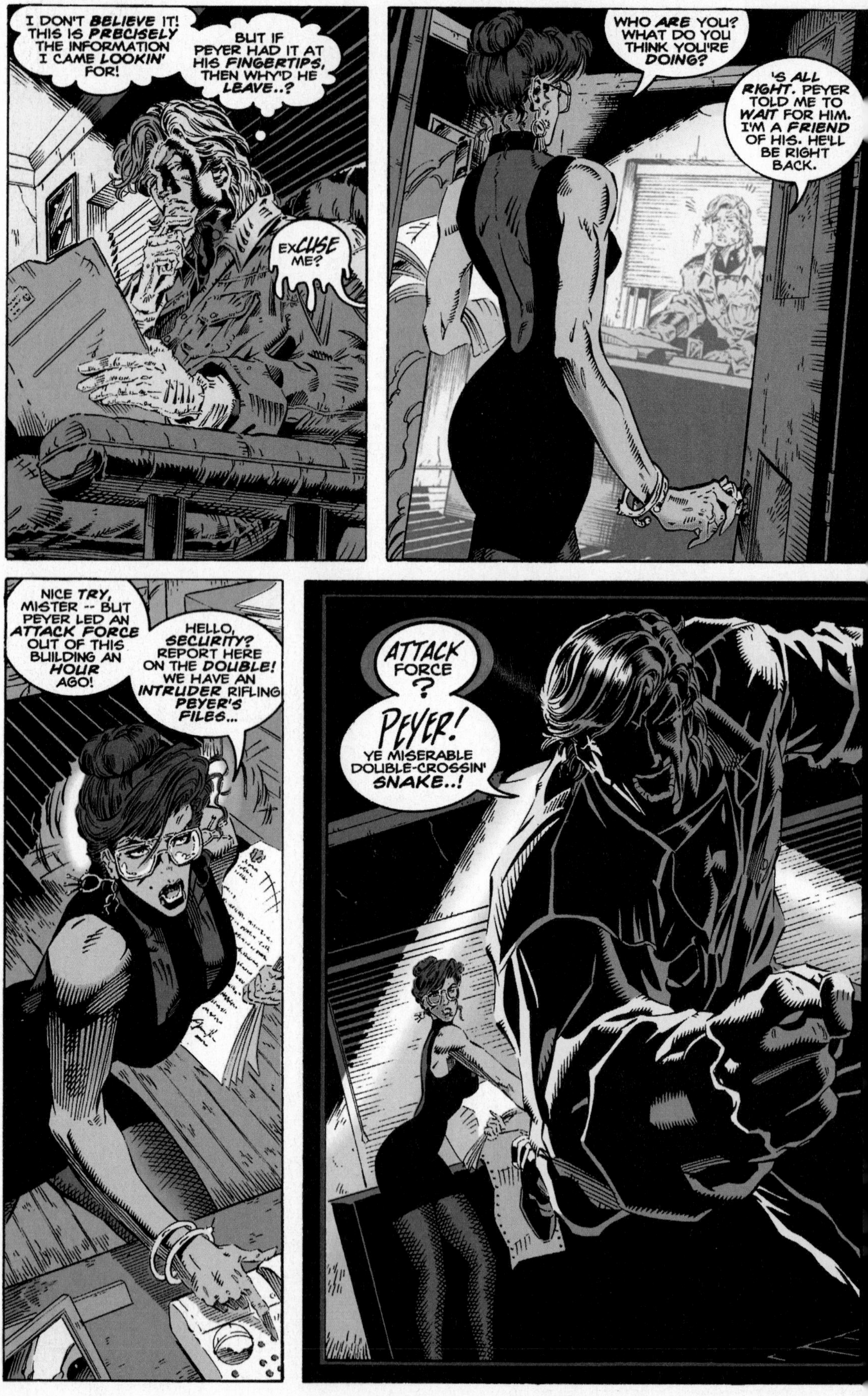
I DON'T BELIEVE IT! THIS IS PRECISELY THE INFORMATION I CAME LOOKIN' FOR!
BUT IF PEYER HAD IT AT HIS FINGERTIPS, THEN WHY'D HE LEAVE..?
EXCUSE ME?
WHO ARE YOU? WHAT DO YOU THINK YOU'RE DOING?
'S ALL RIGHT. PEYER TOLD ME TO WAIT FOR HIM. I'M A FRIEND OF HIS. HE'LL BE RIGHT BACK.
NICE TRY, MISTER -- BUT PEYER LED AN ATTACK FORCE OUT OF THIS BUILDING AN HOUR AGO!
HELLO, SECURITY? REPORT HERE ON THE DOUBLE! WE HAVE AN INTRUDER RIFLING PEYER'S FILES...
ATTACK FORCE?
PEYER! YE MISERABLE DOUBLE-CROSSIN' SNAKE..!

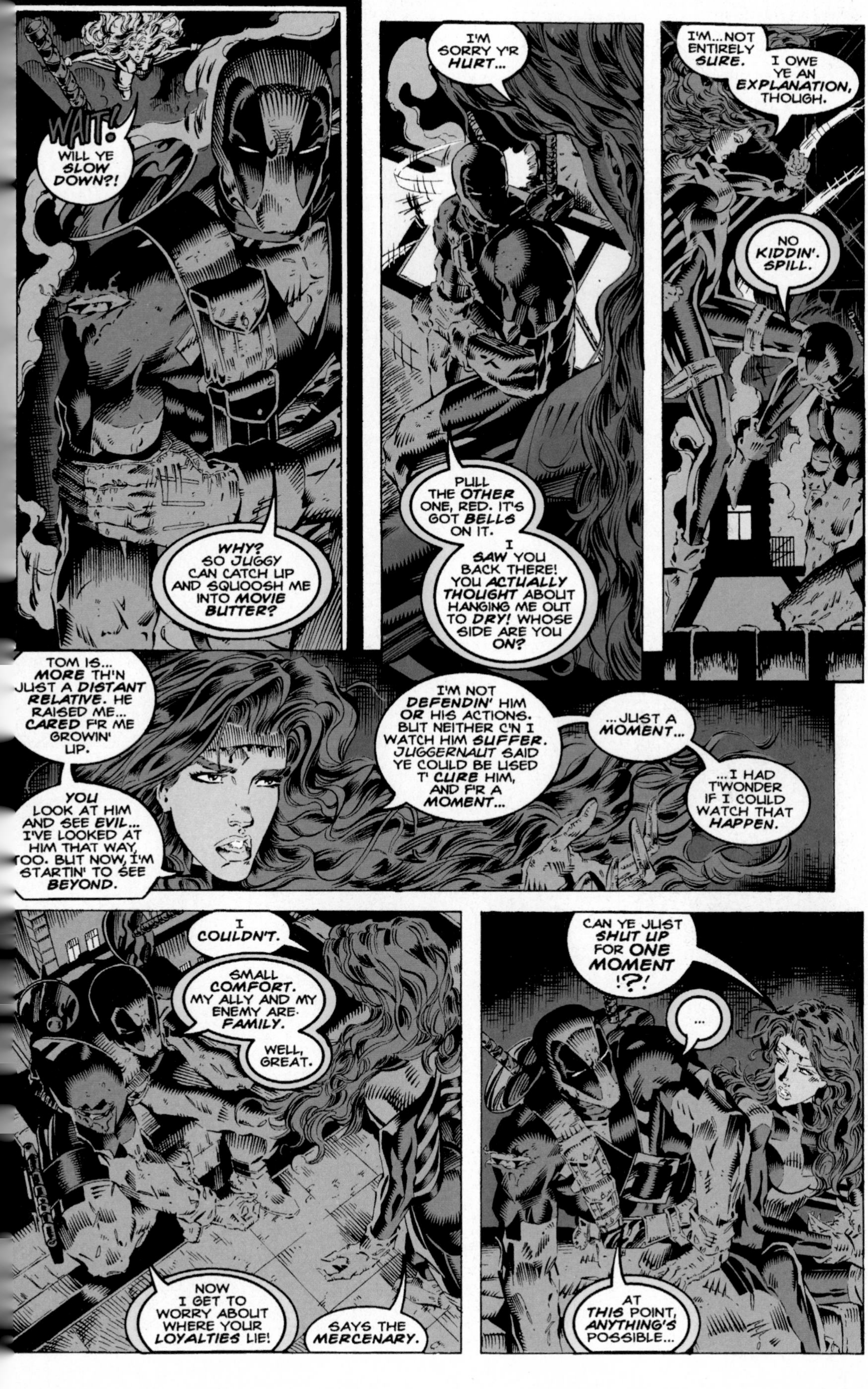
WAIT! WILL YE SLOW DOWN?!
WHY? SO JUGGY CAN CATCH UP AND SQUOOSH ME INTO MOVIE BUTTER?
I'M SORRY Y'R HURT...
PULL THE OTHER ONE, RED. IT'S GOT BELLS ON IT.
I SAW YOU BACK THERE! YOU ACTUALLY THOUGHT ABOUT HANGING ME OUT TO DRY! WHOSE SIDE ARE YOU ON?
I'M...NOT ENTIRELY SURE.
I OWE YE AN EXPLANATION, THOUGH.
NO KIDDIN'. SPILL.
TOM IS... MORE TH'N JUST A DISTANT RELATIVE. HE RAISED ME... CARED F'R ME GROWIN' UP.
YOU LOOK AT HIM AND SEE EVIL... I'VE LOOKED AT HIM THAT WAY, TOO. BUT NOW, I'M STARTIN' TO SEE BEYOND.
I'M NOT DEFENDIN' HIM OR HIS ACTIONS. BUT NEITHER C'N I WATCH HIM SUFFER. JUGGERNAUT SAID YE COULD BE USED T' CURE HIM, AND F'R A MOMENT...
...JUST A MOMENT...
...I HAD T'WONDER IF I COULD WATCH THAT HAPPEN.
I COULDN'T.
SMALL COMFORT. MY ALLY AND MY ENEMY ARE FAMILY.
WELL, GREAT.
NOW I GET TO WORRY ABOUT WHERE YOUR LOYALTIES LIE!
SAYS THE MERCENARY.
CAN YE JUST SHUT UP FOR ONE MOMENT !?!
...
AT THIS POINT, ANYTHING'S POSSIBLE...

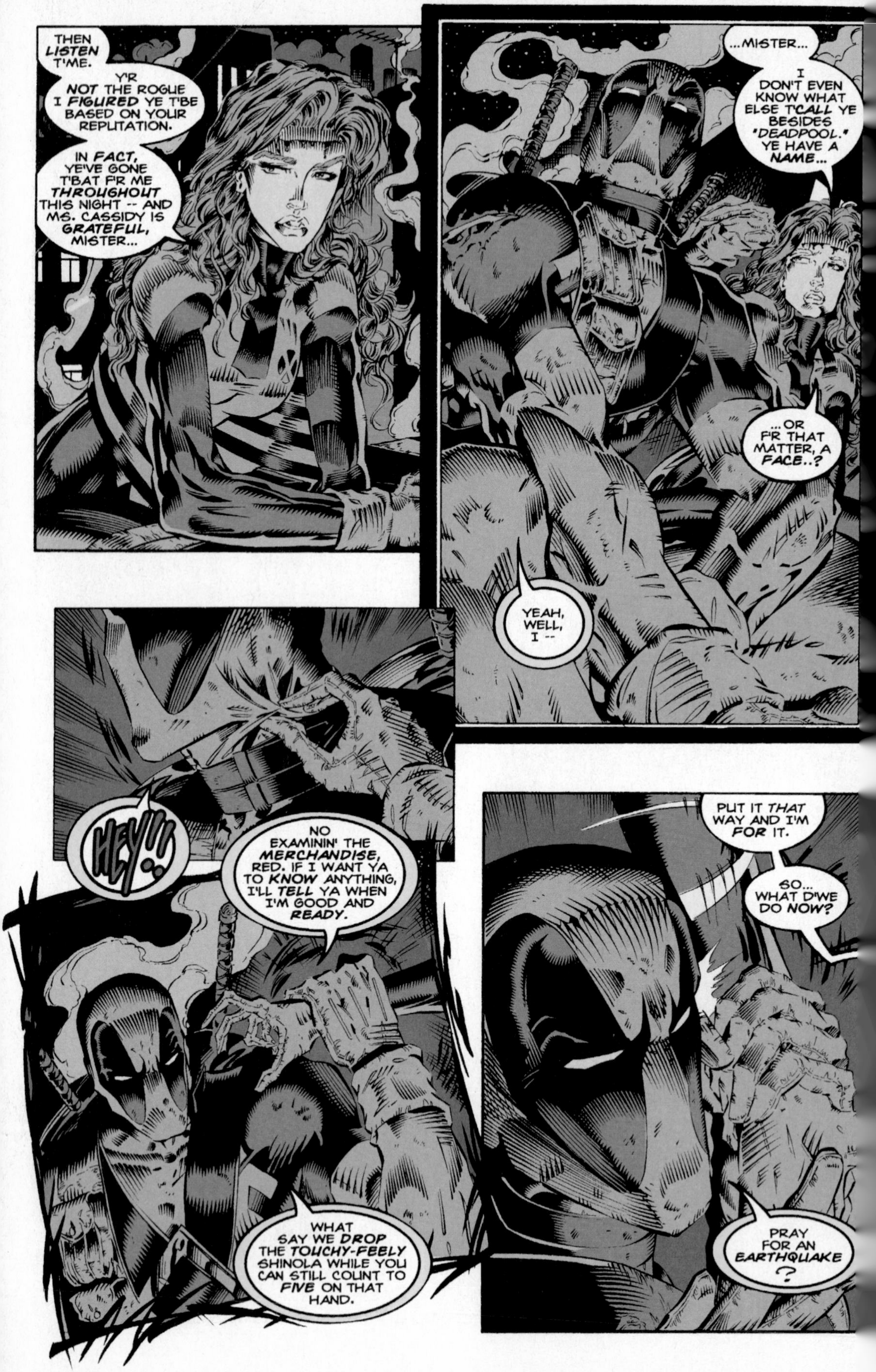
THEN LISTEN T'ME.
Y'R NOT THE ROGUE I FIGURED YE T'BE BASED ON YOUR REPUTATION.
IN FACT, YE'VE GONE T'BAT F'R ME THROUGHOUT THIS NIGHT -- AND MS. CASSIDY IS GRATEFUL, MISTER...
...MISTER...
I DON'T EVEN KNOW WHAT ELSE T'CALL YE BESIDES "DEADPOOL." YE HAVE A NAME...
...OR F'R THAT MATTER, A FACE..?
YEAH, WELL, I --
HEY!!!
NO EXAMININ' THE MERCHANDISE, RED. IF I WANT YA TO KNOW ANYTHING, I'LL TELL YA WHEN I'M GOOD AND READY.
WHAT SAY WE DROP THE TOUCHY-FEELY SHINOLA WHILE YOU CAN STILL COUNT TO FIVE ON THAT HAND.
PUT IT THAT WAY AND I'M FOR IT.
SO... WHAT D'WE DO NOW?
PRAY FOR AN EARTHQUAKE ?

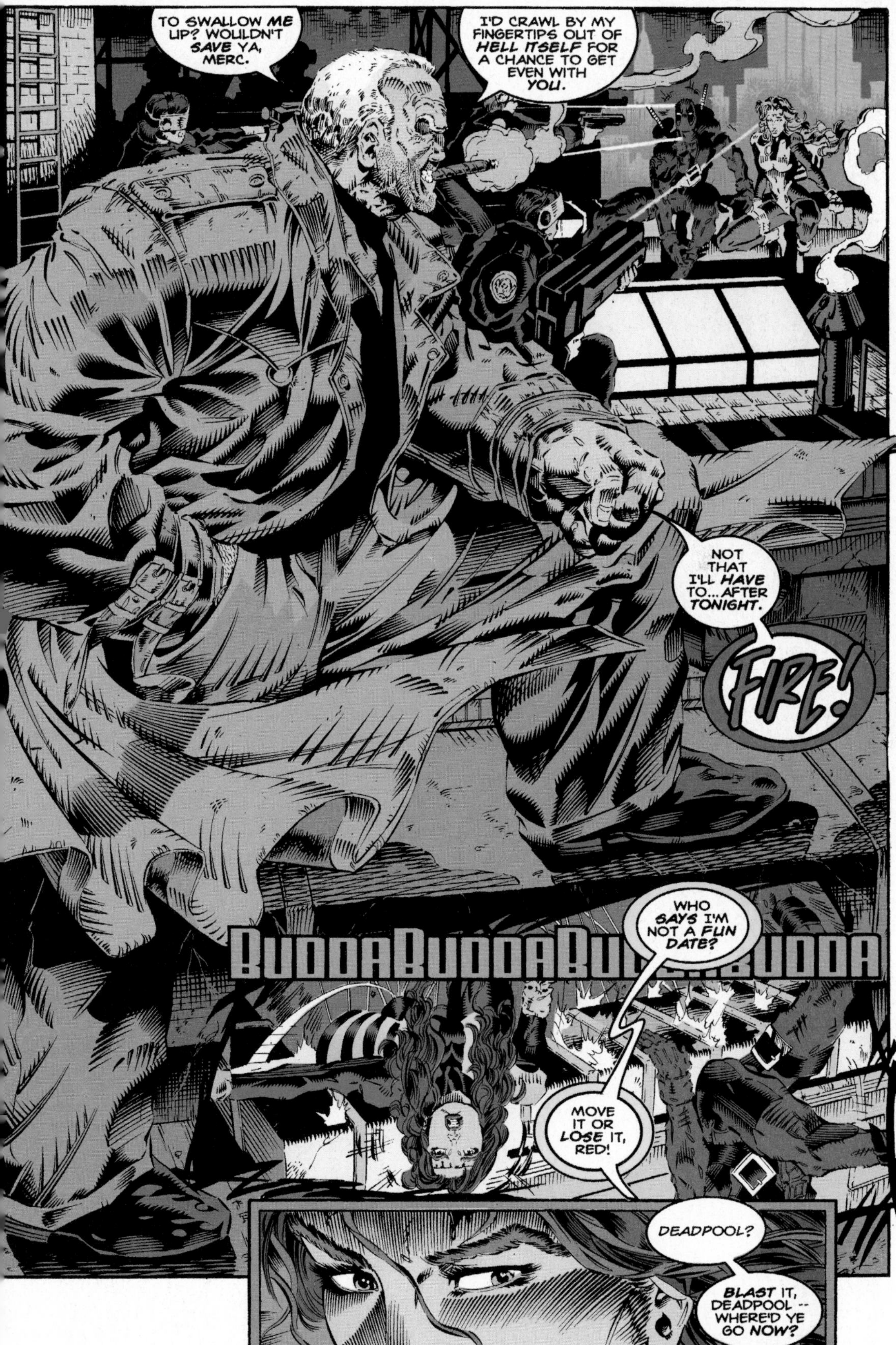

TO SWALLOW ME UP? WOULDN'T SAVE YA, MERC.
I'D CRAWL BY MY FINGERTIPS OUT OF HELL ITSELF FOR A CHANCE TO GET EVEN WITH YOU.
NOT THAT I'LL HAVE TO... AFTER TONIGHT.
FIRE!
WHO SAYS I'M NOT A FUN DATE?
MOVE IT OR LOSE IT, RED!
DEADPOOL?
BLAST IT, DEADPOOL -- WHERE'D YE GO NOW?

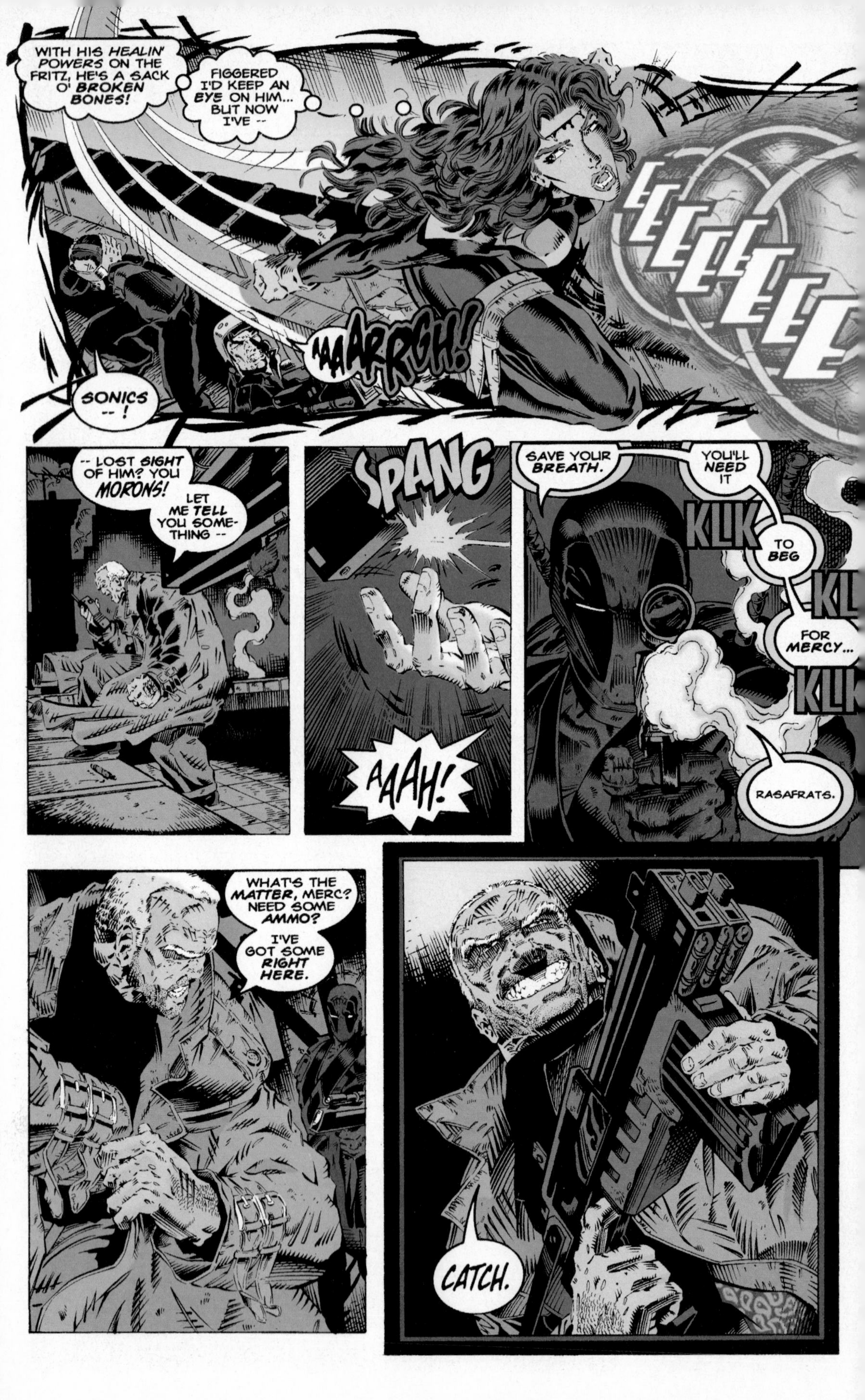
WITH HIS HEALIN' POWERS ON THE FRITZ, HE'S A SACK O' BROKEN BONES!
FIGGERED I'D KEEP AN EYE ON HIM... BUT NOW I'VE --
EEEEEEEEE
AAARRGH!
SONICS -- !
-- LOST SIGHT OF HIM? YOU MORONS!
LET ME TELL YOU SOME-THING --
SPANG
AAAH!
SAVE YOUR BREATH.
YOU'LL NEED IT
KLIK
TO BEG
KLIK
FOR MERCY...
KLIK
RASAFRATS.
WHAT'S THE MATTER, MERC? NEED SOME AMMO?
I'VE GOT SOME RIGHT HERE.
CATCH.

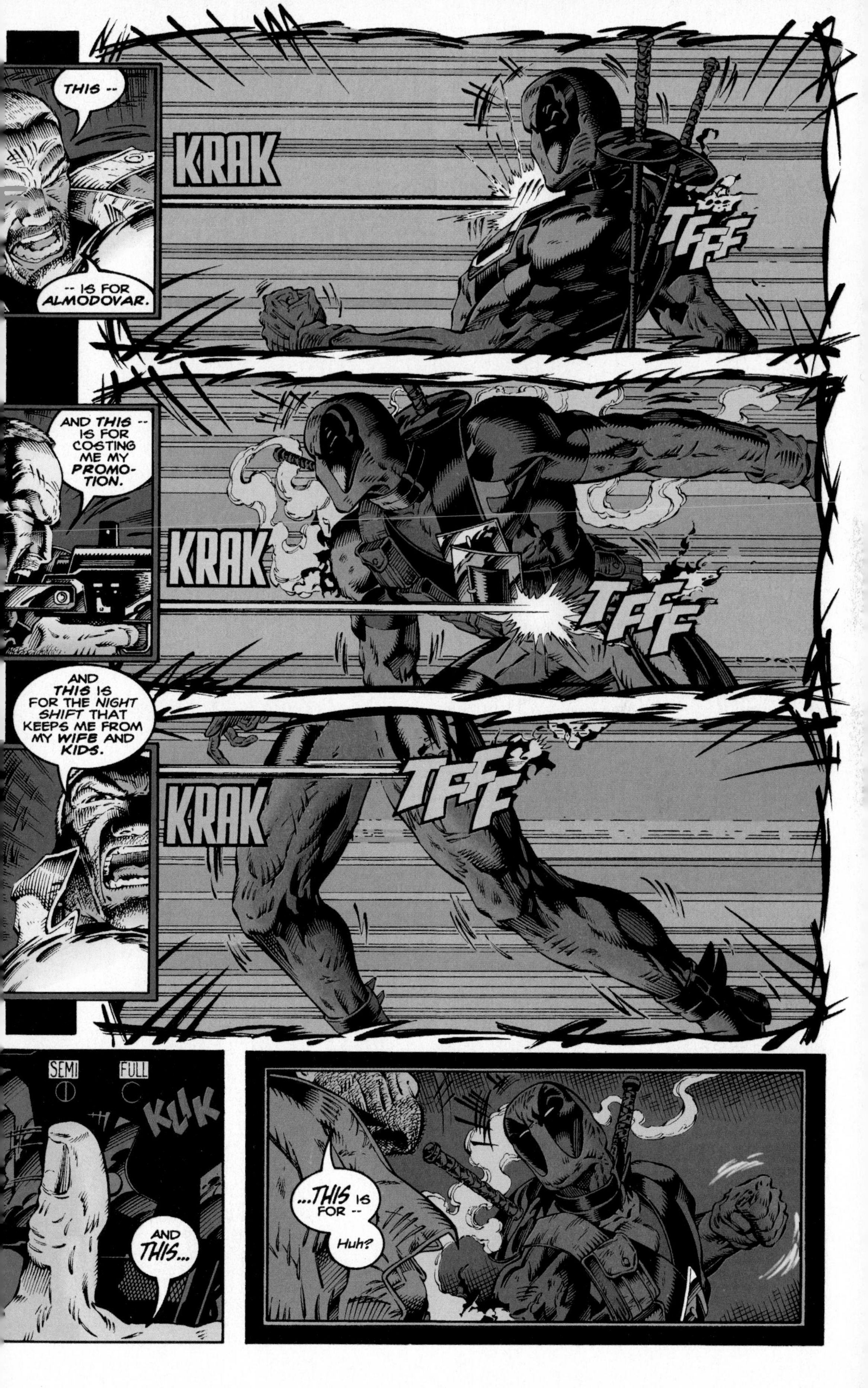
THIS --
KRAK
TFFF
-- IS FOR ALMODOVAR.
AND THIS -- IS FOR COSTING ME MY PROMOTION.
KRAK
TFFF
AND THIS IS FOR THE NIGHT SHIFT THAT KEEPS ME FROM MY WIFE AND KIDS.
KRAK
TFFF
SEMI
FULL
KLIK
AND THIS...
...THIS IS FOR --
Huh?

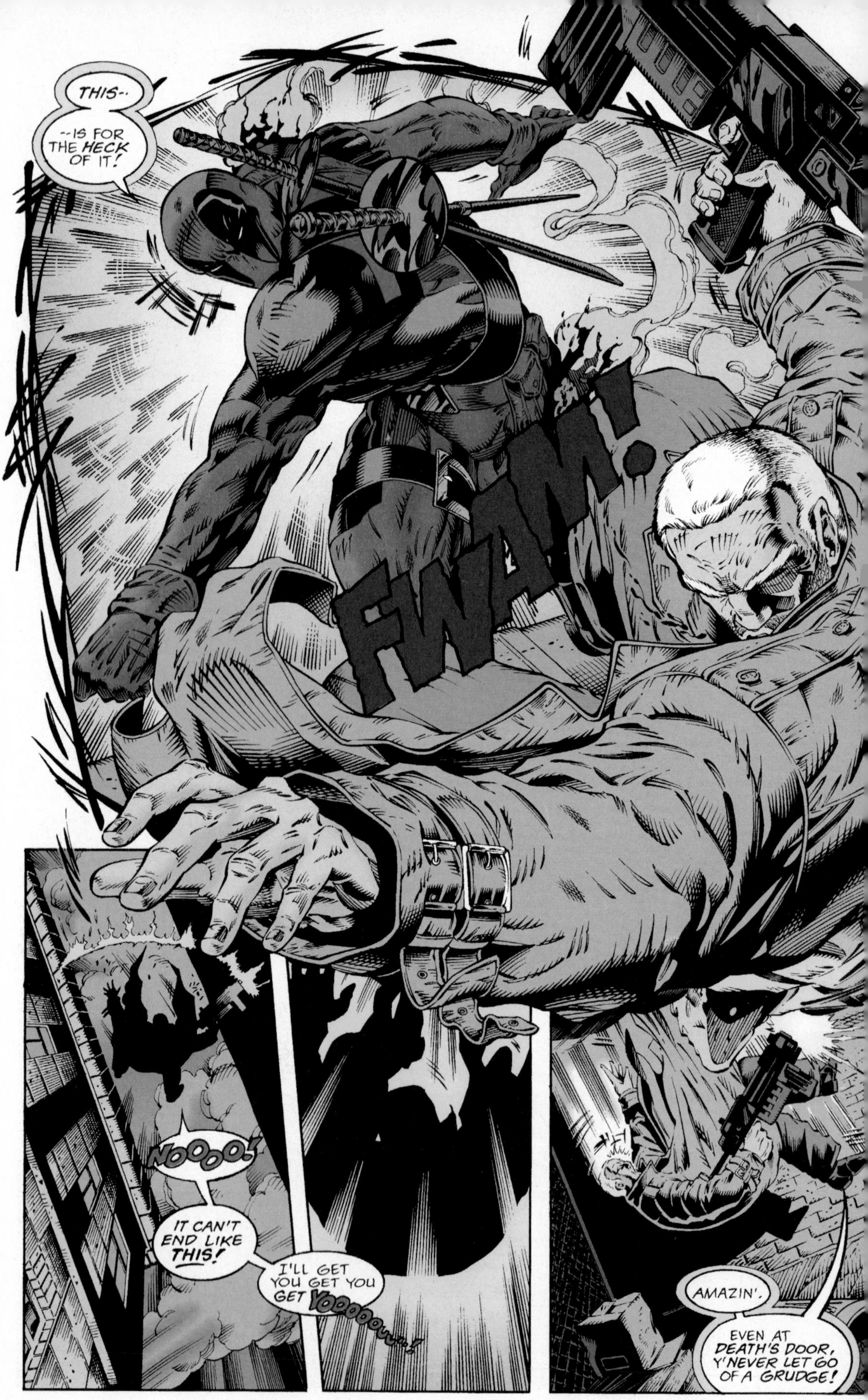

THIS--
--IS FOR THE HECK OF IT!
FWAM!
NOOOO!
IT CAN'T END LIKE THIS!
I'LL GET YOU GET YOU GET YOOOOOUUU--!
AMAZIN'.
EVEN AT DEATH'S DOOR, Y'NEVER LET GO OF A GRUDGE!

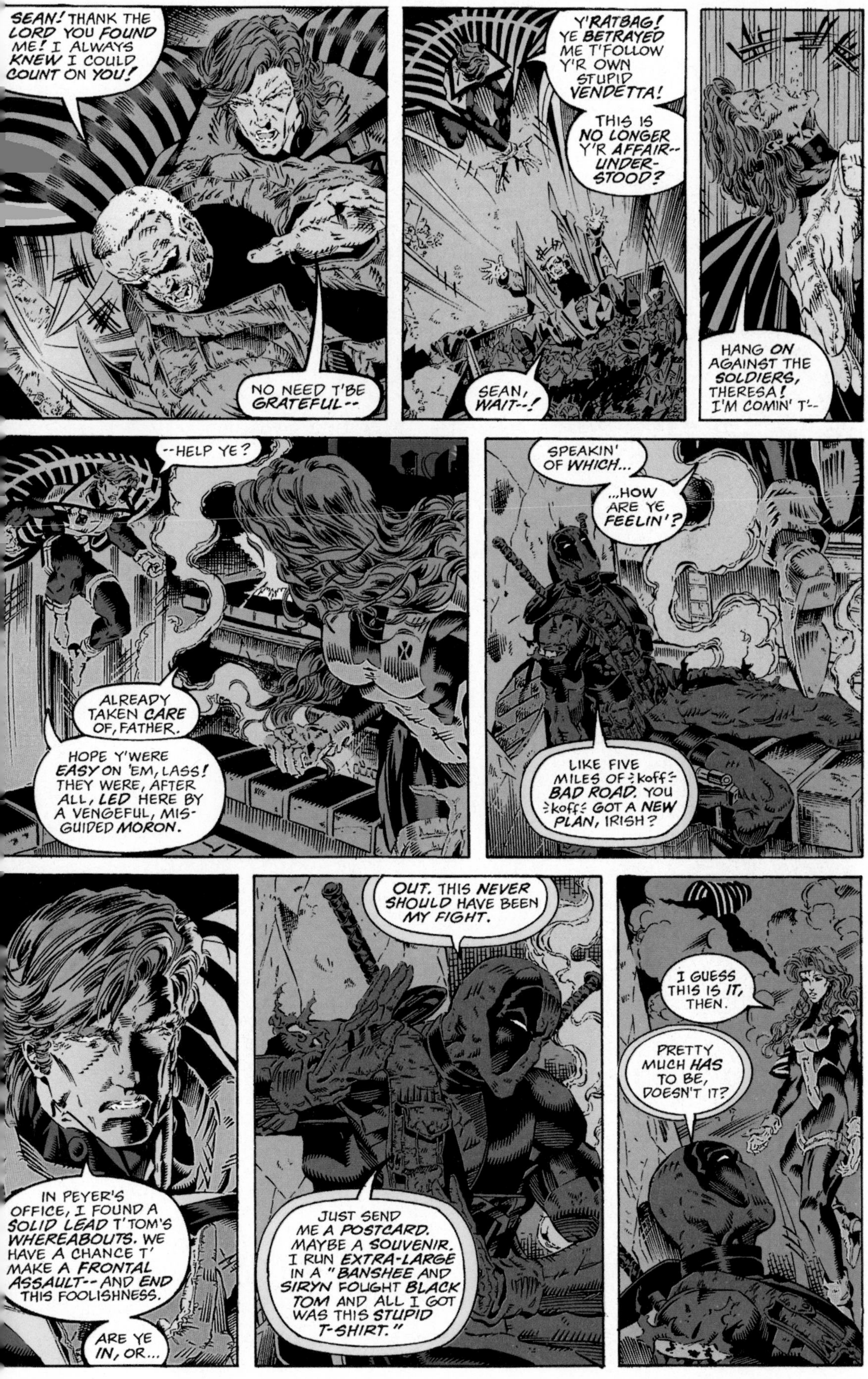
SEAN! THANK THE LORD YOU FOUND ME! I ALWAYS KNEW I COULD COUNT ON YOU!
NO NEED T'BE GRATEFUL--
Y'RATBAG! YE BETRAYED ME T'FOLLOW Y'R OWN STUPID VENDETTA!
THIS IS NO LONGER Y'R AFFAIR--UNDERSTOOD?
SEAN, WAIT--!
HANG ON AGAINST THE SOLDIERS, THERESA! I'M COMIN' T'--
--HELP YE?
ALREADY TAKEN CARE OF, FATHER.
HOPE Y'WERE EASY ON 'EM, LASS! THEY WERE, AFTER ALL, LED HERE BY A VENGEFUL, MISGUIDED MORON.
SPEAKIN' OF WHICH...
...HOW ARE YE FEELIN'?
LIKE FIVE MILES OF koff BAD ROAD. YOU koff GOT A NEW PLAN, IRISH?
IN PEYER'S OFFICE, I FOUND A SOLID LEAD T'TOM'S WHEREABOUTS. WE HAVE A CHANCE T' MAKE A FRONTAL ASSAULT-- AND END THIS FOOLISHNESS.
ARE YE IN, OR...
OUT. THIS NEVER SHOULD HAVE BEEN MY FIGHT.
JUST SEND ME A POSTCARD. MAYBE A SOUVENIR. I RUN EXTRA-LARGE IN A "BANSHEE AND SIRYN FOUGHT BLACK TOM AND ALL I GOT WAS THIS STUPID T-SHIRT."
I GUESS THIS IS IT, THEN.
PRETTY MUCH HAS TO BE, DOESN'T IT?

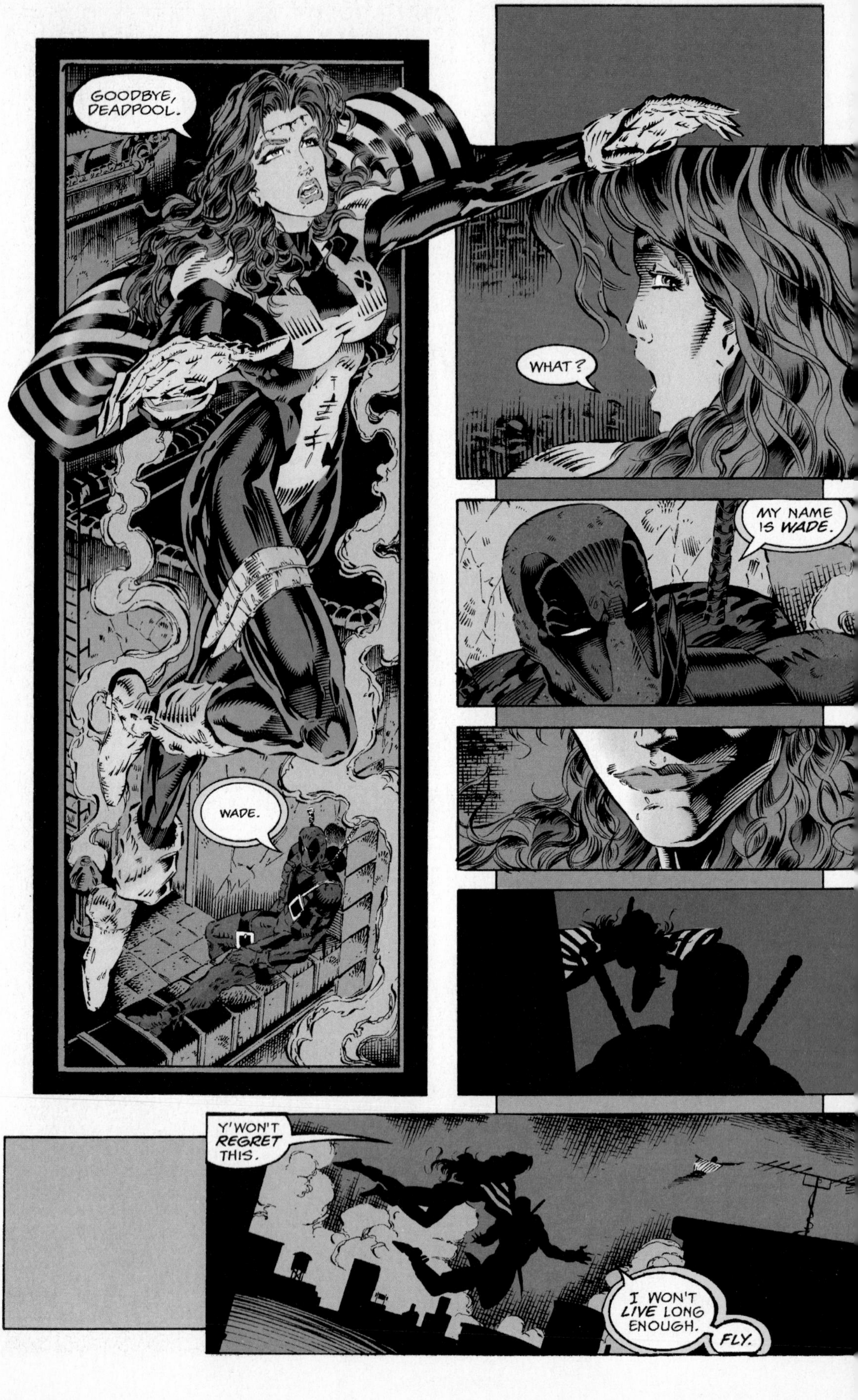
GOODBYE, DEADPOOL.
WADE.
WHAT?
MY NAME IS WADE.
Y'WON'T REGRET THIS.
I WON'T LIVE LONG ENOUGH.
FLY.

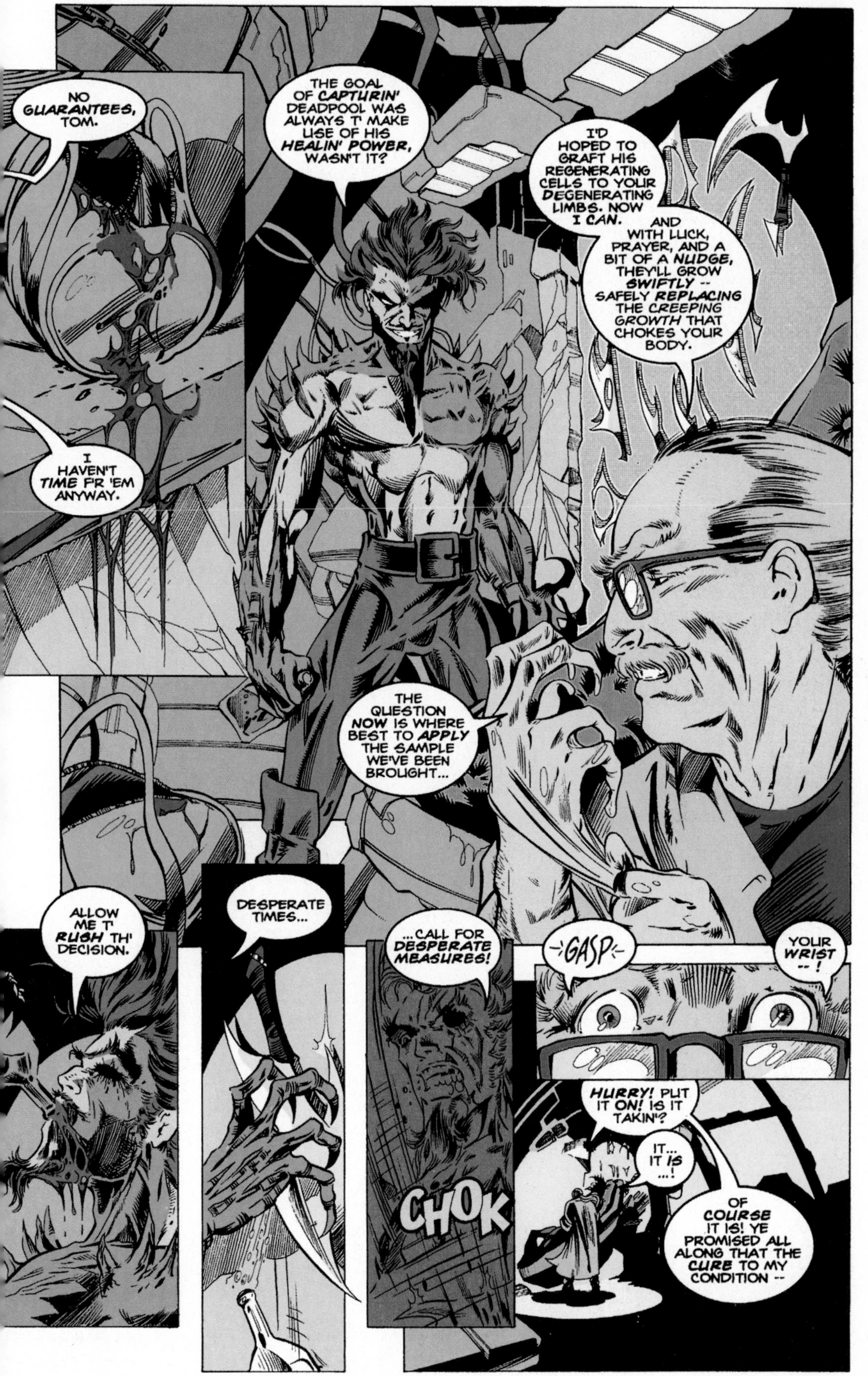
NO GUARANTEES, TOM.
THE GOAL OF CAPTURIN' DEADPOOL WAS ALWAYS T' MAKE USE OF HIS HEALIN' POWER, WASN'T IT?
I'D HOPED TO GRAFT HIS REGENERATING CELLS TO YOUR DEGENERATING LIMBS. NOW I CAN.
AND WITH LUCK, PRAYER, AND A BIT OF A NUDGE, THEY'LL GROW SWIFTLY -- SAFELY REPLACING THE CREEPING GROWTH THAT CHOKES YOUR BODY.
I HAVEN'T TIME FR 'EM ANYWAY.
THE QUESTION NOW IS WHERE BEST TO APPLY THE SAMPLE WE'VE BEEN BROUGHT...
ALLOW ME T' RUSH TH' DECISION.
DESPERATE TIMES...
...CALL FOR DESPERATE MEASURES!
CHOK
GASP
YOUR WRIST -- !
HURRY! PUT IT ON! IS IT TAKIN'?
IT... IT IS ...!
OF COURSE IT IS! YE PROMISED ALL ALONG THAT THE CURE TO MY CONDITION --

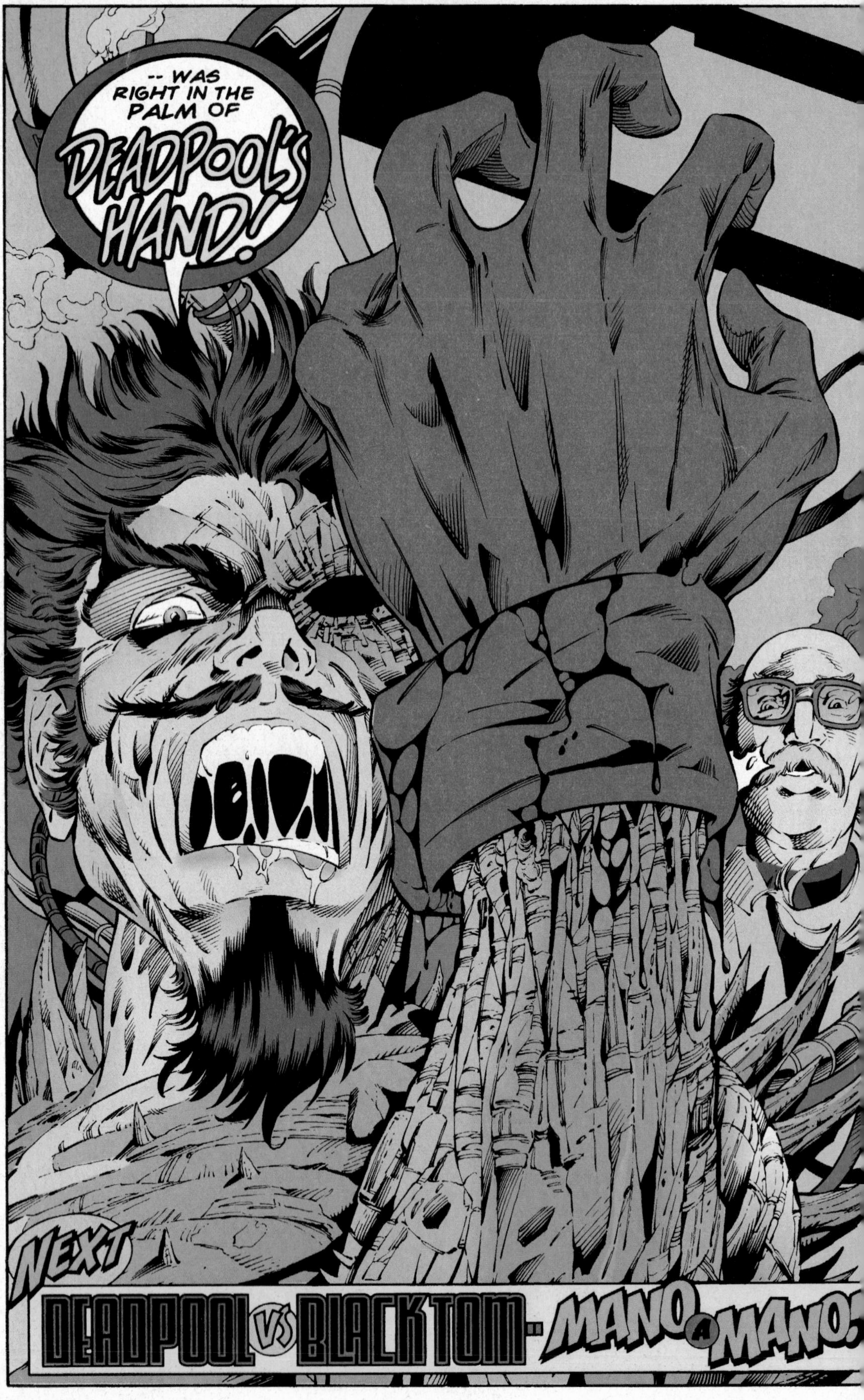
-- WAS RIGHT IN THE PALM OF DEADPOOL'S HAND!
NEXT
DEADPOOL VS BLACK TOM-- MANO A MANO!

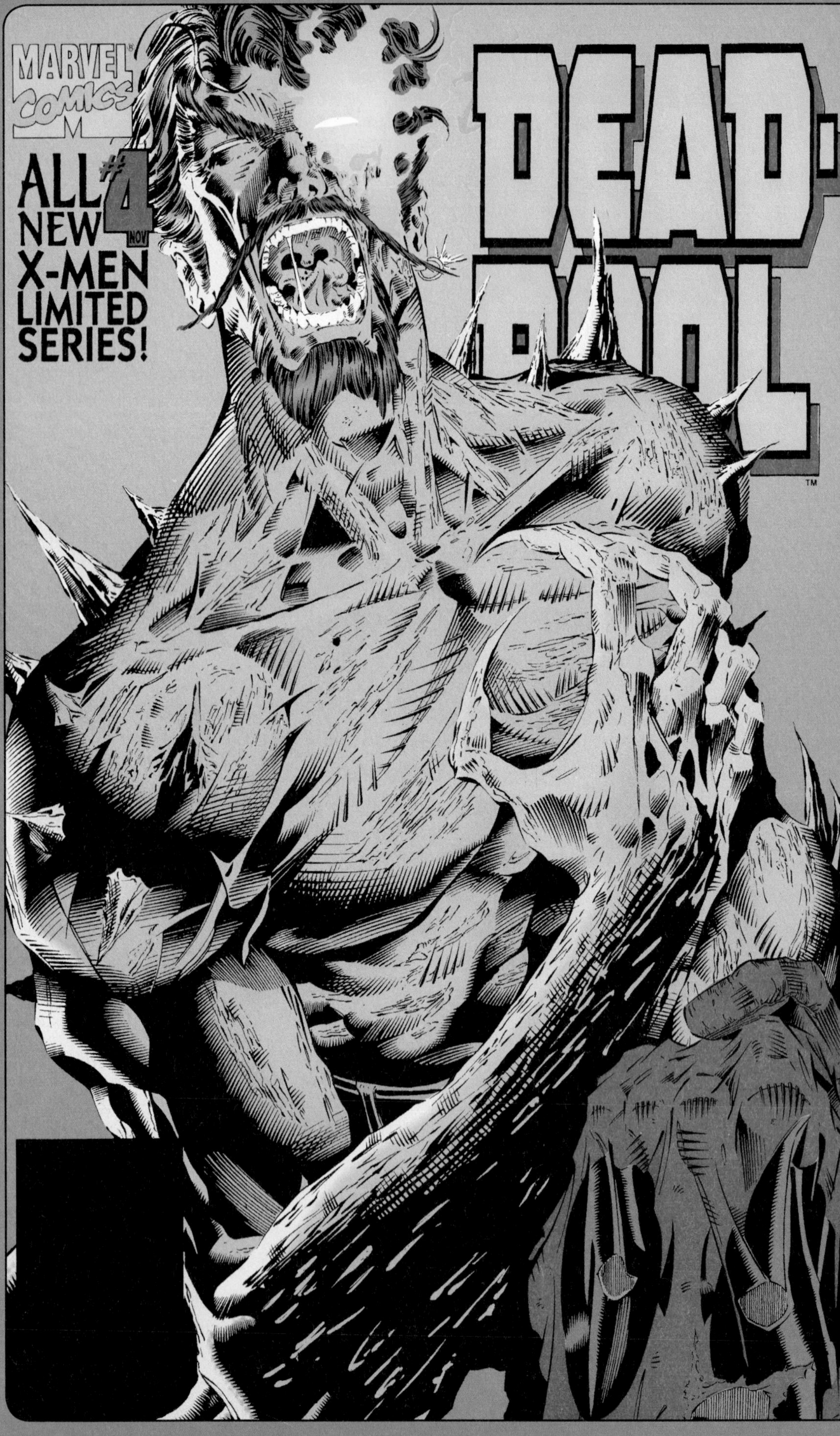
MARVEL COMICS
ALL NEW X-MEN LIMITED SERIES!
#4 NOV
DEAD-POOL™

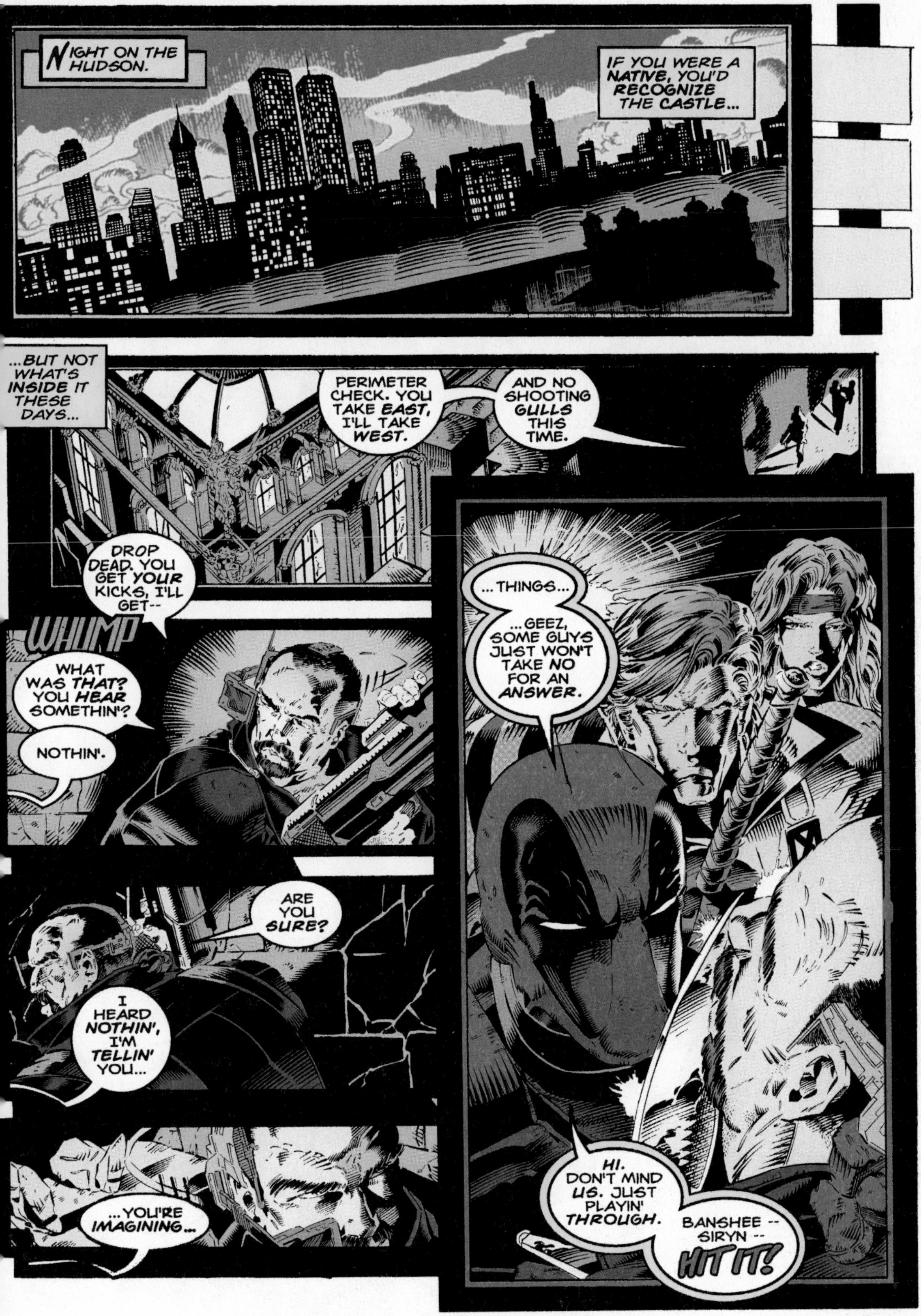

NIGHT ON THE HUDSON.
IF YOU WERE A NATIVE, YOU'D RECOGNIZE THE CASTLE...
...BUT NOT WHAT'S INSIDE IT THESE DAYS...
PERIMETER CHECK. YOU TAKE EAST, I'LL TAKE WEST.
AND NO SHOOTING GULLS THIS TIME.
DROP DEAD. YOU GET YOUR KICKS, I'LL GET--
WHUMP
WHAT WAS THAT? YOU HEAR SOMETHIN'?
NOTHIN'.
ARE YOU SURE?
I HEARD NOTHIN', I'M TELLIN' YOU...
...YOU'RE IMAGINING...
...THINGS...
...GEEZ, SOME GUYS JUST WON'T TAKE NO FOR AN ANSWER.
HI. DON'T MIND US. JUST PLAYIN' THROUGH.
BANSHEE -- SIRYN -- HIT IT!

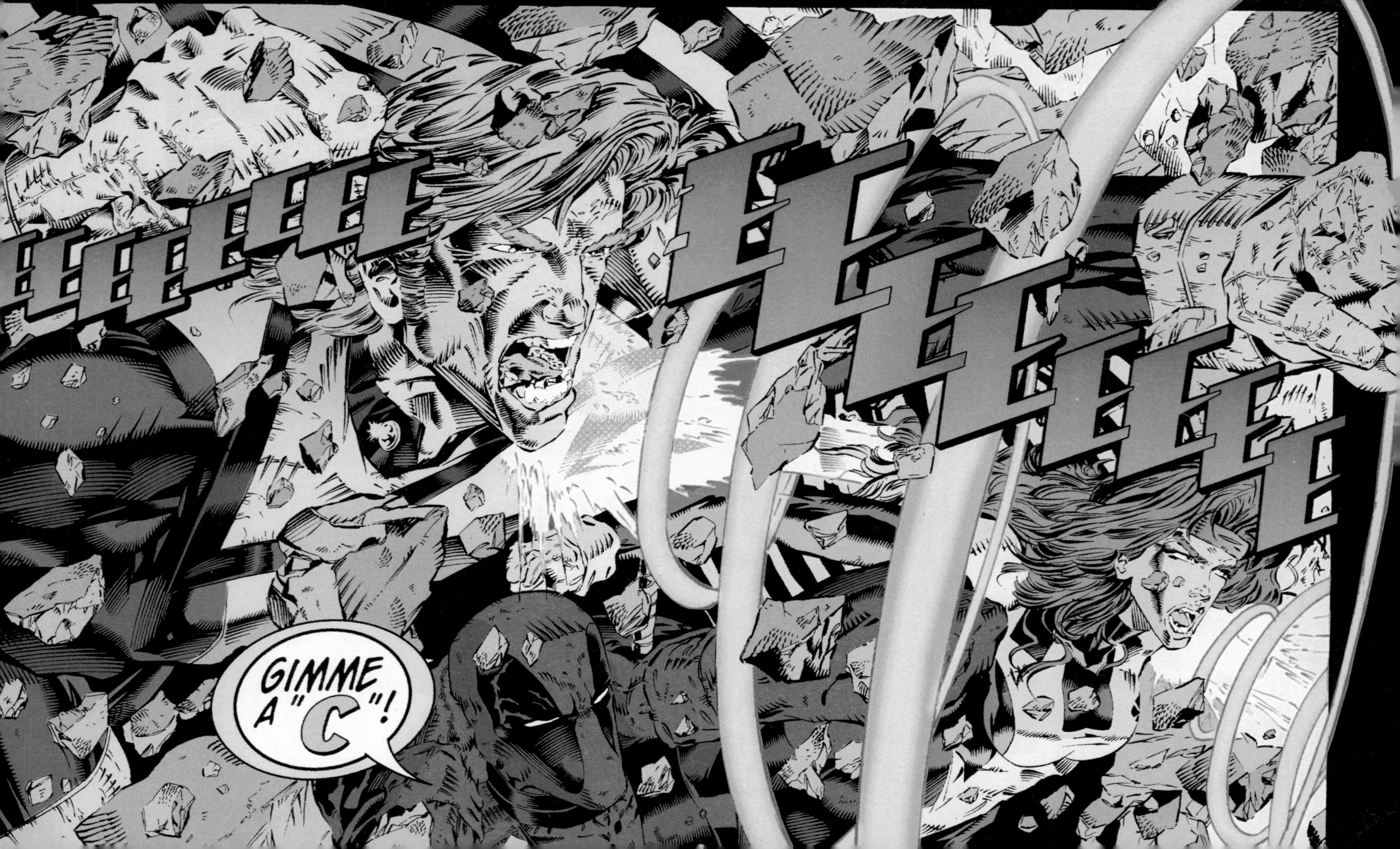
GIMME A "C"!

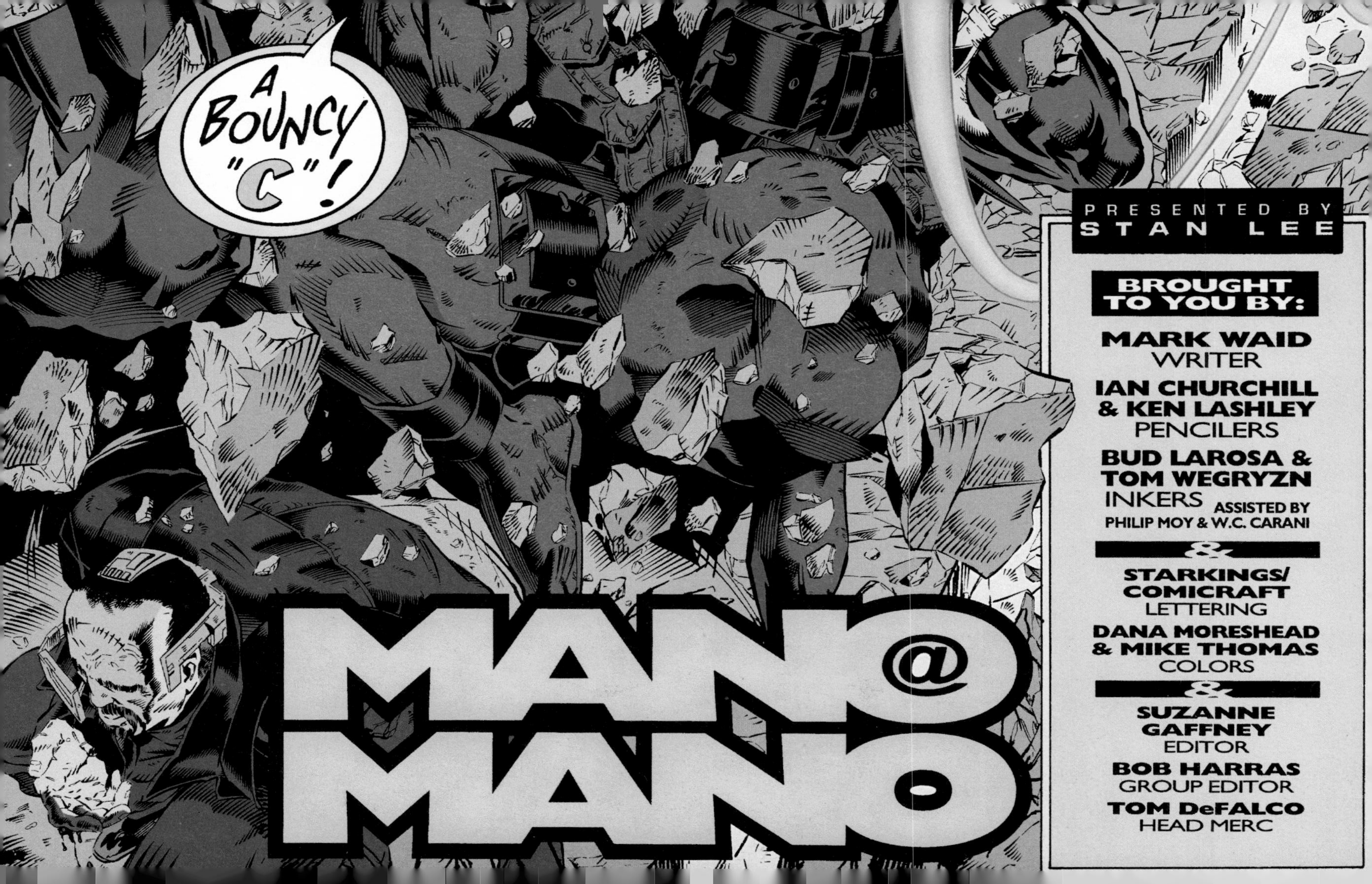
A BOUNCY "C"!
MANO @ MANO
PRESENTED BY STAN LEE
BROUGHT TO YOU BY:
MARK WAID WRITER
IAN CHURCHILL & KEN LASHLEY PENCILERS
BUD LAROSA & TOM WEGRYZN INKERS ASSISTED BY PHILIP MOY & W.C. CARANI
&
STARKINGS/ COMICRAFT LETTERING
DANA MORESHEAD & MIKE THOMAS COLORS
&
SUZANNE GAFFNEY EDITOR
BOB HARRAS GROUP EDITOR
TOM DeFALCO HEAD MERC

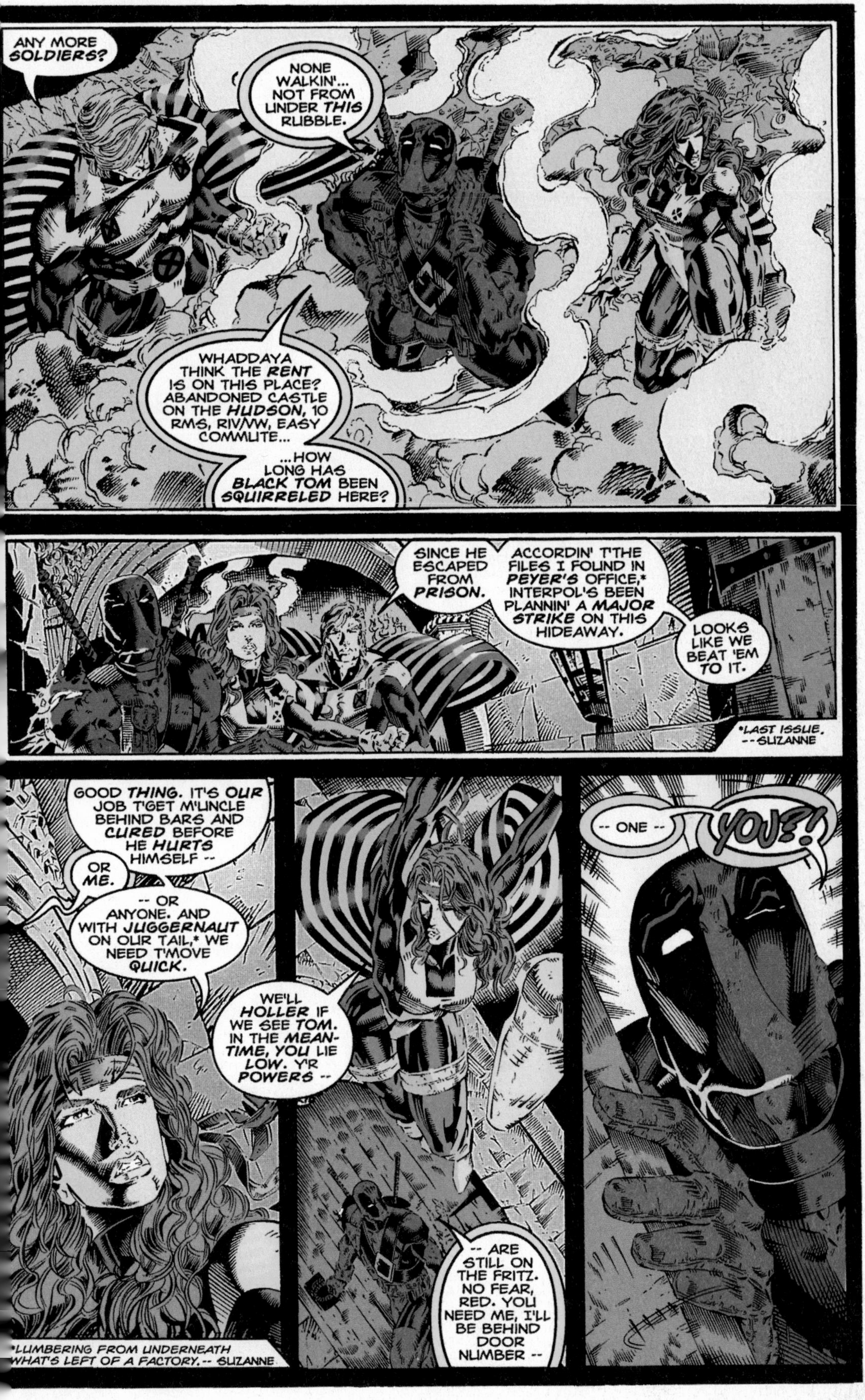
ANY MORE SOLDIERS?
NONE WALKIN'... NOT FROM UNDER THIS RUBBLE.
WHADDAYA THINK THE RENT IS ON THIS PLACE? ABANDONED CASTLE ON THE HUDSON, 10 RMS, RIV/VW, EASY COMMUTE...
...HOW LONG HAS BLACK TOM BEEN SQUIRRELED HERE?
SINCE HE ESCAPED FROM PRISON.
ACCORDIN' T'THE FILES I FOUND IN PEYER'S OFFICE,* INTERPOL'S BEEN PLANNIN' A MAJOR STRIKE ON THIS HIDEAWAY.
LOOKS LIKE WE BEAT 'EM TO IT.
*LAST ISSUE. --SUZANNE
GOOD THING. IT'S OUR JOB T'GET M'UNCLE BEHIND BARS AND CURED BEFORE HE HURTS HIMSELF --
OR ME.
-- OR ANYONE. AND WITH JUGGERNAUT ON OUR TAIL,* WE NEED T'MOVE QUICK.
*LUMBERING FROM UNDERNEATH WHAT'S LEFT OF A FACTORY. -- SUZANNE
WE'LL HOLLER IF WE SEE TOM. IN THE MEAN-TIME, YOU LIE LOW. Y'R POWERS --
-- ARE STILL ON THE FRITZ. NO FEAR, RED. YOU NEED ME, I'LL BE BEHIND DOOR NUMBER --
-- ONE --
YOU?!

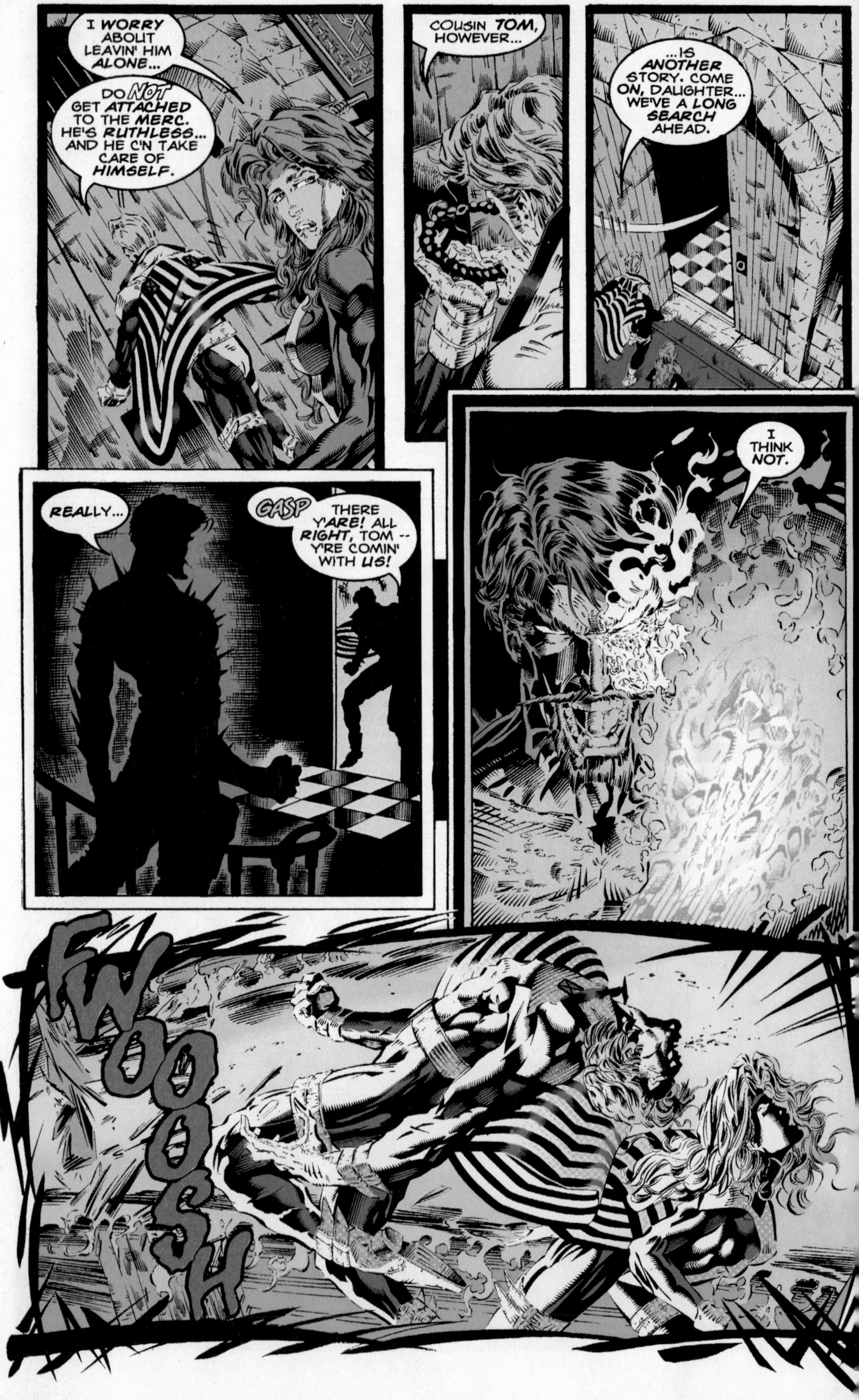
I WORRY ABOUT LEAVIN' HIM ALONE...
DO NOT GET ATTACHED TO THE MERC. HE'S RUTHLESS... AND HE C'N TAKE CARE OF HIMSELF.
COUSIN TOM, HOWEVER...
...IS ANOTHER STORY. COME ON, DAUGHTER... WE'VE A LONG SEARCH AHEAD.
REALLY...
GASP
THERE Y'ARE! ALL RIGHT, TOM -- Y'RE COMIN' WITH US!
I THINK NOT.
FWOOOSH

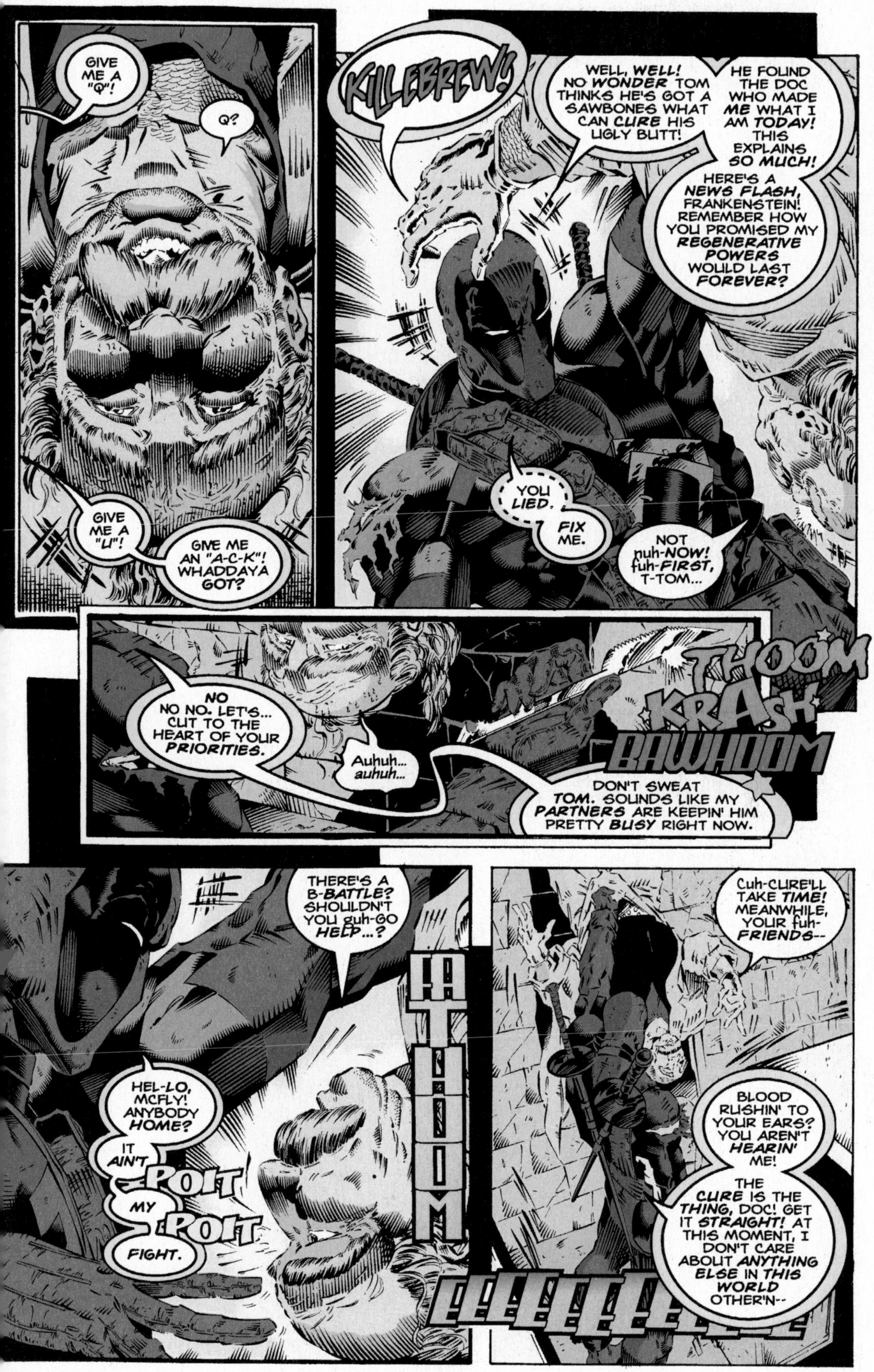
GIVE ME A "Q"!
Q?
GIVE ME A "U"!
GIVE ME AN "A-C-K"! WHADDAYA GOT?
KILLEBREW!
WELL, WELL! NO WONDER TOM THINKS HE'S GOT A SAWBONES WHAT CAN CURE HIS UGLY BUTT!
HE FOUND THE DOC WHO MADE ME WHAT I AM TODAY! THIS EXPLAINS SO MUCH!
HERE'S A NEWS FLASH, FRANKENSTEIN! REMEMBER HOW YOU PROMISED MY REGENERATIVE POWERS WOULD LAST FOREVER?
YOU LIED.
FIX ME.
NOT nuh-NOW! fuh-FIRST, T-TOM...
NO NO NO. LET'S... CUT TO THE HEART OF YOUR PRIORITIES.
Auhuh... auhuh...
THOOM
KRASH
BAWHOOM
DON'T SWEAT TOM. SOUNDS LIKE MY PARTNERS ARE KEEPIN' HIM PRETTY BUSY RIGHT NOW.
THERE'S A B-BATTLE? SHOULDN'T YOU guh-GO HELP...?
HEL-LO, MCFLY! ANYBODY HOME?
IT AIN'T POIT MY POIT FIGHT.
FATHOOM
Cuh-CURE'LL TAKE TIME! MEANWHILE, YOUR fuh-FRIENDS--
BLOOD RUSHIN' TO YOUR EARS? YOU AREN'T HEARIN' ME!
THE CURE IS THE THING, DOC! GET IT STRAIGHT! AT THIS MOMENT, I DON'T CARE ABOUT ANYTHING ELSE IN THIS WORLD OTHER'N--

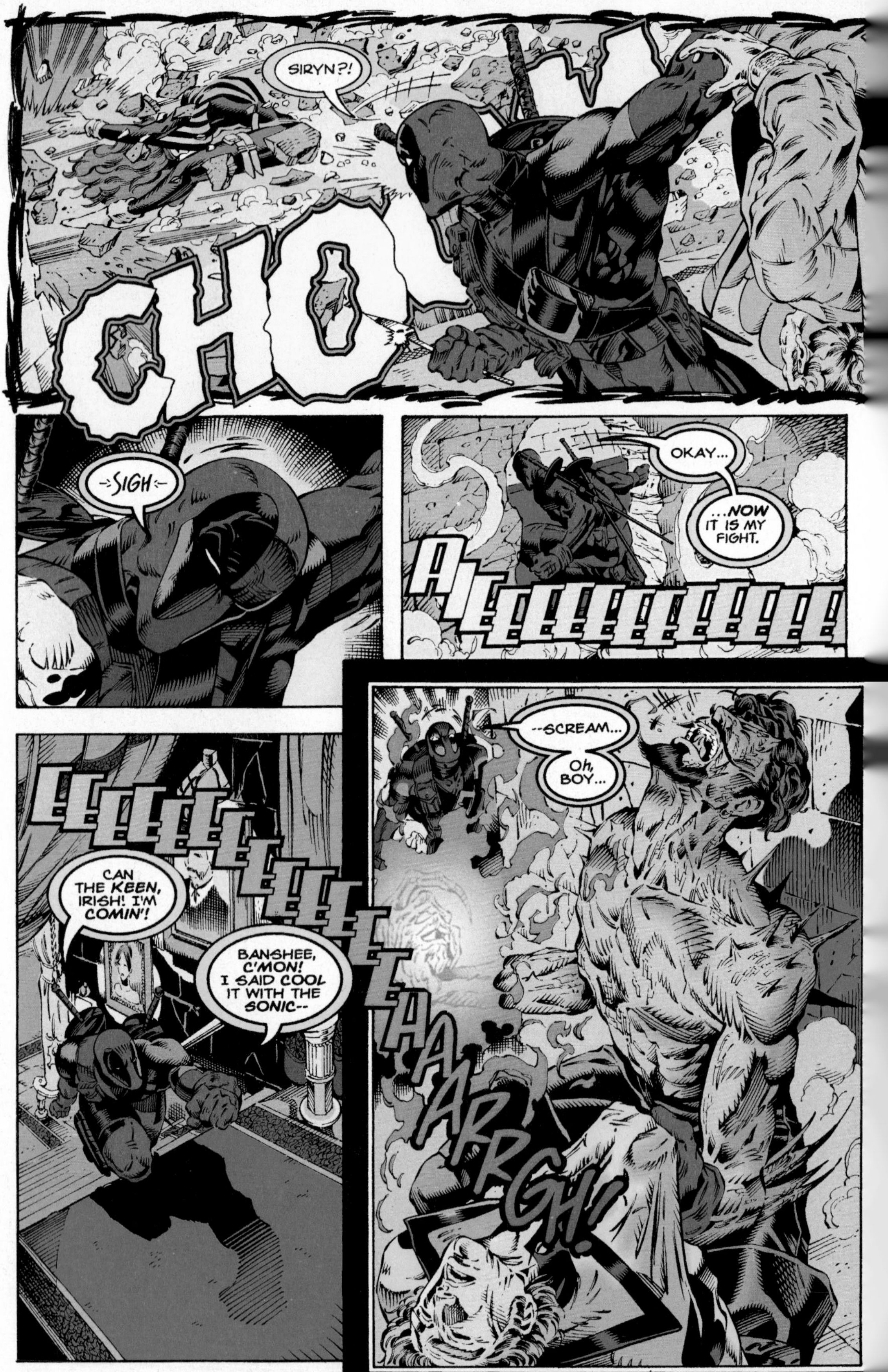
SIRYN?!
CHOOM
-SIGH-
OKAY...
...NOW IT IS MY FIGHT.
AIEEEEEEEEEEE
EEEEEEEEEEEEAAARRGH!
CAN THE KEEN, IRISH! I'M COMIN'!
BANSHEE, C'MON! I SAID COOL IT WITH THE SONIC--
--SCREAM...
OH, BOY...

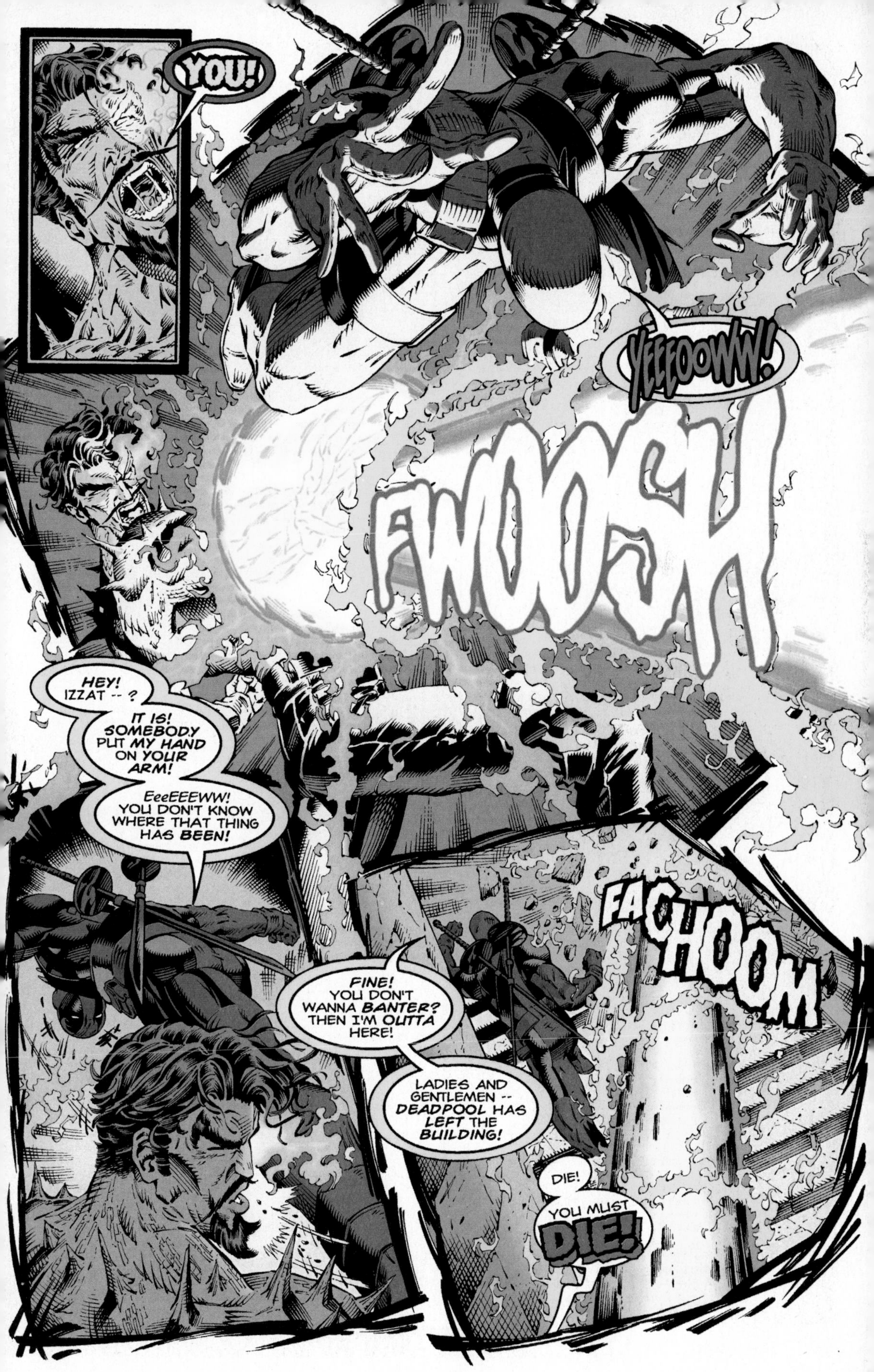
YOU!
YEEEOOWW!
FWOOSH
HEY! IZZAT -- ?
IT IS! SOMEBODY PUT MY HAND ON YOUR ARM!
EeeEEEWW! YOU DON'T KNOW WHERE THAT THING HAS BEEN!
FACHOOM
FINE! YOU DON'T WANNA BANTER? THEN I'M OUTTA HERE!
LADIES AND GENTLEMEN -- DEADPOOL HAS LEFT THE BUILDING!
DIE!
YOU MUST DIE!

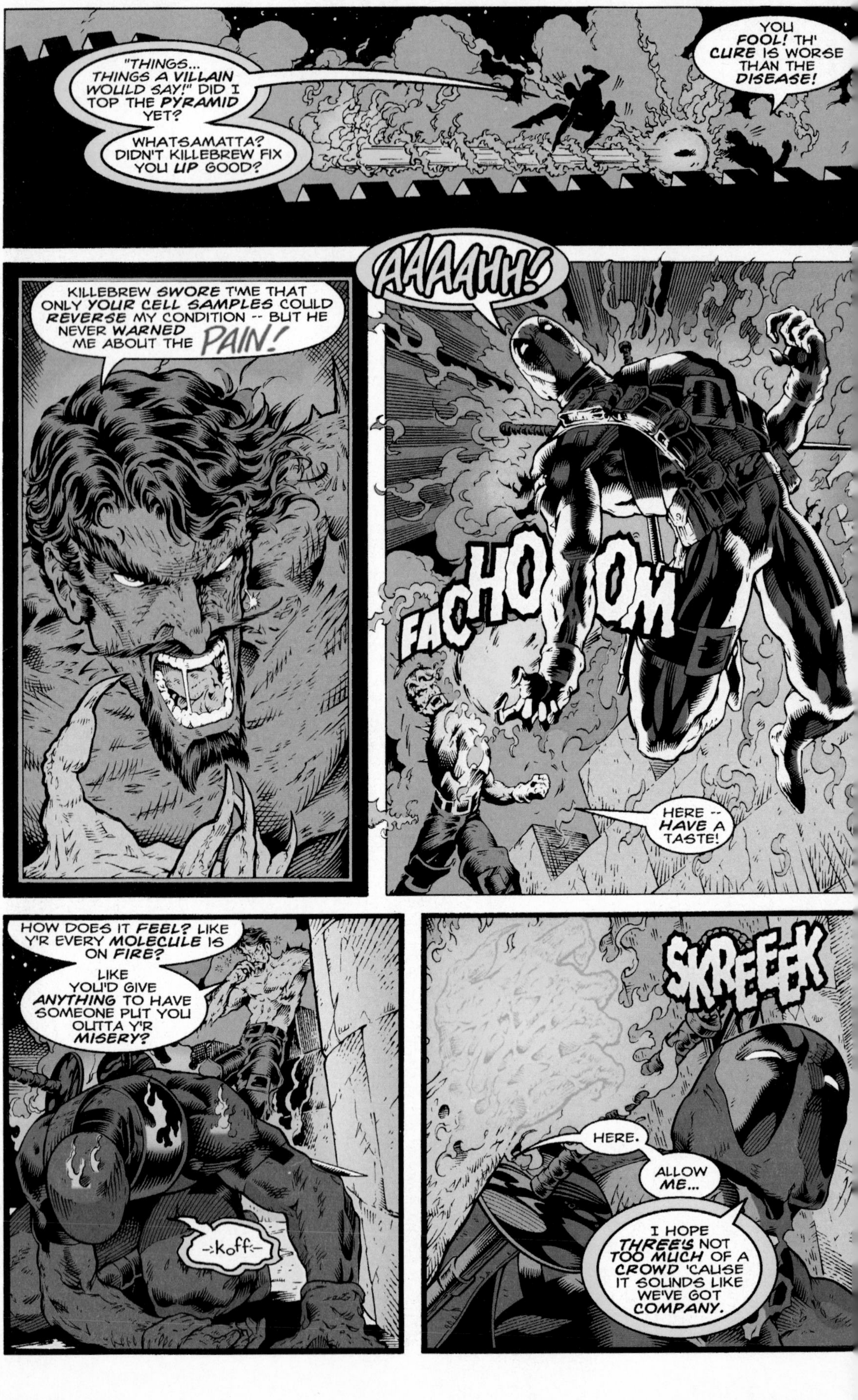

"THINGS... THINGS A VILLAIN WOULD SAY!" DID I TOP THE PYRAMID YET?
WHATSAMATTA? DIDN'T KILLEBREW FIX YOU UP GOOD?
YOU FOOL! TH' CURE IS WORSE THAN THE DISEASE!
KILLEBREW SWORE T'ME THAT ONLY YOUR CELL SAMPLES COULD REVERSE MY CONDITION -- BUT HE NEVER WARNED ME ABOUT THE PAIN!
AAAAHH!
FACHOOOM
HERE -- HAVE A TASTE!
HOW DOES IT FEEL? LIKE Y'R EVERY MOLECULE IS ON FIRE?
LIKE YOU'D GIVE ANYTHING TO HAVE SOMEONE PUT YOU OUTTA Y'R MISERY?
-:koff:-
SKREEEK
HERE.
ALLOW ME...
I HOPE THREE'S NOT TOO MUCH OF A CROWD 'CAUSE IT SOUNDS LIKE WE'VE GOT COMPANY.

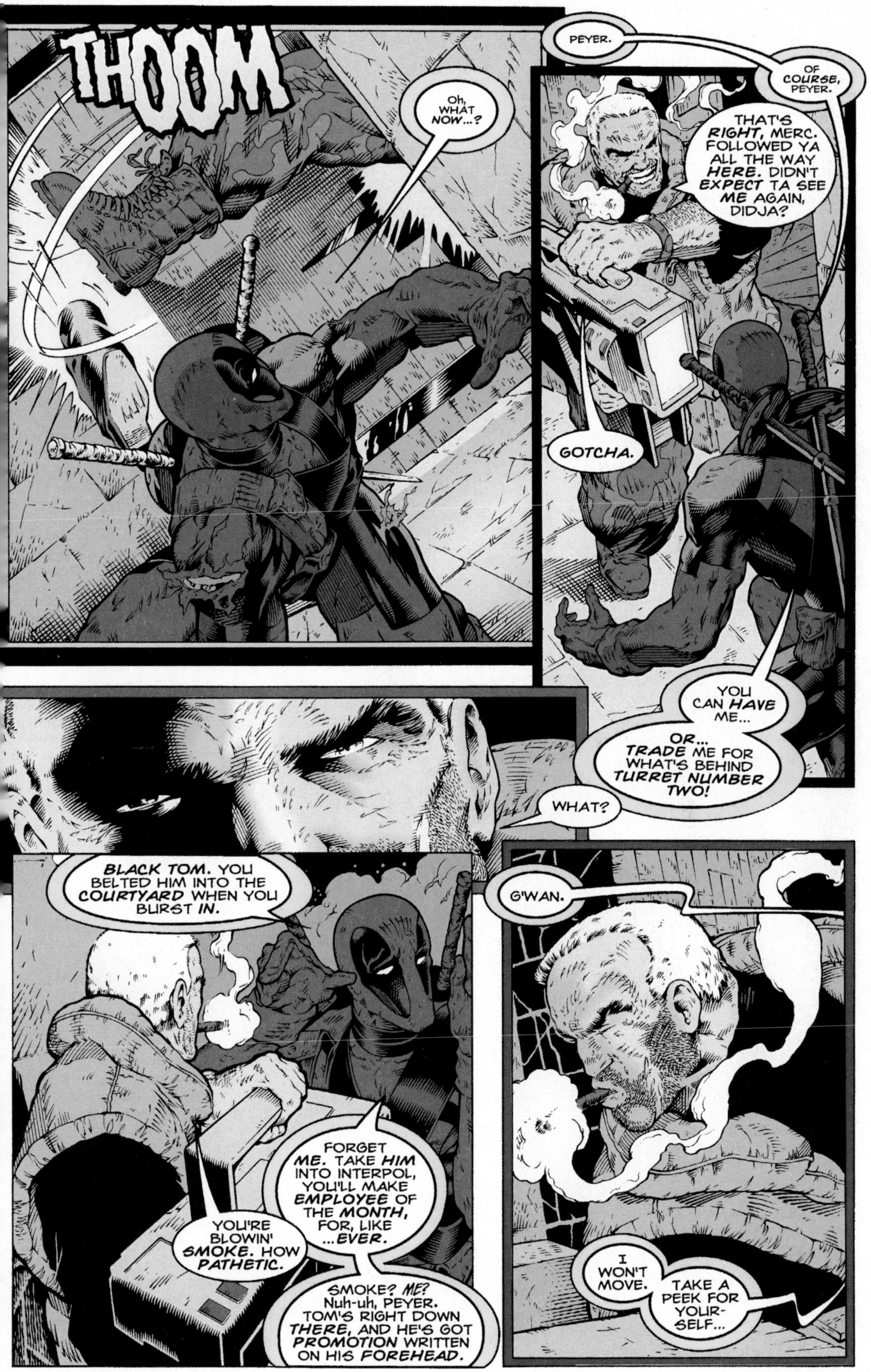
THOOM
Oh, WHAT NOW...?
PEYER.
OF COURSE, PEYER.
THAT'S RIGHT, MERC. FOLLOWED YA ALL THE WAY HERE. DIDN'T EXPECT TA SEE ME AGAIN, DIDJA?
GOTCHA.
YOU CAN HAVE ME...
OR... TRADE ME FOR WHAT'S BEHIND TURRET NUMBER TWO!
WHAT?
BLACK TOM. YOU BELTED HIM INTO THE COURTYARD WHEN YOU BURST IN.
FORGET ME. TAKE HIM INTO INTERPOL, YOU'LL MAKE EMPLOYEE OF THE MONTH, FOR, LIKE ...EVER.
YOU'RE BLOWIN' SMOKE. HOW PATHETIC.
SMOKE? ME? Nuh-uh, PEYER. TOM'S RIGHT DOWN THERE, AND HE'S GOT PROMOTION WRITTEN ON HIS FOREHEAD.
G'WAN.
I WON'T MOVE.
TAKE A PEEK FOR YOUR-SELF...

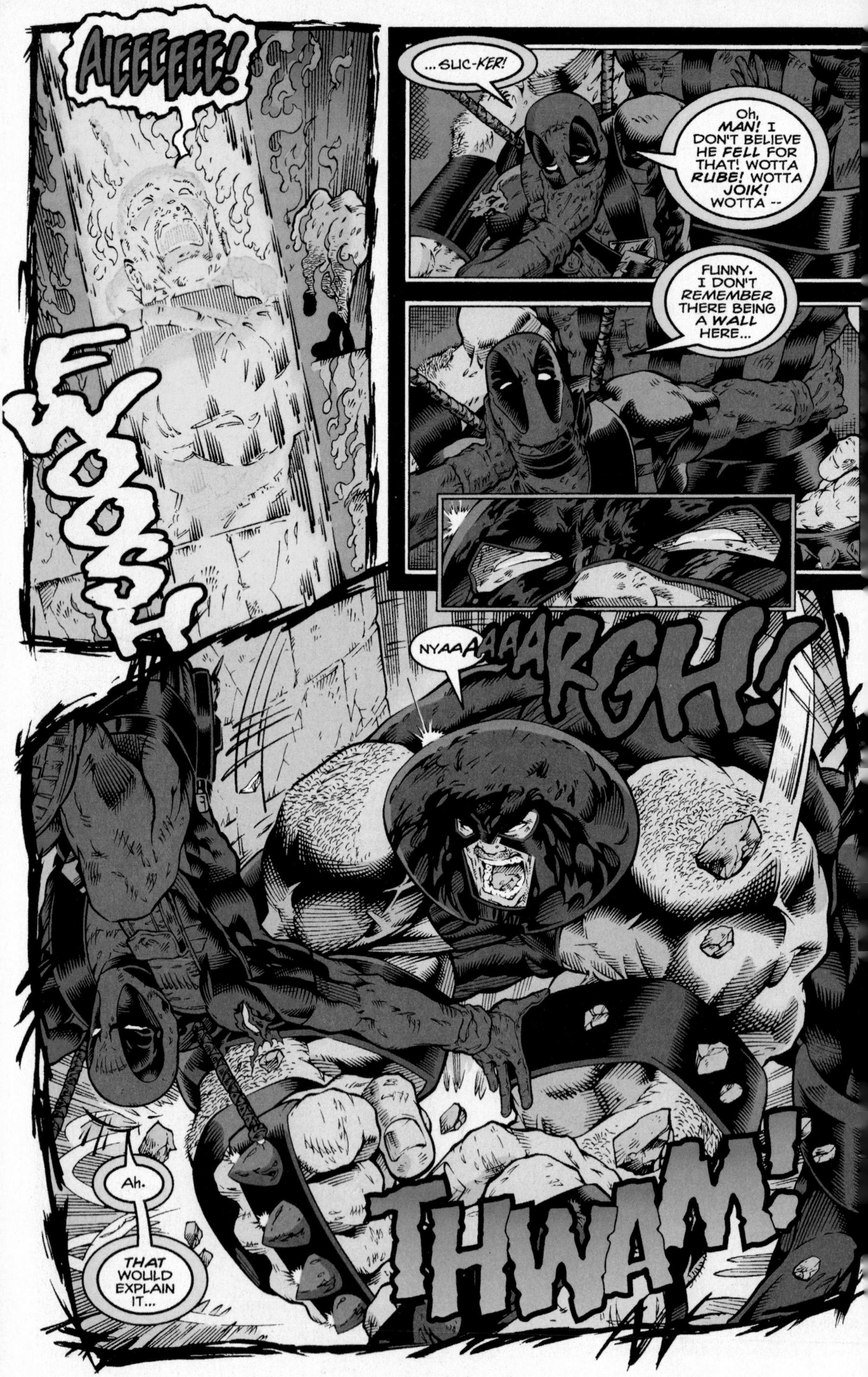
AIEEEEEEE!
FOOOSH!
...SUC-KER!
Oh, MAN! I DON'T BELIEVE HE FELL FOR THAT! WOTTA RUBE! WOTTA JOIK! WOTTA --
FUNNY. I DON'T REMEMBER THERE BEING A WALL HERE...
NYAAAAAARGH!!
Ah.
THAT WOULD EXPLAIN IT...
THWAM!

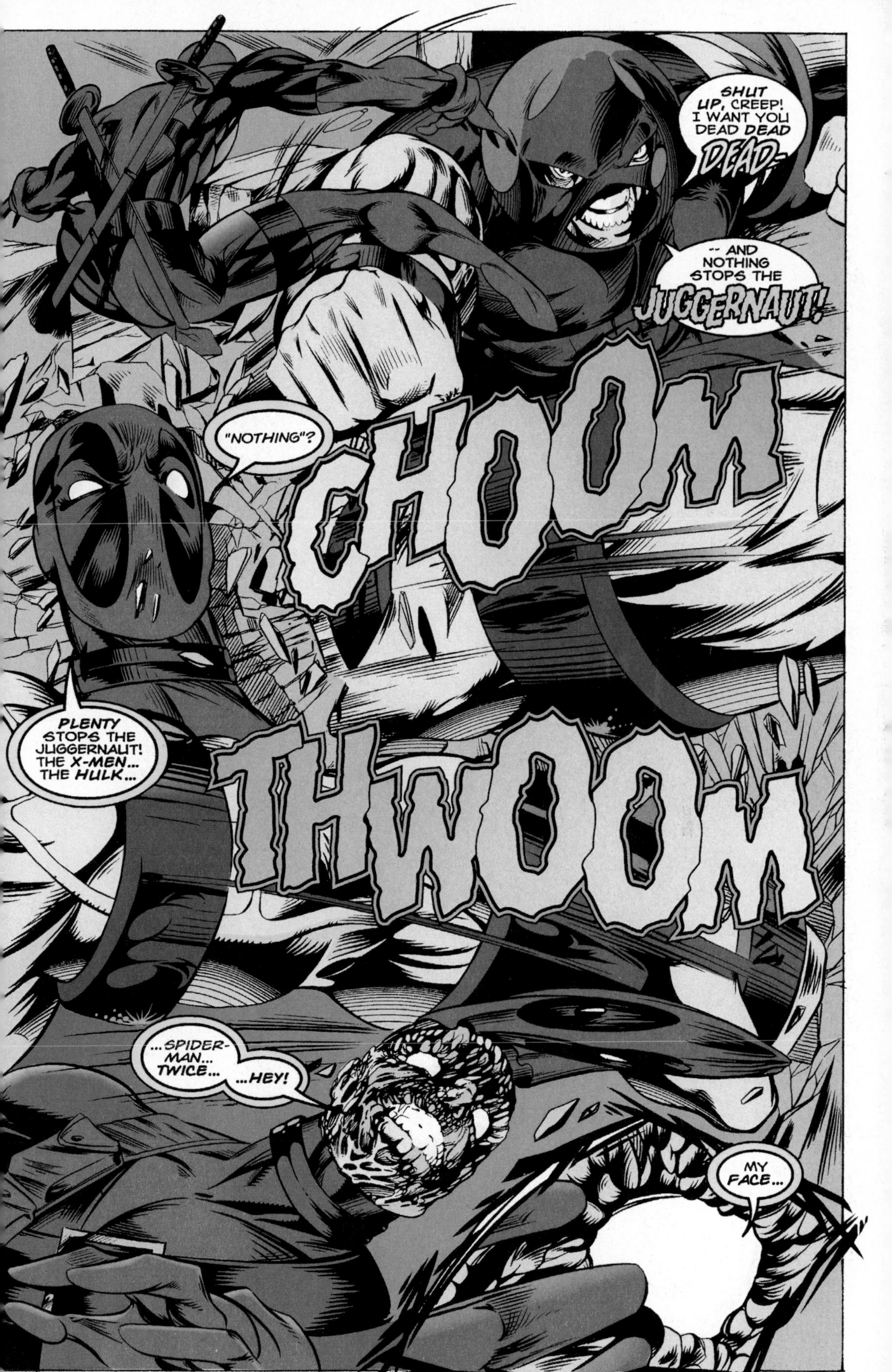
SHUT UP, CREEP! I WANT YOU DEAD DEAD DEAD--
-- AND NOTHING STOPS THE JUGGERNAUT!
"NOTHING"?
CHOOM
THWOOM
PLENTY STOPS THE JUGGERNAUT! THE X-MEN... THE HULK...
...SPIDER-MAN... TWICE...
...HEY!
MY FACE...

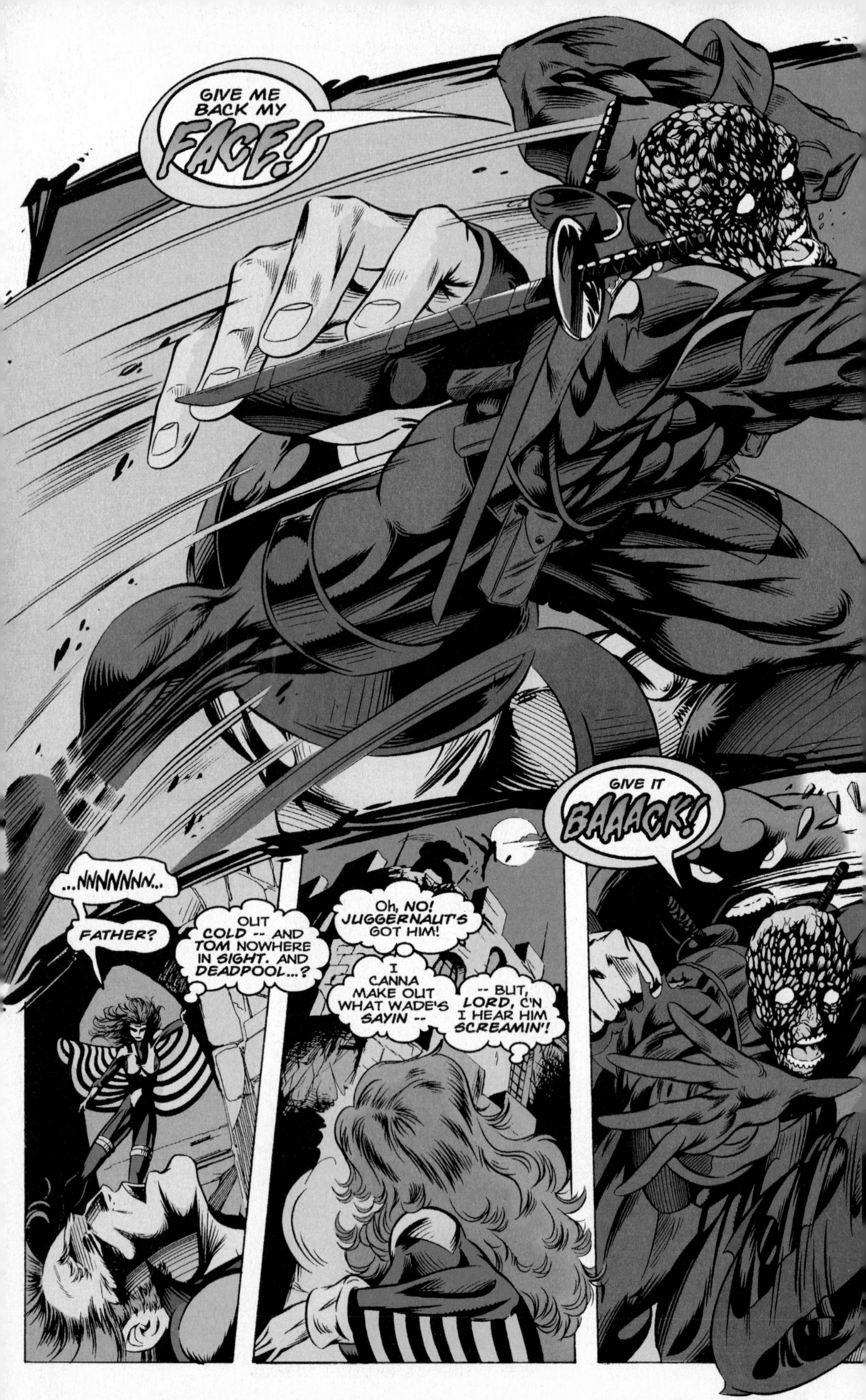
GIVE ME BACK MY FACE!
GIVE IT BAAACK!
...NNNNNNN...
FATHER?
OUT COLD -- AND TOM NOWHERE IN SIGHT. AND DEADPOOL...?
Oh, NO! JUGGERNAUT'S GOT HIM!
I CANNA MAKE OUT WHAT WADE'S SAYIN --
-- BUT, LORD, C'N I HEAR HIM SCREAMIN'!

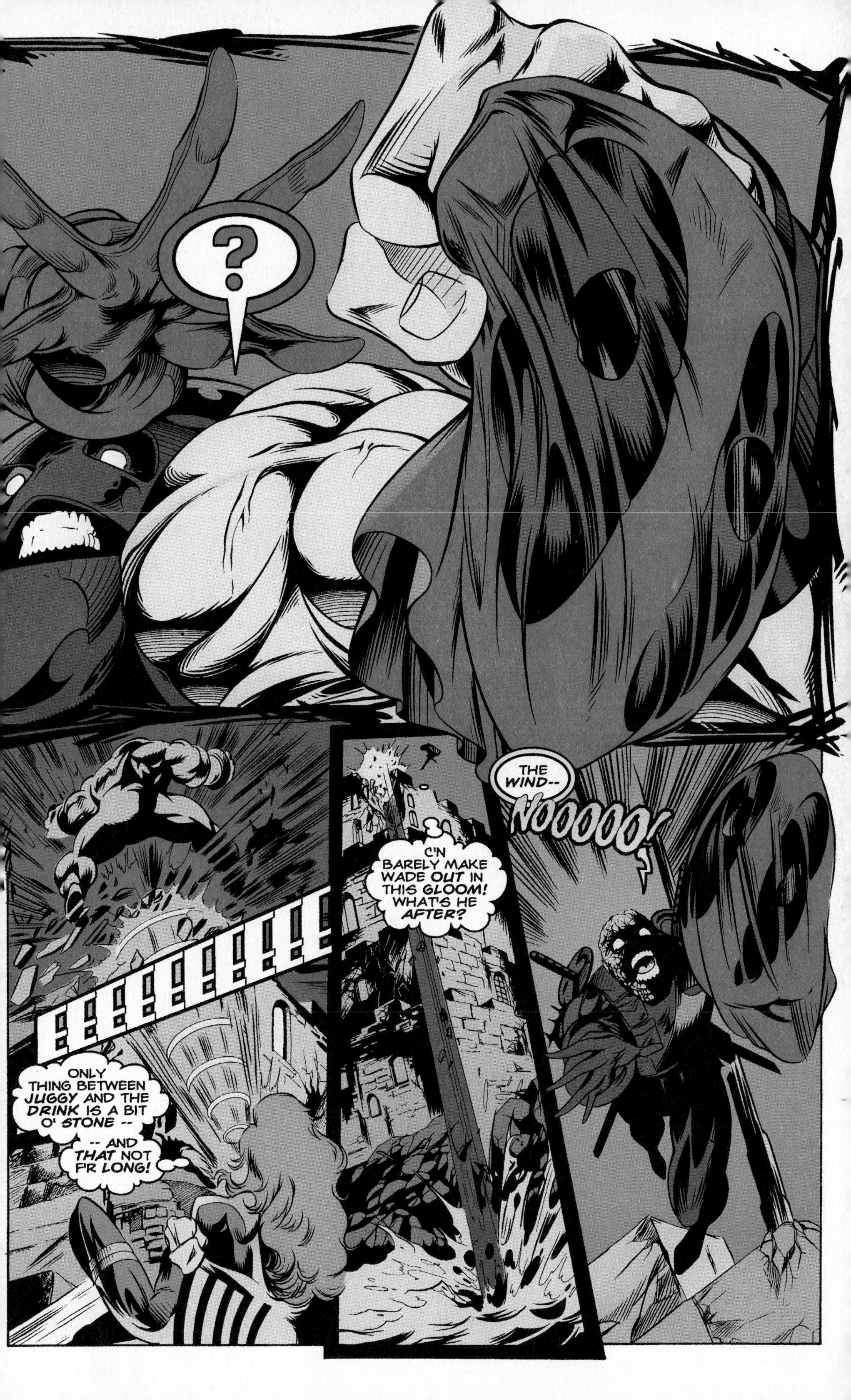

?
EEEEEEEEEEEE
ONLY THING BETWEEN JUGGY AND THE DRINK IS A BIT O' STONE --
-- AND THAT NOT F'R LONG!
C'N BARELY MAKE WADE OUT IN THIS GLOOM! WHAT'S HE AFTER?
THE WIND--
NOOOOO!

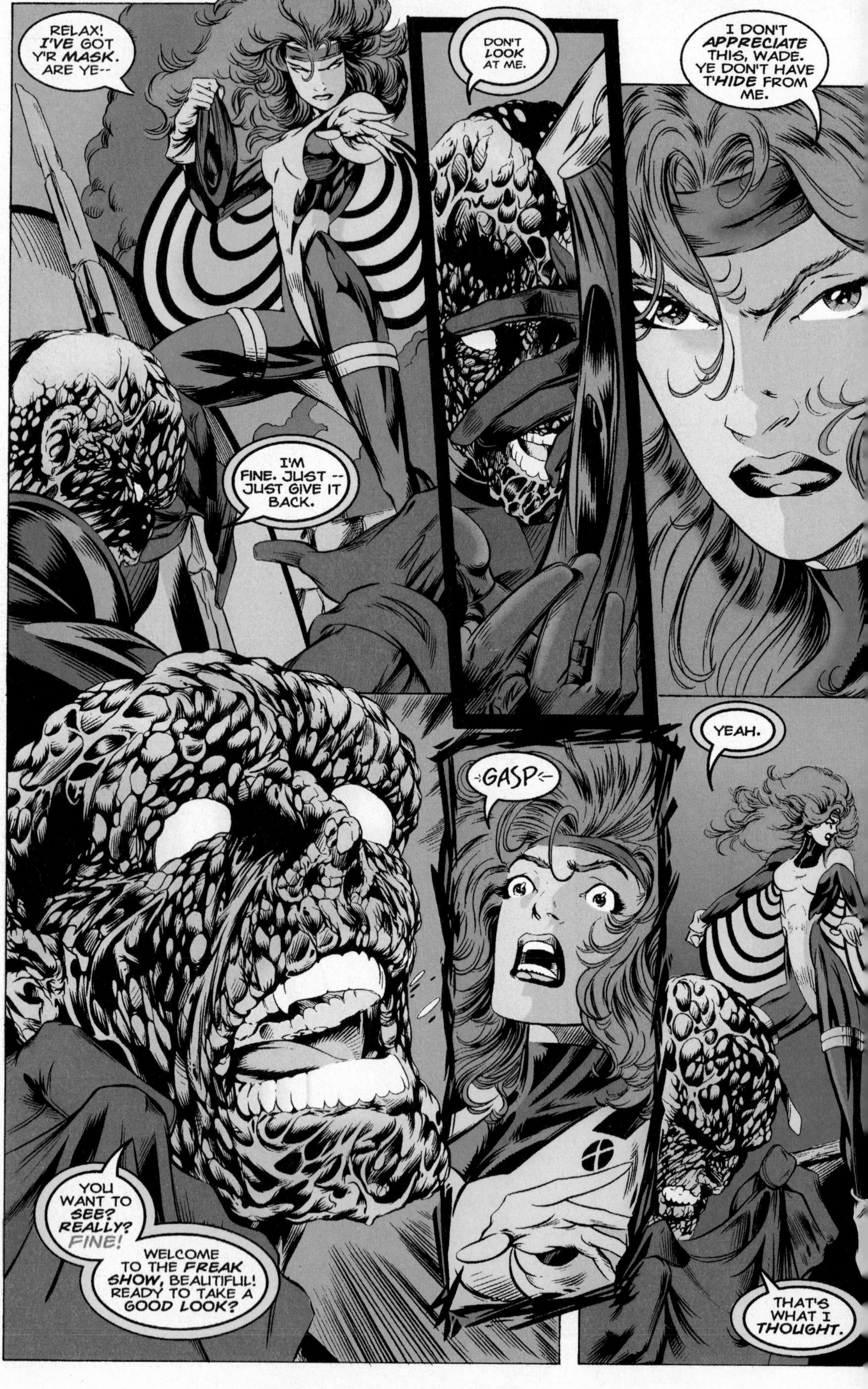
RELAX! I'VE GOT Y'R MASK. ARE YE--
I'M FINE. JUST -- JUST GIVE IT BACK.
DON'T LOOK AT ME.
I DON'T APPRECIATE THIS, WADE. YE DON'T HAVE T'HIDE FROM ME.
YOU WANT TO SEE? REALLY? FINE!
WELCOME TO THE FREAK SHOW, BEAUTIFUL! READY TO TAKE A GOOD LOOK?
GASP
YEAH.
THAT'S WHAT I THOUGHT.

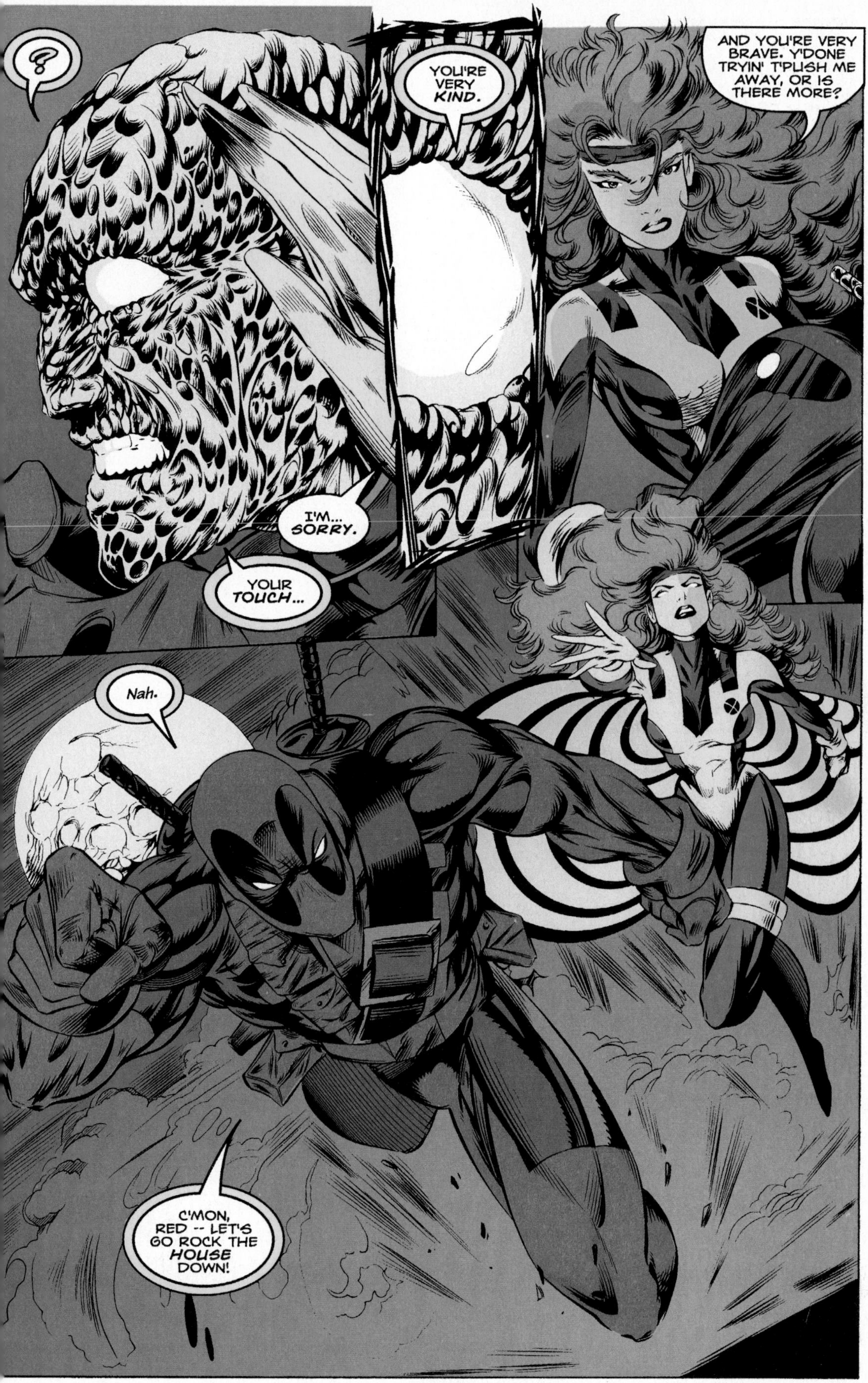
?
YOU'RE VERY KIND.
AND YOU'RE VERY BRAVE. Y'DONE TRYIN' T'PUSH ME AWAY, OR IS THERE MORE?
I'M... SORRY.
YOUR TOUCH...
Nah.
C'MON, RED -- LET'S GO ROCK THE HOUSE DOWN!

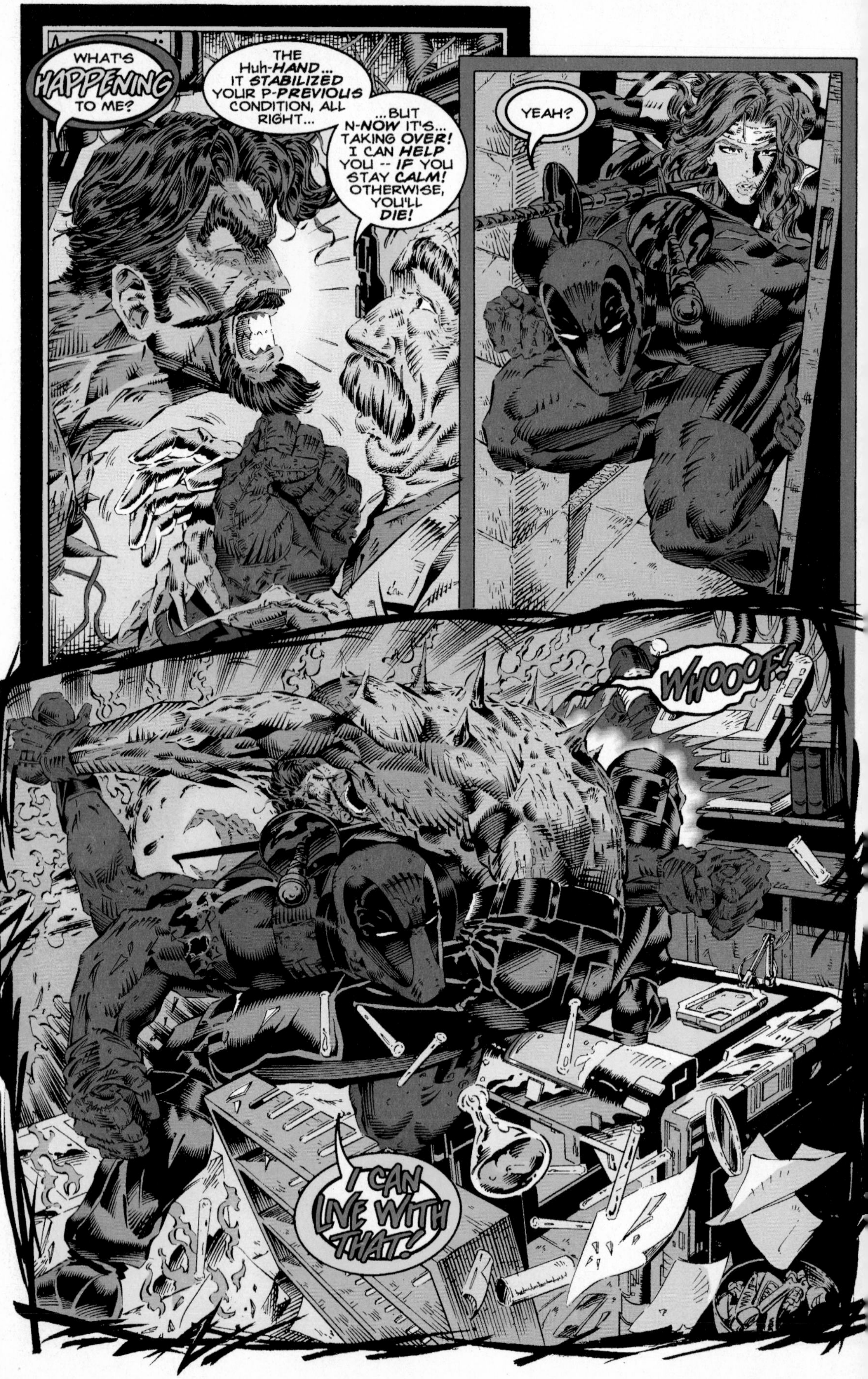
WHAT'S HAPPENING TO ME?
THE Huh-HAND... IT STABILIZED YOUR P-PREVIOUS CONDITION, ALL RIGHT...
...BUT N-NOW IT'S... TAKING OVER! I CAN HELP YOU -- IF YOU STAY CALM! OTHERWISE, YOU'LL DIE!
YEAH?
WHOOOF!
I CAN LIVE WITH THAT!

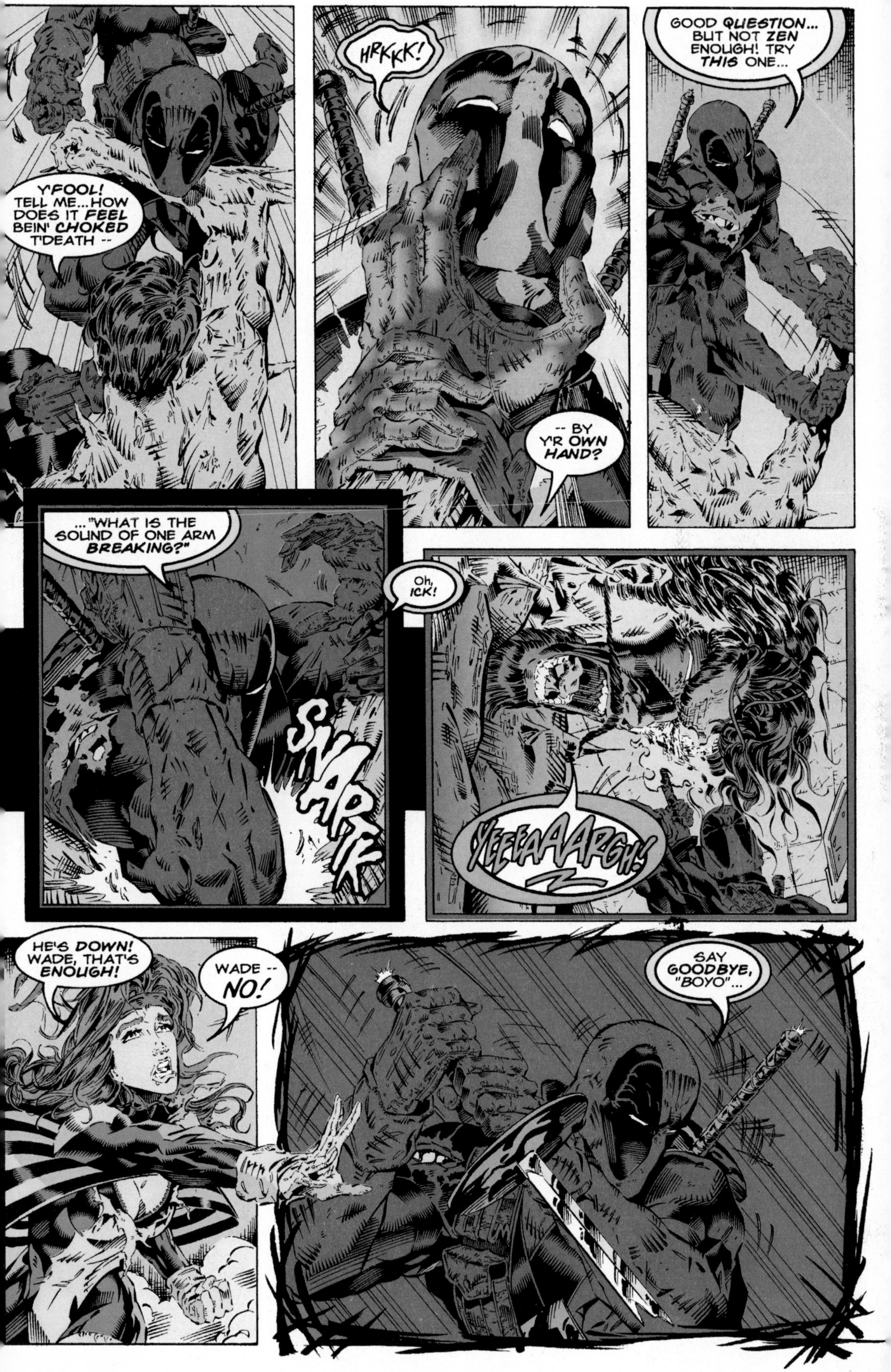

Y'FOOL! TELL ME...HOW DOES IT FEEL BEIN' CHOKED T'DEATH --
HRKKK!
-- BY Y'R OWN HAND?
GOOD QUESTION... BUT NOT ZEN ENOUGH! TRY THIS ONE...
..."WHAT IS THE SOUND OF ONE ARM BREAKING?"
SNAPIK
Oh, ICK!
YEEEAAARGH!
HE'S DOWN! WADE, THAT'S ENOUGH!
WADE -- NO!
SAY GOODBYE, "BOYO"...

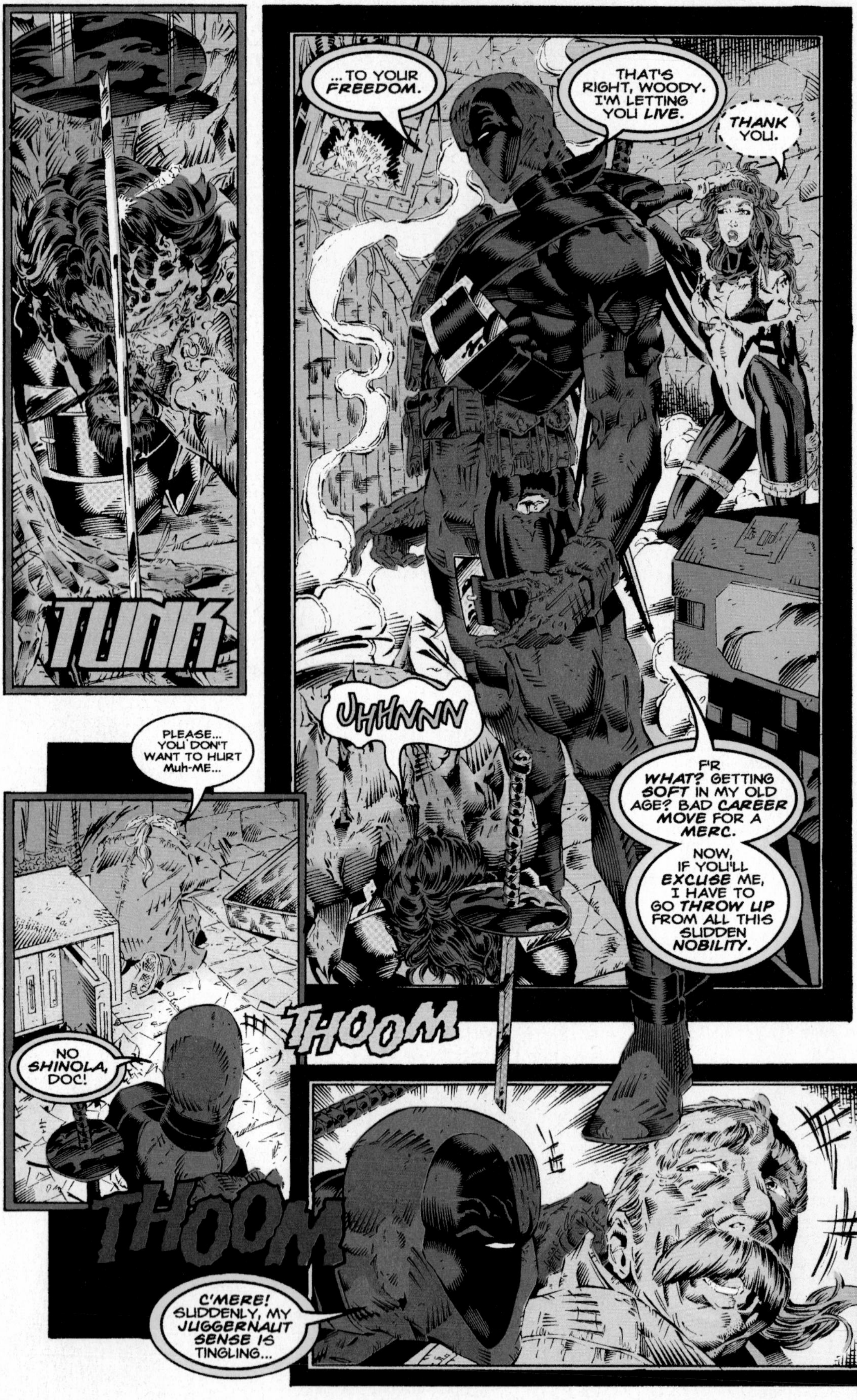
TUNK
...TO YOUR FREEDOM.
THAT'S RIGHT, WOODY. I'M LETTING YOU LIVE.
THANK YOU.
UHHNNN
F'R WHAT? GETTING SOFT IN MY OLD AGE? BAD CAREER MOVE FOR A MERC.
NOW, IF YOU'LL EXCUSE ME, I HAVE TO GO THROW UP FROM ALL THIS SUDDEN NOBILITY.
PLEASE... YOU DON'T WANT TO HURT Muh-ME...
NO SHINOLA, DOC!
THOOM
THOOM
C'MERE! SUDDENLY, MY JUGGERNAUT SENSE IS TINGLING...

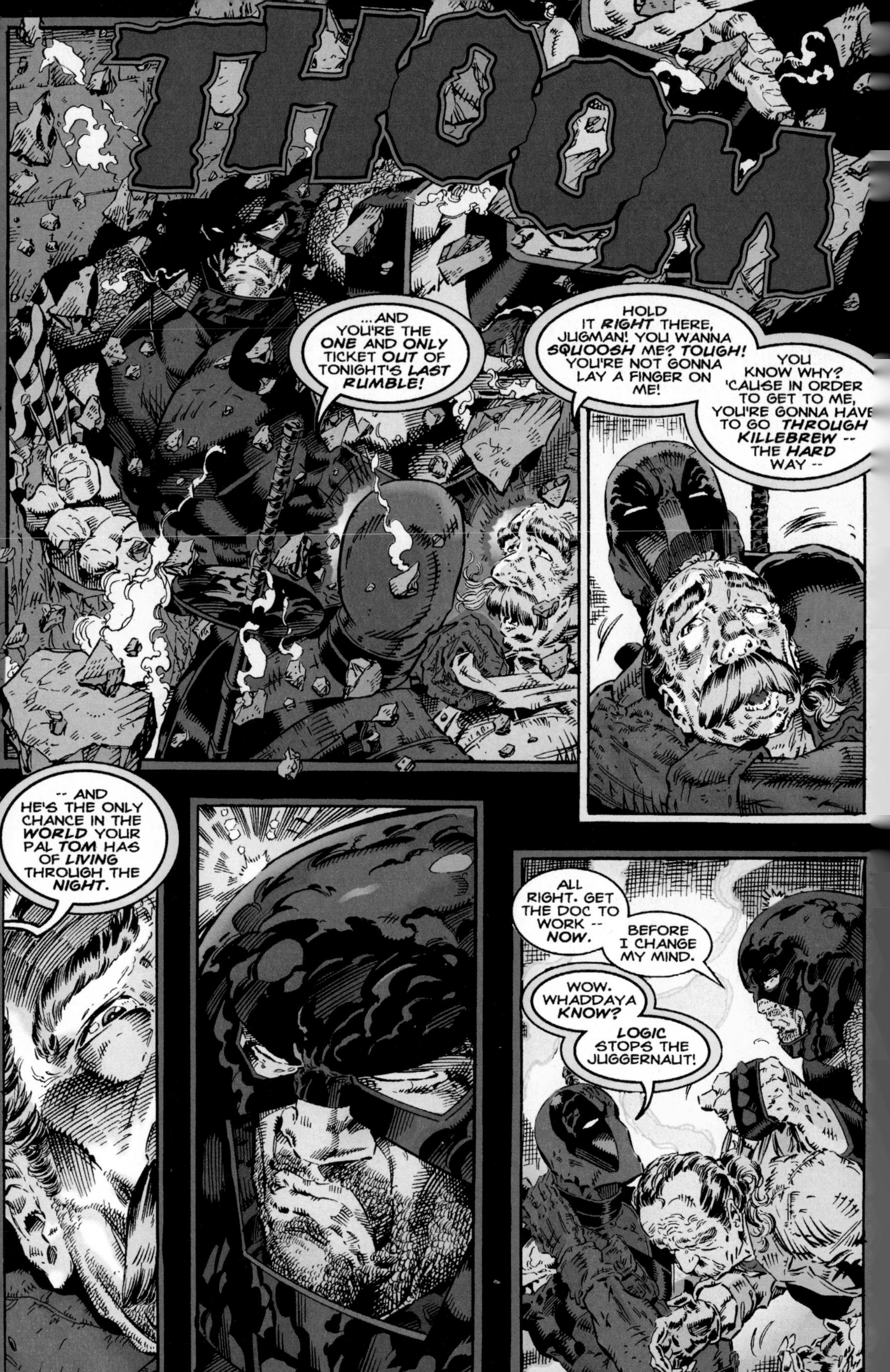
THOOM
...AND YOU'RE THE ONE AND ONLY TICKET OUT OF TONIGHT'S LAST RUMBLE!
HOLD IT RIGHT THERE, JUGMAN! YOU WANNA SQUOOSH ME? TOUGH! YOU'RE NOT GONNA LAY A FINGER ON ME!
YOU KNOW WHY? 'CAUSE IN ORDER TO GET TO ME, YOU'RE GONNA HAVE TO GO THROUGH KILLEBREW -- THE HARD WAY --
-- AND HE'S THE ONLY CHANCE IN THE WORLD YOUR PAL TOM HAS OF LIVING THROUGH THE NIGHT.
ALL RIGHT. GET THE DOC TO WORK -- NOW.
BEFORE I CHANGE MY MIND.
WOW. WHADDAYA KNOW? LOGIC STOPS THE JUGGERNAUT!

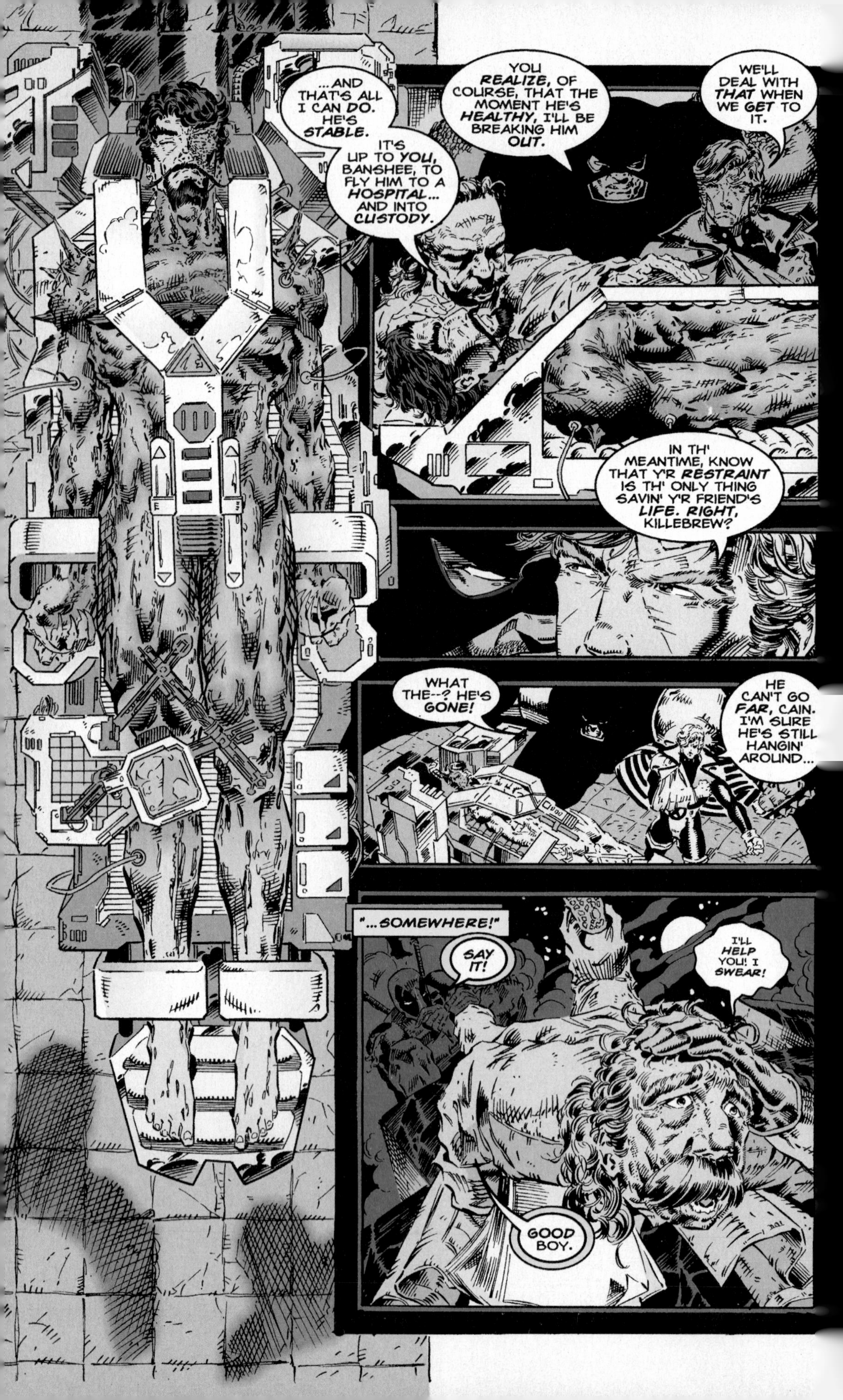
...AND THAT'S ALL I CAN DO. HE'S STABLE.
IT'S UP TO YOU, BANSHEE, TO FLY HIM TO A HOSPITAL... AND INTO CUSTODY.
YOU REALIZE, OF COURSE, THAT THE MOMENT HE'S HEALTHY, I'LL BE BREAKING HIM OUT.
WE'LL DEAL WITH THAT WHEN WE GET TO IT.
IN TH' MEANTIME, KNOW THAT Y'R RESTRAINT IS TH' ONLY THING SAVIN' Y'R FRIEND'S LIFE. RIGHT, KILLEBREW?
WHAT THE--? HE'S GONE!
HE CAN'T GO FAR, CAIN. I'M SURE HE'S STILL HANGIN' AROUND...
"...SOMEWHERE!"
SAY IT!
I'LL HELP YOU! I SWEAR!
GOOD BOY.

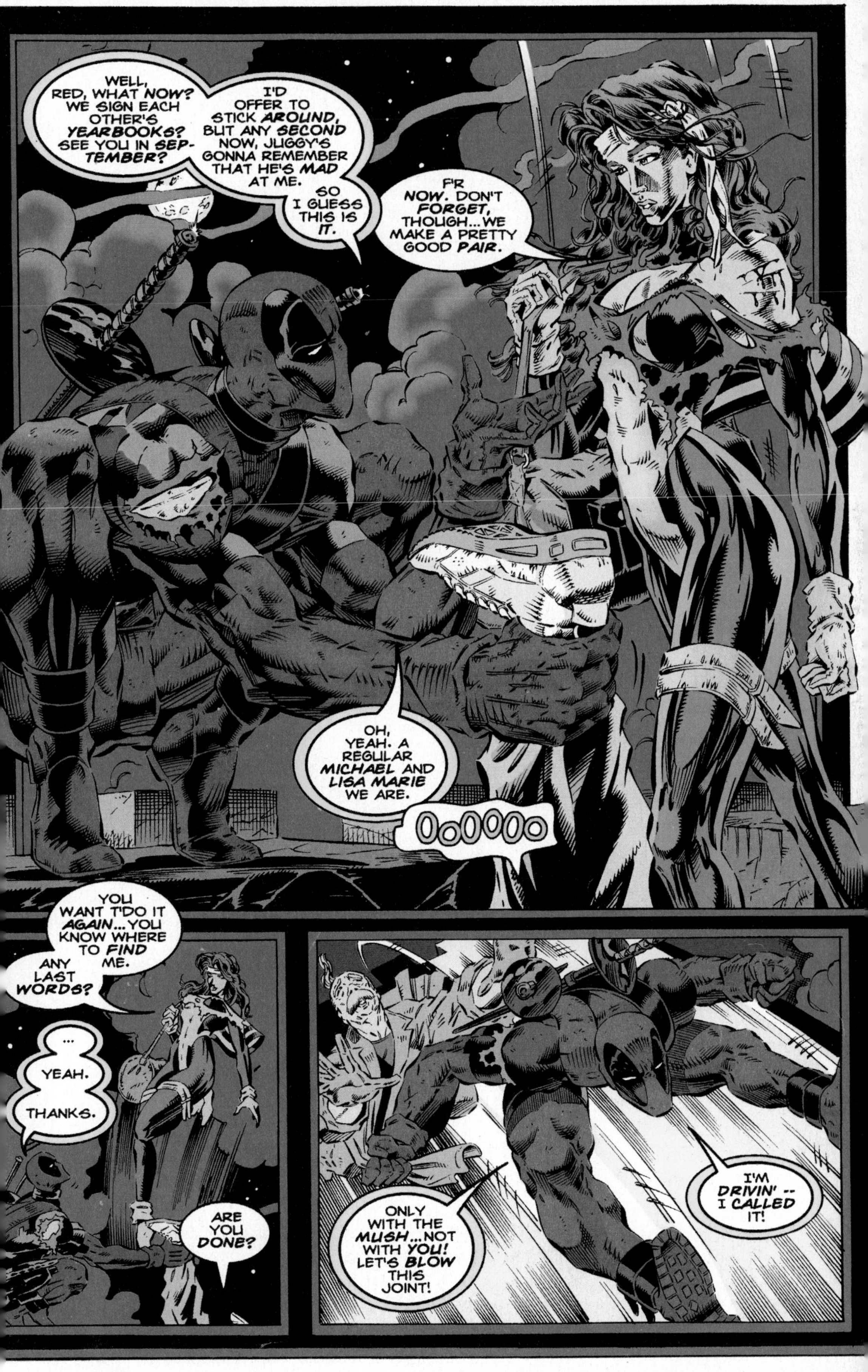
WELL, RED, WHAT NOW? WE SIGN EACH OTHER'S YEARBOOKS? SEE YOU IN SEP-TEMBER?
I'D OFFER TO STICK AROUND, BUT ANY SECOND NOW, JUGGY'S GONNA REMEMBER THAT HE'S MAD AT ME.
SO I GUESS THIS IS IT.
F'R NOW. DON'T FORGET, THOUGH...WE MAKE A PRETTY GOOD PAIR.
OH, YEAH. A REGULAR MICHAEL AND LISA MARIE WE ARE.
OoOOOo
YOU WANT T'DO IT AGAIN...YOU KNOW WHERE TO FIND ME.
ANY LAST WORDS?
...
YEAH.
THANKS.
ARE YOU DONE?
ONLY WITH THE MUSH...NOT WITH YOU! LET'S BLOW THIS JOINT!
I'M DRIVIN' -- I CALLED IT!

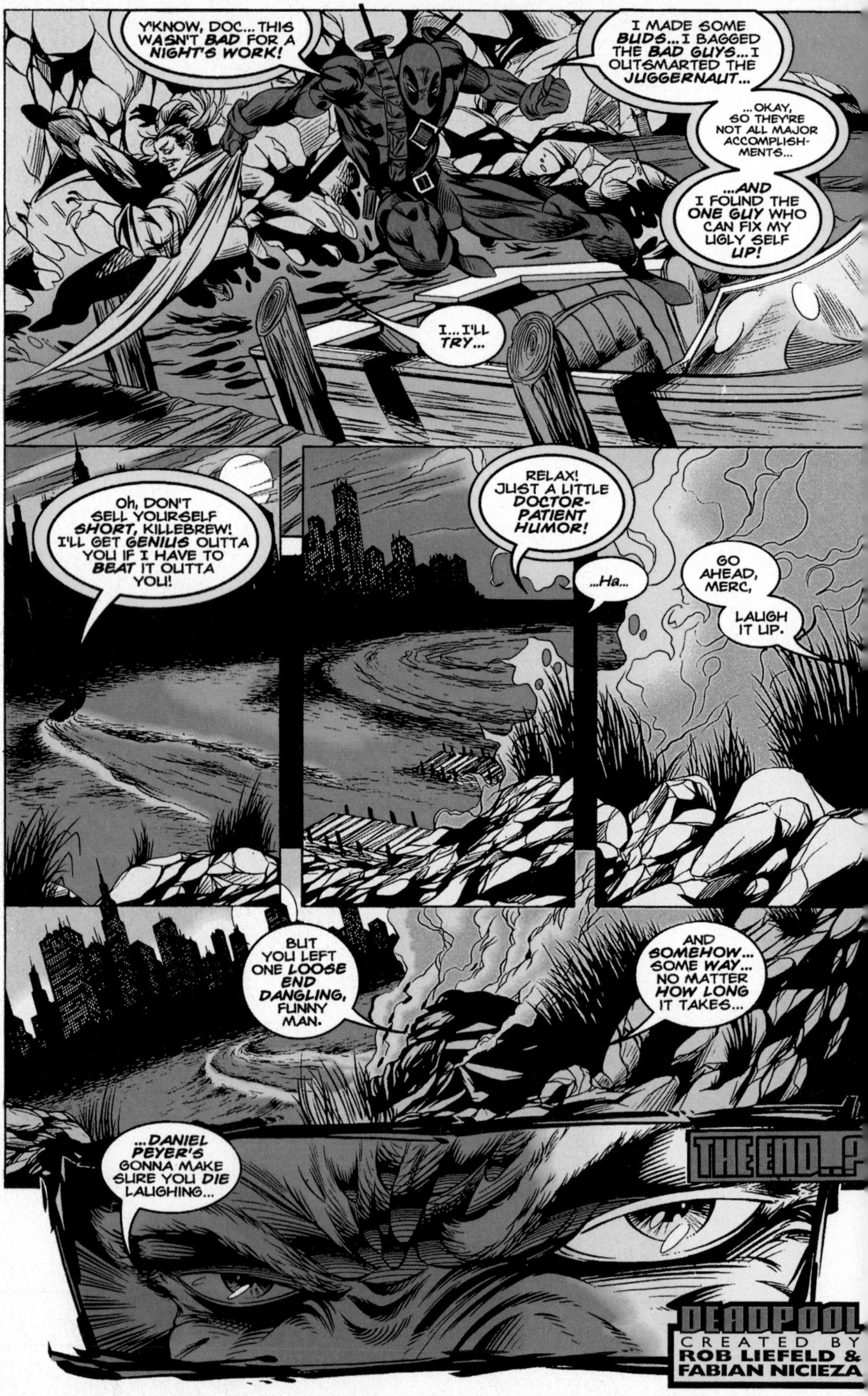

Y'KNOW, DOC... THIS WASN'T BAD FOR A NIGHT'S WORK!
I MADE SOME BUDS... I BAGGED THE BAD GUYS... I OUTSMARTED THE JUGGERNAUT...
...OKAY, SO THEY'RE NOT ALL MAJOR ACCOMPLISH-MENTS...
...AND I FOUND THE ONE GUY WHO CAN FIX MY UGLY SELF UP!
I... I'LL TRY...
Oh, DON'T SELL YOURSELF SHORT, KILLEBREW! I'LL GET GENIUS OUTTA YOU IF I HAVE TO BEAT IT OUTTA YOU!
RELAX! JUST A LITTLE DOCTOR-PATIENT HUMOR!
...Ha...
GO AHEAD, MERC,
LAUGH IT UP.
BUT YOU LEFT ONE LOOSE END DANGLING, FUNNY MAN.
AND SOMEHOW... SOME WAY... NO MATTER HOW LONG IT TAKES...
...DANIEL PEYER'S GONNA MAKE SURE YOU DIE LAUGHING...
THE END..?
DEADPOOL
CREATED BY
ROB LIEFELD &
FABIAN NICIEZA

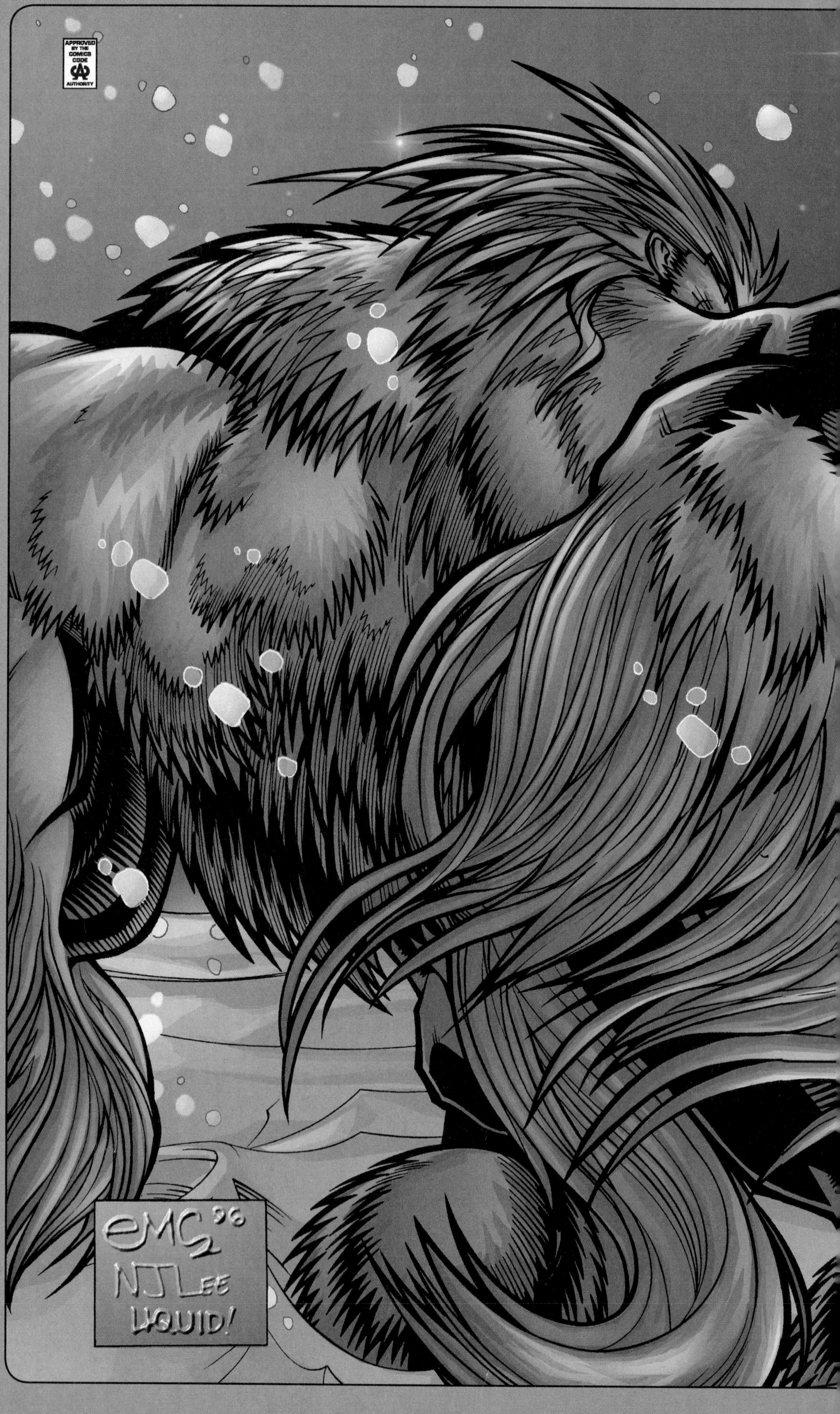
APPROVED BY THE COMICS CODE AUTHORITY
eMC2 96
NJLee
LIQUID!

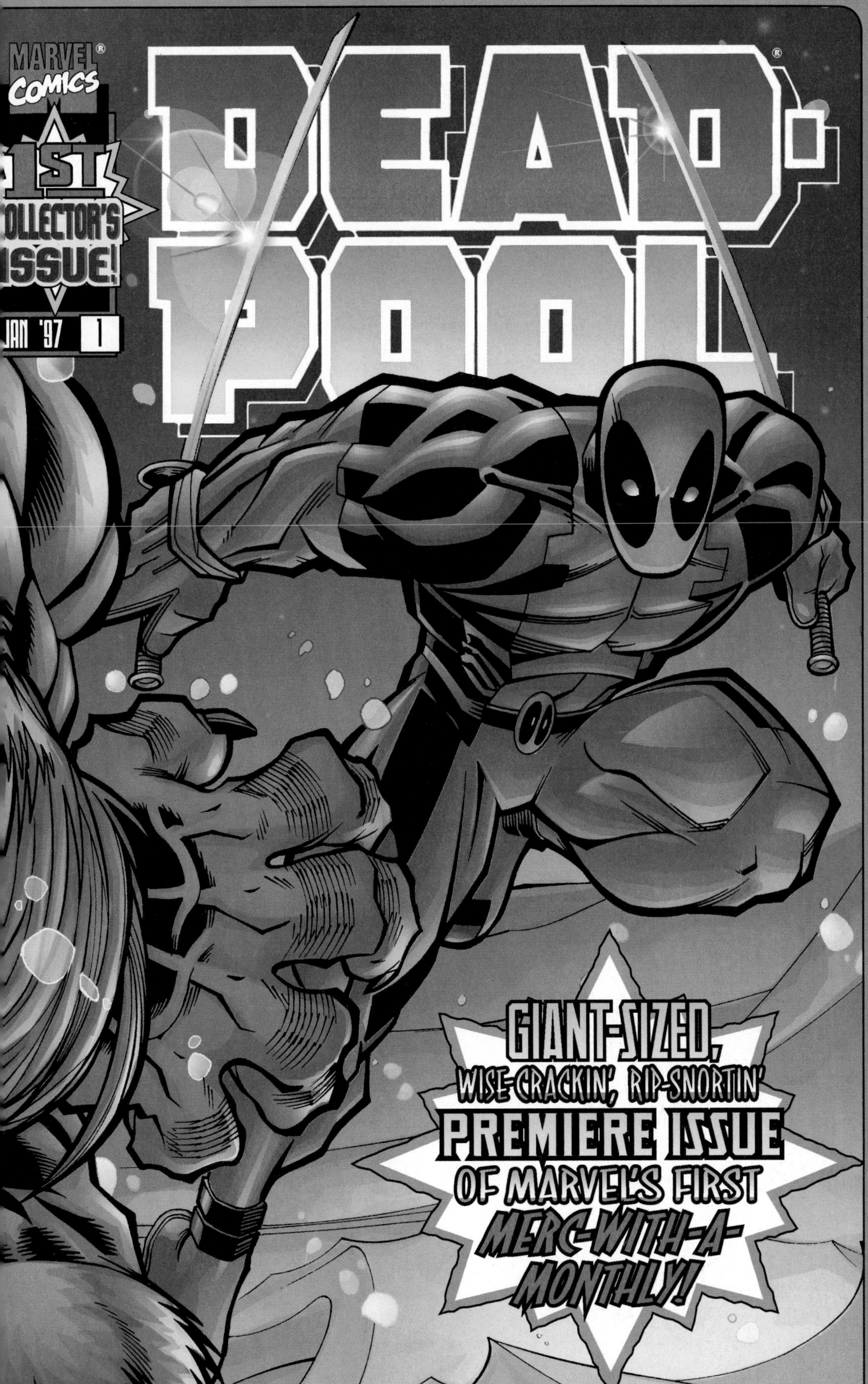
MARVEL COMICS
1ST COLLECTOR'S ISSUE!
JAN '97 1
DEAD-POOL
GIANT-SIZED, WISE-CRACKIN', RIP-SNORTIN' PREMIERE ISSUE OF MARVEL'S FIRST MERC-WITH-A-MONTHLY!

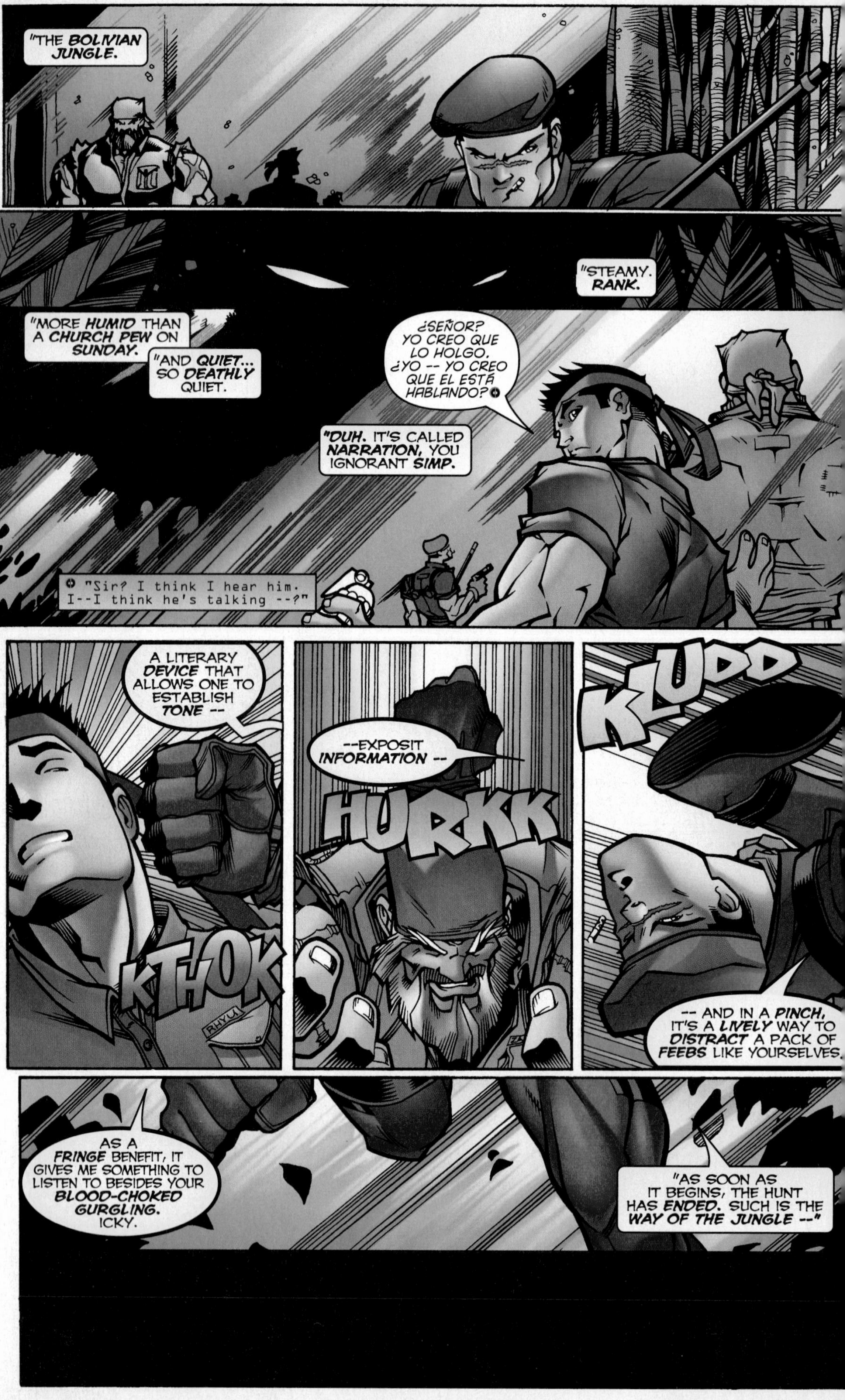

"THE BOLIVIAN JUNGLE.
"STEAMY. RANK.
"MORE HUMID THAN A CHURCH PEW ON SUNDAY.
"AND QUIET... SO DEATHLY QUIET.
¿SEÑOR? YO CREO QUE LO HOLGO. ¿YO -- YO CREO QUE EL ESTÁ HABLANDO?
"DUH. IT'S CALLED NARRATION, YOU IGNORANT SIMP.
"Sir? I think I hear him. I--I think he's talking --?"
A LITERARY DEVICE THAT ALLOWS ONE TO ESTABLISH TONE --
KTHOK
RHYU
--EXPOSIT INFORMATION --
HURKK
KLUDD
-- AND IN A PINCH, IT'S A LIVELY WAY TO DISTRACT A PACK OF FEEBS LIKE YOURSELVES.
AS A FRINGE BENEFIT, IT GIVES ME SOMETHING TO LISTEN TO BESIDES YOUR BLOOD-CHOKED GURGLING. ICKY.
"AS SOON AS IT BEGINS, THE HUNT HAS ENDED. SUCH IS THE WAY OF THE JUNGLE --"

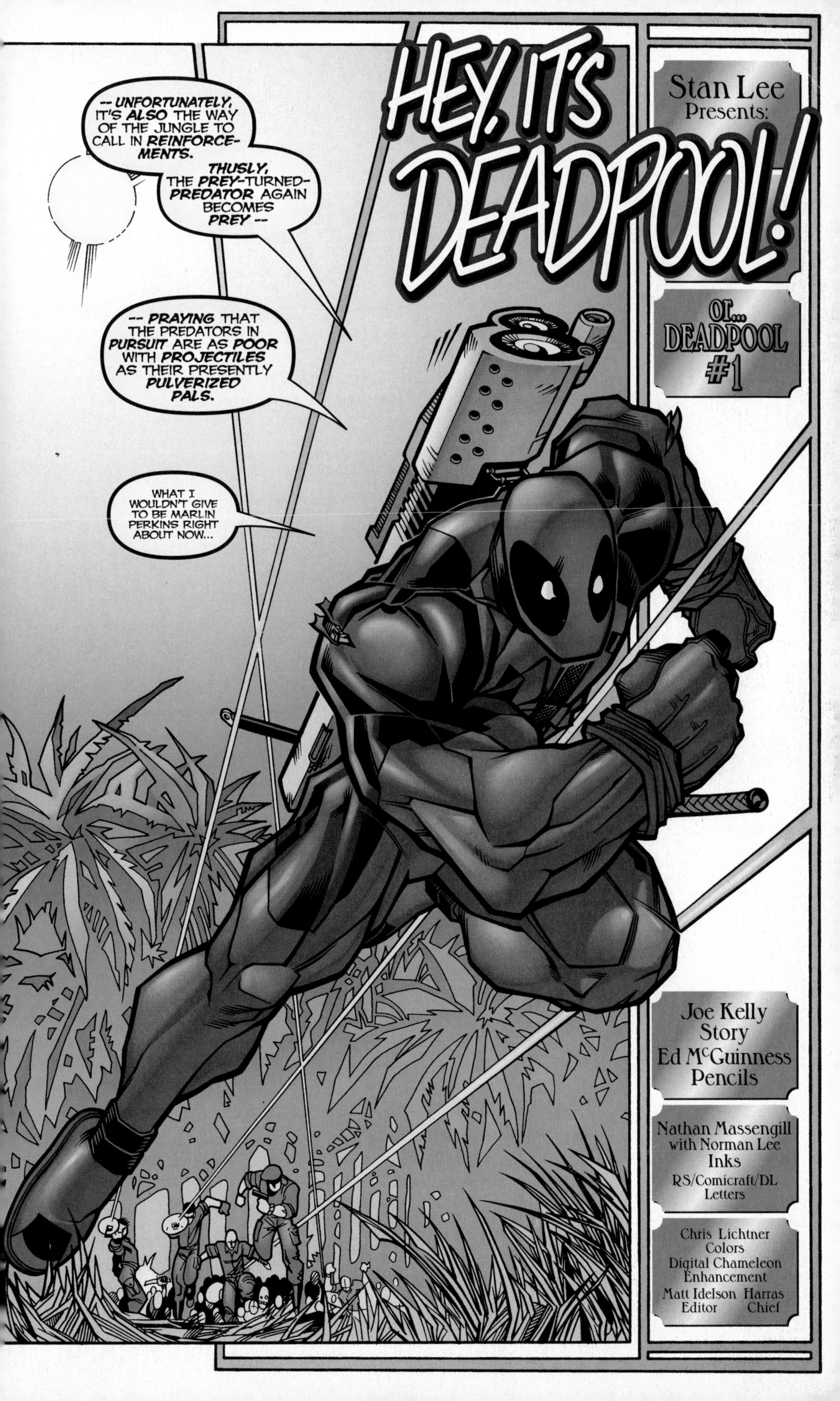

-- UNFORTUNATELY, IT'S ALSO THE WAY OF THE JUNGLE TO CALL IN REINFORCE-MENTS.
THUSLY, THE PREY-TURNED-PREDATOR AGAIN BECOMES PREY --
-- PRAYING THAT THE PREDATORS IN PURSUIT ARE AS POOR WITH PROJECTILES AS THEIR PRESENTLY PULVERIZED PALS.
WHAT I WOULDN'T GIVE TO BE MARLIN PERKINS RIGHT ABOUT NOW...
HEY, IT'S DEADPOOL!
Stan Lee Presents:
or... DEADPOOL #1
Joe Kelly Story
Ed McGuinness Pencils
Nathan Massengill with Norman Lee Inks
RS/Comicraft/DL Letters
Chris Lichtner Colors
Digital Chameleon Enhancement
Matt Idelson Editor
Harras Chief

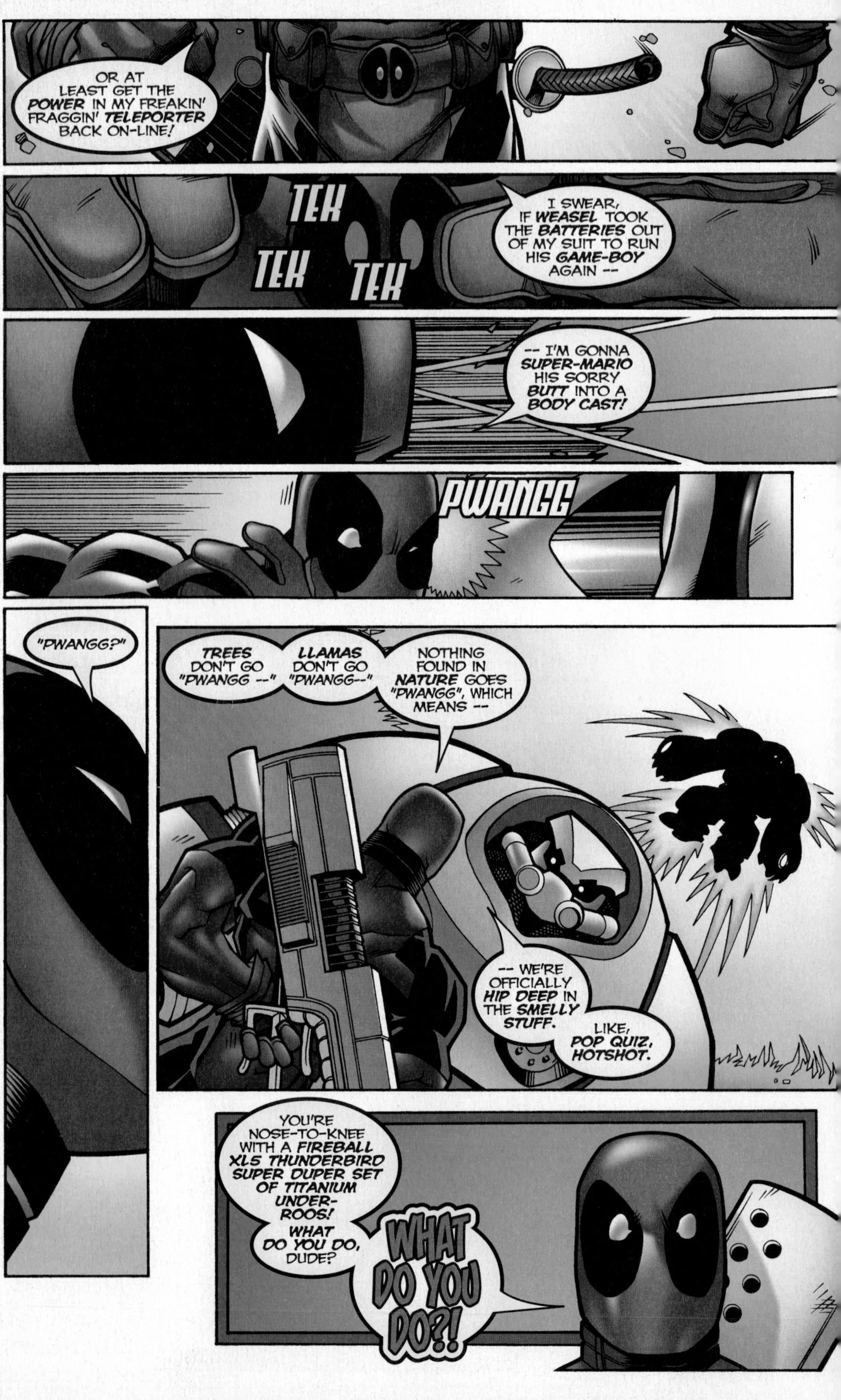

OR AT LEAST GET THE POWER IN MY FREAKIN' FRAGGIN' TELEPORTER BACK ON-LINE!
TEK
TEK
TEK
I SWEAR, IF WEASEL TOOK THE BATTERIES OUT OF MY SUIT TO RUN HIS GAME-BOY AGAIN --
-- I'M GONNA SUPER-MARIO HIS SORRY BUTT INTO A BODY CAST!
PWANGG
"PWANGG?"
TREES DON'T GO "PWANGG --"
LLAMAS DON'T GO "PWANGG--"
NOTHING FOUND IN NATURE GOES "PWANGG", WHICH MEANS --
-- WE'RE OFFICIALLY HIP DEEP IN THE SMELLY STUFF.
LIKE, POP QUIZ, HOTSHOT.
YOU'RE NOSE-TO-KNEE WITH A FIREBALL XL5 THUNDERBIRD SUPER DUPER SET OF TITANIUM UNDER-ROOS! WHAT DO YOU DO, DUDE?
WHAT DO YOU DO?!

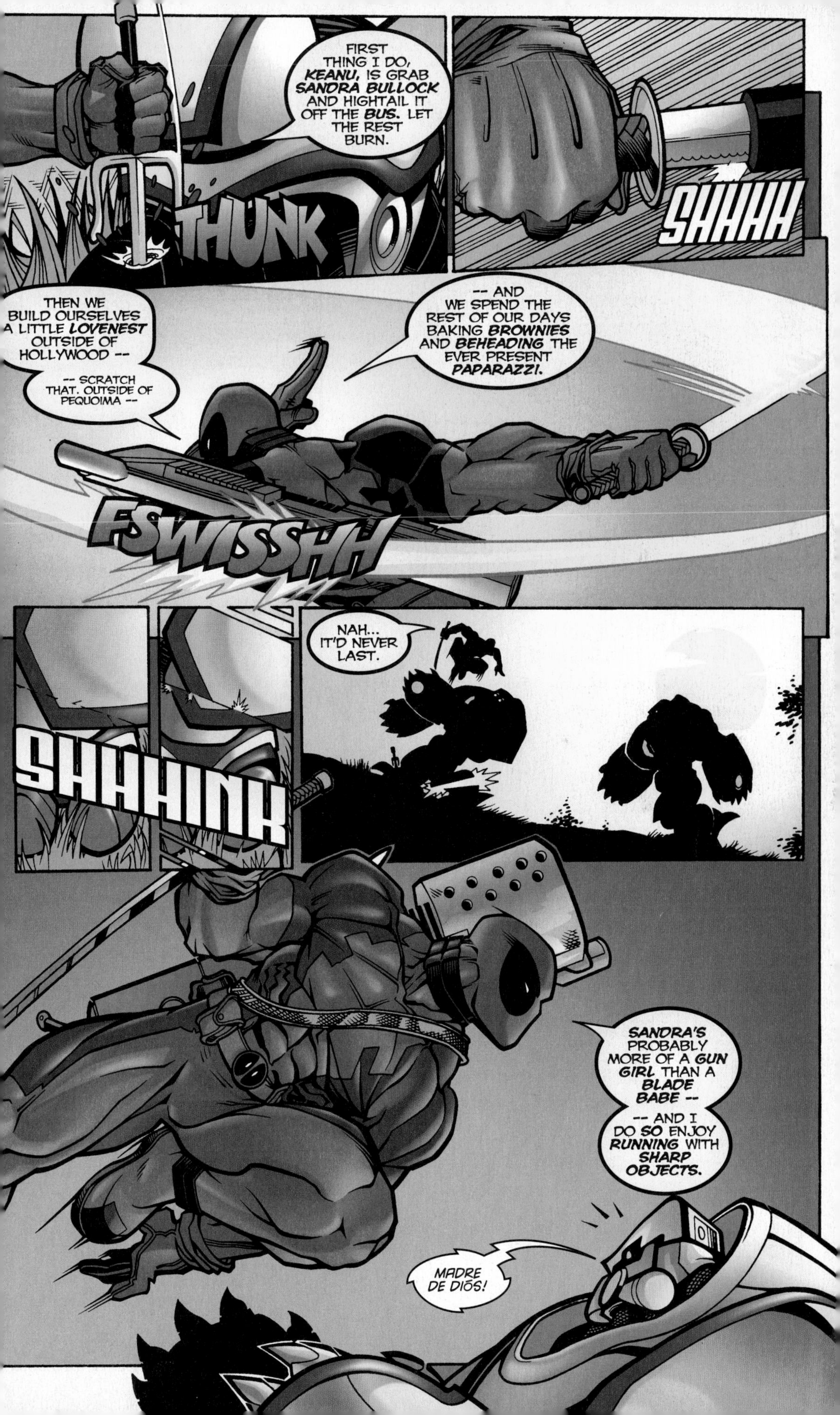
FIRST THING I DO, KEANU, IS GRAB SANDRA BULLOCK AND HIGHTAIL IT OFF THE BUS. LET THE REST BURN.
THUNK
SHHHH
THEN WE BUILD OURSELVES A LITTLE LOVENEST OUTSIDE OF HOLLYWOOD --
-- SCRATCH THAT. OUTSIDE OF PEQUOIMA --
-- AND WE SPEND THE REST OF OUR DAYS BAKING BROWNIES AND BEHEADING THE EVER PRESENT PAPARAZZI.
FSWISSHH
SHHHINK
NAH... IT'D NEVER LAST.
SANDRA'S PROBABLY MORE OF A GUN GIRL THAN A BLADE BABE --
-- AND I DO SO ENJOY RUNNING WITH SHARP OBJECTS.
MADRE DE DIÕS!

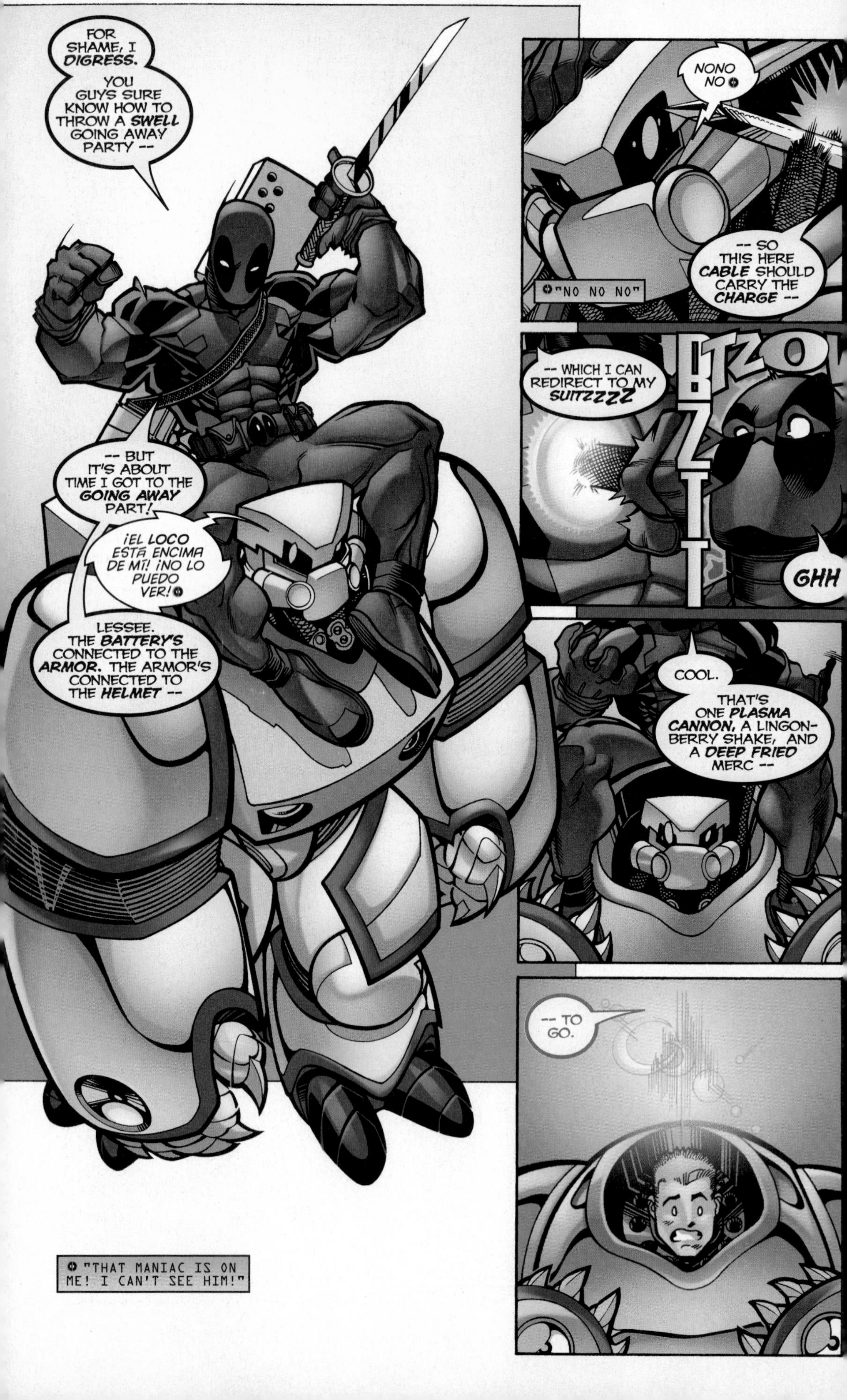

FOR SHAME, I DIGRESS.
YOU GUYS SURE KNOW HOW TO THROW A SWELL GOING AWAY PARTY --
-- BUT IT'S ABOUT TIME I GOT TO THE GOING AWAY PART!
¡EL LOCO ESTÁ ENCIMA DE MÍ! ¡NO LO PUEDO VER!
LESSEE. THE BATTERY'S CONNECTED TO THE ARMOR. THE ARMOR'S CONNECTED TO THE HELMET --
"THAT MANIAC IS ON ME! I CAN'T SEE HIM!"
NONO NO
"NO NO NO"
-- SO THIS HERE CABLE SHOULD CARRY THE CHARGE --
-- WHICH I CAN REDIRECT TO MY SUITZZZZZ
TZOW
BZZIT
GHH
COOL.
THAT'S ONE PLASMA CANNON, A LINGON-BERRY SHAKE, AND A DEEP FRIED MERC --
-- TO GO.

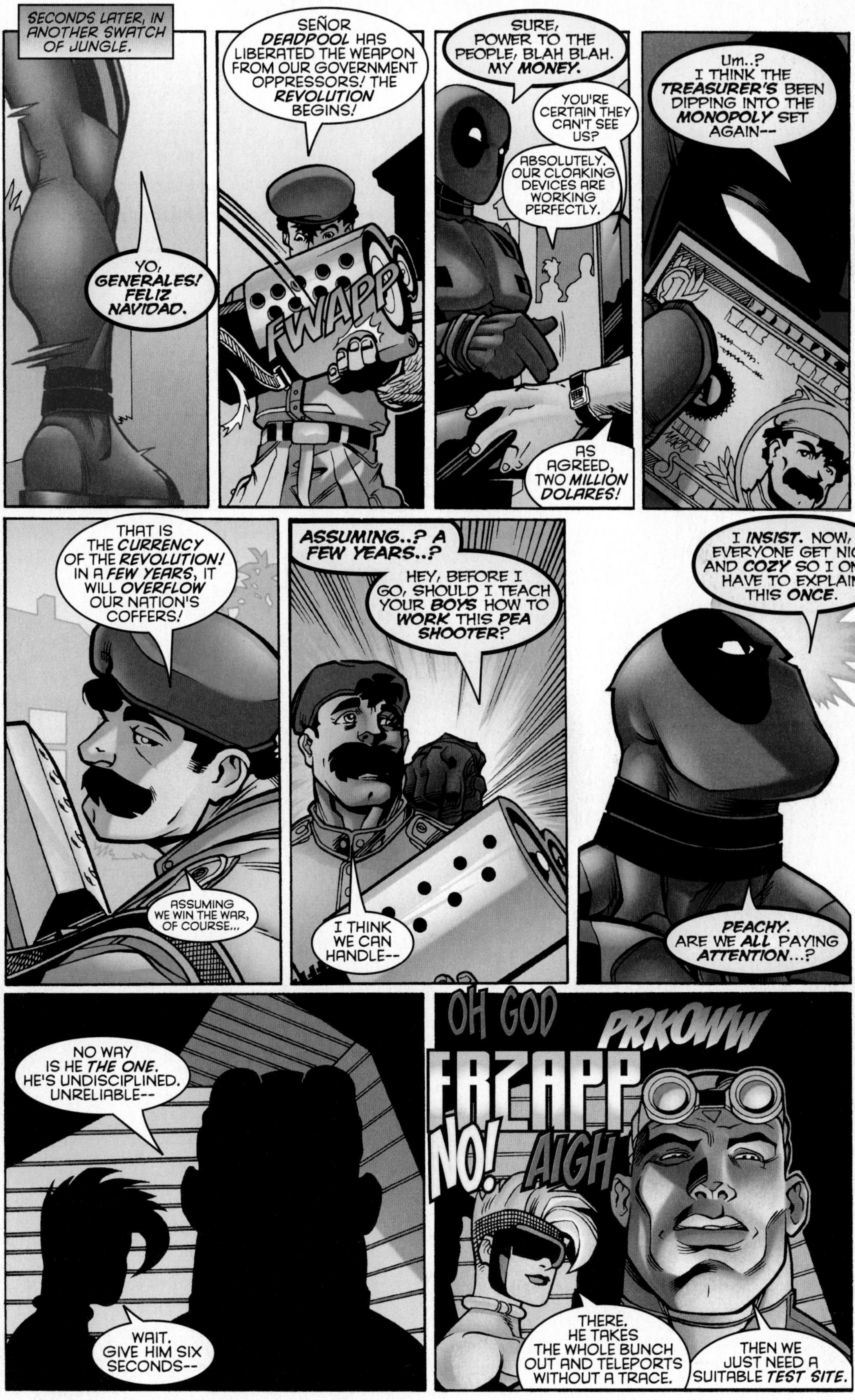
SECONDS LATER, IN ANOTHER SWATCH OF JUNGLE.
YO, GENERALES! FELIZ NAVIDAD.
SEÑOR DEADPOOL HAS LIBERATED THE WEAPON FROM OUR GOVERNMENT OPPRESSORS! THE REVOLUTION BEGINS!
FWAPP
SURE, POWER TO THE PEOPLE, BLAH BLAH. MY MONEY.
YOU'RE CERTAIN THEY CAN'T SEE US?
ABSOLUTELY. OUR CLOAKING DEVICES ARE WORKING PERFECTLY.
AS AGREED, TWO MILLION DOLARES!
Um..? I THINK THE TREASURER'S BEEN DIPPING INTO THE MONOPOLY SET AGAIN--
THAT IS THE CURRENCY OF THE REVOLUTION! IN A FEW YEARS, IT WILL OVERFLOW OUR NATION'S COFFERS!
ASSUMING WE WIN THE WAR, OF COURSE...
ASSUMING..? A FEW YEARS..?
HEY, BEFORE I GO, SHOULD I TEACH YOUR BOYS HOW TO WORK THIS PEA SHOOTER?
I THINK WE CAN HANDLE--
I INSIST. NOW, EVERYONE GET NICE AND COZY SO I ONLY HAVE TO EXPLAIN THIS ONCE.
PEACHY. ARE WE ALL PAYING ATTENTION...?
NO WAY IS HE THE ONE. HE'S UNDISCIPLINED. UNRELIABLE--
WAIT. GIVE HIM SIX SECONDS--
OH GOD
PRKOWW
FRZAPP
NO!
AIGH
THERE. HE TAKES THE WHOLE BUNCH OUT AND TELEPORTS WITHOUT A TRACE.
THEN WE JUST NEED A SUITABLE TEST SITE.

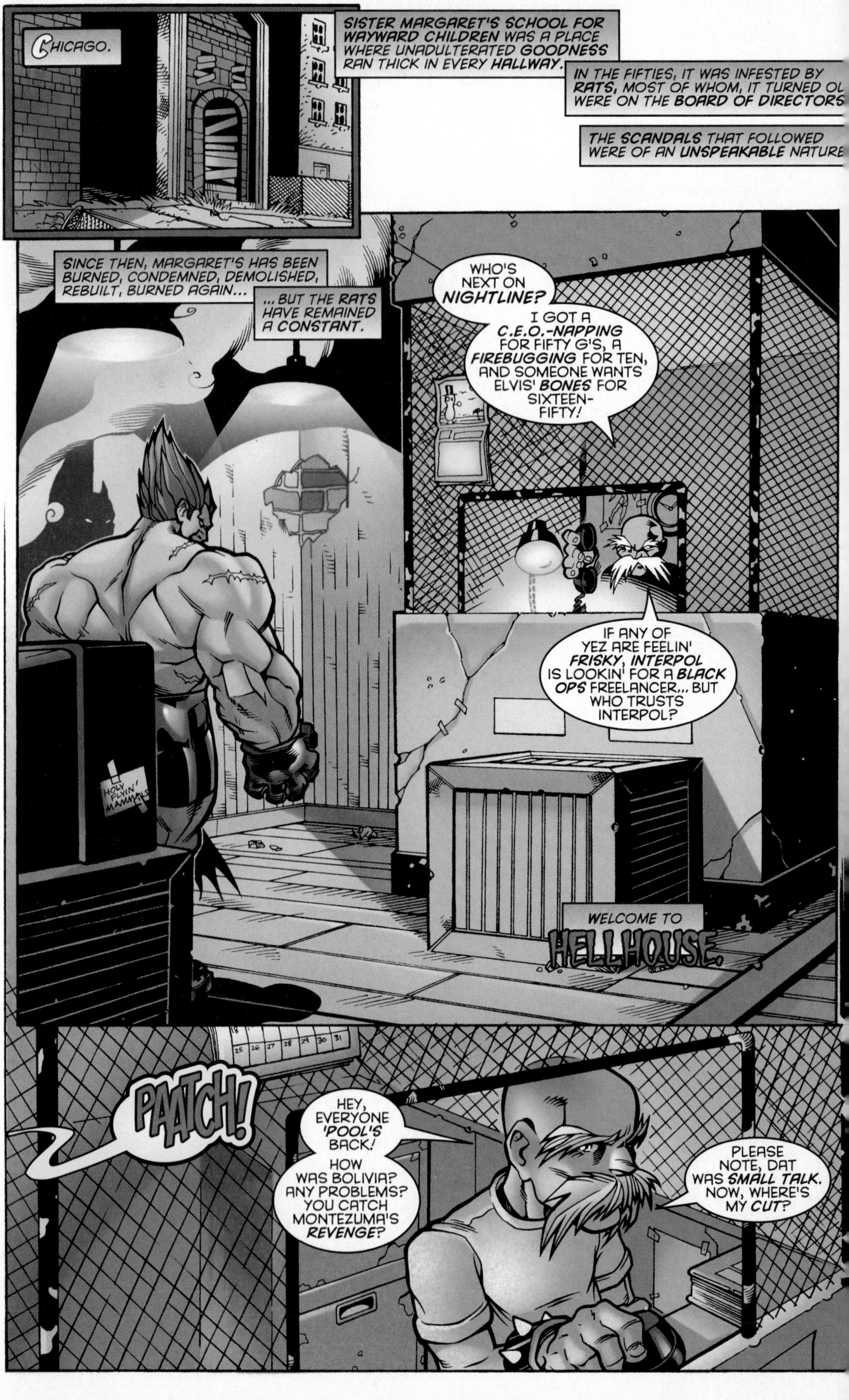
CHICAGO.
SISTER MARGARET'S SCHOOL FOR WAYWARD CHILDREN WAS A PLACE WHERE UNADULTERATED GOODNESS RAN THICK IN EVERY HALLWAY.
IN THE FIFTIES, IT WAS INFESTED BY RATS, MOST OF WHOM, IT TURNED OU WERE ON THE BOARD OF DIRECTORS
THE SCANDALS THAT FOLLOWED WERE OF AN UNSPEAKABLE NATURE
SINCE THEN, MARGARET'S HAS BEEN BURNED, CONDEMNED, DEMOLISHED, REBUILT, BURNED AGAIN...
...BUT THE RATS HAVE REMAINED A CONSTANT.
WHO'S NEXT ON NIGHTLINE?
I GOT A C.E.O.-NAPPING FOR FIFTY G'S, A FIREBUGGING FOR TEN, AND SOMEONE WANTS ELVIS' BONES FOR SIXTEEN-FIFTY!
IF ANY OF YEZ ARE FEELIN' FRISKY, INTERPOL IS LOOKIN' FOR A BLACK OPS FREELANCER... BUT WHO TRUSTS INTERPOL?
HOLY FLYIN' MAMMALS
WELCOME TO HELLHOUSE.
PAATCH!
HEY, EVERYONE 'POOL'S BACK!
HOW WAS BOLIVIA? ANY PROBLEMS? YOU CATCH MONTEZUMA'S REVENGE?
PLEASE NOTE, DAT WAS SMALL TALK. NOW, WHERE'S MY CUT?

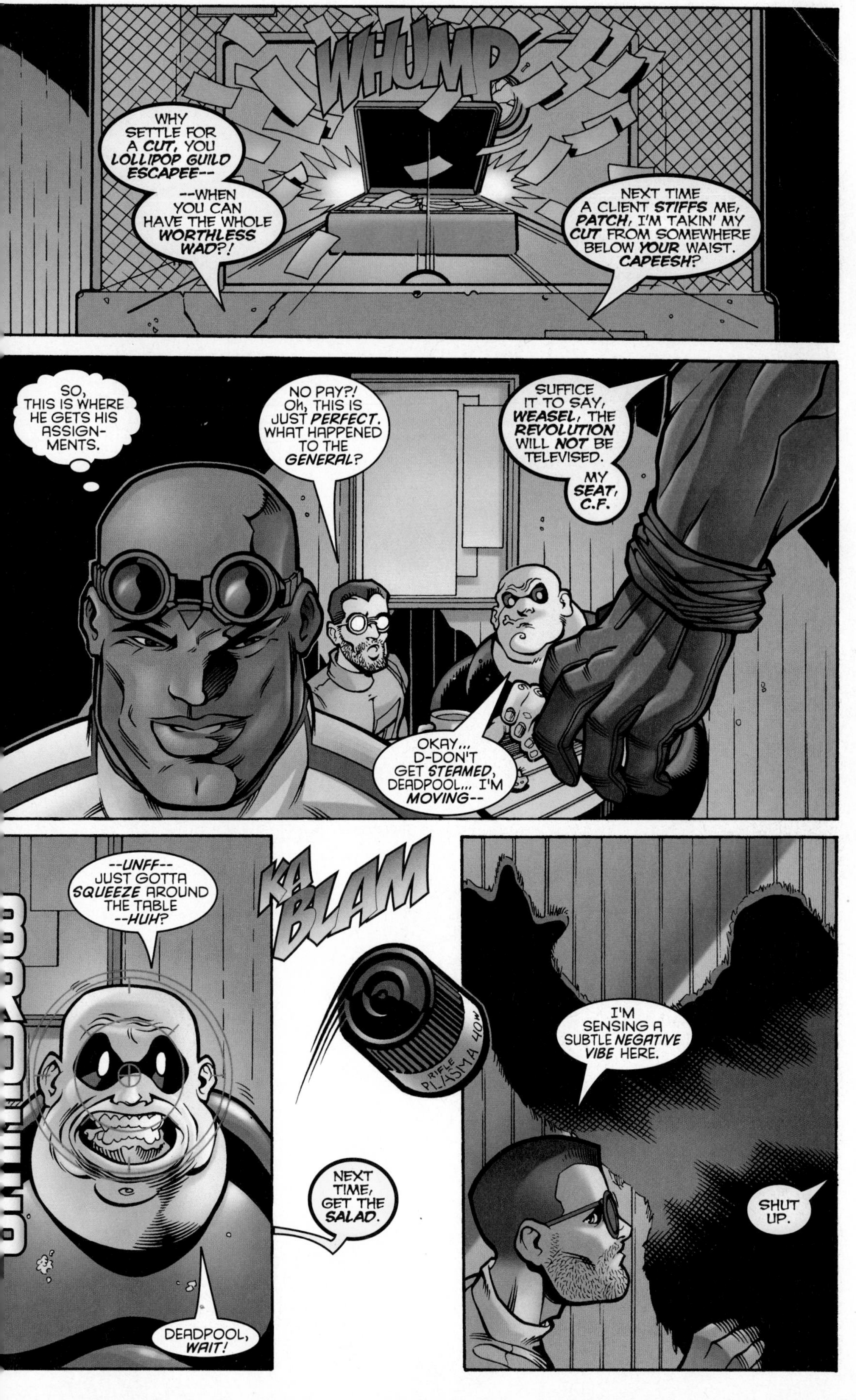
WHUMP
WHY SETTLE FOR A CUT, YOU LOLLIPOP GUILD ESCAPEE--
--WHEN YOU CAN HAVE THE WHOLE WORTHLESS WAD?!
NEXT TIME A CLIENT STIFFS ME, PATCH, I'M TAKIN' MY CUT FROM SOMEWHERE BELOW YOUR WAIST. CAPEESH?
SO, THIS IS WHERE HE GETS HIS ASSIGN-MENTS.
NO PAY?! Oh, THIS IS JUST PERFECT. WHAT HAPPENED TO THE GENERAL?
SUFFICE IT TO SAY, WEASEL, THE REVOLUTION WILL NOT BE TELEVISED.
MY SEAT, C.F.
OKAY... D-DON'T GET STEAMED, DEADPOOL... I'M MOVING--
--UNFF-- JUST GOTTA SQUEEZE AROUND THE TABLE --HUH?
KA BLAM
RIFLE PLASMA 40W
NEXT TIME, GET THE SALAD.
DEADPOOL, WAIT!
I'M SENSING A SUBTLE NEGATIVE VIBE HERE.
SHUT UP.

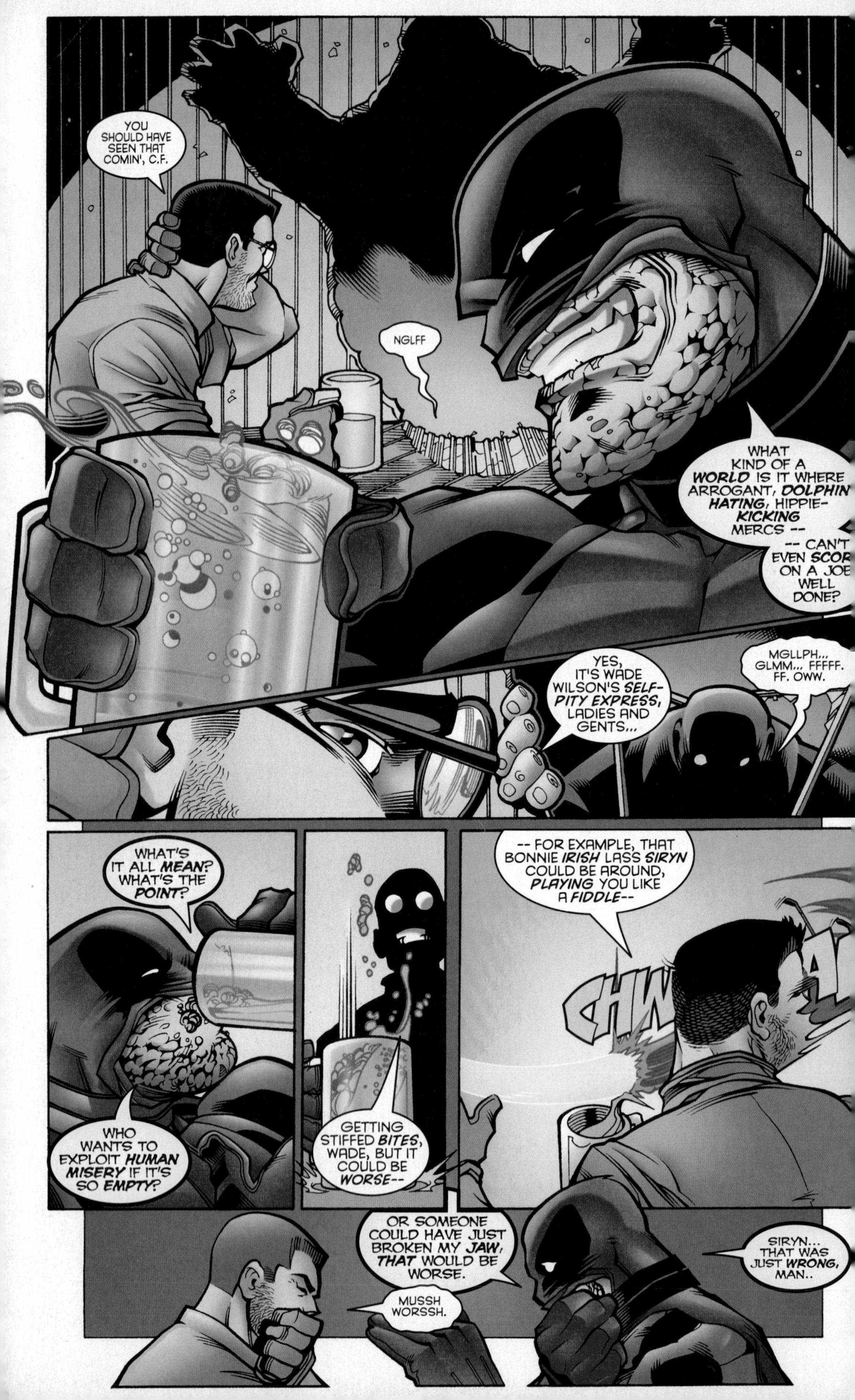
YOU SHOULD HAVE SEEN THAT COMIN', C.F.
NGLFF
WHAT KIND OF A WORLD IS IT WHERE ARROGANT, DOLPHIN HATING, HIPPIE-KICKING MERCS --
-- CAN'T EVEN SCOR ON A JOB WELL DONE?
YES, IT'S WADE WILSON'S SELF-PITY EXPRESS, LADIES AND GENTS...
MGLLPH... GLMM... FFFFF. FF. OWW.
WHAT'S IT ALL MEAN? WHAT'S THE POINT?
WHO WANTS TO EXPLOIT HUMAN MISERY IF IT'S SO EMPTY?
GETTING STIFFED BITES, WADE, BUT IT COULD BE WORSE--
-- FOR EXAMPLE, THAT BONNIE IRISH LASS SIRYN COULD BE AROUND, PLAYING YOU LIKE A FIDDLE--
OR SOMEONE COULD HAVE JUST BROKEN MY JAW, THAT WOULD BE WORSE.
MUSSH WORSSH.
SIRYN... THAT WAS JUST WRONG, MAN..

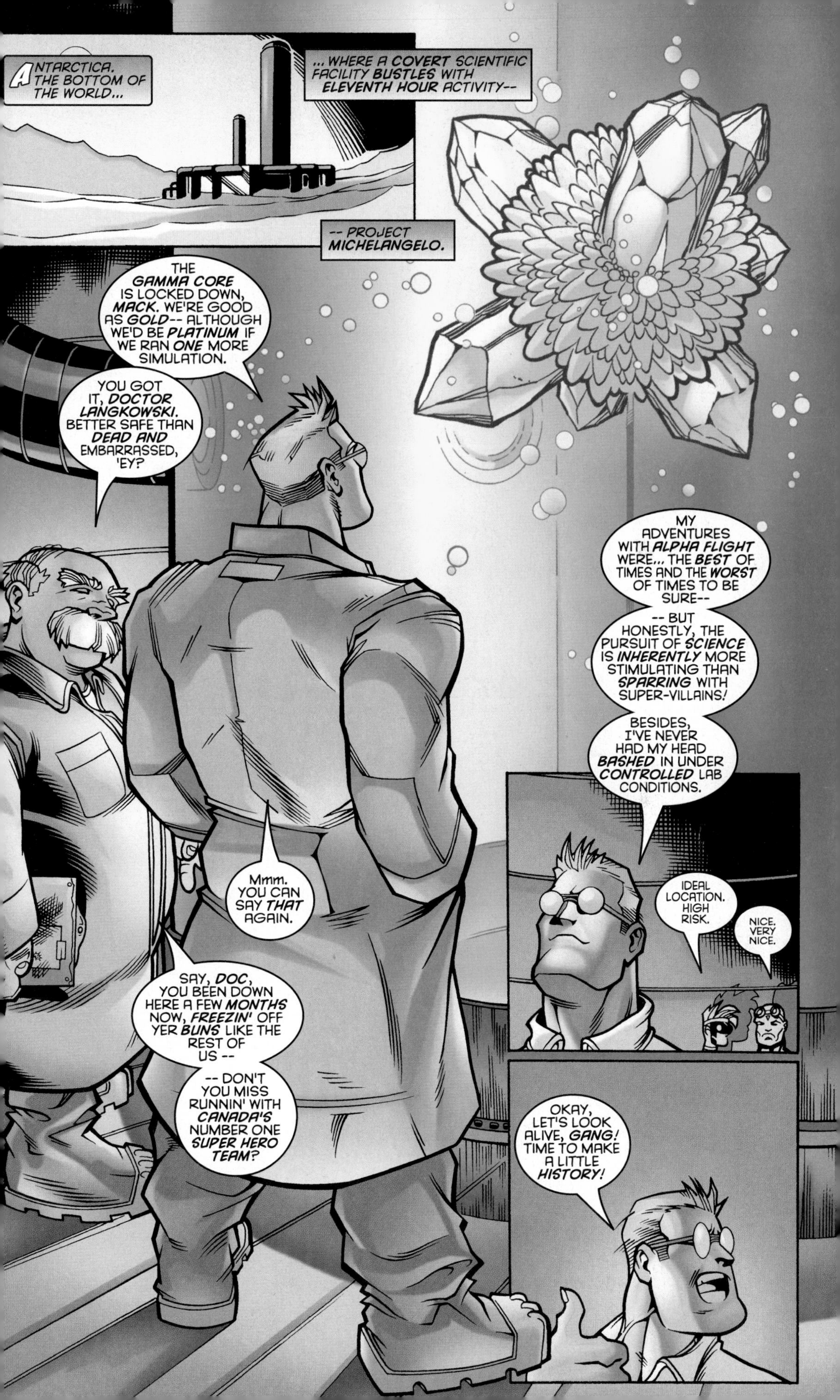

ANTARCTICA. THE BOTTOM OF THE WORLD...
...WHERE A COVERT SCIENTIFIC FACILITY BUSTLES WITH ELEVENTH HOUR ACTIVITY--
--PROJECT MICHELANGELO.
THE GAMMA CORE IS LOCKED DOWN, MACK. WE'RE GOOD AS GOLD-- ALTHOUGH WE'D BE PLATINUM IF WE RAN ONE MORE SIMULATION.
YOU GOT IT, DOCTOR LANGKOWSKI. BETTER SAFE THAN DEAD AND EMBARRASSED, 'EY?
Mmm. YOU CAN SAY THAT AGAIN.
SAY, DOC, YOU BEEN DOWN HERE A FEW MONTHS NOW, FREEZIN' OFF YER BUNS LIKE THE REST OF US --
-- DON'T YOU MISS RUNNIN' WITH CANADA'S NUMBER ONE SUPER HERO TEAM?
MY ADVENTURES WITH ALPHA FLIGHT WERE... THE BEST OF TIMES AND THE WORST OF TIMES TO BE SURE--
-- BUT HONESTLY, THE PURSUIT OF SCIENCE IS INHERENTLY MORE STIMULATING THAN SPARRING WITH SUPER-VILLAINS!
BESIDES, I'VE NEVER HAD MY HEAD BASHED IN UNDER CONTROLLED LAB CONDITIONS.
IDEAL LOCATION. HIGH RISK.
NICE. VERY NICE.
OKAY, LET'S LOOK ALIVE, GANG! TIME TO MAKE A LITTLE HISTORY!

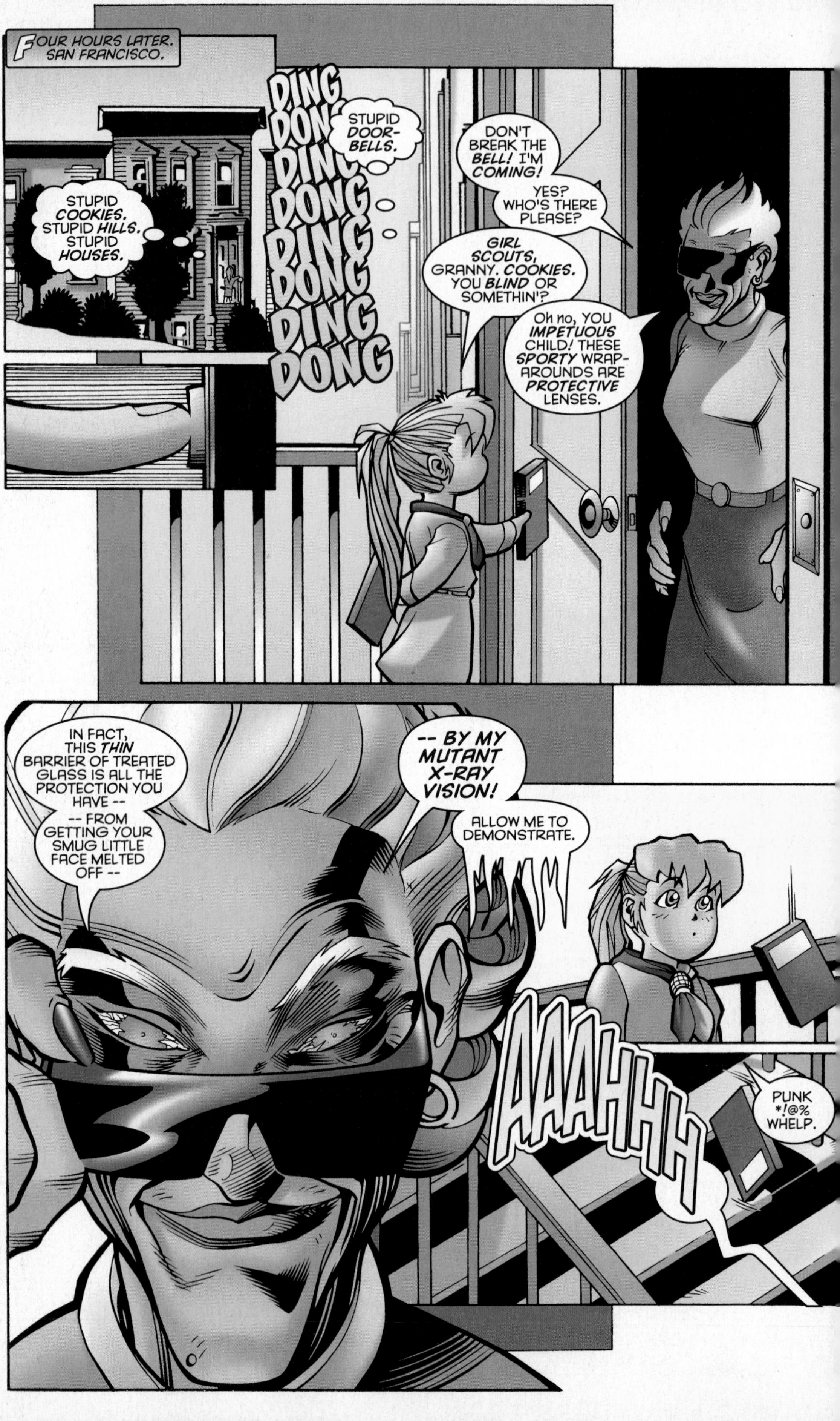
FOUR HOURS LATER. SAN FRANCISCO.
STUPID COOKIES. STUPID HILLS. STUPID HOUSES.
DING DONG DING DONG DING DONG DING DONG
STUPID DOOR-BELLS.
DON'T BREAK THE BELL! I'M COMING!
YES? WHO'S THERE PLEASE?
GIRL SCOUTS, GRANNY. COOKIES. YOU BLIND OR SOMETHIN'?
Oh no, YOU IMPETUOUS CHILD! THESE SPORTY WRAP-AROUNDS ARE PROTECTIVE LENSES.
IN FACT, THIS THIN BARRIER OF TREATED GLASS IS ALL THE PROTECTION YOU HAVE --
-- FROM GETTING YOUR SMUG LITTLE FACE MELTED OFF --
-- BY MY MUTANT X-RAY VISION!
ALLOW ME TO DEMONSTRATE.
AAAHHH
PUNK *!@% WHELP.

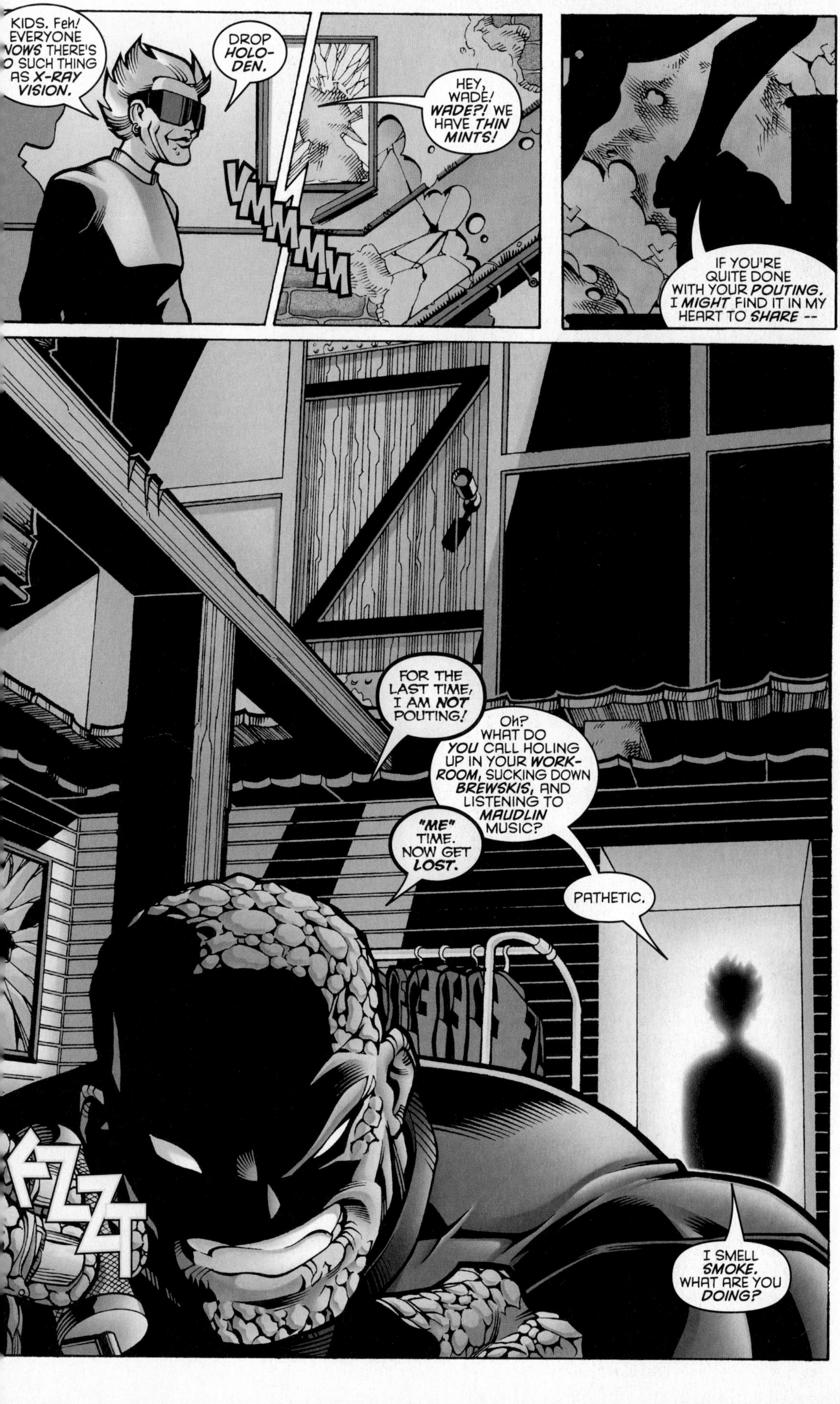
KIDS. Feh! EVERYONE VOWS THERE'S O SUCH THING AS X-RAY VISION.
DROP HOLO-DEN.
VMMMMM
HEY, WADE! WADE?! WE HAVE THIN MINTS!
IF YOU'RE QUITE DONE WITH YOUR POUTING. I MIGHT FIND IT IN MY HEART TO SHARE --
FOR THE LAST TIME, I AM NOT POUTING!
Oh? WHAT DO YOU CALL HOLING UP IN YOUR WORK-ROOM, SUCKING DOWN BREWSKIS, AND LISTENING TO MAUDLIN MUSIC?
"ME" TIME. NOW GET LOST.
PATHETIC.
FZZZT
I SMELL SMOKE. WHAT ARE YOU DOING?

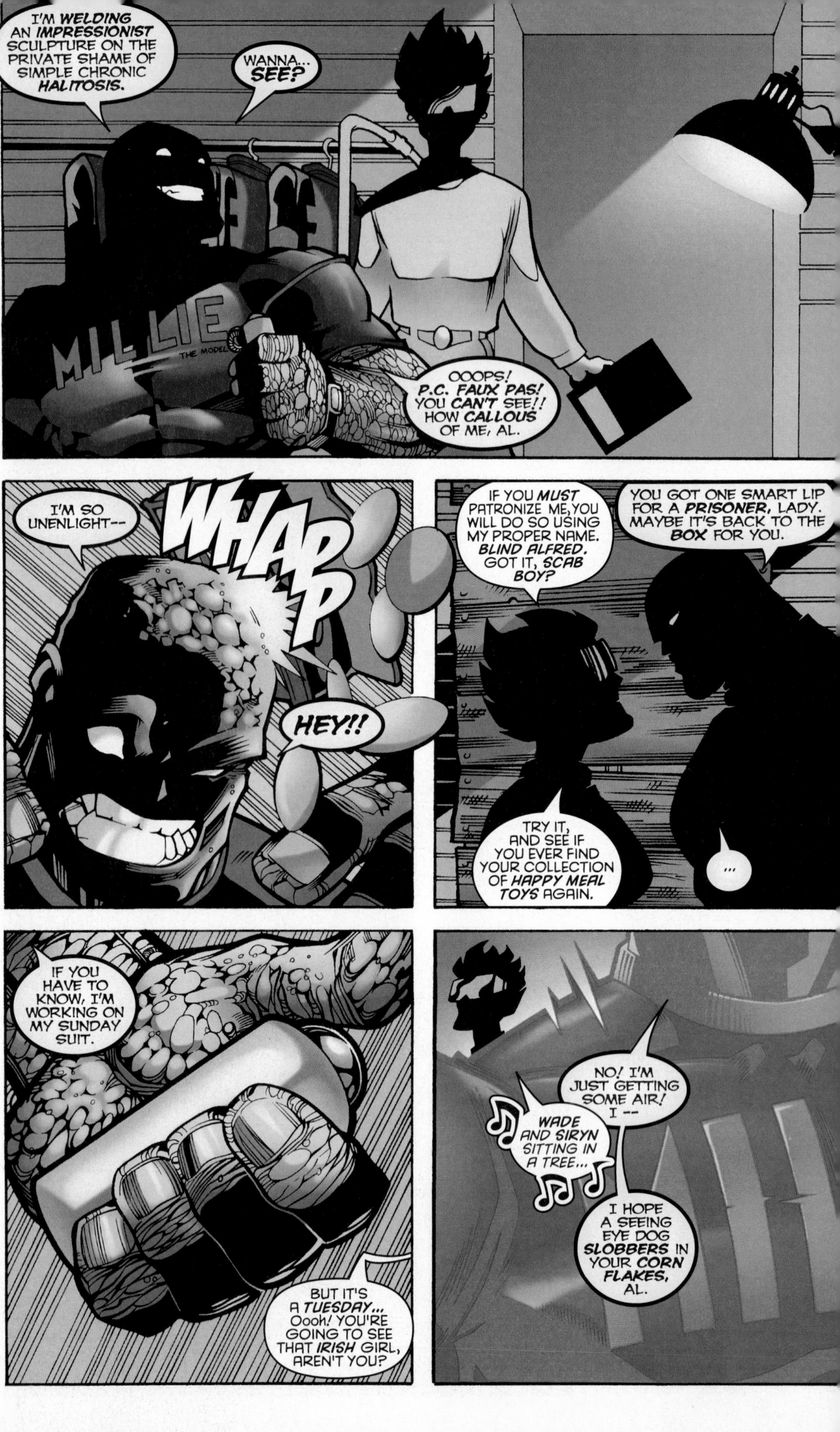

I'M WELDING AN IMPRESSIONIST SCULPTURE ON THE PRIVATE SHAME OF SIMPLE CHRONIC HALITOSIS.
WANNA... SEE?
MILLIE THE MODEL
OOOPS! P.C. FAUX PAS! YOU CAN'T SEE!! HOW CALLOUS OF ME, AL.
I'M SO UNENLIGHT--
WHAP
HEY!!
IF YOU MUST PATRONIZE ME, YOU WILL DO SO USING MY PROPER NAME. BLIND ALFRED. GOT IT, SCAB BOY?
YOU GOT ONE SMART LIP FOR A PRISONER, LADY. MAYBE IT'S BACK TO THE BOX FOR YOU.
TRY IT, AND SEE IF YOU EVER FIND YOUR COLLECTION OF HAPPY MEAL TOYS AGAIN.
...
IF YOU HAVE TO KNOW, I'M WORKING ON MY SUNDAY SUIT.
BUT IT'S A TUESDAY... Oooh! YOU'RE GOING TO SEE THAT IRISH GIRL, AREN'T YOU?
NO! I'M JUST GETTING SOME AIR! I --
WADE AND SIRYN SITTING IN A TREE...
I HOPE A SEEING EYE DOG SLOBBERS IN YOUR CORN FLAKES, AL.

ANTARCTICA.

CORE **ON-LINE.** PREPARING TO ENGAGE IN **FIVE...**

SHOW **TIME.**

...**GAMMA** LEVELS READ STRONG ON **FOUR...** **THREE...**

...**REMOVING** SAFETIES ON **TWO...**

...**CROSSING** FINGERS ON **ONE.**

CL!K

KZZZHK

KA

COME ON... ENGAGE... ENGAGE...

ENGAGE!

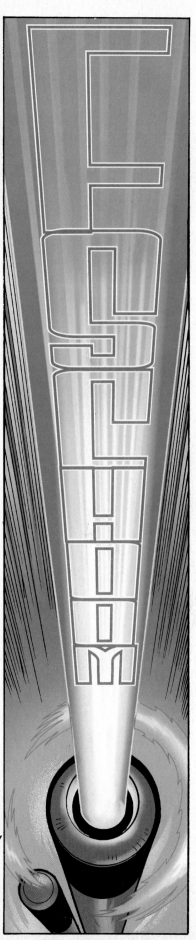

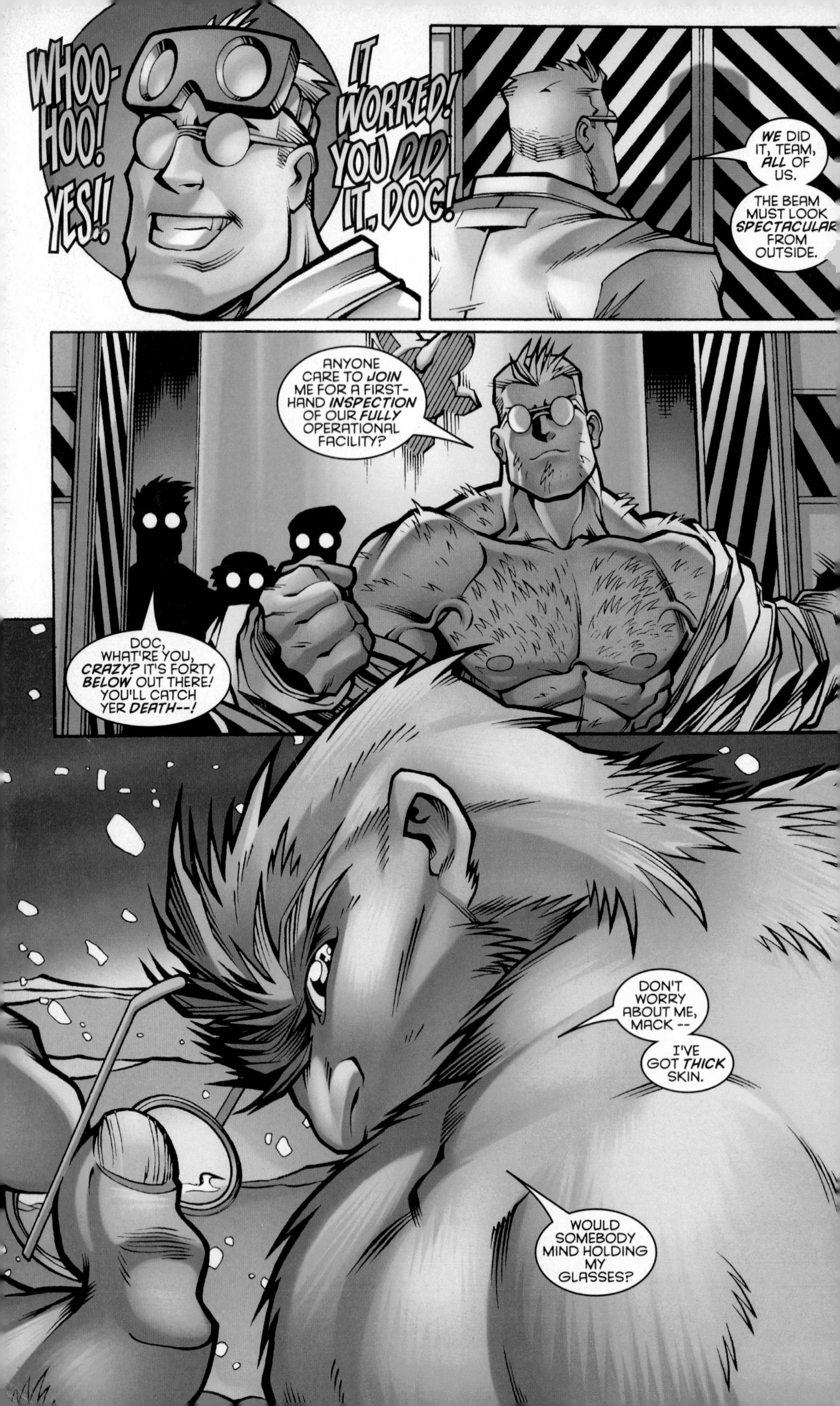
WHOO-HOO! YES!!
IT WORKED! YOU DID IT, DOC!
WE DID IT, TEAM, ALL OF US.
THE BEAM MUST LOOK SPECTACULAR FROM OUTSIDE.
ANYONE CARE TO JOIN ME FOR A FIRST-HAND INSPECTION OF OUR FULLY OPERATIONAL FACILITY?
DOC, WHAT'RE YOU, CRAZY? IT'S FORTY BELOW OUT THERE! YOU'LL CATCH YER DEATH--!
DON'T WORRY ABOUT ME, MACK --
I'VE GOT THICK SKIN.
WOULD SOMEBODY MIND HOLDING MY GLASSES?

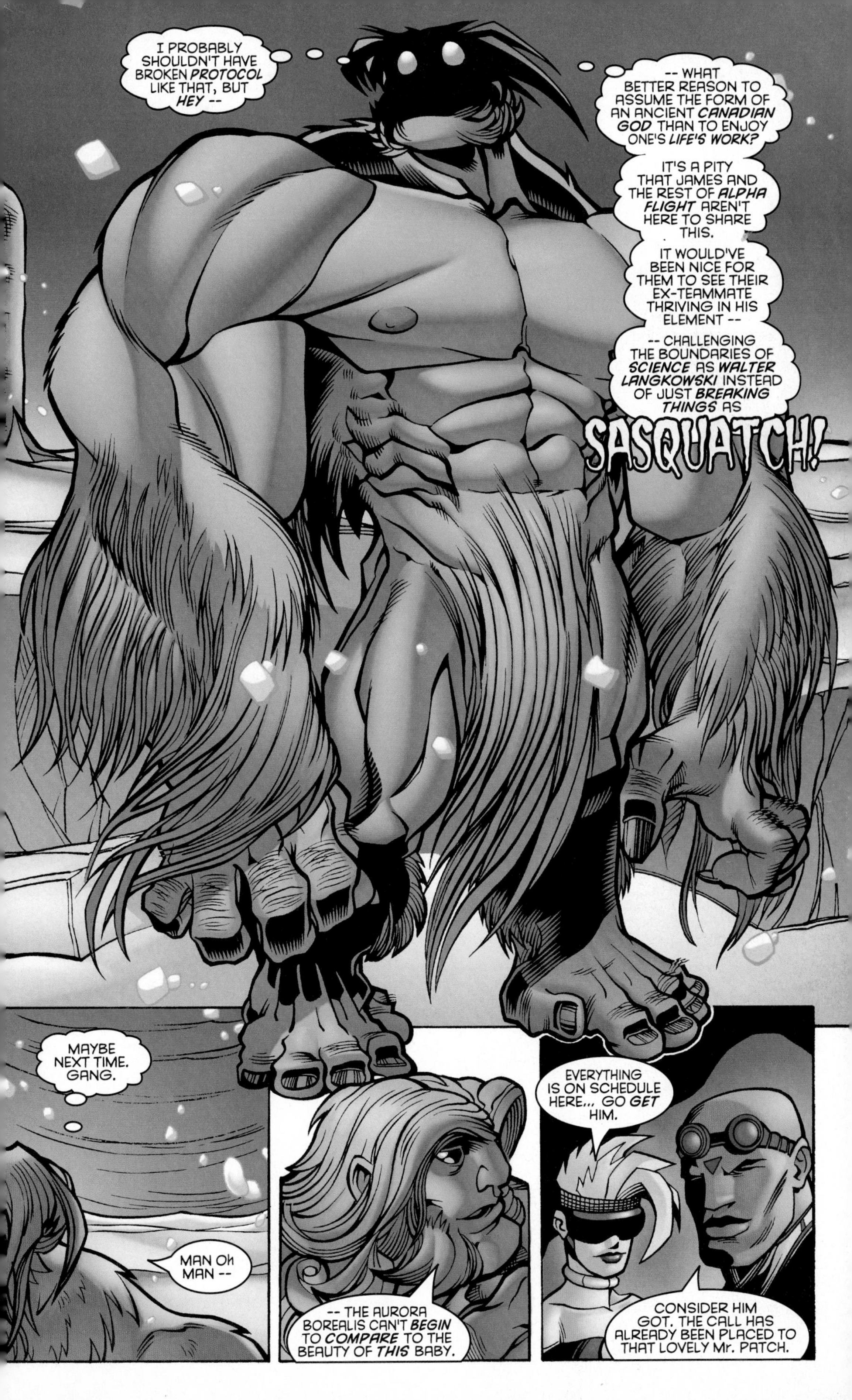

I PROBABLY SHOULDN'T HAVE BROKEN *PROTOCOL* LIKE THAT, BUT *HEY* --
-- WHAT BETTER REASON TO ASSUME THE FORM OF AN ANCIENT *CANADIAN GOD* THAN TO ENJOY ONE'S *LIFE'S WORK?*
IT'S A PITY THAT JAMES AND THE REST OF *ALPHA FLIGHT* AREN'T HERE TO SHARE THIS.
IT WOULD'VE BEEN NICE FOR THEM TO SEE THEIR EX-TEAMMATE THRIVING IN HIS ELEMENT --
-- CHALLENGING THE BOUNDARIES OF *SCIENCE* AS *WALTER LANGKOWSKI* INSTEAD OF JUST *BREAKING THINGS* AS
SASQUATCH!
MAYBE NEXT TIME. GANG.
MAN Oh MAN --
-- THE AURORA BOREALIS CAN'T *BEGIN* TO *COMPARE* TO THE BEAUTY OF *THIS* BABY.
EVERYTHING IS ON SCHEDULE HERE... GO *GET* HIM.
CONSIDER HIM GOT. THE CALL HAS ALREADY BEEN PLACED TO THAT LOVELY Mr. PATCH.

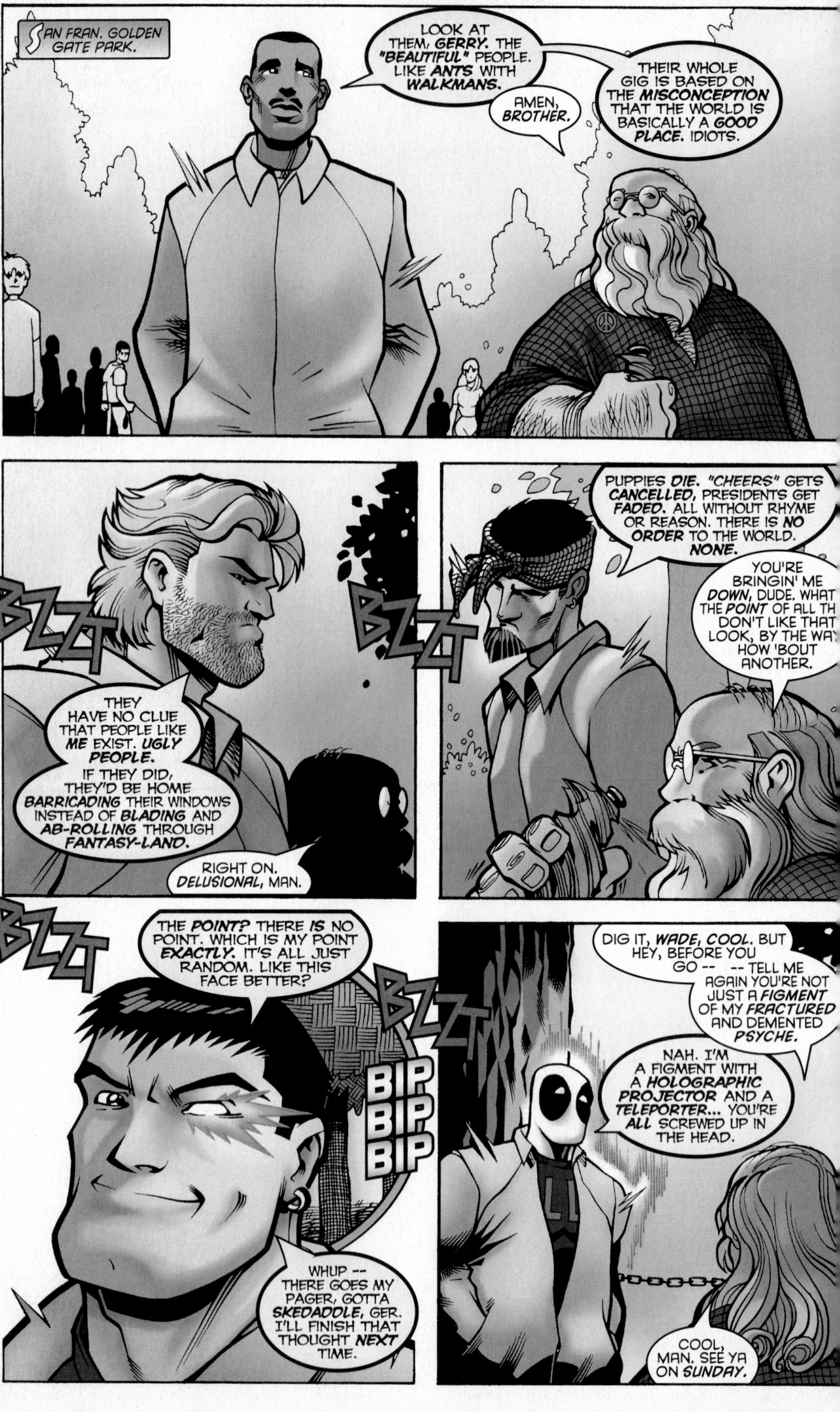
SAN FRAN. GOLDEN GATE PARK.
LOOK AT THEM, GERRY. THE "BEAUTIFUL" PEOPLE. LIKE ANTS WITH WALKMANS.
AMEN, BROTHER.
THEIR WHOLE GIG IS BASED ON THE MISCONCEPTION THAT THE WORLD IS BASICALLY A GOOD PLACE. IDIOTS.
BZZT
THEY HAVE NO CLUE THAT PEOPLE LIKE ME EXIST. UGLY PEOPLE.
IF THEY DID, THEY'D BE HOME BARRICADING THEIR WINDOWS INSTEAD OF BLADING AND AB-ROLLING THROUGH FANTASY-LAND.
RIGHT ON. DELUSIONAL, MAN.
BZZT
PUPPIES DIE. "CHEERS" GETS CANCELLED, PRESIDENTS GET FADED. ALL WITHOUT RHYME OR REASON. THERE IS NO ORDER TO THE WORLD. NONE.
YOU'RE BRINGIN' ME DOWN, DUDE. WHAT THE POINT OF ALL TH DON'T LIKE THAT LOOK, BY THE WA HOW 'BOUT ANOTHER.
BZZT
THE POINT? THERE IS NO POINT. WHICH IS MY POINT EXACTLY. IT'S ALL JUST RANDOM. LIKE THIS FACE BETTER?
BZZT
BIP BIP BIP
WHUP -- THERE GOES MY PAGER, GOTTA SKEDADDLE, GER. I'LL FINISH THAT THOUGHT NEXT TIME.
DIG IT, WADE, COOL. BUT HEY, BEFORE YOU GO -- -- TELL ME AGAIN YOU'RE NOT JUST A FIGMENT OF MY FRACTURED AND DEMENTED PSYCHE.
NAH. I'M A FIGMENT WITH A HOLOGRAPHIC PROJECTOR AND A TELEPORTER... YOU'RE ALL SCREWED UP IN THE HEAD.
COOL, MAN. SEE YA ON SUNDAY.

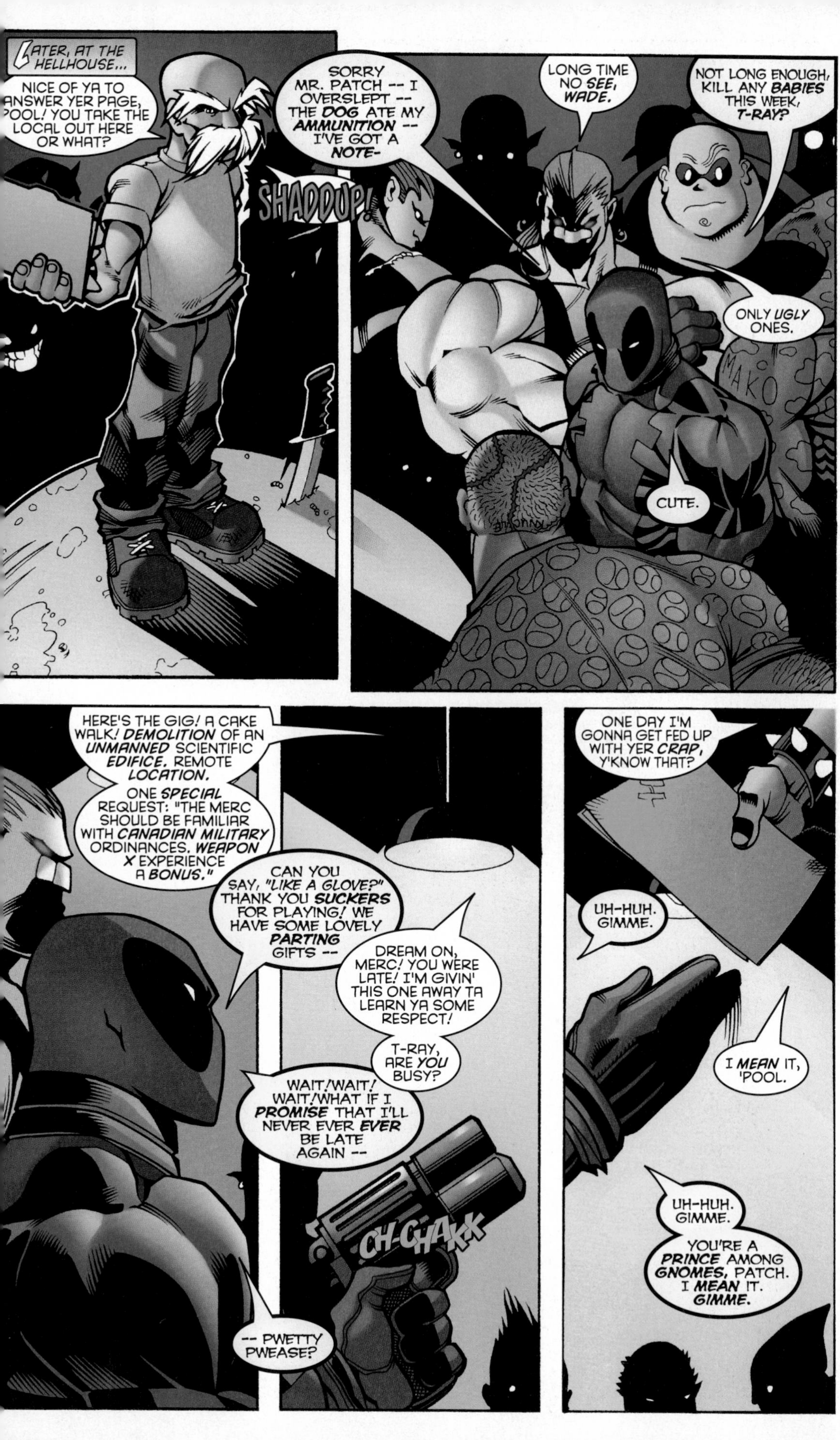
LATER, AT THE HELLHOUSE...
NICE OF YA TO ANSWER YER PAGE, POOL! YOU TAKE THE LOCAL OUT HERE OR WHAT?
SORRY MR. PATCH -- I OVERSLEPT -- THE DOG ATE MY AMMUNITION -- I'VE GOT A NOTE-
SHADDUP!
LONG TIME NO SEE, WADE.
NOT LONG ENOUGH. KILL ANY BABIES THIS WEEK, T-RAY?
ONLY UGLY ONES.
CUTE.
MAKO
HERE'S THE GIG! A CAKE WALK! DEMOLITION OF AN UNMANNED SCIENTIFIC EDIFICE. REMOTE LOCATION.
ONE SPECIAL REQUEST: "THE MERC SHOULD BE FAMILIAR WITH CANADIAN MILITARY ORDINANCES. WEAPON X EXPERIENCE A BONUS."
CAN YOU SAY, "LIKE A GLOVE?" THANK YOU SUCKERS FOR PLAYING! WE HAVE SOME LOVELY PARTING GIFTS --
DREAM ON, MERC! YOU WERE LATE! I'M GIVIN' THIS ONE AWAY TA LEARN YA SOME RESPECT!
T-RAY, ARE YOU BUSY?
WAIT! WAIT! WAIT! WHAT IF I PROMISE THAT I'LL NEVER EVER EVER BE LATE AGAIN --
CH-CHAKK
-- PWETTY PWEASE?
ONE DAY I'M GONNA GET FED UP WITH YER CRAP, Y'KNOW THAT?
UH-HUH. GIMME.
I MEAN IT, 'POOL.
UH-HUH. GIMME.
YOU'RE A PRINCE AMONG GNOMES, PATCH. I MEAN IT. GIMME.

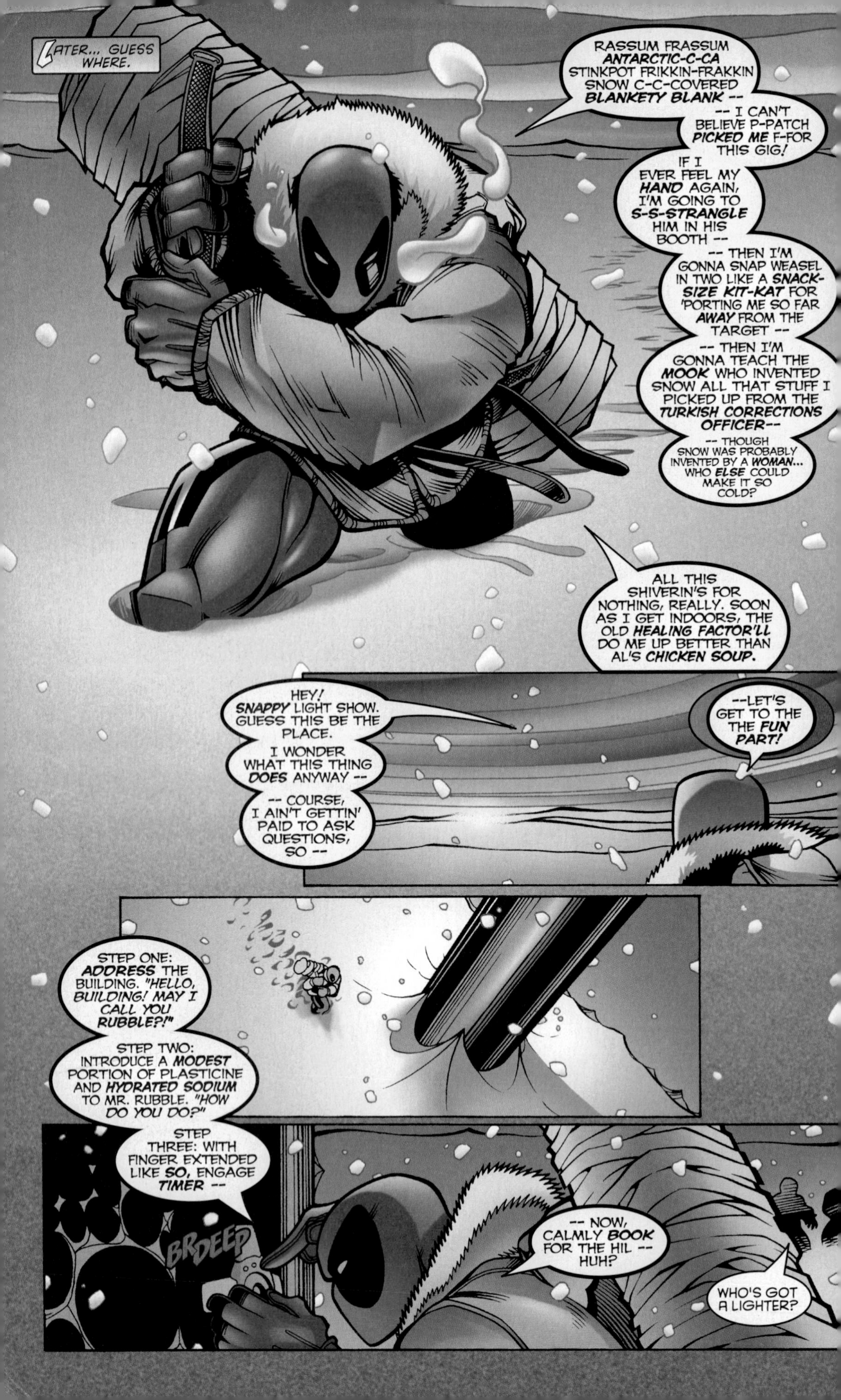
LATER... GUESS WHERE.
RASSUM FRASSUM ANTARCTIC-C-CA STINKPOT FRIKKIN-FRAKKIN SNOW C-C-COVERED BLANKETY BLANK --
-- I CAN'T BELIEVE P-PATCH PICKED ME F-FOR THIS GIG!
IF I EVER FEEL MY HAND AGAIN, I'M GOING TO S-S-STRANGLE HIM IN HIS BOOTH --
-- THEN I'M GONNA SNAP WEASEL IN TWO LIKE A SNACK-SIZE KIT-KAT FOR 'PORTING ME SO FAR AWAY FROM THE TARGET --
-- THEN I'M GONNA TEACH THE MOOK WHO INVENTED SNOW ALL THAT STUFF I PICKED UP FROM THE TURKISH CORRECTIONS OFFICER--
-- THOUGH SNOW WAS PROBABLY INVENTED BY A WOMAN... WHO ELSE COULD MAKE IT SO COLD?
ALL THIS SHIVERIN'S FOR NOTHING, REALLY. SOON AS I GET INDOORS, THE OLD HEALING FACTOR'LL DO ME UP BETTER THAN AL'S CHICKEN SOUP.
HEY! SNAPPY LIGHT SHOW. GUESS THIS BE THE PLACE.
I WONDER WHAT THIS THING DOES ANYWAY --
-- COURSE, I AIN'T GETTIN' PAID TO ASK QUESTIONS, SO --
--LET'S GET TO THE THE FUN PART!
STEP ONE: ADDRESS THE BUILDING. "HELLO, BUILDING! MAY I CALL YOU RUBBLE?!"
STEP TWO: INTRODUCE A MODEST PORTION OF PLASTICINE AND HYDRATED SODIUM TO MR. RUBBLE. "HOW DO YOU DO?"
STEP THREE: WITH FINGER EXTENDED LIKE SO, ENGAGE TIMER --
BRDEEP
-- NOW, CALMLY BOOK FOR THE HIL -- HUH?
WHO'S GOT A LIGHTER?

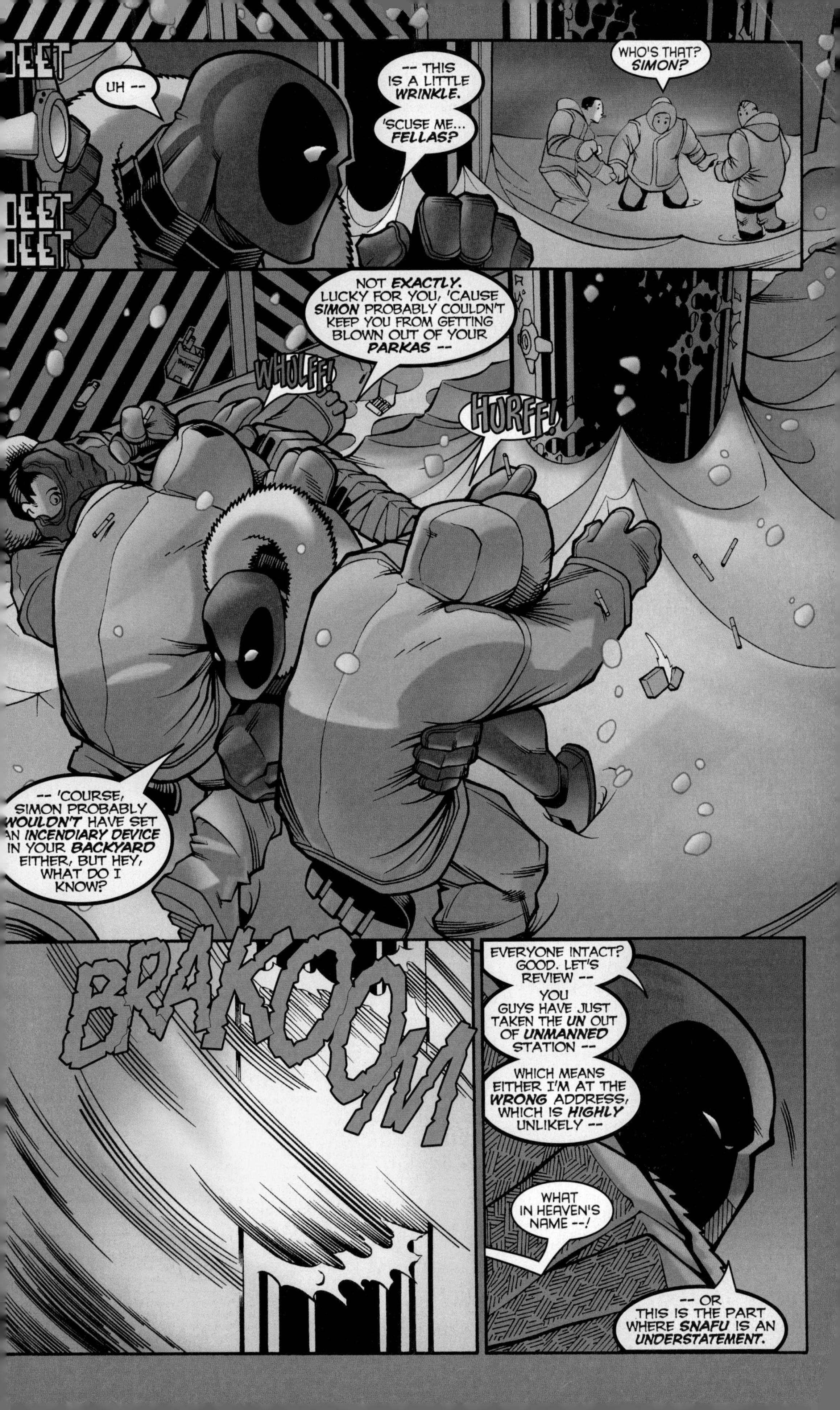
DEET
UH --
-- THIS IS A LITTLE WRINKLE.
'SCUSE ME... FELLAS?
DEET DEET
WHO'S THAT? SIMON?
NOT EXACTLY. LUCKY FOR YOU, 'CAUSE SIMON PROBABLY COULDN'T KEEP YOU FROM GETTING BLOWN OUT OF YOUR PARKAS --
WHOLFF!
HURFF!
-- 'COURSE, SIMON PROBABLY WOULDN'T HAVE SET AN INCENDIARY DEVICE IN YOUR BACKYARD EITHER, BUT HEY, WHAT DO I KNOW?
BRAKOOM
EVERYONE INTACT? GOOD. LET'S REVIEW --
YOU GUYS HAVE JUST TAKEN THE UN OUT OF UNMANNED STATION --
WHICH MEANS EITHER I'M AT THE WRONG ADDRESS, WHICH IS HIGHLY UNLIKELY --
WHAT IN HEAVEN'S NAME --!
-- OR THIS IS THE PART WHERE SNAFU IS AN UNDERSTATEMENT.

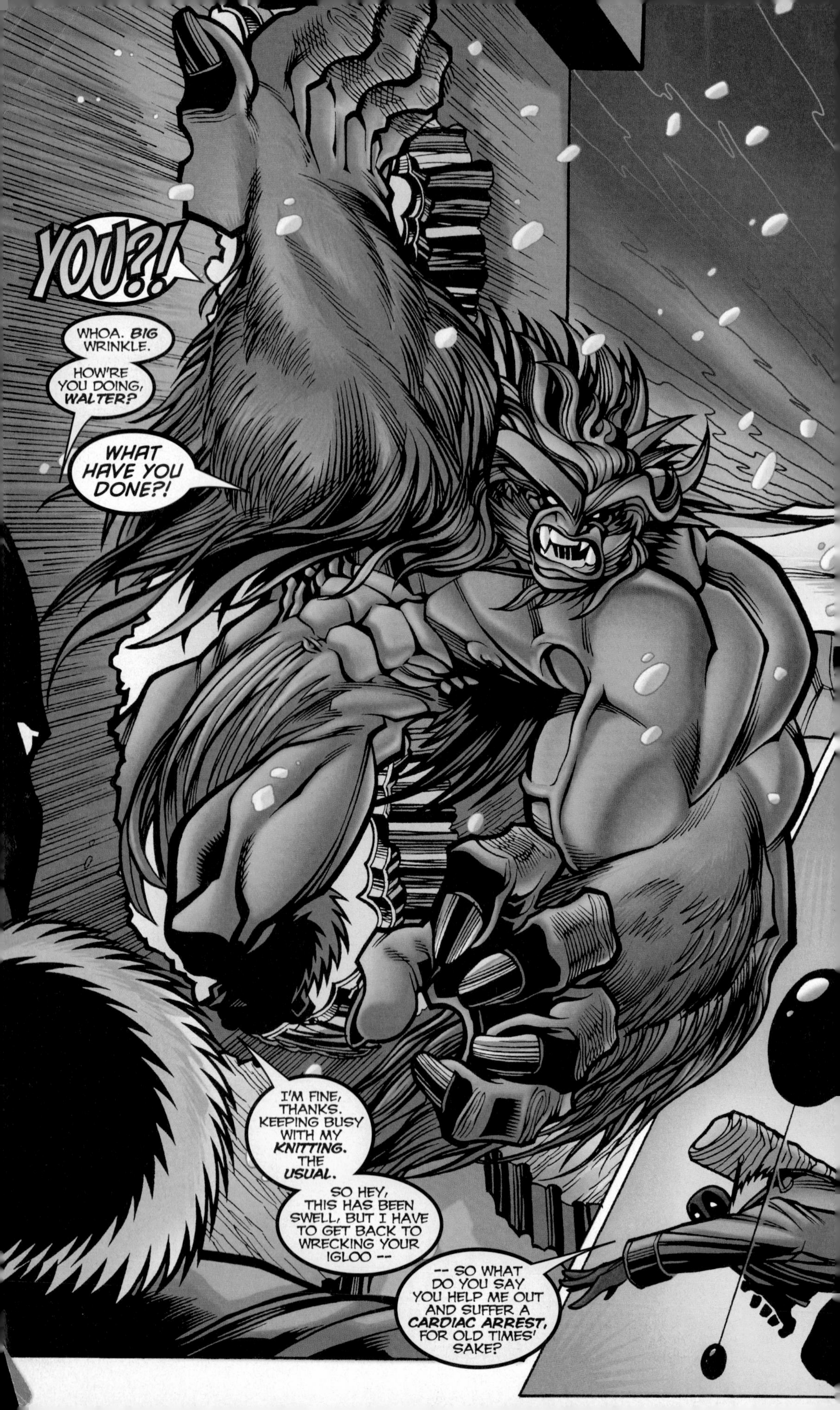
YOU?!
WHOA. BIG WRINKLE.
HOW'RE YOU DOING, WALTER?
WHAT HAVE YOU DONE?!
I'M FINE, THANKS. KEEPING BUSY WITH MY KNITTING. THE USUAL.
SO HEY, THIS HAS BEEN SWELL, BUT I HAVE TO GET BACK TO WRECKING YOUR IGLOO --
-- SO WHAT DO YOU SAY YOU HELP ME OUT AND SUFFER A CARDIAC ARREST, FOR OLD TIMES' SAKE?

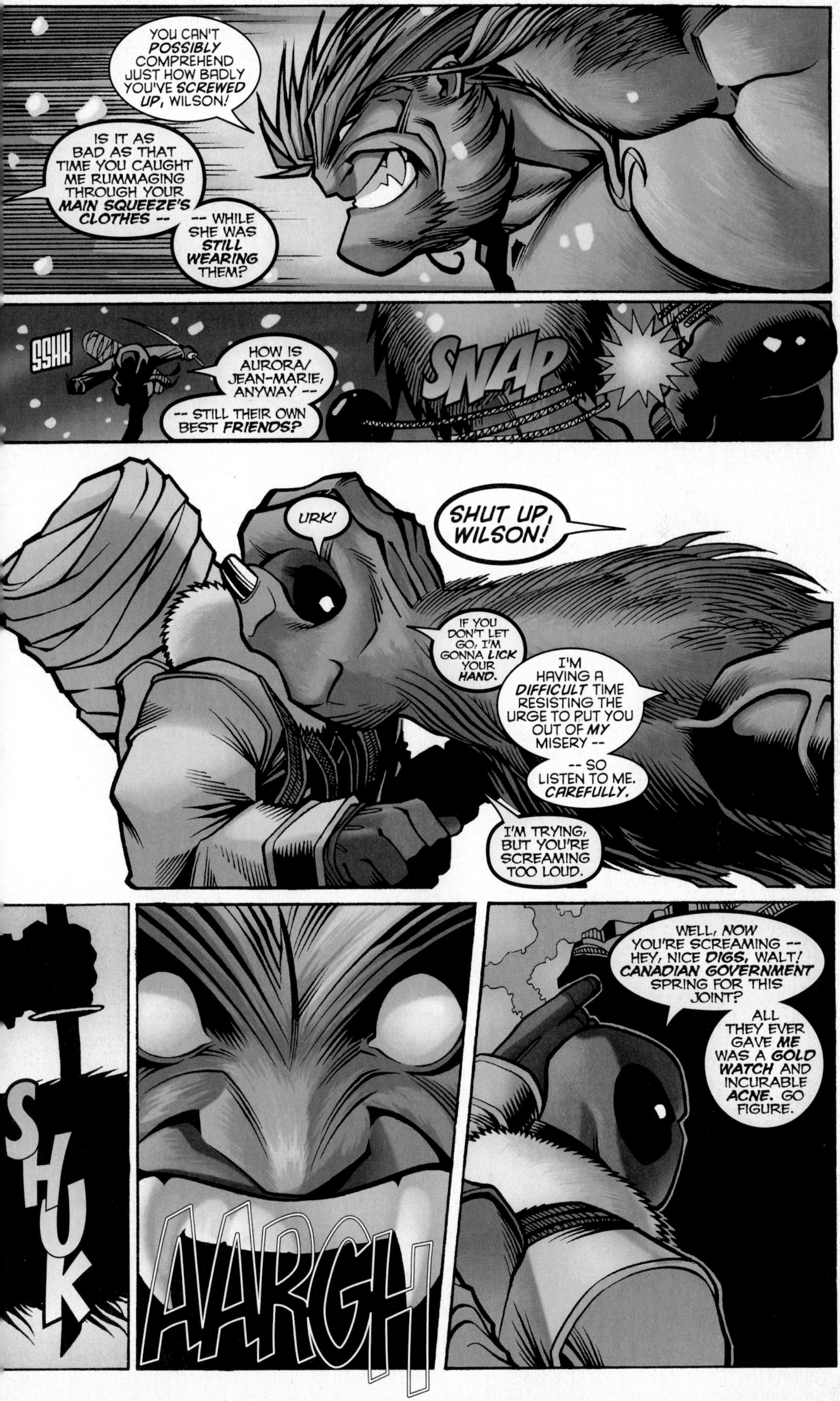

YOU CAN'T POSSIBLY COMPREHEND JUST HOW BADLY YOU'VE SCREWED UP, WILSON!
IS IT AS BAD AS THAT TIME YOU CAUGHT ME RUMMAGING THROUGH YOUR MAIN SQUEEZE'S CLOTHES --
-- WHILE SHE WAS STILL WEARING THEM?
SSHK
HOW IS AURORA/JEAN-MARIE, ANYWAY --
-- STILL THEIR OWN BEST FRIENDS?
SNAP
URK!
SHUT UP, WILSON!
IF YOU DON'T LET GO, I'M GONNA LICK YOUR HAND.
I'M HAVING A DIFFICULT TIME RESISTING THE URGE TO PUT YOU OUT OF MY MISERY --
-- SO LISTEN TO ME. CAREFULLY.
I'M TRYING, BUT YOU'RE SCREAMING TOO LOUD.
SHUK
AARGH
WELL, NOW YOU'RE SCREAMING -- HEY, NICE DIGS, WALT! CANADIAN GOVERNMENT SPRING FOR THIS JOINT?
ALL THEY EVER GAVE ME WAS A GOLD WATCH AND INCURABLE ACNE. GO FIGURE.

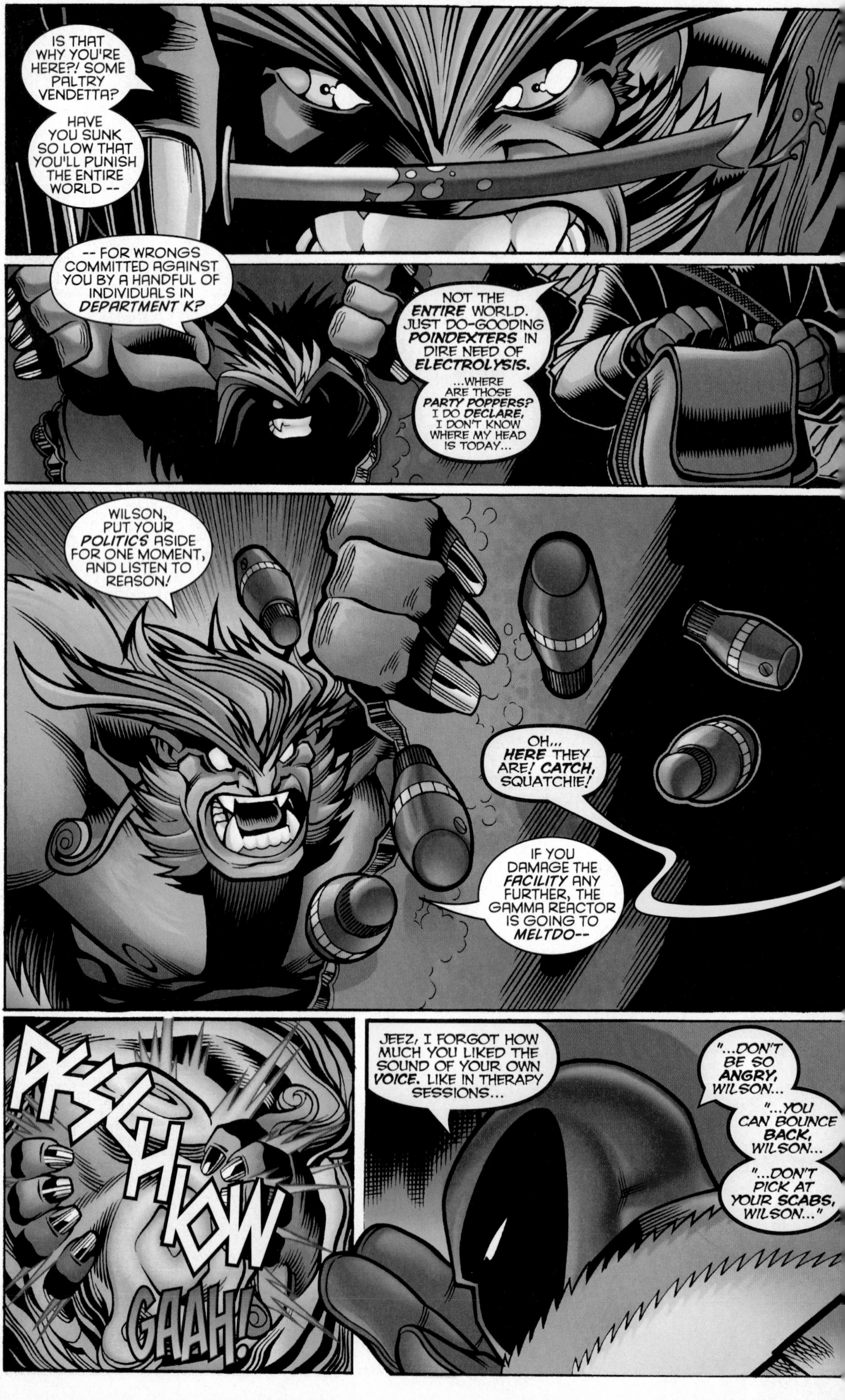
IS THAT WHY YOU'RE HERE?! SOME PALTRY VENDETTA?
HAVE YOU SUNK SO LOW THAT YOU'LL PUNISH THE ENTIRE WORLD --
-- FOR WRONGS COMMITTED AGAINST YOU BY A HANDFUL OF INDIVIDUALS IN DEPARTMENT K?
NOT THE ENTIRE WORLD. JUST DO-GOODING POINDEXTERS IN DIRE NEED OF ELECTROLYSIS.
...WHERE ARE THOSE PARTY POPPERS? I DO DECLARE, I DON'T KNOW WHERE MY HEAD IS TODAY...
WILSON, PUT YOUR POLITICS ASIDE FOR ONE MOMENT, AND LISTEN TO REASON!
OH... HERE THEY ARE! CATCH, SQUATCHIE!
IF YOU DAMAGE THE FACILITY ANY FURTHER, THE GAMMA REACTOR IS GOING TO MELTDO--
DRSCHHOW
GAAH!
JEEZ, I FORGOT HOW MUCH YOU LIKED THE SOUND OF YOUR OWN VOICE. LIKE IN THERAPY SESSIONS...
"...DON'T BE SO ANGRY, WILSON...
"...YOU CAN BOUNCE BACK, WILSON...
"...DON'T PICK AT YOUR SCABS, WILSON..."

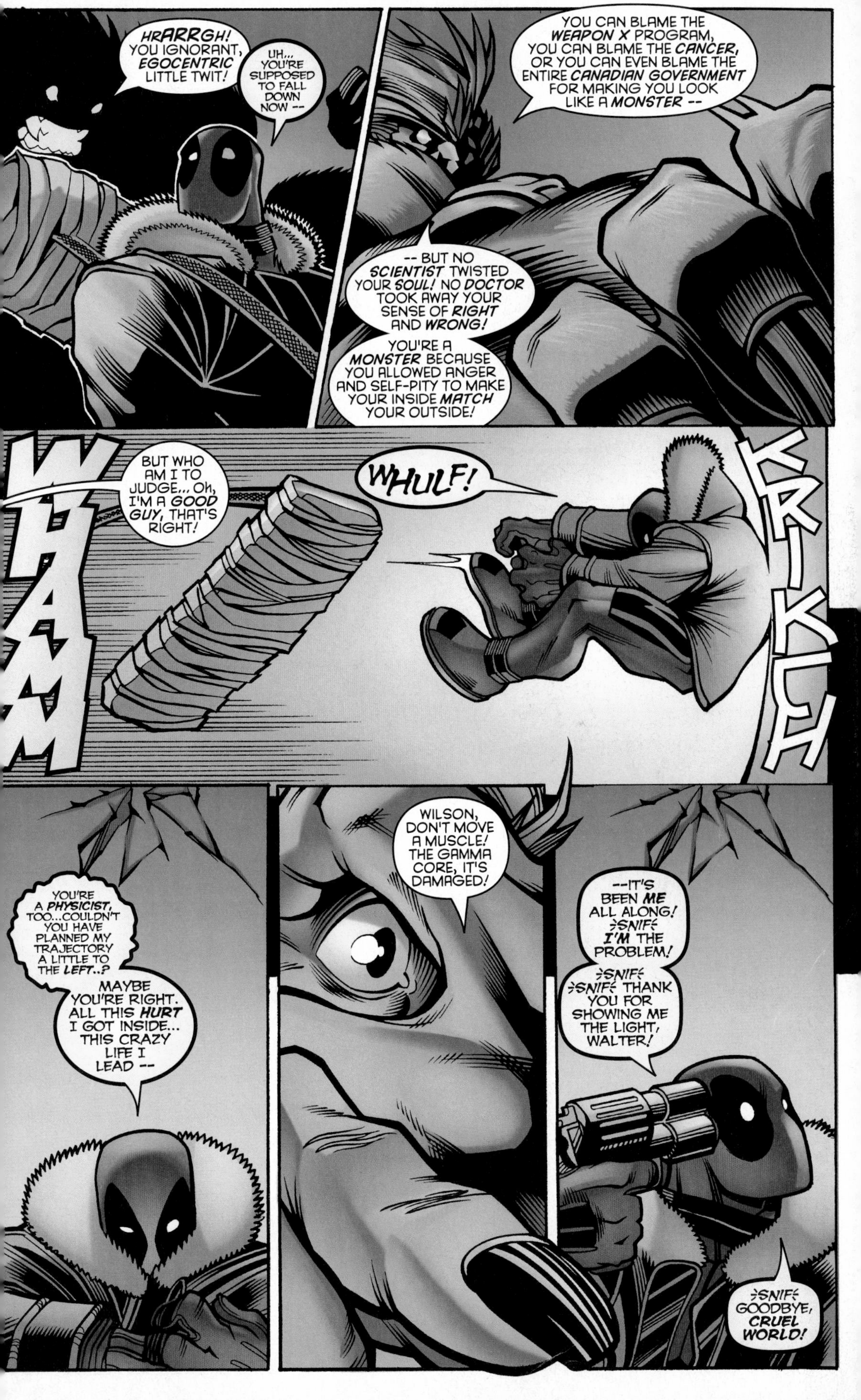
HRARRGH! YOU IGNORANT, EGOCENTRIC LITTLE TWIT!
UH... YOU'RE SUPPOSED TO FALL DOWN NOW --
YOU CAN BLAME THE WEAPON X PROGRAM, YOU CAN BLAME THE CANCER, OR YOU CAN EVEN BLAME THE ENTIRE CANADIAN GOVERNMENT FOR MAKING YOU LOOK LIKE A MONSTER --
-- BUT NO SCIENTIST TWISTED YOUR SOUL! NO DOCTOR TOOK AWAY YOUR SENSE OF RIGHT AND WRONG!
YOU'RE A MONSTER BECAUSE YOU ALLOWED ANGER AND SELF-PITY TO MAKE YOUR INSIDE MATCH YOUR OUTSIDE!
WHAM
BUT WHO AM I TO JUDGE... Oh, I'M A GOOD GUY, THAT'S RIGHT!
WHULF!
KRIKUH
YOU'RE A PHYSICIST, TOO...COULDN'T YOU HAVE PLANNED MY TRAJECTORY A LITTLE TO THE LEFT..?
MAYBE YOU'RE RIGHT. ALL THIS HURT I GOT INSIDE... THIS CRAZY LIFE I LEAD --
WILSON, DON'T MOVE A MUSCLE! THE GAMMA CORE, IT'S DAMAGED!
--IT'S BEEN ME ALL ALONG! SNIF I'M THE PROBLEM!
SNIF SNIF THANK YOU FOR SHOWING ME THE LIGHT, WALTER!
SNIF GOODBYE, CRUEL WORLD!

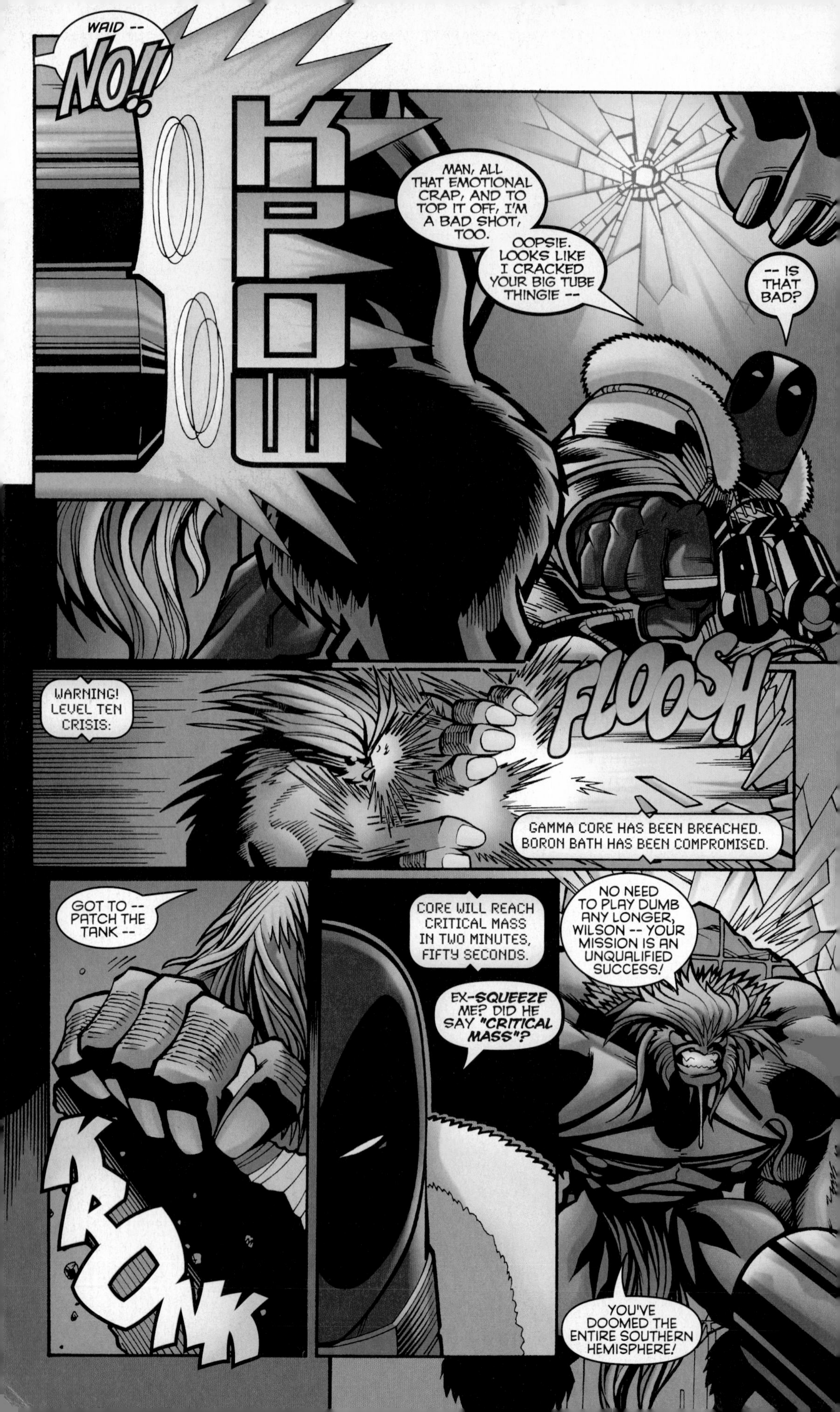
WAID --
NO!!
KPOW
MAN, ALL THAT EMOTIONAL CRAP, AND TO TOP IT OFF, I'M A BAD SHOT, TOO.
OOPSIE. LOOKS LIKE I CRACKED YOUR BIG TUBE THINGIE --
-- IS THAT BAD?
WARNING! LEVEL TEN CRISIS:
FLOOSH
GAMMA CORE HAS BEEN BREACHED. BORON BATH HAS BEEN COMPROMISED.
GOT TO -- PATCH THE TANK --
KRUNK
CORE WILL REACH CRITICAL MASS IN TWO MINUTES, FIFTY SECONDS.
EX-SQUEEZE ME? DID HE SAY "CRITICAL MASS"?
NO NEED TO PLAY DUMB ANY LONGER, WILSON -- YOUR MISSION IS AN UNQUALIFIED SUCCESS!
YOU'VE DOOMED THE ENTIRE SOUTHERN HEMISPHERE!

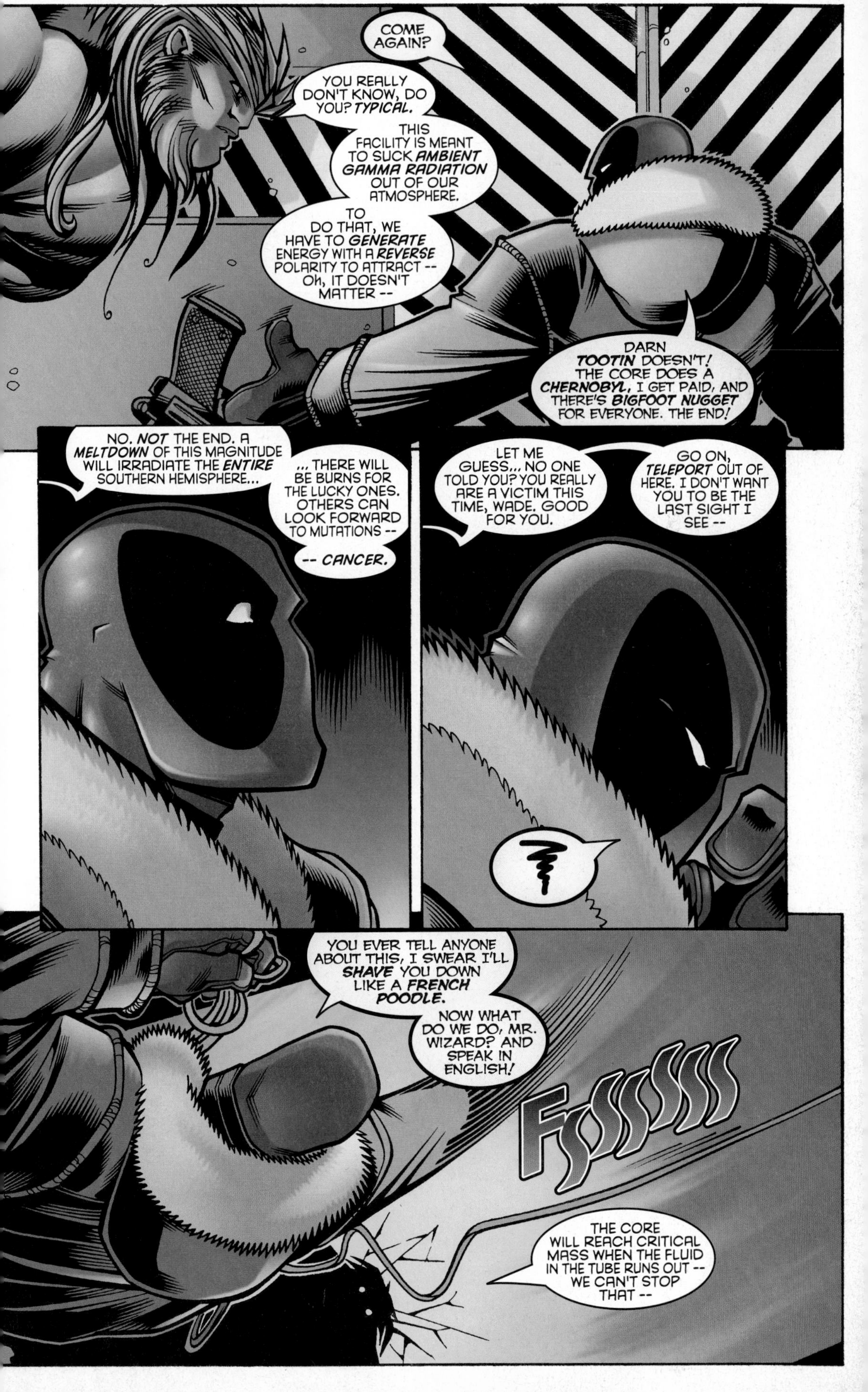
COME AGAIN?
YOU REALLY DON'T KNOW, DO YOU? TYPICAL.
THIS FACILITY IS MEANT TO SUCK AMBIENT GAMMA RADIATION OUT OF OUR ATMOSPHERE.
TO DO THAT, WE HAVE TO GENERATE ENERGY WITH A REVERSE POLARITY TO ATTRACT -- Oh, IT DOESN'T MATTER --
DARN TOOTIN DOESN'T! THE CORE DOES A CHERNOBYL, I GET PAID, AND THERE'S BIGFOOT NUGGET FOR EVERYONE. THE END!
NO. NOT THE END. A MELTDOWN OF THIS MAGNITUDE WILL IRRADIATE THE ENTIRE SOUTHERN HEMISPHERE...
... THERE WILL BE BURNS FOR THE LUCKY ONES. OTHERS CAN LOOK FORWARD TO MUTATIONS --
-- CANCER.
LET ME GUESS... NO ONE TOLD YOU? YOU REALLY ARE A VICTIM THIS TIME, WADE. GOOD FOR YOU.
GO ON, TELEPORT OUT OF HERE. I DON'T WANT YOU TO BE THE LAST SIGHT I SEE --
YOU EVER TELL ANYONE ABOUT THIS, I SWEAR I'LL SHAVE YOU DOWN LIKE A FRENCH POODLE.
NOW WHAT DO WE DO, MR. WIZARD? AND SPEAK IN ENGLISH!
FSSSSSS
THE CORE WILL REACH CRITICAL MASS WHEN THE FLUID IN THE TUBE RUNS OUT -- WE CAN'T STOP THAT --

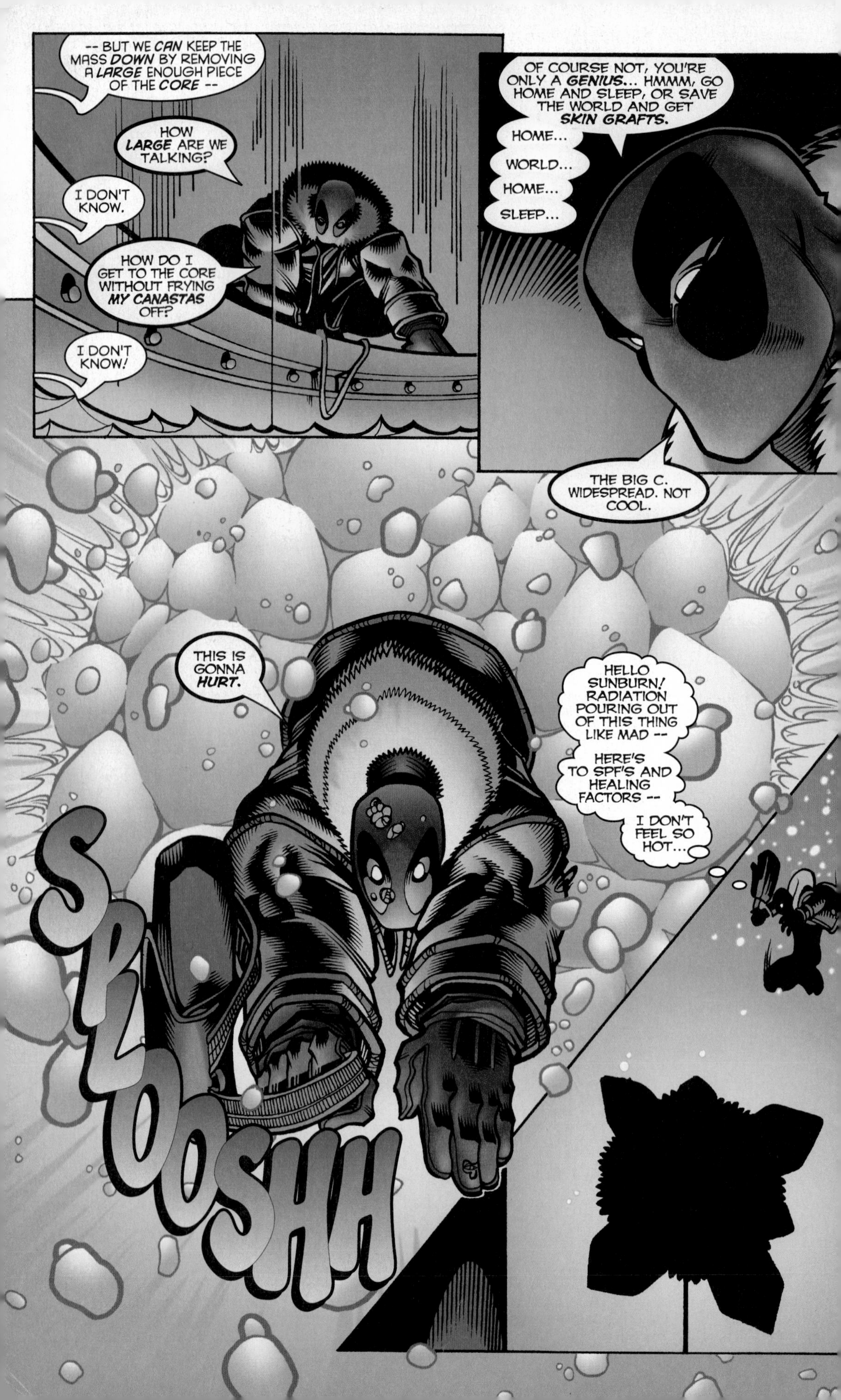
-- BUT WE CAN KEEP THE MASS DOWN BY REMOVING A LARGE ENOUGH PIECE OF THE CORE --
HOW LARGE ARE WE TALKING?
I DON'T KNOW.
HOW DO I GET TO THE CORE WITHOUT FRYING MY CANASTAS OFF?
I DON'T KNOW!
OF COURSE NOT, YOU'RE ONLY A GENIUS... HMMM, GO HOME AND SLEEP, OR SAVE THE WORLD AND GET SKIN GRAFTS.
HOME...
WORLD...
HOME...
SLEEP...
THE BIG C. WIDESPREAD. NOT COOL.
THIS IS GONNA HURT.
SPLOOSHH
HELLO SUNBURN! RADIATION POURING OUT OF THIS THING LIKE MAD --
HERE'S TO SPF'S AND HEALING FACTORS --
I DON'T FEEL SO HOT...

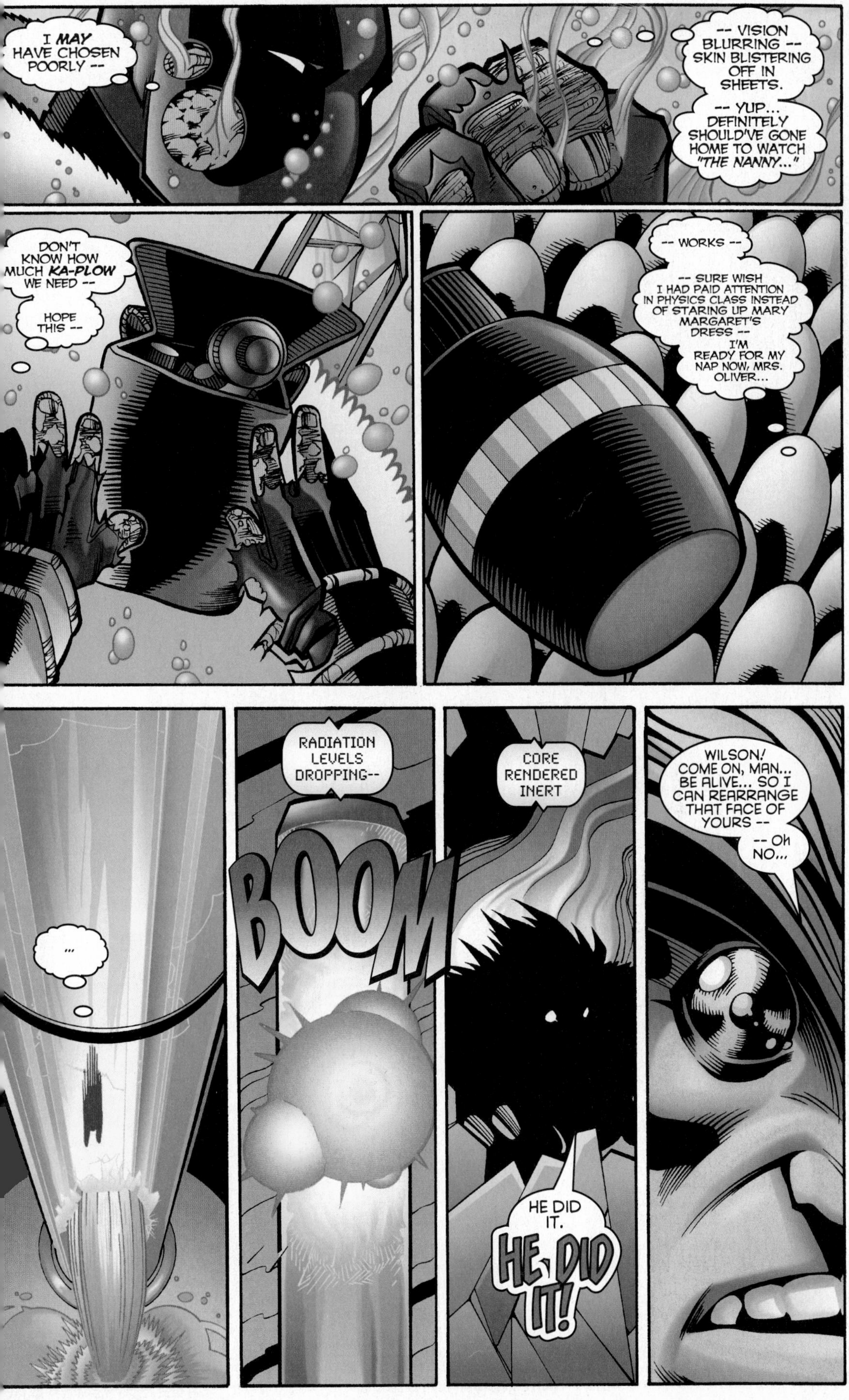
I MAY HAVE CHOSEN POORLY --
-- VISION BLURRING -- SKIN BLISTERING OFF IN SHEETS.
-- YUP... DEFINITELY SHOULD'VE GONE HOME TO WATCH "THE NANNY..."
DON'T KNOW HOW MUCH KA-PLOW WE NEED --
HOPE THIS --
-- WORKS --
-- SURE WISH I HAD PAID ATTENTION IN PHYSICS CLASS INSTEAD OF STARING UP MARY MARGARET'S DRESS --
I'M READY FOR MY NAP NOW, MRS. OLIVER...
...
RADIATION LEVELS DROPPING--
BOOM
CORE RENDERED INERT
HE DID IT.
HE DID IT!
WILSON! COME ON, MAN... BE ALIVE... SO I CAN REARRANGE THAT FACE OF YOURS --
-- OH NO...

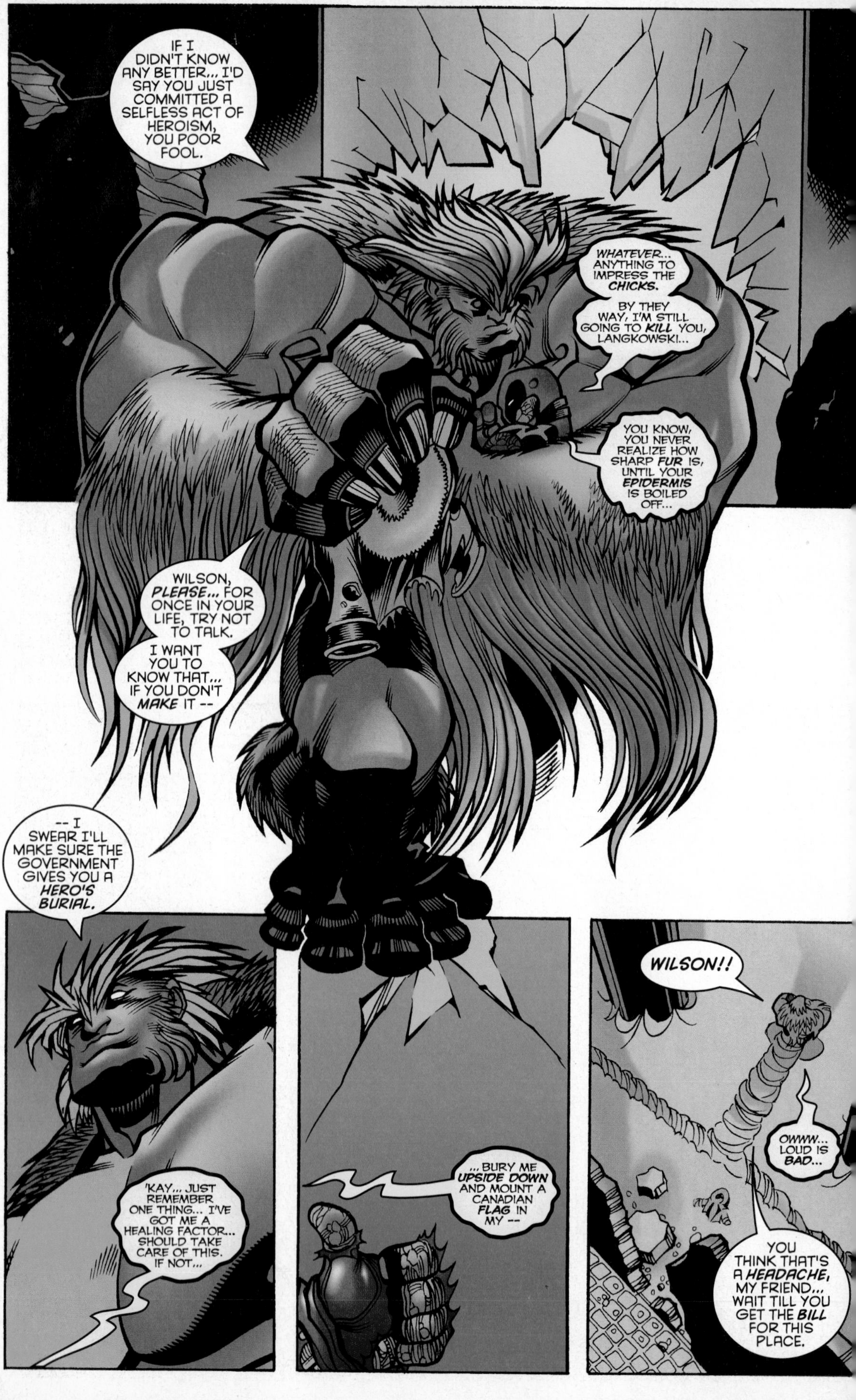
IF I DIDN'T KNOW ANY BETTER... I'D SAY YOU JUST COMMITTED A SELFLESS ACT OF HEROISM, YOU POOR FOOL.
WHATEVER... ANYTHING TO IMPRESS THE CHICKS.
BY THEY WAY, I'M STILL GOING TO KILL YOU, LANGKOWSKI...
YOU KNOW, YOU NEVER REALIZE HOW SHARP FUR IS, UNTIL YOUR EPIDERMIS IS BOILED OFF...
WILSON, PLEASE... FOR ONCE IN YOUR LIFE, TRY NOT TO TALK.
I WANT YOU TO KNOW THAT... IF YOU DON'T MAKE IT --
-- I SWEAR I'LL MAKE SURE THE GOVERNMENT GIVES YOU A HERO'S BURIAL.
'KAY... JUST REMEMBER ONE THING... I'VE GOT ME A HEALING FACTOR... SHOULD TAKE CARE OF THIS. IF NOT...
...BURY ME UPSIDE DOWN AND MOUNT A CANADIAN FLAG IN MY --
WILSON!!
OWWW... LOUD IS BAD...
YOU THINK THAT'S A HEADACHE, MY FRIEND... WAIT TILL YOU GET THE BILL FOR THIS PLACE.

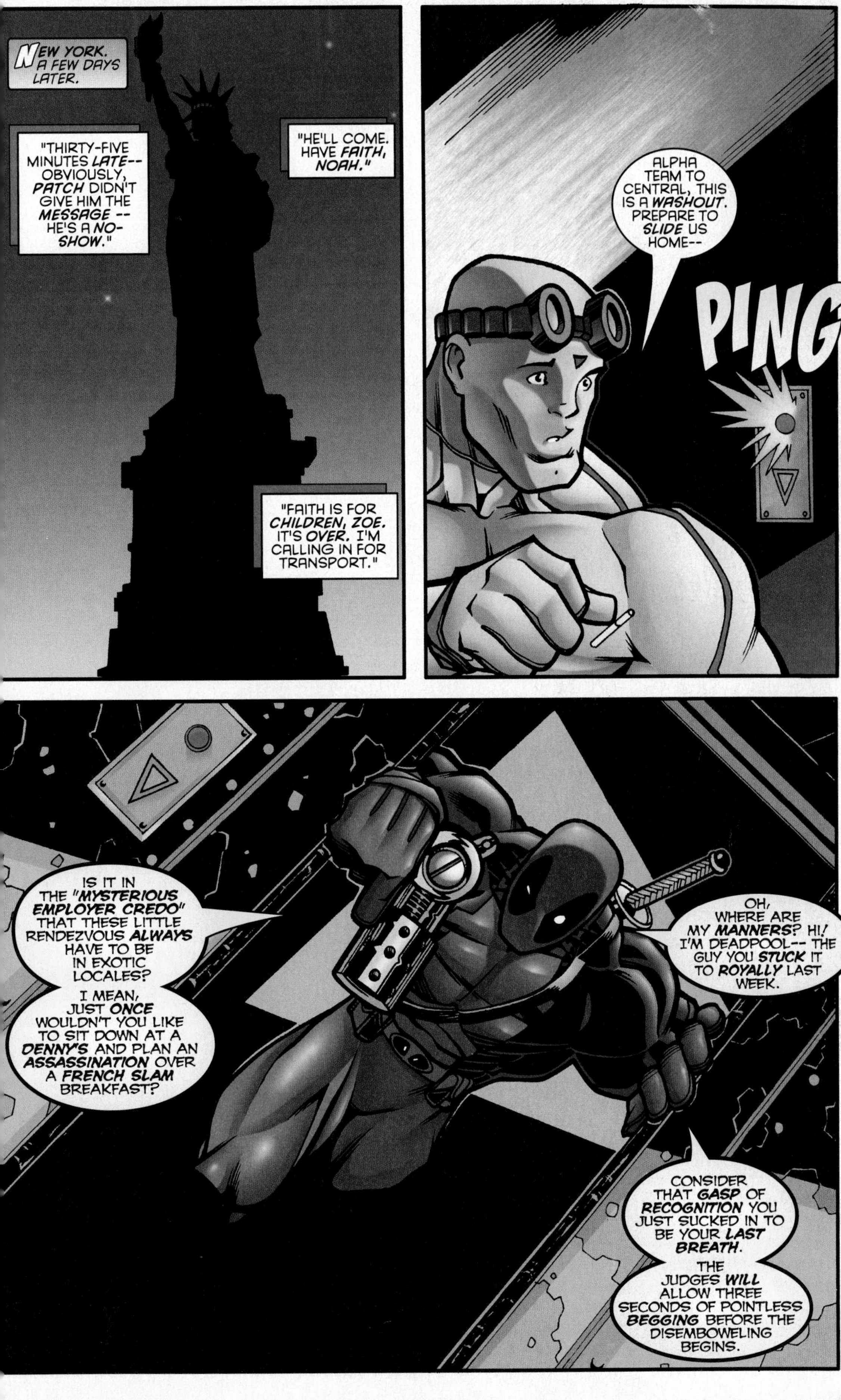
NEW YORK. A FEW DAYS LATER.
"THIRTY-FIVE MINUTES LATE-- OBVIOUSLY, PATCH DIDN'T GIVE HIM THE MESSAGE -- HE'S A NO-SHOW."
"HE'LL COME. HAVE FAITH, NOAH."
"FAITH IS FOR CHILDREN, ZOE. IT'S OVER. I'M CALLING IN FOR TRANSPORT."
ALPHA TEAM TO CENTRAL, THIS IS A WASHOUT. PREPARE TO SLIDE US HOME--
PING
IS IT IN THE "MYSTERIOUS EMPLOYER CREDO" THAT THESE LITTLE RENDEZVOUS ALWAYS HAVE TO BE IN EXOTIC LOCALES?
I MEAN, JUST ONCE WOULDN'T YOU LIKE TO SIT DOWN AT A DENNY'S AND PLAN AN ASSASSINATION OVER A FRENCH SLAM BREAKFAST?
OH, WHERE ARE MY MANNERS? HI! I'M DEADPOOL-- THE GUY YOU STUCK IT TO ROYALLY LAST WEEK.
CONSIDER THAT GASP OF RECOGNITION YOU JUST SUCKED IN TO BE YOUR LAST BREATH.
THE JUDGES WILL ALLOW THREE SECONDS OF POINTLESS BEGGING BEFORE THE DISEMBOWELING BEGINS.

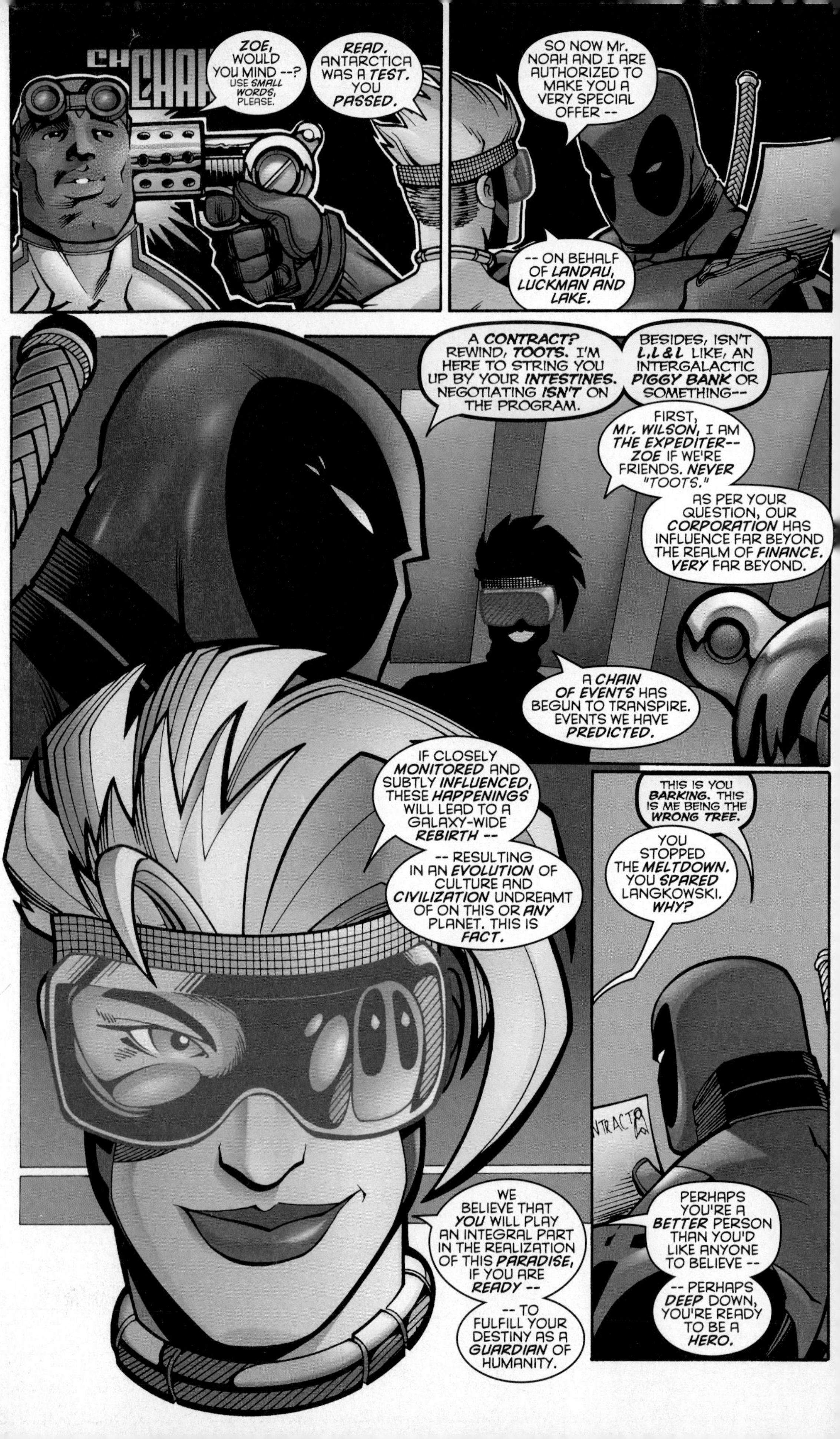
CHCHAK
ZOE, WOULD YOU MIND --? USE SMALL WORDS, PLEASE.
READ. ANTARCTICA WAS A TEST. YOU PASSED.
SO NOW Mr. NOAH AND I ARE AUTHORIZED TO MAKE YOU A VERY SPECIAL OFFER --
-- ON BEHALF OF LANDAU, LUCKMAN AND LAKE.
A CONTRACT? REWIND, TOOTS. I'M HERE TO STRING YOU UP BY YOUR INTESTINES. NEGOTIATING ISN'T ON THE PROGRAM.
BESIDES, ISN'T L,L&L LIKE, AN INTERGALACTIC PIGGY BANK OR SOMETHING--
FIRST, Mr. WILSON, I AM THE EXPEDITER-- ZOE IF WE'RE FRIENDS. NEVER "TOOTS."
AS PER YOUR QUESTION, OUR CORPORATION HAS INFLUENCE FAR BEYOND THE REALM OF FINANCE. VERY FAR BEYOND.
A CHAIN OF EVENTS HAS BEGUN TO TRANSPIRE. EVENTS WE HAVE PREDICTED.
IF CLOSELY MONITORED AND SUBTLY INFLUENCED, THESE HAPPENINGS WILL LEAD TO A GALAXY-WIDE REBIRTH --
-- RESULTING IN AN EVOLUTION OF CULTURE AND CIVILIZATION UNDREAMT OF ON THIS OR ANY PLANET. THIS IS FACT.
WE BELIEVE THAT YOU WILL PLAY AN INTEGRAL PART IN THE REALIZATION OF THIS PARADISE, IF YOU ARE READY --
-- TO FULFILL YOUR DESTINY AS A GUARDIAN OF HUMANITY.
THIS IS YOU BARKING. THIS IS ME BEING THE WRONG TREE.
YOU STOPPED THE MELTDOWN. YOU SPARED LANGKOWSKI. WHY?
NTRACT
PERHAPS YOU'RE A BETTER PERSON THAN YOU'D LIKE ANYONE TO BELIEVE --
-- PERHAPS DEEP DOWN, YOU'RE READY TO BE A HERO.

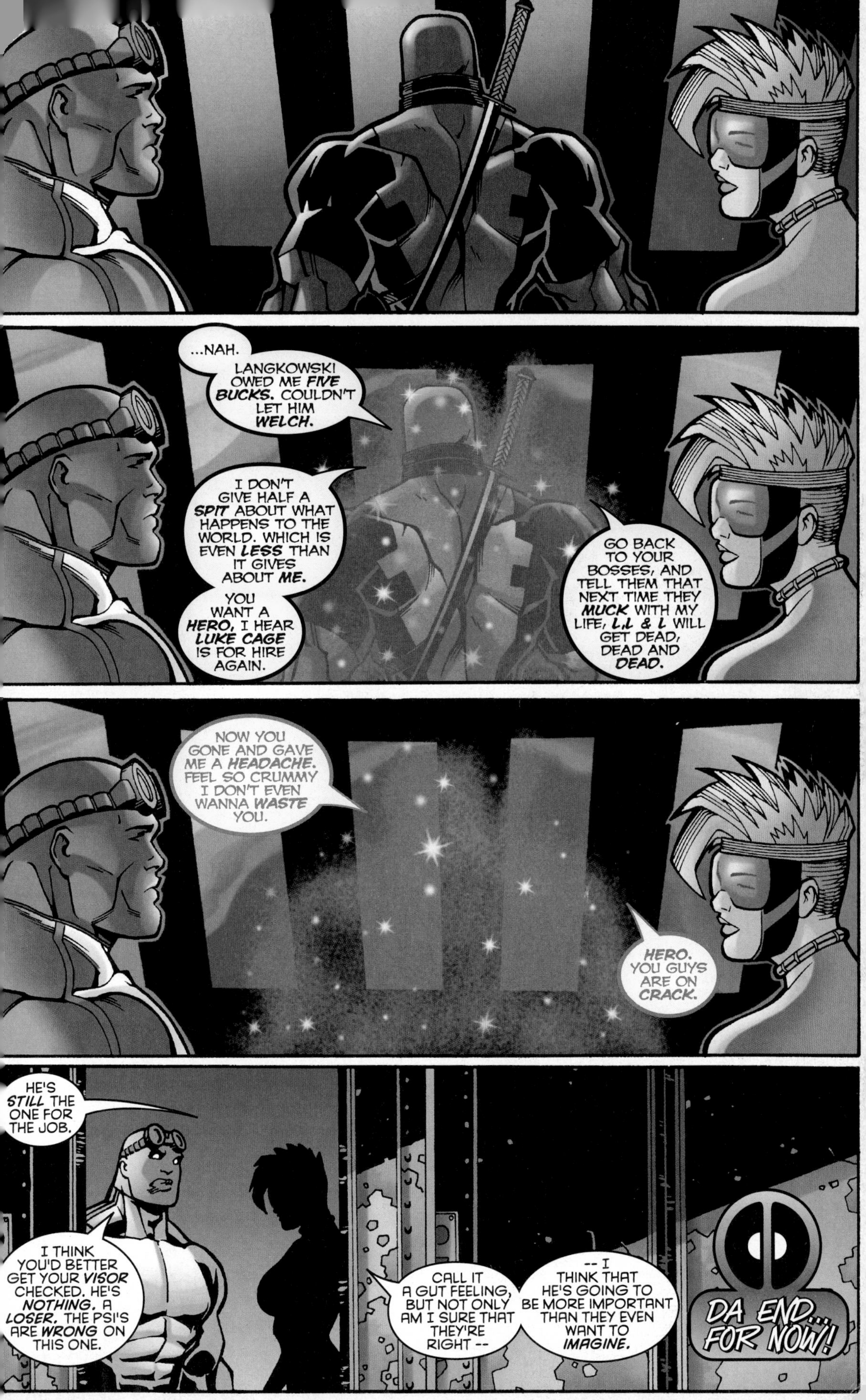
...NAH.
LANGKOWSKI OWED ME FIVE BUCKS. COULDN'T LET HIM WELCH.
I DON'T GIVE HALF A SPIT ABOUT WHAT HAPPENS TO THE WORLD. WHICH IS EVEN LESS THAN IT GIVES ABOUT ME.
YOU WANT A HERO, I HEAR LUKE CAGE IS FOR HIRE AGAIN.
GO BACK TO YOUR BOSSES, AND TELL THEM THAT NEXT TIME THEY MUCK WITH MY LIFE, L,L & L WILL GET DEAD, DEAD AND DEAD.
NOW YOU GONE AND GAVE ME A HEADACHE. FEEL SO CRUMMY I DON'T EVEN WANNA WASTE YOU.
HERO. YOU GUYS ARE ON CRACK.
HE'S STILL THE ONE FOR THE JOB.
I THINK YOU'D BETTER GET YOUR VISOR CHECKED. HE'S NOTHING. A LOSER. THE PSI'S ARE WRONG ON THIS ONE.
CALL IT A GUT FEELING, BUT NOT ONLY AM I SURE THAT THEY'RE RIGHT --
-- I THINK THAT HE'S GOING TO BE MORE IMPORTANT THAN THEY EVEN WANT TO IMAGINE.
DA END... FOR NOW!

BEHIND THE SCENES

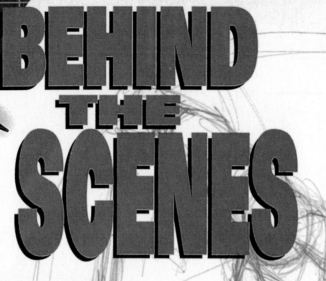

Behind every finished comic there is a story, and the story behind the premiere issue of any series is especially interesting. The assembled creative team must build the framework for what will hopefully be a long series almost from scratch, creating a world inside the Marvel Universe within which the book can grow and thrive. In the case of DEADPOOL, this was especially difficult, since so very little about the character is really known.

Over the next few pages, we're going to take you behind the scenes, showing you a small part of the massive creative and subsequent evolutionary processes that resulted in the book you now hold in your hands.

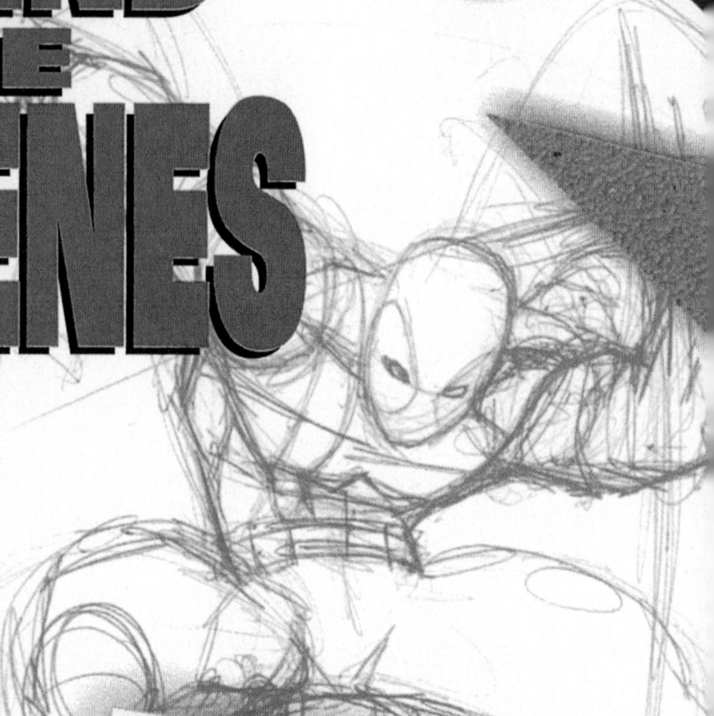

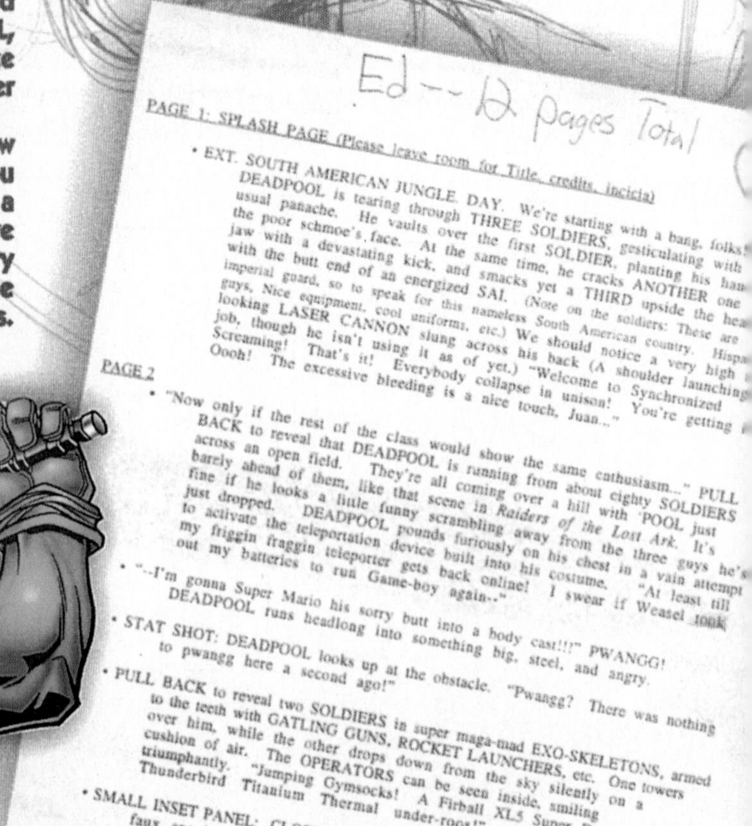

Ed -- 12 pages Total

PAGE 1: SPLASH PAGE (Please leave room for Title, credits, incicia)

• EXT. SOUTH AMERICAN JUNGLE. DAY. We're starting with a bang, folks!
DEADPOOL is tearing through THREE SOLDIERS, gesticulating with
usual panache. He vaults over the first SOLDIER, planting his han
the poor schmoe's face. At the same time, he cracks ANOTHER one
jaw with a devastating kick, and smacks yet a THIRD upside the hea
with the butt end of an energized SAI. (Note on the soldiers: These are
imperial guard, so to speak for this nameless South American country. Hispa
guys. Nice equipment, cool uniforms, etc.) We should notice a very high
looking LASER CANNON slung across his back (A shoulder launching
job, though he isn't using it as of yet.) "Welcome to Synchronized
Screaming! That's it! Everybody collapse in unison! You're getting
Oooh! The excessive bleeding is a nice touch, Juan..."

PAGE 2

• "Now only if the rest of the class would show the same enthusiasm..." PULL
BACK to reveal that DEADPOOL is running from about eighty SOLDIERS
across an open field. They're all coming over a hill with 'POOL just
barely ahead of them, like that scene in *Raiders of the Lost Ark*. It's
fine if he looks a little funny scrambling away from the three guys he's
just dropped. DEADPOOL pounds furiously on his chest in a vain attempt
to activate the teleportation device built into his costume. "At least till
my friggin fraggin teleporter gets back online! I swear if Weasel took
out my batteries to run Game-boy again-."

• "--I'm gonna Super Mario his sorry butt into a body cast!!!" PWANGG!
DEADPOOL runs headlong into something big, steel, and angry.

• STAT SHOT: DEADPOOL looks up at the obstacle. "Pwangg? There was nothing
to pwangg here a second ago!"

• PULL BACK to reveal two SOLDIERS in super maga-mad EXO-SKELETONS, armed
to the teeth with GATLING GUNS, ROCKET LAUNCHERS, etc. One towers
over him, while the other drops down from the sky silently on a
cushion of air. The OPERATORS can be seen inside, smiling
triumphantly. "Jumping Gymsocks! A Firball XL5 Super Duper Set of
Thunderbird Titanium Thermal under-roos!"

• SMALL INSET PANEL: CLOSE ON DEADPOOL as he *McAuley Culkins* his face in
faux anguish. "Whatever will I do??!?"

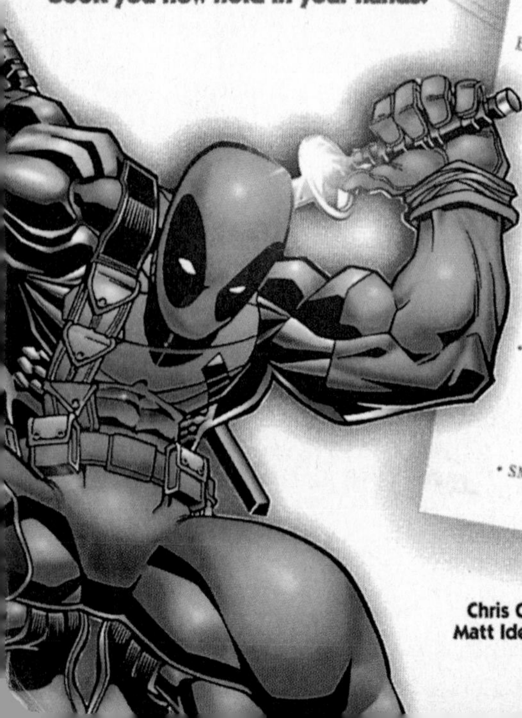

Chris Carroll: Designer
Matt Idelson: Tour Guide

THE STORY

Almost from the outset, it was clear that Landau, Luckman & Lake would be hiring Deadpool to do something bad as a test to see if he was the man for their plans. Originally, writer Joe Kelly envisioned Deadpool being hired to take out the mysterious heads of LL&L themselves. It would be Deadpool's brains that prevented him from pulling the trigger, and Wade Wilson would find himself with a new employer. Editor in chief Bob Harras felt that this was perhaps too cosmic a story for such a down-to-Earth character, and instead suggested using Sasquatch as Deadpool's assigned target. He also thought that Sasquatch and Deadpool doing battle would be an interesting visual. With all that orange and red, it might be a little difficult to make out what's going on, or at least make for a potentially really boring looking page, color-wise. It was quickly decided that having them face off in the snow would make these garish fellows pop out on the page. After that, the revised story quickly fell into place.

In Joe's revised plot, there was a scene that was later cut out in which Langkowski's Gamma Reactor overloads, forcing Langkowski to transform into Sasquatch and save the day. (A) This scene was later cut for dramatic reasons; the story would be better served if it was Deadpool who set off the reactor overload and then had to set things right.

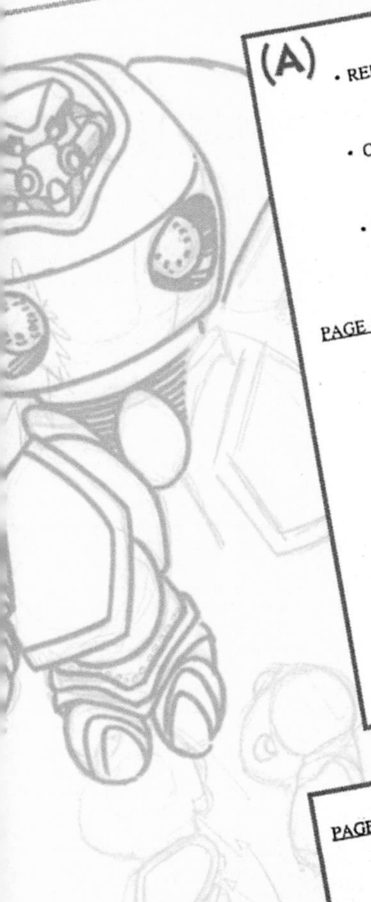

(A)

- REFLECTED IN WALTER'S GLASSES we see the POWER CORE glow with energy. "Gamma levels rising... approaching critical level..." "Steady... Steady..." "Gamma levels at 99% capacity... Doctor--"

- CLOSE ON the controller as WALTER presses a button. The part of the screen we can see reads, "-- DISPERSAL OF GAMMA RADIAT--" "Engage the core NOW!!"

- EXT. THE LAB. POOOOMMM!!! A shaft of energy erupts from the lab into the sky, taking half of the roof with it in a very unexpected explosion!!! (Ed. this is the roof around the tower I'm talking about. The tower itself is still in tact.)

PAGE 11

- INT. THE CORE. Even though the core still pumps out energy, the rest of this massive chamber is in ruins. The roof has caved in, FLAMES are everywhere caused by ENERGY DISCHARGES that fire randomly from the core. SNOW trickles in through the missing roof section. TECHNICIANS and SCIENTISTS run around the room, trying their best to put out the blaze. OTHERS are trapped under debris, hurt, etc. "Someone get to the source!" "Are you crazy!?" "Where are Marsten and Hopper?!?"

- THROUGH THICK SMOKE, a man appears, carrying two unconscious TECHIES, one under each arm. "He's got them!!!" "Everyone! Clear out of here! The core is unstable!"

- WALTER LANGKOWSKI, just a tad cooked by the blast, emerges from the smoke with his men. "Dr. Langkowski has them!!!" "Come on, don't stand there gawking! Get them to med-center!"

(MORE)

PAGE 11 (CONTD.)

- FRANCIS grabs WALTER by the arm as the two men are carried off by other TECHIES. He points upwards towards the explosion. "What are we going to do, Walter?" "You and the rest are going to get to a safe distance while I take care of business here..."

- CLOSE ON WALTER, as he looks upwards towards the hole in the ceiling. He is clearly stunned by what he sees. "While I make sure that there's still a safe distance left to go to!"

In another early plot twist, Deadpool was originally hired for his mission by Noah while atop the Statue of Liberty (B). The scene was cut and replaced with the second Hellhouse scene on page 18. We figured that Deadpool was supposed to get his assignments via the Hellhouse, and it wouldn't make a whole lot of sense for him to be hired by Noah directly. Since this scene served the dual purpose of revealing much of Deadpool's backstory, that function had to be worked into the new scene, and was, in a cleverly constructed moment which also features the first appearance of T-Ray, a fellow merc at the Hellhouse who's going to be causing more than a little trouble in later issues.

(B)

PAGE 18

- EXT. STATUE OF LIBERTY. NIGHT. ATOP THE CROWN. A MAN (NOAH) in shadow, leans on one of the windows, looking out at the water. "Fifteen minutes late... I think he's a no-show."
- CLOSE ON THE WINDOW. The man continues speaking out loud, prepares to light a cigarette. "Central, Prepare to slide me home--"
- KTHINK! A KATANA slices the air right in front of NOAH'S face as he ignites the lighter. The sword splits the Cig perfectly in half. Noah's eyes go wide with surprise. "Why do you high-rollers always choose to meet in such inaccessible locales? Just once I'd like to sit down in Denny's wit the rest of the Schmoes and talk shop over a French Slam breakfast.""Deadpool I presume?"
- COOL SHOT of DEADPOOL as he hangs upside down in front of the WINDOW attatched to a RAPELLING LINE, casually picking at his "fingernails" with the tip of his sword. "Figured I'd sweat you out till I knew who was nearby. SOP, you understand." NOAH holds out a thin DOSSIER f DEADPOOL to peruse. "I knew you were there. I was just testing..." "Ch'yahh, right! As IF!"
- DEADPOOL studies the file intently, though it is clearly upside down. "I file you will find the location and layout of a secret research facili the Antarctic. There's been an accident there.""Love what you di here! Extra points for neatness! Snazzy dress for the cover... wh the bubble gum?"

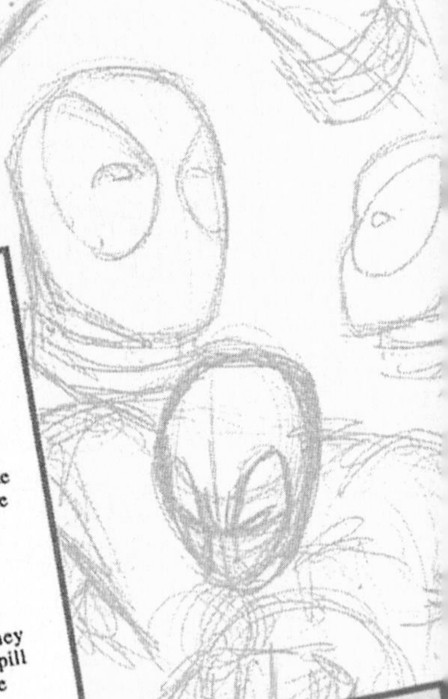

PAGE 19

- DEADPOOL lowers himself onto the ledge, dangling his feet boyishly as NOAH tries to brief him. "Gamma Radiation is spreading at an alarming rate." "Not for nothing, sir. But I fell asleep during nuclear physics... or I was looking up suzi James skirt... either way, I can't stop a three-mile-popsicle."
- REACTION SHOT: DEADPOOL almost drops the file when NOAH sternly explains, "We don't want you to stop it. We want you to help it along." "Ex-squeeze me?" "I represent employers with intrests in the southern hemisphere that are failing miserably--"
- NOAH indicates the DOSSIER, turning it rightside up for DEADPOOL, who sits up suddenly, paying close attention. "--A disaster of this magnitude could ease their pain with an insurance winfall. Loss of life will be restricted to the personnel at the plant, who're dead men anyway. They are willing to pay twenty million dollars to ensure that the Gamma spill runs its course." "Patch said that you requested me personally. Aside from my dashing smile and well defined buttocks, why the special attention?"
- CLOSE ON NOAH, almost smiling. "You have a reputation as a wild card. Whenyou're around, things get broke. That's number one. Number two, your vaunted healing factor makes you resistant to any radiation you'll encounter before the job is done." "Who does your homework? Encyclopedia brown? So much for private medical history... And number three?
- CLOSE ON the DOSSIER, where we see a CANADIAN GOVT. PIC of WALTER LANGKOWSKI. "The man who you'll have to kill to complete the job is an office mate from your Canadian Days."

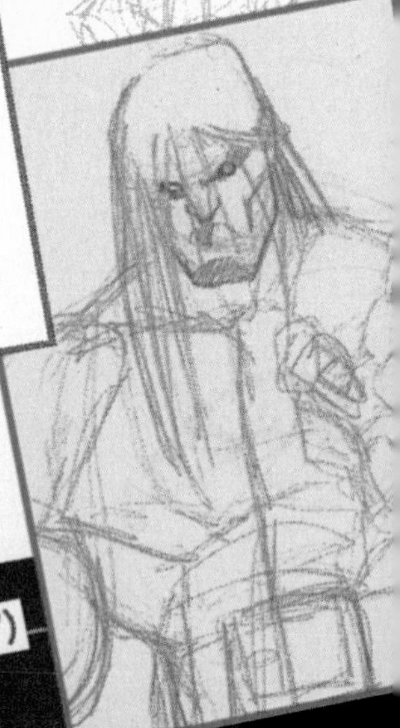

(The Villianous "T-Ray")

THE COVER

The cover of any comic book goes through generations of sketches and revisions before a final design is approved. In this case, the cover was particularly important since this was the first issue of the series. The character had to be well spotlighted, and the logo had to be clear and as unobstructed as possible. To complicate matters further, this was to be a wrap-around cover. The inherent problem with wrap-arounds is that since we're not contending with the logo or tradedress on the backside, the back cover tends to look cooler than the front half.

(1)

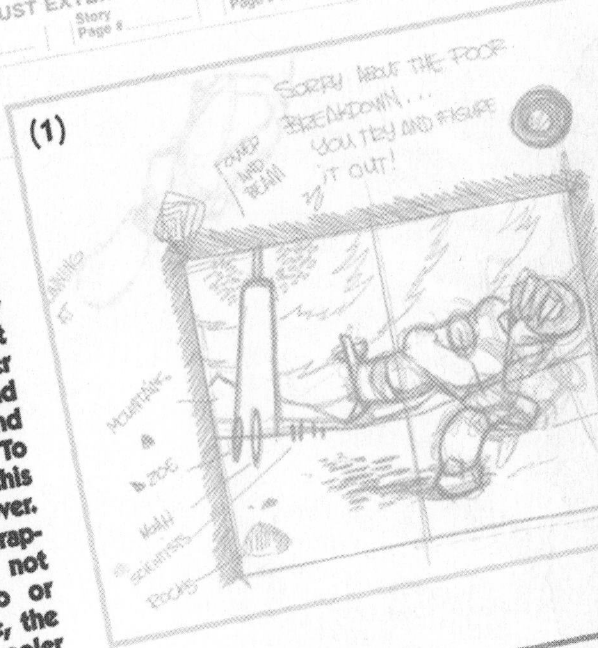
SORRY ABOUT THE POOR BREAKDOWN... YOU TRY AND FIGURE IT OUT!
TOWER AND BEAM
MOUNTAINS
ZOE
NOAH
SCIENTISTS
ROCKS

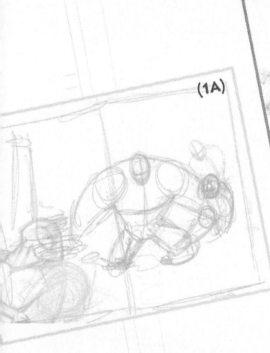

(1A)

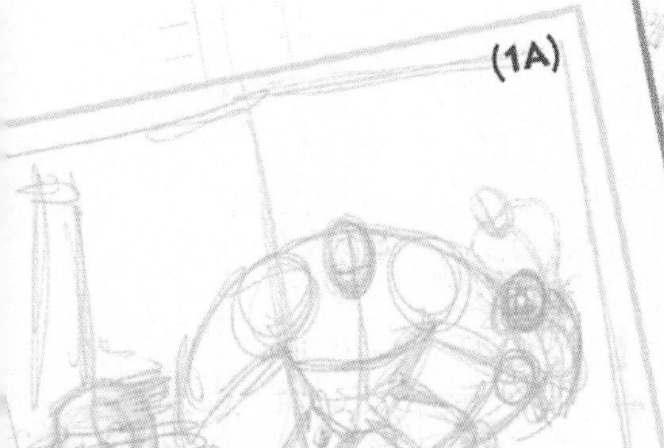

(2)

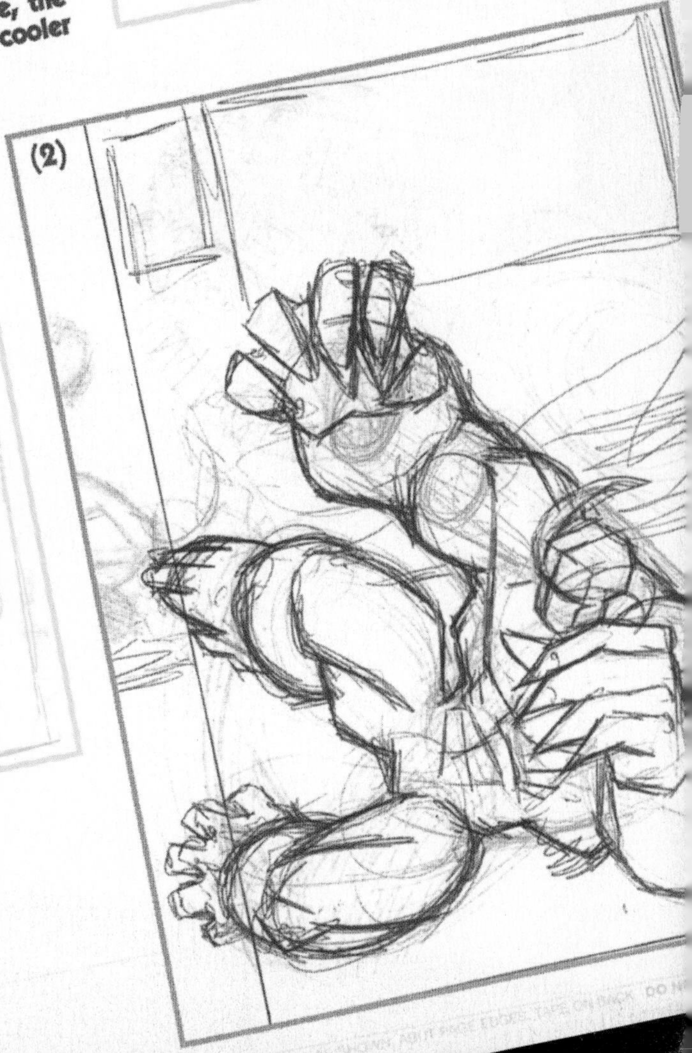

ART PAPER FOR BLEED PAGES (BOOKSHELF FORM... ALL BLEED ART MUST EXTEND T...

Issue

Story
Page #

Page #

Book

(3)

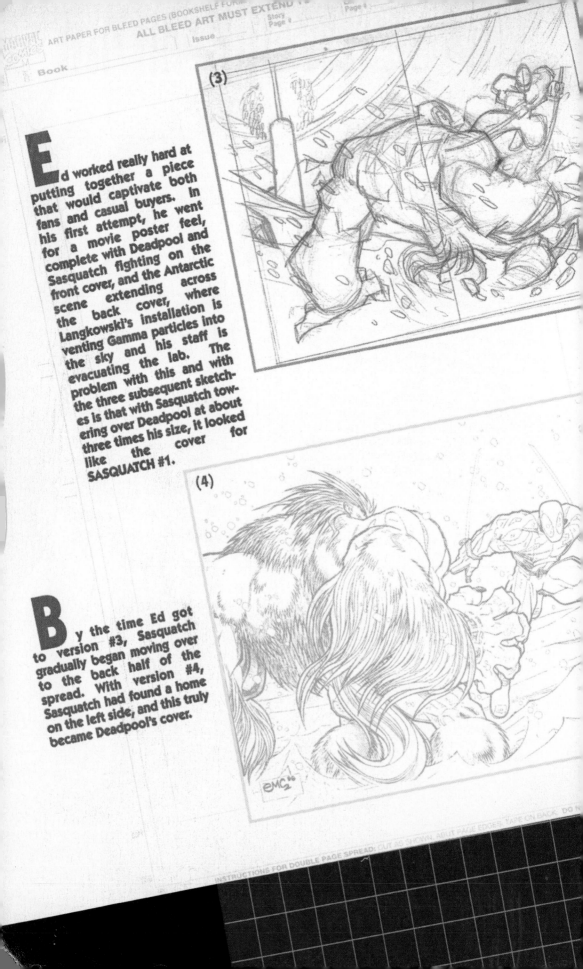

Ed worked really hard at putting together a piece that would captivate both fans and casual buyers. In his first attempt, he went for a movie poster feel, complete with Deadpool and Sasquatch fighting on the front cover, and the Antarctic scene extending across the back cover, where Langkowski's installation is venting Gamma particles into the sky and his staff is evacuating the lab. The problem with this and with the three subsequent sketches is that with Sasquatch towering over Deadpool at about three times his size, it looked like the cover for SASQUATCH #1.

(4)

By the time Ed got to version #3, Sasquatch gradually began moving over to the back half of the spread. With version #4, Sasquatch had found a home on the left side, and this truly became Deadpool's cover.

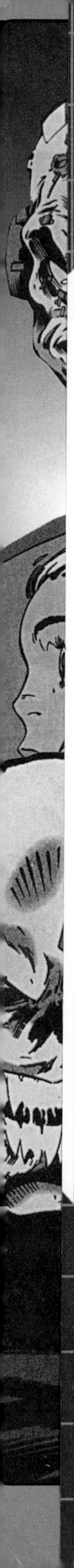

GES (BOOKSHELF FORMAT OR SADDLE STITCH)   AT 67%   ILLUSTRATION QUALITY

ALL BLEED ART MUST EXTEND TO SOLID LINE   KEEP ALL
LETTERING INSIDE
BROKEN-LINE BOX

Story
Page #   Line Up
Page #

IF AT FIRST YOU DON T SUCCEED...

Variations, both large and small, are not confined to just the plotting stage. Change is often the name of the game, particularly when a new series is starting up. With the relentless and unforgiving nature of The Schedule, many are the moments when the inker is called upon to bail out... uh, sorry, *correct* a problem in the pencils.

In this scene, Walter Langkowski has decided to take a trip outdoors to admire his fabulous gamma experiment. Now Walter was *supposed* to transform into Sasquatch as he was undressing. Instead, Ed depicted Walt heading outdoors (panel two), undressing like some kind of streaker (panel three), and finally as Sasquatch in panel four. To fans unfamiliar with the character and his powers, this could be a problem (besides which, watching him transform is kind of cool). No sweat!

Our inker-extraordinaire, Nathan rolled up his sleeves and went to work, give our boy Langkowski some fluffy patches of fur on his face and body in panel three.

Then Chris Lichtner colored the piece, taking into account not just the fur color but changes in Walter's skin color as well, and the problem was solved and none were the wiser (well, until now, anyway).

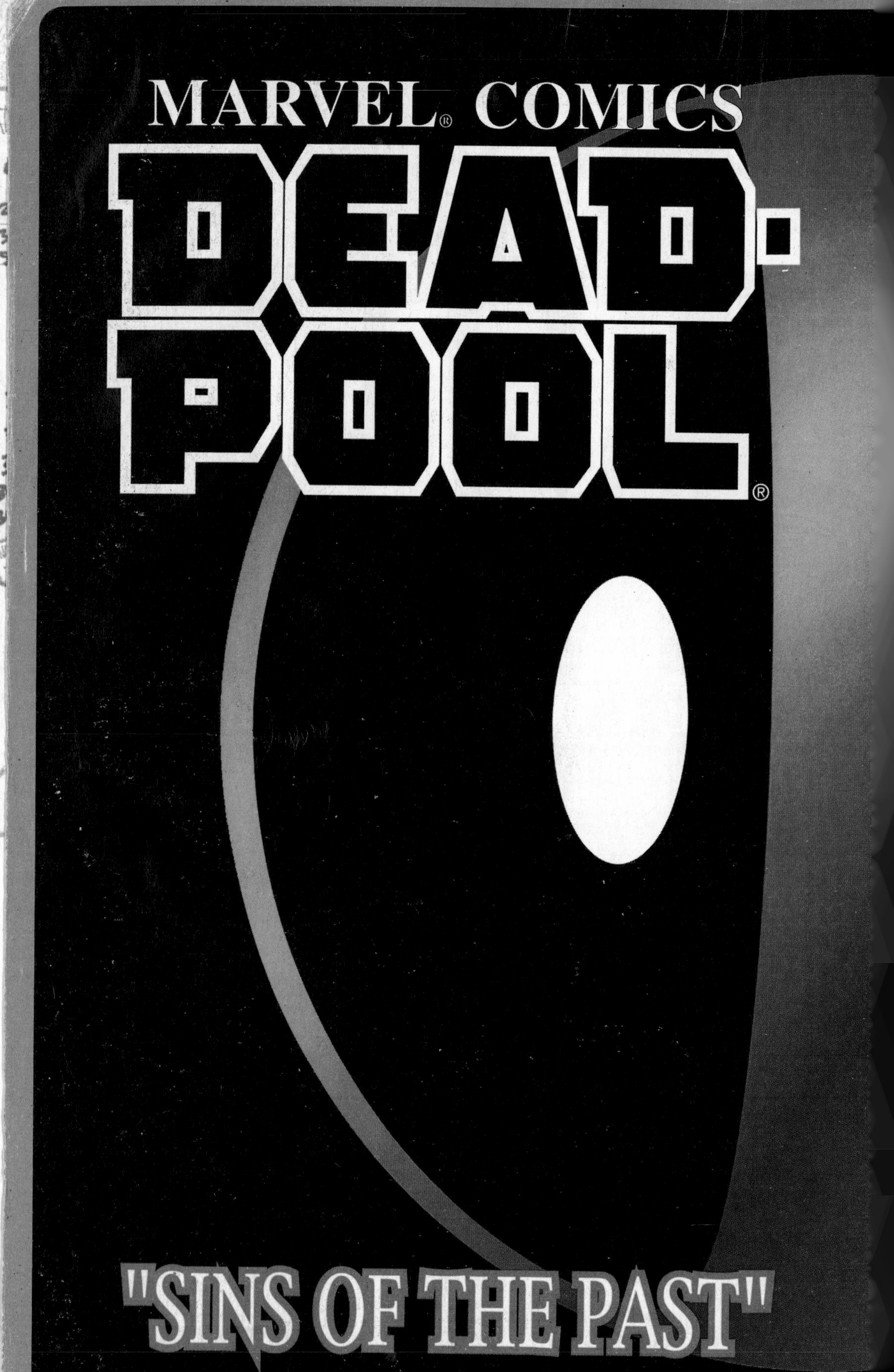
MARVEL® COMICS
DEAD-POOL®
"SINS OF THE PAST"

Deadpool: Sins of the Past TPB Cover